# EDUCATIONAL PSYCHOLOGY

### 3rd edition

# Lee J. Cronbach

*Stanford University*

Under the general editorship of
Ernest R. Hilgard, *Stanford University*

# EDUCATIONAL PSYCHOLOGY

## 3rd edition

HARCOURT BRACE JOVANOVICH, INC.

*New York / San Diego / Chicago / San Francisco / Atlanta*

Lee J. Cronbach
EDUCATIONAL PSYCHOLOGY, 3rd edition

Copyright 1954, © 1962, 1963, 1977 by Harcourt Brace Jovanovich, Inc.

ISBN: 0-15-520883-7

Library of Congress Catalog Card Number: 76-51543

Printed in the United States of America

Illustration credits will be found on p. 859, which is regarded as part of the copyright page.

# PREFACE

How do psychologists think about educational issues? What do they know that helps in planning lessons? What insights can they offer regarding students? These are the questions that an introductory text in educational psychology should answer. But issues, curricula, and student bodies change, and so this book is revised and extended in each decade to treat new questions and to include new findings. The psychological journals and symposia of the 1970s contain much that is significant—about coding, for example, and about effects of rewards. Instructional innovations—open classrooms, bilingual teaching, computers, and so on—are making learning activities far more diversified, offering the teacher far more options. Policy proposals coming from the Panel on Youth, the Project on Classification of Children, and the "open" university (for example) go even further, requiring educators and citizens to reconsider how schooling is organized and what it tries to do.

If texts can get out of date, it is natural to question whether the field has any lasting substance. Can today's educational psychology course offer ideas solid enough to be the foundation for a lifetime of concern with education? From the perspective gained in preparing a third edition, I can give a strongly positive answer. The central principles of the first edition—prepared a quarter of a century ago—are valid and pertinent today. They are still deservedly central in this edition. Insight has developed cumulatively; the thoughts William James and John Dewey set down two generations ago are worth attention alongside the contemporary observations of Herbert Simon and Urie Bronfenbrenner, of Joanna Williams and Patricia Minuchin.

All the specific research findings and implications to be presented are elaborations of three principles:

*Behavior is purposive.* In each act, one sees a sequence of interpretation, provisional try, and response to consequences. Whenever the person actively engages a problematic situation, learning occurs.

*Development is cumulative.* Societal demands set developmental tasks for the person at each age; these generate needs that provide the core of motivation.

*Mental ability is achieved.* "Intelligence" is simply behavior in which concepts, techniques, and attitudes—working together—enable the person to cope with what is unfamiliar. Transfer value is the chief criterion for judging instruction.

This emphasis on transfer, on education for a changing future, goes back to Dewey. As psychologist, as philosopher, and as director of an experimental school, Dewey stressed problem solving and saw purpose and feeling as co-equal in the process with knowledge and reasoning. A second rich heritage comes from E. L. Thorndike, the student of James who showed how to use laboratory techniques and measurements to analyze learning and instruction. His emphasis was on the formation of mental connections, and hence on efficient practice. The two lines of thought are complementary, one integrative and broad, the other analytic and precise. The teacher should think about the school program, and each particular day's work, in both ways.

Both lines of thought enter this book, although on balance it is more Deweyan. Perhaps it will help you in using the book to know its lines of descent. I studied out of Arthur Gates's text in my first course in educational psychology (way back in 1933). Gates's book—a direct descendant of the pioneering text of Thorndike—was a lucid, compact introduction and deservedly influential. When I later taught from the 1948 edition, I found the quality high; but Gates's presentation separated topics I saw as integrally related: development, measurement, intellectual learning, and emotion. And, in the attempt to cover all research findings, with no central model, it had become top-heavy. The "Eight-Year Study," which the Progressive Education Association set up in the 1930s, was an effort in thirty high schools to create and test new curricula and teaching methods reflecting Dewey's principles. I was an intern teacher of math and science in one of those schools, where the curriculum was much influenced by ideas from developmental psychology, and later I served as assistant in Ralph Tyler's evaluation staff for the thirty-school investigation.

At the University of Chicago in 1946 I was assigned the introductory course Tyler had been teaching. He had chosen his course content with an eye on the teacher, not the psychologist. "What are the decisions teachers have to make?" he asked. "What, then, do they need to know from behavioral science?" I adopted this need-to-know criterion for selecting content, but I do not see the educational psychology course as how-to-do-it training. It educates educators, but it also serves citizens who will never teach, and psychology majors who are considering careers in applied psychology. (Nor should an instructor or writer forget that young people seek insight into themselves in every psychology course they take.)

Pressey and Robinson had produced an influential text (*Psychology and the New Education*, 1937, 1944) whose orientation was developmental and social. Their text was eloquent on transfer as the goal of lessons. In the tradition of Dewey, emotional and intellectual activity were treated as inseparable. Oriented to problem-centered teaching though the book was, it was enthusiastic also about educational technology, which meshed with convictions I had formed in developing and evaluating training materials for the Navy. Pressey and Robinson had a fine book, highly teachable. I frankly set out to make my book its successor.

What I particularly wanted to add was an armature—a comprehensive, somewhat systematic view of the process of learning. Trial-and-feedback in significant contexts was the key to learning for Pressey and Robinson, as it had been for Thorndike; emphasizing action, they had remarkably little to say about the learner's purposes and thoughts. I wanted to bring intellectual analysis and the learner's self-direction into the picture. The solution was provided by Hilgard and by Thelen, who were trying to replace the "law of effect" with a happier formulation. "Provisional try with confirmation" seems to do the trick (Chapter 3). A variant formulation—the model of Miller, Galanter, and Pribram (1960)—strongly influenced the cognitive-experimental psychology of recent years. My fortunate early choice of a central scheme thus has made it easy now to incorporate the research of the 1970s, the dominant concept of which is interpretation or structure.

It is with respect to experimental psychology that this book has changed most from the preceding edition. Although I had introduced Piagetian ideas on structure there, not much of the work on the experimental psychology of learning seemed useful for the student of educational psychology. Now, experimenters are speaking of matters clearly relevant to instruction; Chapters 10–13 bring in much of that new work—on discrimination, templates or internal models, organization in memory, applied linguistics, and thought processes.

Always, my own research and field-service efforts have centered upon measurement and its uses. In this aspect of the book the only major change is greater attention to program evaluation. Program evaluations loom so large in educational controversies that some introduction is desirable—for citizens as well as educators. The book takes up evaluation of compensatory education in particular (Chapter 9)—the logic being more important than the results to date. New material on how psychologists collect data on educational questions (Chapters 1, 4, 16) illuminates evaluation and other topics.

With respect to the nature of mental ability and its relevance to teaching, guidance, and social planning, I like to think that this edition sets forth the same views as the second one. The controversies of the past decade have been unproductive, I think (Cronbach, 1969, 1975b); nothing appearing recently is half so valuable to the general student as Gardner's *Excellence* (1960)—or, if icon-oclasm is wanted, Michael Young's *Rise of the Meritocracy* (1958). I have revised my Chapters 8 and 9 to say more about the aspects of the problem that have most confused the public debaters.

Psychological topics cannot be separated. Each important aspect of development—emotional reactions, social learning, reasoning, and so on—affects all the others. This text can be fully comprehended only when taken as a whole. The organization is deliberately repetitive. A topic is introduced in a general overview, or in connection with a classroom example to which it is important. It bobs up from time to time when the text is examining other topics. In due course, it takes the center of the stage and gets a full treatment.

This planned review is one of several means by which I apply principles of educational psychology to the book itself. The questions imbedded in the text are another attempt to assist learning. These invitations to stop and think are placed in the midst of the text to encourage the reader to reflect on one section before going on to the next. Rarely do the preceding pages give the answer directly. The questions call for integration of the content of those pages with other knowledge, as would thinking about any educational problem. There can be many answers to a question; the superior answer will be one that takes more things into account. A good answer will not be a simple yes or no, but will begin, say, "I'd want to know these things before deciding . . ." or "I'd say yes provided that. . . ."

The case reports that appear in some chapters tell a great deal about a single person or classroom, and illustrate topics from other parts of the book. They are based on observations, but they are not accurate scientific reports. Limitations of space have made it necessary to omit detailed information and minor features even in the longer reports. Moreover, to disguise the identity of teachers and students, observed facts have been altered where this could be done without falsifying the picture.

Research described in the text is similarly illustrative. From the many studies that support an important principle, only one or two are reported. The studies selected are those easiest to comprehend or those most important to teachers—preferably both; the conclusions expressed are based on considerable research in addition to those studies. Since the studies reported are chiefly illustrative, there is little reason to remember the details of each. The principles and the general method of attack, as illustrative of psychological investigation, are the important content.

An educational-psychology course ought to clarify the prospective teacher's aims, strengthen his critical abilities and attitudes, widen the range of variables he takes into account, and increase his options. It ought not to "give answers." Teaching is an art, not a technique. Hard-and-fast conclusions do not hold up. I am deeply suspicious of rules for teaching: "Ten ways to reduce forgetting in your class," or "How to motivate disadvantaged adolescents." There is no way to make the teacher's job easy. But teachers respond to challenges.

The profusion of masculine pronouns at the start of the preceding paragraph makes this an appropriate place to say that no sex stereotyping is intended. The coverage of I. L. Child's research in the first edition may have made this the first book in education to bring up the subject of stereotype. The age-old stereotypes of the schoolteacher as female and the college instructor as male are absent from this book. But, because of the shortcomings and awkwardness of the alternatives, I continue, for the most part, to use the convention in which "he" and "his" are general and refer to a person of either gender.

It is a pleasure to acknowledge the assistance of many colleagues. Foremost is E. R. Hilgard, who as editor of the book in all its editions has been an ideal teacher. My experimental-psychologist colleague Robert C. Calfee has given me considerable help in several sections of this edition. Also, he prepared the case report on Mrs. Whittier (p. 97) on the basis of his experience with teachers of reading. Many authors have allowed me to use their work, and often they have provided useful comments or unpublished material. Every chapter of the book was given a critical reading by reviewers, who called my attention to gaps or obscurities in the argument; I trust that I have repaired these. My readers and I owe much individually and collectively to the reviewers—those who preferred to remain anonymous, and those whose names follow: Bruce Biddle, Urie Bronfenbrenner, Courtney Cazden, Donald Cunningham, Robert Glaser, D. Bob Gowin, Robert Havighurst, Alan Kaufman, Walter Kintsch, Kathryn W. Linden, William J. McGuire, Anthony J. Nitko, Barak Rosenshine, Aileen Schoeppe, Lee Shulman, and Bruce Tuckman.

I thank Jack Alexander, Nelly Glenn, and Marcia Linn, of the Palo Alto Unified School District, Menlo-Atherton High School, and Lawrence Hall of Science, respectively, for help in my search for pictures; Olga Baca, Claire Russell, and Jacqueline Libertal for patiently putting untidy drafts into good form; and Phil Ressner, Marilyn Marcus, and Dodie Shaw of Harcourt Brace Jovanovich for their artistic and editorial contributions to the book. Leonard Fisk has prepared an Instructor's Manual with tests, and Barbara Goodson a study guide for students.

If all of us together have succeeded, this book will give prospective teachers an interest in analyzing instructional problems and the confidence that they can devise superior teaching tactics to fit particular contexts. It will give citizens a sense of what education can be, and prospective psychologists a sense of how they can contribute.

Lee J. Cronbach

# CONTENTS

## 3 PROCESSES IN BEHAVIOR AND IN LEARNING   77

## 4 MODES OF INVESTIGATION IN EDUCATIONAL PSYCHOLOGY   109

# PART TWO

## Readiness and Its Development   147

# 5   THE STREAM OF DEVELOPMENT   149

# 6   MOTIVATIONAL DEVELOPMENT: EFFECTS OF HOME AND COMMUNITY   205

# 7  ASSESSING ABILITIES   253

# 8  NATURE AND ORIGINS OF GENERAL ABILITIES   307

## 9 INDIVIDUAL DIFFERENCES AND SCHOOL PRACTICE    351

## PART THREE
### Fundamental Learning Processes    391

## 10 SKILLS    393

# 11 PERCEIVING AND REMEMBERING    441

# 12 THE STUDENT'S COMMUNICATIONS, AND THE SCHOOL'S    489

## 13   PROBLEM SOLVING   543

## PART FOUR

### Planning, Motivation, and Evaluation  591

## 14   PURPOSES AND CONSEQUENCES   593

## THE TEACHER AS CLASSROOM LEADER    647

## ASSESSING PROGRESS IN LEARNING    683

# PART FIVE

## Beliefs, Feelings, and Character    735

# 17 ATTITUDE DEVELOPMENT AND ATTITUDE CHANGE    737

# 18 CHARACTER 783

# EDUCATIONAL PSYCHOLOGY

### 3rd edition

# PART ONE
## How Psychological Inquiry Contributes to Education

**THEMES**

■ Because the psychologist observes systematically, some of his findings raise questions about traditional educational practices and ideas.

□ Psychology offers concepts for the teacher and curriculum-maker to take into account in framing their plans. But just how to proceed in any class depends on the goals of instruction and the characteristics of the students to be taught.

□ The educator can become more effective by acting as an applied scientist, testing his plans carefully. The tryout process is especially well illustrated in educational technology.

■ Judgments about values and assumptions about facts enter into educational decisions. The behavioral sciences contribute to the soundness of both.

□ Three styles of psychology are distinguished: behavioristic, humanistic, and cognitive-developmental. Behaviorism seeks to develop firm conclusions from objective evidence, and avoids discussion of internal psychological processes. Humanistic psychology emphasizes inner feelings and interpretations. Wishing to explain broad phenomena, the humanist accepts a wide variety of data, including naturalistic observation. The cognitive-developmental psychologist sees the person as actively engaging his environment, thinking about his experience, and growing as a result.

**CONCEPTS**

educational research
educational technology
computer-assisted instruction
value judgments
empirical statements
behaviorism
behavioral control

reinforcer
token economy
neobehaviorism
humanistic psychology
cognitive-developmental
   style
cognitive / affective

# PSYCHOLOGICAL VIEWPOINTS

This book is about people and how they learn. Since you have been learning nearly all your life, and watching others learn, our topics will not be foreign to you. Very likely you have taught—in a school, in a recreation group, or in your own family. Even so, psychology can give you new ways of looking at familiar experiences.

Whatever the field, the informed person has two advantages: he or she takes more things into account and uses more varied concepts to organize observations. The boy first beginning to follow baseball looks at the score. As he becomes more sophisticated, he looks at the batter's stance, the manager's tactics in placing the outfielders, and the break on the pitcher's curve ball. The expert in physical education considers all these, then goes on to yet other ways of thinking about the athlete. He thinks of the body as a mechanical system, and is able to analyze motions in terms of the principles of levers and of momentum. He looks on the body as a chemical system, and so is better able to understand fatigue. He gains further insight from the psychology of reaction time and feedback systems. A practitioner can get along without knowing all the principles behind his craft; he adopts tested techniques and improves them by trial and error. The person who in addition knows basic concepts can deal with problems for which there are no standard procedures. He can design improvements instead of having to stumble upon them.

# THE VALUE OF PSYCHOLOGICAL VIEWPOINTS IN EDUCATION

In thinking about teaching, multiple viewpoints are essential. Too often, teachers fall into set ways of looking at school problems. Marie refuses to study, whispers in class, sulks when reproved. The teacher, justifiably annoyed, is tempted to explain Marie's behavior as a character defect: "You can't expect much from a girl like her—she doesn't *want* to learn" or "I've done all I can, but some kids just can't concentrate." Pinning a label on the student serves no purpose well. The teacher should begin to hunt down reasons for the behavior.

Psychological case studies show that (save for a few pathological exceptions) people want to do well and want approval from their associates. When a person does not behave in a constructive way there must be a reason. Perhaps the cause can be discovered and treated directly. If Marie's teacher does not settle for labeling Marie as a "discipline problem" or as "a case of learning disability" but tries to see the class situation as Marie sees it, the two should be on the way to a productive relationship. The teacher's task becomes not one of administering justice, but of studying Marie and finding ways to help her toward *her* goals.

## The Place of Scientific Inquiry

TRADITION AND TEACHING    Most novice teachers aspire to be like their own best teachers. But imitation—a fine way to learn, up to a point—is of little value when conditions change. Teaching methods have been handed down from generation to generation with rather little modification. But today's schools have to operate in conditions no previous generation has seen. Parents who are themselves uneducated and poor are rightly demanding that the schools *teach* their children, instead of dismissing them as incompetent. Teachers are being held accountable for students' performances: the teacher instead of the student may be judged a failure on the basis of test results! Children come to school attuned to the flash and snap of the television commercial; by contrast, even a lesson that lasts only 20 minutes may seem tedious. Students with a wide range of backgrounds, needs, and hopes are seeking education in a wide range of settings, to develop themselves for their own purposes. Students are more inclined today to question what an authority proposes for them.

Traditions give security, stability, and a fund of tested wisdom, but they easily become fossilized. Communities evolve, and educators had better respond by redesigning their roles and procedures. They do have to maintain cultural continuity by teaching appreciation of art forms, ethnic history, longstanding political ideals, and so on. But concepts change, and so do the

meanings given to old facts. The teacher cannot rely on the approaches that worked a few years back.

The present methods of teaching are the result of a long process of trial and error. Trying one method after another is not a bad way to hit upon a superior teaching procedure. Present education is a remote descendant of the successive inspirations of master teachers: Socrates, Comenius, Froebel, and others. Ideas that worked well in the hands of their inventor are imitated in other places. A technique that served Mark Hopkins opposite a single student, or Socrates strolling with a few disciples, is amended—more trials and errors—to fit the bureaucratic schedule of a large school.

QUESTIONS THE PSYCHOLOGIST ASKS  Theory and principle hasten invention. Trial and error has less error in it when new proposals spring from understanding. Psychological concepts contribute to that understanding. If educators (and that includes parents and those who would lead public opinion) have lessons to

# What psychology can you trust?

The statements below illustrate the form of generalizations from psychological research. But do not store the list in your mind as you read it.

- More intelligent children tend to receive less social acceptance from [classmates]. . . . (This is easy to understand, because as is well known, children resent the greater success, higher grades, and teacher acceptance of the more able pupils.)

- If a group of pupils is given a considerable amount of practice and instruction in developing a skill, the pupils will become more alike in that skill. (Certainly, if a group of persons is subjected to a uniform experience, their homogeneity on dimensions relevant to this experience will become greater.) . . . .

- If you want to strengthen a kind of behavior, you should reward it, and if you want to eliminate an erroneous kind of behavior, you should punish it. And if the pupil repeats his error, he should be punished more severely than for the first error. . . .

- The only way to secure transfer of learning from one situation to another is to increase the similarity, or the number of so-called identical elements, between the learning situation and the application situation. (Ever since William James and E. L. Thorndike, we have known that there is no general transfer. . . . [The tasks and problems set in lessons] should therefore be made as much like real life as possible.) . . . .

Since these principles are so obvious, why do educational research workers expend so much effort to ascertain and validate them? And why should such common-sense [and obvious] notions be taught to prospective teachers? . . . These would be legitimate questions except for one noteworthy fact about the list. *Every one of these statements is the direct opposite of what actually has been found by educational psychologists*. More intelligent pupils are *better* accepted by their classmates. Individual differences *increase* with training. . . . One does *not* eliminate undesirable behavior most effectively by punishing it. One *can* foster transfer by getting pupils to learn general concepts and principles in an intellectual discipline.

Hence, I add, tough-minded investigation is needed to detect the fallacies in superficially plausible ideas.

SOURCE: N. L. Gage, *Teacher Effectiveness and Teacher Education: The Search for a Scientific Bias* (Palo Alto, Calif.: Pacific Books, 1972), pp. 144–45.

learn from psychology, what are they? It is impossible to put in a nutshell the content of the remaining chapters, but here are illustrations of the questions for which psychology seeks answers:

- Why do children in the same family, brought up similarly, have different personalities?

- What makes some verbal presentations unnecessarily difficult for the student?

- What experiences produce the sort of person who generates quick, unconventional interpretations?

- Why do people do unwise things—like planting the same crop over and over until the soil is worn out, even when they know this will happen?

- What are the consequences, good and bad, of holding a young person to a high standard?

To answer any such broad question, the psychologist has to subdivide it, collect facts relevant to the resulting subquestions, and then construct explanatory hypotheses that fit the facts.

Educators and laymen formulate their ideas about human development and about schooling out of observation, as psychologists do. The psychologist, however, observes more systematically. Sometimes he merely confirms what everyone "knew." Usually, he reaches a more precise estimate of an effect. By locating conditions under which the effect is strong and other conditions in which it is absent, he offers a better interpretation. Not infrequently, the psychologist discovers that a long-standing belief is wrong, simply because his more objective methods rule out a good deal of bias and error of observation.

EVIDENCE VERSUS JUDGMENT    For all the importance of judgment in the moment-to-moment work of teachers, there is danger in the sentimental view that the judgment of a teacher "with the right spirit" is to be trusted without question. Mistakes in judgment are always with us because information is limited. Moreover, the teacher is likely to give undue weight to some facts while overlooking others that run counter to his sympathies.

Consider, for example, teachers' judgments about student opinion. In one study (Amos & Washington, 1960), junior-high-school students filled out a Problem Check List (p. 241), checking whatever difficulties caused them concern. Each teacher tried to predict how many students would report each of the problems. On the average, the students reported about three times as many worries in the area of health, physical development, money, and work as the teachers expected. Girls, especially, reported many more problems regarding home, family, and boy-girl relations than teachers recognized. Teachers also tended to be wrong in thinking that students lacked interest in school and disliked studies; and they greatly underestimated the number of students afraid of failure and afraid of making mistakes.

Misjudgments make a difference, as a study of reading teachers in an Ohio city showed. Two groups of five teachers, matched in experience and method of teaching, were picked out. The teachers were told that 80 per cent of girls succeed in first-grade reading. Then they were asked what percentage of boys usually succeed. One group said that 80 per cent of boys succeed in reading; others had said that 50 to 60 per cent of boys succeed. The investigator (Palardy, 1969) examined the reading success of students of these teachers during the next year. He adjusted for age and IQ in the final comparison. Moreover, he left out of the analysis students who had done badly on a prereading test in

## FIGURE 1.1

### Teacher expectations affect educational results

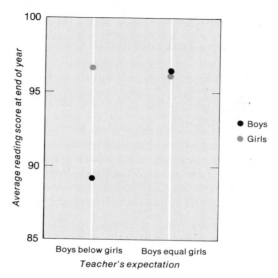

Average reading scores of children having teachers who expected boys and girls to perform equally well or teachers who expected boys to perform less well.

SOURCE: Data from Palardy (1969).

September—so the boys and girls he considered were capable of success. Figure 1.1 shows the average reading scores of these boys and girls in May. It appears that boys fared less well if taught by a teacher who had poor expectations for boys. What caused them to lag was surely neglect rather than direct mistreatment.

Findings like these do not imply that judgments about students should be turned over to machines; the teacher brings to bear an array of facts far richer than research can supply. But such findings do imply that teachers should maintain a critical rather than a trusting attitude toward their judgments. Scientific knowledge improves their judgments without eliminating the need for them.

## The Fruits of Educational Research

RESEARCH AND EDUCATIONAL PRACTICE  The educator usually asks for recommendations, not explanations: "At what age should children begin to study multiplication?" "What program should the high school offer a student whose reading and abstract thinking are poor?" "What is the best sequence of topics in high-school science?" Psychology can rarely give a direct answer to such blunt, practical questions. Indeed, the psychologist must insist that most questions of this kind are unanswerable, that "It depends . . ." The justification for such seeming evasiveness is that it really *does* depend. Different answers fit different schools and different learners, and there is no general recommendation applicable to all cases.

From the very first days of modern American psychology, teachers have been coming to psychology classes with the expectation that they will be handed definite, scientifically proved recipes ready for application. William James's reply to this demand, written in 1899, holds today:

> . . . you make a great, a very great mistake, if you think that psychology, being the science of the mind's laws, is something from which you can deduce definite programmes and schemes and methods of instruction for immediate schoolroom use. Psychology is a science, and teaching is an art; and sciences never generate arts directly out of themselves. An intermediary inventive mind must make the application, by using its originality.

## Technology

"You mene I've bin spending this whol
term with a defektiv reeding machin?"

## Beyond the grasp of science?

Misunderstanding of the claims and purposes of scientific psychology has led to strong objections at times, particularly from those who regard the humanities as the source of wisdom about human affairs. Thus the thoughtful literary critic Gilbert Highet (1950, pp. vii–viii) has said:

> It seems to me very dangerous to apply the aims and methods of science to human beings as individuals. . . . Teaching involves emotions, which cannot be systematically appraised and employed, and human values, which are quite outside the grasp of science. . . . Teaching is not like inducing a chemical reaction: it is more like painting a picture . . . or on a lower level like planting a garden. . . . You must throw your heart into it, you must realize that it cannot all be done by formulas, or you will spoil your work, and your pupils, and yourself.

With all but the very first sentence the psychologist agrees heartily. Values, emotions, and instantaneous judgments are required in teaching, and these succeed in proportion to the depth of the teacher's understanding and compassion. But science and the humanities should join in creating that understanding: The gardener who has set his heart on roses must respect unsentimental facts about soil chemistry. A physicist may know a great deal about the refraction of light and still enjoy a sunset. Every dependable fact about human behavior must be respected by the teacher, even though the facts and measurements of the behavioral scientist are by no means sufficient to dictate what the teacher shall do.

> The science of logic never made a man reason rightly, and the science of ethics . . . never made a man behave rightly. The most such sciences can do is to help us catch ourselves up and check ourselves, if we start to reason or to behave wrongly; and to criticise ourselves more articulately after we have made mistakes. . . . (James, 1907 edition, pp. 7–21.)

Behavioral research is based on sampling. From all the possible conditions under which a question can be studied, the psychologist picks one set for investigation. The results are more secure when repeated studies under other conditions give the same results. The separate studies take on still more significance when combined into a theoretical explanation; this in turn often has practical implications for education. But experimental findings and theories cannot be directly translated into rules for decisions.

Decisions about general policies can be made by a state agency, a local school board, or a curriculum designer. Even when statewide policy is at issue, research cannot itself supply the answer. The psychologist again must say: "It depends." The decision-maker considers the facts that research has turned up, the alternative educational goals, and the likely response the proposal will draw from the public and the profession. The teacher, who must make specific plans, has to consider in addition his own subject-matter and the readiness of his own class. The sound way—at the policy level or at the classroom level—is to act as one does in any applied science: trying various approaches, observing the results, and interpreting what happened.

RESEARCH AND EDUCATIONAL TECHNOLOGY  Loosely, we can trace educational technology back to the invention of the slate and the printing press, or even to those pebbles Demosthenes used in curing a speech impediment. Nor is technical invention to be identified with hardware exclusively. Shakespeare's chronicle plays were entertainment, but they were also a mass medium that heightened the Englishman's nationalism. They taught citizenship as surely as did the televised Watergate hearings.

Some new techniques have been directly inspired by research on behavior. A good example is computer-aided instruction. Some universities now are wired into a system that teaches specific skills or even whole courses. There are, for example, exercises where the computer shows the student what happens when he applies chemical reagents to an "unknown"; the student spends his time interpreting this information and thinking what reagent to apply next, instead of having to spend hours in hands-on filtering and boiling and weighing. Grade schools around the

country are connected by phone to a central computer that presents drills on addition with an efficiency and patience that neither the human teacher nor the printed workbook can match.

The rationale for computer-assisted instruction rests in part on the principle of feedback or reinforcement (p. 89). Clear-cut signals about the appropriateness of responses shape response patterns. The first developments were programmed instructional materials in printed form. Unlike traditional workbooks, these gave instant information as to correctness each time the student filled in a blank or worked a problem. Programs were field-tested before publication. The number of errors at each point showed the writer where revision was needed. Unlike the textbook writer, who does everything from an armchair, or who conducts a casual field trial, the programmer could engineer pages to generate just the desired amount of difficulty. The computer offers considerably greater flexibility than the printed page. In particular, it can choose the next question in the light of the student's last response, just as the Socratic teacher does. Moreover, it seems to maintain student enthusiasm better than printed programs.

The principles in a technologically controlled education are no different from the principles that guide traditional teacher-student instruction. A language laboratory can provide the student with recorded voices speaking at the rate and level that is right for him or her. The language teacher who does not have a laboratory and cannot so fully individualize instruction will be equally concerned with pace, level, and variety of listening activities.

The "engineering" mentioned earlier gives research a unique role in educational technology. A technical device is expensive to produce, and will be used in the same form with thousands or even millions of students. Therefore, it is profitable to check out the details of the instructional material and technique while it is being developed.

The Children's Television Workshop (CTW) is a group of artists and writers; they achieve their results through creative inspiration and craftsmanship. It was CTW that developed Big Bird and the Muppets, not the *Journal of Educational*

Around her waist instead of a belt she wore a worm.

So she waved her wand and her washtub filled with warm water.

# Which letters was "Sesame Street" teaching well?

When the TV program "Sesame Street" was first broadcast, the research staff set up a small experiment in daycare centers. About 200 children were chosen randomly, half of whom viewed the show regularly and half of whom did not. There was a pretest on ability to name letters, and another test three months later. (The gains by the nonviewers were attributable to improvement in test taking, maturation [p. 160], and experience other than "Sesame Street.") With data for all letters (like those shown here for A, R, S, and W), the producers could judge whether the techniques were working at both ages, and whether some letters were being taught less successfully than others.

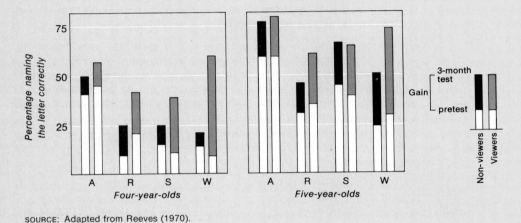

SOURCE: Adapted from Reeves (1970).

*Psychology.* But when CTW was starting work on "Sesame Street" it established a research group under the direction of educational psychologists Edward Palmer (1974) and Gerald Lesser (1976). They tested the artists' ideas as fast as they could be put onto a trial videotape. What did the children in the test audience pay attention to? How long could a sequence continue before it lost attention? Could children tell *W* from *M* after two exposures to Wanda the Witch? After six exposures? (Reeves, 1970.) It was sometimes annoying to the artists to have to compromise their intuitive judgment with the evidence as to how children responded. But the total cost of production and air time, plus the importance of really teaching something, more than justified the cost and trouble of field testing.

**1** Some citizens urge the Board of Education of the State of Harmonia to establish minimum performance standards for high-school graduation. They complain that the diploma now "doesn't mean anything." Since teachers grade permissively, the diploma can be earned merely by staying in school for four years. Other citizens argue that to deny the diploma to some students would make it harder for them to get jobs, and thus might work to the disadvantage of some minorities. Also, making it harder to get through high school would increase the dropout rate so that students who need more education would be less likely to get it. What questions pertinent to the decision regarding performance standards might be answered by psychological or statistical investigations?

2 Junior colleges in Harmonia have similar student bodies and faculties. Three instructional programs were introduced at one or another of the junior colleges. The students were satisfied with their program and the faculty thought that the students learned adequately. If another junior college were to adopt these programs, what further evaluations would it need to carry out?

3 College lectures for large classes would lose little in videotaping. Careful revision could enhance their educational usefulness. If the probability of continued use of taped lectures justified the cost of field-testing and revision, what checks should be made on the preliminary tapes? Consider a history lecture on Roosevelt and the New Deal as an example.

# SCIENTIFIC APPROACHES TO EDUCATIONAL ISSUES

## Bases for Evaluating Assumptions

Educational practices and proposals are based on ideas about both values and facts. Value judgments deal with the desirability and priority of various outcomes. The facts, the empirical base, deal with probabilities; they are the basis for predicting the *likely* outcomes of the proposed action.

JUDGMENTS ABOUT VALUES    The goals of schooling are chosen politically. It is the people in a community who decide, for example, whether the local high school should increase attention to vocational preparation.

The public view of educational goals is illuminated by a continuing scholarly debate. The economist calls attention to the economic decisions that will face future citizens, the classicist speaks of the pertinence of great writings of the past for today's affairs, and so on. The psychologist draws attention to goals that might otherwise be overlooked. For example, he speaks of the motivational outcomes of schooling: changes in the young person's interests, expectation of success, and life aims. The educational psychologist emphasizes social behavior, personal effectiveness, and emotional adjustment just because some other

voices put all the emphasis on "subject-matter." Many people treat schooling as a purely intellectual activity, but successful performance requires a harmonious blend of thought and feeling, of intellect and spirit. These are psychological goals.

The psychologist can also help others define the goals of their educational programs. His research shows, for example, that ability to repeat a fact from the textbook may not imply ability to use the fact, and that ability to solve a problem explained in class does not guarantee success in solving other problems involving the same principle. The psychologist presses educators and policy-makers to be clear about the benefits instruction is intended to produce. He helps planners to state their expectations in such a way that research can test whether the curriculum works.

THE EMPIRICAL BASE OF JUDGMENT   When values are under discussion, the psychologist is one among many more or less expert voices. But when facts or principles describing behavior are under discussion, he has a unique role. Every proponent of educational change argues that following his suggestion will produce certain outcomes. Such statements are empirical in the sense that they can be verified or contradicted by suitable observations. Controlled observations in a laboratory, a classroom, or a community are needed to confirm claims and hopes.

An educational-psychology course provides an opportunity to learn something about research methods in education. The psychologist specializes in observing individuals and in experimenting in order to identify causes of behavior. Developmental psychologists make observations at successive points in a person's life. Some psychologists make case studies in depth, using interviews and observations to understand how the individual views his life situation. All these methods can be adapted to the study of schooling and its effects. Additional techniques have been developed especially for educational studies—methods of classroom observation, for instance.

Behavioral sciences other than psychology are being brought to bear on education. The educational system is studied by the survey techniques of the sociologist, the input-output models of the economist, and the organizational analysis used by the political scientist. The sociologist and anthropologist demonstrate how the person's immediate companions and the larger culture modify behavior. Although topics in this book are developed within a psychological framework, some evidence from these neighboring disciplines will also be considered.

**4** "Assumptions" accepted by those who establish open classrooms were listed by Barth (1970). Are the following statements from Barth's list judgments about values or empirical propositions?

    a. If a child is fully involved in and is having fun with an activity, learning is taking place.

    b. Children have both the competence and the right to make significant decisions concerning their own learning.

    c. There is no minimum body of knowledge essential for everyone to acquire.

**5** The following propositions about knowledge (also from Barth, 1970) are usually endorsed by educators favoring "open classrooms." Can you state a contrary position that some other thoughtful educators would agree with? If so, on what basis can a decision between the alternatives be reached?

    a. The final test of an education is what a man *is*, not what he *knows*.

    b. Knowledge is a function of one's personal integration of experience and therefore does not fall into neatly separate categories or "disciplines."

    c. The structure of knowledge is personal and idiosyncratic.

## Intellectual Styles of Psychologists

Each psychologist works in his own way. His philosophy and theory influence his choice of problem and investigative technique, and the interpretation he offers.

For the sake of highlighting some of the differences, I shall contrast the behavioristic and humanistic orientations. These categories are, however, oversimple. When I lump Skinner and Gagné as behaviorists, or Erikson and Rogers as humanists, I ignore major differences in emphasis and research technique. But if we regard the people placed in the same camp as congenial companions, not as persons who share precisely the same beliefs, we are on safe ground. And, although I dramatize the contrast between the behavioristic and humanistic extremes, most psychologists, including myself, happily use ideas arising from any thoughtful investigator, even though each is most comfortable with the ideas of his nearest intellectual neighbors.

BEHAVIORISM   All psychologists observe behavior. Strict behaviorism places exceptional emphasis on what can be seen, and so, on what can be recorded objectively. Reasoning is cautious, and conclusions are limited to observable behavior. The strict behaviorist speaks only about what a person *does.* He avoids reference to the mind, the feelings, or any other inner state. He speaks of "conduct" (observable), not of "character" (inferred). He discusses motivation in terms of actions chosen and rewards received, not of purposes or satisfactions. He concentrates on aspects of the situation that can be experimentally altered and controlled (Becker et al., 1975).

A major figure in the behavioristic school is B. F. Skinner (1968, 1970). Much of his research and that of his followers has investigated how rewards affect responses. The experimenter sets up conditions in which some one kind of response can be precisely measured. With a young child, a Skinnerian might count acts of dependency, asking whether they increase when an experimenter responds warmly to them.

**Behavior control**

FRED BASSET by Alex Graham, © Associated Newspapers Group Ltd. 1976, Dist. Field Newspaper Syndicate, 1976.

The behavioristic emphasis is summed up in the following assumptions or working hypotheses (adapted from S. White, 1969; in Mussen, 1970, I, pp. 665–66):

- The environment can be unambiguously characterized in terms of stimuli.

- Behavior can be unambiguously characterized in terms of responses. (After a stimulus is presented, an observer can say that the response did or did not occur.)

- A class of stimuli called *reinforcers* can be identified. (The reinforcer may be the grain in the pigeon's cup, or the teacher's nod of approval following the student's response to a question. A reinforcer makes the response it follows more likely in the future.)

- Learning can be completely characterized in terms of couplings among stimuli, responses, and reinforcers.

- Unless there is definite evidence to the contrary, any type of behavior is assumed to be learned, to be open to change when conditions are altered, to be trainable, and to be extinguishable (in the sense that a habit can be wiped out).

Discovering methods for controlling behavior is a major goal of behaviorists. They see the problem as primarily technical; Skinner titled one of his books *The Technology of Teaching* (1968), and programmed instruction was his invention. Behavior dependent on teacher-controlled rewards can be "turned on" and "turned off" by changing the reinforcement. If a child is given candy every time he reads a page, he will keep turning pages. When the candy runs out, he is likely to stop reading fairly quickly if the candy is his sole incentive (Staats, 1973, pp. 203ff.).

Psychologists in the behavioristic tradition have had great success in dealing with some difficult practical problems (boxes). When the reinforcement conditions can be controlled and the desired outcome is definite, behavioristic techniques can work remarkably well.

The strengths of the behaviorist's position appear as weaknesses to his critics. Since he stresses objectivity and external behavior, he says nothing about the subjective aspects of experience. Concerned with what he can control in a research setting, he says nothing about how individuals direct their own behavior. Because he concentrates on concrete details in single acts, he says nothing about broad, long-term aspects of behavior.

Rarely does the behaviorist examine cumulative effects over a school year, much less over a school career. Long-term studies are difficult to pursue in the strict behaviorist fashion, because the person's surroundings are hard to control.

The learner's purposes and his self-fulfillment are hard to discuss in behavioristic language. Such "contents of the mind" are not observable behavior, hence not open to behavioristic study. Behaviorism has little to say about such

## Behavioral control as an aid to learning

Risley and Wolf (1967) describe behavioristic procedures for helping children with abnormal behavior (autism, retardation) develop normal patterns of useful speech. As one example, Risley and Wolf tell how 7-year-old Carey was led to imitate words spoken by the psychologist:

> Imitation must reliably occur immediately after a word is presented before significant advances in speech can be made. Reliable and immediate imitation can be obtained by systematic reinforcement of imitation. The therapist presents a given word every 4–5 seconds. Whenever the child says this word he is reinforced [usually with food]. . . .
>
> Systematically reinforcing an imitated word will increase the frequency with which the child imitates that word, but it may also increase the frequency of non-imitative repetitions of the word. Other verbal utterances such as phrases or snatches of songs may also increase and should be extinguished. The therapist should wait until the child is silent before again presenting the word to be imitated. In this manner only *imitation* is being reinforced. . . .
>
> When the child is reliably and immediately imitating the first word, a new word is introduced, and the above procedure is repeated. The two words are then alternately presented. . . .

**A record of imitative responses**

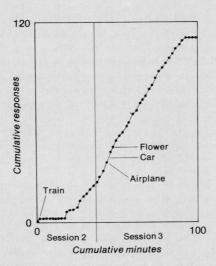

Each dot represents a 2-minute interval. Where Carey imitated during an interval the curve steps upward; thus, the steeper the curve, the more rapid the progress. Midway in Session 3, because Carey was ready for a more advanced task, the therapist shifted to asking him to name objects.

SOURCE: Simplified from Risley & Wolf (1967). © 1967. Reprinted with permission of Pergamon Press Ltd.

[The figure] shows the establishment of control over . . . [Carey's] imitation. From the start of session 2 the word "train" was repeated by the experimenter. The child imitated this word once early in the session, and was reinforced. Sixteen minutes later, during which time he was intermittently having tantrums, he again imitated "train" and was reinforced. After this the rate of imitating the word rapidly increased. Three other words, "flower," "car" and "airplane," were then introduced, and the child imitated each of them on the *first* presentation as well as on each subsequent presentation. Thus, in approximately 30 minutes, control was established over the child's imitative speech.

## The token economy

The "token economy" is a method of managing the classroom in accord with behavioristic principles (O'Leary & Drabman, 1971; Krasner & Krasner, 1973). When a student presents a severe behavior problem, the entire class may be unsettled by his disruptive actions; a class with many such children calls for exceptionally skilled management. The token economy is a plan used to create order in such classes. The teacher introduces a short list of rules of conduct, and tells the students that they will receive tokens when their behavior matches these rules. The tokens are exchanged for candy, ice cream, comics, free time, and so on, the reward depending on the age of the children.

In one application (O'Leary & Becker, 1967), the rules written on the blackboard were: In seat. Face front. Raise hand. Working. Pay attention. Desk clear. When the teacher checked a student and saw that his behavior conformed to the rules, the student was given a token. If the student was misbehaving, the teacher ignored his act. At first the students exchanged the tokens for rewards at the end of each day, then every couple of days, then at longer intervals. Over time, concrete rewards were gradually replaced with more traditional ones, such as praise from the teacher.

In this study, the rate of disruptive behavior (percentage of students out of order at any moment) ranged at the start from 66 to 91 per cent. After the token economy was put into effect, disruptions dropped below 32 per cent. Such dramatic changes are not uncommon.

There are limits to the effectiveness of the technique. The program demands a great deal of work from the teacher, and it is not always easy to wean the student from dependence on the tokens. Improved behavior in one situation does not lead to improved behavior elsewhere; the student who works well in the morning under a token economy may raise a ruckus in the afternoon in another setting.

an educational outcome as appreciating music, since each person develops his own response. Even so, behaviorism may help the teacher of music. It is evident, for example, that no one can appreciate music who cannot discriminate higher from lower tones. And it is behavioristic treatment—a form of conditioning—that has proved able to overcome tone-deafness (Wyatt, 1945). The educator who finds the answers from behaviorism incomplete can nonetheless take advantage of them.

In recent years, a neobehaviorism has appeared. It takes up a broad range of phenomena, and does consider cognitive processes (for example, Bandura, 1974; Thoresen & Mahoney, 1974). Neobehaviorists expand on such terms as "reinforcement" to offer a richer interpretation of learning and behavior, though they still stress objectivity. For instance, they note that reinforcement provides information as well as pleasure. A person learns to anticipate the consequences of his behavior, and it is often this anticipation that changes behavior, rather than the "stamping in" of a stimulus-response connection. A person can arrange his own reinforcement (Thoresen & Mahoney, 1974). Even a student who has never heard of reinforcement theory does this: "When I finish this page of my homework, I'll go to the kitchen and get some ice cream!" The neobehaviorist argues that one gains in self-control as one makes self-reinforcement more deliberate.

Behaviorism is a philosophical position as well as a method of research. It can be contrasted with a view that stresses the internal wellsprings of behavior, that insists that anybody acts as he wants to act, or feels he must act. From this standpoint it makes sense to hold the individual accountable for his behavior. Strict behaviorism turns this position on its head: Human actions are caused by environmental conditions; people act as they do because they have learned what consequences follow their actions. The first point of view stresses thought and internal motives; the second stresses actions and external reinforcement. But neither view is complete in itself.

Thought must be tied to action, motives to consequences. For instance, freedom of self-expression is an ideal of our society. For the behaviorist, "freedom is defined in terms of the number of options available to people and the right to exercise them" (Bandura, 1974, p. 865). In this light, freedom is partly a matter of education because education adds options by extending the person's repertoire of skills.

HUMANISTIC PSYCHOLOGY   The humanistic psychologist prefers the very language the behaviorist avoids. His psychology is particularly concerned with inner states, feelings, aspirations, the self. The humanist sees each person as a self-directing, integrated being, evolving in a unique direction as he interprets his experiences. Although the humanist psychologist, like any other, seeks to ground his reasoning in thorough observation, the subject himself is a key observer. What the person says about present feelings and recollections of past experiences, the humanist takes as prime data. The humanistic psychologist does not break behavior into single actions; he will break up, into units no smaller than a scene of a play, the activity by which a person engages the world.

Whereas the behaviorist usually limits conclusions to what he can be sure of, the humanist risks deeper interpretations. He typically gives a complete answer even if evidence is difficult to pin down and the conclusions partly speculative. Among contemporary humanistic psychologists, one of the most eminent is Erik Erikson, who has drawn on studies of American Indian tribes and of such men as Luther and Gandhi to clarify how one achieves a sense of "identity." Identity: Youth and Crisis (1968) is the current statement of his views. For Erikson, the acts of the person are not to be understood from the outside but are to be examined through the person's eyes. The late Abraham Maslow (1973) took a similar position, equating healthy development with "self-actualization."

*(text continues on p. 26)*

## Artists in the making

Frank Barron set out to learn about the motivation of students preparing for careers in art; his work illustrates one variety of humanistically-oriented psychology. He devotes several chapters to a study of 64 first-year students at the San Francisco Art Institute. His first chapter describes the school, primarily in the words of the students. The chapter gives few specific facts about the program, but gives many impressions about the students' experience. The second chapter presents miniature case studies in the form of interviews with six students. The third brief chapter draws on the interviews to make some general statements about the difference between the men and women in the sample. We can quote only a fraction of the four-page statement by Barron and his teammates Jarrell Kraus, Isabel Conti, and Cynthia Marlowe (1972, pp. 34–37). Note the frequent reliance on *individual* statements.

> We see immediately a dramatic difference when we look at the answers to the question *Do you think of yourself as an artist?* Of those who answered, most of the women said *no* (67%), but most of the men said *yes* (66%). The men already think of themselves as artists. The women are not nearly so ready to view themselves as artists—student artists, perhaps, but not artists, not yet.
>
> When the students were asked, *In comparison to the work of others at the Institute, is your work particularly unique or good?,* another sex difference in answers was noticed. Forty percent of the men but only 17% of the women felt their work was of superior quality. (Perhaps in answering this question in this way the girls are more realistic, but the difference in self-image as an artist is our main concern.) . . .
>
> None of the differences we find between the men's and the women's evaluations of their work would be startling if, in fact, the men did produce better art work. But this is not the case. When all the students' art was rated by a large and varied number of judges, the women's work ranked as highly as the men's did. There were no discrepancies in ability or quality of work based on sex differences. The quality of the women's art work was equally high.
>
> The quality of the women's intensity and commitment to art, however, is not nearly as strong. The men in their interviews make statements like "If I couldn't paint, I would rather die," or "If I couldn't sculpt, I would cement myself into a wall."
>
> Nowhere in any part of the interview do any of the women make such statements. When the question was asked, *How important is your art work to your life as a whole?,* the men answered with ". . . It *is* my life"; ". . . I believe art is the only thing I was born for"; or ". . . I couldn't do anything else. Without painting I couldn't function." . . . Only one woman said her work was "essential" to her life. The rest answered like this:
>
> ". . . It's pretty important."
> ". . . It's half my life, the other half is my future family."
> ". . . I'm not sure yet, but I like it."
> ". . . It's helpful but not an absolute."
> ". . . It's most important right now, maybe when I have my baby that will be another source of growth."
>
> Nowhere in the women's interviews could we find any indication of the passion with which the men approach their work. Some of the men speak of the canvas, colors, and cameras as if they were alive. "My photography isn't separated from my life. The two things aren't separated at all. They can't be." Some see their work as themselves. "I am my work." And for some, their work is an encounter with a lover or a deity.

". . . My painting is the only thing that gives me a real happiness, real ecstasy."

". . . Painting is a love for me. I cannot live if I don't love my old lady [girlfriend] and my painting."

". . . I've passed out painting sometimes, I get so stoned with my work."

". . . Painting to me is like praying."

Such statements reveal a very high degree of motivation and dedication in the men students, a dedication that is just not expressed by women art students. . . .

What becomes of these students? Who will continue? Perhaps it is not surprising that in recent years none of the women graduates of the Art Institute has gone on to have a one-person show. We are still a long way from giving any definitive answers that might explain why the women seem to be less intense in their motivation to become an artist. A contributing reason might be that in this society artistic pursuits are considered feminine. These men have had to overcome the negative associations and the financial strains of being an artist. After all, what could be further from the American ideal than a son who wants to be a painter— unless it is a son who wants to be a ballet dancer? Then, too, many of the women probably will marry and have children, making their creative energies unavailable for work as an artist.

SOURCE: Barron, *Artists in the Making* (New York: Seminar Press, 1972), pp. 34–37.

The traditional humanist—philosopher or classical scholar or essayist—examines the human condition in its broadest aspects. So does the humanistic psychologist. The rigorously objective scientist, who insists on precise facts observed under well-controlled conditions, often has to plead ignorance about the causes of behavior in natural settings. Questions that puzzle the scientist must nevertheless be faced by educators. The humanistic psychologist works in the tradition of the natural sciences. He offers relective answers based chiefly on naturalistic observation. Instead of setting up controlled conditions to get data, he capitalizes on biographical studies, on anthropological studies of whole cultures, on interviews that examine the sources of a person's life style, and even on his own introspections. From these he gains impressions of the broad sweep of individual development; his studies allow him to interpret the individual in a social context. The humanist does not claim to be dispassionate. He is sensitive to the role of value judgments in education and to the values that enter into his own conclusions.

There is in humanistic psychology a romantic strain that values self-expression and deprecates social controls and restrictions. Humanists are likely to echo D. H. Lawrence on "the first great purpose of Democracy: that each man shall be spontaneously himself—each man himself, each woman herself, without any question of equality or inequality entering in at all; and that no man shall try to determine the being of any other man, or of any other woman" (1950, p. 93). This implies that "behavioral objectives" are useful only insofar as the individual is helped to achieve *his or her* goals. Cherishing pluralism, the humanist insists that the goals of education can only be the goals of the individual. Whether one student has achieved "more" than another is, for the humanist, a meaningless question.

Sometimes the emphasis on self-determination in writings on alternative forms of education has suggested that the self can do no wrong. Some of the popular writers on education seem to favor casting students adrift on a chartless sea of permissiveness, but the humanistic psychologist does not. The humanist has strong views about the good life and the good society. He is prepared to judge that some people use freedom badly and some use it well. He is prepared to praise those who develop rounded selves and to condemn others who remain pinched and colorless. While unwilling to "mold" students, he is by no means without standards for judging educational systems by their results.

The behaviorist-humanist dialectic is alive in the minds of most educational psychologists. Research performed under controlled conditions provides firm conclusions about a limited problem. But if "a man never steps twice into the same river," a teacher never steps twice into the same classroom (Cronbach, 1975a). Hence the behaviorist's firm conclusions may or may not fit the ever-changing classroom. The humanist's pronouncements are not limited to specific conditions; a certain vagueness, however, limits their use as guides to everyday decisions.

THE COGNITIVE-DEVELOPMENTAL STYLE   In writing this book I take an intermediate position. I need to discuss interpretations and feelings, so I do not restrict myself as the orthodox behaviorist does. On the other hand, I focus on evidence more than is usual in writings of a humanistic cast. I shall incorporate provocative ideas from writers such as Erikson, Mead, and Friedenberg, but as their personal interpretations rather than as scientific conclusions.

My own view can be described as cognitive-developmental. The first of these terms stresses the *active intellectual* functioning of the person. The second stresses that behavior develops in a *cumulative* fashion. Past history counts as much as present circumstances in explaining behavior. Today's event reverberates out into the person's future.

Cognitive-developmental psychology is not dominated by a few big names. The tradition goes back to the work of John Dewey and Evelyn Dewey as experimental educators and to the child-study movement of G. Stanley Hall. It links up with such current lines of work as the psychology of information processing (Newell & Simon, 1972) and ego psychology (Coelho et al., 1974). It

*(text continues on p. 30)*

# Can training substitute for aptitude?

A portion of the research program of James Greeno and his colleagues illustrates one kind of experiment undertaken by cognitive-developmental psychologists. In the initial study in a series, Greeno's group taught college students the theory and formula for solving problems in binomial probability. They found that the best teaching sequence depended on how much the student already knew (Egan & Greeno, 1973).

A later study (Mayer et al., 1975) varied the student's "background" experimentally and measured the effect of this pretraining on later learning. Students who already knew a lot about probability were excluded from the study. There were four pretraining conditions. As a baseline condition, no pretraining of any kind was given. Students in the second condition memorized formulas, with no explanation. A third group was pretrained on concepts; they read a booklet about binomial probability, but were given no computational procedures. In the fourth group, both formulas and concepts were provided.

After pretraining, students worked through a series of task cards designed to teach them to solve problems in binomial probability. Each problem had eleven subtasks. If the student gave the wrong answer at any step he was shown the correct answer and the correct procedure, before he went on. The investigators noted how many problems the student had to work through before he mastered a step. The student might catch on to one subtask quickly and have trouble with another, even after going through ten problems. Each step required a computation or the use of a concept. Performance during this learning stage is shown in Fig. i. Students who received no pretraining (the topmost bar) made more errors during learning than those who had received pretraining. The groups with pretraining on formulas had little trouble with computational steps, whether or not they had any idea of what the formulas were about. Pretraining on concepts reduced the number of conceptual errors during learning, but it did not help in ap-

**Figure i**
**Errors made during learning**

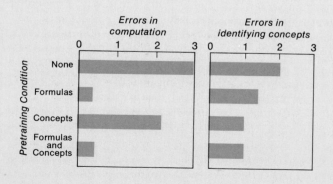

plying the ideas. The students with both kinds of pretraining made the fewest errors *during learning.*

After learning was finished, another test was given. Some of the items required only substitution of numbers into formulas and calculations; others were cast as "story problems."

There was little difference among the groups in performance on the formula problems of the posttest (Fig. ii). The groups pretrained on basic concepts did best on the story problems; they transferred their learning. The students who had grown dependent on memorized formulas could not think through the questions about probability in a new setting.

Putting the whole series of studies together, the authors made this final statement (their p. 350):

> It could be argued that students with low aptitudes should be given instruction emphasizing algorithmic computation, since their overall scores on posttests will probably be higher if that is done. However, the fact that relevant aptitudes appear to involve relatively specific knowledge and skills argues that subjects lacking the necessary background can probably be provided with that background and then given instruction that leads to understanding as well as skillful performance. . . . If students are taught by a method that leaves minimal understanding . . . , then their conceptual preparation for later learning will be more deficient than it was previously. . . .
>
> Subjects whose pretraining involved memorizing a formula, with no attention to its meaning, acquired problem-solving skill rather easily but were considerably deficient in understanding of that material when compared to subjects with different preparation and to subjects with no preparation at all. We take this as evidence that subjects' background experience can seriously affect their perceptions of what new instruction is about and therefore affects subjects' organization of new material.

**Figure ii**
**Success on final test**

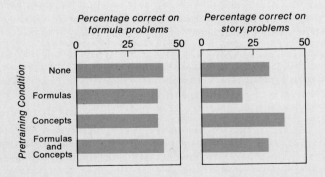

# Philosophical views of psychologists

The following questionnaire items paraphrase or reverse statements made by John Dewey. Dewey, who was a psychologist and the director of an experimental school before he made philosophy his chief life-work, would be classified among cognitive-developmental psychologists. B. B. Brown (1968, p. 126), who developed the questionnaire, obtained responses to Dewey's statements from behaviorist B. F. Skinner and eminent humanistic psychologist Carl Rogers. See if you can guess how Skinner and Rogers responded, and what Dewey originally said. Use + for "I believe this," — for "I don't believe this," 0 for "no belief" or "uncertain."

| Skinner | Rogers | Dewey | |
|---------|--------|-------|---|
| —— | —— | —— | 1. Man's destiny is determined by circumstances of nature which are beyond his control. |
| —— | —— | —— | 2. The value of knowledge lies in its use in the future, in what it can be made to do. |
| —— | —— | —— | 3. Whatever is carried on under the dictates of authority for some disconnected purpose limits intelligence. |
| —— | —— | —— | 4. Practice is subordinate to knowledge; merely a means to it. |
| —— | —— | —— | 5. The mind is a group of "contents" which come from having certain materials presented to it from without. |

(Answers on p. 33.)

views the person as engaged continually in transactions with the world, sensing problems and opportunities, creating solutions, acting to reach personal goals.

Educators think of the cognitive and the affective as quite different aspects of experience. The former refers to understanding, interpretation, and intellectual analysis; its root is a Latin verb the dictionary translates as "become acquainted with." "Affective" (accent the first syllable) is associated with affection—that is, with preferences, interests, and positive feelings. (By extension, it applies to negative feelings as well.) Although the terms do provide distinctive emphases, the contrast is not to be taken seriously; most experiences have both intellectual and emotional elements.

Most writers regard the self-concept as a central aspect of emotional development; but note the word "concept"—it is a signal that we are talking about interpretations. As the person "becomes acquainted with" himself, his views form a system of interrelated ideas about what he can do and about how others regard him. These ideas are loaded with emotion. Emotions are reactions that arise in coping with difficulties or challenges; they are not habits or states of mind.

Alfred Binet or Jean Piaget observes 4-, 6-, and 12-year-olds stringing beads to match a model. They thus learn how thought processes change as the child faces harder tasks. Nancy Bayley or Jean Macfarlane tests the same group of subjects periodically from age 2 to age 40, and learns whether they maintain over that period the ranking in stature or verbal ability or emotionality from early years.

It is not enough to describe changes from one age to another. Development is not the unfolding of a predetermined human nature. Behavior and attitudes evolve in part through encounters with the world; hence the developmental psychologist compares persons living in different conditions. Like the humanist, he is concerned with "natural," uncontrolled conditions. He cannot assemble groups at will. For his studies he has to classify children in terms of social-class background or the parents' style of child rearing. Then he can compare children who have had roughly similar experience.

The cognitive-developmental psychologist employs standardized conditions, under which he can make the observations that permit age-to-age or group-to-group comparisons. Precisely the same laboratory experiment on learning may be carried out, for example, on learners of different ages or different aptitudes. As in Greeno's program of work (box, p. 28), such comparisons precede an attempt to change aptitude.

The cognitive psychologist's interpretation often goes beyond the description of behavior to the underlying mental process. He tries to infer, from the errors made, what is going on in the learner's head. When he speaks of *attention*, for example, he refers to a mental process, not just to the behavioral evidence of eye movements. Encoding, self-criticism, and identification are other inferred mental processes. Concern with internal process is the hallmark of the cognitive-developmental style.

There is a danger in trying to merge contrasting approaches. It may seem at times that the text wobbles without direction from behaviorism to mysticism. When a behavioristic treatment seems appropriate, that will be the style here; when interpretation is needed and the evidence is diffuse, the style will be that of the essayist. This text tries to give a comprehensive account of teaching and learning in the classroom—an account that has room for values and purpose, but one that looks continually for evidence on which to base planning and action.

---

**6** How would behaviorists as a group treat each of the following statements? Would they endorse it, reject it, or have no particular opinion?
- a. It makes little sense to talk of "character"; we ought to be talking about a particular act, such as making contributions to charity.
- b. A speech teacher working with shy adolescents ought to concern himself with identifying purposes that speech serves in their lives and with improving their images of themselves.

c. The proper function of the school is to develop competence; the school should not concern itself with the person's goals and values.

d. The teacher can do a much better job if he knows a good deal about his students' backgrounds and their lives outside of school.

e. The proper question to ask in evaluating instruction is: Was the lesson mastered?

7 How would humanistic psychologists, as a group, treat each of the statements in Question 6?

8 How would cognitive-developmental psychologists, as a group, treat each of the statements in Question 6?

9 Could a humanistic psychologist investigate reinforcement? How would his studies differ from those of the behaviorist?

10 If a behaviorist or a cognitive-developmental psychologist were to study art students, could he investigate their motivation to produce art? What kind of investigation would these psychologists be likely to make?

11 Greeno's study (box, p. 28) was carried out in a short period. In what sense can one say that his research has a developmental aspect?

12 In an educational psychology course, what might be an affective change that the instructor wants to produce in students? Is the change truly one in feelings only, or does it also call for cognitive change?

13 A short title and a description of papers written by psychologists are given below. Where does each fall on a spectrum of psychological styles ranging from behavioristic through cognitive-developmental to humanistic?

a. "Growth of the idea of law in adolescence." Thirty persons at each of several ages from 11 to 18 were asked to describe the government that would be needed in setting up a community on a desert island. Interviewers found that, among other differences, older children placed less stress on the restrictive use of law and greater stress on positive aims (Adelson et al., 1969).

b. "The learning of sharing behavior." Children in a private nursery school and in a residential center for neglected children were given cards with pictures of animals, to be arranged on paper and then colored. One child, specially trained as the experimenter's confederate, worked alongside the child being tested. The experimenter hinted that it would be good to share so that each child could have different kinds of cards. There were two training sessions in which praise was given for sharing; in order to provide a model, the confederate shared and was lavishly praised. All the nursery-school children displayed sharing in a final test; only two-thirds of the other group did (Doland & Adelberg, 1967).

c. "Learning to be free." According to a psychotherapist's records of therapeutic dialogues, the client moves from fearing his inner feelings to a frank recognition of his impulses and values. He moves from a perception of himself as driven by others to a perception of himself as responsible. The increased sense of freedom is threatening; this ambivalence is illustrated by a quotation from one of the case records. The kinds of attitudes and statements on the part of the therapist that facilitate these changes in clients are identified. Ways to produce these same conditions in the classroom in order to facilitate the development of autonomy are suggested (Rogers, 1963).

d. "Reading failure and peer-group status." Seventy-five boys living in a tenement area were interviewed, usually in group sessions where several friends talked about their social lives and values. The school provided a record of the boys' performance on a reading test; it was seen that boys who belonged to street groups were consistently below the average of nonmembers. The conflict between the value system of the school and that of the street (toughness, boldness, social uses of verbal skill) is pointed out. It is suggested that a young male adult who resides in the area be made a part of the school staff as a "cultural intermediary" (Labov & Robins, 1969).

---

Answers to the B. B. Brown questionnaire, p. 30.

|     | Skinner | Rogers | Dewey |
|-----|---------|--------|-------|
| 1.  | +       | −      | −     |
| 2.  | +       | −      | +     |
| 3.  | −       | +      | +     |
| 4.  | −       | +      | −     |
| 5.  | *       | −      | −     |

Note that Dewey's views overlap at points with the behaviorist on the one hand (in a concern for practical accomplishment) and with the humanist on the other (in a concern for autonomy). The cognitive-developmental outlook does allow integration of somewhat conflicting outlooks.

* Skinner made a notation to this effect: "I might accept the point if worded differently."

READING LIST

Carl Bereiter, "A Nonpsychological Approach to Early Compensatory Education," in *Social Class, Race, and Psychological Development,* ed. M. Deutsch, I. Katz, and A. R. Jensen (New York: Holt, Rinehart and Winston, 1968), pp. 337–46.

> Bereiter discusses behavioristic techniques he has used for teaching significant intellectual skills to children with impoverished backgrounds and poor language development. The discussion shows how a research worker can attack a practical problem even when basic theory is confused and unsettled. Despite his title, Bereiter is acting as a psychologist both in his planning and in his evaluation of his procedures. For a critical reaction to Bereiter's ideas, see, in the same volume, pp. 368–72.

Committee on Reading, National Academy of Education, "The Reading Problem" and "A Diagnosis of the National Reading Problem," portions of "Report of the Committee," in *Toward A Literate Society: A Report,* ed. John B. Carroll and Jeanne S. Chall (New York: McGraw-Hill, 1975), pp. 3–27.

> Appraises the American reading problem, discussing where research findings suggest how to improve school programs. The portions selected offer case studies to illustrate the range of student problems and show the practical questions that can be illuminated by formal research.

Robert Glaser, "Educational Psychology and Education," *American Psychologist* 28 (1973), 557–66.

> Educational psychologists "can help create and preserve an experimental mood in education whereby scientists, educators, curriculum designers, teachers, parents, and students feel that they have a direct part in decisions to improve the schools." Glaser points to problems of curriculum and instruction where psychological analysis and field-testing of proposed solutions can be helpful.

William James, "Psychology and the Teaching Art," in *Talks to Teachers on Psychology* (New York: Holt, 1901), pp. 1–14. Excerpted in Torrance and White (see below).

> These pages introduce the first presentation of educational psychology in the American scientific tradition. Compare James's aspirations for educational psychology with those stated in Chapter 1 here.

Lawrence Kohlberg and Rochelle Mayer, "Development as the Aim of Education," *Harvard Educational Review* 42 (1972), 449–96.

> Espouses a progressive education that aims to arrange conditions for active personal development, finding fault with proposals from humanists and behaviorists.

Abraham Maslow, "What Is a Taoist Teacher?" in *Facts and Feelings in the Classroom,* ed. L. J. Rubin (New York: Walker, 1973), pp. 150–67.

> A statement by a leading humanistic psychologist, written shortly before his death, describing his ideal of an education that would facilitate personal and emotional growth. Not all teachers can adopt the requisite "let-be" attitude; growth in the teacher is a first requirement, Maslow says.

B. F. Skinner, "Contingency Management in the Classroom," *Education* 36 (1970), 93–100.

> Contrasts the ideas out of which behaviorism arose with both traditional and prevailing views of education. Describes specific applications of the principle of "contingent reinforcement" in maintaining a businesslike classroom atmosphere and in organizing programmed instruction.

E. Paul Torrance, "The Risk of Being a Great Teacher," in *Issues and Advances in Psychology,* 2nd ed., E. P. Torrance and W. F. White, eds. (Itasca, Ill.: Peacock, 1975), pp. 452–61.

> To be a great teacher, says Torrance, is to perform miracles—but every day, teachers here and there perform such miracles. He illustrates how teachers have helped students change from failures to successes—sometimes through warmth, sometimes through psychological insight, and sometimes through designing imaginative, unconventional lessons.

# WHAT SCHOOLS ARE TRYING TO ACCOMPLISH

Before studying *how* people learn and what can be done to help them learn more, let us discuss *what* they should learn. How to teach and how to judge effectiveness depends upon the outcomes sought. This chapter analyzes, from the perspective of the social sciences, the contribution education makes or could make to the development of the student, and offers a broad list of desirable outcomes. The fundamental question here is, "What must people learn in order to function well in our society?"

An example will illustrate the value of a broad perspective. One student of educational psychology visited a high-school English class to observe teaching procedures and returned with a critical report. "They weren't working on English. Instead of having lessons on sentence structure and things like that, they were sitting with their chairs in a circle listening to reports and talking about them. There didn't seem to be anything they were trying to learn, and I don't see how the teacher thought she was teaching English! That's why students get into the University without knowing how to write." This student reacted with so harsh an opinion because he did not recognize that the teacher had aims beyond improvement of sentence structure.

When the educational psychology students considered carefully what was going on in this high-school session, they found many possible purposes behind the activities. Each activity had a definite aim, as outlined below:

| ACTIVITY | INTENDED OUTCOME |
|---|---|
| The students prepared the reports. | That they learn (one might hope) to use the library, to select material from reference books, and to select topics worthy of emphasis. |
| The students gave the reports and answered questions. When the speaker mumbled or spoke too fast, students who could not follow him requested a repetition. The teacher commented on the organization of the reports. | That they learn to speak to an audience and use good diction and delivery; that they practice thinking on their feet and learn to outline content in a clear, logical fashion. |
| The students reported on feudal England, with much discussion of knightly tradition and courtly love. | That the students learn enough about the scene to understand Chaucer's stories, which they were to take up next; that they develop some interest in the period and learn the source of traditions about manners and romantic love that affect their lives; that they use discussion to clarify their feelings about standards set for men and women in our own day. |
| The students raised questions, discussed the meaning of unclear points, and contributed additional information. | That they learn to examine disagreements and reach conclusions, to think for themselves, and to voice their opinions with confidence. |

At the end of this analysis, the student had changed his view. "Use of the library is certainly something high-school students need to learn, and English classes ought to teach them how to speak and to prepare reports. Studying about the feudal era before reading the stories sounds good too. But I still think that some time—perhaps on other days or later in the year—should be spent on grammar." One could accept this, with the caution that not all formal grammar lessons are profitable.

The function of this chapter is to broaden your conception of the tasks of the school. The theme of the chapter—and of much of the book—is voiced in a famous statement by John Dewey (1938):

Perhaps the greatest of all pedagogical fallacies is the notion that a person learns only what he is studying at the time. Collateral learning in the way of formation of enduring attitudes, of likes and dislikes, may be and often is much more important than the spelling lesson or lesson in geography or history that is learned. For these attitudes are fundamentally what count in the future. The most important thing that can be formed is the desire to go on learning.

What Dewey wrote decades ago is by no means outdated. Bloom (1974, p. 46) says almost the same thing: Alongside the explicit curriculum of school-subject content is an implicit curriculum that "teaches each student who he is in relation to others. . . . [and] his place in the world of people, of ideas and of activities."

Some writings on open education—inspired by a humanistic outlook—reverse the matter, arguing that the *center* of the curriculum is the affective outcomes, that the lessons are mere vehicles for developing resourcefulness, critical thinking, communication skills, and so on (D. Miles, 1975). Collateral

**Collateral learning**

## FIGURE 2.1

**Responses of fifth-graders who had worked in a traditional and in an "open" classroom**

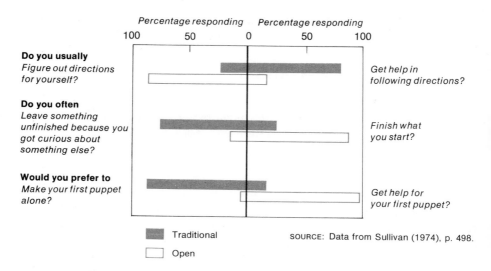

SOURCE: Data from Sullivan (1974), p. 498.

outcomes depend on the style of teaching as well as on the curriculum. Sullivan observed and questioned fifth-graders in two suburban schools. One group had worked throughout the year in a traditional classroom with workbooks and assigned textbooks, seats in rows, and every subject assigned its regular segment of the school day. The "open" classroom used independent projects, group work, flexible schedules, teacher-student planning, and varied materials. The two groups developed markedly different work attitudes, as Fig. 2.1 shows. Asked to write a story, 97 per cent in the traditional class wrote on a factual topic, whereas 88 per cent in the untraditional class wrote a fictional story. As to vividness of writing, the group taught untraditionally outscored the others two to one. Furthermore, they showed themselves at ease when a group of college students visited as observers, whereas the traditional class was shy and hesitant. Generalization is not warranted; traditional styles and "open" classes vary in the techniques used and the effects that result. This report tells us only that two teachers working with similar groups of students shaped the students differently.

1 Bloom identifies the "implicit curriculum" with the affective outcomes of schooling—that is with changes in feelings and attitudes. For Dewey, is collateral learning affective, or does it also include some gains in understanding and skill?

2　Members of a fifth-grade class interview persons who have resided in their community for thirty years, and compile information on what the community was like in former times. What, besides these facts, can the students learn from this activity?

3　Does "collateral learning" take place in professional training—say, in a college course in mechanical engineering or accounting?

# SCHOOLING AS A PART OF SOCIALIZATION

## The Socializing Process

The process of preparing a person for membership in a society is called socialization. Every group of people, whether on the tiniest island of the Pacific or in a modern city, has some plan for changing human raw material into whatever type of adult is needed to make its society run. Human behavior varies from one society to another, being determined by the society's religion, its ideas about proper treatment of other people, its economic system, and its accumulated knowledge. Sometimes children are socialized largely by the parents, as they were on the American frontier. Boys and girls on the frontier acquired knowledge by helping around the homestead and in the hunting field, and at the same time acquired character traits appropriate for that self-reliant life. A more complex society uses more formal institutions to accomplish socialization. In the United States the school is one of the chief agencies of socialization. Inkeles (1969, pp. 615ff.) offers a definition:

> Socialization refers to the process whereby individuals acquire the personal system properties—the knowledge, skills, attitudes, values, needs and motivations, cognitive, affective, and conative [striving] patterns—which shape their adaptation to the physical and sociocultural setting in which they live. The critical test of the success of the socialization process lies in the ability of the individual to perform well in the statuses—that is, to play the roles—in which he may later find himself.

The word "later" in the last sentence can be misinterpreted. People sometimes speak of education as "preparation for life." But educating and socializing activities *are* life. They start at birth and continue all through life. Each activity adds to the richness of living and to the person's fulfillment here and now; if it does not, something is awry in the culture. The activity also does its bit to prepare the person for the opportunities to come—tomorrow, next year, and for years to come.

Although elders arrange for socialization of the young, the process flows in both directions. It has been often noted that in immigrant families the parents are guided by their quickly adapting children. Mead (1970) suggests that, because of today's rapid changes, the young have a special role of inducting the elders of the family into the coming culture. It is most often the young who first stock the fridge with yogurt, put biodegradable detergents on the shopping list, and bring home someone of another race as a guest. And any experienced teacher of adolescents knows that they do about as much to shape the teacher's behavior as the teacher does to shape theirs. Arrow (1974) points to a similar process in industry and business management; it is the recruit fresh out of college who causes the firm to recognize that its techniques and policies are outdated.

The tradition-dominated society introduces the new member to clearly foreseen duties and ceremonies. Everyone knows his or her place. In the modern world, to quote Inkeles (1969, p. 617) again:

> There is no specification as to exactly how many "actors" there are, and their "parts" are only vaguely defined. Indeed there may be no fixed script at all. The play may have never been put on quite in this form before, so that the interplay of the actors is uncertain and difficult. . . . New parts are being added all the time, and old ones cut out. No one is too firmly assigned to any given part, and the actors often improvise their roles as they go along.

Under such circumstances, both socializers and socialized have difficulty in choosing courses of action they will later judge to have been wise. The tribal elders can do little more than help younger people think through the goals in life to which their age group is committing itself. New cultural goals, however, emerge out of the traditions of the society; indeed, the strongest note in many youthful protests is the charge that the practices of today's society do not adequately serve its long-professed ideals. This commitment to ideals is itself a much-desired outcome of socialization.

**4** Is "socialization" the same as "citizenship education"?

**5** Professor Travis is a scholar whose translations of Greek poetry are famous. He is shy, uneasy when he must attend a social gathering or make a public appearance, and so formal and undramatic that undergraduate students avoid his classes. He has never married and spends most of his time happily at work on manuscripts in the library or in discussions with his graduate students. Is it correct to speak of Professor Travis as having been "socialized"?

## The School as Socializing Agency

The responsibility for socialization is shared by many institutions: the home, the church, employers, mass media, and so on. All these agencies promote ideas, skills, and attitudes that help a person function in his culture.

The school can be conceived narrowly as the main dispenser of knowledge and widely useful skills. For instance, everyone should know the system of numerical symbols. The school therefore is asked to teach arithmetic and, more broadly, quantitative thinking. The school is likewise the place where people can acquire an organized conception of the world through geography, science, and history. Significant though this "narrow" responsibility is, a more critical responsibility is to promote socially constructive conduct and attitudes, and to teach the problem-solving skills that aid in reaching social goals and remedying social ills. In these areas the educator supplements the efforts of other socializers. The educator is the one socializer formally under the control of the community, and so is asked to promote those views that the vocal elements in the community favor. The educator is often charged with counteracting the influence of other socializers. If the home teaches religious or racial intolerance, the public school is expected to offset this by teaching tolerance. The school is charged with inspiring socially favored kinds of ambition, community pride, esthetic values, rational handling of conflict, and so on.

To shape young people as the community desires may be to transmit what is outdated or narrow-minded. Holt, Friedenberg, and similar critics suggest that the American educators and student bodies have belittled the values and traditions of Mexican, Chinese, and American Indian elements of the community (see also p. 50). Other critics have blamed the schools for teaching nationalistic attitudes or for glorifying a technological, centralized system when young citizens ought to be challenging its excesses.

Schools do teach beliefs that depart significantly from the common denominator of the community. The young person is attracted—by his instructors and by his roommate's bookshelf—to better literature than his parents typically read. The school introduces children of America Firsters to international perspectives and subdues the historic parochial antipathies: farmer for city dweller, westerner for easterner, and old stock for newcomer. Over the centuries, educators have often had a conscious aim to teach a critical attitude toward society.

Schools even set out to train persons for the role of reformers or agents of change. The missionary, the efficiency expert, the journalist, and the applied social scientist have all been taught that it is a virtue to "shake things up." As an agent of the community, however, the school cannot move much faster than do the groups that hold power in its community, and thus it will always disappoint those who advocate rapid social change.

Educational aims ought, I think, to be derived from the answers to two questions:

- What must a person know to be an effective part of the society or of the better society that education could promote?

- Which of these types of learning can be better attained through the school than through any other agency?

---

**6** The educator is asked to promote the kind of socialization the community mainstream favors. Is this in conflict with the ideal of academic freedom?

**7** Which of the following do you think are being taught adequately by the home and other out-of-school agencies?
   a. Homemaking and parenting
   b. Automobile driving
   c. Recreational skills and interests

**8** What aspects of American life would you examine to determine whether a good job was done by each of the following in the past generation?
   a. The mathematics curriculum
   b. The music curriculum
   c. The vocational agriculture curriculum
   d. Career-guidance activities
   e. The education of lawyers
   f. The teaching of effective spoken language

---

The following pages describe the person who may be considered well socialized in a modern Western culture. I will argue that such a person:

- Solves problems as well as the available facts permit.

- Has some absorbing goals, interests, and sources of satisfaction.

- Is effective in dealing with others, and helps them to lead satisfying lives.

- Has self-respect and warranted self-confidence.

- Wants his actions to be praiseworthy, but examines values critically before conforming to them.

These five qualities do not operate independently. Skill in solving problems, for example, leads to nothing unless the choice of problems is sensible. Moreover, one quality contributes to another: interests to self-respect, self-confidence to problem solving, and so on. This general ideal leaves plenty of room for a person to find his own style and function in life. But an American adult who does not satisfy these requirements is an incomplete and handicapped person.

---

**9** To which aims of socialization can each of the following contribute?
    a. A study of the solar system in Grade VII
    b. Little League baseball
    c. Individual music lessons

**10** To what extent do you think the five qualities listed here ought to be encouraged in
    a. residents of villages in a developing country?
    b. prospective leaders and technicians in a socialist country?

---

## Competence in Solving Problems

Tomorrow's adult will have to cope with events no one foresees today. For example, many workers will fill jobs that did not exist when they were in school. Choices unknown to the last generation will confront tomorrow's citizen as a consequence of inventions, the growth and decay of cities, and shifting social priorities. In such a world each person must find answers for himself, as citizen, parent, and consumer.

**TABLE 2.1**

Attention to social problems in social studies textbooks

| Topical area | Percentage of paragraphs devoted to area | | Percentage of those paragraphs referring to conflict | |
|---|---|---|---|---|
| | Grade III texts | Grade IX texts | Grade III texts | Grade IX texts |
| Distribution of income, goods, and services | 7 | 17 | 8 | 5 |
| Political negotiations and processes | 2 | 24 | 49 | 3 |
| Race and ethnic relations | 4 | 3 | 14 | 15 |
| Ecological practices | 5 | 2 | 49 | 0.3 |

SOURCE: Data from Hess (1974), p. 289.

It has been argued by Hess (1973) that schools and other social machinery do a poor job of promoting thinking about political and social problems. If social mechanisms are working well, Hess says, the system need only persuade the young to accept the practices of adults. That is how American political socialization operates. It builds emotional attachment to the symbols of nationalism and authority long before the child has any intellectual understanding of them. The more conceptual training comes too late and is subtly biased to conceal problems the system faces. Hess and Fox classified paragraphs from prominent social-studies textbooks for Grades III and IX. Table 2.1 gives their findings on two questions: How much attention was given to four social issues? and When a controversial topic came up, was conflict acknowledged? (For example, a reference to the success of a Japanese shopkeeper might or might not mention that, for members of minorities, securing opportunity has been and is a problem.)

The four social issues were barely hinted at in Grade III. In Grade IX, the topics received attention, but with only passing hints that they are areas of current conflict. A conflict, when mentioned, was often pictured as one that had already been largely overcome. Regarding only a minority of conflicts did the texts suggest a need for hard thought and negotiation.

For unforeseeable problems the school can offer neither solutions nor systematic procedures guaranteed to achieve solutions. Yet it must somehow produce a person who is alert to identify problems, able to reduce them to resolvable questions, able to locate and make sense of pertinent information, able to cast off habit and prejudice.

Problem solving calls for emotional resources. A humane identification with other persons enables one to step outside one's own selfish interest. Security in interpersonal relations is needed before one feels free to assert oneself and try out novel ideas.

## Goals and Interests

Living should be more than vegetating. A satisfying life is one in which goals are pursued and reached, and one in which opportunities for diverse experience are seized. The school can prepare the person not merely to be effective but to enjoy being effective. It can give him the skills and knowledge that allow him to find work and play that are personally satisfying. It can make him aware of the higher purposes that can be served by professional work, by community action, or by sensitivity to the needs of the people he deals with. It can help him take pride in craftsmanship, and pleasure in self-expression.

Likewise, schooling enriches his life as a consumer. It opens his eyes to the arts, to the intricacies he can observe in nature, and to the subtleties of personality. Knowledge and skill enable him to glean more satisfaction from travel, from current events, boating, gardening, or whatever he turns his leisure to.

## Effective Relations with Others

Social interaction is a learned skill. One learns to communicate, to sense the reactions of others, to plan group tasks, to hold one's own in the face of opposition. The person who is effective in interpersonal relations trusts and respects
other people. He thinks that they have a will to do good and that their reasoning will be as good as his if they have all the facts. Skill in working with others
rests on a foundation of emotional security, on ability to interpret the behavior
of associates, and on concern for the welfare of the group.

## Confidence and Self-Respect

The person who aims low or who gives up at the first difficulty is handicapped.
For him, accepting failure is less unpleasant than continuing to try. If he felt
that he would satisfy his wants by persisting, he would consider the effort
worth making.

The school and home can make a person confident that his efforts will
bring him to his goals, and confident that if sometimes he tries and fails he will
not be scolded or ridiculed. Respect for one's own capabilities develops continuously. Through successful performance, the school beginner learns that he can
succeed at reading; at the same time, he builds faith that he can cope with academic tasks generally.

It is normal to try things one cannot finish. That experience is still educative; one wins partial successes and, at worst, one learns how to face difficulty.
What breaks the spirit is not the instance of failure, but criticism that generates
a sense of unworthiness. Adults who discourage a child's initiative may "keep
him out of trouble," but they thereby cramp his style. One who dares not take
chances does not become an autonomous, responsible person.

## Acceptance of Social Values

The choices of a thoughtful person hinge on his values. One set of values familiar in the United States emphasizes ambition, civic responsibility, and respect for truth. But some segments of society place other values first. Some of
the competing systems are based on pleasure: "Have fun while you can." Some
are based on spiritual values; kindness is placed above cleverness, and inner
peace above achievement.

Values determine what problems one thinks about and what solutions one
accepts. Someone who shares values with other persons receives and gives respect, and can resolve disagreements rationally. A group without shared values
disintegrates as members pull in different directions.

Psychopaths, some criminals, and some delinquents become rebels and live
by a code of "every man for himself." Others who outwardly conform may secretly wish to violate various standards of behavior. A person who does not be-

lieve in the values he publicly conforms to must deceive others and perhaps himself. Neurotic disorders arise out of just such internal conflicts.

The socialized person adopts the value system of his group, but this does not mean that he cannot challenge it. The successful reformer usually shares many of the traditional values of the community. Because he respects others in the community and shares many of their commitments, he can stand behind proposals that would be heresy if put forward by an outsider.

The goal of socialization is not a uniform set of attitudes imposed on all. The American ideal is that people who consider religion, for example, the key to life will live alongside those who have no religious convictions, each respecting the other. Fundamentally, *each person must do what he thinks is right, and must be willing to defend his position to his group.*

Even in the midst of pluralism, in a time when majority values are changing, the school can usefully teach certain basic values such as consideration for others, trustworthiness, and rationality in argument. The school can make a student more aware of his own values and of how those values are influenced by others. This allows for diversity. Students will develop their own priorities among the values the culture accepts. These choices may reflect their home backgrounds, the model their friends set, or the kinds of success they experience.

---

**11** Amish parents wished to withdraw their children from the community high school because they feared that the school would undermine allegiance to their traditional ways. The Supreme Court ruled that to give up two years of compulsory schooling—on the grounds of religious freedom—did not sacrifice any compelling community interest. This case represents a conflict between the parents' view of what the child should become and the model offered by the larger community. Is it possible for a child to choose for himself whether he will live in his home community (where religious values are strong) or to move into a less isolated, more materialistic world? If your answer is "Yes," at what age should a child be given this latitude?

**12** The founder of behavioristic psychology, John Watson (1928, pp. 186–187), summarized his aims in socialization as follows:

> We have tried to sketch . . . a child as free as possible of sensitivities to people and one who, almost from birth, is relatively independent of the family situation. Above all, we have tried to create a problem-solving child. We believe that a problem-solving technique . . . plus boundless absorption in activity . . . have worked in many civilizations of the past and . . . will work equally well in . . . the future.

    a. What sort of school program would be consistent with Watson's goals? What sort would he criticize?

    b. Some would argue that Watson was seeking to prepare the child for a world that no longer exists. What do you think?

*(questions continue on p. 51)*

## Should the schools be committed to a traditional "Anglo-American" ethic?

Nicholas Hobbs speaks for a study group commissioned by the United States government to review policies and practices affecting exceptional children. (See Chapter 9 in this book.) His group challenges the viewpoint that identifies the exceptional or deviant child by traditional standards. He first mentions Herbert Spencer's influence on American thought—in particular the concept of "survival of the fittest" with its implication that the unfit could survive only as objects of charity. He goes on:

> Certain religious codes also served to justify and shape some of the basic attitudes and behavior patterns of the Protestant majority. Early New England was largely a Puritan society, and the doctrine of predestination had a powerful and pervasive influence (Erikson, 1966). According to this doctrine, salvation is a gift of God and not a result of the deeds of man. God's chosen ones are inspired to attain to positions of wealth and power through the rational and efficient use of their time and energy, through their willingness to control distracting impulses and to delay gratification in the service of productivity, and through their thriftiness and ambition. The elect could be identified by their success and social position and the damned by their lowly circumstances. The rich and established were obviously (the argument went) virtuous and favored by God; the poor and disenfranchised were obviously sinful and morally deficient. Poverty and dependency were looked upon as disgraceful, and relief measures were viewed as encouraging weakness of character. Economic self-sufficiency, which came to be equated with success and virtue, became a primary societal goal for the individual. . . .
>
> What can be said, then, about what it means to be "normal" or "acceptable" in our culture? First, it seems to mean that one is prepared to participate, in an independent fashion, in one specific cultural milieu, what has been referred to as the "Anglo-American mainstream". . . . The norm is essentially a monocultural one. The "rules whose infractions constitute deviance" have been made largely by a single group, the custodians of the Protestant, Anglo-Saxon culture. Within the framework of the monocultural rules, the following characteristics can be identified as normal, good, and acceptable:
>
> 1. to be rational
> 2. to be efficient in the use of one's time and energy
> 3. to control distracting impulses and to delay gratification in the service of productivity
> 4. to value work over play
> 5. to be thrifty
> 6. to be economically and socially successful and ambitious
> 7. to be independent and self-reliant
> 8. to be physically whole, healthy, and attractive
> 9. to be white
> 10. to be native-born
> 11. to be Protestant
> 12. to be intellectually superior
> 13. to inhibit aggressive and sexual behaviors except in specially defined situations
> 14. to be fluent in American English

SOURCE: Hobbs (1975a), pp. 24, 25, and 28–29. Format altered.

13 At what point does the Hobbs list of "monocultural rules" (box) differ from the characteristics of the socialized person emphasized in this chapter? (Consider omissions as well as inclusions.)

14 The Hobbs list is said to reflect an Anglo-American, Protestant view. What alternative views would you expect to find in other cultures? (Consider both developed and underdeveloped, Asian and Latin countries.)

15 The Hobbs panel is obviously critical of this set of standards. Disregarding Items 9–11, how do you think they would justify the view that this list does *not* describe a "normal, good, acceptable" pattern for members of a minority in the United States who will interact with the English-speaking community?

## AUTONOMY AS A CRUCIAL VALUE

Among all the aspects of a philosophy of life, the one given greatest attention in recent psychology and sociology has to do with independence. Each research group has its own jargon, and much the same ideas turn up in findings on "autonomy," "the achievement ethic," "sense of efficacy," "internal control," "responsibility," "future orientation," and so on. Each phrase refers to a slightly different set of questions about behavior or feelings.

Mead (p. 52) contrasts orientations toward the past (tradition), toward the present (hedonism), and toward the future (achievement) as a source of gratification. Tradition does not loom large in American affairs, but the other two philosophies are strongly represented.

Many a person who finds life hard and pleasures few will seize the present moment because he does not expect tomorrow to be better. He will not invest in making his future better. Feeling that unpredictable outside forces—"fate"—dominate one's life spawns passivity. An autonomous person, in contrast, believes that *he* controls his fate, that he earns his own rewards and misfortunes. The sense of autonomy or efficacy has much in common with the so-called Protestant ethic, but the attitude is equally significant in Japan, in some Catholic countries, and in modern Russia. Douvan and Adelson (1966, pp. 331ff.) did find contrasts, however, in the predominant attitudes among United States Protestant and Catholic adolescents of the same social class.

In a developing country moving from an agricultural economy toward industrialization many traditional attitudes interfere with learning and productivity. Sociologists and anthropologists speak of "modern" attitudes held by the

## Conflicting values among teachers

Mead (1951) notes three "types" of value system and personal style among American teachers:

The "child-nurse," who helps the learner to be himself and enjoy his present activities.

The "parent," who works for success and wants to prepare the child to succeed in the uncharted future.

The "grandparent," whose memories run far back and who enjoys bringing children to appreciate their traditions.

This classification is an analogy from Mead's observations in other cultures. In some Indian tribes children are reared chiefly by grandparents. Samoans leave children in the charge of older sisters. The "efficient, profit-seeking" fishermen of the South Pacific Admiralty Islands are the socializers, keeping the children beside them as they do their own tasks.

As Mead sees it, the teacher of the "child-nurse" type—typically, a female—finds her satisfaction in sharing the child's joy. Anything that makes school life less pleasant to the child, she too finds unacceptable. She fulfills her own needs by participating in the group's episodic, entertaining, unsystematic, uncriticized activities. The teacher of the "parent" type has found satisfaction and prestige in moving ahead and meeting new challenges. This teacher expresses his or her own motivations when preaching progress and ambition. The students are

> ... to acquire habits of hygiene and of industry, to apply themselves diligently to prepare to succeed, and to make the sacrifices necessary to success, to turn a deaf ear to the immediate impulse, to shatter any tradition which seems to block the path to the goal, but to shatter it . . . [as an] entrepreneur.

Finally, Mead characterizes the teacher who serves as does the grandparent in the Indian tribes. This teacher, who has found stability and pleasure in the arts and traditions, stresses the immutable past. This teacher cares little about whether or not the material is "useful" in solving practical problems.

> The gifted teacher of the classics conveys to the child a sense of the roundedness and relatedness of life, of the way in which each period repeats in its own way an old story that has already been written in a more gracious and finished way in the past. Any budding desire to explore the new, to make new conquests, can be gently, benignly reduced to the expected, by a reference to Diogenes or to Alexander.

persons who are making the transition successfully. Schools, industrial-training programs, newspapers, and speeches by public men try to transmit these new values so that the talents of the people can be brought into use. The new values conflict with traditional emphases on rituals, on luck, on family cohesion, and on following in one's father's or mother's footsteps, as the Inkeles-Smith questionnaire (p. 54) suggests. Members of a society change their thinking as the society's institutions take modern form. Individuals who cling to the older values have fewer opportunities and may become an underprivileged, "backward" segment of the nation. In Nigeria, Argentina, Israel, and other countries, a straight-line relationship is found: with more education, more acceptance of the modern attitude (Inkeles & Smith, 1974).

Precisely the same conflict of traditional attitudes with the requirements of a productive nation is found in an advanced nation as it tries to bring all its segments equally into the mainstream. Reasonable mastery of schoolwork is needed if a person is to become employable; moreover, mastery gives the person a sense of competence. The achievement level reached by an American student body seems to depend at least as much on the students' sense of efficacy as on expenditure per student, racial integration, family background, or even interest in schoolwork. This was the finding of Coleman's national survey *Equality of Educational Opportunity* (J. S. Coleman et al., 1966). Among both whites and blacks, superior school achievement went with a stronger sense of efficacy.

In schools where achievement is high, the students tend to respond "No" to these statements from a "sense of efficacy" questionnaire:

---

**Good luck is more important than hard work for success.**

**Every time I try to get ahead, something or somebody stops me.**

**People like me don't have a very good chance to be successful in life.**

---

A slum child who feels that things are stacked against him very likely sees his world as it really is; some part of his response reflects unpleasant facts. But some part reflects a discouragement out of proportion to the facts. (See also pp. 221 and 607.)

According to Coleman, belief in personal efficacy is contagious. And so is the opposite—resigned submission to fate. A student body whose majority is committed to autonomy and achievement nurtures self-reliance and striving in individuals who would remain passive in another social environment. Defeatism and fatalism are less common among black students who are in fully integrated schools. Blacks seem to have, on the average, a poorer impression of their own ability when in a school with a white majority. Even so, black achievement tends (other things being equal) to be at its best in schools where the majority of students are white. Katz (1968, p. 65) sums up the finding: "A modest self-concept is not detrimental to Negro academic performance, provided children can depend upon the environment to dispense rewards in a fair and equitable way"—that is to say, so long as they learn that achievement *is* rewarding.

BEHAVIOR OF MEN MOTIVATED TO ACHIEVE   Persons with strong achievement motivation or a strong sense of efficacy respond differently from others to the incentives offered in school and in work. Those high in such variables probably can be expected to achieve more. The solid research findings come almost entirely from males, however. For reasons that are little more than speculative at present (p. 609) and that may be changing rapidly in American society, findings on this motive in females are weak and inconsistent.

The usual measure of motivation to achieve (often labeled "need for achievement" and abbreviated nAch) is obtained by asking the person to make up a story, telling what might be happening in a picture. Men with strong nAch tell stories of challenge and triumph over obstacles. Men with strong affiliative needs make up stories about friendly, mutually supportive interactions. Kelly et al. (1973) had college freshmen work in pairs to assemble Tinkertoy rockets. The researchers established three experimental groups: cooperative, individual, and competitive. In the cooperative condition, a 50-cent reward was given to both team members if their total output reached a team standard. In the second condition, a person could get the reward by meeting a one-person standard—both men in the pair could gain the reward, or neither, or just one. On the competitive teams, the reward went to the student who produced more

## FIGURE 2.2

Response, under three motivational conditions,
of men high and low in motivation to achieve

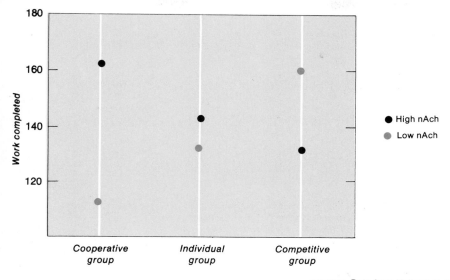

SOURCE: Data from Kelly et al. (1973).

than his partner. The results (Fig. 2.2) show that men with strong achievement motivation responded best in a cooperative setting, whereas men with low achievement motivation did their best in the competitive condition. This finding helps dispel the mistaken notion that motivation to achieve is synonymous with motivation to beat out others. Kelly et al. collected no data on affiliation motivation.

Elizabeth French (1958) showed that the reward has to fit with the personality to be fully effective. She assigned men to two types of teams. Some teams were made up of men selected to be high in nAch and weak in affiliative motivation. Others were made up of men with the reverse pattern. (No study was made of men high on both or low on both.) French had each team arrange phrases and sentences provided by the experimenter to make a sensible story. Each of twenty phrases was written on a card, and each man was handed five of the cards. The men could reconstruct the story only by effective communication. Halfway through the task, French interrupted to praise the teams. Half of them she praised for working efficiently. She drew attention to things they had been doing that reflected intelligent organization (for example, using grammatical cues to fit sentences together). She praised the other half of the teams for their friendly spirit. The teams then went back to work. The final story was judged for completeness and correctness. The average scores, for eight groups

## FIGURE 2.3

Response to praise as a function of personal motivation

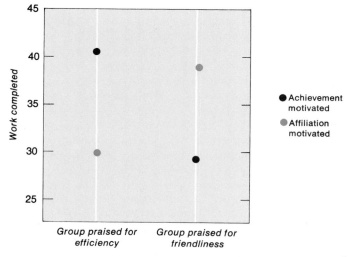

● Achievement motivated

● Affiliation motivated

SOURCE: E. French (1958).

of each type, are shown in Fig. 2.3. The men with achievement motivation were obviously impatient when told how fine their social conduct was, but they listened keenly when the investigator talked about their efficiency. And the men who valued affiliation worked better after being told that they were in a friendly group! Praise improves performance most when it speaks to the values of the individual.

SCHOOL POLICY   As we shall see in later chapters, schools modify motivation. The school should not shape those with a predisposition toward achievement into efficiency experts, nor should it foster only the social skills of the affiliation-minded. The school has to balance between respecting the student's personal style and pushing him toward maximum effectiveness as a member of society. The democratic society loses vitality when a block of its members suppress ideas for the sake of harmony. Educators can properly aspire to fire the enthusiasm of young people for what they can accomplish in life.

16   Some psychologists classify persons by whether their gratification lies in reflecting on the past, in living for the present, or in visualizing what they can attain in the future. Relate these orientations to Mead's types, and to the modernity scale of Inkeles and Smith.

17   Can one be autonomous—in responsible command of one's own fate—and not be motivated to achieve?

18  Closely associated with a sense of efficacy is a willingness to work for future rewards, to postpone gratification. Could one have an achieving society without this willingness among the people?

19  Many critics decry the quality of life in contemporary, industrialized America. To be consistent must that critic reject the values described as "modern" by Smith and Inkeles?

# MAKING EDUCATIONAL AIMS CLEAR AND EXPLICIT

Purposes of education are often stated in general language—for example: "to develop literacy," "to promote good character," "to increase sensitivity to beauty in nature and in man-made objects." Our stated aims of socialization have been equally broad. Such statements, helpful to start discussion, are inadequate for planning or evaluating instruction. Everyone can read his own preferences into a general statement, leaving disagreements hidden and unresolved.

Even an apparently tangible outcome such as literacy can be given many interpretations. Some educators expect only that graduates will be able to gain the plain sense of everyday communications. Others would ask for full understanding of a communication (together with its emotional overtones) and ability to criticize its logic. The less ambitious educator stresses mechanics; the more ambitious educator sees reading as an active interchange between reader's mind and author's thought.

Ambiguities are even greater when we turn to goals related to life style. For example, what is "good character"? That the term has more than one meaning is dramatically illustrated by Bronfenbrenner (1970). The Soviet home and school push the young person to work for the welfare of the groups to which he belongs; the primary good is loyalty to and service through the collective. One of the models presented to schoolchildren is Pavlik Morozov, a boy who denounced his father to a court when the father violated government agricultural regulations. We need not look so far as Russia for a contrast. Within the same American community, parents who agree that "the school should develop character" are likely to disagree on what is really desired.

One might describe what a school is trying to do in terms of the "offerings": by saying, for example, that the ninth-grade program includes English, world history, general science, and physical education, plus one of several electives. But this communicates next to nothing. The English course may devote its time to written expression or to literature. If the latter, the literature may be *Canterbury Tales, Lord of the Flies,* or science fiction. One communicates more by describing class activities, as on p. 38. The intended outcomes still remain to be inferred.

The merit of an educational program lies in its outcomes. If students taught *the teacher's* interpretation do not learn how to interpret literature for themselves, the teacher has shortchanged them. If students are encouraged to make their own varied interpretations of an author's intent, yet end the course believing that each interpretation is as good as every other, again their teacher has failed.

Some identify the goals of the school with the outcomes represented by tasks in nationally distributed standard tests, but the educator ought not to let the test define what he is to teach. Published tests lag behind the curriculum. They embody aims accepted for a long time by most schools, underemphasizing many modern aims. Thus, standard tests in science give only limited attention to inquiry skills, and few put as much weight on ecology as today's lessons do. The only way an educator can keep his target in view is to state the full range of outcomes he is aiming toward, whether they appear in a test or not.

It is natural for teachers to employ general phrases—"Susan understands how the number system is organized" or "is able to appreciate and criticize an author's viewpoint." Aims stated abstractly are adequate for some purposes: the first phrase does imply a concern for going beyond adept computation. Still, it is not clear *what* Susan learned.

In any systematic effort to improve instruction by research and development, the psychologist presses the educator to identify the kind of behavior that is consistent with his broad aims. When a psychologist evaluates a program, he relies in large part on behavior observed after a period of instruction. So he has to know what to observe.

"Behavioral objectives" can profitably be used in planning instruction also, if the educator chooses a form of objective that fits the program. We shall describe two forms of objective. The first, fostered particularly by behaviorists, calls for detailed lists of specific outcomes. The cognitive-developmental style of behavioral objective is more open, but it too asks that intended outcomes be put in a form that leaves little ambiguity.

## How the Behaviorist Formulates Training Objectives

A behavioristic definition of an objective has two elements; it identifies a kind of situation likely to be encountered, and it describes the desired response. Consider teaching a child to bat a ball. What the batter is to learn has to be spelled out before the training plan can cover it fully and before anyone can verify that the training works. The "situation" consists of one or another pitch the player is likely to encounter. The "response" may be described in terms of the result: "Will knock the ball out of the infield $x$ per cent of the time." Or it may be described in terms of actions: "Will shift weight to the forward foot as he swings." Objectives differ with the stage of learning. At first the coach may

## Micro-objectives, behaviorist style

a. Given the context "The _____ flower is pretty," the child can provide an adjective or adjectival phrase.[1] (The child is not to learn the word *adjective*.)

b. The child recognizes the structural spelling pattern of the double consonant—*latter, totter*, etc. vs. *later, toter*)—and can successfully read words containing it.[1]

c. The student will solve any problem of the form $3 + 4 = \square$ with sums under 11, using a set of problem-solving operations.[2]

d. The student will write a story of ten sentences or more about a field trip.[2]

e. At the end of the school year, the preschool student will be able to accomplish a two-footed jump—beginning with both feet parallel, using the arms for forward thrust, and landing with both feet together.[3]

f. Upon completion of a six-week training session, the student will have improved his grip strength by at least five pounds as measured by a dynamometer.[3]

g. Given a drawing of the interior of the human torso, the student can correctly identify the vital organs.[4]

h. The student indicates that he would feel confident if he were hired to do a job requiring considerable use of the arithmetic he has studied in school.[4]

SOURCES: [1]Ball & Bogatz (1973). [2]Becker et al. (1975). [3]Harrow (1972). [4]Scannell & Tracy (1975).

---

be concerned only with the response to straight, soft pitches. As the batter becomes more expert, the coach wants him to react in specific ways to hard, soft, fast, and slow pitches.

Sometimes the person designing instruction can foresee fairly exactly the situations in which the student will use what he learns, and can specify what the student should do. Such instruction I refer to as "training." In preparing an apprentice worker for a specific job as assembler, for example, the instructor knows precisely what the duties will be. Skills such as typewriting or handwriting or conjugating the French verb *être* can be defined sharply for school purposes.

A training program is improved by analyzing act by act, judgment by judgment, just what the trained person should be able to do, and then planning exercises, correction procedures, and so on to teach the discriminations and acts needed in the performance. Psychologists working on military-training problems have effectively used this kind of task analysis to guide design of training equipment such as flight simulators. When psychologists turned to educational research after World War II, they found similar planning useful in programmed instruction and computer-guided instruction. The educational technologists usually have adopted the behaviorist position, concerning themselves with observable acts rather than mental processes and feelings.

The behaviorist generally takes the following approach in preparing a list of objectives:

- The content or skill to be mastered is broken down into specific acts or verbal associations.

- The class of situations is defined narrowly, so that one response serves for all the situations in the class.

- A particular response or class of responses is defined as correct or desirable.

- A standard of adequate performance is stated (for example, "When the pitch is straight and soft, and the batter swings, the bat will drive the ball forward 90 per cent of the time." Or ". . . will drive the ball past the infield 90 per cent of the time"). The first standard is suitable for a beginner. Once that standard is met, the second standard becomes the next target.

- The situations mentioned in the objectives are quite similar to those encountered in the lessons.

- The list of objectives, as a whole, attempts to include all of the outcomes the body of instruction is intended to produce.

## Behavioristic objectives for several kinds of learning

On p. 94 I will introduce Gagné's system for classifying kinds of learning. Gagné and Briggs (1974, p. 85) recommend that teachers use behavioral objectives in designing curricula and evaluating results, and show how behavioral statements can be offered for each major type of instructional outcome. Gagné's list of "types of learning" (Table 3.1, p. 95) matches only approximately the set of categories shown below, since complex performance may combine several types of learning.

| | Verb | Example |
|---|---|---|
| **Intellectual Skill** | | |
| Discrimination | DISCRIMINATES | discriminates, by matching, the French sounds of "u" and "ou" |
| Concrete Concept | IDENTIFIES | identifies, by naming, the root, leaf, and stem of representative plants |
| Defined Concept | CLASSIFIES | classifies, by using a definition, the concept "family" |
| Rule | DEMONSTRATES | demonstrates, by solving verbally stated examples, the addition of positive and negative numbers |
| Higher-order Rule (Problem-Solving) | GENERATES | generates, by synthesizing applicable rules, a paragraph describing a person's actions in a situation of fear |
| Cognitive Strategy | ORIGINATES | originates a solution to the reduction of air pollution, by applying model of gaseous diffusion |
| Information | STATES | states orally the major issues in the Presidential campaign of 1932 |
| Motor Skill | EXECUTES | executes backing a car into driveway |
| Attitude | CHOOSES | chooses playing golf as a leisure activity |

SOURCE: *Principles of Instructional Design* by Robert M. Gagné and Lester J. Briggs. Copyright © 1974 by Holt, Rinehart and Winston, Inc. Reprinted by permission of Holt, Rinehart and Winston.

One may state intended outcomes for a course or for a unit within the course, or even for a 15-minute fragment of instructional material (for example, what is to be learned from a single-concept film loop). Some writers state objectives in the behaviorist style for the whole school program (that is, listing all that the graduate should be able to do). To do this, one has to omit important kinds of development or fall back on generalized statements.

The behaviorist favors making a verb the key element in the goal statement: "recall," "paraphrase," and so on. The verb usually does make for definiteness, as is seen in the Gagné-Briggs examples (box). If the student is told that an objective for the unit is "to be able to give three examples of 'diminishing returns'," he knows how to prepare himself and can test his own mastery.

In listing intended outcomes at the course level, the educator is wise to describe a standard of overall proficiency rather than the component acts the instructor will take as day-to-day objectives. The instructor of a course in typing, for example, is likely to state that after $x$ months of instruction he wants the learner to type forty words per minute, with not more than two errors per hundred words. This instructor will have such subordinate objectives as "His hands will come to rest with the little finger of the left hand over the A key."

Psychologists frequently organize objectives into *hierarchies*, putting at the lower levels the subobjectives that contribute to the whole task. Gagné in particular has demonstrated the usefulness of hierarchical analysis in mathematical tasks such as the calculation of binomial probabilities. Greeno's teaching materials (p. 28) were organized on the basis of such a breakdown of the performance and learning sequence. A comparatively simple hierarchy of objectives developed by Barbara Hollingsworth for skill in tennis is shown in Fig. 2.4. As you can see, six of the seven second-tier objectives remain to be expanded. And each lowest-tier objective describes a task that can be further analyzed. There is no point in descending to trivial detail, but it is not trivial to recognize that "stand properly" contains at least two elements: locating the correct place relative to baseline and center line, and positioning feet appropriately. Such a

**FIGURE 2.4**

Portion of a hierarchy of objectives in playing tennis

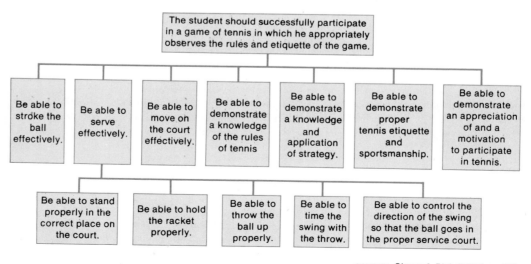

SOURCE: Singer & Dick (1974), p. 326.

hierarchy may mistakenly suggest that the beginner must master the first-tier acts before he can perform at the next higher level. Just how to divide effort between higher tasks ("wholes") and subordinate objectives will receive attention in Chapter 10. There is no simple answer.

TYPICAL RESPONSE DISTINGUISHED FROM ABILITY    To develop an ability is only a beginning. There is no merit in teaching a child how to write legibly if in the end he scrawls all his papers except the penmanship exercises. The first purpose of training is to develop ability to act in a particular way. The second is often to make the ability "second nature," so that the student uses the ability with ease when a situation calls for it. The person who states an objective—in the behaviorist style or any other—ought to be clear whether he is after a "can do" or a "will do" performance. Some objectives stress ability: "When directed to do so, the student can correct errors of spelling and grammar in a simple business letter." Some objectives emphasize what the person is expected to do—that is, what his typical behavior is to be. For example: "Whenever the student writes a simple business letter, he will, on his own, correct any errors of spelling and grammar." The difference is not trivial. If the student can produce an error-free letter for the teacher to mark, this shows only that the ability objective has been reached. The behaviorist's set of objectives do often include typical behavior: desired work practices, attention habits, and so on. Also, he may list acts he wants to discourage.

It is convenient to speak of typical responses as "habits," but the educator rarely wants an invariant response. The educator hopes that the student will make a response appropriate to the situation. Not many educators would want the student to use formal sentence structure all the time. Rather, the student should choose a degree of formality appropriate to the situation. Only in the loosest sense could one ask that the student "make a habit" of reading Shakespeare with enjoyment; but the educator will be interested in increasing the frequency with which the student does this. The question of what is typical then becomes: When an occasion for this response arises, what is the probability that this person will respond in the manner suggested?

The category of typical behavior includes affective outcomes (p. 30). What the student tells us may or may not be evidence of his true feelings, so the behaviorist prefers to state affective outcomes in terms of observable performance. When the educator says that he wants the student to "value" reading, the behaviorist looks for actions that indicate a positive attitude. Hence, instead of using the vague word "value," he may list the following as behavioral indicators (for about Grade IV):

Will fairly often turn to the bookshelf for reading matter when he has free time.

When asked about a book he has read, will indicate parts he particularly enjoyed and state why.

When in need of information, will often search in books for it or ask for suggestions of suitable material.

**20** Compare the objectives in the box on p. 59 with the features of the behavioristic style described on p. 60. Where one of the features is not specified, can the missing information be inferred from the statement? If not, is the statement unacceptably ambiguous?

**21** The ideal for an objective in the behavioristic style is a statement so unambiguous that if two testers were to decide independently whether each student has attained the objective, their yes-or-no reports on any student would agree. How close do the objectives listed by Gagné and Briggs come to this ideal?

**22** Restate the objective "Will be able to read simple music" in a form that satisfies the ideal stated in Question 21. Consider a level of skill appropriate for introductory instruction at age 6–7, and assume that the children have experience in playing familiar tunes on a xylophone.

**23** Is it possible to express, in terms of one or more behavioral objectives, the aim: "To increase sensitivity to beauty in nature"?

**24** Elaborate the hierarchy in Fig. 2.4 with respect to
    a. "Stroke the ball effectively."
    b. "Knowledge of the rules." (Make this more behavioral!)

**25** In Fig. 2.4, the objective regarding etiquette and sportsmanship was stated in "can do" form (p. 63). Restate it as a typical-behavior objective. Does it make any difference which of these two objectives teacher and student have in mind?

## The Cognitive-Developmental Style for Stating Objectives

Developmental objectives are less precise, broader, and more concerned with transfer than most behavioristic objectives. Instead of listing acts or habits to be acquired, the educator can state how he would like the learner to function after a period of instruction. The developmental psychologist, instead of thinking, for example, about the specific lessons in arithmetic the student will take up this year, emphasizes his gradual progress in general mathematical understanding and proficiency.

TRANSFER OBJECTIVES   When experience in one situation enables a person to cope with a novel situation later, we say that his learning from the first setting has *transferred*. A student of French is to learn to express himself in everyday situations. This is a vague statement, but there is no way to list all those occasions for transfer from the lessons. Without trying to list all the situations as a behaviorist would, one can specify the objective by illustrating suitable levels of accomplishment: If asked for directions, the learner will give them with sufficient clarity for a 12-year-old French child to follow. Or ... will be able to carry out transactions such as renting an automobile. Descriptions such as these are clear, yet do not catalog the phrases the person is to have at his command. Students saying different things could complete the car-renting transaction. Though no ideal response is specified, one can judge that the objective has been attained.

Traditional school subjects can, at their best, develop abilities that apply widely. Thus, much of the recent curriculum reform in mathematics has been intended to develop insight into the nature of mathematics and skill in mathematical analysis (Kohl, 1974). The "base-5 arithmetic" of the new math has no *direct* use; it is introduced in order to promote mathematical imagination and insight. It is hoped that the graduates of a modern program will not only be able to compute but will have some ability to analyze any information that has

## Transfer

*"Okay, Joey ... put in your penny an' we'll get off one at a time so Margaret can figger out how much we weigh."*

"Dennis the Menace" used courtesy of Hank Ketcham and © 1975 by Field Newspaper Syndicate, T.M.

mathematical regularity. Likewise, the teaching of literature is supposed to develop broadly useful techniques and attitudes. The class that comes to understand and enjoy *The Merchant of Venice* has gained something. That immediate objective is far less significant, however, than the transfer objective of a richer response to all manner of good literature.

Transfer is not confined within subject-matter lines. It is reasonable to hope that the study of literature, for example, will contribute to an understanding of all the arts, and to an understanding of human relationships. Effects of instruction that transcend subject-matter boundaries are especially significant. A work attitude that catches errors in the making, social attitudes such as respect for other persons and for other nationalities—these and many similar attainments are the by-products of instruction that had other daily and monthly objectives. These by-products are what Dewey referred to as "collateral learning." Such inner processes cannot be fully identified with behavior, though their existence can be inferred from what the person does and says.

"Education of the whole person" can easily become a hollow slogan, but the phrase can remind us that behavior depends on much more than the acquisition of ideas. Even the college that has thought of education as purely intellectual will fail in its purposes unless it concerns itself with typical behavior and personality. As Nevitt Sanford (1962, pp. 36–37) emphasizes:

> One could say that education . . . has as its sole object the inculcation of skills and knowledge respecting civilization, society, and culture. . . . [But] students may learn a great deal without changing their personalities in any important way. . . . A person might put great resources of academic learning into the service of his need to exhibit himself and to score points at the expense of the less well tutored. . . . The difference between the uneducated anti-Semite and the educated one would be that the former might engage in overt actions against the Jews while the latter could invent clever remarks in parlor discussions, or perhaps write learned essays on why the Jews "get themselves into so much trouble." In short, the person who is educated in the narrow sense of this word has been given a set of terms in which to carry out his functions as a personality; if he is immature or psychopathic he may now display these characteristics in an educated way.

BREADTH OF THE STATED OBJECTIVES    The educator who thinks in developmental terms can make clear the kinds of responses he is concerned with and the standards by which they are to be judged, even when he cannot specify them in detail. He takes more or less this approach in his statement of objectives for a lesson or course:

- A few broad, important outcomes (often four to seven) for a course or program are listed. Each outcome describes a kind of competence ("Can interpret scientific data") or attitude ("Is interested in understanding natural phenomena") or typical behavior pattern.

- For each objective, situations are identified in which one can observe whether the student acts in the manner the objective calls for.

## Objectives for social development, ages 3–6

Burton White and Jean Carew Watts (1973, pp. 10ff.) proposed the following as reasonable objectives for early education. (They also offer a list of cognitive abilities, which I have not reproduced.) In the list below, the distinction between ability and typical response is not sharply maintained; one wants the child to develop the ability and also to use it as occasion arises.

   a. To get and maintain the attention of adults in socially acceptable ways.
   b. To use abilities as resources (making a request, making a demand, gesturing, pointing).
   c. To express both affection and hostility to adults.
   d. To assume control in peer-related activities (give suggestions, orient and direct, . . .). Also, . . . to follow the lead of peers.
   e. To express both affection and hostility to peers.
   f. To compete with peers.
   g. To praise oneself and/or show pride in one's accomplishments.
   h. To involve oneself in adult role-playing behaviors or to otherwise express the desire to grow up (for instance, to act out a typical adult activity).

- The characteristics of desirable responses are stated. (For example, a good interpretation of data agrees with the data, recognizes the inexactness of measurements, avoids unwarranted remarks about causation, and so on.) But the "correct response" need not be specified; judgment and personal values lead to legitimate diversity of response.

- Responses, arguments, actions, or conceptions are thought of as varying from crude and simplified to complex, subtle, and articulated. Hence the same *kind* of behavior is a developmental objective for many levels of schooling, with a new standard of performance expected at each level.

- The outcomes are cross-classified into broad categories of response and content. (For example, within the subject of biology, one is to interpret data about genetics, public health, evolution, and so on.) Not all the content will have been covered in the lessons.

- Each kind of behavioral outcome is illustrated for the sake of clarity, but no exhaustive listing of situations and responses is attempted.

Just how closely particular statements fit this form depends on the purpose of the communication. The science objectives (box, p. 68) were stated only briefly, concrete exercises to fit the objectives being worked out later.

The educator need not stick to one style of objective. A short list of rather broad objectives is best suited to general discussions of curriculum, particularly when members of the community are involved. A detailed list of micro-objectives is likely to be useful when designing details of instruction, particularly when the same instructional program will be refined and used repeatedly. The social philosopher will prefer to think in terms of broad, comparatively open objectives; the technologist will require performance specifications. Most subject-matter is part philosophy and part technology, and the teacher should speak each language as occasion arises.

**26**  Which of our "aims of socialization" (p. 45) could be restated as behavioral objectives?

**27**  There is a French proverb that runs something like this: "Education is what remains when you have forgotten the lessons you studied." What does the proverb imply regarding the aims the school should be concerned with? Can the view of the proverb be expressed in behavioral objectives?

**28**  We cited, as an objective in the behaviorist style, "To be able to give three examples of 'diminishing returns'." Will satisfactory performance show that the student's understanding is transferable? How could the objective be reworded to make it a transfer objective and not a recall objective?

**29**  How would a behaviorist react to the objectives suggested for humanistic education (box, p. 70)? Which would he consider reasonable kinds of goals? Which would he find acceptable in form of statement?

*(questions continue on p. 70)*

## II. UNDERSTAND AND APPLY THE FUNDAMENTAL ASPECTS OF SCIENCE IN A WIDE RANGE OF PROBLEM SITUATIONS

### C. Understand and apply conceptual schemes

1. Use available evidence in interpreting land features.

For example, makes inferences bearing on the age of the earth's crust from evidence seen in sedimentary layers exposed in a road cut.

Age 9     Understands that a particular rock has not always been in its present location and may not always be there; understands that upper layers were formed most recently.

Age 13    Understands that the layers of rock are of varying composition (sandstone, limestone, etc.); explains that the layers were deposited in a succession; explains that the layers may have been formed by different processes.

Age 17 and Adult    Interprets a sequence of events from the sequence of deposits or other geologic features; speculates about the relative ages of rocks (an intrusion is younger than layers intruded, folding would have occurred later than deposition of the folded layers, etc.).

SOURCE: National Assessment of Educational Progress (1972), pp. 25–26 and 32–33.

## Formal objectives to suit humanistic education

The humanistic educator, with his concern for the individual's self-direction, sometimes protests that it is wrong to "set objectives." To demonstrate that "open education" is also concerned with specifiable changes in the child, Rathbone (1972, p. 530) offers a list of "desired outcomes" that fit this philosophy:

> The child will take responsibility for his own decisions and actions.
> The child will be autonomous, acting and making decisions independently.
> The child will have the ability and desire to set his own goals.
> The child will possess self-discipline and will not need externally applied discipline.
> The child will learn self-direction as a basis for organizing his life; he will be self-actualizing.
> The child will have a capacity for long-term involvement at learning tasks of his own choosing.
> The child will possess a willingness to experiment; he will demonstrate an ability to seek new solutions and new problems.
> The child will have self-confidence.
> The child will exhibit trust in himself and others.
> The child will feel free; he will be socially and intellectually adaptable.
> The child will feel comfortable with and confident of his own learning processes.
> The child will be in touch with his own inner impulses; he will not fear fantasy or feeling.
> The child will value the ethic of open education.

**30** Consider the objective: "The child will exhibit trust in himself and others." Is it possible to put this in a more formal cognitive-developmental style by stating situations where the response can be observed, and stating characteristics of a desirable response?

**31** Prepare a few objectives for family-life education (Grade IX) in both the behavioristic and cognitive-developmental styles.

## THE SCHOOL AND SOCIAL OPPORTUNITY

The school has functions in society other than instruction. The college, for example, is seen by many as a place to make contacts useful in the business world. Formal education in the United States, some say, reflects a more-or-less conscious effort to hold young people off the labor market. Preschools thrive because parents need child-care services. In a book concerned primarily with instruction we need not say much about the school as a cog in the socio-economic wheel. But one social function—the regulation of social mobility—is so linked to psychological concepts and techniques as to deserve preliminary attention here. (See also Chapters 7–9.)

Teachers are rightly proud of their efforts to help young people rise in the world. Nearly every society is stratified to some degree. Some persons have greater power and higher standards of living. American society provides for considerable mobility: "poor boy to President" is a tradition rather than a myth. The school has been seen from the earliest days of this nation as the doorway to opportunity. The motive has been less a concern for social justice than a conviction that power should be placed in the hands of able and motivated persons. Thus Thomas Jefferson, as early as 1779, proposed for Virginia a scheme of state scholarships, awarded and renewed on the basis of careful examinations. These would enable a number of poor boys who performed excellently in school to continue through the university. Jefferson sought to replace an "aristocracy of wealth and birth" with a "natural aristocracy." For the young Lincoln with his law book before the cabin fire, and the young Hoover working his way through Stanford to become a mining engineer, learning was the gateway to a profession. The college became still more the path to prominence as corporations turned to colleges to fill junior-executive positions for which college studies had little direct relevance.

The school is a sorting agency. It has the power to raise some persons in each generation toward the top and to push others out into routine jobs and "common man" status. As Gardner (1961, p. 71) put it, "Who should go to college?" translates itself into "Who is going to manage the society?" The school record becomes a stamp of approval not just on intellectual performance but on the person as a whole.

The school fosters upward mobility by identifying able youngsters and encouraging them to prepare for an occupation higher than that of their parents. To some extent it also determines who will move downward; even well-to-do and influential parents can offer only limited advantages to the person who does not meet school requirements and so is discouraged. The education one achieves has some correspondence to that of one's parents.

The fact that a man's ranking within the occupational hierarchy corresponds only roughly to that of his father is evidence of considerable mobility. The strength of that relation for today's men is about what it was a generation or two back. The correlation coefficient (p. 134) is about 0.40. Even with the great extension of schooling, mobility of males is no greater than in 1900 (Blau & Duncan, 1967; Jencks & Riesman, 1968). No similar analysis of the smaller number of women in careers has been made.

The relation of schooling to men's occupational mobility is demonstrated in Fig. 2.5 (p. 72). Occupations were given scores representing their prestige; for example, the range 80–84 included college faculty members, electrical engineers, and pharmacists, while 60–64 included stenographers, real estate agents,

## FIGURE 2.5

### Relation of men's occupational mobility to amount of schooling

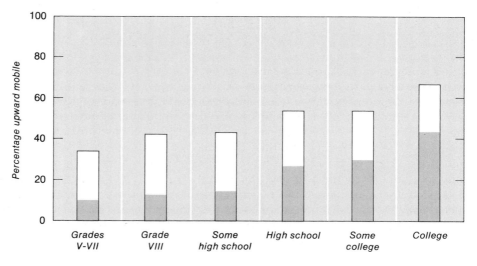

Shaded area represents percentage "mobile upward, long distance" (see text). Upward mobility is determined by comparing prestige ratings of father's and son's occupations.

SOURCE: Data from Blau & Duncan (1967), p. 499.

and photoengravers. A man's mobility was judged by comparing the score of his occupation with that of his father. A photoengraver's son who became a chemist would be counted as mobile upward, short distance; if he became a lawyer or judge he was mobile upward, long distance. The figure shows that upward mobility was far more common among those who completed more education—this even though the college group, tending to be from wealthier homes, had rather little room for upward movement. Young men whose fathers held low-status jobs typically left school early and took low-status jobs like those of their fathers. Those who started college but did not complete it had no more net mobility than high-school graduates. Evidently, college was unsatisfying to them; possibly, their entry into college reflected their parents' affluence and ambitions for them, not their own motivation.

The system of schooling that contributes to social stratification and selection is open to attack, and it unquestionably needs modification. The British sociologist Michael Young, in his mock history *The Rise of the Meritocracy, 1870–2033*, condemned the very ideal of "the progress of all through the leadership of the wisest and best," which was once cherished by progressives everywhere (Young, 1958).

## How open is the system?

Sociologists study social processes by a statistical technique known as path analysis. The findings represented in the figure below are from such a study and can be understood without going into technical detail. Each number alongside a straight line indicates—on the zero-to-one scale of correlation coefficients (see p. 134)—how much *direct* influence one factor has on a later variable. The numbers alongside curved lines indicate a relationship without suggesting causality.

Occupational level depends heavily on education, little on any other identified factor. Motivational factors such as interests are among the "other influences" that all together carry heavy weight. Education depends on ability, as we would expect. The two companion weights for parental characteristics indicate that, among young men of equal ability, the ones with family advantages stay in school longer. The figure of 0.8 for "other influences" is important. It tells us that who gets to stay in school is not primarily determined by ability, nor is it primarily determined by ability and family status combined. Who stays longest in school depends on financial resources other than the father's salary, and on a variety of motivational factors. Some influences, such as receiving special encouragement from a science teacher or the early death of the family breadwinner, have to be considered as "luck," good or bad.

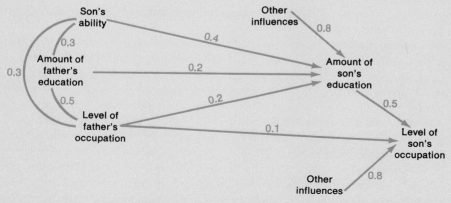

The numerals at the left are correlations, with ability measured by a general-ability test in late adolescence. The other numerals are standardized regression coefficients. Where coefficients were less than 0.1, lines were omitted.

SOURCE: Adapted from Duncan et al. (1972), p. 103.

The educator should think through his beliefs about the distribution of wealth and living standards, about the respect accorded persons playing different essential roles in the community, and about the equities involved in compensatory devices. (On special admission rules for subpopulations who have had poor opportunities, see Cronbach, 1976.)

School procedures that affect the flow of talent may not be dealing with the most important characteristics. Admission procedures may be entirely fair, or in some subtle way they may give an advantage to children from wealthier homes. Certifying examinations may truly identify students who are ready for professional responsibility, or may reward applicants who have crammed their heads with sterile book-learning.

As a specific example of the way educators' decisions favor one talent rather than another, consider the program in arithmetic. (See also pp. 300–03.) Some children find distasteful the traditional teaching that emphasizes following a model procedure perfectly. This training develops computational skills, but it repels children who dislike routine work—including the very ones most likely to become excellent mathematicians. The true mathematician (as distinguished from the bookkeeper and the surveyor) works intuitively rather than by rule; he grapples with a vague problem and imaginatively constructs plausible solutions (Polya, 1954). Arithmetic teaching that encourages the use of intuition may discover talent in some children who appear mediocre when taught conventionally.

Educational selection cannot be dispensed with. The problem is to be sure that, among those who apply for a certain kind of training, the selection is made fairly and reasonably. Psychologists have done much to develop selection procedures and have a special responsibility for making sure that such procedures are used properly.

When there is a direct relation between a school task and a job, then school performance is a proper basis for selection. A student who has trouble in spelling is likely to be a poor typist, so it is sensible to select good spellers to be trained as typists. Selection on the basis of a spelling test would be harder to justify if a remedial course could turn a poor speller into an adequate one. But in fact, a generalized weakness in spelling is not easy to remedy. Suppose we shift the example to the poor reader. A reading test would select students more likely to succeed. Reading usually does respond to an intensive remedial effort, especially where the deficiency is one of speed rather than of vocabulary or comprehension. If a poor reader wants to become a typist, the school could wisely help him qualify by offering him special work in reading.

 READING LIST

Richard C. Anderson and Gerald W. Faust, "Behavioral Objectives," in *Educational Psychology: The Science of Instruction and Learning* (New York: Dodd, Mead, 1973), pp. 13–56.

> This chapter gives the arguments for formal statement of objectives in a behavioristic form. It will be particularly helpful in showing how a curriculum can be regarded as a chain of objectives to be attained one by one.

H. S. Broudy, "Mastery," in *Language and Concepts in Education,* ed. B. O. Smith and Robert O. Ennis (Chicago: Rand McNally, 1961), pp. 72–84.

> A philosopher distinguishes types of knowledge and skill, and discusses how teachers should judge whether or not a pupil has a high degree of mastery of them.

Alex Inkeles, "Social Structure and Socialization," in *Handbook of Socialization Theory and Research,* ed. D. A. Goslin (Chicago: Rand McNally, 1969), pp. 615–32.

> A description, from the sociological and anthropological viewpoint, of the kinds of socialization that occur at different ages and in different cultures. According to Inkeles, what is taught depends on ecological, economic, and political aspects of the system; these shape both the goals of socializers and their practices.

David C. McClelland, "Testing for Competence Rather Than 'Intelligence'," *American Psychologist* 28 (1973), 1–14.

> An eminent psychologist protests that success in school is an arbitrary basis for limiting opportunity. In his view, success in school has little to do with excellence (or adequacy) of performance "in life," and academic excellence is conditioned more by family background than by any superiority in the person. McClelland proposes a radical change in policies for allocating educational opportunity.

Sylvia Scribner and Michael Cole, "Cognitive Consequences of Formal and Informal Schooling," *Science* 182 (1973), 553–59.

> Education in school differs from the informal transmission of culture found in homes and in traditional societies. Having observed and tested children and adults in many countries, Scribner and Cole report the consequences of each type of socialization. They find that formal methods lead to important gains in ability to think, through a learning-to-learn process. The formal methods, they say, are unlikely to serve poor and Third-World children unless the lessons are brought into closer contact with everyday reality.

George D. Spindler, *The Transmission of American Culture* (Cambridge: Harvard University Press, 1959), 51 pp.

> Each teacher expresses achievement values or affiliative values in his educational theory and practice. Spindler quotes from a well-motivated teacher whose identification with superior ability and achievement is so great that he is unable to be encouraging and sympathetic to children from poor Mexican-American families. The teacher's biases color even his remarks to students on the value of studying typewriting.

**THEMES**

■ Whether a response made during a learning episode is retained or abandoned depends on the consequences of the response. What happens in an episode depends first of all on the student's readiness: physical, intellectual, and motivational. Secondly, it depends on the situation: the physical surroundings, the social environment, and the work itself.

■ Having interpreted the situation, the student chooses a trial response. If the act brings the consequences he expected, the response is confirmed and it will probably be used in the future in similar situations.

☐ A single episode changes the person only a little, but development is the cumulation of these small changes. The student changes not only in knowledge of the lesson or the skill practiced but also in more general skill, beliefs, and feelings.

■ Learning refers to any relatively permanent change in behavior that results from experience. Psychologists classify learning into a number of types, ranging from simple interpretation of a signal to complex problem solving.

■ In planning and directing lessons, the teacher should arrange matters so that each activity in the learning cycle goes well. Considering the several elements helps in organizing curriculum materials, in taking individual differences into account, in arousing motivation, and in evaluating.

**CONCEPTS**

*readiness*            *provisional try*
*abilities*            *consequences*
*habits*               *feedback*
*attitudes*            *learning*
*traits / states*      *stimulus*
*interpretation*       *reinforcement*

# PROCESSES IN
# BEHAVIOR
# AND IN LEARNING

This chapter gives a concentrated description of classroom learning; the central ideas will be explained more fully throughout the book.

Teaching occurs in many places and in many styles. In a conventional classroom, of course. But also in a factory, a home, or a park. Television advertising and motion pictures teach. The student may be a 40-year-old preparing for a new career, or a 2-year-old. The subject-matter may be Israeli folk dancing, bricklaying, or computer programming. The teacher may be a paraprofessional, another student, or a computer terminal. The course of study may have every detail worked out in advance, or it may be improvised on the spot.

To identify the conditions that affect learning and the processes that go on during learning, the kaleidoscopic events of the classroom are divided into episodes. An episode is a brief, rather arbitrary interval during which a meaningful sequence of connected events takes place. An episode may be the lecturer's two-minute presentation of a single point, or the brief interchange when the teacher looks over the student's shoulder as he works. It may be the track star's practice run of a mile under her coach's eye, or a half-hour demonstration of setting up a loom. We focus in turn on the state of affairs at the beginning of an episode, the events that occur as it proceeds, and conditions at the end.

Later we shall be more concerned with the way the effects of successive experiences accumulate, perhaps over weeks or months, to change what the person does and is.

# INITIAL CONDITIONS OF A LEARNING EPISODE

At the beginning of the episode, we consider the readiness of the student for the opportunities to be offered, and the situation he is in.

## Characteristics That Make Up Readiness

What the student brings to the situation depends on his stable characteristics (traits) and his physical and mental state at the moment. Readiness refers to all the traits that contribute to success in a situation. Traits can be classified as abilities, habits, and concepts and attitudes. Abilities refer to skills and knowledge. Habits are responses or styles of response that the student typically employs in a certain situation. Concepts and attitudes include beliefs, feelings, and aims in life.

ABILITIES   Abilities encompass the entire repertoire of actions the student can perform. He knows certain facts, understands certain words, possesses certain skills, solves certain kinds of problems, and so on. He has abilities directly related to the subject-matter and he also has skills of learning from books, from laboratory work, and from vigorous classroom discussion. He can do far more than his behavior in the classroom usually reveals.

Both specific and general abilities are important. Memorizing a dozen middle-game strategies carries a chess player only a little way; he also needs to develop a general ability to think strategically. But specifics count too. During the day a student uses a host of specific abilities: tying a square knot, converting miles to kilometers, sewing a fine seam, locating Nicaragua on a map. No

---

**Characteristics of the person**

Traits
   Abilities
   Habits
   Concepts and attitudes
States
   Health
   Mood
   Arousal
   Mental set

amount of general verbal ability will enable the student to appreciate Gray's phrase "some mute, inglorious Milton" if he has never heard specifically of *Paradise Lost*.

HABITS    Ability refers to an action the student can take when he wishes. Habit refers to the kind of action the student is *likely* to take. The distinction is that made in Chapter 2 (p. 63) between customary or typical responses and available responses. Nothing more need be said here.

CONCEPTS AND ATTITUDES    I put attitudes and concepts together here, as both terms refer to beliefs and interpretations. In a class, each student is likely to have his own concept of the elements that enter into the lesson. He has a concept of reading, for example, as drudgery, a difficult task, one that offers few rewards—or as a pleasure, something he wants to do better, something he can master. We could similarly speak of his concept of the teacher, of authority, of the capitalistic system, or of the power and limits of the scientific method. Concepts shade over into attitudes, and no sharp distinction is required. The term *attitude* more often implies an emotionally loaded belief.

Particularly important are a person's beliefs about himself. From his early years, the growing child develops a concept of what he can do or is likely to do and of how others regard him. Some of his strengths he values, others he sees as of no importance. Shortcomings that loom large in one person's self-image cause another no pain: "I never could carry a tune!"

STATES    The temporary physical and psychological condition of the person may affect his readiness on a particular day or at a particular moment. Psychologists, for example, are thinking of a trait when they speak of "the anxious person"; but it is obvious that an individual is more anxious on some occasions than others, and therefore a distinction between *trait anxiety* and *state anxiety* is made (p. 211).

The effects of health, fatigue, and available energy on the student's schoolwork are obvious. His mood likewise conditions his readiness to put forth effort, to criticize himself, to take advantage of class discussion, and so on.

*Arousal* is a term used to distinguish different levels of attentiveness. One student is drowsy and notes only a fraction of what goes on around him; another is passively taking in the most striking elements of the scene; and a third is entirely alert, trying to capture every scrap of information. The teacher's first task is often to arouse.

*Mental set* refers to the ideas and interests that are close to the surface in a student's mind at a given time. We may say, for example, that a student is "set" to complete his assignment as fast as he can, in order to get on to something more pleasurable. A student who has just heard a great deal about pollution may be "set" to pay attention to an argument against industrial expansion and to disregard an argument on the other side.

1 What are "appropriate habits for learning" from
   a. the demonstration a golf instructor gives?
   b. reading a dialogue of Socrates?
   c. a programmed text in high-school biology that covers the classification of vertebrates?

2 Illustrate ability, habit, and attitude as seen in the acts of a teacher in a particular course.

3 Does it make sense to speak of a five-year-old's "readiness for school," or is readiness specific to particular lessons and classroom practices?

## The Situation

By *situation* we mean the people, things, and occurrences that surround the student, specifically including the teacher, the task set for the student, and the physical and social environment.

| Aspects of the situation |
| --- |
| Physical environment<br>Social environment<br>  Teacher<br>  Peers<br>Task<br>  Materials<br>  Directions |

THE TEACHER   In most classrooms, the teacher is at the center of the students' attention a good fraction of the time. He tells the student what he should be working on, provides explanations to ponder or facts to remember, demonstrates actions to be followed, and does much to set the emotional tone of social interactions. Some classrooms have several teachers or teacher-aides, each having a slightly different style, each winning the special trust of a different subset of the students. Some teachers arrange class activities so that the work goes on for an hour or even for several successive hours with little attention to the teacher. This is a common mode in the shop class, where every student is hard at work completing his own project of the month, and it can occur in most upper-grade and high-school classrooms if the teacher chooses to carry out instruction through group projects. In that event the task, rather than the teacher, does most to regulate behavior.

## FIGURE 3.1

**A classroom organized to encourage movement and diversity**

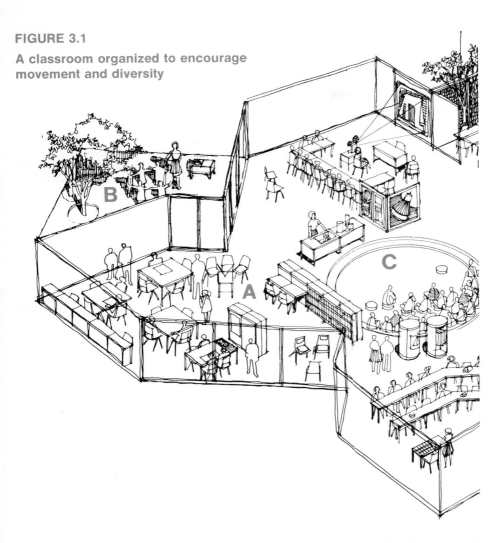

Shown is half of a plan for a multigrade unit. Several groups are at work simultaneously, and some students are working independently. *A* identifies one of several perimeter learning areas that can be used by small groups or individuals; *B*, one of several outdoor work areas; and *C*, one of the central areas for large working groups.

SOURCE: R. Gross & J. Murphy, *Educational Change and Architectural Consequences.* © 1968 Educational Facilities Laboratories, pp. 50–51.

THE TASK   The student sets to work on the assignment as he interprets it. In effect, he has in mind an ordered list of tasks to be worked through and a set of procedures to be followed. The teacher's instructions at this moment and those from the past are only a part of the task specification. The student is also guided by other rules of which neither he nor the teacher is fully conscious—

## The fourth-grade room at Adams

The room was large, light, and functional. The up-to-date equipment included such items as a telephone to the school office, public address system, drinking fountain, and new movable table desks and chairs. The room was painted a pastel color. Shouting and moments of silence were a structural necessity since the acoustics were very poor: sounds in the room bounced off the walls and competed with assorted noises in the street.

The table desks and chairs (38 in Year I, 30 in Year II) were arranged in lengthwise contiguous group areas. This arrangement permitted the children a wider visual field than they had when sitting in formal rows and made it easier for them to talk to each other. The tables, though movable, were never rearranged; the chairs were occasionally moved about and the children changed seats for sectional work.

The teacher's desk was placed catty-cornered facing the children. In addition to the desk and the flag, the loudspeaker was also visible at the front of the room. One feature, unique to the classroom in the first year, was a "bad child's seat." Placed near the door at the front of the room, its occupant was clearly revealed to anyone outside when the door was open.

There was a painting area near the sink. A newspaper was often put under the easel.

The room had an air of immaculate neatness, especially notable in the first year. Also in the first year* there was a little-used research table, complete with a lettered sign, RESEARCH, and there was a placard, THINK, on the teacher's desk.

There were no plants, flowers, or animals in the room.

Many displays covered the walls, all carefully arranged by the teacher and mounted on large sheets of colored paper. Displays about current curriculum and charts made by the teacher emphasized rules and procedures to be used in ongoing projects. A large Mercator map of the world, captioned "The World We Live In," dominated one wall. All displays were similarly captioned, looked very neat, and showed no signs of being handled. There were newspaper and magazine clippings brought by teacher and children, mounted under the caption "What's New in the World." There were many examples of children's work.

*The teacher in charge of the room changed at the end of the first year of the authors' observation.

unspoken conventions about what to do and how. The stated task might be: "Do the first ten exercises on page 42." The unstated side-conditions include how much time it is reasonable to spend on the effort, what standards define adequate performance, what help he can legitimately seek, and so on.

THE PHYSICAL AND SOCIAL SURROUNDINGS The physical features of the room affect learning. Is it comfortable and cheerful? Can the student find a quiet spot when he needs to think about his paper on how pearls are formed? Can everyone see the demonstration of how an electromagnet works?

Rows of seats facing the teacher's desk foster one style of discussion; chairs the students can place to suit themselves foster another. And facilities

## The fourth-grade room at Dickens

The high-ceilinged, large room needed a coat of paint; the plaster was cracking on the walls. The room got dark in the early afternoon and the lights had to be turned on. The acoustics were good and street noises did not interfere (as they did in the Adams classroom). The 31 movable table desks and chairs were arranged in contiguous rows but were moved about often as the need arose.

There was a good-sized free area at the front of the room which was used for a reading circle and other activities and generally reinforced the free use of space in this classroom. There was a painting and craft area with an easel which stood on a piece of linoleum (presumably easy to clean).

Cotton curtains, which the children had helped to make and which they had decorated with crayon drawings, adorned the windows. Later in the year the children made new curtains crayoned with additional scenes of the city, seen on another trip. Because of these touches, the Dickens classroom had an intimate personal quality: it was the children's own room crowded with their things.

Along shelves at the back of the room and on the window sills were plants, three or four fish tanks, and several turtles. Some children were responsible for taking care of these, others checked on their progress, still others took only a casual interest in them. As in all the public school classrooms, authority symbols tended to be at the front of the room: the teacher's desk, the flag. The teacher's desk was placed somewhat off-center.

There was no telephone or public-address system and the blackboard showed as much evidence of children's use as of the teacher's.

All available wall space was covered with displays. Many children's products were pinned up. One might see, for example, children's crayon drawings of the surrounding neighborhood based on a recent trip. Charts, printed by the teacher, related to current projects. An ever-changing bulletin board contained clippings from newspapers and magazines dealing with current national and international events. The bulletin board items revealed children's handling, were finger-worn and creased; they looked as if they had been objects of a good deal of use and interest.

SOURCE: Both boxes from *The Psychological Impact of School Experience: A Comparative Study of Nine-Year-Old Children in Contrasting Schools,* by Patricia Minuchin, Barbara Biber, Edna Shapiro, & Herbert Zimiles et al., pp. 93–94. © 1969 by Basic Books, Inc., Publishers, New York.

communicate values. The science wing of Blaketon High School has clean, well-equipped classrooms; the humanities wing has decrepit furniture and dingy walls. The student does not have to be told in words what Blaketon adults consider important. One classroom wall has attractive displays; another is a jumble of old clippings and bulletins. The former commands attention and teaches; the latter conveys only the message, "Who cares?" A seminar table has an obvious "head" and "foot" (but the cagey teacher will take a seat along the side, breaking the stereotype).

In both the elementary grades and the university, the "action zone" is up front. Students seated closer to the front and perhaps those nearer the midline pay more attention, participate more actively, and learn more (Brophy & Good,

1974, pp. 21–23). One college instructor, impressed by the differences between front-row and back-row participation in a class of 70 students, rotated the seating. Every Monday, students moved one row forward, the previous week's front-row students taking the back seats. The environment was changed for every student, without spending a dime for remodeling. According to Brophy and Good, Daum (in an unpublished study) obtained some evidence that such reseating improves learning of the less able students.

Classmates are an influential part of the situation. They look on each other as models, almost as social mirrors. After age 6 to 8, peer evaluations carry more weight than those of teachers—for better or worse. Student interaction opens the way to mutual help and encouragement (Chapter 15). But when few students are genuinely motivated, slackness infects everyone.

---

**4** "It's tough to tell a high school from a prison" is the title of an article by two social scientists (Haney & Zimbardo, 1975). Referring to the "oppressive" appearance, the fences and bleak corridors, they say:

> To the extent that a message can be translated from the high school's architectural medium, the language is clear: This place values regularity, order, and control over creativity, spontaneity, and freedom.

a. To what extent is it appropriate for a high school to value regularity over spontaneity?

b. What architectural features that promote spontaneity would also enable the school to do its instructional job?

5  In what ways do the classrooms described in the boxes (pp. 82 and 83) convey different messages to the children about the goals of learning and about how they should work?

6  What style of instruction, discussion, and social interaction does the classroom in Fig. 3.1 foster?

# DURING THE EPISODE: ACTION AND REACTION

The action of the student during the episode can be viewed as a series of events (Fig. 3.2, p. 86). The conception is that the learner is engaged in solving a problem, thinking out what to do and reacting intelligently to the outcome. He is not passively waiting to be "conditioned." The central concept—that of the provisional try—is borrowed from E. R. Hilgard:

> Many learning situations require the selection of one or another possible modes of action in order to reach a goal. Because alternatives are selected one after another until the correct one is stumbled upon, this learning is commonly described as trial and error. . . .
>
> The alternative (to a trial-and-error description) is that the original behavior is not the running-off of earlier habits in the new situation but a *genuine attempt at discovering* the route to the goal. Past experience is used, but in a manner appropriate to the present. Such an interpretation makes the original adjustment a *provisional try,* to be confirmed or denied by its success or failure. (1956, pp. 336, 343ff.)

First, the student perceives the situation; he sees some part of what is before him. Next, he envisions what he might do. After considering possible courses of action, he tries one, provisionally. The act may be a movement or overt comment, or it may be internal (as in silent reading). As he acts and evaluates immediately thereafter, the student examines the consequences of his action. If the consequences match his expectation (or are even more satisfactory), he will move on to further activity. If the consequences are less satisfactory, he may review the situation, reinterpret it, and try another action. He may, instead, persist in the original unrewarding course of action. Trial and adjustment (or failure to adjust) continue until the student is satisfied or gives up.

FIGURE 3.2

What happens during an episode

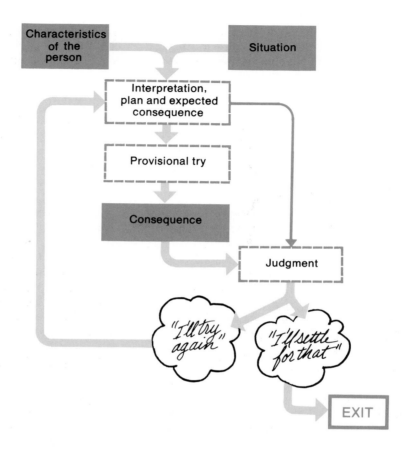

## Perceiving and Interpreting

Perception is the initial act of taking in the situation; interpretation goes on to analyze and predict. The student has to ask, in effect: What consequences are possible or likely in this situation? What options are open, and where will each one lead?

The teacher can promote accurate perception. Perception is more likely to be accurate when a student knows what to look for in a situation, and when the significant features of the task stand out clearly. The teacher can help the student to identify relevant information and interpret it properly—for example, by pointing out which string of notes in the sheet music is to be read as a phrase.

| Interpretation |
| --- |
| Attention and perception<br>Recognition of possibilities; some of them become goals<br>Use of concepts to analyze, then to form a plan<br>Visualization of intended response and expected consequence |

Shown a picture of the human body, with arteries traced out in red and veins in blue, some students add relatively little to the basic stimulus; they perceive a complex web of red and blue lines and leave it at that. Others try to organize the picture, perhaps by following the main trunks of each network, or by noting that the branches tend to spread outward from the heart. Before the teacher utters a word of explanation, some students have thought more than others about what they are seeing.

Such interpretations differ because each student has his own stock of memories and concepts. His expectations and goals also play a part in the interpretation. He imagines what he can hope to achieve. Task requirements point a general direction, but the student identifies what end results and rewards lie down the path. He judges whether they are worth much or little effort and he envisions steps that could lead to the goal. For instance, asked to work ten mathematical exercises, Joe considers his job finished as soon as he has answers that look reasonable. Whether the answers are correct Joe leaves to fate. Jack wants all of his answers correct, and devises a way to check his work. Jeff wants his answers to be right, but sees no way to check. Jerry knows that the execises are easily within his reach, but the task is too easy to stir him to an effort.

Much of the interpretation is hidden from the teacher's view unless it is deliberately called into the open. A teacher, after a meticulous description of an assignment, may think it enough to ask "Have you any questions?" But this assumes that the student can recognize when he has misunderstood. It might be better to have the student say back what is to be done. It is impractical to do this all the time, but it can be of great value when a student seems to have trouble getting started.

## Making a Provisional Try

What the person chooses to do, and indeed *whether* he chooses to act, depends on the events and outcomes he foresees. In familiar actions there is a half-conscious, perhaps instantaneous process of sizing up alternatives and consequences. When unsure what will actually result, the person nonetheless can estimate that he will like the consequences of action A better than the consequences of action B. So he picks A as his trial response.

*"If I never TRY nothin' . . . how am I gonna find out
what I can get away with?"*

"Dennis the Menace" used courtesy of Hank Ketcham and
© 1976 by Field Newspaper Syndicate, T.M.®

In the task that calls for a long sequence of acts—such as writing a paper—the student may envision a whole train of possible steps to take, or he may see just one step ahead. Either way, the response is a series of actions, modified from moment to moment as the early consequences become evident. Even a simple one-sentence recitation may be altered in midstream if the student thinks the teacher frowned on hearing his first words.

We speak of the response as a provisional try to emphasize the tentative, experimental nature of plans and actions (E. R. Hilgard, 1956; G. Miller et al., 1960). A plan is tried out and revised. Walking in the hills, you strike out cross-country toward a distant crest. A concealed fence or a swampy area forces you to reinterpret and to choose a new route. Possibly you have to give up hope of reaching the crest and pick a new objective. Even without obstacles, you make small changes in pace and direction at each step, accommodating yourself to the slope, the footing, and the vegetation.

Actions to cope with a novel problem are obviously provisional; one is well aware of the uncertainty of one's plan. Even in a confident act anticipating and correcting take place. You scarcely need to plan your route from your bedroom to your dining room, having made the trip many times. Even so, the trial-and-correction mode is still in operation. When some housecleaning activity closes off your usual path, you adjust in mid-movement.

The fact that actions are provisional is the key to learning. In matching what actually results with what he anticipated, the person not only corrects his present action but stores up a modified interpretation so that he can act more efficiently when the situation recurs.

RECOGNIZING CONSEQUENCES: THE FEEDBACK PROCESS   Information about the nature and consequences of one's acts is spoken of as *feedback*. Consequences include the learner's direct perception of what he is doing, the objective, observable effects he produces, and the comments of others concerning his acts.

A bowler moves forward and releases the ball. Sense receptors in his muscles tell him instantly that the movement was or was not right. As the ball rolls down the alley, its path offers additional information. The ball finally strikes the pins, they fall and settle, and the lights show how many pins are still standing. From the bench an onlooker gives a word of praise or sympathy. A knowledgeable observer perhaps can tell the bowler just what he did right or how to improve his swing. All these messages can influence his next try.

The first source of feedback is the learner himself. If he judges soundly how well he did and connects the result to the interpretations he made, he gains command of the material and becomes more self-reliant.

When feedback comes from an observer, its timing, specificity, and emotional flavor all matter. Promptness has obvious advantages, but a teacher with 25 or more students, each busy on several projects, is hard put to keep each student fully informed about his progress.

At each moment the teacher decides whose action needs a prompt reaction and whose action can wait. Sharon, for the first time, puts her shoulders into the swing of her bat. She misses, but the teacher shouts to her that her swing was right, to try the same power on the next pitch. The teacher's prompt reaction to Sharon on that try was vital.

Specific comments are more helpful than general ones. A letter grade on a project tells a student nothing about what he has done right. The student needs to know where he went wrong, and where he hit on a technique worth trying again.

| Consequences |
| --- |
| Sensory information from the response itself<br>Effects on the physical environment and task materials<br>Responses of others |

A teacher's comment is more than a cognitive message to the student. Even the most objective evaluation has emotional overtones. The student's emotional reactions depend on how he reads the message and on what message he expected. The teacher says, "Your project looks O.K." This satisfies one student; another, with a higher expectation, is disappointed because he gets the idea that his work was barely passable. Nuances count.

JUDGMENT OF CONSEQUENCES    When a provisional try goes well, expectations are confirmed. This phrase is more accurate than saying that the person "succeeds." The undersized boy's hope may be to do well enough during his turn at bat to ward off caustic comments from the other players. Even striking out may be an occasion for self-congratulation if he hits a respectable foul ball beyond first base. The try confirms his hope (maybe a faint one) that he can have a tolerable experience on the playing field; so he is more likely to come out for baseball another day.

Confirming an expectation also confirms the initial interpretation, setting the stage for a similar action another time. The alternative, of course, is "contradiction of expectations" (which makes better psychological sense than "failure"). According to the norms of the game, the boy who struck out failed; but he did not fail psychologically. His performance was "what he expected." Sometimes a "success" contradicts expectations, too, and alters the way one perceives the world and oneself thereafter.

| Judgment of consequences |
| --- |
| Expectations confirmed, *or*<br>Expectations contradicted<br>Result accepted, *or*<br>Result not accepted; a further try follows |

Teachers can arrange conditions that favor persistence rather than withdrawal. Sometimes they will encourage withdrawal, however, as a healthy choice. The teacher needs to consider how realistic it is for the student to pursue the goal, whether his withdrawal will lead to self-deprecation, and how valuable are the alternative activities that he could turn to. It is when a student habitually reacts to failure by quitting that a teacher should become concerned. No single episode says much about the student, but his characteristic response to difficulty (flexibility, perseverance, indecision, retreat) says a good deal about his mental health.

7  Can the term "provisional try" be applied to each of the following?
   a. Carl, who is four, stumbles and bumps his elbow. He cries and a nearby adult picks him up and comforts him.
   b. Asked the moral of the fable that has just been read to the fifth-graders, Cynthia says dully, "I don't know."

   c. Asked to carry the attendance report to the main office, Beryl does, going directly and returning promptly.

   d. A fisherman hangs his line over the side of the dock and settles back for a long lazy afternoon.

**8**  In a college lecture class in history, do interpretations, tries, and consequences occur during the class hour? In what ways can the instructor increase the amount of trying, within the lecture format?

**9**  Token rewards can appear artificial to both teacher and student. How can a teacher amplify the *natural* consequences of a student's actions, so that these provide effective feedback?

## Outcomes

Instructional outcomes are usually measured over months or years, and those that enter the school records cover a broad territory: a summary measure of science achievement, a grade representing the quality of a semester's compositions, and so on. One sees little day-to-day movement in such a global characteristic as science achievement. But even a single episode makes some difference. Although the permanent residue of any one episode is modest, the accumulation over numerous episodes constitutes the very essence of educational growth.

    The experience the student has may alter his mood or intensify it. If he is apprehensive before going off the diving board, his experience may deepen his wish to withdraw from the risky situation or—if he does better than he expected—may dispel some of his tension. Similarly, other temporary states such as arousal and mental set may be modified or strengthened by the experience. The lasting consequence of the episode is that, to at least some slight degree, the person gains ability or, fixing on a wrong idea, declines in ability; or he entrenches a habit that will either help or hinder him in his work. Changes in ability are sometimes dramatic, as when the person gains insight and steps up to a new level of interpretation. Changes in habits are far more gradual. When the person's plan works out, his interpretations about the situation and about

| Outcomes |
| --- |
| Mood and arousal<br>Abilities<br>Habits<br>Concepts and attitudes about elements in the situation<br>Concepts and attitudes about the self |

his own power to cope with it are confirmed. When the plan does not work out, he may be forced to modify his concept of some element in the situation or of his own competence. All these changes modify the student's readiness for dealing with situations that will be encountered a bit later.

The teacher has to be alert to the changes that an episode may produce in students. Mr. Dolan has been trying for days to explain odd and even numbers to his first-graders. Today a student suddenly makes an illuminating remark: "With an even number of things, you can sort them into pairs, and you wind up with nothing left over. With an odd number of things, you always have one left over!" Mr. Dolan encourages discussion of this insight. When he returns to odds and evens the next day, most students have a better grasp of the topic.

## CATEGORIES OF LEARNING

A person has learned something if his response now is different from what it was earlier in much the same situation. The term *learning* is usually reserved for a relatively permanent change in behavior, interpretation, or emotional response as a result of experience. A chance event or momentary lapse is not learning, nor do we include temporary, reversible changes due to drugs, boredom, fatigue, and so on. On the other hand, the term is not restricted to the response that becomes fixed with practice. A change in the probability of a certain response—Dennis complains now on only half the occasions when carrots are served—is a sign of learning.

Changes deriving directly from growth rather than experience (such as being able to lift heavier objects) are not referred to as learned behavior. Most developmental change combines physical growth with practice in using one's new powers.

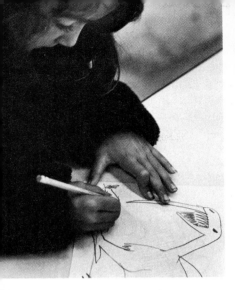
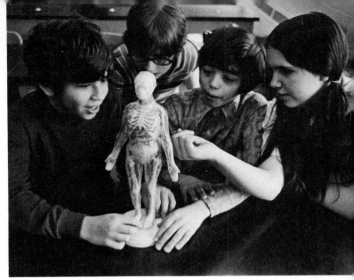

## Stimulus, response, and reinforcement

Research has generated a variety of theoretical concepts for coming to grips with learning phenomena. Behaviorists usually speak in terms of stimulus, response, and reinforcement. These concepts closely parallel the broader concepts of situation, provisional try, and evaluation of consequences. And the learning theorist speaks of "trials" where I have spoken of episodes. Each such trial consists of one presentation of the stimulus, a response, and some reinforcing act by the experimenter.

A stimulus is something sensed by the person in his physical environment. (The stimulus may also be internal—the stretch of a muscle, for example). The classroom situation includes numerous potential stimuli, only a few of which come to the student's attention. The potential stimuli before the first-grader as he looks at a page in his reader include pictures and printed words. But if he cannot read, the effective stimulus for whatever he does is probably the picture.

A response is a reaction as simple as a reflex blink, or as complex as a judge's choice between the arguments of opposing lawyers. A response may be overt and readily observed, or internal and difficult to detect.

Reinforcement refers to anything coming after a response that affects the probability of the response recurring. Feedback, consequences, and reinforcement are overlapping concepts. Reinforcement frequently carries connotations of reward or punishment from outside. According to reinforcement theory, it is the positive, rewarding event following a response that makes that response likely to be repeated. Irregular reinforcement can be effective. A child asking for money to buy ice cream may be denied it nine times out of ten, and yet persist in his response.

## Gagné's Types of Learning

Types of learning are described by various authors (for example, Hilgard & Bower, 1974; Gagné, 1970). Each author's system classifies learning according to the kinds of responses being connected, what they are being connected to, and what prior learning each new response builds upon. In addition to classifying, taxonomies generally rank types of learning from simple to complex. The kinds are distinguished in terms of their psychological properties.

Gagné's (1970) taxonomy, suggested by experimental research on learning, sets forth eight categories (Table 3.1). Each kind of learning is presumed to be unique, in the sense that each follows its own particular principles. The several kinds of learning can proceed independently.

Gagné's system illustrates how experimental psychologists have divided up the investigation of learning—some examine signal learning, others look at problem solving, and so on. Today learning theory is in flux. The psychologist who studies problem solving may also be interested in how the student collects the basic facts, how he forms concepts, how he evolves principles, and how

*(text continues on p. 96)*

**TABLE 3.1**
Gagné's categories of learning

| Type | Task | Examples | |
|------|------|----------|---|
| | | *"Stimulus"* | *"Response"* |
| Signal learning | Connect response to stimulus. | Flash of lightning | Expect thunder; faster heart beat. |
| | | "Now it's time for reading." | Expect failure; stomach-ache. |
| Stimulus-response learning | Connect response to stimulus. | "Shake hands with your uncle." | Extend hand toward adult. [Receives smile.] |
| | | "Ready for spelling." | Pick up pencil and prepare to write. [Teacher says, "Good!"] |
| Chaining | Connect two or more overt responses. | Slide behind wheel of car. | Put key in ignition and depress accelerator. |
| | | "Your social security number?" | "555-37-9182." (in one breath!) |
| Verbal association | Connect a verbal label to a distinctive stimulus. | "What is French for *match*?" | "L'allumette." |
| | | | "Hawk." |
| Discrimination learning | Connect a different response to each of two similar stimuli. | Hearing an A♭ | "That's a clarinet." |
| | | | "The *Western* robin is at left." |
| Concept learning | Place several dissimilar stimuli in same class. | "Which are the mammals?" | Point to man, whale, giraffe, etc. |
| | | "What rhymes with *tough*?" | "Stuff, enough, huff . . ." |
| Principle learning | Learn a relation between two or more concepts. | "Why does a hot-air balloon rise?" or "Why is it hot at the ceiling?" | "Gases expand and become lighter when heated." |
| Problem solving | Use principles to plan a response. | "Design a stage setting for the first act of *Cyrano*." | Analyze the first act of *Cyrano*; combine with knowledge of principles of stage design. |

## Stimulus-response learning

*"Then someone yelled 'Stop, thief!' and, like a dope, I stopped."*

Drawing by Leonard Dove; © 1955 The New Yorker Magazine, Inc.

he puts all the preceding to work in solving the problem. Gagné's recent work, like the approach in this text, makes little effort to keep the types of learning distinct. My analysis emphasizes the similarities among the processes. In Chapter 11, for example, I treat discrimination and concept learning as much the same; elaborating the meaning of a concept such as *stratosphere* is much like what Gagné classifies as learning of principles.

**10** What aspects of a potential stimulus (box, p. 94) are likely to determine whether a student actually becomes aware of it? How does the answer depend on the characteristics of the student? The actions of the teacher?

**11** Which of Gagné's categories seem to include aspects of the learning of attitudes?

**12** The performances that Gagné lists seem to be best described as abilities. Which of his categories also apply to the shaping of typical behavior?

**13** Where might the types of learning in Gagné's system be found in the study of each of these school subjects?
  a. auto mechanics
  b. nutrition
  c. American government
  d. science for kindergartners
  e. music appreciation

# LEARNING PROCESSES SEEN IN THE CLASSROOM

## A Reading Class

Learning in the classroom shows the features discussed above, as two examples will show. The first is a reading class.

It is midmorning reading period in Mrs. Whittier's class. About 25 children are present, six of them across the table from Mrs. Whittier. The others are scattered in groups of two to six. The room is fairly quiet. Most students are practicing word-attack skills in their workbooks, while a few are reading library books. A sixth-grade tutor is helping a second-grader in one corner.

Some students are much further along in the workbook than others. Some have completed many "extra" exercises; others none. The overall quality of the work seems high. The children seem to know what they are doing; they readily answer questions such as "What will you do when you finish this?" "How can you find out whether your work is right?"

Mrs. Whittier has her six boys working on word-attack, each on a different page in the workbook. She checks the work in a regular, almost rhythmic pattern, turning to a new student after a 20- to 30-second interval; each student gets her attention about every three minutes. As she turns to each boy, she comments on what he has done since she last spoke to him, and calls attention to anything that appears questionable: "Why don't you see if that's right?" (And sometimes the student is actually right.) She usually ends with a word of praise: "I think you're going to finish your 'contract' today." "You got that word right this time. You had trouble with it yesterday." "Your writing on this page is very neat."

Occasionally a student from another table comes to Mrs. Whittier's side, waits until she is free, and then asks a question. A brief comment takes care of one problem; another student is told to talk with a friend at her table who can probably help her. Two examples of individual teaching are given in the boxes.

As time goes on, there is more noise and movement. Children complete their assignments and go to the learning station to check their work. There is social interaction in the station area; students compare notes and seek advice about answers that do not check out. Some cluster around the bookshelves to pick out books for "free" reading.

Ten minutes pass and Mrs. Whittier announces: "Time for the Blue team!" Much movement and chatter as the boys break into two groups and go to tables on the other side of the room. Two boys and three girls take places at the teacher's table. Within two minutes the new group is discussing with her their interpretations of a story they had been reading.

ANALYSIS   How does the preceding account relate to the description of classroom learning presented in Figure 3.2? With regard to readiness, motivation appears to be strong. Students vary considerably in reading skill, but all seem to be working hard and progressing. The account focuses largely on what was called "action" in Figure 3.2. The episode of Paul and the boat picture (box) illustrates the interpretation process. Not to mark the picture made good sense, given his interpretation of it as "ship." Mrs. Whittier's question led Paul to try another interpretation, which in turn led to an alternative action.

With regard to situation, Mrs. Whittier's class is organized so that each student can move ahead at his own rate, but still get prompt feedback. In the small groups, Mrs. Whittier trains the students in skills of attention and inter-

## Terry learns to learn

Teachers often take the "long way round," for good reason. In the following dialogue, Mrs. Whittier could have answered Teresa's initial question by spelling the word for her. The roundabout method led Teresa to use a technique that she will apply in the future to resolve many spelling problems for herself. She learned the answer to "How do you spell *snapping*?" But she also learned an answer to "How do you cope with a spelling problem?" to replace her old response: "Ask Mrs. Whittier." Teresa is learning how to learn spelling.

"I'm writing a story about the turtle we found yesterday, and I'm not sure how to spell *snapping*."
"How do you think it's spelled?"
"I don't know."
"How does it start?"
"S?"
"Right. What comes next?"
"S . . . n . . . a . . . p? I'm not sure what comes next."
"What do you think is next?"
". . . i . . . n . . . g? That's what I wrote down, but it doesn't look right."
"How would you pronounce the word you have spelled there?"
"Sn-ay-ping—that doesn't make sense . . . Oh! You need two p's—snapping. O.K., I've got it."

## Paul revises an interpretation

When Mrs. Whittier got around to Paul, he was marking pictures in his workbook, picking out the pictured objects whose names began with the same sound as *boy.* She saw that he had marked all the *b* pictures except for that of a sailboat; hence this dialogue:

"What is this picture?"
"A ship."
"Does it have another name, Paul?"
"Huh? . . . Oh yeah, *boat.* I see! That starts with *b* too."
"That's right. You got all the others right, and didn't mark any that didn't start with *b.* That's pretty good. Why don't you try the next page?"

pretation. By responding to a student's question with a question of her own, she discovers what is on the student's mind and encourages him to ask himself such questions in the future. Each student is clear about what the teacher expects of him, but he also has considerable control over his classroom experiences. He knows what resources are available and how to gain access to what he needs.

 **14** In Mr. Craig's class, students are quiet and apparently intent on their reading workbooks. But they are scattered widely, one or two per table. Mr. Craig moves about the area, responding to individual students who raise their hands. He kneels in turn beside each student, chatting quietly for a minute or two. There is no group work; the students study individually, and Mr. Craig attends to requests for help one by one.

How are the differences between Mrs. Whittier's and Mr. Craig's class organization likely to affect the learning situation? Which do you think will make the teaching more effective?

## A Typing Class

Typing is a skill, hence easily observed, and every student is expected to learn much the same responses. Mr. Wells's high-school typing class contained about 30 students, most of them juniors and seniors. On the opening day of the semester, Mr. Wells's inquiry revealed that few students had ever worked with the typewriter. He let them spend several days exploring the machine. By feeding paper into it, they learned what the paper guide was for and how it could be used. Mr. Wells made no attempt to point out all the knobs and adjustments; only when students asked how to obtain a certain result did he introduce his knowledge. By the end of the week, the group was at home with the machine and turning out small messages with considerable satisfaction. But the novelty was wearing off, hunt-and-peck was becoming tedious, and several class members were wasting time. An observer might have cast a critical eye on the students' bad techniques of performance—poor posture, watching the keyboard, using the index finger for all keys, and the like.

At this point, Mr. Wells described good typing procedure. Had he demonstrated posture and hand placement the first day, he would have found students far more eager to start punching keys than to worry about refinements. As they discovered that their methods were slow and tedious, they became more ready to hear about efficient procedures.

Mr. Wells now taught formally the positions of the fingers. Beginning with the "home" positions—a-s-d-f and j-k-l-;—students performed a limited number of exercises to practice locating the keys. After a few trials with each letter, they began to type words. As new letters were introduced, Mr. Wells encouraged students to make lists of words they could type with those letters. One student would prepare a list (typing it, of course) and give it to his neighbor to practice on. Students also practiced by composing directly on the machine. New letters were brought in rapidly. By the end of the third week all letters were in use, though most students had to search for them on the keyboard.

Mr. Wells left students largely to themselves while they were finding their way around the keyboard, practicing lists of simple sentences. He allowed them to look for letters whose location they did not recall, and called attention only to gross lapses from posture and fingering methods.

By the end of the fourth week, differences in performance were sizable. Some students were at home with all three rows of the keyboard and gaining speed steadily. Others were shaky in their knowledge of the less-used keys, and a few were confused about even the letters first introduced. For students having trouble with common letters, Mr. Wells provided lists of words that used chiefly those letters. As they became proficient, students moved ahead to more complicated words and sentences. Variations for the sake of interest and technique were introduced at times; for example, to encourage prompt stroking, Mr. Wells occasionally dictated a series of letters that the class typed in unison.

As soon as students had mastered the keyboard well enough to type words without marked pauses to search for letters, class time was given chiefly to practice from continuous copy. Students were urged to work as fast as they comfortably could, even if they made errors. At this time also, Mr. Wells introduced weekly 3-minute speed tests. Each student kept a record of the number of words typed on the test and charted his progress from week to week. Many were still slow, but every student could see that he was much better than he had been at the start of the course.

As each student moved from word practice to straight copy, Mr. Wells's work became more varied. He observed each student and drew attention to incorrect posture, faulty attack on the keys, and similar errors that earlier he had let pass without comment. He began to insist that the students type without looking at the keyboard.

Martha had been a laggard throughout and now was markedly confused. Observing her carefully, Mr. Wells found that Martha knew the approximate location of the letter *u*, for instance, but could not put her finger on it directly. Unless Martha looked at the keys, she could only try some letter in the general region, and so she hit *y* or *i* frequently instead of *u*. She was quite erratic in finger placement; for example, she used either her first or second finger for *h*. Since she never knew by feel where her hand was on the keyboard, she could not always land on *u* by reaching out with the first finger. Mr. Wells corrected this by watching Martha as she practiced and warning her whenever she let her hands wander from the proper home position. Once persuaded that using the correct finger was just as important as striking the correct key, she reduced her errors and began to overtake the class. But the majority remained well ahead of her, and she continued to be somewhat discouraged. This difficulty might have been avoided if Mr. Wells had checked on individuals early in their practice to correct serious faults before they became fixed.

According to the tests, a few students seemed to be stalled at a particular level, making no improvement for several weeks. Some seemed merely to be having difficulty because their memory for certain letters was uncertain, and Mr. Wells concluded that further practice would correct that. Others were inefficient in practice. To two students he suggested practice using any work they wished to bring in instead of preplanned drills; there was an immediate increase in their interest and progress.

James, on the other hand, did not respond to attempts to interest him, saying that he did not care whether he learned typing or not. James was taking the course only because he had a free hour at that time and could find no class that better fitted his plan to finish high school and go to work in his father's store. Mr. Wells, unable to arouse James to real effort, decided that nagging would be unwise. James, for his part, put in his time dutifully and created no disturbance. Neither Mr. Wells nor James, however, was satisfied. This problem could be solved only by better counseling or a more diversified curriculum.

Olive had gone into a slump when the class began work on normal copy. She used excellent stroking and had a good knowledge of the keyboard, but her typing was hesitant because she had to read each complicated word from the copy letter by letter. Other students could hold the word in mind and type it straight off with only occasional hesitation. Olive, however, had always been a poor speller, so that thinking of the word as a whole did not permit her to type it. Mr. Wells was unable to bring Olive to the level of the rest of the class on standard copy. By giving her more practice on simple words, he was able to develop her typing skills. A supplementary study of spelling, worked out by Mr. Wells with Olive's English teacher, brought some improvement, but her spelling vocabulary remained so low that her typing was seriously handicapped.

ANALYSIS   Mr. Wells took much care to provide a situation where typing could be learned through practice, where students could react to the task of typing in a natural setting. They practiced from copy rather than by repeatedly typing a memorized sentence about "the quick brown fox." The copy was not nonsense; instead, it resembled what they would later type outside the course. The situation was not, however, identical to typing in an office. For example, early in the course Mr. Wells had students make up their own word lists so that having to look at unfamiliar copy would not complicate their task. Teachers generally must modify, not duplicate, out-of-school situations.

Students varied. Some were more mature and better coordinated; some were better prepared in such fundamentals as reading and spelling; some had better attitudes toward their work, more patience, and better concentration.

Students had goals to which success in typing could contribute, so that good performance became a goal in itself. There were those who looked forward to using typing as a way of earning a living; with each week's progress they gained pride in seeing themselves as nearly independent and self-supporting. Others were striving to win praise from the teacher or to feel superior to the group. Students' goals determine how they react to difficulties. The student with a great need to excel, for example, is likely to become demoralized if he fails to make progress. Mr. Wells tried to make it possible for each student to fulfill his own individual wishes.

The process of action and reaction can be observed in single acts. At a microscopic level, each time a finger strikes a key a full range of cognitive operations from perception through evaluation is engaged. At the beginning of the course, the student had to think about each letter, locate it on the keyboard, decide which finger to strike the key with. If the student was looking at the paper, he saw immediately whether he was right or wrong. With practice, he learned to type sequences—syllables, familiar words, and even phrases. Typing speed increased, and the student paid more attention to the substance of what he was typing.

Each student was evaluating his performance over days and weeks, relative to his own goals and to the behavior of other students in the class. He decided how much effort to spend on typing and how much on other interests. This is another level of interpretation and provisional try.

Students charted their progress in the weekly tests. This feedback was especially important to those who had trouble making reasonable progress. They saw fairly quickly that something was wrong, and decided, with Mr. Wells's guidance, what to do about it. James decided to give up, since he saw no real value in learning to type. Thanks partly to Mr. Wells's interest and skill, Martha and Olive became fairly competent typists.

 **15** What steps did Mr. Wells take to adjust his teaching to individual differences?

## Tasks of the Teacher

How a teacher handles his class varies with the teacher, the subject-matter, and the age, ability, and interests of the students. But some concerns arise in all teaching: selecting and organizing curriculum materials, providing for individual differences, motivating students, and evaluating student performance and program effectiveness.

ORGANIZING CURRICULUM MATERIALS   Arranging a learning situation requires decisions about topics, materials, and activities. In what order will the topics be presented? How rapidly will new ideas be introduced? What are the provisions for review and for pulling together diverse ideas and concepts? One teacher decides to start with an overview of the course, then fills in details and finishes with an integrative summary. Another lets the course unfold more freely—knowing what has to be covered, but letting circumstances dictate the order.

Mrs. Whittier relied largely on commercial workbooks to teach word attack. The materials determined the kinds of tasks presented to students, and the order. Monitoring each student's rate of progress, Mrs. Whittier kept him working at a reasonable rate. To teach comprehension and vocabulary, on the other hand, she relied on library books and group conversation—a nearly unorganized set of lessons.

Mr. Wells's decisions shaped the curriculum of the typing class. He chose to introduce students to real "tasks" early in the course. Each student had considerable freedom to work on copy that meant something to him. Mr. Wells introduced letters in groups corresponding to rows of the keyboard. He did this quickly; some students might have been less confused if new letters had been introduced more slowly.

A plan of instruction is an informal experiment designed by the teacher from his knowledge of the subject-matter and his understanding of the students. He must act as a research worker, attending to control of significant factors and careful measurement. He can do this by thoughtful variation in the curriculum and close observation of student reactions. This supplies evidence about what works and what needs changing. Mr. Wells adjusted his plans, for example, by giving special practice lists to students having trouble with certain letters.

TAKING INDIVIDUAL DIFFERENCES INTO ACCOUNT  Students differ in interests, long-term goals, ability, social effectiveness, personality, and other respects. Some are so atypical that they require intensive study. But for virtually every student there comes a time when his needs warrant special consideration.

"Individualized instruction" is a term much used today. To some it means that the teacher works with only one student at a time, or that he tailors a program of instruction for each student. Neither approach is practical. However, it does make sense for the teacher to keep track of each student's progress, and to try to ensure that no low-achieving student or gifted student gets lost in the crowd.

Casual observation might suggest that Mr. Wells was conducting his typing class through whole-group instruction. Not so. He examined patterns of

## Individual differences

"Priscilla's Pop" by Al Vermeer. Reprinted by permission of Newspaper Enterprise Association (NEA).

errors and suggested practice exercises designed to remedy each student's difficulties. He allowed students considerable freedom in what they practiced and in how rapidly they moved to an advanced technique. The activities were different for every student. Similarly, in Mrs. Whittier's reading class the students proceeded through the workbooks at their own rate. Once a student had successfully completed a set of exercises, he was to read a library book of his choosing and to report on what he had read. This task, requiring little personal attention from the teacher, let the student deepen his skill while pursuing his own interests.

AROUSING MOTIVATION    The most direct way to motivate a student is to convince him that a task is worth his while and that he can succeed with a reasonable investment of time and effort. This process begins with picking the right tasks—matching the curriculum to individual readiness. Both student and teacher benefit from open discussion of the student's goals, of where he stands in relation to those goals, and of what his next step might be. More conventional devices—marks, praise, pressure—have less sustained power than well-defined purposes the student accepts as important to him.

Mr. Wells assumed that students wanted to learn to type and would try to learn so long as they felt they were making progress. His "rewards" were built upon the students' accomplishments. He relied also on social satisfactions. Letting students write messages to each other added interest in the early weeks when the going was tough. There was no way to motivate James; he saw no reason to learn typing. With Mr. Wells's concurrence, he put forth only as much effort as was needed to keep out of trouble.

Mrs. Whittier's students came to reading with high motivation. Reading was important to their parents, and the students knew that their parents would be happy when they learned to read. Their older brothers and sisters read and enjoyed it. And they saw the better readers in their group using the skill. Mrs. Whittier used every opportunity to remind a student of things he was doing well.

EVALUATING  For classroom evaluation, the teacher collects evidence about a student's state of learning and uses that evidence to decide what to work on next. The goals of instruction have to be clear, the evidence adequate and reliable, and the standards for judgment reasonable. Evaluation provides the teacher a sound basis for an instructional program; it also lets the student know how well he is doing and where he might do better.

Evaluation is sometimes mistakenly thought to be the same thing as testing. Tests do serve a useful purpose. But observing a student as he works and talking with him about how he is tackling a problem is often more useful evidence than a test score. Mr. Wells kept track of typing speeds with weekly tests, along with other information. He watched *how* students typed as well as measuring *how much,* knowing that speed might remain fairly constant while a student was making significant gains in form. He ignored some points that other teachers would assess. He was not concerned with how the students organized their desks, nor with how they spaced the letters on a page. He did not try to find out how tired a student felt after a typing session, though this might have suggested the need for a change in posture.

When to evaluate is an important decision. Mr. Wells did not measure speed of typing until students had gained a reasonable amount of skill, on the assumption that an earlier test would have been discouraging. In some cases he delayed more than might seem wise, after the fact. Martha had practiced an inefficient hand placement many times before Mr. Wells noticed the problem. Correcting the problem took longer as a result because the bad habit was strongly established.

Mrs. Whittier also had to consider timing of evaluation. When students progress at their own rates, the gap between fast and slow ones widens. The above-average second-grader, for example, works through books too difficult to be used by the whole class. The student who moves more slowly is left behind. Under these conditions, it was important that Mrs. Whittier gather evidence about each student's progress nearly every day. Formal tests at wide intervals are not enough to guide teaching.

---

**16**  Comment on the following statement: "Individualization of instruction requires continuous and precise evaluation."

**17**  How is *motivation* being used in the following statements? Does each of the following sentences embody the same concept of motivation?
   a. "Motivating students is the most important job of a teacher."
   b. "If a student lacks motivation there is little a teacher can do about it."
   c. " 'Lack of motivation' is an excuse to cover poor teaching."
   d. "As long as a student performs well, it does not matter whether he is motivated or not."

Jack A. Adams, "A Closed-Loop Theory of Motor Learning," *Journal of Motor Behavior* 3 (1971), 111–49.

> A meaty paper illustrating how a psychologist develops and defends a theory of learning. The topic is motor skills (my Chapter 10), and most of what Adams says can be understood by a reader with little training in psychology. His theory is close to the point of view in this chapter, with an emphasis on the relation between what the learner intends to do (interpretation, anticipated consequences) and feedback. Adams brings out the subtle differences between this kind of theory and a more behavioristic stimulus-response-reinforcement theory.

Richard C. Atkinson, "Teaching Children to Read Using a Computer," *American Psychologist* 29 (1974), 169–78.

> Practical procedures used in designing and revising a system of teaching reading with the aid of a teletypewriter and audio headset are described. The computer can respond to what the child types and can itself type messages or send prerecorded audio messages ("Great!"). Atkinson shows how design of the instruction depends upon a theory of learning.

Robert M. Gagné, Introduction and "The Processes of Learning," in *Essentials of Learning for Instruction,* expanded edition (Hinsdale, Ill.: Dryden Press, 1974), pp. 1–47.

> Offers an information-processing model like the one in this chapter, and introduces comparatively formal ideas regarding some parts of the process.

Omar Khayyam Moore and Alan R. Anderson, "An Application of the Four Principles," in *Handbook of Socialization Theory and Research,* ed. D. A. Goslin (Chicago: Rand McNally, 1969), pp. 592–609.

> Describes unusual classroom activities (including a "talking typewriter") for the 6-year-old, to illustrate a pedagogy that emphasizes discovery and progressive responsibility. Although the principles (their p. 585) are worded in terms of the "environment," the authors are primarily concerned with the learner's interpretations, tries, and use of consequences.

Leonard J. West, *Implications of Research for Teaching Typewriting,* Delta Pi Epsilon Research Bulletin No. 4 (St. Peter, Minn.: Gustavus Adolphus College, 1974). 38 pp.

> Illustrates the numerous specific decisions required of a teacher in selecting practice materials, guiding practice, and evaluating progress. West relies heavily on task analysis and on experimental comparisons of alternative techniques of teaching.

■ The experimenter sets up controlled conditions and compares the success of groups of similar composition under those conditions.

■ The experimenter compares group averages and variation among members within groups. When he reports a difference, he also reports the probability of finding a similar difference if the experiment is repeated

□ To conduct an experiment under real classroom conditions it may be necessary to sacrifice some control. The classroom study makes possible valuable observations on classroom events and student responses; these supplement formal comparison of averages.

■ In intensive case study, the investigator tries to formulate a theory about the person studied, not a generally applicable one. He collects a range of information about the person, much of it descriptive and informal.

■ Differences that already exist—between persons or groups—are examined by assessing the correlation between measures of two characteristics. A young child ability is positively correlated with the amount of support he gets from his mother, for example. This finding suggests, but does not prove, that more materna support promotes faster intellectual development.

■ Since a response depends on characteristics of both person and situation, it is useful to examine how the two work together, asking what kind of person does best in each instructional condition.

| | |
|---|---|
| *random assignment* | *statistical significance* |
| *treatment* | *true experiment* / |
| *experimental group* / | *quasi experiment* |
| *control group* | *case study* |
| *mean* | *correlational study* |
| *standard deviation* | *correlation coefficient* |
| *normal distribution* | *interaction of person and situatio* |

# 4

# MODES OF INVESTIGATION IN EDUCATIONAL PSYCHOLOGY

This chapter examines the logic of educational research by means of illustrative studies. The content of the studies is also to be noted; many of them will reappear in later chapters. No doubt you have studied experiments in other psychology courses, but a review will be useful. We also take up a case study by a humanistic psychologist, as well as the correlational method prominent in developmental psychology. Finally, we will look at research combining the experimental and correlational methods.

## EXPERIMENTS ON LEARNING IN ARTIFICIAL CONDITIONS

In a formal experiment, the investigator fixes the conditions in which the person works according to a systematic plan. Two or more sets of conditions are contrasted. The experimenter may manipulate the lighting, or the percentage of the hour that the student works independently, or the order in which examples and principles are presented. The arranged conditions are spoken of as a *treatment*. Most experiments have at least two such treatments, with different subjects assigned to each. Another kind of experiment puts just one group through two or more treatments. To test the effect of caffeine on motor performance, for example, one might give students coffee on one day and decaffeinated coffee on another.

In some experiments conditions are artificial, whereas others are carried out in the usual educational setting. The central distinction between artificial experiments and what this book calls classroom experiments is that in the latter a *normal* course of study is presented in two (or more) versions or under two procedures. Both teachers and students are playing for keeps. The artificial experiment may be conducted in a classroom, of course, perhaps with a brief task that resembles a school lesson.

Artificial conditions in a brief experiment allow the investigator a large degree of control over what happens to the subject. Such experiments leave the reader uncertain about how similar treatments will work in regular teaching, where conditions will not duplicate the artificial ones.

## A Two-Group Example: Training Children to Copy Forms

One of the skills basic to the learning of reading is the ability to identify the shapes of letters. It has often been suggested that children who have difficulty in making this visual discrimination can learn to do so if they start by tracing the shapes, bringing the touch and muscular senses into play. Because previous research had left in doubt the effectiveness of methods such as this, Joanna Williams (1975) set up a controlled study with 20 children, aged 48 months to 66 months, from low-income homes.

Instead of training on letters (which some children might already have become acquainted with), Williams used "letter-like" forms (Fig. 4.1). To assess the training Williams used two kinds of test. Her Reproduction Test used three of the forms. A specimen of one of the forms was placed in front of the child for him to copy on unruled paper. After the child had copied each form in turn, two of the forms were exposed at one time to be copied again. Finally, all three forms were displayed together for him to copy. The Reproduction score (maximum of 12) took into account accuracy and overall appearance.

Williams's Discrimination Test (maximum score of 48) was a multiple-choice task. In the simplest item, the child was given a strip showing one of the standard shapes along with four transformations of it. The child, handed another copy of the shape on a separate card, was asked to find which figure on the strip exactly matched it.

On a random basis, half the boys and half the girls were assigned to the experimental group and half to a control group. Both groups took the tests on

## FIGURE 4.1

Letter-like forms used in laboratory studies of reading, with some of their transformations

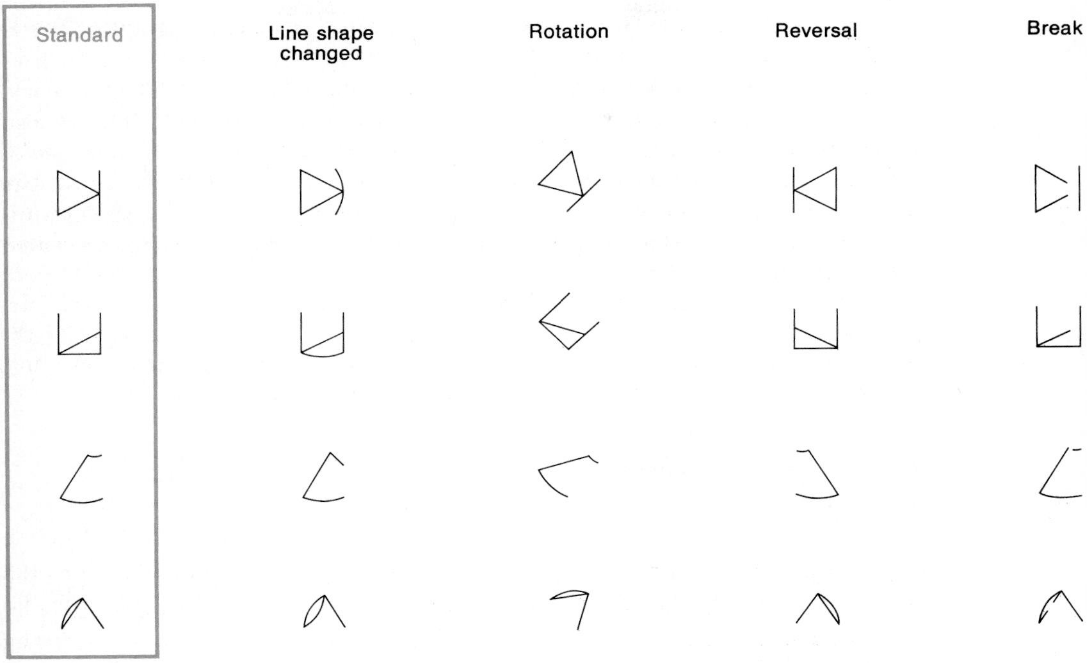

| Standard | Line shape changed | Rotation | Reversal | Break |
|---|---|---|---|---|

SOURCE: Adapted from Gibson et al. (1962), p. 898. Copyright 1962 by the American Psychological Association. Reprinted by permission.

two occasions a week apart. In the interim the Control children participated in the usual activities of their daycare center, with no training; the Experimental children were given 15 minutes of training on three days during the week. The Reproduction training consisted simply of practice in copying the three forms used in the pretest. The experimenter showed how to correct any errors. The Experimentals took their second test the day after the last training session. The posttest averages* were as follows:

| | Experimental group | Control group |
|---|---|---|
| Reproduction Test | 43.5 | 27.0 |
| Discrimination Test | 6.1 | 6.2 |

* Williams reported an adjusted average, but for our purposes the adjustment procedure can be ignored.

There are two obvious conclusions: Experimentals did better on the Reproduction posttest; there was no difference on the Discrimination test. (This last statement ignores the superiority of 0.1 in the Control group. In any comparison, small differences arise by chance. It is more sensible to ignore them than to try to explain them.)

The results seem to mean that training children in copying produces better copying, but has no direct effect on their ability to make comparisons such as the child has to make in recognizing that $b$ in his primer is not $d$. That is to say, training in copying did not "transfer" into better discrimination. Williams also asked another question about transfer: Does practice in copying one set of forms improve ability to copy other unpracticed forms? For this purpose she made up a second pair of posttests, like the original Reproduction and Discrimination tests except that, on the final test day, the children were presented forms they had never seen. The average scores were as follows (change from the other test is shown in parentheses):

|  | Experimental group | Control group |
|---|---|---|
| Reproduction Test | 33.3 (−10.2) | 30.6 (+3.6) |
| Discrimination Test | 6.4 (+0.3) | 6.3 (+0.1) |

Again, we can disregard the small effects (though the gain of 3.6 in the Control group may not be a matter of chance alone). The important point is that the Experimental children were very little better than the Controls at reproducing unfamiliar forms.

Several points in Williams's technique deserve emphasis:

- An untreated control group was the basis for comparison. If Williams had collected data only on trained subjects, she would perhaps have given the training credit for any progress found. But just the experience of taking the first test probably improved scores by some amount. Finding out how well the control group could do, aided only by that "practice effect" on the test, provided a proper baseline against which to judge the experimental group's final performance.

- The membership of the two groups was controlled. Williams kept the sexes in balance in the two groups and tried to balance out other possible differences by random assignment.

- There were four tests. One was direct, and the other three were transfer tests. Often a treatment that improves one outcome is powerless to improve some other important outcome, and sometimes it can actually impair the second kind of performance. Only multiple measurement could clarify just what it was that changed. We shall see the same benefit from multiple measurement in most of the other studies presented in this chapter.

Williams's study has two major limitations: the training was extremely brief, and the sample was small. Brief training is characteristic of laboratory experiments; the results do leave open the possibility that more extended training in the Reproduction task would benefit ability to discriminate. As for the small size, Williams made a deliberate gamble. To train more children would have made the experiment more costly, but would have produced more dependable results. Fortunately, the results here not only seemed clear-cut, but seemed to clear up contradictions among previous studies. It is certain, however, that if the experiment were repeated with 20 other children, the average test scores would not be identical to those Williams found.

1   What would be wrong with conducting an experiment in which the training is given to the children who seem most to need it, keeping the other children as a control group?

2   What reasons lead investigators to keep laboratory studies brief?

## A Four-Group Example: Training in Copying and Discrimination

To get us started, I greatly simplified the story of Williams's experiment; she actually compared 40 children, divided among four groups. Some psychologists had argued that the way to improve perception is to train directly on visual perception; and to check out this suggestion Williams developed a procedure for discrimination training. One group of children (also randomly selected) was given practice on precisely the task that constituted the Discrimination Test: matching a standard form to one form in a row or (as in the harder items in the test) matching a pair or a three-form set. The training used the same forms as those in the pretest.

Williams was investigating two factors in (possible causes of) improvement: practice in copying and practice in matching. She therefore set up a factorial experiment; such an experiment considers the causes in all possible combinations. For Williams, this required four groups:

Control group (neither factor present)

Reproduction group (copying factor present)

Discrimination group (matching factor present)

Combination group (both factors present)

This is called a 2 × 2 (or 2-by-2) design. Far more complicated sets of contrasts can be built up. In each training session for the Combination subjects, Williams divided the time half and half between copying and matching.

## The uses of artificiality

When we take up motor skills in Chapter 10, we will consider the evidence that "mental practice"—thinking about the action while the body does not move—is often beneficial. Although most experiments have the subjects practice some familiar sport, Rawlings et al. (1972) set up an experiment in which subjects fol-

lowed, with an electrical probe, a target that revolved once per second. Rawlings chose this device (called a pursuit rotor) both to get precise measurement and to make certain that the skill being taught was equally unfamiliar to everyone.

The first experiment was conducted on 24 college women. Eight of them (Group A) had twenty-five 30-second trials on each of ten days. During the 30-second rest between trials, they were required to read color names aloud so

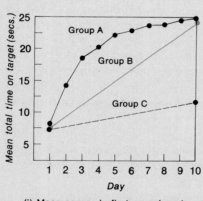

**(i) Mean scores in first experiment**

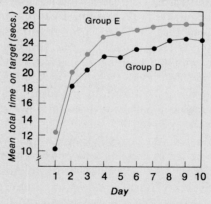

**(ii) Mean scores in second experiment**

| | |
|---|---|
| Groups A and D | Physical practice plus color naming |
| Group B | Mental practice on Days 2-9 |
| Group C | Color naming only on Days 2–9 |
| Group E | Physical practice plus mental practice |

that they could not think about the motor task. The controls (Group C) went through this procedure on Day 1 and Day 10, but did only the color naming on Days 2–9. Group B, the mental-practice group, spent Days 2–9 imagining that they were practicing the pursuit task, making no movements but imaging the movements. The scores in Chart i show that mental practice really worked, though it is something of a fluke that it worked as well as physical practice: as you see, final scores (Day 10) were the same for both groups (A and B). The result is psychologically important because it seemed to disprove the belief that mental practice works only with tasks that have a large symbolic element, such as sorting mail into boxes.

The second experiment (Chart ii) used 20 males. Ten of them (Group D) had the same treatment as those in Group A in the other experiment—physical practice plus color naming. The other ten used the 30-second rest pauses to do mental practice. This second group (E) took a lead on Day 1 that they held until the end of the experiment.

The results of the Reproduction and Discrimination tests (Fig. 4.2, p. 116) again show the usefulness of measuring several outcomes. The findings are as follows:

On reproduction of practiced forms: good results for training that included the Reproduction factor; results from Discrimination training little better than under the Control condition alone.

On reproduction of unfamiliar forms: differences among the three kinds of training slight, but all a bit better than the Control group.

On discrimination of practiced forms: groups with Discrimination training markedly better than Combination groups; groups without practice in matching much weaker.

On discrimination of unfamiliar forms: same pattern as with practiced forms.

The general conclusion is what a psychological experiment on learning often finds: Students learn what they practice. Insofar as this small experiment can indicate, practice in perceptual discrimination teaches perceptual discrimination, practice in copying teaches copying. But transfer was not absent. Practice on one set of forms had some effect on matching or copying of other forms. Transfer in work methods and attention habits accounts for such gains;

## FIGURE 4.2

### Mean scores on four measures in Williams's experiment

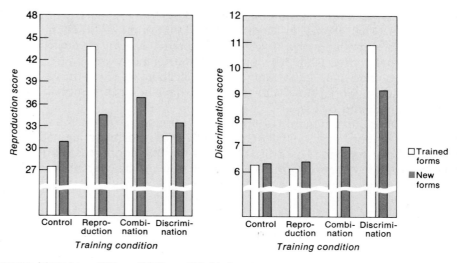

SOURCE: Adapted from Williams (1975), pp. 793–94. Copyright 1975 by the American Psychological Association. Reprinted by permission. Figures have been redrawn.

such collateral learning comes slowly and less surely than gains from direct training on specific responses to a particular repeated stimulus.

Williams, on the basis of this and other experiments she conducted, concluded that tactile-kinesthetic training is unlikely to improve perception, although it seems relevant to a motor performance such as handwriting. Later (p. 444) we shall see results showing a positive effect on visual learning of training with tactile-kinesthetic cues, in a laboratory experiment with conditions different from those of Williams's study.

**3** If you wanted a class to spend 15 minutes a day on training, and considered reproduction and discrimination equally important, how much time would you spend on each?

**4** Photographs are to be used to teach bird recognition. Three decisions need to be made: (1) whether to show the bird in motion, (2) whether to show it in color, and (3) how long to present each bird—15 seconds, 30 seconds, or 1 minute. The total training time is fixed.
   a. How would a factorial experiment be planned to answer these questions?
   b. Would the factorial experiment have any advantage over three separate experiments, one on each causal factor?
   c. What measure or measures would be reasonable to assess the results of the training?

**5** In the second Rawlings experiment (box, p. 115), how many days of practice time did mental practice save? That is, when did the mental-practice group reach the level it took the Controls ten days to reach?

**6** Can you argue from the second Rawlings experiment that mental practice is primarily useful in building intellectual understanding of a task, and not in promoting physical skill?

## Some Statistical Concepts

From time to time in this book you will need some statistical vocabulary in order to follow an argument having practical significance. Moreover, when you read research reports in psychology or education you will encounter statistical procedures. The basic ideas are much the same no matter which statistical technique is actually used in a study; as a matter of fact, in analyzing her study, Williams used procedures I shall not describe.

THE MEAN    The first question one asks is, "How well did the group do?" The investigator most often calculates the arithmetic average; that is, he adds up the scores and divides by the number of scores. This is referred to as the *mean* in research reports. (Another statistic that we shall encounter a time or two in this book—the median—is also a kind of average. It is determined by locating the middle score in the group—the score that half the group surpasses.)

THE MEAN SQUARE AND THE STANDARD DEVIATION    Readers often want to know how widely the group spreads. This could be described by giving the highest and lowest scores, or by calculating how far each score is from the mean and averaging those distances. The standard deviation (s.d.), however, is the most common index of within-group variation.

The first step in calculating standard deviation is to square the deviation (from the mean) for each person. If the mean is 9.2 and Ellen scores 10.0, the deviation is 0.8 and the square is 0.64. One takes the average of those squares to get the "mean square." (Do not try to remember that term. And do not pay attention to my white lie about taking "the average" of the squares. Modern technique divides the sum of the squares by an adjusted value instead of the number of persons; this can be ignored here.)

The square root of the mean square is the standard deviation. It is a kind of average of the distances of the individuals from the group mean.

THE NORMAL DISTRIBUTION    If a report supplies the mean and the standard deviation, the reader can form an impression about the whole set of data. He does this by assuming that the scores have what is called a normal distribution. Some scores come close to a normal distribution and some depart from it (p. 310). But as a rough approximation it serves well.

FIGURE 4.3

Normal distribution

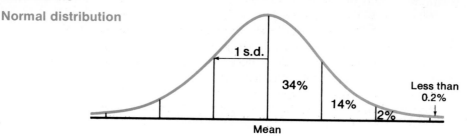

1 s.d.

34%

14%

2%

Less than
0.2%

Mean

SOURCE: Cronbach, *Essentials of Psychological Testing* (New York: Harper & Row, 1970).

Figure 4.3 shows what fraction of the scores in a normal distribution fall within each section of the score scale, where each section is one standard deviation wide. This is a bit much to keep in mind, so it is helpful to memorize these rules:

> Within one standard deviation of the average are approximately 68 per cent of the scores (about two-thirds).

> Within two standard deviations of the average are approximately 95 per cent of the scores (all but one-twentieth).

The count, of course, includes persons on both sides of the average.

The average Reproduction score in Williams's Discrimination group was 33. The standard deviation was close to 5. Now that I have told you that, you can visualize a distribution with two-thirds of the subjects between 28 and 38, and with 95 per cent of the subjects between 23 and 43. Recall that the Control mean was 30; thus, a large fraction of the Discrimination group—something like 25 or 30 per cent—did worse than the average Control subject on this test.

STATISTICAL SIGNIFICANCE    Williams's experiment was small. As I have said, the mean of each group would be likely to change if the experiment were repeated on a fresh sample of children. The experimenter or his reader always has to ask: Did the groups differ enough to show that something other than chance variation was probably at work? The investigator answers by making a statement about *significance*. This is a frequent word in research reports, and it is easy to misunderstand. Let me explain as directly as possible.

The discrimination group had a mean of 33; the Controls had a mean of 30. We know that the difference in another investigation would probably not be 3.0. Could it be 0.0? −3.0? Let us ask a preliminary question. How much can we expect the Discrimination mean to change?

If we did the study over and over on fresh samples, each study would produce a mean score for a Discrimination group. Those means would form a distribution that is close to normal. To estimate *its* standard deviation, you would *divide* the original mean square *by the size of the group*, and take the square root. Williams's mean square was close to 25 and she had ten cases per group; the square root of 2.5 is 1.6. If means of samples vary with an s.d. of 1.6, it would not be at all surprising if the first sample were one or two points away from the mean of all samples. Similar reasoning says that the Control group could—just because of accidents of sampling—be one or two points from the combined mean of all Control samples.

We come to "What if?" questions. What if the Control and Discrimination treatments really have the same effect, and both would produce scores of 31.5 in a very large sample? Would it be likely that if we took ten children at random and calculated their average score, the mean would be as high as 33? Certainly! A mean of 33 is less than one s.d. away from 31.5 in the distribution of sample means. Conclusion: the Discrimination training is not "significantly" better than the Control training. If the experiment were repeated, there is a good chance that the Control mean would be higher than the Discrimination mean.

Whether a difference of three points is called significant depends on two things: variation within each group and group size. If persons within the group have almost the same score, then we would expect those in another sample to have about the same score. So results would fluctuate little. And even if individuals vary widely, averages over large groups fluctuate little. So large experiments give stable results.

The experimenter proceeds formally in his analysis. We shall not look at details of the procedure. If the true difference were zero, a difference of a certain age would occur no more than 5 per cent of the time. If the difference he observed is at least that large, he calls it "significant at the 5 per cent level"; or he puts an asterisk beside it and adds the footnote "$p < .05$." (Other percentages are also used. Thus, Williams said: "Performance on forms that had been used in training was superior to that on untrained forms ... $p < .01$.")

An experimenter is usually conservative in his judgments. When uncertain about a result, he repeats the study with more subjects or otherwise improves the experiment. Eventually, he will either establish a dependable effect or will be convinced that there is none. A research program accumulates evidence and looks for consistent patterns. The "flash in the pan"—the difference observed only once—is dropped from consideration.

The practical significance of differences requires as much thought as the statistical significance. Discrimination training was superior to Combination training in improving discrimination of unpracticed forms. The educator pondering the practical significance would have to consider whether the difference of 2 points on a scale of 12 is important enough to offset the other values of Combination training. A difference can be statistically significant without being important, and vice versa.

# Means and standard deviations in a study of two classroom reward structures

R. Wheeler and F. L. Ryan (1973) set up an 18-day experiment. Guided by a workbook, students in Grades V and VI carried out inquiry activities about the life of the Iban people of Borneo. In one class, students worked individually, knowing that the six best notebooks turned in would earn a prize; in the other class, students worked in teams of five or six, in a group-competitive condition (called "cooperative" by Wheeler and Ryan). In the latter, duplicate prizes were promised to all members of whichever team made the notebook that was judged best. An achievement test showed no important difference between treatments.

Attitude measures were also collected. In the table, P indicates the extent to which the student described his teacher as fostering cooperative practices. ("The teacher tells students to share ideas.") $AT_{ss}$ indicates the student's liking for social studies, and $AT_{coop}$ indicates his liking for working in a team rather than on an individual task. Anxiety had been measured at the start of the experiment; the attitude questionnaires were administered at the end. The analysis considered separately the students above and below the median on anxiety. What conclusions do the means and s.d.'s suggest to you?

**Means and standard deviations for perceptions (P), attitudes toward social studies ($AT_{ss}$), and attitudes toward cooperation ($AT_{coop}$)**

| Group treatment | P | | $AT_{ss}$ | | $AT_{coop}$ | |
| --- | --- | --- | --- | --- | --- | --- |
| | M | SD | M | SD | M | SD |
| High anxiety (cooperative, $n = 14$) | 32.71 | 2.62 | 16.07 | 2.70 | 16.29 | 2.52 |
| Low anxiety (cooperative, $n = 15$) | 33.53 | 2.33 | 15.73 | 2.05 | 17.13 | 1.77 |
| High anxiety (competitive, $n = 14$) | 17.21 | 6.62 | 13.57 | 4.72 | 11.86 | 3.90 |
| Low anxiety (competitive, $n = 15$) | 15.07 | 3.57 | 14.13 | 3.44 | 12.20 | 2.67 |

SOURCE: Wheeler & Ryan (1973). Copyright 1973 by the American Psychological Association. Reprinted by permission.

**7** The Wheeler-Ryan experiment (box) found that the contrast between group competition and individual competition was significant, but anxiety effects were not statistically significant. What does this statement add to the information in the table?

**8** E. Kaplan (1966) compared a Head Start group with a control group on two coordination tasks (among other measures). Performance was scored on a scale from 1 (poor) to 5 (good). The scores were distributed as follows:

| | Performance Level (coloring task) | | | | | Performance Level (cutting task) | | | | |
|---|---|---|---|---|---|---|---|---|---|---|
| | 1 | 2 | 3 | 4 | 5 | 1 | 2 | 3 | 4 | 5 |
| In Head Start | 8 | 2 | 3 | 6 | 16 | 5 | 4 | 5 | 5 | 16 |
| Not in Head Start | 17 | 5 | 3 | 2 | 8 | 7 | 7 | 8 | 5 | 8 |

There were 35 children in each group. Kaplan found the difference on the coloring task "statistically significant," but that on the cutting task not significant. How important is this statement to the reader?

**9** The reading rates of representative college freshmen might range from 250 to 600 words per minute. Would you expect the average score to divide the group in half? Suppose we measure instead the time required to read one thousand words. Would the average for this divide the group in half?

# EXPERIMENTS ON LEARNING IN THE CLASSROOM

To make a formal test of an educational proposal, research is needed under classroom conditions and over a fairly extended period. It is generally difficult to maintain a high degree of experimental control in the field.

A true experiment is one in which contrasting treatments are applied to groups that differ only by chance at the start of the study. To investigate classroom learning, the preferred plan is to form groups at random, or perhaps to pair the subjects according to ability and then split the pairs at random to build up the groups. Each group then is given one kind of instruction. When students cannot be assigned individually, whole classes can be assigned to treatments randomly—assuming that the school is interested in making the experimental test. Initial differences between the classes are often so large as to blur the comparison, unless many classes are used.

Practical problems make compromises necessary in classroom research. Some compromises preserve the randomness of the true experiment, as, for example:

- Carrying out the treatment separately from the regular schoolwork by taking the subject off to a laboratory room.

- Keeping the experiment short. (Perhaps one interrupts the classwork for only a single hour to apply a short treatment; or perhaps for 30 minutes on each of ten days.)

Letting teachers or students volunteer for a particular treatment is less desirable. Initial differences between volunteers and nonvolunteers may distort conclusions. Groups formed by haphazard assignment cannot be called equivalent. Findings of quasi experiments (studies that compare nonrandom groups) are open to question (Riecken & Boruch, 1974; see also Chap. 9).*

The illustration of classroom research given below is a classic. Rigorous techniques were applied on an exceptional scale. Whole classes—not individual students—were assigned to treatments. So many classrooms were used that initial differences probably balanced out.

Educators frequently ask the research worker to find the answer to a question of the form: "Is Method A better than Method B?" Is programmed instruction better than a textbook? phonics better than "look-and-say"? and so on. The experiment to be discussed appears at first to be of that type, but it actually has a factorial design, with qualitative observation added to the statistics. When we have examined the investigators' conclusions, we will be in a position to consider why the educator ought not ask simple A-versus-B questions.

## Example: Two Ways to Subtract

The study is concerned with subtraction. There are two ways to subtract 27 from 91 (Fig. 4.4). In the first method (D), one "decomposes" the larger number. You cannot take 7 from 1 but you can take 7 from 11. To do this you decompose, or *borrow,* 10 from 90 to create $10 + 1 = 11$ in the right-hand column. Then you subtract in each column, 7 from 11, and 20 from 80.

The equal additions (EA) method has been widely used in the British Isles. Again you need 11 if you are to subtract 7. The EA method creates 11 by *adding* 10 to both terms. You add 10 to the 1 in the top number, and to offset it add 10 to 27 in the bottom number. Then subtract.

Do those who learn by EA subtract more accurately and rapidly than those taught to borrow? Brownell and Moser (1949) set out to determine which method to teach, introducing the experiment into the regular grade-school instruction. Forty-one third-grade teachers agreed to cooperate, and their classes were divided at random into four groups. Two groups of classes were taught the D procedure and two groups were taught the EA procedure. Why *two* D

---

* Certain rarely used procedures enable one to reach valid conclusions from nonequivalent groups (D. T. Campbell, 1969).

## FIGURE 4.4

**Two ways to subtract**

Decomposition (D)    Equal Additions (EA)

$$\begin{array}{r} {}^8\!9\,'1 \\ 2\,7 \\ \hline 6\,4 \end{array} \qquad \begin{array}{r} 9\,'1 \\ {}^3\!2\,7 \\ \hline 6\,4 \end{array}$$

groups? The investigators made the astute prediction that what matters is not the subtraction technique but how it is taught. So half the D classes were taught in a rote, mechanical fashion to carry out the rules of borrowing; in the remaining D classes the teachers made a great effort to explain the logic behind the procedure. Similarly, half the EA classes were taught by rote, and half were given explanation as well as demonstration and practice. This was a 2-by-2 design like that of Williams (p. 113).

Performance in subtracting two-digit numbers was tested after several weeks of lessons. Brownell and Moser gave the same test in all classes and calculated averages for the treatments. As shown in Fig. 4.5 (Panel i), the most successful group was the one that learned the decomposition method through a meaningful explanation. Consider this group as a standard; the bar clear across the box shows its average as 100 per cent. The other three groups were not far

## FIGURE 4.5

**Results with four methods of teaching subtraction**

Each group is compared with the average performance in the D-meaningful group.

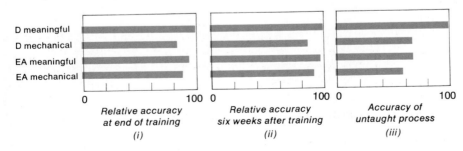

| | | |
|---|---|---|
| D meaningful | | |
| D mechanical | | |
| EA meaningful | | |
| EA mechanical | | |

Relative accuracy at end of training (i)    Relative accuracy six weeks after training (ii)    Accuracy of untaught process (iii)

SOURCE: Data from Brownell & Moser (1949).

behind; even the least successful group scored almost 80 per cent as high as the best group. The differences between the three runners-up were small.

Immediate achievement is not the best measure of long-run educational effectiveness; long-term performance and transfer are more important. So Brownell and Moser did what every evaluator ought to do if he can. First they tested retention six weeks after the instruction stopped. Second, they asked the students to extend their skill to a new task. The training had been on two-digit numbers. The "transfer" task asked them to subtract three-digit numbers (for example, 247 from 533) without additional training.

The results (Panels ii and iii) are again presented with the D-meaningful group as the standard of comparison. You can see that when the students were retested on the same task, meaningfulness was the only variable that mattered. But on the transfer task, there is an interaction: decomposition taught meaningfully generated more flexible mastery of subtraction. It is not surprising that rote teaching produces less durable and less flexible learning.

EA-with-explanation showed up rather badly in the end, apparently because the children did not really understand the process. Teachers reported that their best efforts to explain EA left students confused, whereas the decomposition idea was easy to put across. Meaningful instruction, then, is not a *procedure*; meaning comes out of what the learner does with the instructional stimuli.

This was borne out most strikingly when Brownell and Moser considered schools separately. In schools where arithmetic had been taught meaningfully in Grades II and III, the third-graders made good use of the explanations. They asked penetrating questions of the teacher and even worked out explanations for themselves. Third-graders in other schools had been taught arithmetic mechanically in the first two years, and they could not take advantage of explanations when these were offered. The children had not learned that numerical relations can make sense. They were at a disadvantage intellectually because of the training provided by their first teachers.

## Asking Good Questions

The investigator often has to reinterpret the question the educator asks. If someone had carried out the D-versus-EA comparison by itself, he would have found that the methods made almost no difference—*if* the teachers he studied used mechanical instruction. And if he had called for meaningful instruction, he still would have found little difference, unless he measured outcomes beyond direct, immediate mastery. Even the Brownell-Moser experiment would have given a less sound conclusion if the investigators had not looked at school-by-school reports, and so come to understand that explanations worked well only *after* pupils had learned to make sense of arithmetic. An over-simple conclusion is to be expected whenever an experiment sets up a horse race between competing educational formulas.

## A classroom comparison of instructional aids

The study described here is a bit more elaborate than most classroom tryouts by teachers, but the simple experimental design produces a clear comparison—within the limits of a small, brief study.

Strang (1973) wanted to know how much help self-instructional aids could give in vocational training. He prepared slides showing 20 steps in repairing an automobile distributor. The vocational student—working individually at a bench with a distributor, tools, and replacement parts—had his own projector. He could call up a slide when he reached the step it displayed. The instructor stood by to give advice (a "prompt") when the student asked for help.

Strang had four groups of 12 boys, assigned at random. The treatments were as follows:

A. Slides only
B. Slides plus text (A text paragraph—about 75 words per step—described what the slide showed. It was provided for the student to read along with the slide.)
C. Slide plus tape (When the slide was projected, the student heard a recording of the same words the B group saw in print.)
D. Slides plus text plus tape (In addition to Treatment C, the student had the printed text to refer to.)

At the end of the session, the student was asked to repeat the whole operation without the pictures or words to refer to. If he failed at a step, the instructor prompted him and marked down one error. The following average scores and times are left for you to interpret (Questions 15 and 16). All values are rounded off, to simplify.

|  | Treatment | | | |
|---|---|---|---|---|
|  | A | B | C | D |
| Number of prompts required during instructional run | 7 | 2 | 1 | 1 |
| Time (minutes) required for instructional run | 19 | 30 | 24 | 23 |
| Number of errors on test run (prompts required) | 0.6 | 0.8 | 1.1 | 0.8 |

An instructional plan or device is one part of a system. Its effectiveness will depend upon the harmony with which all parts of the system work together. How much mileage a brand of gasoline gives depends on the car in which it is burned, the way the engine is tuned, the style of the driver, and so on. The mileage one gets from an educational innovation likewise depends on the past development of the students, the way they are tuned to respond to the instruction, and the style of the teacher. Even the administrative procedure of the school (rigid schedules? letter grades?) and the physical structure of the classroom can make a difference. It is for this reason that educational research can give no cook-proof recipes. There have been attempts from time to time to work out mass-produced instruction that cannot go wrong. The term *teacher-proof* has even been used as an advertising slogan for instructional materials.

The following observation regarding "Sesame Street" in daycare centers for 4-year-olds reminds us that uniform instructional materials do not mean uniform instruction: What children take from TV depends on factors beyond the producer's control. One group sits docilely; the adult leader shushes them when any murmur or handclap threatens "to distract from the lesson." Another group is ajump with excitement, shouting out the letters and numbers they recognize, beating the characters on the screen to the intellectual punch-line, taking in the experience through voicebox and muscle as well as through eye and ear. It is hard to believe that learning is the same in both groups. An educational activity operates as a system, and it is the judgment of the teacher (or the self-directing learner) that keeps the system at top efficiency.

---

**10** In a college dormitory, a short course of assertiveness training is offered, on a voluntary basis, to women. A psychology major proposes to evaluate its effectiveness by observing the assertive behavior of the women after they have taken the course, comparing them with women in the dorm who did not take it. What initial differences in the groups might account for any differences the psychology student observes following the training?

**11** Two procedures have been used for evaluating TV programs like "Sesame Street." One is to compare the development of children in the year the program is introduced with the development of similar children observed a year earlier (who could not have seen it). The other is to arrange a true experiment by providing TV sets and scheduling regular viewing in a randomly selected group of daycare centers, leaving other centers without TV. In what sense is each of these designs a compromise with the ideal plan of investigation?

**12** Students who do poorly on verbal reasoning tests often show average ability or even superior ability in rote-learning experiments. Does the Brownell-Moser research support the idea of dividing children according to ability and using rote methods to teach subtraction to the ones who learn well by rote?

**13** A mathematics teacher suggests that the equal-addition method should be taught rather than the decompositon method, because EA can be applied logically when a negative number is to be subtracted from a positive number. (This task is a stumbling block in algebra.) Moreover, this teacher suggests an explanation in terms of "steps along the number line" that he thinks makes EA meaningful to third-graders. His argument illustrates that even a careful, large-scale study can be challenged by a teacher who points to a teaching method or an outcome the first study did not investigate.

Does this kind of challenge suggest that educational experiments are useless?

14  Research is being designed to compare two summer programs for preschoolers. Both programs aim to foster language development. Investigator A proposes to assign the children, from six neighborhoods, between programs strictly at random. Investigator B plans to hold discussions with community leaders and parents and to follow their advice in assigning individual children. Investigator C plans to assign neighborhood blocks to programs, all the children in a program to come from the same neighborhood. The first investigator is proposing a true experiment, the other two, quasi experiments.

What advantages and disadvantages do you see in each of these plans? What further alternatives can you suggest?

15  Assume that the result in Strang's experiment (box, p. 125) would be confirmed in a study with many more boys. On the basis of this evidence, which of the methods appears to be the best for general instructional use? Assume that the cost of having one projector per student is acceptable, and that an instructor would monitor several students at adjacent benches simultaneously.

16  What explanation can you suggest for Strang's findings? How did evidence on more than one effect of the treatment help you in your interpretation?

17  An experiment compared two courses on how to diagnose handicapped children. Commenting on the study, McKeachie and Kulik (1975, p. 176) express regret that the test items providing the final evidence of effectiveness were prepared by the persons who wrote one of the courses. Explain their discontent.

## A CASE STUDY: HIDDEN DEPENDENCY

In the case study, one individual is thoroughly studied, usually by tests, interviews, and observations. Sometimes the case reports are by-products of therapeutic and remedial work, and sometimes they are part of systematic investigations. Nevitt Sanford's (1966) report on Mack is a useful example.

At the time of the study—in the 1940s—Mack was a 24-year-old college freshman preparing for a law career. The son of a retired working man, Mack had worked as a responsible clerk for some time to save money for college. Mack rose in DeMolay, a youth organization, to a high post—Master Councillor; his schoolmates elected him vice-president of the high-school student body; in business school he was president.

Though Mack belongs to a previous generation, people like him are to be found today (as is seen in a briefer case report by Adelson, in Kagan & Coles,

1971). It seems reasonable, therefore, to write about Mack at age 24 in the present tense. The report on Mack is especially instructive because, for all his weaknesses in personality and character, his surface behavior is that of a model student and future citizen. He exemplifies many principles of emotional and attitudinal development that later chapters will examine.

Mack's salient problems center on attitudes toward authority and his sex role. What he feels that he is (his self-concept) conflicts with what he thinks he should be (his ideal for himself). He has always tried to suppress his doubts about himself, and he has learned just those attitudes and styles of action that make this suppression easier. Here we can only summarize the psychologist's explanation of Mack's development, giving none of the detailed evidence from which Sanford reasoned.

The most basic forces shaping Mack's history were his relations with his parents and his weak physical constitution. Mack was loved by his mother and in early childhood got some affection from her. Mack's father was fifty years older than he, emotionally distant but demanding good conduct. As Mack recalls him, he was unambitious and sternly honest. (Having a charge account, in his view, took unfair advantage of the merchant.) Mack's chance of gaining secure affection was wrecked by his mother's death while Mack was still a child. This left Mack in the care of a sister only four years older than he, and of an aunt with a separate home.

From the age of 12, Mack was in poor health: first anemia, later, stomach trouble. During most of his adolescence he was weak and unable to exert himself. His illness perhaps had psychological causes. It appears that Mack would like to depend on someone and to be free not to strive; perhaps illness was a useful way of withdrawing when he could not quit outright.

Mack had good relations with boys. With girls, he says, he was "always the backward boy." At age 24, Mack was dating a teacher. He told the interviewer (Sanford, 1966, p. 143):

> I hope to get married to the girl I'm going with now. She is an awfully nice companion. Most girls are interested only in a good time and want fellows with lots of money to spend. . . . I talked with . . . [her uncle] about an automobile that she was interested in. I looked it over for her, since I knew something about cars, and told her it was in good condition. I got started going with her that way. I found out that she wasn't interested in money, but was interested in me in spite of my discharge from the army, my poor health and prospects. She's just very good—not beautiful, but a tremendously nice personality. . . . She has a nice figure and is very wholesome. When we get married depends on circumstances. It's quite a responsibility. . . . We're both at the proper age. I intend to work part-time. I don't like her teaching; I like to support my wife. . . . She is a good cook, and that is an asset, what with my stomach condition.

This is hardly the enthusiasm one might expect in a prospective bridegroom.

As Sanford pieced together Mack's attitudes and history, he arrived at the "stream of influence" pictured (much simplified) in Fig. 4.6.

## FIGURE 4.6

### Forces forming Mack's attitudes

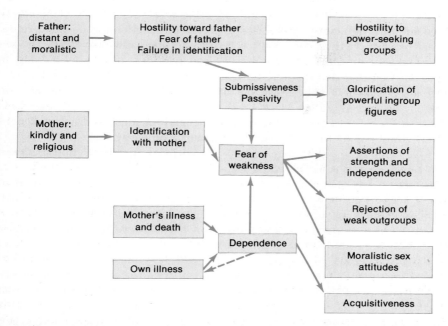

SOURCE: Figure adapted from R. Nevitt Sanford, in T. W. Adorno et al., *The Authoritarian Personality* (New York: Harper & Row, 1950), p. 801.

Mack responded to his impersonal father with both admiration and hostility. Mack did not feel free to violate his father's wishes or to attack him, yet he had no wish to follow his father's ways. Unable to rebel or to identify fully, Mack submitted to his father's authority; a dutiful person is safe from punishment. Mack now reacts to other men in the same way.

He admires and approves of distinguished and powerful figures, including certain prominent military figures. He sees every organization as a hierarchy of power, composed of the lowly, who are directed, and the key figures, who rule. Having repressed his hostility toward "father figures," he thinks of prominent and powerful men as benign, just, and supporting. Mack is an appeaser, hoping to win some measure of acceptance from the powerful figures whose potential to crush him he covertly fears. Mack criticizes anyone who is scrambling for power, suspicious of anyone who would try to get ahead of him. This is one underpinning of his antiminority feelings, for he thinks minority groups are plotting to gain power.

Mack's mother, while alive, communicated religious values. She saw to it that her children attended Sunday school, and Mack accepted some of the teachings. He speaks of God with conviction and reads the Bible thoughtfully. Mack's mother was a model he could imitate. She did not threaten as his father did.

All the forces in Mack's life came together in a hunger for dependency. If he could only get more love, instead of the little attention his bed-ridden mother could give. If he could only return to her care, after her death left him to the hurried ministrations of his sister and his aunt. If, sick as he was, he could only be comforted and told to take life easy.

Fear of weakness pulls Mack out of the role of spineless conformer. Dependency was punished by Mack's father to the point where Mack dared not express it. To be physically strong became a conscious ideal, and he could not—cannot—admit having the dependency wishes of a little boy.

Given this deep-seated conflict between an ideal of strength and a craving to be cared for and directed, what does Mack do? He stresses the symbols of independence and strength: he finds pleasure in a good rifle, insists on being the sole support of his wife, and is tough and aggressive in presenting his political views. Abhorring softness in himself, he condemns it in others. To the persecuted, he is unsympathetic. He must push them away, and find reasons to condemn them rather than align himself with them.

Sex is dangerous. Mack has not succeeded in any previous affectional relation, and his tone in speaking of his present girlfriend is remarkably unimpassioned. Mack seems to lack respect for women as individuals, yet he is nearly ready to marry. This is understood by seeing that Mack thinks of two kinds of women—to quote Sanford (p. 156)—"the 'bad,' weak, dangerous, exploitive, sexual woman who drags one down, and the good, wholesome, asexual one who gives." Mack is able to accept the schoolteacher; he can think of her as pure and mothering, inspiring rather than exciting.

Mack's wish that women would take care of him is part of his more general wish to get things from the world. Having property is important; he is quick to praise those who help him get ahead. At the same time he holds his grasping in check, for he has the conventional disapproval of selfishness. Mack's strongest desire is "to raise myself physically, financially, and socially." But he is too fearful to contend against established power. Law is an ideally chosen route of advancement where he can be on the side of authority and where his training will "unlock doors." Competition disturbs him: nearly twenty years later, he still recalls that in the seventh grade a girl defeated him in a spelling match. A trend-spotter, he likes to see who or what will be powerful and climb onto that bandwagon. He wants to be carried to a position of power.

COMMENT    Sanford's case study was retrospective and used the interview to capture information about Mack's development. Other case studies, and some statistical studies, follow the individual as he grows, collecting new information each year. This was Piaget's procedure in his work on intellectual development (Chap. 8). Another example is Fein's report (1976) on the development

## FIGURE 4.7

## Portion of a case study of intellectual development

Coiling lines become deliberate circle configurations, continuous lines which start at one point and return to that point.

Circle configurations are elaborated with additional circles and with lines radiating to and from their centers, creating a vertical-horizontal relationship at their intersection with the perimeter. These become representational: father, mother, dog, cat, house, birthday cake.

circular formation and vertical-horizontal lines permit formation of the first
se.

Refinement: the horse receives four legs - - only four.

First deviations from the vertical-horizontal are used for ears and legs in opposing diagonal directions. The new diagonals immediately unify head and neck and create a new shape.

The unification of the head and neck is applied to contain the whole horse within one unbroken outline.

Problems of leg-spacing and length are solved.

The new diagonal directions of line allow the horse to run.

A learning plateau provides time to consolidate, and to enrich the horse's gear and markings.

Heidi's last major construction before her sixth birthday is to extend the horse's head toward the ground, "so he can eat."

SOURCE: *Heidi's Horse,* text by Sylvia Fein, drawings by Heidi Scheuber (Pleasant Hill, Calif.: Exelrod Press, 1976), pp. 58–59.

Jean Piaget

of drawing. By collecting all the drawings that Heidi made from age 2 to age 15, Fein was able to offer a detailed account of the changes in Heidi's rendering of horses (which played a large part in her life). Figure 4.7, a page of Fein's report, sums up developments from age 3½ to 6. Structures are mastered, combined, and then gradually refined. As in most case studies, Fein's analysis was rich in detail; for an example, see pp. 582–83.

The case study is entirely different from the experiment in its style. The experimenter states a definite question or hypothesis and collects information in a limited range of situations. The case analyst takes information wherever he can find it, and formulates his hypotheses after he gets to know his subject. The experimenter relies on objective measurement. The case study may take numerical information into account. (Sanford did have some test scores on Mack.) But the information that means most in a case study is likely to be unique to the subject, and qualitative rather than numerical. The conclusions in a case study are a daring exercise in constructing a theory to fit the individual. There is no assumption that another boy with a stern father and no mother would turn out as Mack did, and no way to verify the conclusions drawn about Mack. A case study resembles historical research more than experimental science.

**18** What would be gained or lost, in studying a case like that of Mack, if the investigator restricted himself to behavioral observations, making no use of interviews and the like?

**19** In what ways may the bias of the interviewer and analyst affect the findings of a case study? If the same psychologist were to conduct an experiment, could his bias affect the finding or report in any way?

**20** Case studies made by a staff psychologist can help a school or college to serve the individual studied. But in what way can reports of previous case studies help educators serve a student who has not been the subject of a case study?

# CORRELATIONAL RESEARCH

A correlational study sorts out persons who differ in one respect and determines how much they differ in other respects. In an experimental study, the psychologist creates a difference between groups of subjects by his treatment of them, and then measures the resulting difference in outcome. In a correlational study, the differences the psychologist observes were created by previous biological and social influences. The effect of home background upon emotional adjustment, for example, is studied by comparing children who already differ in home background. The psychologist cannot arrange for randomly chosen children to have a particular home experience, as would be required in an experiment.

A correlational study asks what goes with what. Following up the study of Mack, someone might suggest the principle: Boys reared without a mother have strong dependency needs. This is an hypothesis about correlation of mother-absence and dependency. It would be necessary to observe many boys reared in motherless homes, and many boys reared with both parents but otherwise similar in background to the first group. One would assess the dependency needs of all the boys. If the average dependency need were higher in the former group, this would confirm that dependency need is correlated with absence of the mother. Of course, not *every* boy who loses his mother has strong dependency needs; the correlation would only point to a probability.

The correlation coefficient, which I am about to describe, is a common method of summary, but not all correlational research uses that statistic. Brownell and Moser, when they related previous mathematics instruction to ability to follow a new explanation, were reporting a correlational finding about students who were taught decomposition meaningfully. This part of the study was correlational because the key variable, prior instruction, was not controlled by the investigator. The Blau-Duncan study (Fig. 2.5, p. 72) was also correlational; it asked what degree of social mobility went with what level of education.

## Interpreting Correlation Coefficients

The correlation between two variables can be examined most easily in a scattergram. Figure 4.8 shows scattergrams for 20 hypothetical students who have taken reading and mathematics tests. We know how much they weigh and how many hours per day they say they spend watching television for entertainment. Panel i shows the relation of reading to mathematics. Each dot represents the scores of one student. For instance, one student had a score of 5 in mathematics and 28 in reading (indicated by the arrow in Panel i). The scattergram shows that superior reading goes with superior math in this sample. The strength of such a relation is conveniently summarized by the correlation coefficient, which

**Correlation**

*"Show me a man who gets consistent A's and I'll show you a man who is neglecting his team."*

Drawing by Leonard Dove; © 1956 The New Yorker Magazine, Inc.

## FIGURE 4.8

Scattergrams showing three levels of correlation

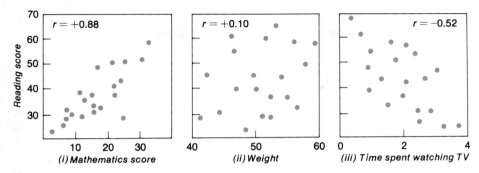

(i) Mathematics score  (ii) Weight  (iii) Time spent watching TV

is a number between 1.00 and −1.00. We are not concerned here with how to calculate a correlation coefficient; our concern is its meaning. In Figure 4.8, reading and mathematics scores are strongly and positively related. The relationship is not perfect, so the correlation coefficient does not reach 1.00; it is calculated to be 0.88. (Or, in short, $r = 0.88$.)

Panel ii relates weight to reading. A student's weight tells little or nothing about his reading ability. In these data $r = 0.10$, very close to zero. Even if correlation is absent in the population, a positive or negative correlation is usually found in a small sample because of random variability. Hence, just as a reader of research learns to question the statistical significance of an observed mean, he should also realize that a correlation may arise by chance.

Panel iii relates reading to TV watching. This time the relationship is negative: the more TV watching, the poorer the student's reading; $r = -0.52$.

The size of the correlation indicates its strength—the degree to which one measure can be predicted from the other.

## Example: Correlates of Honest Behavior

Mussen et al. (1970) tested the honesty* of sixth-graders from lower-middle-class homes and correlated this with other variables. Honesty was measured by a "ray-gun" test (developed by Grinder) in which the child fires a light-gun at a moving target; scores are displayed automatically as in an amusement-gallery machine. The machine is preprogrammed to display a final score that falls short of the prizewinning level. The child reports his or her own score to the investigator (who has left the room). Thus, the child has a chance to report a falsely high score.

_____

* Their findings on altruism were also interesting.

The Mussen analysis compared those who cheated with those who did not. The measures included in Table 4.1 are of several kinds, all common in research on children's personality: (1) Children were asked to describe classmates by answering confidentially such questions as "Who are the ones who always play fair in games?" Several questions of this sort were combined into the honesty-reputation score. (2) The child's feelings about himself were elicited with a questionnaire; for example:

---

**I am proud of my schoolwork:**

**Most of the time** _____ **Sometimes** _____ **Hardly ever** _____

---

This led to a self-esteem score. (3) The mother of each child was interviewed about her attitudes and techniques of child handling.

Two technical points are to be made about this analysis. First, note the number of cases (N) at the top of each column. This warns that results are from a small group. In a sample of this size, a correlation given as 0.29 might, in a very large sample, fall anywhere from 0.09 to 0.49. The reader should ignore modest differences between correlations in these data; with 40 to 50 cases, only large differences are statistically significant. The difference between 0.29 and 0.27 ("Honesty reputation") is clearly trivial, and even the difference between 0.27 and 0.49 (in the right-hand column) might not be found in a second sample. The second noteworthy point is signaled by the asterisks. The figures so marked imply a trustworthy relation in the direction indicated. In this sample, coefficients outside

TABLE 4.1

Correlations of honesty with other variables for sixth-grade boys and girls

| Measure correlated with honesty on the ray-gun test | Boys N = 43 | Girls N = 49 |
| --- | --- | --- |
| Honesty reputation | 0.29* | 0.27* |
| IQ | −0.10 | −0.07 |
| Information from self-description: | | |
| Self-esteem score | −0.36* | — |
| "Kids pick on me" | 0.43* | — |
| Mother's statement: | | |
| "I am easygoing and relaxed with my child. | −0.52* | 0.49* |
| "I make sure I know where my child is and what he is doing." | 0.28* | −0.56* |
| "I let my child make many decisions for himself." | — | 0.36* |

SOURCE: Data from Mussen et al. (1970).
A dash indicates a correlation not significantly different from zero; the authors did not report the actual value.
*p < .05

## Intellectual development in various homes

Three-year-olds were given the Stanford-Binet test, a measure of all-around intellectual development. Their scores were correlated with six ratings of the child's home, made at three earlier ages following observations and interviews with the mother. The homes represented the range of homes in the community.

| Variable rated | Correlation with ability at 36 months | | |
| --- | --- | --- | --- |
| | Age of child when variable was rated | | |
| | 6 months | 12 months | 24 months |
| Mother emotionally and verbally responsive | 0.25 | 0.39 | 0.50 |
| Mother avoids restriction and punishment | 0.24 | 0.24 | 0.41 |
| Physical and temporal environment well organized | 0.40 | 0.39 | 0.41 |
| Appropriate play materials provided | 0.41 | 0.56 | 0.64 |
| Mother involved with child | 0.32 | 0.47 | 0.54 |
| Daily stimulation is varied | 0.30 | 0.28 | 0.50 |

SOURCE: After Elardo et al. (1975).

the range −0.20 to 0.20 (a 40-point range around zero) differ significantly from zero, so they get an asterisk. The critical range depends on the sample size; these investigators decided to accept a 5 per cent error rate (see p. 119). The coefficient of 0.43 among boys for the statement "Kids pick on me" is sufficiently large that a positive relation would probably be found again if the study were repeated. The coefficient of −0.10 between IQ and honesty is essentially a finding of no relationship.

What do the significant relations in Table 4.1 indicate? Boys who did not cheat tended to have good reputations. But these honest boys had lower-than-average self-esteem and felt that others picked on them. Strikingly, the relation between maternal style and honesty was reversed among girls. The maternal style that produced an honest boy tended to produce a girl who was relatively likely to cheat. Mussen et al. gave a theoretical interpretation that we cannot treat adequately here. Broadly, their interpretation (their pp. 189ff.) was that by age 11 "dependence on external authority and compliance with regulations may be regarded as feminine sex-typed characteristics. . . . Honest behavior, as measured by performance with the ray-gun, is essentially compliance with rules and is thus compatible with the [traditional] feminine sex role, less compatible with the masculine."

Presenting psychological conclusions becomes awkward when one has to qualify each generalization by mentioning age differences, sex differences, and social-class differences. In the Mussen study, sex of child interacts with maternal style. Complications such as this are the rule (Cronbach, 1975a). As a psychological investigation proceeds, it moves from studies on mixed collections of subjects and narrows down the findings—ultimately to one age, one sex, and one cultural group

## Does superior civic knowledge go with democratic beliefs?

An opinion poll of high-school seniors included a short test on knowledge of current events and of the historical background of major political concepts. It also included questions about beliefs in (among other topics): liberties protected by the Bill of Rights, "fascist" ideology (glorification of government and the powerful, of strong-handed law and order, and so on), and manifest anticommunism (support for loyalty oaths, suppression of the communist arguments).

For a sample of one thousand students questioned in 1951–52, the following correlations were calculated (Horton, 1963, p. 44):

|  | Knowledge | Civil liberties | Fascism | Anticommunism |
|---|---|---|---|---|
|  |  | Belief in | | |
| Belief in civil liberties | 0.18 |  |  |  |
| Belief in fascism | −0.12 | −0.36 |  |  |
| Belief in anticommunism | −0.23 | −0.34 | 0.27 |  |

These numbers give the impression that relationships are weak (even though all are statistically significant). But allowance has to be made for error of measurement. As will be made clear later (Chaps. 7 and 16), individual scores would

change if a longer test were used. Chance effects due to incomplete measurement hold down correlations. Horton adjusted the correlations he had calculated directly to allow for this. The reliability coefficient (Chap. 7) of each measure was near 0.50, where 1.00 implies complete information on the variable tested.

The figures below are estimates of the correlations that would be found if a fully adequate set of tests was used.

|  | Knowledge | Belief in Civil liberties | Belief in Fascism | Belief in Anticommunism |
|---|---|---|---|---|
| Belief in civil liberties | 0.33 | | | |
| Belief in fascism | −0.24 | −0.67 | | |
| Belief in anticommunism | −0.45 | −0.66 | 0.56 | |

The corrections change the story. Related beliefs are substantially intercorrelated. Knowledge does have some relation (not necessarily causal!) to beliefs. Students with beliefs more in line with what the school teaches were, on the average, a little better informed on social matters.

at a time. This refined analysis often makes possible persuasive explanations for what first appear as sheer inconsistencies. Here, the argument is that—in the generation when the study was made—the nurturant mother developed a "feminine" girl and a "masculine" boy. Each was shaped to the then-traditional cultural demands upon each sex. Further, it is argued that the culture was placing a different value on honesty in each sex.

Causal inferences based on correlations are risky. It seemed natural to conclude in the foregoing arguments that the maternal attitude was a cause of the child's honest or dishonest behavior. But A can be related to B in three ways: A may cause B, B may cause A, or both may have a common cause—C. Indeed, back-and-forth causation can occur.

In the present example, a boy's aggressive masculinity and no-holds-barred striving would perhaps cause his mother not to be easygoing and relaxed. To speculate a bit more rashly, perhaps mothers closer to the borderline of poverty are less easygoing, and boys closer to that line more insistent on gaining the prize offered for a good score. If so, poverty could be a factor C, generating both of the characteristics whose correlation was observed.

21  Honesty reputation correlated 0.62 with IQ among boys and 0.44 among girls (p < .05). What does this mean? Try to reconcile this finding with the related facts in Table 4.1.

22  Correlational research is frequently carried out in the course of developing standard tests. The DAT battery (p. 288) is used for guiding

secondary-school students, and the following correlations are among the many reported in the publisher's manual. Student marks in biology were correlated with the subtests—Verbal, Abstract, and so on—of the aptitude battery, which had been taken before the course began.

| | Verbal | Abstract | Mechanical | Spatial |
|---|---|---|---|---|
| Bartlesville, Okla. | | | | |
| (N = 140) | 0.58* | 0.38* | 0.28* | 0.22* |
| Ralston, Neb. | | | | |
| (N = 55) | 0.54* | 0.35* | 0.47* | 0.25 |

* p < .05

   a. Why is 0.22 starred in the top row and 0.25, a larger value, not starred in the bottom row?

   b. Does it appear that these four aptitudes are equally important, or is there evidence that proficiency in biology depends more on some abilities than others?

   c. Do the tested abilities seem to explain fully why some students get high grades and others do not?

**23** What conclusions are suggested by the correlations in the box on intellectual development (p. 137)? Are the relationships plausible?

**24** How would the correlations in the second row ("12 months") be changed if the home had been rated on "Amount of restriction and punishment"?

**25** Why is it important that the homes represented the normal range in the community?

**26** In Horton's study (box, p. 138) there was a scale of "Marxist" attitudes, most of them statements proposing that the government take over control of business enterprises. The words *Marx* and *communism* did not appear in the statements. The "Marxist" beliefs correlated 0.45 (adjusted correlation) with belief in suppression of communist arguments. What explanation can you suggest for the fact that this correlation was positive rather than negative? The Marxism score correlated −0.43 (adjusted) with knowledge, −0.46 with belief in civil liberties, and 0.64 with fascist views.

**27** With a correlation of −0.66 between anticommunist (McCarthyite) beliefs and belief in civil liberties, would it be possible to find students who strongly advocate freedom of speech for all but communists?

**28** What explanation for the correlation of knowledge and attitudes (box) can you offer, other than that greater knowledge generates attitudes more in line with what the school teaches?

# STUDYING INTERACTION OF PERSON AND SITUATION

Behavior is determined both by the characteristics of the person and the characteristics of the situation (D. Hunt & E. Sullivan, 1974). To investigate the combined effect of person and situation, one has to combine the experimental and correlational methods into what is called an *interaction study*. Brownell and Moser reported an interactive effect of meaningfulness and previous experience, and Mussen et al. reported that the effect of maternal nurturance depended on the gender of the child. Now we shall see how a Person × Situation interaction can be brought out in a formal experiment.

Such a study starts with a measure of one or more characteristics of the person (Cronbach & Snow, 1976). This pretest is usually referred to as an aptitude measure, but it could be a personality measure, a report on family background, or something similar. The experimenter divides the group, preferably at random, and administers a planned treatment to each group. At the end of the study he measures the outcomes, and examines two questions. First, the usual question of the experimenter: Is the average in one treatment group higher than in the other? Second, the question usual in correlational research: What trend relates pretest to outcome? But this trend may differ from treatment to treatment. To examine that shift is to look for an interaction.

## Example: Student Style and Teacher Style

Do independent students respond better to teachers who allow their independence free rein? Do teachers who allow independence get better results from more independent students? Domino thought so. To get evidence, he first (1968) carried out a pilot study using a correlational design. He administered a personality test to a large number of college students, obtained information on the teaching styles of a number of their instructors, and collected the grades made by the students. He sorted the instructors into two groups, according to whether they encouraged student independence or laid out specific plans for students to follow. The teacher who required conformity made more specific assignments, required attendance, and employed class time to work through a predetermined outline. The teacher who placed responsibility on the students allowed them more latitude in choosing projects, made attendance optional, and allowed more class time for student views. There was no manipulation of treatment; teachers were sorted on the basis of the style they habitually followed.

The evidence strongly suggested that independent students do better with instructors who encourage independence. The evidence was inconclusive, however. Course marks might only indicate what kind of student each instructor tended to reward, not who learned most. And the differences in student performance might be due to the nature of each course, rather than to differences in teaching style. Domino therefore went on (1971) to a manipulative experiment.

He had tested the freshman class on the California Personality Inventory, which can be scored to measure "achievement through conformance" (Ac) and "achievement through independence" (Ai). The High-Ac student is one who checks statements such as the following as true of him:

---
**I have a very strong desire to be a success in the world.**

**I always try to do at least a little better than what is expected of me.**

---

He is one who strives to meet standards set for him by others. The High-Ai student is more independent and more attracted to intellectual complexity. He is distinguished less by the statements he accepts than by his rejecting, for example, the following:

---
**It is annoying to listen to a lecturer who cannot make up his mind as to what he really believes.**

**I like to plan a home study-schedule and then follow it.**

---

The two scales are moderately correlated, but one can find students who combine High Ac with Low Ai, and vice versa. Domino carried out his study in the sophomore-year psychology course, confining his sample to students in the middle range of intellectual ability. He located 50 with the High-Low pattern and 50 with the Low-High pattern. These were assigned to sections of the introductory psychology course, so that each section was made up of one type of student.

The instructor who taught all four sections was not told the basis for assigning students. He agreed, for the purpose of the experiment, to teach two sections in an unstructured style that encouraged independence and two in a structured manner to which students had to conform. The design of the study, then, employed the four sections listed in Table 4.2.

The test at the end of the semester was the same in all sections; there were factual multiple-choice items plus essay questions calling for imagination and the ability to reason. Domino also recorded the course grade, along with measures of originality of thought and student satisfaction.

Table 4.2 summarizes the chief results. To permit easy reading, the average in each section is expressed as a percentage of the average score in whichever section scored highest. This technique is open to certain objections, but here, as in the Brownell-Moser study, it gives a quick impression of complicated results. Sections 1 and 4, where instructor style matched the student's personal style, ranked ahead of the other sections on three of the four measures. The exception is the measure of original thinking, where the conforming students did badly regardless of instructor style.

No sweeping conclusion can be drawn from only a pair of studies. Domino's findings suggest strongly, however, that the independent achiever would do best to

## TABLE 4.2

Outcomes in four sections of a psychology course

| Section | Student style | Instructor style | Exam | Mean outcome* | | |
| | | | | Course grade | Originality of thought | Student satisfaction |
|---|---|---|---|---|---|---|
| 1 | Independent (High Ai, Low Ac) | Informal | 98 | 100 | 99 | 100 |
| 2 | Independent (High Ai, Low Ac) | Structured | 87 | 83 | 100 | 88 |
| 3 | Conforming (Low Ai, High Ac) | Informal | 78 | 66 | 65 | 82 |
| 4 | Conforming (Low Ai, High Ac) | Structured | 100 | 89 | 59 | 94 |

SOURCE: Adapted from Domino (1971). Copyright 1975 by the American Psychological Association. Reprinted by permission.
* Expressed as a percentage of the highest average score.

sign up with an instructor who fosters independence in the classroom, and that the person who achieves through conforming will do better with an instructor who lays out clear requirements. (For related studies, see p. 702; also Brophy & Good, 1974, pp. 244ff.; and Cronbach & Snow, 1977, Chap. 13.)

If Domino had carried out a two-group experiment with a mixture of students, he would have concluded that neither the informal style nor the structured style of teaching produces superior results on the average. (The net difference is very small when Sections 1 and 4 combined are compared with 2 and 3 combined.) A correlational study could have been carried out by mixing all four sections into one analysis. Without control over the assignment of students to teachers, the correlation might have reflected natural selection in the choice of teachers by students. Only the interaction design combines the control of a manipulative experiment with the analysis of relationships between type of student and type of instruction.

 **29** What was the advantage or disadvantage of each of these features of Domino's design?
   a. One teacher taught all four sections.
   b. All students were drawn from the same ability range.
   c. The instructor was not told how sections were formed.

**30** In an evaluation of Head Start it was found that, in "traditional pre-school programs" (with much emphasis on self-expression and little in the way of planned lessons), children from relatively well-to-do homes seemed to prosper more than in programs with a structured curriculum. The reverse was true for very poor children (Bissell, 1973). Not all the evidence on the point is consistent. If this finding were to be confirmed by additional research, how could educational planners make use of the finding?

**4** READING LIST

Thomas X. Barber, "Pitfalls in Research," in *Second Handbook of Research on Teaching,* ed. R. M. W. Travers (Chicago: Rand McNally, 1973), pp. 382–404.

Barber illustrates errors introduced into data on social and educational research by preconceptions or loose techniques. He suggests controls, but urges users of research to place confidence in ideas that emerge from multiple studies carried out by persons with different theoretical views.

Lee J. Cronbach, "Beyond the Two Disciplines of Scientific Psychology," *American Psychologist* 30 (1975a), 116–27.

I said in Chapter 1 that the answer to almost any educational question begins "It depends . . ." This is equally true in engineering applications of physical science, but it calls into question the extent to which scientific "laws" can be the basis for application. This article illustrates the critical importance of interactions, and calls for more attention to the context in which the psychologist observes his subject.

Richard I. Evans et al., "Fear Arousal, Persuasion, and Actual versus Implied Behavior Change," *Journal of Personality and Social Psychology* 16 (1970), 220–27.

Physical education students in junior high schools were exposed to propaganda for thorough toothbrushing. Messages varied in the degree to which fears of tooth decay were aroused. The experiment gives a particularly clear example of the value of multiple-outcome measures. The failure to use random assignment made analysis difficult.

Jean Piaget, "Developmental Use of 'Because' in the Reasoning of the Child," in *Piaget Sampler,* ed. Sarah F. Campbell (New York: Wiley, 1976), pp. 17–36.

> This carefully edited excerpt from Piaget's early book *Judgment and Reasoning in the Child* illustrates his highly influential method of investigation. It combines features of the case study and the correlational method: Piaget collected over 10,000 remarks made by children of ages 3 to 7, and identified in them the characteristic logic associated with each stage of development.

Henry W. Riecken et al., "Experimentation as a Method of Program Planning and Evaluation," in *Social Experimentation,* ed. H. W. Riecken and R. F. Boruch (New York: Academic Press, 1974), pp. 1–12.

> Advocates the use of randomized field experiments to check on the effectiveness of social programs. The studies described include an experiment on release of prisoners without bail, the evaluation of a physics curriculum, and a study of whether an enriched diet in infancy would raise mental ability.

Philip Zimbardo and Ebbe B. Ebbeson, "Critically Analyzing the Conceptualization, Methodology, and Interpretation of Attitude Change Research," Chapter 4 in *Influencing Attitudes and Changing Behavior* (Reading, Mass.: Addison-Wesley, 1969), pp. 39–62.

> Some unusual experiments and field studies on persuasive techniques are examined in detail to show the nonspecialist reader how he can reason from data instead of accepting the author's conclusion uncritically.

# PART TWO
## Readiness and Its Development

# THE STREAM OF DEVELOPMENT

Readiness is the central concern behind such questions as: "What works of literature are appropriate for junior high school?" "In what grade should fractions be introduced?" "Can Stephen succeed in a precollege curriculum?" Chapters 5–9 consider how readiness develops, how to judge readiness, and how the school can use information on readiness. How to promote readiness is an element in all subsequent chapters on instruction. Readiness is affected by the learner's biological equipment, ideas and skills, habits, and attitudes and values. Some people speak of readiness as being present or absent; thus "Alix is ready for the study of French, but Rachel is not." This oversimplifies. Readiness is not readiness merely for certain subject-matter. The learner is ready or unready for the total learning situation, taking into account the method of teaching and the satisfactions offered, as well as for the subject-matter. One can learn French at age 2 under certain conditions of instruction, and not until high school under others. A student who will fail under one instructional procedure can profit from some other procedure directed to the same ultimate outcome.

The student who lacks readiness for the instruction ordinarily scheduled at his age is ready for *some* learning experience. To speak of what he lacks is to miss the point. Information on readiness guides the teacher's attempts to match instruction to the student. The teacher should be acquainted with all aspects of development and with all periods of life. What went on before the student enters this teacher's classroom affects what he can and will do, and what happens to him here must be judged in terms of what it contributes to his subsequent readiness.

Four principles will be illustrated over and over in this and later chapters:

- All aspects of development interact. When the normal sequence is interrupted in any way, effects are to be seen throughout the child's development. A developmental achievement in one sphere of life is likely to be reflected in responsiveness to opportunities of other kinds. Thus social development influences intellectual activities and learning. Achieving competence in abstract thinking opens the way to new political attitudes. And emotional adjustment radiates into better eating, better sleep, and better problem solving.

- Physiological maturing prepares one to profit from experience. Biological changes, especially in the nervous system, influence what one can learn. Children who differ in rate of maturing have different experiences and develop different personalities.

- Experiences have a cumulative effect. Each experience affects one's reaction to the next similar situation. One success makes the next more likely; a series of successes snowballs, building up readiness for advanced activities of a similar kind. Cumulation of failures holds back development.

- There are formative periods in life in which readiness for a particular activity is established (or retarded—see box, p. 186). The period in which a person first has a chance to engage in an activity is especially important. The formative period for physical skill is, roughly, from age 1 to age 4. From the first crawl through the "runabout age," the child is establishing coordination and developing confidence or timidity. A chief formative period for attitudes toward one's intellectual abilities and toward school is the first year or so of schooling. Success, failure, challenge, and conflict at that time precondition the reaction to all later schooling.

Inadequate development at one age need not blight a child's life; a later opportunity may enable him to offset early setbacks. It ordinarily takes special effort and skilled teaching, however, to eradicate responses acquired during the formative period and practiced thereafter. The timing of a formative period is as much determined by the culture as by biological nature.

---

1 Show that physical, intellectual, and attitudinal characteristics would all be of concern in teaching:
    a. handwriting
    b. high-school English
    c. auto mechanics

2 A fourth-grade girl of average-to-superior mental ability is chosen by her group to take the principal part in a play they are presenting. She does well and is praised for her acting. What effect is this likely

to have on her future behavior? How will she be affected by the time she reaches high school if she has further experiences of this sort?

3  Comment on this statement: "Readiness is more important in the elementary-school classroom than in high school or college."

# PHYSICAL MATURING AS THE BASE OF READINESS

Children grow at different rates and develop different physiques. The direct effect of these differences is seen in the children's ability to play games and to hold their own. The indirect social and psychological effects are even more important. Physical immaturity, poor coordination, or biochemical abnormalities can interfere with any type of learning. The child who tires readily, for example, will have a shorter span of concentration, will be more upset by difficulty, and will be less willing to persevere. He should have extra help and should, where possible, be given tasks he can complete in a relatively short time. When trouble signs appear, the school should make certain that the student gets a medical examination; proper diagnosis may suggest a change of diet or a medical treatment that will restore the energy level to normal.

Physical superiority tends to have a beneficial effect on personality. Physically competent children gain social assurance. The child with a slight physique or poor coordination finds himself unwanted when his playmates are choosing teams. Physical size is particularly important to the boy, whose strength affects all of his social relationships. Around age 12, his social influence is closely related to how well the other boys think he can fight. Stronger boys are superior in spirit and appearance, and more masculine.

One's attitude toward one's physical endowments is an element in self-confidence at all ages. During adolescence in particular, boys tend to compare themselves with athletes, and girls with actresses. The judgment of self is complicated by many false ideas, such as a person's notion that he is unattractive because he wears glasses. A large proportion of adolescents are at some time disturbed about one or another physical characteristic. Tallness in girls, shortness in boys, and fatness in either sex lead the list of causes of discontent.

Some body builds are associated with a good image and some with a bad image. A youngster is likely to worry if he is far from the good image. A "good image" for the girl is intermediate between the bony and the plump extremes. Preadolescent girls, shown three silhouettes of different body builds, typically associated the medium figure with labels like "best friend," "helps others," and "smart." They rarely associated good labels with the lightweight silhouette, matching it with "fights," "worries," "gets teased," "lonely," "argues." (The peer expectation can make such predictions come true.) As for the third, heavy body type, the commonest adjectives were "quiet," "clean," and "weak"—a nothing personality (Staffieri, 1972).

Physical superiority does not necessarily lead to superior development as a person. Sometimes the large boy is overbearing and unpopular. A relatively small adolescent who is attractive and mature may be popular with both sexes. The effect of a physical characteristic depends upon the meaning attached to it by the person and his group.

## Normal Trends in Physical Development

SIZE   Change in height and weight is most striking in early adolescence. Adolescence sees great increase in height, change from childish to adult body proportions, change in the sexual organs, change in glandular functions, and change in voice. The child in effect acquires a new body, which can do new things and admit him to new social relationships. These biological changes extend over several years and have no definite beginning or end point. It is customary to consider the appearance of adult sexual characteristics as the start of adolescence. This development, known as puberty, is dramatically signaled for the girl by the first menstruation (menarche), and less suddenly for the boy by the appearance of pubic hair. The child does not leap into adolescence. The physiological and social changes are gradual.

## FIGURE 5.1

Growth in a motor performance with age

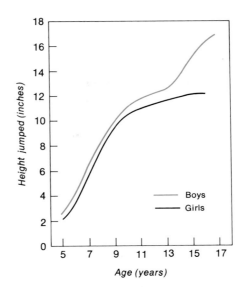

SOURCE: Data from column "Jump and Reach (inches)," Table 24.1, Espenschade & Eckert, *Science and Medicine of Exercise and Sport*, 2d Edition, ed. Johnson & Buskirk (New York: Harper & Row, 1974), p. 329.

Growth is more than enlargement. Parts of the body change in relative size, glands take on new functions, and innumerable changes take place in the body's microanatomy and biochemistry. A decline in metabolic rate, for example, might cause a girl to put on fat, creating consequent difficulties in her adjustment.

Height grows rather steadily during childhood, slowing a bit before the spurt at puberty. In middle childhood, the averages for the two sexes on most physical measures are about the same. In adolescence, males become taller, heavier, and stronger than females. Figure 5.1 gives a representative comparison. (See also Oxendine, 1968, pp. 150–51.)

TIMING OF ADOLESCENT CHANGES   Girls enter the adolescent cycle ahead of boys. The peak growth for the girl comes somewhere between ages 10 and 15, most often at about 12—two years ahead of the average boy. The more rapid growth of girls presents special problems during Grades V–VIII. Physically, the typical girl is at this time as mature as the boy two grades ahead. The girl who matures early has less in common with her classmates than at any other time in her school life.

The average age of puberty apparently has changed. Medical records indicate that, in Western countries, puberty now occurs about three years earlier than in 1880, a shift of four months per decade (Tanner, in Mussen, 1970, I, p. 146; 1974). This shift has occurred among poorer families, not among the well-to-do, and the most recent figures indicate that any further shift is likely to be small (Panel on Youth, 1974, p. 97; Zacharias et al., 1976). The probable explanation is that substandard nutrition and health care delayed maturing among the poor in former times, but that this deficit has been removed by a better standard of living.

INDIVIDUAL DIFFERENCES    Both before and after puberty, persons of the same age and sex differ markedly. Some girls enter adolescence at age 10, and a few do not make the transition until six years later. Among boys, even some high-school juniors are still children physically. Whatever the quality measured, some children are physically like the average child two years older, and some like the average child two years younger.

Cross-sectional comparisons (made by measuring children of different ages in the same manner) often produce distributions like those in Fig. 5.2. In one task, the child was to trace simple geometric figures (diamonds, triangles) onto a thin sheet laid atop a printed specimen. Accuracy of reproduction was scored by a point system. The distribution shows a spread at age 5, but at later ages the majority performed almost perfectly. Age 5–6 appears to be the period when this task is brought under control. Progress requires mastery of the pencil, perceptual accuracy, and self-control. The more difficult freehand drawing task (right-hand column) required the child to draw a diamond or triangle like the printed specimen, without tracing. Again, rapid progress is made at age 5–6, but perfection is approached slowly over many years. (See Birch & Lefford, 1971, for a detailed breakdown of progress in subskills, which advanced at different times.)

Most of the traits that concern teachers have something like a "normal distribution" (p. 117), as is the case in Fig. 5.2. The curves become *nonnormal* only as students begin to bump against the upper end of the scoring scale. Both physical and mental measures are likely to have somewhat symmetrical distributions, high in the middle, when the scale is open-ended.

By remembering that measures of individual differences are distributed more or less normally, we avoid two mistakes. One is to recognize only deviations in an undesirable direction. Too often, individual attention is given just to the students who are behind the group. The normal curve reminds us that superiority is about as common as inferiority. The second mistake is to think of "normal," "inferior," and "superior" groups as distinct. Nearly all the qualities of concern to teachers have continuous distributions. There are no gaps in the height distribution, separating "tall" from "normal"; nor in the mental-test distribution, between bright and normal. Whenever "exceptional" children are selected for special treatment, the dividing line is arbitrary. Considerable variation remains within each group.

The normal distribution is a useful working concept, but not an exact law. The specific shape of a distribution depends on the trait and the method of measurement. It takes only a little mathematics to show that in a group where height in centimeters has a strictly normal distribution, body volume in cubic centimeters does not. With regard to abilities and other psychological characteristics, the test items chosen make a difference in the distribution. Note also

## FIGURE 5.2

Progress, with age, in two coordination tasks

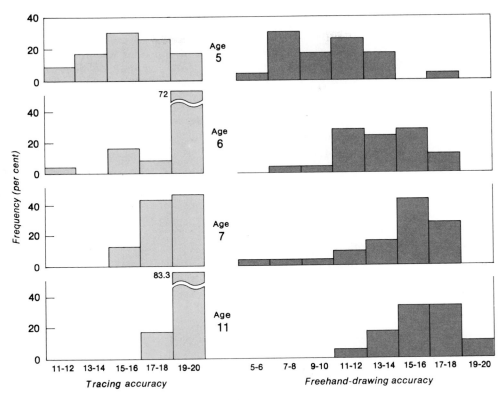

SOURCE: Data from Birch & Lefford (1971), pp. 21, 22.

that equal differences in size may not be equally important. Being four inches above the average height is much more distressing for a girl of 14 than being four inches below average.

The child who is advanced in some physical characteristic has a good chance of remaining above average; for example, height at ages 4 through 10 correlates at least 0.75 with height at maturity (Tanner, in Mussen, 1970, I, p. 136). Despite this consistency, positions shift considerably from year to year. Some children spurt in size or strength while others seem to be marking time. Illness or an emotional upset may impair not only physical development but all learning and social adjustment. Physical characteristics give no indication of mental ability or probable academic success. The correlation of academic abilities with size, strength, and measures of skeletal maturity is usually positive, but no greater than 0.25 (Scottish Council, 1953; Klausmeier et al., 1958).

## Anxiety over physique

The unathletic, lanky boy, unable, perhaps, to hold his own in the pre-adolescent rough and tumble, gets still further pushed to the wall at adolescence, as he sees others shoot up while he remains nearly stationary in growth. Even boys several years younger now suddenly surpass him in size and athletic skill. . . . The late developer at adolescence may sometimes have doubts about whether he will ever develop his body properly and whether he will be as well endowed sexually as those others he has seen developing around him. At a deeper level the lack of development may act as a trigger to reverberate fears accumulated deeper in the mind during the early years of life. (Tanner, in Mussen, 1970, I, p. 110.)

This fear has an ironic side, implied by the evidence in Fig. 5.3. The boy of lanky build, four inches shorter at age 14 than a classmate who had the same height at 11 as he did, is likely again to match him in height by 17.

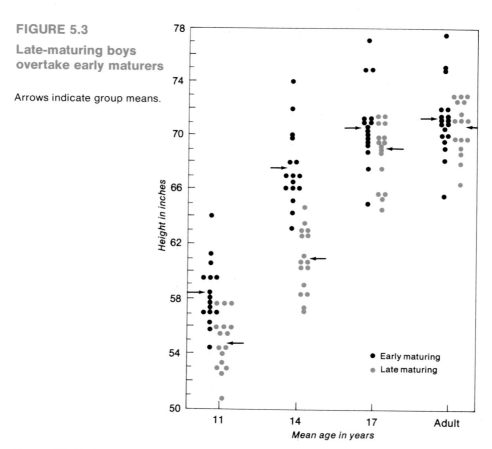

**FIGURE 5.3**

**Late-maturing boys overtake early maturers**

Arrows indicate group means.

SOURCE: After M. C. Jones & N. Bayley (1950). Copyright 1950 by the American Psychological Association. Reproduced by permission.

The social consequences of delayed puberty are long-lasting (M. C. Jones & N. Bayley, 1950; Clausen, 1975). The early-maturing boys become far "smoother" socially: each success gives confidence and prestige, which helps them further. At a ninth-grade graduation party they come at a sophisticated late hour, they dance well and daringly, and act condescendingly. Boys of the same age who are not as far into physical adolescence show childish, bouncing enthusiasm, giggling, and silliness. They do not dance well or know how to talk to girls. They are not popular, do not succeed in athletics, and are not chosen for class office. They are apt to be troublesome to teachers. They tend to be restless, energetic, and bossy. Twelve out of 18 late maturers were rated by observers as having a strong desire to attack others by ridicule and criticism, an indicator of insecurity found only half as often among early maturers. By age 17, the late maturers (even though well into adolescence) are straining to be popular and to be accepted in groups (Mussen & Jones, 1958).

Early maturers and later maturers do not differ in professional success, but they do differ as persons. It is far more common for early maturers to describe themselves, on a questionnaire at age 30, as relatively high in responsibility, sociability, dominance, and self-control. Others depend on them for advice and reassurance: they are influential. The psychologists judge them to be somewhat better adjusted. Indeed, those males who matured early are consistently ahead in personality-trait comparisons at age 30. The only criticism that might be made is that they tend to be a bit stuffy and inflexible in their easily won adjustment. Their superiority is a psychological by-product of a biological advantage; the early maturer is physically ready in early adolescence to take a full part in a new social environment and to learn from it (Jones, 1957, 1965; Peskin & Livson, 1972).

The years around puberty are stressful for girls, the peak tension evidently coming in the year or so immediately before menarche. Frequent disturbing dreams are reported by 39 per cent of the girls two years before menarche, and by only 9 per cent two years after. There is a prepubertal peak of shyness, emotional dependence, and irritability (Macfarlane et al., 1954). The early-maturing girl has more of these problems than the late maturer. In Grades V and VI her interest turns to boys, but she gets no encouragement from the boys in her class. She is socially out of step until Grades VII–IX. By age 17, the early-maturing girl is likely to be superior in self-acceptance and poise. In high school, it is the late-maturing girl who is at a disadvantage; in college and in adulthood also, the early-maturing girl is better adjusted than the late maturer (Faust, 1960; Jones & Mussen, 1958; Peskin & Livson, 1972; Weatherley, 1964).

---

**4** Account for the fact that the early-maturing girl gains in popularity and adjustment between the ages of 12 and 17.

**5** The present trend in child rearing and in schooling is to reduce the distinctions in treatment between boys and girls. If this continues, is it likely to change the pattern of adolescent concerns from that described in the text?

6 What methods can be suggested for dealing with the girl who reaches puberty while in Grade V and loses interest in the activities of her classmates?

7 Should all students move into high school at the same age? Would it be wiser to make this transfer according to individual physical maturity?

8 Which of the following characteristics seem likely to be normally distributed among 9-year-old boys?
   a. Ability to whistle a tune
   b. Ability to count to 500
   c. Cheerfulness
   d. Finger dexterity, such as is used in tying knots
   e. Respect for authority

## Educational Implications of Growth

Because feelings about physical characteristics play an important role in personality development, the instructional program should help each student to appreciate his own qualities. For example, primary pupils can be taught to place proper valuation on differences in size. Rearing a family of animals can convey that one's size is usually like that of one's parents, and that small size is not a mark of inferiority. Curriculum material urging certain foods "to make you big" suggests that the child who is not big has something to apologize for.

The program of physical activity should be varied. Small boys and girls can perform well in sports where size is less important than agility. With suitable roles to play, even awkward children can achieve self-respect, as in the following incident:

> John went with his class and teacher one spring day across the neighboring fields to gather specimens for their aquarium. The children clustered along the bank of a stream seeking to catch the prized crayfish. Only the nimble-fingered had occasional successes.
>
> John, clumsy of body and slow in reaction time, after five minutes of no success turned to the teacher and said, "Don't you think it would be a good idea if I gathered some moss and leaves to line the baskets we are going to carry these crayfish in?" The teacher nodded approval of this suggestion and John, accompanied by a half dozen others, set happily about the task. In other sections of the teacher's record about John, we find him holding the tape for racing matches or refereeing a game (C. Tryon & W. Henry, 1950, p. 157).

Where competitive sports are the only ones that count, the school intensifies the adjustment problems of the undersized and underskilled child. Interscholastic competition in basketball for 11-year-olds, for instance, stresses the difference between those who are "good enough for the team" and those who are not. The less able boys have little chance to develop fundamental skills. Some of the undersized or clumsy preadolescents will be tall and well coordinated five years later, so that the competitive program is not ideal even for developing champions. Discouraging the less adept boys cuts out some who might be star performers in high school and college if they were given an early start. A physical education program that offers rewards only to the large, fast, and adept is as inimical to the development of all as is an academic program in which the dull find nothing they can do right. Varied sports calling on different types of physical readiness are needed; activities that minimize comparison and competition should be part of the program.

Because of the wide range in size at any age, and the differences in maturity at adolescence, it is valuable to arrange activities so that students of different ages can mingle and sort themselves into groups of corresponding development. To relax the graded structure of the elementary school so that a child can work with others a year or two "ahead" or "behind" in age has been highly desirable in this respect. Even where classrooms remain age-structured, recreational and community activities based on interests and skills help both the more mature and the less mature to participate in a satisfying way.

## Neural Maturation

The neurophysiology and biochemistry of the brain and nervous system change as the child grows older, and these have much to do with performance and learning. But our knowledge of these physiological topics is seriously incomplete, and in any event we would no more expect the teacher to apply them directly than we would expect the chef to become an expert in food chemistry. The teacher needs only to be aware of the significance of neural development and of the interpretations that have been made of the findings.

The brain changes in size and structure. One important change is the deposit of a fatty substance myelin, which appears to act as an insulator between the nerve cells, thus permitting more precise control of motor responses. The microanatomy also changes: nerve-cell endings branch and lengthen, more fibers connect the trunk with the brain, and, in general, the system becomes more complexly connected. It was once thought that brain development was largely complete by middle childhood. But the evidence now indicates that myelin deposits, brain structure, and brain-wave patterns continue to develop in adolescence and perhaps in adulthood (Yakovlev & Lecours, 1967; Eichorn, in Mussen, 1970, I, p. 248). As the brain changes, new performance becomes possible, hence intellectual growth, even after schooling begins, is probably biological in part.

Many changes seem to be an unfolding of prepatterned structures that can be counted upon to appear, given normal health, nutrition, and stimulation. The biological pacing of structural changes inevitably paces the development of

## Should every child start school at the same age?

After testing the readiness of Gary Brock (not his real name), the school staff advised his parents to hold him out of kindergarten for a year. The staff had observed him at play, interviewed him, and given him a short test (oral and simple manual tasks). This test, the Denver Developmental Screening Test, covers aspects of physical, social, and intellectual maturity considered important in kindergarten work.

The case became controversial, as the following comments from two letters to *Newsweek* show.

> I have rarely felt such outrage as I did after reading about the subjection of Gary Brock to the kindergarten "entrance examinations" in _____ and the use of those tests to determine that Gary is not "ready" for kindergarten. . . .
>
> Schools exist for children, and the goal of education is facilitation of *individual* development, not the production of persons who think and act alike according to a "norm." The elementary school of _____ has an obligation to all children in the district; the issue is not the "readiness" of the children, but the "readiness" of the school to administer to all 5-year-olds—including Gary Brock.

> To put 5-year-old Gary in kindergarten now may be to invite failure for his entire schooling. In many cases, a year's wait takes a child from the bottom of the class to the top, simply because he has had time to develop his pre-school skills. Success at 6 is better than struggle at 5.

These letters pose the policy question sharply. Confronting them makes a good introduction to these chapters on readiness. Do not be misled by side issues. Gary was black, but not poor; his father was a highly skilled worker and they lived in a well-to-do suburb. Race seemed not be an issue; the four others judged "not ready" for kindergarten on that occasion were whites. Whether the

performance; this is referred to as *maturation.* More formally, a maturation process is one where the timing of emergence of some characteristic, and its form, are controlled primarily by the genes (Eichorn & H. Jones, 1958). Note the word "primarily"; every physical and behavioral characteristic depends to some extent on diet, exercise, maternal care, and other aspects of environment.

If under normal conditions brain structures unfold in some largely predetermined manner, this should influence the timing of instruction. Certain acts might develop without being taught; others might be easier to teach when the child is older. Radical experiments testing this hypothesis can be tried in the animal laboratory. One investigator raised salamanders in an anesthetic solution to see if preventing movement in this way delayed the development of swimming reactions. At the age when normal salamanders swim, the anesthetic was allowed to wear off; swimming appeared promptly. This suggests that the swimming response merely "unfolds" biologically. Other functions also can ap-

school used the best possible test and procedure can be set aside at this moment, since the same issues would arise if the test items or technique were altered to meet the specific criticisms.

Assume that Gary got the best possible psychological examination. Now, what do you think of these letters?

pear without being developed through experience, so long as the nutrients for biological development are supplied. (For a review, see Carmichael, in Mussen, 1970, I, pp. 447–64.)

A second stream of evidence from animals points in the opposite direction. Rats have been reared in barren environments that offered little variation in stimulation and little opportunity to explore. Other rats have been reared in complex environments with elaborate runways and "toys." In the rich environment the rats developed heavier brains and greater enzyme activity. And these physical characteristics are in turn associated with faster maze learning. Hence richer experience promoted physical and mental development. Lack of experience retarded development, as shown by the poor progress of the rats in the barren environment. The difference between environments mattered more for some genetic strains of rats than others. (For a review of these studies, see Thompson & Grusec, in Mussen, 1970, I, pp. 565–654.)

Experiments with a variety of techniques on many animal species have amply confirmed both biological "unfolding" in the absence of experience and behavioral damage resulting from a restriction on experience. Which is more important depends on the complexity of the organism and on the kind of behavior under consideration.

It is hard to know what animal research may imply for educators. Humans are not just like lower animals, and the tasks we want them to learn are not much like the tasks assigned to laboratory animals. A generation ago, the predominant findings indicated that structures unfold without stimulation. *Maturation* was the big word in educational circles. Readiness would come about in its own good time, the educator was told; no purpose would be served by stimulation in advance of readiness. Today's two-sided evidence on animals makes it clear that "wait for maturation" is not a biological law to which educators must bow.

Neurological studies of humans establish the role of stimulation during a formative period in promoting even biological maturing. For example, Riesen (1960) found that physiological development of the retina proceeds normally only if the eyes are used early in life. This is dramatically evidenced in persons born blind whose sight is later made normal by an operation. Such a person, who has had no opportunity to compare patterns in childhood, finds it very difficult to make such discriminations when he finally can see (von Senden, 1960; Gregory & Wallace, 1963). A young adult with vision blocked by cataracts was cured by an operation. Although she was intelligent, having succeeded in completing high school while blind, after the operation she could not learn to rec-

TABLE 5.1
Effect of enriched environment on appearance of attentive responses

| Response | In control group | In experimental groups, relative to controls | |
| --- | --- | --- | --- |
| | | Massive enrichment | Moderate enrichment |
| Swipes at object | 65 | same | 10 days earlier |
| Both hands raised | 80 | 10 days earlier | 15 days earlier |
| Hands brought to midline and clasped | 95 | same | 10 days earlier |
| Torso turned toward object | 105 | same | 10 days earlier |
| Full upward reach | 145 | 50 days earlier | 60 days earlier |

*Median age of appearance (days)**

SOURCE: Data from B. White (1967).
*These values, taken from a chart and based on small groups, are rounded to the nearest five days.

ognize the faces of her associates. Hebb (1958, p. 123) extends such findings into the general conclusion that "perceptual development depends essentially on exposure to the patterned stimulation of the early environment. . . . It is rare that an adult learns a [new] language so well that he can pass in every respect as a native. . . . One's 'ear' for the rhythms and nuances of speech must be acquired early." Despite the fact that some developments are highly dependent upon biological processes, a normal range of varied experience appears to be necessary if these processes are to do their work.

A kind of counterpart to the salamander experiment is the practice among the Hopi of strapping the child to a cradle board. Despite the fact that this gives him no opportunity for crawling, the child develops walking in a normal manner when the usual age arrives (Dennis & Dennis, 1940). But a later study in Tehran (Dennis, 1960) showed that in some ways experience does make a difference in walking. Children in an Iranian orphanage spent their time in a dimly lighted room, mostly in their beds. Their walking was severely delayed; the majority did not walk even by age 3. The barren environment and lack of incentive in Tehran provided more of a handicap than the physical restriction of the Hopi, whose environment provided stimulation.

## Early Stimulation and Instruction: Pro and Con

Once, the preschool years were seen as a period of physical and not intellectual growth. Delaying instruction until age 6 was considered both kindly and efficient. More recent research has established that the child works actively on his environment from the first weeks of life. In the process, he develops skill in comparing, classifying, and anticipating the effects of his acts. Observations of infants show the child gradually stabilizing his attention on objects within his visual field, and later (typically by five months of age) learning to coordinate and direct his reach. How much stimulation he gets affects his rate of development.

STIMULATION IN THE CRADLE  Burton White (1967) compared three groups of normal, healthy infants. In the institutions where they were being cared for he arranged three distinct treatments:

Controls. The children were left alone save for basic care as needed. They could see little of interest from their cribs, where they lay on their backs. Crib fittings were white. (Some of the children were "handled" during the first month.)

Massive-enrichment group. The children were picked up and handled for 20 minutes per day during the first month. Through the next three months, they were placed in the prone position three times a daily. Objects of various shapes and colors were hung over the cribs where the infants, lying face-up, could see them. Crib fittings were multicolored.

Moderate-enrichment group. The children were picked up and handled for 20 minutes per day during first month. After this, for a month, two patterned forms were suspended six inches above their eyes. During the final two months, objects like those used for massive enrichment were hung over the crib.

White observed how actions develop, and sometimes introduced an object to test attentiveness. A few of his findings appear in Table 5.1. Reaching developed much earlier when stimulation was provided. Limited amounts of stimulation had as much effect as massive stimulation, which perhaps overloaded the child. Research of this kind is still primitive, but other studies support White's view that the initial information-processing activities of the child are "plastic." Adjusting the environment in cradle days gives the parent a first opportunity to educate the intellect.

MATURATION AND EDUCATIONAL POLICY    Some writers suggest that the early years are all-important for development. I do not take so extreme a position. Development is cumulative. Much happens in the first few years, but there is no age at which development or learning has to stop. Psychologically significant developments occur at age 12 or 25 or 40.

Public educational planning deploys limited resources over much of a person's life span. How large a fraction of the effort to invest in early education is hard to decide, for several reasons:

- The "richest" environment may not be the best one; increase in stimulation often has little effect and can even retard development.

- A push at an early age is insufficient. A burst of stimulation has little permanent meaning unless followed up by opportunity and stimulation to accomplish the tasks of later ages.

- What one person should learn may be unimportant for another. The earlier instruction is attempted, the less is known about what the person should learn in order to live his own life at *its* best.

Most experimental trials of intensive stimulation or instruction are of short duration. Brief training almost invariably puts the experimental group of children ahead of the control group, but the salient question is whether the advantage lasts. As time passes, the gap between those who were Controls and Experimentals ordinarily decreases, and it may disappear entirely (p. 354). Such evidence seems to support the view (box, p. 166) that instruction "in advance of maturation" is a waste of effort.

The well-known Hilgard study is representative of these findings. Two-year-olds received 12 weeks of training and practice in cutting with scissors and in similar skills (J. R. Hilgard, 1932). Each child in Group A had from 25 to 30 practice periods. Group B, of the same age, was trained only during the last week of the experiment. As Fig. 5.4 shows, children in Group B gained a great deal between December and April just from growth and everyday experience. Four sessions of

## FIGURE 5.4

### Children may learn faster when training is delayed

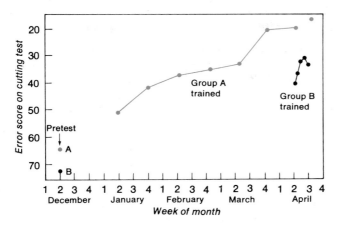

SOURCE: After J. R. Hilgard (1932).

specific training in April produced almost as much gain as Group A had achieved from mid-January to mid-March. The children in Group B, more mature, profited more from their initial training. Nonetheless, the group with longer training was more proficient in the end. The question is principally one of efficiency; if a parent or teacher has to invest more effort to accomplish the same results when training is started earlier, the early effort may not be justified.

It has at times been suggested that early training is actually harmful. A child learning at a comparatively early age would probably perform the task in a different way from one who started when more mature. For example, perhaps a child taught to add at age 5 would often fall back on such techniques as counting on his fingers, whereas an 8-year-old could hold combinations in his head. Crude techniques, adopted early and practiced repeatedly, would perhaps be hard to eliminate, leaving the child who started earlier at a disadvantage by age 10. Credible as this argument is, there is simply no research support for it. To be sure, less mature learners use less mature techniques; but they progress to mature techniques as they grow older, if properly taught.

Many critics fear that undertaking difficult activities early puts undue stress on the child. Most tasks will be easier later rather than earlier, and hence can be mastered later with less anxiety and less sense of inadequacy. Those promoting early learning should keep this warning in mind, but there is no evidence that early stimulation and opportunity to practice do harm—unless there is heavy pressure for excellence.

Experimental evidence such as Hilgard's is not a sufficient basis for discouraging early instruction. An experimenter's treatment is not of long dura-

## Does early education serve any purpose?

An expert on Piagetian theories (pp. 336, 364), David Elkind (1971, pp. 22–24), takes a conservative position in the passage reproduced below. The proper question to hold in mind is: What evidence would refute his statements?

> What is the evidence that preschool instruction has lasting effects upon mental growth and development? The answer is, in brief, that there is none. To prove the point one needs longitudinal data on adults who did not have preschool instruction but who were equal in every other regard to children receiving such instruction. With the exception of the Montessori schools, however, the preschool instruction programs have not been in existence long enough to provide any evidence on the lastingness of their effects. Indeed, most of the earlier work on the effects of nursery school education . . . has shown that significant positive effects are hard to demonstrate when adequate experimental controls are employed. . . . no one, to my knowledge, has done a longitudinal study of adult Montessori graduates. . . .
>
> I am sure that someone will object at this point that studies of mental growth such as those of Bloom (1964) suggest that half the individual's intellectual potential is realized by age 4. Does this not mean that the preschool period is important for intellectual growth and that interventions during this period will have lasting effects? Not necessarily, if we look at the facts in a somewhat different way. Bloom writes, "Both types of data suggest that in terms of intelligence measured at age 17, about 50 percent of the development takes place between conception and age 4, about 30 percent between ages 4 and 8, and about 20 percent between ages 8 and 17" (Bloom, 1964). Now an equally feasible implication of this statement is quite in contradiction to that of preschool instruction. If, it might be argued, the child has only 50 percent of his intellectual ability at age 4 but 80 percent at age 8, why not delay his education 3 years so that he can more fully profit from instruction? With 80 percent of his ability he is likely to learn more quickly

tion. In genuine instruction, one maintains the initial learning not only by further opportunities for practice but by building advanced skills upon the base first laid down. The late starters then are far less likely to overtake the precociously trained group. If one were to teach the 3-year-old to read, for example, this would open the way for his continued intellectual growth, provided that he enjoys reading and so pursues it without pressure during the years 3 to 6. We can teach normal children to read at age 3 by techniques that are not stressful and seem to do no harm (Fowler, 1961; Durkin, 1966). One cannot recommend the practice, however, without considering carefully the cost of the techniques that have to be used and recognizing that time given to reading must be withdrawn from other activities significant for development.

WHEN TO LEARN A SECOND LANGUAGE    How considerations of policy and practicality enter into the educator's thinking about biological findings is illustrated by proposals for teaching a second language early. In a Montreal experiment (box, p. 371), an entire school program from kindergarten to Grade VI, for chil-

and efficiently and is not as likely to learn in ways that he will need to unlearn later. That is to say, without stretching the facts, it is possible to interpret the Bloom statement as implying that instruction should *not* be introduced into the preschool program.

Not only is there no clear cut longitudinal data to support the claims of the last-ingness of preschool instruction, there is evidence in the opposite direction. . . . [Research findings] suggest a negative correlation between early physical matura-tion and later intellectual attainments. Animals are capable of achieving early some skills (a dog or a chimp will be housebroken before a child is toilet trained) but perhaps at the expense of not being able to attain other skills at all. This data suggests the hypothesis that *the longer we delay formal instruction, up to certain limits, the greater the period of plasticity and the higher the ultimate level of achievement.* There is at least as much evidence and theory in support of this hy-pothesis as there is in favor of the early instruction proposition. Certainly, from the Piagetian perspective there are "optimal periods" for the growth of particular mental structures which cannot be rushed.

Please understand, I am not arguing against the benefits of preschool enrich-ment for children. Even preschool instruction may be of value for those disadvan-taged children who do not benefit from what Strodtbeck (1967) called the "hidden curriculum of the middle-class home." What I am arguing is that there is no evi-dence for the *long-term effects* of either preschool instruction or enrichment.*

With respect to Bloom's observation (quoted by Elkind above), Bloom might rea-sonably have said that *individual differences* in final standing are half determined by age 4. But a person has certainly not by that age acquired half the concepts he will ultimately, nor has he developed half his adult ability to reason logically.

* See pp. 361ff.

dren from English-speaking, lower-middle-class homes, was successfully con-ducted in French.

The eminent neurosurgeon Wilder Penfield, drawing on anatomical rather than experimental evidence, has argued that the older brain is unable to learn some things it could have learned at an early age. Specifically, "for the pur-poses of learning languages, the human brain becomes progressively stiff and rigid after the age of nine" (Penfield & Roberts, 1959, p. 236). Particularly dur-ing the second year of life, the child is building, through practice, the neural connections required to pronounce syllables. Simultaneously, he builds neural "programs"—systems of interconnections—to produce speech rhythm and sen-tence structure.

This word *program* will play an important part in discussions of complex performance (p. 398). An electric computer is controlled by a program, that is, a sequence of orders telling the machine what steps to take next, at what instant to send an impulse through a particular circuit. A similar sequence of orders controls movements by which the diaphragm, voicebox, and mouth shape a sound. The program is like a well-designed football play: each player has his assignment, and if he comes in at the correct instant the play succeeds.

Practice at the right age develops circuits or programs that on demand bring forth, by a coordinated sequence of rapid actions, the sounds and structures of the language. The child develops a basic program only for the sounds of his own language. It is quite difficult to train the older person to pronounce new sounds; he most often speaks a French word by putting together the sounds from his native language that come close to the French sounds. The Hawaiian language possesses only seven consonants (h, k, l, m, n, p, w). When Europeans arrived, islanders who as children had learned no language save Hawaiian found it necessary to say "Mele Kalikimaka" as their best approximation to "Merry Christmas." If Penfield is correct, the child learning a language before age 10 does so by creating *new* circuits in the syllable-producing areas of the brain; the older person can only recombine the syllable-circuits of his first tongue. Consequently, the person who acquires a second language in high school or college is unlikely to speak it without an accent.

A biological finding is not in itself a basis for educational policy. It does warn us that in delaying instruction we might miss the boat, letting the child drift past the point where he can most easily form certain neural circuits. But this does not in itself make the case for early instruction. One has to be clear about what is to be gained. Presumably, teaching a second language early will improve pronunciation, but perfect pronunciation seems not to be of great importance for an American who will speak a second language only as a traveler. Nothing in Penfield's data implies that delaying instruction impairs one's ability, as an adult, to comprehend a second language or to formulate thoughts in it. Only by interpreting instructional experiments in the light of educational values can one decide on the timing of instruction.

Early instruction in a second language in Montreal is worthwhile because of the setting. Montreal is a bilingual city in which commercial affairs are dominated by the French majority. Parents who do not speak French feel themselves to be at a disadvantage. They encourage instruction in French so that their children can succeed in an increasingly French Quebec. This, plus the availability of the needed teachers and cultural supports, makes the program practical in Montreal. The same values and supports are not to be found at present in communities in the United States, except where English is taught as a second language.

---

**9** What, if anything, in the remarks of Penfield and in the Montreal experience, is relevant to discussions about whether to conduct early school programs for Chicano children in Spanish rather than English? To discussions about bilingual schooling that also exposes the Anglo classmates of the Chicanos to instruction in Spanish?

**10** A maze task requires a person to study a printed square maze until he can trace the path from center to exit, without entering a blind alley. A certain maze of high complexity contains ten choice points. Suppose it is found that children never solve this task on the first trial before age 12. Would this imply that the performance requires some biological maturation that occurs around age 11?

**11** Group A in the Hilgard experiment (p. 164), with 30 training sessions, finished at a higher level than Group B, with four sessions. If other studies confirm this finding, does it argue for training the 2-year-old in cutting?

# CULTURAL PRESSURES AND OPPORTUNITIES

The stimulation and constraints imposed by a culture encourage certain activities and discourage others, thus shaping mental development, interests, tastes, and character. In one setting, children grow into the New Guinea tribesmen who are gentle, contented, and possess only simple arts and skills. Another setting develops the competitive, aggressive Alaskan Indian who works to humiliate and subjugate rivals.

The stimulation available becomes richer and deeper with age, in at least four significant ways. There is, first, the obvious expansion of geographical range from cradle to community to far corners of the world. Second is the culture represented in language and the experiences that language conveys vicariously. Third is the increasing variety of agents who mold thinking. The child's parents are his first guides, but relatives and teachers, the communications media, and, above all, persons of his own age take on increasing importance. Fourth, additional roles open. In a social gathering, the young child is likely to be confined to passing the cookie plate and responding pleasantly to the guests. In later years, he is expected to respond with sensible remarks that move the conversation forward, and by mid-adolescence it is appropriate for him to initiate topics of serious conversation. While this expansion continues into adulthood, at some age the process is reversed. Waning health and lessened physical strength begin to restrict the older person, and his family and job make smaller demands. These changes too require learning new roles and finding new sources of satisfaction.

## The Environment Widens

The infant's first environment is little more than his mother's face and voice. As his maturation permits him to focus his eyes, reach, sit up, and creep about,

he widens the range he can explore. American children ordinarily make plentiful contacts with others of like age during the years from 2 to 5. Sarah learns about conflict and power when Billy wants the tricycle. The child learns that he or she is "too little" to enter certain activities; even at this age, a social role is defined. Babyhood has its pleasures as well as its restrictions. The child may cling to its indulgence and protection. Witness Robin, age 3, who tells his mother solemnly after a misdemeanor: "You won't spank me. I'm too little to understand."

Entrance into school, whether at age 3 or age 6, is a significant step toward independence. Before that, most activities are linked to the home and supervised by a parent. In school a child enters a life over which parents have little control. He makes his way among strangers and joins social groups on his own.

The preschool child deals almost entirely with events and objects within his immediate experience, but stories, television, and the like begin to acquaint him with the wider world, as do reading and his wider exploration of the community after age 6. The Western drama communicates, along with the excitement of horses and guns, a dozen cultural values and taboos. Stereotyped though it is, it acquaints the child with motives he might never observe in his daily life—greed, revenge, public service—and lines up his emotions on the side of justice and property rights (and violence). Such stimulation stretches the child's horizon across the earth's surface, backward into history, and forward into time and space.

Out of increased physical interaction with the environment comes a firmer intellectual grasp (p. 328). The same event carries a meaning for the older child different from that for the younger one. This is illustrated by children's responses to questions about the flag (Weinstein, 1957). At 5, the child sees the flag as an object with pretty colors; he knows of no connection between flags and nations. A year later, he associates flags with the idea of "good" and "bad" countries. By 8 or 9, he is aware that there are flags for many governments, and he begins to speak of ideas of honor, loyalty, and pride in connection with the flag. By age 12, his vague ideas coalesce into a reasoned concept. He sees the flag as an agreed symbol of a people and their government.

LANGUAGE MULTIPLIES ABILITIES    Language serves as a telescope and a time machine, bringing experiences the child could never crowd into his own lifetime. Language multiplies memory by packing an experience into a verbal capsule that is readily stored. Linguistic devices—the number system and the abstract concepts of the disciplines—make it possible to define and solve problems precisely, without wasteful trial and error.

The child's ordinary exposure to speech in home and playgroup assures that he will pick up speech. This process, as it occurs naturally, is often not very efficient; some homes equip the child with a far more effective language than others do.

**12**  James Coleman (1972) sees today's society as "information-rich." Thanks to television and other media, as well as his own travel, the child comes to school with far more knowledge of the world, of technology, and so on than used to be the case. Does this change make it unimportant for the school to extend the child's horizon through vicarious experience?

## The Child's Social Group Expands

The circle of others who influence one's life is constantly widening. Three categories of persons have a socializing influence: those in power who present explicit demands and reward compliance (authority figures), those who present an image of behavior that can be copied (models), and those companions whose favorable and unfavorable reactions are rewarding or punishing.

The infant begins with one chief socializer, his mother. The way mother and child interact is highly significant. B. White and Watts (1973) observed how mothers treated children at ages 1–3 and related that information to the children's social and intellectual competence. The mothers of more competent children interacted more with them, and interacted in a more intellectualized manner. The best results, as White and Watts report, are seen in homes that facilitate the child's explorations. In time, the child passes into the care of teachers; nowadays, this is likely to happen at a rather early age. Three-year-olds coming from homes where their autonomous exploration is encouraged often experience something of a shock when confronted by a preschool teacher who aims to plan their activities. But sooner or later the child does have to come to terms with a planful teacher.

By age 8, other models are at least as important as parents and teachers. The American child is likely to spend 20 hours per week before a television set, which presents models of heroes, models of consumption, and models of social protest. Though television is a strong socializing influence, much of what it offers is directed by no philosophy of socialization and controlled by no community purpose.

PEER INFLUENCES   Peers (persons of the child's own age and status) are powerful sources of reward. Since the power to reward is in itself the power to demand, the peer group acts as an authority figure. Unlike other authority figures—parents, teachers, older brothers and sisters, bosses—the peer group is not delegated its authority by the adult culture. The peer group represents its own interests and values, even working in opposition to the more official socializers. Here, for example, is the plaintive report of a university faculty who arranged a "Talent Series" of concert artists as a contribution to the cultural development of students:

> It was once considered fashionable—"the thing to do"—to attend the Talent Series. Those who did not attend were just not quite "in style." Undergraduate attitudes have changed. Of 1,900 season tickets sold this year, only 200 were sold to undergraduates. In contrast, special programs such as rock concerts are patronized almost exclusively by undergraduates. About 4,200 of the 5,000 who attended a recent rock concert were undergraduates. Are students redefining what is cultural? Who is to say that the Cleveland Orchestra is "cultural" while a rock band is not?

Peers first enter the child's life as models whose actions suggest provisional responses; if Timmy is playing in the snow, Sharon wants to go out, too. This suggestive force is gradually transformed into a positive need for doing things with others and being accepted by them. In the preschool years, children pair off in ever-changing small groups. There is little group spirit and the child is not inclined to subordinate his own impulses to the will of the group (Hartup, in Mussen, 1970, II, p. 374). As intellectual development makes it possible for a larger group to operate effectively, group spirit emerges and group approval becomes a near-coercive force.

Peers are increasingly influential in child and adolescent development when the society becomes urbanized, family ties weaken, and neighbors interact less. As early as Grade VII, American youngsters spend twice as much of their free time with peers as with their parents (Condry et al., 1968). Peers are more significant in American childhood than in some other countries. Boehm

(1957) presented probes such as this in Geneva, Switzerland, and in Winnetka, Illinois:

---

**A group of children of your age want to give a surprise birthday party for their scout leader. One boy has accepted the responsibility of decorating the room. He wonders whom he could ask for advice.**

---

In interviews, 70 per cent of the Swiss children insisted that teachers and parents always give the best advice. Only 7 per cent of the Americans considered teachers' advice superior to that of an artistically talented student.

Some persons suppress their own judgments when they hear a different opinion from peers. Such conforming is rare at preschool ages, and strong during middle childhood; it decreases gradually in adolescence. The peak of conformity—at least as judged by the test described on p. 212—comes at about age 13 (Hartup, in Mussen, 1970, II, pp. 406–11). After that, the superior reasoning power of the adolescent gives him a basis for security when in opposition.

## Roles Become More Varied

Each setting into which the person moves calls for new relationships and styles of response; each experience is a training ground for future roles. The 5-year-old who takes a turn at "show and tell" is learning a new role; in passing out drawing materials, he practices another. Social competence at any age is made up of those roles one is able to perform with a reasonable degree of comfort. One can master alternative styles of behavior—aggressive or passive, nurturant or critical, and so on. This makes it possible to play roles that seem to call for different "personalities." Social roles are defined by the group; in this sense they are sockets into which a person must fit. Within the role, one has much latitude to write one's own lines.

With new roles, power increases. Few choices are allowed before age 3. The parent chooses the child's food, tells him when to go out and when to play indoors, is firm against his wandering about the neighborhood. Gradually, restrictions are removed. The child selects his games and his playmates; he decides which of his clothes he will wear and how he will spend his allowance. He may be consulted about how the family will spend Sunday afternoon or what project his class will next undertake. By adolescence, the boy or girl has considerable freedom in choosing activities and may be allowed to spend, on clothes or recreation, amounts that are substantial in relation to the family income.

COMMUNITY DIFFERENCES    Communities differ in the roles open to individuals and the opportunities for learning the roles provide. In a small town, the 10-

year-old has a good chance to do things that "mean something" to the adult community—making an announcement in a church meeting, playing Little League ball before a neighborhood audience, helping in a UNICEF campaign. In a metropolis there is little chance for joining in activities significant to the adult community.

Barker and Schoggen (1973) compared two towns with populations of about 1,000: "Midwest," Kansas, and "Yoredale," in rural Yorkshire, England (both pseudonyms). They counted all the roles essential to community activities—participant roles as distinct from audience or customer roles. In a year's time, the Kansas residents fill, on the average, three times as many responsible roles as those in Yorkshire. There is more activity in Midwest and fewer people to carry it on. The distribution by ages showed that Midwest gave especially great opportunity to adolescents. The authors speak of a "melting pot" system of child rearing in Midwest and an "enlightened colonial system" in Yoredale (pp. 404 ff.).

> According to the Midwest system, children are best prepared for adulthood by participating in a wide variety of the town's settings. Midwesterners think that it is of particular benefit to children to undertake tasks that are important and difficult for them before they can discharge the tasks with complete adequacy. . . . This responsible participation involves sharing of power with adults. . . .
>
> According to the Yoredale system, children are best prepared for adulthood by removing them from the general, public settings and placing them in [special] . . . settings under the direction of experts. . . . children are not welcomed into some community settings because they do not have the requisite skills and attitudes to take their places smoothly. . . . In terms of the Colonial System metaphor, Yoredale children are the underdeveloped people of the town, and Yoredale adults are the responsible bearers of a higher culture.

What is true of Midwest may not be true of all towns in the United States, and it certainly is not true in metropolitan areas. Urban crowding and suburban sprawl force activities into a bureaucratic mold; the amateur cannot drift easily in and out of the community activities as in Midwest. Moreover, the structure reduces the number of significant roles to be played relative to the number of inhabitants.

Coleman (1972) argues that the large American community does not allow young persons sufficient chance to contribute to real enterprises. The schools, he says, ought to be much less concerned with conveying knowledge; it is sufficient to teach how to locate information as needed. Coleman would make the schools' major task that of engaging young people in economically productive teamwork or community service (box, p. 197).

Individuals are encouraged to adopt different roles, partly by the expectations of their families and subculture, partly in recognition of physical characteristics and aptitudes.

SEX ROLES  The most notable differentiation of persons is along sex lines. From infancy, boys and girls are traditionally offered different toys and games; the 5-year-old knows that boats are for boys and dollhouses for girls. Nowadays girls are more often encouraged to prepare themselves for what were once masculine roles. Some boys are encouraged to develop skills in nurturance that were once left to the female, but on the whole, boys are pressed to "act like boys" (Maccoby & Jacklin, 1974, p. 339).

Sex differences in abilities are not great during the preadolescent years but there are appreciable sex differences in school performance. Girls are more compliant and receive higher grades, though boys outdo girls in tasks that have a mathematical or spatial aspect (Maccoby & Jacklin, 1974; see also p. 287). When a mathematical problem is cast in terms of laying out areas of a garden, girls do better than they do if the same problem is given in abstract form. Kagan (1964, p. 157) makes the following interpretation:

> It seems that the typical female believes that the ability to solve problems involving geometry, physics, logic, or arithmetic is a uniquely masculine skill, and her motivation to attack such problems is low. The decreased involvement may reflect the fact that the girl's self-esteem is not at stake in such problems, or the fact that she is potentially threatened by the possibility that . . . unusual excellence on such tasks may be equated with a loss of femininity.

All such remarks, of course, relate to statistical trends; some girls will hold their own with boys in any pursuit of which they are physically capable.

Just as dolls and dishes are seen as feminine, so the school and its tasks tend to be viewed as feminine during the early grades. Not just the teacher, but

**Role training**

"BOYS DON'T WRESTLE WITH GIRLS!"

"DID YA HEAR *THAT,* GINA? GET *OFFA* ME!"

"Dennis the Menace" used courtesy Hank Ketcham and © 1975 Field Newspaper Syndicate, T.M.®

## Heidi sees herself in many roles

Heidi, living in a comfortable suburban setting, is a devoted horsewoman and, in her drawings, appears as show rider and as cowgirl with lasso. But at age 8½ she is conscious of her many other roles, present and potential. Through these drawings she is discovering herself, expressing and elaborating her self-concept.

even the desks and books and blackboards take on a feminine connotation, Kagan finds. (The effect is not so strong when some of the faculty are male.) A boy concerned with demonstrating his masculinity can be expected to limit his commitment when the tasks he is given seem girlish. Fewer boys than girls succeed in first-grade reading; lukewarm commitment is one plausible explanation. Strikingly, in an experiment where beginning reading was taught primarily through interaction with a computer terminal, few boys failed. In later grades the boy's vocational, practical orientation, together with "masculine" connotations of tough-minded reasoning, tends to increase commitment to schoolwork.

SOURCE: *Heidi's Horse*, text by Sylvia Fein, drawings by Heidi Scheuber (Pleasant Hill, Calif.: Exelrod Press, 1976), pp. 81 and 83.

A school can set up conditions that reduce stereotypes of behavior appropriate to boys or girls. Minuchin et al. (1969) probed the inner attitudes of 9-year-old girls who were from rather well-to-do families in traditional and "modern" schools. The traditional image—"I think I want to be like my mother; I don't want to work"—came up fairly often in the traditional schools and in one modern school. In the other modern school, no girl said this sort of thing. The girl from that school foresaw a future in which her activities would express her own interests. She was liberated from some of the developmental pressures that operate to push boys in one direction and girls in another.

**13** Some people describe personality as a collection of habits; others as a repertoire of roles the person can play. Which concept do you most often use?

**14** A teacher plays many roles during the school day. Illustrate this.

**15** How would a 15-year-old in Yoredale differ from a 15-year-old in Midwest?

**16** Barker regards the Midwestern "use" of children in community affairs as a heritage from the underpopulated frontier, where children were needed to carry out community functions. What does this imply regarding the function of the school today in Midwest and in a crowded American city?

**17** Socialization performed in the schools today, says Coleman, emphasizes "the narcissistic goal of self-improvement." Do you consider that a just description? Should the emphasis be changed?

## Developmental Tasks

In its normal activities, the culture takes for granted that a person of a given age and sex will have command of certain roles. The person who has not mastered one of these roles to the point of feeling comfortable in it is at a serious disadvantage. Learning these roles constitutes a timed series of developmental tasks. The culture provides opportunities for each generation to master a given task through the institutions and activities open at a certain age level. The person who for some reason misses the opportunity finds it comparatively difficult to make up the deficit later. To take a not-too-fundamental example, Americans normally can drive a car safely by age 18. Driver training is offered at ages 14–17. Attaining a driver's license opens the way to pursue preferred activities, and hence to self-development, during later adolescence. One can learn to drive later, but by that time he may have missed out on a lot of adolescent activity. That is the kind of thing that makes accomplishing a developmental task so nearly obligatory. The culture, in defining for the person the role he should master, provides a natural and most powerful motivation. As Havighurst (1953, p. 5) has put it:

> When the body is ripe, and society requires, and the self is ready to achieve a certain task, the teachable moment has come. Efforts at teaching which would have been largely wasted if they had come earlier give gratifying results when they come at the *teachable moment*.

Table 5.2 summarizes, by age periods, major developmental tasks in the United States. The periods correspond to major changes in behavior and social role (English, 1957; C. Gordon, 1971), but the divisions are not sharp. Development is continuous, and there is no overnight change at any birthday.

What the culture expects at a given age changes as the job market changes, or new styles of family life develop, or more rapid maturing ripens interests earlier. The past decade has seen significant alteration in the options open to youth—demonstrated in the shift of the age for voting and holding property to 18—and in changing sexual mores.

The timing of tasks, and the relative emphasis, varies from one subculture to another. Table 5.2 probably fits the well-to-do suburban family best. A table drawn up for an Amish community or a tribal group of American Indians would be different in content and timing. As was observed in Yoredale, some communities postpone responsibility and independence. Some cultures differentiate more sharply between sexes, and some—notably the mainland Chinese (Bronfenbrenner, 1975)—replace the ideal of individual self-reliance with the ideal of community interdependence. Whatever the cultural specifics, a pattern of steadily advancing expectations is seen everywhere.

EARLY ADOLESCENCE AS AN EXAMPLE    Discussing entries in the row for ages 12–15 will acquaint you with the table. In early adolescence, the young person increasingly takes on an individual identity. At earlier ages, schooling covered about the same ground for everyone; now it begins to branch. A new time in life is signaled by the onset of puberty, and the adolescent is self-consciously aware that he is expected to act in a new way.

There is some hazard in generalizing about "early adolescence" (or any other age) in a time of rapid social change. On the one hand, the developmental agenda of early adolescence today seem to reflect the same biological and cultural realities as in previous decades (Kagan & Coles, 1972). But it is also true that the behavior typical at a certain age changes from decade to decade. Indeed, Nesselroade and Baltes (1974) found that the average for 15-year-olds on a personality measure shifted in the short span from 1970 to 1972. Their sample was limited to a few West Virginia communities, but similar questions put to a nationwide sample of slightly older youth in the same years showed similar trends (Yankelovich, 1974, pp. 66, 68). As is usual, the averages on extroversion and dominance increased from age 12 to age 15. The adolescents who reached age 15 in 1972 were more extroverted than the 15-year-olds of an earlier year; such a difference was also found at other ages. From 1970 to 1972, holding age constant, the trend was to more extroversion, less impulse control, more autonomy, and much less motivation to achieve. If these trends continue over several years, adolescent behavior will be quite different by 1980. But the trend may already have been reversed by a change in social forces; only new data can tell.*

Early adolescence is the period, above all, of learning to be autonomous: to define oneself, to set one's own goals, to make one's own decisions. Until this age, the parents have expected the child to trust them, and usually he has done so.

---

* Another trend, occurring prior to adolescence, deserves mention. Eron et al. (1974) found that aggression scores among 9-year-old girls in the 1970s match those of boys, and are far higher than among similar girls 10–15 years earlier.

**TABLE 5.2**

Developmental tasks from infancy to adulthood in the United States

| Age (years) | Physical landmarks | Characterization | Need for affec |
|---|---|---|---|
| 0–1½ (Infancy) | Creeps by age 1 | Dependent; learns to interpret sensory impressions | Establish feeding schedule, weani develop confider in adult care |
| 2–4 (Early childhood) | Walks and talks by age 2 | Energetic play; social regulation imposed with or without understanding | Accept newborn brother or sister form secure ider cation with like-s parent |
| 5–9 (Early schooling) | | Adapts to organization; develops tool skills; evaluates self comparatively | |
| 10–11 (Middle childhood) | | Stable group activities; projects extending over longer periods | |
| 12–15 (Early adolescence) | Puberty: Girls 10–14, Boys 12–16 | Reasons systematically; dating begins; increased sense of unique personality, planning for future | |
| 16–23 (Youth) | | Direct preparation for work; sexual intimacy; tension between youth culture and adult expectation | Form close comr ship with membe of opposite sex; tain sex adjustme |
| 24–28 (Transition) | | Establishes own home; settles into career path | Devote self to inf (women, sometim men) |

| Need for secure relation with authority | Need for approval by peers | Need for autonomy | Need for competence and self-respect |
| --- | --- | --- | --- |
| | | | Master objects within reach; gain eye-hand coordination |
| Accept rules, schedules, denial of wishes; begin to understand principles behind regulations | Develop social skills: share, take turns, inhibit aggression; learn property rights | Accept separation from parent; express own desires via requests; successfully make demands on others | Accept and meet parental performance standards; successfully make demands on environment |
| Accept rules and procedures; control emotions; understand rights of others; accept teacher as model and guide | Care for own appearance; win acceptance in school group; develop play skills | | Succeed in schoolwork; master physical skills for games; accept own physical characteristics, aptitude for school |
| Make effort toward school achievement | Learn style respected by own-sex peers; accept group code; learn to compete within the code | Carry on tasks without supervision; enjoy own industriousness; accept some conflict with authority | Develop interests; find means of earning pocket money |
| Accept more impersonal direction in departmentalized school; hold self to schedule | Gain acceptance from opposite sex; acquire new sex-appropriate skills and styles | Find satisfaction in nonfamily recreations; search for own views on basic issues | Accept own body, role of own sex; accept own abilities and talents; settle on some interests that define one's individuality |
| Carry out tasks assigned in general terms | | Take responsibility for car, job; take stands on political matters; make decisions despite parental opposition | Find general vocational direction and demonstrate ability; develop vocational skill; find part-time job |
| Apply standards set by authority to own work with minimal supervision | | Plan with mate | Establish self securely in job |

There has been no significant divergence between parents' views and peers' views. The adolescent becomes aware of outside standards that differ from those of his parents and incorporates some of them as his own. He begins to question parental rulings on conduct, parental views on political themes, and parents' rights to impose their aspirations on him. As Blos (in Kagan & Coles, 1972) puts it:

> . . . the child passes, gradually and persistently, from the highly personal family envelope to the eminently impersonal societal envelope. In this transition we witness the steady arousal of affective responses to social, moral, and spiritual issues. . . . The personal and intimate ties of love and hate which were the heartbeat of the child's social matrix become slowly replaced by immersion into the anonymity of society. . . . Personal intimacy and emotional bonds become a matter of personal choice.

Table 5.2 has no entry under "need for affection" for this age, as no new hurdles appear. Security in the family should have been established years earlier, and affectional ties can be casual at this time. The main emotional problem of this period is to draw away from the family. The affection of the family is needed just as before, but maintaining it is not a new "task."

It is in self-esteem (last column) that the most critical developments of this period are found. I have already spoken of the changes puberty brings and of the problems of social adjustment that come with delayed growth or other departures from the cultural ideal. Adolescents clearly work to make the most of their physical resources: improving their complexions, building up their physiques, and so on. Some come fully to accept their physical selves, while others cannot escape a feeling of inferiority.

The years of puberty are likely to be stressful, and signs of tension become evident even in boys and girls who had previously been stable. This is normal, not alarming. Those young people who seem to take early adolescence in stride, remaining self-controlled and emotionally steady, often turn out to be below average in adjustment as adults. The adolescent boys who turn irritable, and the girls who lose confidence for a time, are the ones most likely to turn out poised and dependable in the long run. It appears that to experience some degree of crisis in adolescence is a sign of coping and relearning; bland equilibrium is sometimes a sign of rigidity and insensitivity (Peskin & Livson, 1972).

Early adolescence is a period of opening up one's life and sensing the possibilities it offers, before the hard choices of later adolescence begin. The adolescent is offered a wide range of options. The middle grades abound with curricular and extracurricular options: music of all kinds, photography, sports, stamps, movies, books, clothing, woodworking, rockhounding, pen pals around the world, and so on.

Far richer options are available in some communities than others, sometimes because of poverty and isolation, and sometimes because community agencies lack imagination or resources. Adolescents from affluent homes are free to take advantage of the options, while those from other homes may be caring for younger members of their family—or just drifting in the neighborhood, if that is the normal after-school activity in their set. Where budgets and energy are available, the school can break into this vicious circle.

Often a school allots a reasonable part of the day, in the upper grades, to exploratory activities. This curriculum plan fits Erikson's (1964) well-known conception of adolescence as a *"psychosocial moratorium* during which the individual through free role experimentation may find a niche in some section of his society, a niche which is firmly defined and yet seems to be uniquely made for him." By "moratorium" Erikson means that there is little demand for serious production outside of the chief school subjects. The teenager can pick up interests and set them down without an admission of failure. He is not expected to have an accomplishment to show.

The normal 12-year-old has just attained the ability to organize matters logically, to envision alternatives and eliminate them systematically. He can entertain propositions that conflict with reality—"All three-legged snakes are purple; I am hiding a three-legged snake. Can you guess its color?" Kagan (in Kagan & Coles, 1972) shows that this logic exposes more fundamental conflicts between facts ("The world contains many unhappy people") and beliefs instilled by the parents ("God loves man"). With regard to religion, parental and civic authority, and personal conduct, the shell of belief in simple truisms cracks, as the teenager and his group bear down upon them with their new logical tools. The young adolescent resolves intellectual conflicts forcefully, often simplistically. Asked to comment on a law that is not working out, he is likely to propose sterner enforcement instead of proposing to amend the law (Adelson, in Kagan & Coles, 1972). During early adolescence, the youngster learns to temper this ruthless logic and learns to bring multiple considerations, including the conflicting motives of discontented parties, into a temperate balance.

New roles

"I hate to see her leaving childhood so soon. This year,
she said 'The Nutcracker' was a bummer."

Drawing by Donald Reilly; © 1974 The New Yorker Magazine, Inc.

Working to a standard and directing one's own work has always been a developmental task for this age. In school, algebra, foreign language, English composition, and other studies demand concentrated effort. Conflict arises because these studies seem irrelevant to young people; the courses are urged upon the student as the means by which he can attain a successful, satisfying *later* life. Diligent work at whatever task the school sets is demanded not only of the college-bound but also of those headed for blue-collar work, because employers make the school's report of good work habits a passport to employability even at the industrial workbench.

**18** As one task in early adolescence, Table 5.2 lists "search for own views on basic issues." What forces impel such a search? What penalties does the person suffer if he neglects this task?

**19** Add two rows to Table 5.2 listing developmental tasks that you think would be important in middle maturity (ages 40–50) and at retirement (ages 60–70). In middle maturity, children are leaving the home, occupational skill and economic power are at their height, and physical powers are beginning to fade. At retirement, loss of occupation and health are major concerns.

# THE DEVELOPMENT AND SATISFACTION OF NEEDS

Each major developmental task is related to one or more continuing needs. A single task, such as courtship, is part of a long process of satisfying the need for affection. A need is a broad motive that makes certain types of goals attractive and important to the individual. The emphasis is on continuing patterns of motivation, whereas words such as *goal, purpose,* and *motive* usually refer more to the specific motivation in a particular episode.

Whenever a person acts, he is presumably trying to attain a goal, and the goals chosen on various occasions often seem to have a common element. The goals people seem to be rushing toward at noon on a given day are remarkably diverse in location and substance, but they all have to do with eating. We can summarize this consistency by speaking of a need for food.

The sources of positive motivation (and also of troublesome behavior) important for school purposes are needs for affection, for secure relations with authority, for peer approval, autonomy, and competence and self-respect. This list is not exhaustive, nor is it the only way to describe and classify motives. Some writers compress the list to three or four needs, and some expand it to twenty or more.

This text omits "tissue needs"—for food, oxygen, or avoidance of pain—even though physiological sources of motivation are important in school. A chronically hungry child is as lacking in readiness to learn as a child who lacks affection. Such truths require no elaboration here.

## Need for Affection

Close affectional ties with a few persons provide the chief satisfaction of living for most Americans. The home and family are central institutions, to which work, community participation, and creative activities are secondary. While achievement can be satisfying in itself, most people find greater pleasure in the appreciation given by family and friends. Many people do not find a way to fulfill the need for affection. Among the adults and children who require help from clinical psychologists, the feeling of rejection is a common trouble.

The developments that bear most directly on affection are grouped in one column of Table 5.2. The need for affection is manifested early. In the baby's first months he is engulfed in a meaningless swirl of sensations. Many are unpleasant: hunger, wetness, muscular cramping. His mother attends to these, and her tender, smiling care accompanies the routines that give him comfort. Soon the infant begins to show pleasure in the presence of his mother and stops crying when she appears. He has learned to find affection gratifying and to want it when it is absent. At seven months of age, attachment to the mother should be well advanced (Ainsworth, 1973).

## Failure in a developmental task: "irreversible catastrophe"?

### Edgar Friedenberg comments on Erik Erikson's *Childhood and Society* (1964):

> Erikson stresses . . . that catastrophe is irreversible. . . . An infant who has good reason to distrust his mother in the sense that she just is not there when needed, that she lets him down and cools him out, is not really going to trust anybody—ever—because he will not know what trust feels like; and the occasions that might evoke it will terrify him. . . . Furthermore, this privation will warp all his subsequent stages of growth. If he cannot really trust himself, he will whine and cringe when a more confident child would be walking and talking; then, in his first play group, he will cower uncertainly away from situations that other children would delightedly explore, and so on. Failure at any stage tends to precipitate failure in each of the later ones cumulatively; success at any stage brightens chances at a later one. However, a person who achieves success at a later stage after protracted earlier failure is not repaired and made whole. We all know children who bustle about with great bursts of industry at school, simply to cover up years of fussy neglect by parents who had no confidence in them and no interest in anything about them but their achievement. These are often the children whom teachers select to direct traffic at school crossings. In later life they may become assistant district attorneys, or efficient and officious obstetricians who are careful, for the sake of the infant, not to give the laboring mother as much sedation as she thinks she needs. But development usually works out less neatly.

SOURCE: Friedenberg (1965), p. 2. Reprinted with permission of *The New York Review of Books*. Copyright © 1965 Nyrev, Inc.

Successful establishment of attachment in the first year promotes independence in the second. The secure child is more ready to explore his environment and so can develop faster. ("Dependency" sounds much like attachment, but there is a distinction: The attached child is at ease with a parent in the background; the dependent infant is ill at ease unless the parent is close, protecting him from all risk by her guidance.)

The father increases in importance as a model and a source of approval, especially for the boy. The warmer the relation, especially at about age 3, the more quickly and confidently the boy develops the masculine qualities of the "real boy" (Bronson, 1959; Mussen & Distler, 1960). A major part of Mack's trouble (p. 127), you will recall, stemmed from his inability to relate warmly to his father.

The child who feels accepted and wanted during the preschool years usually remains trusting as he works out later social relationships. In late adolescence, the person comes to depend on a partner of his own age for emotional assurance and purpose. Achieving a stable and satisfying marriage requires faith in the unwavering affection of the mate. As in childhood, security is threatened if disagreements on routine decisions lead to a feeling that one's partner will withdraw his love. Affectional security established with the parents helps one to establish emotional security in adult relationships. Even in adulthood, the person is still meeting new affectional demands and learning new roles.

In the activities related to affection, five principles applying to all social needs are illustrated:

- An experience associated with other gratifications comes to be desired for itself. This is how social needs are learned. Although a learned motive may have an instinctive base (this is difficult to investigate), its strength and the goals sought are a product of experience.

- From time to time, changes in a person's social surroundings and in the demands upon him make it impossible for him to satisfy his needs by the actions that formerly satisfied them.

- If a person fails to master the developmental tasks at one age, satisfying the same need at later ages is more difficult.

- The development of a person is interlocked with the needs and development of others around him.

- Development continues throughout life. Important adjustments and learning remain to be accomplished in adulthood (Havighurst, 1968; Vaillant & McArthur, 1972).

**20** Friedenberg's gloss on Erikson (box) suggests that a person who is seriously maladjusted can never recover. Are his remarks fully in accord with our principles here and on p. 150?

**21** Illustrate how the five principles just listed apply to developing one's identity as a member of one's sex.

## Need for Secure Relations with Authority

Authority figures are ever-present: parents, teachers, superiors on the job, building inspectors and other representatives of public authority. With all such figures the person must establish a working relation appropriate to his age. There is a place for obedience, there is a place for using one's own judgment despite what authority recommends, and there is a place for outright rebellion. As the person develops, he finds his own balance between the pressures from designated authority, the more diffuse pressures from his circle of associates, the force of reality, and his own impulses. Ideally, the person will become comfortable with authority so that interactions are neither slavish nor tinged with guilt-ridden antagonism.

The infant, beginning to explore his home, encounters prohibitions and regulations. Pretty as the vase is, he must not touch. He must pick up his toys before he may eat. If, during the first five years, he often balks and gets around the prohibitions, he concludes that adult mandates can be disregarded. If severely punished, he comes to see authorities as arbitrary and threatening. A more wholesome resolution to the conflict between desires and restrictions is for the child to learn that parental judgments are consistent and predictable.

A home with firm standards gives the child a set of norms. If parents are absent much of the time or indifferent, the child has less chance to work out the inevitable conflicts between his own impulses and the standards of others. It is found that among middle-class adolescents, initiative and responsibility are greater if there is considerable parent-child interaction, and less if the parents are remote. Absence of the father—who is generally charged more with regulation and less with nurturance than the mother—is particularly significant (Bronfenbrenner, 1961; Barclay & Cusumano, 1967). The child reared without a father is far more susceptible to the influence of peers, more often passive, and more inclined toward a compliant delinquency. According to the 1960 census, some 40 per cent of homes among the urban poor were without a male head; the figure dropped to about 5 per cent in homes where the income exceeded $3,000 (Sebald, 1968).

The child who learns at home to be rigidly obedient or to act on his own momentary impulses is prepared to react similarly to the more impersonal authority at school. If he thinks of parents as willing to hear his suggestions and willing to modify rules when he can give a good reason, he will try these approaches with other adults.

The techniques of leadership and control used by the teacher make it easy for some children to adapt, and hard for others. If the teacher reduces rules to the minimum in order to give children experience in planning and self-regulation, some children make good use of their opportunity. Children who have learned to do just what an adult wants, however, become insecure when the teacher does not state definite goals.

Boys are especially likely to be in conflict with teachers because boisterous, vigorous activity disturbs the classroom. Yet in middle childhood these traits are encouraged by peers and, more subtly, by parents. Classroom observers find that boys are far more often criticized for misbehavior, or warned against misbehavior, than girls. This perhaps reflects spilled energy and poor impulse control more than an urge to act in the wrong direction. Boys not only are more likely to call out an answer out of turn, but are more likely to wave their hands for recognition (Brophy, 1972; Brophy & Good, 1973).

Attitudes toward authority have much continuity. Macfarlane et al. (1954) found overdependency more persistent than any other personality problem over the ages 5 to 14. Attitudes toward school authority carry over into relations with superiors on an adult job (see also p. 129). But there is also change. Boys, especially, change their coping styles as they move into adolescence and adulthood (Kagan & Moss, 1962).

---

 **22** A third-grade teacher appoints monitors to keep records of children who talk, drop papers on the floor, and so on. What will the monitors learn from this experience?

---

## Need for Approval of Peers

Accepted patterns of social behavior change as the character of the social group changes. The young child plays with one or two other children at a time. His games are loosely organized; everyone may be playing with blocks, but Jeff stops work on Mary's tower to pile blocks in Joe's wagon. Then Joe wants to pull the wagon before it is loaded. Children adjust by falling into dominant or submissive roles. Parents and preschool teachers suggest interpretations and ways of acting: sharing, asking the owner of a toy for permission, acknowledging that Joe had the wagon first and is for the moment in charge. During this early period, children are expected to become aware of others' feelings and to act so others will also be happy.

Failure in these early encounters can have a lasting effect. Crandall and Battle (1970) rated young adults on academic efforts (such as how much time they put into study and whether they had selected hard academic programs). Records on this group, reared on farms and in small towns in Ohio, had been collected from early childhood. Those who were strivers in their twenties had been somewhat unusual even at age 3. At that early age, they were less accepted by peers ($r = -0.62$) and were comparatively dependent on adults. In the first school years, they were notably perfectionist in their schoolwork. Perhaps a smooth social life prior to school turns the child more toward his peers, so that the tasks set by adults count for less in his life.

Middle childhood is a period of increasingly stable social relations. *Mutual* choices (liking given and received) rise. About 80 per cent in Grades III to VI participate in at least one such pairing; in Grades VII to XII the percentage is near 90 (Gronlund, 1959, p. 108). Group members come to be "typed" in middle childhood: the one who is good at ball games, the bully, the one everybody teases, and so on. Reputations become harder and harder to change, and the flow of social rewards responds as much to reputation as to behavior. The popular and able child can be irritable and uncooperative for a time without losing status. The outcast can be cheerful and helpful without being accepted. Eron et al. (1974) report that third-graders identified as aggressive by their peers tend to be rated similarly ten years later ($r = 0.38$ for boys, 0.47 for girls).

Acceptance depends on what active roles the child takes, and how. The restrained, inhibited child figures less in the group and receives less support from it. Popularity goes to those who best contribute to the goals of group activity. In choosing a work partner, a child often picks one who can help with the specific assignment but who is not generally popular. The child tends to select as partner someone above him in ability, but not too far above. Even the relatively unpopular student has some talents that can make him a sought-after partner, if the teacher arranges an activity that calls for his assets.

By Grade III, some children have learned skills of making friends and communicating with peers; these children are the more popular ones. Gottman et al. (1975), having found this skill difference, suggest that direct training on the skills can increase the child's popularity.

The popular child can more easily be creative because others are unlikely to make fun of him. Encouraged to communicate, he develops more varied, more connected, and more meaningful language. The popular child sent to the store on an errand stops by a friend's house, takes him along, and so gains one more bit of social experience. The child who is uncertain of his reception by others simply does the errand, with no loitering to exchange gossip and hence no social learning. Likewise, the child who feels accepted converts schoolwork into a social activity while the insecure child works by himself.

GROUP STRUCTURE    Popularity is not just a matter of being "in the swim." The social life of a school is a complicated flow of main currents, isolated eddies, and backwaters. Each student finds his best friends in a particular pool, and the nature of that subgroup does much to shape his actions. One counselor traced friendship patterns in a large suburban high school. Each student was asked to name his three best friends. Figure 5.5 diagrams the choices among boys in Grade XII. (The great majority of the choices were of boys in the same grade.)

In this school, each year-group tended to be a self-contained system with limited influence on the next. High-school teachers often observe that "this year's junior class has its own personality"—eager or apathetic, keen on dances or passing them up, centered on school affairs or interested chiefly in out-of-school clubs. This may depend on the style of the student pacesetters, on the history of the earliest class parties in Grade IX, or on the energy and talent of the class adviser. Classroom-to-classroom differences are similarly found in the lower grades, and also in medical schools and graduate seminars.

FIGURE 5.5

Sociogram for twelfth-grade boys

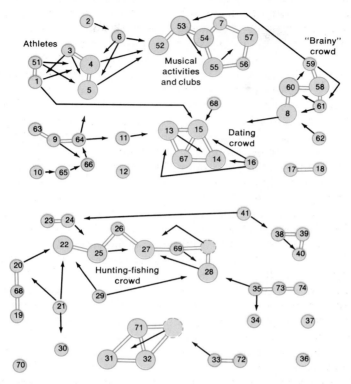

Each boy was asked to name his three best friends. A double line indicates a mutual choice. Where fewer than three choices are shown, the boy chose someone in another grade or school, or a twelfth-grade girl, or someone who did not take part. Numbers are arbitrary, but those above 50 designate boys who went on to college. Large circles are for boys who were chosen three or more times; broken circles are for boys in another grade who were members of the group.

SOURCE: Adapted from C. W. Gordon (1957).

As in many large groups, distinct clusters of social influence appeared within the class charted in Fig. 5.5. One group dominated the school clubs and musical activities, the athletes associated chiefly with each other, and in a third section of the chart we find a studious crowd. Each crowd valued and encouraged certain things: the athletes were driving to the next town to find girls and beer while the "intellectuals" were exchanging notes about the extra-credit math problem. Four of the five in the studious corner of the class went to college, and in the activity group, six of the seven; but only one of the daters and one of the athletes went to college.

Each clique tended to have its own academic level: the studious group in the top fifth of the class, the athletes in the lowest fifth, and the hunting-fishing crowd at or slightly below the average. These outdoor sportsmen took little part in school activities. The scholars in this class were active participants.

Details of Fig. 5.5 should be noted. Some (for example, Boy 36) were never chosen and chose no one in the sex-grade group.

CONFLICT OF YOUTH AND ADULT CULTURES    Even in the preschool, one can observe the child caught between the adults' disapproval of fighting and his peers' expectation that he will stand up for himself. Adolescents are in frequent disagreement with adults about dress, language, and the importance of study. In one of many studies of this point, Marks (1954) found that the most popular adolescent girls hold more attitudes of which parents disapprove than less popular girls. The young tend to be more committed to political and social equality, and see no reason to suppress opinions that challenge tradition (D. Sears, 1969, p. 392). The young person is proud to be a member of the fresh team pouring onto the field, and the ever-popular refrain about "times a-changin'" inevitably carries a rebuke to the parental generation.

At one time, young people were likely to move rather abruptly from the role of the student, subordinated to parents and high-school teachers, into the role of worker and homemaker. Recent years have seen drastic changes in social expectations and attitudes; many developmental tasks have been rescheduled from the late teens to the middle twenties. The period of "youth" is now rather long, and a distinct "youth culture" is recognized by social observers (Keniston, 1970). The Panel on Youth (1974, pp. 112ff.) lists five core characteristics of the youth culture:

- A closed system. The young person tends to use his or her companions and youth-oriented mass communications as the principal sources of models and standards.

- Psychic attachment. Emotional ties are found primarily with a selected group of peers, these ties being much stronger than family ties. Even young people living together as couples are tied more to friends than used to be the case in the first years of marriage.

- Press toward autonomy. The desire for independence is augmented by the symbolic figures in the youth culture who dramatize protest or self-determination.

- Concern for the underdog. This is expressed chiefly in political contexts.

- Interest in change.

These characteristics by definition increase the distance of young people from their elders and from institutions (including the school) that took shape in an older generation.

Conflict between generations is easily exaggerated (L. E. Thomas, 1974). The following quotation summarizes typical research results:

> The adolescent's own values, in some respects, seem to be a compromise between the values of his parents and those of his peers as he sees them; further, his expectations about his subsequent adult values clearly approach those of his parents as perceived by him. Thus whatever the gap between the generations, youth has every intention of bridging it. (J. D. Campbell, 1964, p. 315.)

The civil rights protests of 1964, during which Campbell was writing, have been succeeded by wider movements. Then and now, adolescents ranged from revolutionary to complacent. It is significant that the students most active in recent social protest tend to be from liberal homes where the parents have preached the virtues of independent thought and social criticism (Flacks, 1970; L. E. Thomas, 1971).

**Conflict of generations**

*"Can't that kid ever stay home? When I was his age, you didn't catch me gallivanting around night after night to every damned fertility rite on the island."*

Drawing by Whitney Darrow, Jr.; © 1957 The New Yorker Magazine, Inc.

A national survey (Yankelovich, 1969) questioned youths and their parents with regard to various traditional beliefs. The responses to each question fall into about the same pattern. One question was: Will hard work always pay off? The percentage of yes responses was 85 per cent among parents of noncollege youth; 79 per cent among noncollege youth; 76 per cent among parents of college youth; and 56 per cent among college youth. Thus, the noncollege youth had moved away from tradition about as far as college parents had; the college youth—as a group—were further down the same path. Yankelovich thinks of college youth as the "pacesetters" who test new viewpoints (and sometimes discard them). What they accept, others are likely to accept after a few years have passed. Thus, in a 1973 survey of noncollege youth, Yankelovich (1974, p. 26) found the percentage saying "hard work always pays off" had dropped to 56 per cent, from the 1969 figure of 79 per cent; that is, their attitudes lagged just four years behind those of college youth. This is not to say that movement is always in one direction; on some issues, at some times, college youth swing back toward an older view.

Throughout the 1950s, college youth were criticized for their conformity; in the early 1970s, it was suggested that a whole new breed of self-actualizing youth had emerged. Although changes in student bodies are requiring shifts in curriculum and teaching style, the amount of change from 1950 to 1970 is remarkably small. Charles Morris has described thirteen "ways of life" or value systems, each in a lengthy paragraph. In 1950 and in 1970, ratings of the values were obtained from comparable groups of college students (Morris & Small, 1971). The mean ratings for several preferred outlooks are listed in Table 5.3. The one great change was the drop in concern for traditional culture—the values of Mead's "grandmother" (p. 52). And today's women are less (!) interested in a life of active problem solving, according to these data. The diversity

TABLE 5.3

College student values in 1950 and 1970

| | Rating* | | | |
| | Men | | Women | |
| Outlook | 1950 | 1970 | 1950 | 1970 |
|---|---|---|---|---|
| Integrate action, enjoyment, contemplation | 5.58 | 5.39 | 5.84 | 5.53 |
| Preserve the best that man has attained | 5.06 | 3.79 | 5.16 | 3.73 |
| Show sympathetic concern for others | 4.22 | 4.37 | 4.43 | 4.55 |
| Constantly master changing conditions | 4.88 | 4.43 | 4.77 | 3.87 |
| Live with wholesome, carefree enjoyment | 4.53 | 4.40 | 4.42 | 4.43 |

SOURCE: Data from Morris & Small (1971).
*Numbers indicate average rating on a 1-to-7 scale (7 high).

within each generation is conspicuous. Young people endorse radically varying choices: Except for the "little-bit-of-everything" philosophy represented in the first line of the table, no value is given a top rating by more than 10 per cent of either sex.

The conflict of generations is in large part a symptom of the struggle to achieve maturity and to be recognized as mature. Although young people cherish their independent views, they are not hostile toward their parents. In fact young people, when asked about their political beliefs and those of their parents, indicate greater agreement than actually exists (D. Sears, 1968, p. 380). High-school boys typically report that their fathers are helpful and competent, that they find much satisfaction in their homes, and that they share many of their parents' values (Offer, 1969). Hot disagreements in the family serve mostly the function of testing strength or demonstrating that independence is being achieved. To quote Erikson:

> True, it gratifies them that parents are dismayed by their appearances, for the display is really a declaration insisting on some positive identity. . . . such nonconformism, in turn, is a plea for fraternal [peer] confirmation and thus acquires a new ritualized character that is part of the paradox of all rebellious identity formation. (1968, pp. 27-28.)

Open rebellion erupts in colleges and high schools with a frequency alarming to elders; this has been happening for centuries. Rebellion is not primarily a clash between generational values; rather, it is a struggle over domination itself. A survey of seven thousand students in junior and senior high schools (de Cecco et al., 1970) found that only six per cent of student complaints centered on the larger social scene of racial inequity and military policy. Fifty-two per cent of the expressed protests had to do with the "arbitrariness" of teachers and principals, and with the unwillingness of adults to negotiate. Frustration, because parliament and king turned a deaf ear to attempts to gain a larger share of influence, was the source of the American Revolution; the restiveness of today's students seems to have a similar origin (M. B. Smith, 1968, p. 313ff.).Typical of the incidents the young people object to is a principal's insistence that students not sit on school steps and grounds. Students not in class should go to the lunchroom, he orders. But the lunchroom offers a hundred seats—in a school that has thousands of students.

Allowing children and adolescents to share decisions with adults is not abdication of responsibility; it has a positive educative function. What M. B. Smith says (1968, pp. 314-15) about parents applies to educators:

> The authoritarian parent who uses his age status for the naked assertion of power over his children gets dependence and passive resistance; maybe, if he is lucky, revolt. The wise nurture of competence in the young would seem to call for a deliberate progressive sharing of power and responsibility as the growing competence of the child enables him to use it. A little faster, perhaps, than is securely warranted by what the child can do: good "parentalism," unlike conventional paternalism, sees to it that the child has real problems and challenges to face, and that his solutions are his own.

The foregoing remarks on the blind spots of the parental generation are not an endorsement of all youthful protest. Fairmindedness does not require the adult to sympathize with those who find infantile gratification in kicking their elders' shins, or to read righteousness into mob emotions. Even during the heated protests of the Vietnam period, however, the actions of most protestors, most of the time, were guided by conscience (Haan, 1975).

**23** What does Figure 5.5 (p. 191) tell about Boy 6, whose grades and participation are above average? Why is the sociometric information of interest to his teachers?

**24** Which is more nearly correct: "A student's values determine the friends he chooses" or "A student's friends determine his values"? Defend your answer.

**25** Why does M. B. Smith, in the quotation above, think revolt a sign that the parent he speaks of is "lucky"?

**26** Smith compares student protest movements to militancy among colonial peoples and American blacks. He sees all these as oppressed groups now gaining power but having no previous experience, as a group, in ways of exercising it. Lacking experience, they set goals that are unrealistic and bound to be frustrated. "Given competition among the leadership elite in the outrageousness of their claims, and given the predictable 'backlash' from whoever constitute the relevant Establishment, the potentialities for continued explosive violence are very great indeed." (1968, p. 314.) To what extent does Smith's analogy seem valid? What might a high-school principal do to make explosive protest less likely?

**27** In the Morris-Small survey (Table 5.3) the following question was asked in 1970 (but not in 1950): "Do you feel that our society is satisfactory for the development and expression of your own abilities and wishes?" The response divided as follows in both sexes: 43 per cent yes, 49 per cent no, 8 per cent mixed. Do you consider this a realistic response? Could educators do anything to raise the proportion of yes responses in the next decade?

## Need for Autonomy

Even the young child develops interests of his own and occupies himself for long periods, if he is not frightened into undue dependency. With satisfaction in these activities and confidence that no harm will come to him, he can accept the absence of his mother. By the age of 6, he leaves the sheltering home for a full day of school. There, he should be an autonomous member of the group. He will learn to fit in with group plans, but he should learn also to disagree

## New institutions for youth?

The Panel on Youth of the President's Science Advisory Committee (1974), quoted on the youth culture on p. 192, was established under the chairmanship of James Coleman to advise policy-makers regarding needed changes in social institutions. This panel, while respecting the desire for autonomy, viewed with alarm the increasing isolation of young people from social institutions. It called for institutional changes that would have the effect of redistributing developmental tasks.

The panel suggested that schooling should no longer be a full-time occupation in the later teens. The reduction of hours of schooling per day would fit into the trend, already evident, of returning to part-time formal education in the middle years of life. The panel proposed that young people spend much of their time in work settings and community action groups, side by side with adults. This is less a proposal for youth employment than a proposal to educate them about work in a work team.

One move in this direction is the agreement of the *Detroit Free Press* to allow students to spend several days in the newsroom and manufacturing plant, helping where they could (Bronfenbrenner, 1974b).

As an alternative to reducing the hours of schooling, the panel entertains the idea of inserting into the school program "noncognitive" activities—attractive group tasks in which young people and their teachers could cooperate. They point to Outward Bound, 4-H Club projects, and the Neighborhood Youth Corps as possible points of departure for school programs. The important point about these activities is the large degree of responsibility for performance that devolves upon the young participant. He is a doer more than a student, even though the activity can educate him in many ways.

and obtain a hearing for his reasons. Havighurst and More (1953, p. 87) mention the following as indicators that the 9-year-old is making adequate progress toward autonomy, "changing from a morality of constraint to one of consent."

- Works for an hour or more at tasks which interest him. . . .

- Occasionally shows displeasure at the arbitrary way in which parents, teachers, and other authority figures direct his behavior; expresses rebellion by such actions as disregarding commands, disobeying rules occasionally, arguing with adults. . . .

- Works for the approval of teachers, but is not slavishly dependent on such approval as motivation for doing his best.

Autonomy is fostered by the widening environment. As a child mingles with children from other homes and with community groups, his interests and activities are less tied to his family. He carries on with limited supervision. He has more frequent occasion to go among strangers, and his assurance is the outgrowth of his experience, over many years, that as he enters a new group he is treated pleasantly.

The continuity of development is remarkable. Schoeppe and Havighurst (1952) found that the degree to which a child had attained emotional independence from others by age 10 correlated 0.78 with independence at 16. Consistency was equally great with regard to ability to establish relations with peers, to master intellectual requirements, and to make ethical judgments. The age-to-age correlation of ratings on mastery of an appropriate sex role was much lower—0.42; this process is much less continuous. It is worth noting also that success in one psychosocial task is only moderately correlated with success in another task at the same age; in the Schoeppe-Havighurst ratings, emotional independence correlated around 0.45 with conscientiousness, for example.

## Need for Competence and Self-Respect

The happy, effective person is committed to goals, active in his approach to living, accepting of his real limitations but otherwise hopeful of the future. Whereas the needs discussed to this point are inherently social, competence has to do with the person's interaction with all reality. A sense of competence and satisfaction in achievement are learned through interaction with things as well as with people. Desire for competence has much to do with motivation to achieve, but achievement can be competitive striving, an effort to impress one's parents, or an expression of insecurity.

Learning to control one's environment is a source of pleasure (R. W. White, 1960; M. B. Smith, 1968; Harter, 1974). Much of the gratification lies in being able to predict the change one's act will produce; to conquer uncertainty is an adventure. Taking stairs three at a time is fun even though there is a bit of risk.

The desire for competence exists quite apart from socially induced ideals regarding achievement. Some of the compelling evidence of this comes from animals. Animals solve mechanical problems to escape confinement or to get food. Animals also like just to manipulate pieces of equipment (Harlow et al., 1950, on monkeys; Kavanau, 1967, on mice): Nail a hasp and staple to the cage wall. Put a hook through it, and push a pin into a hole so that the hook is blocked in place. Monkeys will learn to disassemble the device, and will do so time after time, though they get no prize and are left with nothing save the parts of the device hanging on the wall. (Prizes, indeed, can be counterproductive; see p. 623.) At all ages, play is action that is in some ways familiar, in some ways unfamiliar, and thus leads always to new ground and enlarges competence. Interest wanes when challenge is lost. The game of tic-tac-toe loses its charm when one has learned all the moves and countermoves; no crossword addict fills in the same puzzle twice. The satisfaction found in manipulating objects has its counterpart in manipulating abstractions. The preschool child is observed making long strings of rhymes, or singing a song in which the same phrase is put to one tune after another. This is joy in invention, reinforced by no reward except that of performance itself. The act has a goal in that the person strives toward a certain orderliness or equilibrium (Piaget, 1957; see also Berlyne, 1960, p. 301). The child prefers rhyme to an unconstrained sequence of words. He makes his games more difficult for himself by adopting rules. But he is more interested in arranging events than in finding "correct" solutions (Harter, 1975). The contribution of this exploratory way of living to intellectual development cannot be overestimated.

As the child approaches school age and more tasks are set for him, the motivation to explore and master things for their own sake becomes overlaid with ideas of duty and approval. The child's early joy in exploratory learning can be stamped out when school and home make a puritanical distinction between work and play. "Fooling around" with indefinite aim is perhaps the essence of creativity. The key to producing more curious, more inventive adults may lie in cultivating a playful attitude toward topics the school now treats with somber dedication to "the right answer."

The child's work is evaluated, praised, criticized. He acquires standards by which to judge himself and an ideal of what a good person ought to do. If his performance and conduct are usually accepted and he makes steady improve-

## Intellectual work is fun

The story of Blaise Pascal (1623–1662) illustrates intellectual effort and intellectual growth motivated solely by the enjoyment of competence. Pascal was a genius, but the same process is observed in other children when the conditions are right. Pascal's father was a nobleman actively engaged in government and a promoter of the new scientific interests of the period. He was also intensely interested in his son. The statement below comes from C. M. Cox's collection of childhood histories of intellectually eminent men (Cox, 1926, p. 691); some of her statements are quoted from biographies of Pascal.

> Pascal early showed much interest in his surroundings and "wanted to know a reason for everything." . . . Even at an early age he took great pleasure in conversations upon the subject of natural science.
>
> His genius for geometry made its appearance before he was 12 years old and in an extraordinary manner. His father wished him to learn languages before undertaking mathematics and in consequence put away all his books on the subject and refrained from mentioning it in his son's presence. "This precaution did not prevent the child's curiosity from being aroused, however, and he begged his father to teach him mathematics. . . . He refused [though he did tell the boy that it was the way of making accurate figures and studying their relation to each other]. At the same time he forbade his son ever to think or speak of it again." Pascal, however, began to dream over the subject and . . . he used to mark with charcoal on the walls of his playroom, seeking a means of making a circle perfectly round and a triangle whose sides and angles were all equal. He discovered these things for himself and then began to seek the relationship which existed between them. He did not know any mathematical terms and so he made up his own, calling circles *rounds*, lines *bars*, etc. Using these names he made axioms and finally developed perfect demonstrations . . . until he had come to the thirty-second proposition of Euclid ("the sum of the angles of a triangle . . ."). One day the father came in unexpectedly and asked his son what he was doing. The child explained, showing him some demonstrations he had made. . . . The father left the room, without saying a word, and unbosomed himself in tears of joy to a friend who lived close by.

SOURCE: *The Early Mental Traits of Three Hundred Geniuses*, by Catharine Morris Cox, *Genetic Studies of Genius*, vol. II, edited by Lewis M. Terman (Stanford: Stanford University Press, 1926), p. 691.

ment toward the ideal, he comes to believe that he is good. If he seems never to come near the ideal, he sprouts a sense of inadequacy. Self-respect does not mean smugness. A healthy self-concept is, "I am able to meet present demands upon me, and where I want to do better, I am able to improve." Supportive responses from others do much to promote self-development.

Being labeled a failure instills a sense of unworthiness that eliminates trying. Many Americans have never developed even the most elementary skill in drawing because, during childhood, they learned that others considered them deficient as artists.

No single incident and no single type of failure destroys the sense of worth. After failure in one activity, the child tries others. But when a child encounters criticism over and over, either because he does poorly or because adults hold very high standards for him, he learns to think of himself as inadequate. He tackles a new job as if he were licked before he started. Constructive criticism helps him to accept his impulses as reasonable without approving his conduct. It shows him a better way to deal with impulses: "Yes, I know you were very angry at Tommy, but the next time you feel that way you had better just go play elsewhere."

The needs listed in this chapter (affection, secure relations with authority, approval by peers, autonomy, and competence and self-respect) may be compared with the qualities of the socialized person of Chapter 2: competence in problem solving, confidence and self-respect, effective relations with others, goals and interests, and acceptance of social values. How well students are satisfying these needs should be considered in evaluating the school.

---

**28** What relevance to understanding Pascal's motivation does each of these facts have?
    a. His mother died when he was three years old.
    b. His father personally supervised his education from age 3.
    c. His father's acquaintances showed amazement and delight at the child's questions and conversation from an early age.
    d. His father refused to instruct him in mathematics.

**29** What does each of the following generalizations suggest to a person choosing suitable excursions for the preschool child?
    a. The child learns from interacting with his environment.
    b. Enjoyment comes from variation that shows new possibilities in a familiar situation.
    c. Creativity is the expression of one's own purposes.

**30** Rohwer (1971) challenges the relevance of grade-school curricula, contending that what the student does in his daily lessons rarely makes any contribution to the tasks he faces in home, peer group, and community. To be sure, the 10-year-old rarely has occasion outside of school to perform long division or to name the Great Lakes. But what about collateral outcomes? Does participation in lessons and tests on conventional curricula make a difference in the young person's performance of his out-of-school tasks?

**31** An elementary school has numerous service positions (safety squad, stage crew, library assistants, milk distributors, student council, and so on). These positions are regarded as honors to be earned by successful academic work during the preceding school year. In general, the oldest and most responsible students are chosen. What assumptions are reflected in this method of filling positions? How can these positions be assigned so as to make a greater contribution to student development?

**32** Many communities have experimented recently with student tutors, reporting considerable success (National Commission, 1974, Chap. 3). A student a few grades above the tutee works with him in his own classroom or at an outside meeting place, perhaps giving remedial lessons or perhaps giving a motivational orientation. Often both tutor and tutee are from a minority group. Assuming that the tutor has sufficient support from the school system so that he can see that he is achieving results, which of *his* needs does the activity serve?

**5** READING LIST

[Dorothy Eichorn et al.], "Biological, Psychological, and Socio-Cultural Aspects of Adolescence and Youth," in *Youth: Transition to Adulthood,* Panel on Youth (Chicago: University of Chicago Press, 1974), pp. 91–111.

> The report (prepared for the President's Science Advisory Committee) raises questions about the fit of present social institutions to the development of young people. The section for which Eichorn took chief responsibility summarizes the relevant facts of development, which the policy sections of the document then take into account.

David Elkind, "Erik Erikson's Eight Ages of Man," *New York Times Magazine,* April 5, 1970, pp. 25–27. Also in Biehler (1972), and Kagan & Coles (1972).

> Erikson's theory derives from his psychoanalytic training, his work with maladjusted youth, and his observations. Erikson is a noted humanistic psychologist whose theory of stages is an alternative way of describing the sequence of developmental tasks. Elkind gives some information on Erikson as a person and on his lines of research, as well as summarizing his system.

Jerome Kagan, "A Conception of Early Adolescence," *Daedalus* 100 (1971), 997–1012.

> Kagan emphasizes that the newly coalesced reasoning powers of the 12-year-old cause him to question the truisms of childhood. This loss of certainty generates emotional problems and disaffection for the school. Illustrative quotations from interviews with students bolster the argument.

Abraham H. Maslow, "A Theory of Human Motivation," in *Motivation and Personality,* 2d ed. (New York: Harper & Row, 1970), pp. 80–106. Also in Biehler (1972), Hamachek (1976).

> A textbook chapter on the development of needs. Maslow's list of needs is not identical to mine; he separates basic needs (physical wants and safety) from needs related to belonging, self-esteem, and self-actualization. The principles of Chapter 5 are further illustrated in his account.

M. Brewster Smith, "Competence and Socialization," in *Socialization and Society,* ed. John A. Clausen (Boston: Little, Brown, 1968), pp. 270–320.

> Smith discusses competence as a life style intimately related to self-satisfaction and mental health. He summarizes research on home and school practices that foster reality-oriented rather than competitive striving.

# MOTIVATIONAL DEVELOPMENT: EFFECTS OF HOME AND COMMUNITY

Chapter 5 repeatedly noted that *individual* courses of development differ. Educational planners, and teachers carrying out their daily work, have to be continually concerned with these differences, simply because a plan that fits the average student of a given age fits almost no one well. The character of individual differences, their origins, their assessment, and ways of adapting schooling in the light of them will be the concerns in the next four chapters, starting with motivation and personality.

## PSYCHOLOGICAL DIFFERENCES AMONG HOMES

Personality and intellectual skills originate in the home, and the home remains an important force during the school years. To the psychologist, the most important aspect of a home is not the parents' wealth or educational level; it is the emotional atmosphere the parents establish. Stimulating, supportive homes can be found at every level of society. (Even within one socioeconomic category, homes are far from alike.) Each home has an individuality, neither totally good nor totally bad, that leaves a unique impression on the child. The home makes it easy for the child to master some developmental tasks and inadvertently makes development along other lines harder.

Homes differ in many respects: warmth, encouragement of independence, pressure for achievement, and so on. Warm parents express their own love and encourage the child to express *his* feelings; family members react to each other on an emotional level, their feelings alive and open. Warmth is not the same as indulgence. The indulgent parent protects the child from difficulty, rarely demanding that he take responsibility or meet standards. At the opposite extreme is hostile rejection: the parent dislikes the child and is continually critical and punitive.

In some homes the child has little influence and little freedom. In other homes (often called *democratic*), policies are worked out between parent and child, or are explained carefully. Giving the child a share in decisions is not permissiveness; the permissive home bows to the whim of the child.

Traits of homes combine. One might find a coldly democratic home, or a warm autocratic home where there is strong pressure for excellence. Nor is a single home perfectly consistent. Isolated practices gleaned from Spock's "baby book" are grafted onto the ethnic traditions, value orientations, and emotional needs of the parents. Thus, in families moving upward from the lower class, mothers allowed children food on demand when experts popularized permissiveness. Their anxiety regarding their own status, however, led them to maintain strict control over the child's aggression. They were not psychologically free to be permissive across the board (R. Sears, 1950).

## FIGURE 6.1

### Traits of preschool children as a function of parental style

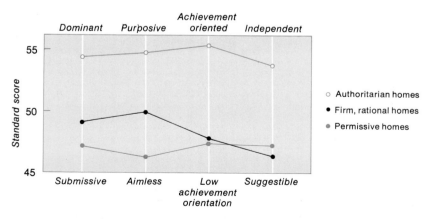

For groups with unequal numbers of boys and girls, data have been weighted to compensate.

SOURCE: Data from Baumrind, in Pick (1973), p. 18.

Generalizations about the effects of parent behavior require much qualification. Any generalization refers to a statistical trend, not a certain outcome. The same parental style has different effects at different ages, and different effects on boys and girls (p. 210).

## Providing Emotional Support

The warmth of the home is evidently the most important factor in promoting the child's adjustment. The consequences of a cold, rejecting home appear in early infancy and continue: feeding problems, slow development of age-appropriate behavior, and language difficulties. Lisping, baby talk, and other speech disorders, and some reading difficulties as late as Grade V can be traced back to rejection or overprotection in early childhood (McCarthy, 1959; Wood, 1946). Sluggish educational progress in the upper grades, even after a good start in school, can be a consequence of strains in the home (Thayer, 1970).

A steady flow of affection and care during the first two years gives the child assurance and protection. This makes it possible for him to act confidently, knowing that he has sympathy and help to fall back on. In addition, it makes him value his mother's approval. This desire to be approved extends later to his father also. In the warm home the child identifies with his parents; that is, he adopts many of their acts as his own trial responses and uses their standards to guide his conduct. Early development of conscience can be expected in the warm home. In such a home, when the child acts "improperly" there is no direct punishment. Rather, the parents distance themselves, making sure that warmth and attention do not reward the act (R. Sears et al., 1957). The child in that home learns to regulate himself instead of waiting for external pressure.

The consequences of rejection are hard to predict. In a rejecting home, nothing the child does brings parental support. He is unable to develop affectional security and a clear understanding of how to behave. His likely safety play is to become dependent even in matters where normal children regulate themselves (Maccoby & Masters, in Mussen, 1970, II, p. 140). Children referred for psychotherapy frequently come from families where the mother gives little affection and support, and the father is passive and powerless. The mother is herself badly adjusted: resentful of her burdens, inclined to accuse others of imposing on her, and secretly wishing for more affection than she receives. The greater the mother's unfulfilled need for love and help, the less she can free her child to express such needs (Chance, 1959, p. 154). The emotionally underprivileged child may become aggressive, or passive and dependent, or inhibited and withdrawn.

A long-term study in New York City found that daycare children who had been apathetic and inhibited at age 5 learned poorly in the early grades. Those who had been defiant and resistant at age 5, however, did nearly as well in Grades I and II as their seemingly adjusted classmates (M. Kohn & B. Rosman, 1972).

## Fostering Autonomy

A formative period for autonomy comes when parents begin to impose regulations and demands. When it is time for weaning, for playing alone, or for sharing attention with a brother or sister, the relation with the parent is placed under strain. The infant crying for food controlled his mother; now he finds that *she* wishes to control *him*. His wants are fulfilled only occasionally, tasks are set for him, and when he seeks help he may be scolded for "acting like a baby." Ideally, initial dependence gives way to an alternation between dependence and independence, according to what is reasonable in the immediate situation.

The child has to discriminate which situations call for an independent role. Discrimination is fostered by the warm home that is consistent and explicit in its requirements. Such a home imposes demands and rewards compliance, but it also encourages self-direction. It defines spheres of activity where the child is subject *neither* to criticism nor to directive praise. Dependent responses that are inappropriate generate no care and approval in that home, and simply fade out (R. Sears et al., 1957, p. 256; Baumrind, 1973).

**Dependent response**

*"How many times must you be told not to follow Mommy too closely?"*

## Barbara Singer: An overmanaged child

Barbara Singer's home is subtly autocratic, even though her parents "believe in democracy." The Singers think they want to make Barbara independent; she is encouraged to voice her opinions and to make her own decisions. But Mrs. Singer, who feels inadequate to her executive's-wife role, cannot risk Barbara's becoming truly independent. The Singers have climbed from modest origins, and they fear that Barbara may be "contaminated" by any attitude that does not contribute to social status. If one of Barbara's companions makes an unconventional proposal, Mrs. Singer makes the child seem inferior or ridiculous by casual hints; Barbara can usually be counted upon to drop that friendship. Barbara has been taught to be reserved in social relations, not to share her bicycle because "ordinary children don't take care of nice things such as you have." She has had swimming lessons, dancing lessons, music lessons, even roller-skating lessons—anything to give her polish. Under these doting but determined parents, Barbara finds it easy to conform. Says the observer:

> She has developed into a neat, prim, adult-child, smug and self-satisfied. She . . . takes it for granted that in the intellectual area she can do whatever she sets out to do. . . . She realizes that she is unpopular with other children in general and is experiencing a social isolation that makes her miserable and confused. Admittedly the brightest child in her class, she knows so well how little her scholarship contributes toward popularity that she is contemptuous of this success, in fact, almost resents it. (Baldwin et al., 1945, p. 420.)

Homes that combine firmness with opportunities for independence produce boys who, in Grades III to VI, are superior in schoolwork, successful as leaders, and friendly. Neither independence training nor firm discipline alone leads to such desirable development (Hoffman et al., 1960; Radin, 1972). In another study, adolescent boys were placed under a firm adult leader who set out interesting activities but gave no chance for self-expression. The ones who adjusted to the leader's demands were those from firm and warm homes (Lewin, 1946, p. 837; see also p. 752). They had learned that cooperating with authority works out well. They had no need to rebel just to prove a point.

Homes differ in the degree to which they encourage autonomy. Some parents are eager to have the 8-year-old circulate through the town by himself, others are reluctant. Some parents demand from the adolescent a full account of his social plans, and some give him no supervision. Excessive supervision may reflect parental anxiety (box). Regarding autonomy and social class, see p. 220.

Training can go wrong in many ways (Maccoby & Masters, in Mussen, 1970, II, pp. 134–38). Strenuous pressure for compliance can cause the child to overreact toward either slavishness or rebellious independence. Inconsistent discipline or reward for dependent acts can delay maturity and make the eventual shift to self-direction more difficult. Dependency tends also to be high

among those who have been often rewarded *and* often punished for dependent behavior. Cases of "school phobia" (panicky resistance to going to school, often accompanied by physical upset) are traceable to homes where the mother keeps the child so dependent that he feels threatened when on his own.

As was mentioned earlier, effects differ with the age and sex of the child. The long-term effect on females of protection and restraint or maternal hostility at ages up to 3 is a tendency toward withdrawal in adulthood and lack of motivation to achieve; restrictiveness on males at ages up to 3 produces a comparatively independent adult. Restrictiveness at 3–10 inhibits development of adult male independence, but seems to have no consistent effect on the female (Kagan & Moss, 1960; Maccoby & Masters, in Mussen, 1970, II, p. 139).

INCONSISTENCY AS A SOURCE OF ANXIETY    Frustrating the preschool child's impulses to act dependently creates an *approach-avoidance* conflict. The child desires help and encouragement, so he is tempted to approach the strong adult. But he expects criticism or punishment for clinging to adults; that threat holds him back. Similar conflict arises even at later ages, when he wishes to express his own views and follow his own plans yet anticipates unpleasantness when he violates the wishes of authority. A temporary conflict generates a state of anxiety; everyone experiences such conflicts from time to time. The person who repeatedly experiences threat (from real dangers or misperceptions) is anxious most of the time; this is called *trait anxiety,* as distinct from *state anxiety* (Spielberger, 1972). A person with a high level of trait anxiety is not equally disturbed in all settings, however. For some people, anxiety peaks in social situations, whereas for others intellectual demands are the chief threat.

When inconsistent gratification and punishment instill anxiety, behavior is altered in several ways:

- The anxious child is less sensitive to the subtle cues that would help him to identify where dependency is acceptable.

- The anxious child acts to reduce his anxiety about what will happen. He must escape uncertainty at all costs. When he goes to one extreme or the other, consequences are predictable even if not pleasant. Conflict over dependency is often resolved by rushing headlong toward violent, irrational independence or slavish dependence.

- The erratically gratified need becomes stronger.

- The need generalizes widely, determining response in situations quite unlike those in which it originated.

Conflicts are minimized for the young person when adults impose consistent demands. The world is stable and one can cope if the rules and the penalties for breaking the rules are the same from week to week. But if behavior that is viewed indulgently on one occasion is treated harshly another time, one cannot come to terms with authority. When investigators related the maturity of adolescents to the atmosphere of their homes, the two home variables that correlated highest (around 0.60) with maturity were consistency and mutual trust (Peck & Havighurst, 1960, p. 107). This speaks for setting standards in the home, not for leniency. Adolescents from more egalitarian but more permissive families had many good qualities: cheerfulness, sensitivity, ability to express feelings; but they tended to be less responsible and less ready to meet quite ordinary demands of school authority (Devereux, 1970). Evidence in the early years (Fig. 6.1) points to the same conclusion.

Many delinquent adolescents are youngsters who, unable to find the path to approval, have resolved their conflict by exaggerated independence (Fig. 6.2). In school they resist influence from both peers and teachers: avoiding help, not seeking praise, making nuisances of themselves by tossing paper airplanes and

FIGURE 6.2

Feelings about parents generalize

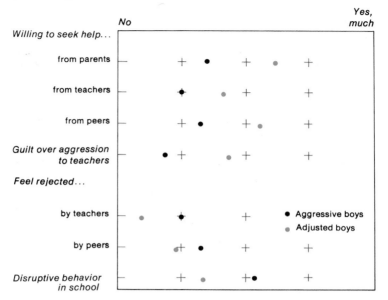

SOURCE: Data from Bandura & Walters (1959).

conspicuously breaking rules. Beneath this bravado is considerable anxiety, as we see in this reply of one boy asked how he feels about getting help from a teacher or counselor: "I just don't like it. I just, I don't know. I just don't like asking them for help. I don't want to. I don't know why. I just don't like it." The adult world is an enemy camp to be avoided.

Children made anxious by the penalties for independence conform to an excessive degree. They dare not be independent. One laboratory test of conformity presents an intellectual problem (estimating which of three lines is longest, say). The subject is seated among several other persons who are confederates of the experimenter and have been coached to give the wrong answer. A person who cannot risk being different denies the evidence of his eyes in order to stay in harmony with the group. College students who conform to peers' opinions in this manner recall their parents as harsh and restrictive (Mussen & Kagan, 1958).

Some children who have been disciplined sternly at home positively demand strong adult direction outside the home. Frenkel-Brunswik (1955) has described one such 11-year-old who felt threatened by authority but nonetheless preferred strict teachers. Demands reduced his anxiety because they told him what to do to avoid trouble. His fears were so great that he could not trust the teacher who offered freedom and reassurance.

The effect of the autocratic home was described by Frenkel-Brunswik (her pp. 383–84) as follows:

> Family relations in such homes are commonly based on roles clearly defined in terms of demands and submission. Execution of obligations rather than affection is the basis of smooth functioning. Furthermore, there is a stress on stereotyped behavior and on adherence to a set of conventional and rigid rules. The intimidating, punitive, and paralyzing influence of an overdisciplined, totalitarian home atmosphere may well exert a decisive influence upon the thinking and creativity of the growing child.
>
> The rules are bound to be beyond the scope and understanding of the child. To compel the child into an obedience of the rules which he is thus unable to internalize may be considered one of the major interferences with the development of a clear-cut personal identity.
>
> It seems to be largely the resultant fear and dependency which discourage conscious criticism and which lead to an unquestioning acceptance of punishment. . . . [But] children who seem most unquestioningly to accept parental authority at the same time tend to harbor an underlying resentment. . . . The existing surface conformity . . . [is] devoid of genuine affection.

This is reminiscent of Sanford's statements about Mack (p. 127), as is only natural, since Frenkel-Brunswik was one of Sanford's colleagues in that investigation.

1 To what aspects of personality other than anxiety does it make sense to apply the "trait-versus-state" distinction?

2 "It is wrong to speak of anxiety as a 'trait.' 'High trait anxiety' is merely shorthand for 'this person is conditioned to react to a great number of stimuli with state anxiety.'" Does this remark make sense?

3 What practices in the school might "erratically gratify" a need?

4 What acts of the 3-year-old in a preschool or daycare center are to be regarded as "dependent acts"? Distinguish these from appropriate use of adult help and friendship.

## Encouraging Achievement

The psychologist distinguishes motivation "to achieve" from motivation to comply with the demands of school. The person motivated to achieve enjoys the struggle for competence. He enjoys both intellectual and nonintellectual challenges. His self-respect is attached to growing competence and responsibility. He competes vigorously, puts forth effort beyond that demanded, persists when a task is difficult, and rejects unsound opinions from associates. "Disrespect [for parents] is not nearly so serious a vice for the subjects high in achievement motivation as is lack of courage. Courage is apparently symbolic for them of their independent, self-reliant achievement urges" (McClelland et al., 1953, p. 286).

On the whole, the active, democratic family that encourages self-expression and experimentation seems to produce a preschool child with greater-than-average curiosity (Baldwin, 1949; Pentony, 1956). Changes in mental test scores also reflect the family style. We shall examine this evidence later (p. 322).

Generalization about the antecedents of achievement motivation must again be made with caution. The mother's effect on a son may be the reverse of her effect on a daughter. And a tactic that fosters growth in early years may have the opposite effect at age 8 (Crandall, 1969).

Greater competitiveness, excitability, and impatience go with a surge in intellectual self-reliance. Such faults can be tolerated for a time, because at later ages it will be easier to acquire control than to acquire spontaneity. In fact, these "faults" promise good adjustment; recall the Kohn-Rosman finding (p. 207). E. Werner (1959) compared the histories of men who made good adjustments by age 30, despite serious stress in their lives, with those of men who showed permanently the effects of the stress. At age 5, those who were to become well-adjusted men had been more active, more turbulent, and more dominant. These traits characterize the boy who as an adult will be highly motivated to achieve (Ryder, 1967). In the girl, a calmer variant of the same active, independent style foreshadows both adjustment and motivation to achieve.

**Achievement motivation**

*"Good-o! Sally and her father get the same answer we do."*

Some homes directly train ability to learn and motivation to learn (Wolf, 1964; Freeberg & Payne, 1967). Emphasis on intellectual achievement has a powerful effect. Even in the cradle, the child begins to hear of the importance of learning, as in the Jewish lullaby:

> The Law shall baby learn,
> Great books shall my Yankele write.

The parents who foster achievement motivation create learning situations for the child and help him extend his competence. They may go so far as to teach the rudiments of reading and arithmetic. Their efforts reflect both the value they place on education and their high expectations for the child. The consequence, of course, is a child equipped with the attitudes and skills that make for success in the primary school.

The home that generates achievement motivation is the home where the parents care passionately about what the child accomplishes. Rosen and d'Andrade (1959) observed equally able boys with high and low drive toward achievement. Visiting in the home, they asked the boy to take tests in the presence of both parents, the parents being free to talk with the boy when and how they wished. Some parents urged the child forward, others gave specific hints and directions. Compared with parents of boys with low drive, mothers of achievement-motivated boys expressed more warmth, gave fewer specific directions, stated higher expectations regarding the boy's score, and when the task requirements were indefinite, demanded more from him.

Mothers and fathers have different influences. Achievement motivation tends to be stronger where an achievement-oriented mother dominates the home. According to Rosen and d'Andrade, mothers of achievement-motivated boys become highly involved in their performance and highly demanding. Compared with mothers of unmotivated boys, "these mothers are likely to give their sons more option as to exactly what to do, [but] they give them less option about doing something and doing it well." The fathers put on *less* pressure than fathers of unmotivated boys. A powerful father who demands that his son meet *his* standards is seemingly perceived as an invincible competitor, so that the boy is unwilling to accept the challenge. A demanding mother, on the other hand, is evidently seen as a source of attainable reward. These results were generally confirmed in Brazil, Turkey, and Holland (Rosen, 1962; Bradburn, 1963; Hermans et al., 1972).

Striving may express enjoyment of competence, or insecurity. Some homes generate anxiety by their steady pressure for accomplishment (box, p. 186). Their child may feel that he will lose affection if he does not do well in school. Anxious, he may strive more than is reasonable. He may be irrationally competitive or unable to accept anything short of perfection. Sometimes the symptom is prodigious effort. In any college class, there is likely to be a student whose papers are twice the length called for. This greater volume is not entirely to his credit. It is usually a sign that his insecurity forces him to go on and on after the job is really finished. Even when praised, he experiences no fulfillment. On a treadmill, he must run furiously toward the next goal and the next.

## Promoting Cognitive Development

Apart from any intent to stimulate the intellect, the way some parents talk and the things they talk about provide rich models. Other parents are poorer intellectual models. The observations on this point are summarized by J. McV. Hunt (1969, pp. 205–06), who says that the parents of poor children

> typically spend less time in verbal interaction with them than do the parents of the middle class. When they are communicating with their children, these parents verbalize in sequences substantially shorter than those of middle-class parents. . . .
>
> What parents of poverty talk about may be another factor. Their talk may be rich in emotional content and in the similes of such content, but highly lacking in what calls upon the child to abstract such aspects of objects as their color, their shape, and their size. . . . What these parents talk about is lacking in prepositional relationships, causal explanations, and concepts of space, time, and justice. The parents of the slums . . . seldom discuss with their children the whys of decisions or the outcomes of various kinds of action. . . . On the contrary, when the children of the poor ask questions or talk out, their parents typically respond with "shut up" without saying why.

Much is written about the role of the home in *early* development, but parents also count in later intellectual growth. P. A. Jones (1972) gave a nonverbal mental test to Canadian boys around age 11 and picked out a normal-to-superior set. Then he judged their language development from vocabulary, sentence complexity, and so on. Those with poorer verbal development tended to come from less well-to-do homes, but the best predictor was the opportunity to use language in the home. Active conversation, materials to read, and parents whose reading set an example were making a contribution to the boy's verbal proficiency even at age 11. Parental pressure for achievement is a more significant variable in promoting verbal development than parental education. This pressure is usually greater on first-borns than on later-borns. In a group of United States 11-year-olds, the ones who were eldest children were experiencing greater pressure than the ones who had older brothers or sisters, and their development was somewhat greater (Marjoribanks & Walberg, 1975).

# CHARACTERISTICS OF CULTURAL SUBGROUPS

## Social Status and Its Correlates

The American community is an aggregation of groups identified by religion, race or ethnic background, and economic level. A person's group membership influences how others react to him, and each group perpetuates a certain style of conduct and certain attitudes. There is a gradation from the upper-crust families (old money, long-standing prestige) through the professional and man-agerial families, through the middle ranks of trained workers (white- and blue-collar), down to the semiskilled and unskilled levels and finally to the chroni-cally unemployed. (I ignore the sociologist's distinction between social "status" and social "class"; where I say "lower class" a sociologist might say "low SES" [socioeconomic status] and the person might describe himself as "working class.")

In speaking about characteristics of social classes and ethnic groups I do not suggest that a school tailor programs to fit the demographic characteristics of its student body. The same aims of socialization are relevant to all segments of society. But teachers have to understand the forces influencing individual students.

Every paragraph in this section carries an unspoken qualification: On any variable save income, a subcommunity spans almost the entire range of the larger community. Many persons placed in the middle class (or any other level) according to their income, education, and responsibilities have not adopted the tastes of their neighbors. There are regional and rural-urban differences. Some differences within a class group are associated with occupational, religious, or ethnic identifications, particularly when social conflict has heightened the sense of group identity in a certain time and place. Despite the other causes, and de-spite the uniqueness of each family, children's experiences are appreciably as-sociated with their social class.

Families have an image of their place in the community. They know that certain neighborhoods are "better" than theirs and certain neighborhoods worse; and that some institutions (churches, recreation centers, clothing stores) serve "their kind" of person (R. Coleman & B. Neugarten, 1971). This is not a matter of discrimination on the part of the institution, but rather of institutional appeals that attract some persons and alienate others. The person who chooses a lunch counter rather than a more dignified restaurant is choosing a place where he is "at home." When one's choice of associates is significantly deter-mined by shared tastes, it is not surprising that the cultural group should de-velop its own preferences. Some magazines find their circulation predominantly among upper-middles, some among lower-middles. So also for television pro-grams, for styles in art and decorating, for spectator sports. To recognize this patterning is not to deny the openness in the system. Opera in the park is free to all comers, and lower-class members attend, but not in proportion to their number. Advertising and word-of-mouth contagion may spread bowling or tennis over the whole social spectrum, but they do not wipe out the correlation of participation with social class.

Family SES directly conditions a child's life chances: a better or worse diet, more or less financial support for his education, and so on. But the more pro-found effects are mediated through the intellectual and emotional climate of the home. A student body that is predominantly lower class may not respond to the appeals that have worked well with the middle-class students who tradi-tionally populated high schools and colleges. The low morale in inner-city

FIGURE 6.3

Qualities fathers desire in their children

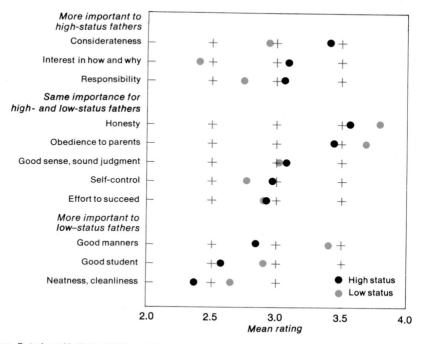

SOURCE: Data from M. Kohn (1969), p. 50.

schools arises in part from the inadequacies of the schools, and in part from limitations in the students. Beyond this, friction and discouragement are fostered by the disparity between the attitudes developed in the home and the attitudes the school expects.

VALUES AND CHILD-REARING PRACTICES   The social classes differ in their demands upon children, particularly in their emphasis upon independence. A national survey (M. Kohn, 1969) sampled representative fathers of children aged 3–15, and classified them by occupational level. Each father ranked a set of values according to their importance in a child of his son's (daughter's) age. The ranks were recoded on a 1-to-5 scale, obtaining the averages plotted in Fig. 6.3. (For an average of 4.0, all the fathers in the group would have had to place the item among the top three, and for an average of 2.0, in the lowest three. There was, of course, too much variation within each group for averages to reach the extremes.)

Middle-class fathers cared more about responsibility, considerateness, and interest in the how and why of things. Lower-class fathers put more weight on manners, neatness, and studiousness. The poor do care about schooling; but they define it to emphasize conformity and mastery of minimum essentials. Expectations stated for boys and girls were similar in this study, save that neatness was more desired of girls.

Kohn analyzed the data by ethnic background and religion. A composite score was made up to represent the value placed on self-direction. It correlated with background variables as follows (Kohn, p. 62):

0.30 with social class (holding constant race, religion, national background)

0.13 with national background (holding constant class and religion)

0.06 with religion (holding constant class and national background)

0.07 with the black-white classification (holding class and religion constant)

Thus social class related far more closely to valuing self-direction than race or religion. The social-class trend was the same among blacks as among whites (Kohn, p. 60). Figure 6.4 displays some of the averages. The ratings for religious groups have been adjusted to offset social-class differences in the makeup of the groups.

FIGURE 6.4

Parental values according to race and religion

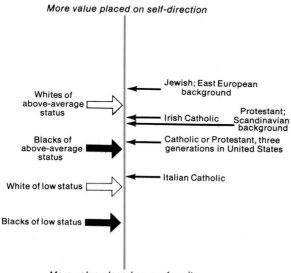

SOURCE: Data from M. Kohn (1969), pp. 60 and 64.

Higher-status homes have higher aspirations for their children and encourage them to seek more education. The combination of motivation and financial backing has a powerful effect. Among high-school boys of superior ability, about half of those of low SES entered college, according to one survey in the early 1960s. About 90 per cent of the able boys of high SES entered college (Flanagan & Cooley, 1966).

The middle class teaches its children to get ahead, not merely to get by. It teaches, moreover, that work is a vehicle for gratification and self-expression. In a survey of employed youth between ages 16 and 25, Yankelovich (1974) found that, when asked what they wanted in a job, all social groups gave somewhat similar answers. On some items, however, the college-educated professionals and junior executives gave answers that contrasted with the answers of blue-collar workers (with noncollege white-collar workers in between). For example, "chance to use your mind" was mentioned as important by 80 per cent of the professionals and by 68 per cent of the blue-collar group. Similarly for "as much responsibility as you can handle": 56 per cent versus 37 per cent. For "good pay" the percentages were 53 and 65; this was the only response the blue-collar workers gave greater weight to. Success in life, of course, is not occupational success alone. Most of the young people Yankelovich questioned said that their main satisfaction comes from social relations outside the job. This sentiment was almost as strong among the young professionals as among blue-collar workers.

The best single source of information on child-rearing practices of middle- and lower-class parents is a summary by Bronfenbrenner (1958; see also Hess, in Mussen, II, 1970). Bronfenbrenner compiled evidence collected in various communities over a 25-year period. Over the years, middle-class parents became more permissive, more ready to accept the child's emotional impulses. In the 1950s and 1960s they were somewhat more permissive than lower-class mothers with respect to training of infants, and more permissive toward the child's speech, interest in sex, and aggressiveness. Middle-class parents used "psychological" methods of discipline, such as appeal to conscience and reasoning. In the lower class, physical punishment was relatively common, and children were managed by blunt orders more than discussion.

Middle-class parents expected the child to accept more responsibilities in the home and to take care of himself at an earlier age; the parental pressures were task-oriented rather than conduct-oriented. It is the home on a higher educational and economic level that encourages the adolescent to share in planning family activities and listens to his opinions with respect. In the upper-class home the child is taken more seriously, allowed to exercise his judgment on things that matter to his parents. This trains for autonomy.

Middle-class children have a greater sense that they can influence their own fate (pp. 51 and 188). This is a realistic perception, but it is also a motivational force. Middle-class children are more responsive to verbal and symbolic rewards and more ready to accept "delayed gratification" (see also p. 800). They will work on a task that stretches out over a period of days for the sake of a larger achievement. The whole middle-class regimen of daily events on a regular schedule is foreign to many a lower-class home. All in all, the lower-class child is ill-attuned to the demands made by the school and the gratifications usually available there (J. McV. Hunt, 1969, pp. 208ff.).

Comprehensive reports on the values and attitudes of the extremely poor are lacking, but they seem to have achieved none of the "aims of socialization" set forth in Chapter 2. Merely to survive in their circumstances shows some competence in problem solving, but they are ill-prepared to cope with modern complexities. Compared to the working-class average, they have low self-esteem and are in no position to pursue positive interests. They tend to be strangers in their own communities and to have an unstable family life; they are at odds with and distrustful of the larger society. In their difficult circumstances, they have few prospects, few options, and little reason for cheer. Hence they tend to become passive and withdrawn (Hess, in Mussen, 1970, II, pp. 464–68).

---

5 The middle class tends to be future-oriented whereas the lower class "lives in the present." What causes can you suggest for this disparity? Do you see any connection with Mead's "three types of educators" (p. 52)?

---

## Minority Groups

Cultural differences between "old American" groups and such minorities as blacks, Chicanos, and Asian-Americans have been much discussed in recent years, but adequate descriptions—current and objective—are not available. Also, descriptions of minority-group samples are hard to interpret. A departure from the national norm may indicate a specific ethnic factor, or it may be adequately accounted for in terms of social class. Even when an attempt is made to match ethnic samples on social class, the comparison is suspect. A sample of black ministers is likely to differ from a sample of white ministers in the same state with respect to education and economic position, yet the typical research procedure would treat them as alike in "socioeconomic status."

With many variables, social class makes a far greater difference than ethnicity (among persons living in the same community). When one classifies persons in the same SES group into ethnic subgroups, he usually finds only small differences in the average views of the subgroups. In the Kohn data on fathers' values, the black-white classification and the national origins of families had much less significance than social class (Fig. 6.4). To be sure, the marked concern for autonomy among Jews and Scandinavians and the comparative lack of concern among Italians and blacks have been confirmed repeatedly. Note, however, that the higher-status blacks emphasized autonomy more than the lower-status whites. Precisely the same trend appeared in direct measures of motivation to achieve among adolescents in these two categories (Rosen, 1959). Typically complex relations are illustrated in Fig. 6.5, which reports a survey in four Chicago high schools (Paton et al., 1973). Both economic level and intellectual emphasis in the home were considered in identifying "highs" and "lows." As can be seen, the blacks at least matched the whites of similar background in statements on self-respect and sense of responsibility, but (not unrealistically) the blacks more often said that their success was influenced by external forces. Somewhat larger differences between beliefs of the adult poor were reported by N. Johnson and P. Sanday (1971), the blacks showing less positive attitudes.

Ethnic subcultures encourage particular motivational patterns. For example, some American Indian groups socialize their children to cooperate and not compete; this leaves the child unwilling to respond to some of the appeals teachers use (box). The Zuñi child is taught that the group should do well, but

**FIGURE 6.5**

**Attitudes of high-school students as a function of home background**

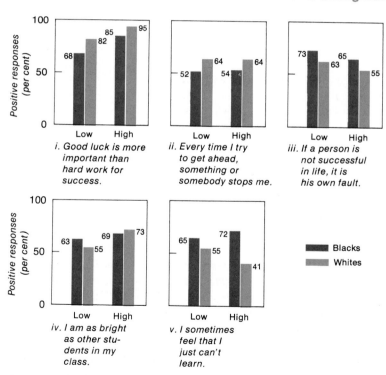

Answers taken as positive are *No, No, Yes, Yes, No* for Parts i to v, respectively.

SOURCE: Data from Paton et al. (1973), p. 89.

## Student behavior, Kwakiutl style

Classroom assignments were frequently perceived as a group task. My worksheets and practice papers were treated as though any class was a secretarial pool—older and brighter pupils did papers for younger or slower ones, sometimes because the assignments were difficult, sometimes because they were fun. My pupils, as a class, were organized to cope with me collectively, while I was trying to cope with them individually. . . .

One of the most successful classroom activities of the year was the exchange of a series of letters between the older pupils and a sixth-grade class in a California school. As the exchange of letters progressed, some members of the class began receiving more letters than others. Those who received many letters farmed out the excess and had other pupils write the replies. . . .

There was some tendency to help the slower children of one's age or ability group. Such help differs from the help given to younger pupils. . . . [It] served to keep a pupil from appearing too inadequate in the eyes of the teacher.

SOURCE: Wolcott (1974), pp. 413–14. Wolcott, an anthropologist, served as a teacher for a year in a one-room school at Blackfish Village, British Columbia.

that he should not act to put himself ahead of other members. There is the story of the teacher new to the Indian school who asked the children to work an arithmetic exercise at the blackboard, and to turn around when finished. The children carefully paced themselves so that all would turn at once.

Chicano children are said to be loyal to the group and unmotivated to work for their individual advantage, but this is one of those stereotypes that magnifies a statistical tendency. McClintock (1974) used an experimental game where competitive acts benefited one player at the expense of another, whereas cooperation brought a better *total* reward to the two players. Chicano children made fewer competitive responses than whites, but this difference was less impressive than the similarity. In Grade VI, for example, the percentages were 73 for "Anglos" and 64 for Chicanos. Justin (1970) reported that Chicano high-school seniors had less sense of personal control over their fates than Anglos, and less willingness to delay gratification. The distributions overlapped a great deal, and if Justin had equated for social class, the difference might have vanished.

The question of whether there is a distinctive black culture in the United States, with distinctive effects on personality, is hard to view objectively. Statistical or observational reports on black and white groups generally do not take social class into account adequately. The Hess-Shipman observations on black mothers (p. 494) should be noted: child-rearing practices varied with the social-class scale just as they do among whites. The case studies of black families assembled by C. V. Willie (1974) show large social-class differences. The middle-class families he describes as "affluent conformists," with a strong emphasis on education and a "Puritan orientation toward work and success." The working class, the "innovative marginals," are struggling economically. Keeping afloat

# Inside the home of a poor black child

It is all too easy to generalize about lower-class children or ghetto children. Jules Henry (1971) has provided an antidote. Henry described two first-graders, David and Rachel, both black, both poor, both living in a crowded housing project. David's home matches the worst of the stereotypes: halls smelling of urine, disorganized to the point where the child has no permanent sleeping place, no play, little verbal communication, tensions between mother and children that erupt in spankings. In contrast, here is Rachel's background, as described by Henry.

> Rachel is one of five children and lives with her father and mother. Father, an unskilled worker, is a family man, but seems rather aloof from the children. Mrs. Potter was observed to be always deeply involved in them.
>
> The Potters' apartment has four rooms: a combination living-room and kitchen-dining area and three bedrooms. The apartment is always neat and the furniture is so arranged as to make a clear distinction between living-room and dining-kitchen areas. The front area presents the family "front" but the rear rooms are drab and bare. The children all have permanent bedroom assignments. Only members of the nuclear family live in the apartment. . . .
>
> Both Mr. and Mrs. Potter are stable figures in the lives of their children. Mrs. Potter has frequent, intimate, and affectionate contact with them. The father is absent from the house during work and watches TV in the evening. Mrs. Potter is a housewife and Mr. Potter is definitely a "family man." There is a very warm relationship between Mrs. Potter and her children, and she appears sure of her position as an authority and as a nurturant figure. Rachel spontaneously includes her mother in her play.
>
> [Rachel and several playmates are jumping rope.] R: "Mama, let me see you jump rope." Mrs. Potter smiled, said O.K., and jumped rope. . . . At one point Rachel said, "I'm going to make six mice with cheese," and her mother said, "Mice with cheese. Show me how you draw that, Rachel." And Rachel began. When she finished she went to show her mother. . . .
>
> [Rachel and several of her friends are playing school.]. . . Rachel was telling the other kids that, "When I finish this you're going to have to draw it," and her mother said, "They're going to have to draw it, but you didn't draw that. Alice drew that." And Rachel said, "I know it, but I'm the teacher. They're supposed to do what I say." . . .
>
> Mrs. Potter's intervention is in the framework of positive learning: she teaches Rachel the right thing to do—not to be selfish, to give other children a chance (fair play), not to try to run things. She intervenes in the interest of moral learning and justice. Her intervention is nonviolent and she does not threaten.

SOURCE: *Anthropological Perspectives in Education*, ed. Murray L. Wax. © 1971 by Basic Books Inc., Publishers, New York.

leaves them with little energy or resources for their children. The "struggling" poor lack stability, hope, and trust, though they try to give emotional support to their children. When social class is equated and the sexes are pooled, black-white differences in values disappear (Rokeach, 1973, p. 70). Likewise for personality measures. Although some investigators report that blacks have a lower average sense of efficacy, for example, than whites, other studies with similar measures report no difference or even a difference in the opposite direction (Edwards, 1974; see also Fig. 6.5).

Ethnic identity is a powerful force in the life of the individual and often has a powerful effect on the school community. Much of the thrust of recent movements to recognize minority interests has been to increase pride in ethnic identification. When black children see pictures on the front page of blacks who have been given political and business responsibility, or when they see a black student-body president, they gain a sense of their own potentiality. The school can contribute to this pride and capitalize on it.

Serious questions arise when ethnic identification is glorified to the point of cutting a subgroup off from the mainstream. Gunnar Myrdal is the Swedish sociologist whose *An American Dilemma* (1944) fired the opening gun in the modern battle to eliminate the barriers of caste. He has recently (1974) expressed considerable doubt about proposals promoting different cultural ideals for different ethnic groups. These movements, he says, serve conservative and even reactionary interests because they evade the crucial problems of power and money. Anything that convinces ethnic-group members that they should live outside the mainstream of influence and participation is likely to prolong

their position of disadvantage. A young Chicano instructor, working in a Mexican-American studies program, said this:

> I encourage these students to think of themselves as creators and producers. They hear so much that the Spanish culture is a culture of the heart, not of the mind. I tell them that they are the inheritors of two great cultures of the mind, the Spanish and the Mayan. I tell them that they can work up to their traditions and have both the virtues of the heart and the mind.

This is ethnic identification in service to individual potential and to full participation in society.

Educational opportunities for minorities have changed considerably in recent years; indeed, the fraction of black youth entering higher education in the 1970s matches that of white youth. This does not imply that equality has been attained, as the statistic does not distinguish advanced trade schools from universities, nor competent faculties from marginal ones. Still, the statistic makes clear that blacks are interested in education. Black parents want good schools and want their children to take advantage of them. However, most of them see the primary aim of schooling as vocational preparation, and see reading, arithmetic, and the like as the first steps in that preparation. This understandable motivation may leave them unenthusiastic about the broad kind of education that enriches the person's life.

As W. E. DuBois pointed out two generations ago in a famous dispute with Booker T. Washington, there is a social danger in allowing the black community to concentrate on vocational skills while the whites are acquiring the liberal arts.

This issue is not peculiar to the black community. Over the years the schools have maintained a balance. The high school first expanded to offer vocational training to the sons of immigrants. Once this appeal was holding such youth in school, courses in citizenship, science, and the arts were made a regular part of their program. A fully integrated school will no doubt offer a diversified program; the risk is that when courses are selected a kind of self-segregation will occur. We do not have systematic comparisons of educational attitudes of black parents (and their youngsters) with attitudes of other groups of similar social status.

---

**6** Mexican-American students are likely to leave high school before finishing. What conflicts between the reward system of the school and their motivations might partly account for this? What could the school do to increase their satisfaction in school?

**7** What might account for the trend on the "feel I can learn" item in Fig. 6.5 (p. 222), where advantaged whites tended to give negative responses?

---

One of the really exciting moments in every teacher's life comes when he sits at his desk in an empty classroom and waits for his new class to appear. One minute the places are empty; a bell rings, and the room begins to swarm. Some students come in laughing pairs and chattering clusters. Some enter singly, shy and silent. Two boys rush in, one chasing the other with evident intent to crown him with a book. The glances of the teacher, sizing up the students, are matched by their glances in his direction and their behind-the-hand exchange of impressions.

To the layman, the students seem much alike. True, there are differences in dress, and some children are quieter than others. But when you put together 30 fourth-graders, all much of a size, with much the same social development, eager and giving voice to their vitality, the first impression is one of homogeneity. At higher levels of education, selection makes for even greater uniformity.

The thoughts of the teacher, however, quickly dismiss the seeming uniformities. In this group, he knows, will be some who have difficulties in learn-

ing, and others so quick mentally that they will be bored by tasks that challenge most of the class. One of the boys in this group will choose the teacher as a close friend and rely on the teacher for the support he does not get at home. And there is likely to be a student who feels less attractive than the others, whose self-respect must be bolstered.

In judging the readiness for classwork, the teacher will consider each individual's developmental success. Teachers find it easy to think *separately* about intellectual development, social adjustment, and other elements. It is harder to recognize how these relate to each other.

Only a case study that integrates information from observations, other teachers, tests and questionnaires, and interviews can give a reasonably full psychological picture of a student. Case studies have appeared at earlier points (Mack, p. 127; Barbara Singer, p. 209). One further case, Bill Chelten, will show how many of the concepts of Chapters 5 and 6 enter into interpretations.

## Bill Chelten: A Bright Boy

The following case report describes a tenth-grade boy. Bill Chelten is well toward the top of the group in tested intelligence. But all his grades are B's or C's. His file from previous years—he is now a high-school sophomore—shows that many teachers have complained of his indifference or his inability to concentrate. Consistent patterns of behavior appear in the following incidents reported by an observer.

*Bill is belligerent and out of step.*

His German teacher opens class with a comment on the deadline for an assignment. Bill calls out, "But you said that wasn't due till Thursday!" The other pupils squelch him with polite and impolite comments that it is due Tuesday and everyone else knows it. Bill subsides, mumbling to himself. Minutes later, pupils are reading orally in turn from the prepared assignment. No one else has trouble, but when Bill's turn comes, he falters repeatedly, knowing much of the passage but requiring help on several words. When helped, he says petulantly, "I can *translate* it, but it still doesn't make sense." Two minutes later, when called on again, he has no idea what is to be read next. As soon as the oral work is done, Bill reopens the matter of the assignment with "We voted for *Thursday* last week." The class in chorus: "We voted for Tuesday." Bill: "Well, let's vote again." The teacher firmly ends the debate and introduces a new activity. (Fifteen minutes of class time are covered by these incidents.)

*Bill volunteers occasionally, apparently with real interest.*

In English, he follows up the teacher's comment on Sweden with a long story about smorgasbord. Another time he offers to run a motion-picture projector. He volunteers to report to the German class about a book he has been reading.

*Bill does not work seriously on group activities.*

When the class is discussing ways to improve the school, five or six of the boys offer facetious comments; Bill says the school should put in an elevator. When the boys are practicing basketball, Bill tosses the ball in a perfunctory manner, seeming not to try or care. The observer comments, "On one occasion he astonished me by offering to answer three questions in regular geometry work. The only reason I could see was that, because the rest of the class was stumped, he found it a chance to show off."

If we translate Bill's actions into the needs they represent, it appears that autonomy is important to him. He continually argues with the teacher or with the group. He dawdles through assigned work, but is quick to participate when he can do so voluntarily. His favorite subject is art, where the teacher allows individual choice of projects. Apart from that, his only continuing interest is his pet cocker spaniel and all related topics; he talks seriously of studying veterinary medicine. Bill is not warmly accepted by his classmates, though they tolerate his quarreling and horseplay. He has few habits that win approval from peers or adults. His self-respect and self-confidence are hard to judge. While his moments of lively participation are a favorable sign, the reports that he dislikes criticism and puts off difficult jobs are unfavorable.

The crucial element in Bill's development seems to be his relations with his parents. There has been conflict over many matters and for several years: arguments over his clothes, restriction on his excessive reading, criticism of his schoolwork, and distress over his unwillingness to become a physician like his father. Bill's parents have visited the school repeatedly to learn how he is doing and what the school is doing for him. Dr. Chelten is a prominent local personage and expects others to accept his ideas. He is as blunt as Bill and has much to say about what is wrong with the school. Mostly, his criticism centers on the fact that Bill does not have homework every night and that Bill is studying local community problems instead of American history. From the Cheltens' comments, it is clear that they expect much of Bill and keep steady pressure on him.

Conversations with Bill's elementary-school teachers confirm the hunch that Bill has had trouble in peer relations and in developing independence. During his early school years, Bill worked hard and well. He was quiet and alert. His social relations were less successful: he had few close friends and tended to work alone. One factor impeding his social development was his comparative clumsiness. He did not play games well and seemed hesitant to take part in them after the fourth grade. Even now he is chubby and underdeveloped. From Grades VII to IX he was noted for squabbling, but now in Grade X his behavior is comparatively peaceable. He still quarrels with any authority, but he criticizes classmates less. His original conformity gave way over a period of years to his present combination of intractability and indifference. No one noticed a sharp break, but the cooperative boy his fourth-grade teacher recalls does not resemble Bill in Grade X.

Sole cause

*"She's utterly lacking in group integration."*

Drawing by Robt. Day; © 1940, 1968 The New Yorker Magazine, Inc.

As his growing interests and intelligence led him to make demands his parents would not accede to, Bill set out to test his strength against theirs. Defeated on every ground by their firmness and power, he found no way of being independent and retaining their approval. Dr. and Mrs. Chelten criticize Bill steadily, but they cannot make him work. His stubborn and ill-conceived resistance—an assertion of his will—makes his life harder. Partly because his ability keeps him from falling far behind, partly because the teachers encourage his initiative, he is better adjusted to school than he was last year. If he begins to succeed in some activity and enjoy it, he may devote himself to purposeful work and accept his parents' pressure as a cross to be borne. Or he may become more and more a social outcast, lose his present spontaneous interest, and find neither success nor happiness.

Since Bill's fight for independence is a fight for self-respect, it is not surprising that he creates an issue in school whenever the opportunity arises. His English teacher chose *David Copperfield* for the class to study, and when Bill protested that he had already read the book, she insisted that he reread it with the class. He continued to cause friction throughout the semester; the teacher had chosen the one tactic most likely to set Bill in opposition. The only teachers who could get a good response were those who gave him a chance to demonstrate independence. (This study was made by my students some time ago. Bill is now in his forties and a success in his work. What career do you guess he is in? For the answer, see the note at end of this chapter.)

Three principles are helpful in diagnosing behavior:

Any action is an attempt to satisfy some need.

Consistent behavior patterns run through the student's actions in many situations. These patterns are stable over long periods of time.

Any pattern is the resultant of many causes, and any single cause may lead to many different adaptations.

Bill's belligerence is annoying, and the teacher's first impulse may be to put him in his place and end the trouble. But if Bill's unruly behavior expresses an urgent need, stamping out his trial responses may be like tying down the safety valve on a boiler. The tension is sure to explode in some other action, perhaps more harmful than his argumentativeness. If the teacher looks for the need that is the cardinal cause of Bill's unusual behavior, perhaps this need can be satisfied in some legitimate way, substituting a desirable and successful act for the disturbing one. Such a strategy of "diagnose—then work on the cause" was followed by the teachers who discovered that Bill was striving for independence and encouraged him to take initiative. They allowed him to satisfy his need in a way that contributed to class progress.

Instead of looking for basic needs, some teachers try to deal with the surface behavior directly. This rarely works. When Bill is punished for speaking out of turn or for voicing his opinions, he becomes even more convinced that adults are against him. Thus he becomes less ready to discuss his problems with them, and less likely to volunteer helpful ideas in class. If a student who does failing work is punished by being required to repeat courses, he is made more unhappy but not more adequate.

The English teacher who demands that Bill reread *David Copperfield* thwarts his campaign for independence. In fact, this teacher thought she was performing a service by "teaching Bill that he must do as he is told," though this was the tactic that had failed for Bill's father. Instead, she might recognize Bill's need for independence and try to teach him how to be independent and cooperative at the same time. For example, Bill might be allowed to read *Great Expectations* or *Oliver Twist*. Then, in class discussion, whenever a question about plot or character development arose in connection with *David*, Bill could be asked to tell how Dickens handled similar dramatic themes in the other novel. Bill would thus have a chance to be independent and yet remain an important member of the group. Such a solution can come only when the teacher discovers the dominant aim in the student's striving, as reaching for independence is at this time for Bill.

**8** How else might Bill's personality have developed, given his ability and his parents' motives?

**9** Describe the German class incident (p. 228) in terms of the elements in learning. What was Bill trying to attain? Why did he use this trial response? What did he learn from the incident?

**10** Each of the following statements was made by one of Bill's tenth-grade teachers. How do you account for the wide differences? Which statement do you agree with?

"Bill has a chip on his shoulder and is frustrated within himself. His manner is really a defense."

"Somewhere along the line he has got the idea that he is so intelligent he does not need to put forth any effort. No one knows what Bill's IQ is better than Bill."

"Bill is very personable, an excellent scholar, and well adjusted. He had trouble last year, but now he's found his place in the group."

**11** One prominent technique for handling deviant behavior in the classroom is *behavior modification*, the systematic reinforcement of desired behavior (pp. 20 and 624).
  a. Did Bill offer opportunities for applying reinforcement?
  b. Some critics argue that behavior modification deals with the symptoms on the surface of the personality but neglects underlying causes. Could teachers handle Bill better by giving attention to more basic causes of his classroom behavior?

## Observing Students

Skill in observing and interpreting behavior is developed through training in sound procedures and through experience. The need for training in observation is indicated by Prescott's list (1957, p. 100) of common shortcomings when teachers judge students:

1. Faulty knowledge. They employ mistaken ideas about human behavior and development.
2. Uncritical acceptance of data. They accept rumors and prejudiced descriptions as facts; they do not distinguish between fact and opinion.

3. Leaping to conclusions. They draw conclusions from a single incident, neglecting facts that would cast doubt on the generalization.
4. Overlooking situational modifiers. They observe some frequent reaction (for example, timidity) and interpret it as characteristic, failing to recognize which situations do and which do not elicit that reaction.
5. Confusing hypothesis with fact. Having interpreted a few incidents as reflecting some cause, they accept that suspected cause as a fact without collecting sufficient evidence.
6. Excessive certainty. They accept interpretations as established truths when the facts establish only a probability of truth. This closes their minds and freezes their attitudes.
7. Oversimplification. When they identify one probable cause, they accept this as the sole and sufficient cause for the entire behavior pattern.
8. Emotional thinking. In drawing conclusions, they give excessive weight to incidents that have disturbed them.
9. Projection of their own experience. They reason from their own experience, not realizing that the experience behind the learner's behavior may have been quite different.
10. Expressing their own needs in interpretation. Teachers attribute to students motives that the teachers, to justify their own feelings, "want" them to have. (For example, a teacher may see a student as hostile to justify the teacher's own insecurity and antagonism.)

To avoid these errors, a teacher is advised to be objective. This means particularly: Begin with a factual description of behavior rather than with statements about traits or causes. Postpone value judgments. Premature interpretation often causes the observer to report falsely what the student does. From watching Bill in his German class, an observer might remember only: "Bill is lazy. He kept trying to get out of finishing his work on time." This is a poor description, for the total picture shows plenty of energy and effort. Recollections of this kind are superficial. Suppose one person reports, "Bill is lazy," while another one says, "I saw Bill and he is energetic"; contradictory impressions cannot be reconciled. Uncolored factual descriptions of each situation and Bill's behavior in it can be put together into a valid image.

One excellent procedure is to accumulate a folder of anecdotal records describing significant incidents factually. A detailed written record is especially helpful in comparing situations to which the student responds differently, to see what conditions may account for the seeming inconsistency. An observation report ought to mention the date, locality, and general activity. A note that says "Tom got into trouble because he shoved Mark in class" is unrevealing. If given the full facts—that all the students were writing papers and that both of the boys had finished ten minutes before the pushing began—a counselor can understand Tom's boredom and can suggest ways of preventing trouble in the future.

In recording an incident, it is often wise to put down a preliminary interpretation and carefully note it as such, by putting the interpretation in brackets, as in the passage quoted in the box (p. 235).

The observer should see the individual student in a wide range of situations and also call on what other persons know. The teacher sees behavior in one classroom, but needs to know about the student's entire life. How does he react to other adults? How when there is no adult leader? Some of the most revealing information comes from watching the students in the cafeteria, in the hall before school, or in the bleachers at a basketball game. This does not require the teacher to skulk behind pillars like a fictional detective. Students behave naturally in the presence of an observer, so long as he does not stare at his target or pointedly take notes.

The teacher should welcome information about the student's home and his nonschool activities. A visit to the home or merely a stroll down the block where the student lives adds to the teacher's knowledge of his background. Although often tinged with deceptive biases, reports from other teachers provide essential information. A medical report or information from a social agency may shed light on behavior in school.

When many incidents have been recorded, consistent patterns come out. This process never fails to amaze beginning observers. The first time they see a youngster, they form an impression and think they understand him. A few observations later, they have found so many inconsistencies that they cannot imagine an underlying unity. When records are made in many situations, consistent relationships do emerge. Bill is troublesome and quarrelsome, but there are contrasting moments when he takes initiative and helps the teacher. When we see how those situations differ, we arrive at his unifying pattern: Bill is negativistic when *required* to do something.

The observer's first impressions are of surface characteristics. These characteristics—tenseness, aggressiveness, devotion to sports, and so on—have slight explanatory value; primarily, they define the problem to be studied. As soon as there is sufficient evidence to support a preliminary characterization, it is desirable to start thinking about causes. Causal thinking counteracts any tendency to regard traits as fixed and difficulties as beyond help. If probable causes are identified, treatment suggestions follow. Early in his observation of a student, the teacher should make a list of possible causes. This list should be wide-ranging and speculative. Bill's difficulties may stem in part from retarded physical development, insecurity in relations with girls, inefficient study skills, or a dozen other sources. Subsequent observation and tests can be directed to verify the hypotheses listed. Only a broad list offers the teacher a good chance of turning up the truly critical information. As facts accumulate, some hypotheses are found unreasonable and others are given support. At the same time, as it becomes clearer which situations bring out desired behavior and which ones trigger undesirable responses, the teacher revises his description of the student.

Anyone who knows the practical situation in which teachers operate is skeptical about proposals to make case studies. Teachers who want to do the best possible job sometimes feel guilty when they realize that they never get around to making individual studies. Just what can a busy teacher hope to do? It is good training to make one or two full-scale case studies. By such work, a

## Anecdotal record

The form and value of anecdotal records is illustrated by this memorandum from an educational psychology student who was studying Clark, an orthopedically handicapped 12-year-old:

> After lunch, before the class had been called to order, James asked the teacher if he could show the fossil rocks he had brought from home during the lunch hour. She consented, and he talked for two or three minutes, holding up the rocks. Clark said nothing during this, but, like the others, he watched Jim closely. [Seemed much interested.] When Jim was finished, the teacher took two of the boys to get books from across the hall, and the group as a whole became noisy. Clark got up, went across the room to Jim's place, and engaged him in conversation while handling the fossils. As Miss Gordon came back, he turned and started for his seat. Mike stuck out his foot and Clark stumbled slightly over it. Clark looked apologetically at Miss Gordon, made a face at Mike, and took his seat. [I don't think he was embarrassed at being out of his seat, but he knew he should go back. Mike seemed to be teasing Clark; Clark was good-natured about the tripping. Maybe Mike was trying to get Clark in trouble.]

This one incident offers information on Clark's intellectual interests, his relations with other pupils, and his security in his relations with the teacher.

teacher learns how to extract information from minor incidents, and sees for himself how behavior is organized into consistent patterns. After this initial experience, however, teachers rarely make formal studies. The teacher ought to record key incidents that he observes in the course of his regular activities. The teacher should not think only of "problem cases." Students who function well in their daily affairs need guidance also, and an accurate record of representative behavior lays the groundwork for truly personalized assistance. Ordinarily, the teacher observes everyone as opportunity permits, but looks deliberately for facts about one or two students at a time. In this way, the teacher's limited time is concentrated effectively. The high-school teacher has a more impersonal relationship with most students than the elementary-school teacher. But responding to the student as an individual is no less important in the later grades or, for that matter, in graduate school. Hence every teacher ought to develop skill in observing and interpreting the characteristic patterns of his students.

Coming to understand the individual is a professional responsibility for the teacher no less than for the physician and the minister, but the community is less prepared to trust teachers. Only a fine line separates a professional conversation—say, about Bill's difficulties with his parents—from a gossip session. Even the most objective appraisal ("Mrs. Larsen seems somewhat too concerned over Carol's school achievement") might be resented by Mrs. Larsen. Lawyers representing parent groups have recently argued that cumulative records can prejudice the child's future teachers, and that as a safeguard, all school files should be open to the parents for inspection. This would make it inadvisable for the school to keep written records going beyond objectively measured aspects of performance, and would make it harder for teachers to do a sensitive job. (We shall consider some evidence on teacher bias on p. 159.) Legal restrictions, however, will not reduce the importance of thinking about the student as a person. With or without legal constraint, the teacher's inquiries ought to be restricted by good taste and by a sense of what the community will accept.

Some of the techniques social scientists use to study individuals can invade privacy even in impersonal research studies. Invasion of privacy is even more at issue when signed responses are collected by the student's teacher (Westin, 1967). A questionnaire handed to the fourth-grader, for example, may ask how well he gets along with his parents or even how well the parents get along with each other. Many parents find such questions objectionable, especially if the school does not explain how the information can help the school do its job. Sometimes, with the best of motives, the school gives the preadolescent a questionnaire intended to spot delinquent tendencies. The more valid such a test is, the closer it comes to asking the youngster to incriminate himself. At best, such tests are valid only on a statistical basis; hence they may blacken the youngster's reputation undeservedly.

Some of the challenges to the study of individuals come from political conservatives who insist that the child's personality is the concern only of his parents, and that schools should stick to the three Rs. In Chapters 2 and 5, I have taken a different position. But the relevance of the student's personality to the teacher's task does not make the issue of privacy less weighty. Various policies can be used to continue inquiry and yet keep it within legitimate bounds. Ordinarily, counselors and others with specialized training are allowed wider latitude in their inquiries. Questions are usually proper so long as the person tested understands and approves the use to be made of the information. Allowing the student to respond or not, as he wishes, is consistent with this standard. It is a healthy practice to keep parents informed about proposed questionnaires and personal inquiries. Some schools go so far as to require the parent's written consent before the student is asked any questions on personality and home background. General policies to guide the use of tests and questionnaires in socially sensitive situations have been suggested by professional organizations (American Psychological Association, 1974; Goslin, 1970).

---

 **12** One set of recommended standards (Goslin, 1970, p. 20) refers to a category of data consisting of "verified information of clear importance, but not absolutely necessary to the school, over time, in helping the child or in protecting others." This would include health data, family background information, systematic teacher reports on behavior, and aptitude tests. With regard to this category the report makes two recommendations: (1) "unnecessary data should be eliminated when the student moves from elementary school to junior high or from junior high to high school"; (2) "the records should be destroyed, or at least stripped of any label that would identify the individual, when the student leaves school." What arguments can you give for and against each of these policies?

**13** Of the ten errors listed by Prescott (p. 232), which might be overcome by appropriate training?

**14** One of the principal devices in training teachers to interpret behavior is to ask them to list as many possible explanations as they can for the behavior pattern observed, even if the explanations are conflicting. Which of the ten errors might this device overcome?

## Obtaining Peer Judgments

Some students are left on the sidelines when sports or parties are starting; some are popular and in demand; some are "natural leaders." Information about social relations helps the teacher to understand tensions in the group and sometimes suggests how he can intervene helpfully. That Sara is high-strung and sometimes quarrelsome has already drawn the teacher's attention. When he finds that Sara and Julie are rivals in popularity and leadership and notes that Sara's outbreaks always occur when Julie is getting the spotlight, he knows that a new social pattern will have to emerge before Sara's tension can subside.

Teachers have found it profitable to make formal studies of the social structure and of students' reputations. If a student's peers think of him as uncooperative, for example, that is important information—even if, in fact, he cooperates as well as others. An undeserved reputation can still influence adjustment. Collecting peer judgments is legitimate *if* constructive use will be made of the results. The method should not be used where students are likely to find it intrusive or threatening. Teachers use two formal procedures, peer ratings and the sociogram, to find out what his fellows think about a student.

PEER RATINGS    Peer ratings have been collected at all levels, from the primary room to the college dormitory, with directions and questions modified to fit the group. A form offers a series of descriptions worded in student language, with instructions to match them to members of the group. For young children, the directions may be cast in "Guess Who" form. Usually the rater is free to put no name, one name, or several names after the item. With intermediate-grade children, the descriptions might include these:

Here is someone who likes to talk a lot, always has something to say.
Here is someone who always seems rather sad, worried, or unhappy, who hardly ever laughs or smiles.
Here is a girl who likes to read boys' books, play boys' games, or would prefer to be a boy. (Cunningham et al., 1951, pp. 419–22.)

Ordinarily, responses are left unsigned. The teacher or counselor explains why the questions are being asked. The plan is likely to backfire into complaints unless the students like the teacher and welcome his personal interest.

The teacher should pay no attention if a given child is mentioned two or three times as "a poor sport," since such random mentions do not show a crystallized reputation. But if a third of the class nominates Patrick as a poor sport, the information is significant. It does not show that Patrick *is* a poor sport; perhaps he does not know how to play the games, or perhaps the others judge him unfairly. The remedy may be to work on Patrick's behavior, or it may be to develop group acceptance of him.

The teacher will find differences between his view and the group view. Teachers identifying class leaders may give undue attention to brighter students or to the ones they like, only to find that the students themselves name a much less conspicuous boy as the one who has good ideas about what to do and who can take charge and get things done.

THE SOCIOGRAM    The sociogram, such as that for the boys in Fig. 5.5 (p. 191), portrays social structure. To obtain the needed information, one may request each student to write his own name and the names of three, four, or five best friends. The teacher then prepares a chart, drawing arrows to connect each person with the persons he chose. The first sketch is jumbled. Once the names are rearranged to put mutual friends together and to shorten the lines between choices as much as possible, a well-defined network appears. Always, several "stars" receive more than their proportionate share of choices, and others ("isolates") receive none.

The structure often comes as a surprise to the teacher. Because 30 students means 435 possible pairings, the teacher can perceive only a part of the elaborate social structure of his class. He has spotted certain chums and certain rivalries, and knows that Jane is going around with Emily's crowd this fall. The sociogram brings the relations into view like a microscope turned abruptly into sharp focus. Jane is seen to be on the outskirts of Emily's crowd, able to count on friendship only from Emily and ignored by the other four. The quiet Ann seems to follow the dashing Carol around, but the sociogram shows her as the real "star," whom everyone thinks of as a friend. The teacher had seen Bonnie and Bella as indistinguishable, well-mannered girls. Yet Bonnie now shows up as a member of a warmly knit social group, while Bella is no one's close friend.

Again, the teacher must convince the students that the inquiry is to help them rather than to pry into their affairs. Ordinarily, the teacher explains frankly that if he knows their friends, he can understand them better, plan occasions for them to work with their friends, and so make life pleasanter. Often the inquiry is connected with an immediate problem: for example, "We are going to work in committees for the next two weeks. Please list the five people you would most like to work with. I'll arrange for you to have as many of your choices as I can." To maintain confidence, the choices should really be used in making up committees. Good work is obtained from such compatible committee members; moreover, the teacher who notes that Charles wants to work with Bruce and Mike can put him on their committee and give him a chance to build a friendship.

If the same group remains together from year to year, peer ratings are likely to be quite stable. Even when the membership of the group changes, as in going from an elementary school to a junior high where groups are shuffled together and reformed, the year-to-year correlation is 0.50–0.60 (Roff, et al., 1972). Individual popularity is most likely to shift when the teacher plans activities to promote the acceptance of underchosen children. Change is not always for the better. Sometimes a popular person slips as he fails to adapt his social techniques to the shifting interests and ideals of the group.

Even though popularity is not very changeable, the friendship linkages are continually shifting (Taba, 1955b, p. 62). Especially if the teacher gives students a chance to work together and help each other, the sociogram may shift from one with cliques and rival stars to one where choices spread over the whole group, with no tight clusters or cleavages.

A sociometric survey of the school or the grade group sheds light on the extent to which the school community is socially integrated. Thus, in Westlake High School, an all-white school in a prosperous residential neighborhood of a city, 19 per cent of the girls and 37 per cent of the boys were chosen by no one. This frequent social isolation reflected the influence of out-of-school clubs and sororities in which newcomers, less wealthy students, and those of a minority religion had no place. An uninspired program of school activities in which only the athletics appealed to the boys was a contributing factor. Upon inquiry, it was found that students frequently transferred away from Westlake because they were "miserably unhappy" (Taba, 1955a). The sociometric survey, by detecting an unhealthy social atmosphere, encourages a deeper inquiry and remedial action. Survey results may also be reassuring. In an elementary school studied by Taba, the staff anticipated a cleavage between Jewish and Gentile children that did not appear in friendship choices.

15  If a girl who shows a loss of social acceptance turns to reading as an outlet, what is best for the teacher to do?

16  May a frequently chosen student be maladjusted?

17  What further inquiries are needed before modifying the Westlake program? What changes in the program might be desirable?

18  Considering either primary, junior-high-school, or college students, write several peer-rating descriptions that would give the teacher significant information.

## The Student's View of Himself

Just as his classmates' image of him is a reality that affects the student, so is his *self*-image important. If he considers himself unattractive in appearance or below average in ability, that will influence his responses whether or not his belief is justified. Teachers can make some inferences about the student's self-concept from his actions, and some further hints will come from conversations with the student. Pencil-paper questionnaires collect information quickly, in a similar form, for every student.

Although these questionnaires have had considerable use in research they have not proved to be very profitable in the hands of teachers. Responses are distorted by the student's desire to make a good impression (or, sometimes, to

**FIGURE 6.6**

**A self-concept questionnaire**

NAME    Howard                                                                  DATE  Fall, Fifth Grac

Check (✓) the number from 1 to 5 which most nearly indicates how you feel about the following school subjects and activities.  After checking a number you may wish to write at the side to further explain your choice.  If your class does not have any of the following subjects or activities please leave a blank space.  Be sure that numbers 1 and 5 are used.

| | 5 Like very much | 4 Like some-times | 3 OK but not wild about | 2 Dislike some-times | 1 Dislike very much | Comments |
|---|---|---|---|---|---|---|
| 1. Arithmetic drill on fundamentals (mechanics, such as +, ÷, −, ×) | | | | | ✓ | |
| 2. Solving problems in arithmetic | | ✓ | | | | |
| 3. Foreign language | ✓ | | | | | |
| 4. Playing games, singing in foreign language | | ✓ | | | | |
| 5. Health facts | | | | | | |
| 6. Personal and world health problems | | | | | | |
| 7. Spelling workbook | | | ✓ | | | |
| 8. Spelling words in everyday writing | | | | ✓ | | |
| 9. Handwriting − formal drill | | | | | ✓ | |
| 10. Being careful of handwriting in everyday writing | | | ✓ | | | |
| 11. Creative poetry (making up poetry) | | | | | ✓ | |
| 12. Learning specific art techniques | ✓ | | | | | |
| 13. Creative art and construction − using own ideas | | | ✓ | | | |
| 14. Having long periods in which to do work more thoroughly | | | ✓ | | | |
| 15. Taking tests − achievement | ✓ | | | | | |
| 16. Giving reports | ✓ | | | | | |
| 17. Being given responsibilities and special jobs (officer, monitor, student council, etc.) | ✓ | | | | | |
| 18. Discussing how individual work went in class discussion (evaluating) | ✓ | | | | | |
| 19. Discussing how class work went in class discussion (evaluating) | | ✓ | | | | |
| 20. Teacher keeping strict control and quiet | | | ✓ | | | |
| 21. Letting people talk and move around as much as they like | | | | | ✓ | |
| 22. Major sports | | | | | ✓ | |
| 23. Recreational reading | ✓ | | | | | |
| 80. Individual study based on your own interest | ✓ | | | | | |

SOURCE: Pauline S. Sears and Vivian S. Sherman, *In Pursuit of Self-Esteem: Case Studies of Eight Elementary School Children* (Belmont, Calif.: Wadsworth, 1964), p. 68. © 1964 by Wadsworth Publishing Company, Inc., Belmont, California 94002. Reprinted by permission of the publisher. The questionnaire form is not to be reproduced without permission of its authors.

fly a distress flag that will get him attention). The more complicated instruments can be interpreted only by a person with specialized training; some school counselors and school psychologists, of course, do make considerable use of personality tests. In a mass testing program, issues involving respect for privacy (p. 236) are likely to arise.

PROBLEM CHECKLISTS   Teachers can make good use of the so-called problem inventory or checklist in those situations where relations between teachers and students are fairly open. Applying such an instrument in a junior high school can indicate what problem areas most concern the students as a group (p. 9) and can locate especially troubled students for whom counseling conferences are advisable.

Typical items from the Mooney Problem Checklist (junior-high level)* are:

> Don't get enough sleep
> Not good looking
> Afraid of tests
> So often feel restless in classes
> Being treated as an outsider
> Ill at ease at social affairs
> Giving in to temptations
> Not having as much fun as other kids have
> Family worried about money

There are other forms of the checklist for senior-high, college, and adult groups.

One may count the number of checkmarks in such areas as health and physical development, school, home, economic security, and boy-girl relations. The number of checks made by an individual is not an accurate indication of degree of disturbance. Adjustment may be drastically upset by a single problem. The most effective use of the checklist is to find out *what* concerns the student. The problems may be such that the teacher can provide direct help, or they may be beyond any solution the school can suggest.

Even when the teacher can give no practical help, he may do substantial good merely by encouraging the student to talk further about his problem. Students generally welcome the chance to discuss their worries with a mature person. A common reaction to a counseling conference is, "Thanks very much. Just talking about the problem made me feel better." Youngsters sometimes hesitate to talk with their parents about a problem, particularly when their struggle for independence is near its height or when their parents seem remote. A teacher whose attitude makes clear his readiness to listen will find much demand for that service.

---

*Items copyright 1950 by The Psychological Corporation. Reproduced by permission.

## Howard as others saw him

Howard, very bright, had skipped from Grade I to Grade III. Pauline Sears and Vivian Sherman (1964, pp. 97–113) studied Howard at length, with tests, observations, and interviews of those who knew him. Here are some of their impressions. Compare them with Howard's self-description in Fig. 6.6.

Mr. Salton, Howard's fifth-grade teacher, speaks of him as "very immature . . . the stereotyped academic little boy with the college vocabulary. . . . Has had it fairly easy in his school years and seems to think everything that is done is going to be easy for him." Mr. Salton complains that Howard fools around and turns in sloppy-looking papers. But the work is good, except that Howard writes less than he should.

Howard threatens Mr. Salton a bit by checking out the accuracy of whatever the teacher says in the science lesson. Says Mr. Salton: "Relations with me is an area in which Howard could improve. He is displaying behavior [that] . . . he knows is antagonizing to me. . . ." Yet Howard says that Mr. Salton is helpful, understanding, and easy to get along with.

Howard is a poor performer in sports.

Howard does not seek out social relations, and as a result he does not spend much time with any other child. He seems not to be unfriendly, just detached. Observer's notes: ". . . unhappy, bored, rebellious . . . rarely showed any enthusiasm or excitement . . . constant frown." "He gave the appearance of a peculiar, bespectacled old man, seriously and efficiently engaged in business of importance to him. . . ."

The positive self-concept seen in the fall questionnaire (Fig. 6.6, p. 240) dropped considerably when Howard filled out the questionnaire again in the spring.

SELF-CONCEPT QUESTIONNAIRES  Teachers confuse success with adjustment, and may assume that the student whose classwork is good has no problems. Sarason et al. (1960, p. 265) report:

> If a child is bright, highly motivated, and clearly adequate to his classwork, it is difficult for his teacher to believe that this child may be highly anxious about his abilities and his classwork. We have had occasion many times to discuss high anxiety children with their teachers, and, particularly in the case of the bright child, we have encountered a reaction of near-disbelief that such a child answered the [anxiety] questionnaires as he did.

Questionnaires to assess the self-concept are widely used in evaluating programs that are intended to improve adjustment and confidence, including guidance programs and programs of compensatory education. The forms are also used to identify individuals who may be maladjusted. One such form is shown in Fig. 6.6 (p. 240). Useful though they are both in statistical studies and in the hands of psychological testers, questionnaires like these cannot be trusted as accounts of either the adjustment or the inner feelings of individuals (see also p. 745). Howard reports self-satisfaction, but the information in the box suggests that he is not getting what he should out of school and life.

**19** How do you interpret the discrepancy between Fig. 6.6 and the information in the box? Do you think Howard was reporting his judgments of himself honestly?

**20** The Buros *Mental Measurements Yearbook* (1972; see p. 265) describes personality questionnaires and provides critical reviews. Examine and discuss the review of one of the following:
    a. California Psychological Inventory (ages 13–adult)
    b. Junior Eysenck Personality Inventory (ages 7–15)
    c. Thomas Self-Concept Values Test (ages 3–9)
Would it be desirable to use this test in school? If so, in what grade? Who should interpret it and for what purposes?

**21** In evaluating a preschool program intended to improve readiness for school, would it be appropriate to assess each child's personality systematically, at the end of the program? (Assume that the evaluator plans to use the scores only to judge the program and will not pass them on to parents or teachers.)

**22** Questionnaire measures of adjustment usually have low correlations with the number of peer choices a student receives. Why?

## Evaluating Adjustment

As the teacher comes to know the students, he will form opinions about the student's degree of adjustment, whether he uses personality measures or not. He must do so in order to decide whether he should put more pressure on him or less, draw him more into the group or allow him to pursue his independent activities, and so on. It would be wrong for the teacher to fix on one model of personality as ideal for everyone of a given age, but it is equally wrong to make no judgments. Some personalities are healthier than others, and even the teacher who considers the student's personality none of his business will be affecting that personality by his actions.

To start the discussion, I invite you to examine your present opinions about traits that might be considered undesirable. On a sheet of paper, write three columns of numbers: 1–10, 11–26, 27–36. Then arrange the following traits or acts in order of their seriousness, assigning rank 1 to the most serious.

| | | |
|---|---|---|
| Carelessness | Inquisitiveness | Sullenness |
| Cheating | Interrupting | Suspiciousness |
| Cruelty, bullying | Masturbation | Tardiness |
| Destroying materials | Profanity | Tattling |
| Disobedience | Obscene notes, talk | Temper tantrums |
| Domineering | Restlessness | Thoughtlessness |
| Dreaminess | Shyness | Truancy |
| Enuresis | Silliness, smartness | Unhappiness |
| Fearfulness | Smoking | Unreliability |
| Heterosexual activity | Stealing | Unsocial withdrawing |
| Imaginative lying | Stubbornness | Untruthfulness |
| Impertinence | Suggestibility | Whispering |

Do not devote much effort to working out a precise order in the middle column, but give careful attention to rankings at each end of the list. Base your judgment solely on how serious, *as a sign of emotional disturbance and possible breakdown*, repeated acts of this kind would be in a 10- to 12-year-old. (Later you will have a chance to compare your ranking with a ranking by experts.)

Mental health is not synonymous with being "socialized" or "contented." The foregoing text emphasized disturbance and risk of breakdown. All the school does for a student is wasted if, in the end, emotional conflicts incapacitate him. A socialized person is a contributor and a problem-solver. He uses his knowledge and skill to act wisely on his environment. Excessive timidity or aggressiveness can prevent him from making this contribution. The adjusted person is one who commits himself to a consistent set of goals and uses his energies effectively in working toward them. I emphasize effectiveness; the person who is consistently effective, and so fulfills his needs, will be happy as well.

The items you have just ranked have been used in a number of studies of professional opinions. Authorities on emotional development have ranked the symptoms. While the ranking varies a little from study to study, depending on its date and the experts chosen, the consensus is always much like that shown in the box (p. 246). Unhappiness is rated most serious of all signs in that list, thoughtlessness the least serious. Compare that ranking with yours, and think about any large discrepancy.

This list serves as a summary of what mental hygienists judge to be symptomatic of bad adjustment—that is, likely to foreshadow breakdown or serious malfunctioning. The traits most serious in the eyes of the experts are signs of unhappiness and tension. Violent discharge of emotion (direct or displaced) is represented by cruelty and tantrums. Withdrawal and repression are indicated by several traits high on the list: unsocial withdrawing, fearfulness, shyness.

The experts are concerned when the person has recurring trouble in relations with others or in meeting everyday demands. A person can have trouble, however, and still respond to life toughly and optimistically. Serious emotional strain is implied when cheerfulness gives way to depression and passivity replaces vigor. Most of the symptoms rated very serious in this list show lack of confidence and lack of constructive effort. Current thought among psychiatrists and many clinical psychologists is summarized in the description Linn et al. (1969, p. 299) give for *dysfunction.* Dysfunction, they say, suggests

discontent and unhappiness, accompanied by negative self-regarding attitudes ... handicapping anxiety and other pathological interpersonal functions that reduce flexibility in coping with stressful situations or achieving self-actualization in what is to that person a significant role. . . . Dysfunction is seen as coping with either personal, interpersonal, or geographic environment in a maladaptive manner.

## How experts judge symptoms of adjustment

| Most Serious | Least Serious |
|---|---|
| Unhappiness | Whispering |
| Fearfulness | Profanity |
| Unsocial withdrawing | Smoking |
| Cruelty, bullying | Interrupting |
| Enuresis | Tardiness |
| Shyness | Heterosexual activity |
| Suspiciousness | Masturbation |
| Suggestibility | Carelessness |
| Temper tantrums | Inquisitiveness |
| Domineering | Thoughtlessness |

SOURCE: Henderson (1949). See also Lessing et al. (1973).

The school and community disapprove of many of the actions on the "least serious" list. The student should learn to avoid most of them. But do these actions imply personality disturbance? The question is not whether profanity, say, is morally good or bad. The question asked is empirical: Is this act especially common among those who show a progressive disorganization of personality? The experts say no. Smoking, profanity, whispering, sex experimentation are all tried by normal children at one time or another. The act is disapproved, or it is approved by their social group; they develop their ultimate responses accordingly. Interrupting, inquisitiveness, and whispering are signs of energy and eagerness. They may inconvenience others, but they are not signs of something basically wrong.

---

**23** Each of the following was rated by psychiatrists as not indicating serious maladjustment (Lessing et al., 1973). Why not?
   a. Is boisterous, rowdy.
   b. Demands a lot of attention.
   c. Finds it hard to talk to certain people.
   d. Is worried about being sexually underdeveloped (ages 12–18).

**24** Sometimes a person is described as "thin-skinned; sensitive to anything that can be construed as an interpersonal slight." Block (1971) reports that, among females, this trait has virtually no stability from adolescence to adulthood. Can the school therefore dismiss the trait as a transient stage of maladjustment?

---

# IMPLICATIONS OF PERSONALITY TRAITS FOR SUCCESS

Success in school or success in life is not appreciably correlated with any personality measure. To be sure, some personality measures overlap with ability measures: for example, an anxiety questionnaire is certain to correlate with past achievement when it includes items such as "I worry about my schoolwork." The question is whether combining the personality measure with the ability measure predicts success better than the ability measure does by itself. No personality measure—of anxiety, of self-concept, of motivation to achieve, of interest, and so on—appears to improve practical prediction of performance or learning. Correlations show up in occasional studies, but no relation to overall achievement emerges consistently. Trait measures do predict satisfaction with school or with a certain career. Also, as in the Domino study (p. 141), they predict learning under particular kinds of instruction.

The failure of prediction does not mean that personality makes no difference. It is simple generalizations that break down. One might think that maladjustment would make failure likely. But Mack (p. 127) met demands successfully in part because of his fears.

In a series of studies in and around Berkeley, California, children and their families were studied intensively for many years, and follow-up tests and interviews were conducted when the subjects were in their thirties. Studies I discuss elsewhere (pp. 157, 189; Fig. 8.2) drew on these data. Here, let us consider how adult characteristics related to observations in childhood and adolescence (Macfarlane, 1963; Honzik, 1967; J. Block, 1971).

Some aspects of performance were consistent. Certain ratings made by observers and interviewers in high school correlated as high as 0.70 with ratings made 20 years later (Block, 1971, pp. 302ff.).* For men, highly stable traits were the presence of a wide range of interests; a high degree of intellectual capacity; taking pride in being "objective," rational; and being unable to delay gratification. In sum, the male who was rational and intellectual early was that way later; the male who was impulsive and subjective early was that way later. The list of stable items for women was not quite the same, but again differences in intellectualization were stable. The one striking contrast is that degree of autonomy was stable for women ($r = 0.68$), not for men ($r = 0.27$). In both sexes the unstable items (correlations near zero) had to do with emotional responses. Evidently a person's style of expressing tensions and his or her style in interpersonal relations change radically over the years.

---

*These are correlations derived from an unusual form of rating that poses certain difficulties of interpretation. The correlations are adjusted to compensate for inaccuracy of the judgments.

Psychologists were often wrong in predicting later success of the adolescents (Macfarlane, 1963). About half of the subjects turned out a good deal better than the psychologists seeing them as adolescents had expected. Predictions regarding overcontrolled adolescents were sound. These people formed a defensive life style early and took few opportunities to change it. Sound forecasts were made also for a few extremely immature adolescent boys who had suffered from inconsistent treatment at home; many of them, seen as adults, were on the road to alcoholism. On the other hand, some of the athletes and belles of the ball, adjusted and popular in their teens, were leading depressed adult lives. They could not find an adult activity half so gratifying as their teenage careers.

The successes that contradicted gloomy predictions came where good resources were present in adolescence despite maladjustment to circumstances. One early-maturing girl, large and awkward in adolescence, went through years of unhappiness—and then "caught fire" in a college course during her junior year. Once she started to enjoy her work she had the motivation to study and to make a successful career and a happy life as a mother. Another student, finishing high school as "a listless oddball" with mediocre grades and an IQ of 100, managed to prepare himself as an architect and is now enjoying great success in career, home, and community. In Block's compilation, perhaps most surprising was a group of boys who could be described in high school as plebeian: not bright, not interesting, from average homes, inclined to withdraw, negativistic. As adults, ensconced in creditable second-rank positions (such as *assistant* manager), they were members of the local service clubs, middle-of-the-road Republicans, fathers in stable families (with more children than most). They were calm, cheerful, dependable. I suspect that their cheerlessness in adolescence arose from the offerings of the high school, in which they found nothing to interest them.

These surprises do not contradict the principle that development is continuous and cumulative. The personalities of these young-adult Babbitts grew out of their high-school personalities; but as adults they found niches where they could be themselves happily. A person's style does evolve. He learns new ways to cope (Haan, 1974). Sometimes marriage provides a sense of worth that was lacking when the person was earlier working to satisfy others or no one. Yet the new pattern is woven in part out of the tensions and self-concepts laid down in the earlier period. Though the swan has all-new feathers, his time as an ugly duckling can be traced in his emotional life. (Once again, we recall Mack as an example.)

Even in the short run, it is hard to predict behavior from knowledge about personality. Prediction fails in part because people are flexible enough to override their "personalities." They can act cheerful when they feel sad, can key themselves up for an exam when they would like to run from it, can join a protesting group even though (or because) they are conformers at heart.

Educational situations vary. Prediction is difficult without knowledge of the person's instructional program. We learned from Domino that the performance of the student with high achievement motivation depends on the tactics of his instructor. To explain Mack's success, the psychologist had to consider Mack's fear of dependency *along with* his passivity and his identification with the powerful. Mack organized his life so as to be independent and assertive within the Establishment. Another person who scored the same as Mack on Ac and Ai might have taken an anti-Establishment route that would produce a poorer record of achievement. A person prone to anxiety may retreat from ambiguous, potentially troublesome situations. But another with the same internal stress may reduce the risks by working hard and taking great pains to check what he does as he proceeds. It might improve prediction of success to take many traits into account at once; but even then, general prediction does not work out (Mischel, 1973). A psychologist who has studied a person thoroughly can say little about his response to school "in general" or about his success in an otherwise unspecified "engineering career." The psychologist *can* make some educationally suggestive predictions about his probable response to *particular* situations. This specificity is hard to document statistically, but a piece of evidence turns up here and there. You will recall Frenkel-Brunswik's description (p. 213) of children who come out of an autocratic home. Haggard (1957) examined a group of bright adolescents with these same symptoms: they were fearful of authority, untrusting, passive, rule-bound, lacking in independent judgment. Their school records showed excellent performance in just two areas: spelling and the mechanics of English. They were near the average in the kinds of achievement that require one to depart from rules and rely on one's own judgment. These unadjusted students had "readiness" for typical instruction in spelling and language, subjects that call for diligent study rather than understanding.

25 Suppose it were found that the man whose personality resembles Mack's tends to succeed in the practice of law to a much greater extent than the man who is more secure and self-accepting. Would it be a good idea to use this information in selecting applicants for law school? In selecting graduates fresh out of law school to join a firm? In advising college students whether to consider a career in law?

26 How might the trait of aggressiveness contribute to the success of some persons and interfere with the success of others? Would situational variables make a difference?

27 Could the high school have served better the boys described as plebeians?

Now in his early forties, Bill Chelten (p. 228) is a nationally prominent executive, head of a large enterprise.

# 6 READING LIST

Howard S. Becker, "Social Class Variations in the Teacher-Pupil Relationship," *Journal of Educational Sociology* 25 (1952), 451–65.

> Interviews with sixty Chicago schoolteachers indicate how children from different backgrounds appear to the teacher, and what problems of classroom discipline and motivation he encounters. Read these reports closely to decide whether the problems are inevitable or are aggravated by school policies and the teacher's attitudes.

Ira J. Gordon, "Assessing the Child's Personality," in *Studying the Child in School* (New York: Wiley, 1966), pp. 89–111.

> Gordon describes the techniques teachers can use—questionnaire, observation, examination of children's writings—to learn more about their personalities and adjustment. Similar techniques can be used at the high-school level. Gordon reproduces complete questionnaires for appraising the self-concept.

Dorothy Lee, "Developing the Drive to Learn and the Questioning Mind," in *Freeing the Capacity to Learn,* ed. A. Frazier (Washington: Association for Supervision and Curriculum Development, 1960), pp. 10–21.

> An anthropologist describes how cultures with strongly established intellectual values—the Oglala Sioux and the eastern European Jews—conveyed those values to the child. These methods succeeded in spite of a faulty educational system.

Jean Walker Macfarlane, "From Infancy to Adulthood," *Childhood Education* 39 (1963), 336–42. Also in Clarizio (1974).

> The several long-term follow-up studies conducted at the Institute of Human Development in Berkeley have contributed much to our knowledge of the continuity of individual differences. Here one of the chief investigators discusses how persons in middle adulthood departed from the predictions that might have been made on the basis of their adjustment and ambition while in school.

Dane G. Prugh, Mary Engel, and William C. Morse, "Definitions and Case Examples," extract from "Emotional Disturbance in Children," in *Issues in the Classification of Children,* vol. 1, ed. N. Hobbs (San Francisco: Jossey-Bass, 1975), pp. 287–96.

> Illustrates the range of emotional reactions found in young people, from healthy responses to a developmental crisis to psychosis.

George D. Spindler, "Beth Anne—A Case Study of Culturally Defined Adjustment and Teacher Perceptions," in *Education and Cultural Process,* ed. G. D. Spindler (New York: Holt, Rinehart and Winston, 1974), pp. 139–53.

> Tells the ironic story of an enterprise in which the teachers of a school set out to learn about their "best-adjusted" children. Beth Anne, selected by the teachers as well adjusted, proved to be a mass of tensions. Beth Anne's defensive motivation was put to work to earn a good school record, at considerable personal cost. Spindler blames her parents' false values, and the teachers' lack of perception, on the "tyranny" of the culture they identify with. Spindler's account illustrates some personality tests and the sociometric technique.

Charles V. Willie, "The Black Family and Social Class," *American Journal of Orthopsychiatry* 44 (1974), 50–60.

> Willie studies the black family as a part of the black community, instead of comparing it to the white family. On the basis of two hundred case studies, he describes family activities and attitudes typical of three income levels.

# ASSESSING ABILITIES

This chapter describes tests used in appraising readiness and in guidance, and describes the relation of abilities to each other and to success. Then I return to a theme from Chapter 2—the school as sorting agency—and examine the guidance policies of schools. Chapter 16 will deal with tests used daily and weekly as a part of instruction and in end-of-year evaluation. Many concepts introduced here will be treated more thoroughly in that chapter.

The teacher has full responsibility for the tests he constructs, and is responsible for making good use of published tests for his subject-field and grade. Scores on tests given for guidance purposes, which are usually made available to the teacher, are helpful in individualizing instruction. Tabulations of the means for class and for school are pertinent to curriculum and policy decisions.

Appraising study skills involves few assumptions and requires little background. This chapter starts with tests of study skills, then turns to tests of "intelligence"—that is, of scholastic aptitude. These tests were invented in the years before 1920, and ever since, laymen and psychologists have been debating what they mean and whether they are fair or introduce bias into educational decisions (Cronbach, 1975b). Chapters 7–9 have much to say about these controversies. After you hear the full story, you may decide that such tests are not a good basis for guiding selection, counseling, and instruction. I shall try, however, to point out the special role certain kinds of "intelligence" tests can play in practical affairs.

Even educators who do not rely on intelligence tests need to think about the research based on them. These tests have contributed a vast body of evidence about individual differences. Comparable studies have at times been made with measures of achievement in reading and other subjects, and these less extensive studies consistently turn up similar findings. Virtually every sound conclusion based on the general mental test is equally true for a comprehensive measure of achievement.

# MEASURING TOOL SKILLS

In every grade, inadequate skills of learning—"tool skills"—cause difficulty for some students. In preschool, some children have not learned to attend to instructions, whereas others have. In the early grades, attending to detail becomes important. In Grades IV and beyond, language skills are the foremost require-

## Locating the elements in "poor reading"

Sometimes a diagnostic report identifies just a few key problems, but Ben had difficulties of all types. The psychologists observed that Ben was emotionally disturbed by reading tasks. Ben's mother felt that her having held a job during Ben's early years left him neglected. Ben's vision had long been faulty; at the time of this diagnostic study, he had just acquired glasses that brought his sight to the normal level. The following extracts from the report of the reading specialist (Otto et al., 1973, pp. 93–95) indicate the faults identified and describe a few of the targeted remedial techniques. Ben gained a reasonable command of the most basic skills in a few weeks.

Ben was instructed in reading for a period of time by his mother, who used a system of intensive phonics instruction. The method includes a series of flash cards with many groups of letters to be memorized. . . . [It] appears likely that a certain amount of confusion would result if a disabled reader were required to memorize the many combinations. It would seem that increased tension and greater frustration would come from trying to learn the combinations and being unable to do so. Ben himself says, "When Mom tried to help me it seems my reading got worse."

. . . [At] the clinic, considerable time was spent in administering formal and informal tests in order to determine specifically the nature of his reading disability and its degree of severity. Ben demonstrated a need for: (1) systematic instruction in the basic reading skills at the primer level; (2) better knowledge of the manuscript alphabet, upper and lower case; (3) multiple methods of word attack; (4)

ment. Others required for educational success include skills in computation, written expression, planning of study, locating information, capitalizing on instructional demonstrations, and reorganizing information into meaningful structures.

## Reading

Educators once took it for granted that high-school and college students could read well enough. Actually, a large fraction of students—even those not particularly "disadvantaged"—are struggling along without the reading skills they need. A textbook assignment that the efficient reader can understand in 30 minutes requires two or three times as long for others in the same college class. In Grades IV–IX, some students are close to being nonreaders.

The teacher can identify some poor readers from their confused contribution in class discussion. He can locate more of them by taking each student off in a corner to hear him read orally. Even a simple group test in which each one marks his place after five minutes of silent reading gives useful information. But a formal test tells more about individuals and about the group.

A commercially published test is convenient, uniform, and satisfactorily precise. Moreover, such tests are issued in comparable forms for different

elimination of reversals such as d and b, q and p, f and j; (5) knowledge of consonant blends; (6) practice in reading stories at his level; and (7) many success experiences.

Ben learned the short vowel sounds with the aid of pictures representing the sound (apple, elephant, Indian, octopus, and umbrella). He referred to these when he could not remember. . . . [Before using] Kirk's Remedial Reading Drills, . . . the short vowel sound was introduced and discussed. Then Ben was asked to read the words in the drill, which were rather simple (i.e., sat, mat, cap, can, sad). In all, there were forty words in Drill I. Ben read the words without error and wrote the words when dictated, missing only one.

Ben practiced printing the alphabet . . . [after] a test revealed that he was confused about the order of the alphabet and the correct shapes of certain letters. He improved with practice.

Ben has developed an overanalytical, letter-by-letter approach to attacking all words. To encourage sight recognition of frequently used words, . . . [a list] of preprimer and primer words was studied with the aid of a tachistoscope [an apparatus for brief controlled exposure]. By the end of the summer program, Ben was able to recall about 85 percent of the words as sight words. Configuration clues were also explained and Ben was encouraged to use them when appropriate. . . .

Ben needs practice in reading fluently and easily in a relaxed situation from materials at the primer level. Perhaps a teacher could be released to give Ben individual instruction in the basic reading skills for about thirty minutes a day.

SOURCE: Corrective and Remedial Teaching by Otto, McMenemy & Smith. Copyright © 1973 by Houghton Mifflin Company. Used by permission of the publisher.

grades, enabling the teacher to collect evidence of a student's progress over the years. The published test is accompanied by tables based on nationwide samples; these enable the teacher to compare his class with other classes in the same grade. When a class reads less well than the norm, the teacher may have to use simpler reading materials than are usual in that grade. If a group is superior, the teacher will not hesitate to offer comparatively difficult reading matter.

Reading tests come in many styles. One test measures speed in reading simple sentences. Another requires comprehension of difficult passages. Some call upon knowledge of uncommon words. In the middle grades and beyond, students who do well on one reading test can be expected to perform adequately on another, though proficiency varies somewhat from task to task (p. 254). For assessing readiness early in the year, the most appropriate test is one whose reading tasks resemble those to be demanded by the materials and methods of instruction.

Before the teacher can help a poor reader, the nature of the student's difficulties has to be pinned down. Some students comprehend well enough but cover the page too slowly. Some who read simple material fluently are baffled by an unfamiliar word, not knowing how to "sound it out" so that they can recognize it. A "poor reader" need not be poor across the board.

Defining faults exactly is referred to as *diagnosis* (box). The standardized test that picks out poor readers should be followed by an analytic study of them. Once the weaknesses are identified, remedial instruction can be planned. Diagnosis in education is concerned not so much with what lies behind faults as with specifying the bad habits and missing skills that hinder the student now.

One step in the diagnosis of reading difficulties is to listen carefully as the student reads aloud, noting errors or pauses. Another everyday technique is to have the student read a page silently and give a brief summary. The page should be one that he could read orally with little trouble. Then failure to identify main points and excessive reliance on the words of the original show that the student has not thought sufficiently while reading.

A specialist in remedial reading uses more highly developed techniques. For example, ability to turn unfamiliar words into sounds can be judged by having the student read any hard passage, but a diagnostician is likely to have a special test list. He would confront college students with artificial words such as *plithograte* and *bineracious;* the student who can break up such visual monstrosities and reassemble the right sounds has excellent "word attack" skills and can surely recognize the printed form of any word he has in his speaking vocabulary. Another diagnostic trick is to have the student read from a book that is lying flat on the table, the observer sitting opposite and watching the reader's eyes in a mirror (also on the table). A skilled reader takes in several words at a glance. His eyes pause only three or four times in each line, and rarely have to jump back to recheck a phrase. The reader whose eyes pause six or more times in each line has not learned to take in whole words or phrases at a glance. Published reading tests help in diagnosis when they offer subscores representing parts of the reading process; but the diagnostician has to supplement these tests with direct observation.

A teacher becomes adept at diagnosing reading (or any other subject) through experience and special training. Because reading failures have been studied intensively for several decades, much is known about diagnosis and remediation. Many techniques used by a reading expert can be adopted by the classroom teacher, although the teacher rarely has time to give the individual supervision required by a reader far below the class norm. Referral of such a child to a reading specialist for thorough diagnosis and special exercises is advisable even when the teacher is able to identify some of the child's problems.

A diagnosis made by the classroom teacher or a specialist helps in selecting focused instructional exercises aimed at developing whatever subskills are weak or absent. Thus, an exercise can be designed to train the student in judging the meaning of a word from its context, in breaking a long word into syllables, or in skimming to get main ideas without reading every word. Once the student understands it, he can polish the technique by practicing it in his everyday reading, usually without a long course of special exercises.

1  Are the purposes of the teacher who tests achievement at the end of the term the same as the purposes of the teacher who tests the same students at the beginning of the next term? Should the tests used on the two occasions be similar?

2  One can distinguish between a student's reading vocabulary, his hearing vocabulary, and his speaking vocabulary. How might an observer or tester measure the size of each of these? Why might a word in the hearing vocabulary not be present in the speaking vocabulary? In the reading vocabulary?

3  *Reading readiness* tests check the five- or six-year-old's ability to compare forms, to compare sounds, to recognize letter shapes, and so on. If these skills are not adequately developed, the child is given training to develop them. Those children who score well, on the other hand, are started directly in reading instruction. A critic (Weber, 1974, p. 9) says:

> . . . these tests . . . do more harm than good. It would be wiser to begin formal reading instruction, as some schools do, by attempting to teach all children the same things, without prejudging or predicting their success. Then, after perhaps a half-year or a year, the pupils could be grouped for further instruction on the basis of their demonstrated achievement.

What justification for readiness testing can be offered? Considering both sides of the issue, what is your conclusion?

## Other Prerequisite Achievements

Summary statements about readiness are often made in terms of scores, but it is important to realize that performance is made up of acts and regulated by concepts. Development has a global side and a specific side. The child becomes generally better at paying attention and combining concepts or acts. He also grasps particular concepts and movements, and stores them up. In targeting instruction, a first step is to identify the specifics that are or are not in the child's repertoire. Table 7.1 is an illustrative list of concepts that Francis Palmer (1969) used in cataloging what 2-year-old black boys entering a preschool program

**TABLE 7.1**

**Concepts in the repertoire of some 2-year-olds**

| Percentage responding correctly | Concept |
| --- | --- |
| 80–89 | on top of<br>into |
| 70–79 | (none in the list used) |
| 60–69 | open<br>out of<br>closed |
| 50–59 | wet |
| 40–49 | down<br>circle<br>full |
| 30–39 | little<br>square<br>empty |
| 20–29 | fat<br>heavy<br>short |
| 10–20 | smooth<br>biggest<br>slow |

SOURCE: F. Palmer (1969), p. 48.
In the full list, more than three concepts fell in each interval below 50 per cent in Palmer's sample of children from impoverished homes. Sixteen concepts fell in the 20–29 per cent range.

knew. The tests—"Give me the *empty* cup"—required the child to understand words but not to say them. The preschool child will know many (not all) of the high-ranking concepts, and he may know a few of those far down the list. The more of them he knows, the more he can profit from conversation. Once the teacher knows which ones the child has in his store, the remainder of the list outlines a curriculum for him.

Information about the older student's mastery of fundamentals can and should be obtained from the reports of previous teachers, but such reports are indefinite at best. Jeff's low mark in arithmetic last year is no more than a warning to the algebra teacher. A descriptive memorandum left in the file by the previous teacher is almost as limited. "Needs drill in fundamentals" gives little guidance. It may be what the teacher writes when the student is erratic in adding (which may not truly indicate that drill is appropriate). The same phrase may be just an exasperated substitute for, "I've tried my best and can't determine where his difficulty lies." Jeff's algebra teacher wants to know more: Is the trouble in Jeff's ability to think through problems, in his computation skills, or in his grasp of particular topics, such as percentage? The teacher has to make his own analysis of students to detect weaknesses that will block progress.

No student is just "poor in arithmetic" or "unable to spell." Even a seemingly general weakness can be broken into a list of critically important faults. If the teacher can locate where the student goes off the track, he can reteach the

**Diagnosis**

*"He's too sick for today's arithmetic test, but well
enough for tomorrow's spelling test."*

Roir—Rothco Cartoons

critical response. Ralph, in bookkeeping, tries to find percentages by guessing which number to divide into the other. The teacher who discovers this fault in procedure has a manageable task of reteaching; there is no hope for Ralph if his teacher does not see beyond "Ralph is weak in arithmetic."

Observation is usually the best basis for the teacher's diagnosis. If an algebra student is confused, the teacher should observe him as he works (preferably aloud). Faulty reading and interpretation of problems, weakness in fundamental concepts, failure to organize work, or erratic computation will be noticed. Skill in diagnostic observation is one of the chief differences between a person who merely knows his subject and one who can teach it well.

Some intellectual difficulties are beyond the teacher's power to diagnose. Nelson (1961) discusses subtle brain damage that will remain unrecognized unless the teacher asks for a specialist's assessment. One sign is writing disturbances. Nelson mentions a 12-year-old who was asked to write from dictation "The weather becomes cold in winter," and wrote "The wearthe become cold in wather." Less severe symptoms of brain damage include short attention span, inflexibility of ideas, and poor sound discrimination. When students show unusual symptoms, the teacher is likely to require the help of physicians, psychologists, speech pathologists, and other special consultants.

**4**  What specific difficulties might be mentioned in a record describing a student who is poor in written expression?

**5**  Does "diagnosing" spelling mean anything other than listing all the words a student misses?

## Study Skills and Work Methods

There are many identifiable skills of study. Map-reading, for example, has quite specific components. The student must comprehend a number of conventions: the placement of *North* at the top of the map, the use of color to indicate altitude, and so on. He has to decode distances with the aid of the scale. In more advanced work, he must allow for distortions of shape introduced by projection. Students fail to profit as they should from their reading in geography until they are taught such skills.

The teacher can take advantage of pertinent measuring instruments such as the "Work-Study Skills" section of the Iowa Tests of Basic Skills (Fig. 7.1). The version designed for Grades I–VIII, contains sections on reading maps; on reading graphs, tables, and charts; and on using indexes and dictionaries. The test also measures language skills and mathematical skills. An instrument of this character

**FIGURE 7.1**

**Items for testing map-reading skills of eighth-graders**

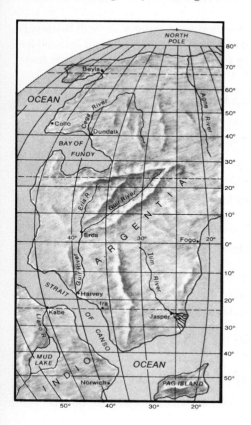

**Which city is located nearest the equator?**

1) Beyla     3) Dundalk
2) Collo     4) Fogo

**Where is the point 23°N. and 34°W. located?**

1) In the ocean
2) In the mountains
3) In a bay
4) On an island

**Which of the following is a true statement about Argentia?**

1) Its western boundary is approximately 57° W.
2) The northern part of the continent is in the Tropics.
3) No part of it lies south of the equator.
4) Much of the western coast is mountainous.

**Which city is farthest east, Beyla or Dundalk?**

1) Dundalk
2) Beyla
3) They are both the same.
4) One cannot tell from the map.

SOURCE: Iowa Tests of Basic Skills, Form 6.
Copyright © 1971 by the University of Iowa.
Reproduced by permission. Map is reduced.

is often administered to every student in a school at the start of the year. All the scores together (the *profile*) indicate the skills in which the student's readiness is well advanced and those in which he needs special help.

Again, informal observations can supplement tests or substitute for them. The teacher who finds a class confused about distances among the American colonies may suspect poor map-reading as a cause; he can check this by an informal exercise. A small assignment in which information must be located reveals gaps in library skills. (Activities to improve such skills will be discussed in Chapters 10–15.)

In some ways more important, and much harder to identify and remedy, are faulty *habits* of work. High-school and college students fail to schedule adequate time for study. Some who organize a theme well for an English class neglect to outline their thoughts before writing a report in another subject. Students check arithmetic in the mathematics classes, where it is demanded, yet turn in erroneous computations in the science laboratory rather than take the trouble of checking.

Making the student critical of his own study practices is usually an objective in Grades IV through VII, but faults persist even in college students. A questionnaire in which the student describes his customary methods of work, a log in which he records his study activities, critical inspection of work in progress—all can be useful in the self-appraisal.

Several studies have compared the questionnaire reports of high achievers and low achievers who have similar mental ability. Among high-school and college students, H. D. Carter (1958) found that the effective students were much more likely to use the following techniques:

> Trying to foresee questions that might be asked about a reading assignment.
>
> Planning an orderly sequence for papers and essay test answers.
>
> Looking for relationships among ideas, within a subject, and from one subject to another.
>
> Drilling oneself deliberately on details in foreign language and geography.
>
> Studying alone when possible.
>
> Studying by reciting material to oneself.
>
> Studying each subject nearly every day.

These statements, put together, picture an active as well as diligent intellectual attack. The effective student tries to understand as much of his assignment as he can, and only then turns to memorization of elusive details (box).

Some techniques that imply diligence but not skilled attack are associated with inferior attainment:

> Repeated reading of the assignment.
>
> Writing down rules of grammar or summaries of chapters of novels.

Copying extensive notes from books.

Talking the lesson over with another person.

There is an air of busywork about these activities; they involve far less deliberate processing of the material to be learned than do the tactics of effective students. Ineffective students find it hard to concentrate because their work seems purposeless or hopelessly difficult. They ignore part of the assigned work if they do not expect to be tested on it. Preoccupied with details, they lose sight of central themes. They wait until the last minute to write a paper, instead of allowing it to mature through successive outlines and drafts. In sum, they are unable to discriminate where to put their effort.

Bad study habits are in large measure created by teaching that rewards mindless work.

> In a social studies class of an elementary school in a well-to-do suburb of one of our great eastern cities, I saw groups of twelve-year-old children doing a "project" on the southeastern states. Each team was gathering facts that might eventually end up on a ... chart.... The fact-gathering was atomized and episodic. Here were the industrial products of North Carolina. There was the list of the five principal cities of Georgia. I asked the children of one team what life would be like and what people would worry about in a place where the principal products were peanuts, cotton, and peaches. The question was greeted as "unfair." (Bruner, 1959.)

## Sense of proportion as an aid to study

College students flock to reading clinics because they are unable to cover their assignments. Perry (1959) describes those coming to the reading clinic at Harvard. They rank in the top 15 per cent of all college freshmen in the nation in reading ability. They work diligently. But when asked to sit down and study a chapter of history as he would for an assignment, only one student in ten makes any effort to look ahead, to read the chapter summary first, or to make sense of the chapter as a whole before slogging off into the marsh of facts.

Further evidence that the students cannot judge what learning is worthwhile appeared when they were asked to grade two essay responses to this test question:

> From 1066–1272, the Norman and Angevin kings laid the foundations of English self-government both by their strengths and by their weaknesses. Discuss. (Twenty minutes)

One essay was as factual as an encyclopedia and as little pointed toward the quotation: any fact, about any king, tossed onto the collection plate. The other was a neat essay going to the heart of the question, with no names of kings or dates of incidents on display. About a third of the students thought the first essay deserved a higher grade, or preferred the second essay and gave the wrong reason. "A C-minus," says Perry, "for the attainment of useless knowledge is perhaps less of a kindness in the long run than congratulations for effort and a clean E for expending it in the wrong game."

**6** The task presented in Fig. 7.1 is a measure of skill for students who have been taught, in geography, to interpret the globe. For the student who has not studied such diagrams it is more nearly an intelligence test. Is it fair to apply the test to both kinds of students as a measure of readiness?

**7** Some students need the ability to read shop drawings. List several specific skills included in this type of readiness.

**8** What explanations can be suggested for the fact that writing down rules of grammar is associated with ineffective study?

## TEST CHARACTERISTICS

Having discussed a few types of tests used in appraising student readiness, I turn to general statements about testing principles. I shall say a few things about mental tests even though their content and purposes have not yet been discussed; descriptive information enters at p. 276.

A person deciding whether to use a test, and which of the available tests of a given kind to employ, must ask two questions:

Does the test give the information I want? That is, is it relevant to my purposes? (*Validity*)

Is the test sufficiently precise? (*Reliability*)

It should be clear from the way the questions are phrased that a test satisfactory for one educational use may not be adequate for another. For example, the simple observations of reading that serve the teacher's week-by-week diagnostic purposes are unreliable, both because they are performed quickly and because the teacher's impressionistic judgment will sometimes be wrong. Even so, they are of great help in devising instructional plans; when they do generate a false suggestion, the plan can be altered with no great waste of effort. Where the decision is not easily reversed—for example, a decision that a student should be moved into a special room for the retarded—only a thorough and precise analysis will suffice.

The purpose in giving a certain test may be primarily descriptive or primarily predictive, or some combination of the two. In college admissions, where the purpose of testing is prediction, the relevant evidence of validity would be that predictions based on the test actually come true. We return to validation of predictions later in the chapter; at this point we concentrate on the validity and reliability of descriptive statements based on tests.

When a test is intended to describe behavior, the question about validity—that is, about relevance—amounts to asking whether the person has been observed in appropriate tasks. The question about reliability amounts to asking whether the sample of behavior taken by the test is large enough to give an accurate measure. However, a test is of no value if it is precise but irrelevant.

## The Test As a Work Sample

A miner who wants to know if there is enough gold in some ore to make it worth bringing to market takes a sample of the ore. When a consumer organization wants to know whether a certain brand of canned peaches is Grade A or Grade B, it samples the total pack of peaches. From the sample the quality of the whole is judged. The teacher who wants to know about all of a student's performance must be content with observing a sample. Testing procedures of psychologists and educators are based on the work-sample principle. Out of all the tasks or topics in an area, a small sample is presented as a test. It is essential that the sample be representative of the defined area (a matter of validity), and large enough so that the results are little affected by accidental factors (a matter of reliability).

Because tests do not always give dependable information, teachers selecting and using tests should take advantage of critical reviews. A review describes a test, gives an expert evaluation of its content and the evidence supporting its interpretation, and summarizes uses for which the test can be recommended. The most important source of reviews is the *Mental Measurements Yearbook,* edited by O. K. Buros (1972 and earlier), which covers tests of personality, achievement, and mental abilities. In a test review, the most important issues are those concerned with validity.

VALIDITY   The tasks in an educational test should represent the domain it intends to measure. A test given to appraise basic competence at the start of the year clearly should appraise the kinds of skill and knowledge the subsequent lessons will call upon. A social studies teacher might use the Iowa test (Fig. 7.1) to determine who is likely to have difficulty in using maps during his course. The test is appropriate only if the map-reading skills required by the test are to be used in the classwork. If technical geographic vocabulary (*Tropic of Capricorn, meridian*) will be needed in class discussions, items covering that vocabulary help to measure readiness. If, instead, the class will be studying trade routes, perhaps items on estimation of distances should appear in the work sample.

A published achievement test covers a broad range of subject-matter. Content is selected by a sampling process akin to drawing ore from various parts of the mountain or drawing the peaches to be examined from different boxes. If the tasks presented by a test are a sample of the situations the student will en-

## Do similar tests tell the same story?

One principal of a small school (Knezevich, 1946) wondered how accurate IQs from a group test were. He investigated by giving the sophomores two similar tests a month apart—first the Henmon-Nelson Test, then the California Test of Mental Maturity. Here is a summary of the IQs:

| Name | Henmon-Nelson | California | Difference |
|---|---|---|---|
| 1. Axton, Doug | 95 | 80 | −15 |
| 2. Barnes, Glenn | 119 | 121 | 2 |
| 3. Borden, May | 109 | 110 | 1 |
| 4. Charles, Ernest | 88 | 86 | −2 |
| 5. Davis, Marshall | 96 | 93 | −3 |
| 6. Duncan, James | 91 | 98 | 7 |
| 7. Edgerton, Dorothy | 87 | 85 | −2 |
| 8. Filson, Donald | 117 | 92 | −25 |
| 9. Gorham, Helen | 98 | 95 | −3 |
| 10. Grant, Lloyd | 127 | 115 | −12 |
| 11. Harris, Cora | 103 | 87 | −16 |
| 12. Howard, Francis | 69 | 107 | 38 |
| 13. Hurt, George | 124 | 106 | −18 |
| 14. Kirk, George | 108 | 104 | −4 |
| 15. Lawrence, Kenneth | 99 | 103 | 4 |
| 16. Lee, Max | 102 | 87 | −15 |
| 17. Logan, Gertrude | 99 | 97 | −2 |
| 18. Meadow, Adolph | 99 | 104 | 5 |
| 19. Olsen, Ralph | 110 | 100 | −10 |
| 20. Petersen, Lola | 118 | 118 | 0 |
| 21. Pollack, Mary | 107 | 99 | −8 |
| 22. Sanders, Willa | 103 | 94 | −9 |
| 23. Smith, Viola | 105 | 88 | −17 |
| 24. Stroup, Guy | 95 | 84 | −11 |
| 25. Tanner, Charles | 93 | 83 | −10 |
| 26. Thompson, Jerry | 101 | 92 | −9 |
| 27. Vance, Marie | 122 | 116 | −6 |
| 28. Wilson, William | 123 | 114 | −9 |

If only the first test had been given, teachers would expect Doug Axton to do normal work. If they had only the second measure, they would probably regard him as a borderline case, unable to carry a regular high-school program. Francis Howard is certain to have learning problems according to the first measure, but is classed as normal by the second. Two reading tests or two English tests would disagree to about the same extent.

counter in the future, and the responses credited are like those needed in the future, the test is a valid basis for description. The judgment about validity is based primarily on the content of the test—the items, and what the scorer or observer looks for in the response. Consequently, we speak of *content validity*. (The content validity of course examinations will be discussed further in Chapter 16. Another important aspect of interpretation—stability over time—is discussed in Chapter 8.)

RELIABILITY   No sample gives perfect information. A test presents only a fraction of the questions that might be asked. Any single test is only an estimate based on a sample of performance; other questions, another day, or another examiner would produce a somewhat different score. Accuracy of interpretation is increased by using especially long tests, by retesting when there is reason to regard a score as unrepresentative of a student's ability, and by considering the score alongside other factors about ability.

Test publishers report information on test accuracy in the form of a standard error of measurement and a reliability coefficient. At this point I give just enough background for you to interpret such information. Chapter 8 examines typical findings on reliability. Chapter 16 (p. 699) has more to say about the accuracy of tests teachers construct.

A person would be measured far more reliably by an average of many equivalent tests given on many days. The more test scores combined in his average, the more nearly it approaches what can be called his "true" score. The error of measurement in an observed score is the difference between it and the person's true score. The average error is zero, since errors are both positive and negative. Since it is impractical to measure a person exhaustively, his true score is unknown, and so is the error in a particular score.

The tester can find out how large *typical* errors are, however. A standard deviation (p. 117) indicates how widely a set of numbers scatter. The standard error of a test is simply the standard deviation of errors of measurement. By making certain assumptions, we can estimate this from a study that applies the measure twice to the same persons. The standard error of the IQs in the box is about seven points. (When two forms of the *same* mental test are given, the standard error is likely to be smaller, perhaps five IQ points.)

Students who have true scores of 120, for example, will have observed scores that scatter on both sides of 120. How much the scores scatter is described by the rule used earlier with standard deviations: About two-thirds will fall within one standard error of the true score; about 95 per cent will fall within two standard errors of the true score. With a standard error of 7 points, and a true score of 120, about two-thirds of the observed scores will fall between 113 and 127 (120 − 7, 120 + 7). Only 5 per cent are expected to fall outside the range 106–134 (120 ± 14).

The test user looks up the standard error in the test manual. When the standard error is given as seven score points, the user is warned that a difference of three or four points between two students means nothing; their scores are wandering around the true values and the difference might be reversed on another test. (Consider Marshall Davis and James Duncan in the box.) The user is also given a basis for interpretation: for example, a person with an IQ well above average, such as 120, is most unlikely to have a true IQ of 100 or lower; but the user cannot be sure that the true IQ is better than 110.

All this sounds rather technical. The important thing is to be aware that the true score is unknown and unknowable. A measurement locates a region with shadowy boundaries within which the person probably falls; it does not locate him at an exact point. For practical purposes, the person who reads in a test manual "The standard error of measurement is $x$ points" need only remember that errors up to $x$ points are common, and that errors as large as $3x$ occur very rarely.

The standard error and the standard deviation together enable us to calculate the reliability coefficient. Another way to calculate this coefficient is simply to correlate the two independent measurements. For the best published tests of ability, coefficients are near 0.90 for two forms of the test given a week or so apart. The interpretation of such coefficients is discussed more fully on p. 308. For now, I add only that short tests or tests much affected by the person's mood have relatively large standard errors and rather low coefficients. (A test with a small standard error will have a low coefficient if the persons under study are nearly uniform in performance. The low coefficient indicates that the test does not give accurate *rankings*.)

A test with moderate reliability is often worth using. It can give useful predictions. It can raise questions to be pursued in further work with the individual. It can give a go-ahead for students who are clearly proficient, while leaving decisions about the remaining students to be determined by a more thorough test.

---

**9** Is a composition on the assigned topic "A Happy Holiday" a valid and accurate work sample of ability to write well?

**10** How would the concepts of validity and reliability apply to the following statement by a teacher: "According to what I observe, when Julie is supposed to be studying, her attention is on her work only about half the time."

**11** Suppose that the standard error of the Henmon-Nelson IQ is 6 points. How many of the students in Knezevich's study (box, p. 266) evidently had true Henmon-Nelson IQs below 100?

**12** Colleges usually ask the high school to provide a rating of seniors who apply for admission. How can the reliability and validity of such information be studied? What factors would lower the accuracy of ratings?

---

# Norms

In selection and guidance, test scores are generally compared to norms. (Regarding norms in evaluation, see p. 726.) If, on an interest questionnaire, Anna expresses liking for 18 "persuasive" activities (soliciting funds, selling subscriptions, convincing voters) out of 30, we cannot immediately say whether this is an unusually strong interest or a weak one. No one enjoys every activity in a category. The counselor therefore takes the responses of others into account. If Anna's 18 is much above average for girls of her age, we can think of her as exceptionally likely to enjoy persuasive activity. But the average is not the sole basis for judgment. It could be argued that liking only 18 out of 30 activities is a rather low level of enthusiasm, even though *comparatively* it is high (Cronbach, 1970, p. 487).

The teacher using a published test often has recourse to norms based on a national sample from the same age and grade. Such norms show how difficult the test proved to be for typical students. They guard against the teacher's possible tendency to have unreasonably high expectations for his class.

The norm table given by the publisher converts the student's raw score to a grade equivalent, an age equivalent, a percentile, or a standard score. The raw score is the number obtained by applying the scoring key to the test. Usually it is a count of the number of right answers.

If Fred's reading matches that of the average beginning third-grader, his score could be reported as a grade equivalent of 3.0. (See also p. 729.) If it matches the average of 9-year-olds, his age-equivalent score is 9.0. The mental age (MA) is an age-equivalent scale. A child's MA is the age at which the average child earns the same raw score as he does.

The percentile scale is the one most often useful to teachers. The percentile scale is a ranking, expressed on a scale from 1 (low) to 99. A raw score at the sixtieth percentile exceeds the raw scores of 60 per cent of the persons in the reference group. One may calculate percentile standing within a single class, or within a national sample of students from a certain grade, and so on.

Another reference scale, not as often encountered by teachers, is the standard score. On the usual standard score scale, the average raw score is arbitrarily set equal to 50, and whatever raw score is one standard deviation (s.d.) above the average is converted to a standard score of 60. A standard score of 80, then, is immediately interpretable as falling 3 s.d. above the mean of the reference group.

Standard scores serve much the same purpose as percentiles. When scores are normally distributed (p. 117), the two correspond as shown in Fig. 7.2. The figure also shows that IQs are a type of standard score. Instead of setting the average equal to 50, the IQ scale sets it at 100. And instead of adding 10 points for each standard deviation, the IQ scale adds 16 points. An IQ of 132 indicates that the student's raw score is two s.d. above the mean for his age group. (This unique scale has a 60-year history; the quotient was originally obtained in a different manner. The only reason for using the IQ scale rather than percentiles or ordinary standard scores is that teachers and laymen are now familiar with IQs.)

Figure 7.2 is helpful in answering such questions as these:

Jeff's IQ is 120. His mechanical comprehension is reported as at the 80th percentile. How do these scores compare?

Is Jerry's standard score of 75 on a test of modern-language aptitude unusual?

Equal steps on the standard score scale do not correspond to equal steps on the percentile scale. A shift from the 95th to the 99th percentile ordinarily implies a large difference in standard score and in raw score. Because there are few cases toward the extremes of the distribution, neighboring ranks represent sizable differences in ability.

Both the standard score and the percentile compare the student's performance to that of others of the same age or grade. So does the IQ. In comparing students of *mixed* age, the raw score or the mental age serves better. Consider three girls in Grade VI. Ethel is 10½ years old, Ruth is 12, and Joan is 13. (Such differences arise through variation in admission and promotion policies, transfers from school to school and loss of time through illness, and other causes.) If these girls solve exactly the same problems on a scholastic aptitude test, they will have the same raw score and the same MA—say, 13. According to this test, they have equal readiness for the school year to come. Whereas their minds seem well matched at present, their standard scores and IQs differ

## FIGURE 7.2

### Relations among three score scales

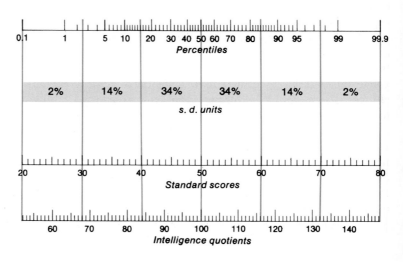

because each girl is compared to a different age group. Ethel's IQ is about 120, Ruth's is 107, and Joan's is 100. When the group is uniform in age, of course, the IQ ranks the girls the same as the raw score or the MA does.

Children with the same MA are not "just alike" mentally. A child of low IQ earns most of his points from test items that call for trainable responses. A younger child of average IQ can earn the same number of points by passing more of the items that require adaptation and judgment. The performance of the two at this time is scored as a tie, but they are not winning the same events.

**13** MAs of 12-year-olds spread much more widely than those of 6-year-olds. Why?

**14** Interpret each of the scores in the following statements as fully as possible using Figure 7.2.
  a. Pete is at the 40th percentile for his grade.
  b. Steve has a standard score of 75.
  c. Mike has an IQ of 110 and is 10 years old.

**15** Both Donna and Lita have grade-equivalent scores of 7.0. Donna is in Grade IV and Lita in Grade X. Are they equal in ability?

## Motivational Influences in Ability Tests

The score on an "ability test" reflects feelings and habits. The student asked to trace the path through a printed maze, for example, may be painstakingly cautious and earn a poor time score. Or the student may recklessly cut across corners—because he wants to get the test over with or because he does not realize that inaccuracy will be penalized.

The ability test has to be regarded as a sample of what the person does in a school setting, where he is responding with ordinary school motivation. For the great majority of children who have become adjusted to school, this motivation is adequate to elicit a sample of the student's normal efficiency. If the student is resistant to authority, however—as might be true of a delinquent sent in for a psychological examination—or if he is too cautious, his score is likely to suffer. The test has accurately assessed his performance under test conditions. It is likely that on another test he would do much the same. It is also likely that he will have difficulty in other encounters with authority where his resistance or overcaution impair performance. While the test gave valid data, the interpretation that the person "lacks ability" is not to be trusted. The fact is that he did not *display* ability.

A child who would be able to do what is called for if he made the right kind of effort may "fail" a test. Sioux Indian children seem to be unable to report the content of simple pictures, whereas white children from lower-middle-class homes could do this task easily. When the abilities of the Sioux children were eventually brought out by a patient examiner, it turned out that they could interpret pictures without difficulty (Elkind, 1969).

Labov (1970) makes a similar report about the ghetto black. When questioned in a standardized but nonthreatening situation, even when the interviewer himself is black, the 8-year-old is likely to convey an impression of poor intellectual and linguistic development. He gives one-word answers and rarely develops a thought. But what happens when the interviewer goes round to the child's home and starts a conversation when he, the boy, and one or two of his friends are lounging on the floor around a heap of potato chips? Then the boy turns out to be fluent—though he talks in the ghetto dialect. The ghetto child, says Labov, sees formal interactions (including conversations at school) as encounters with an inimical culture. Feeling that open expression of his thoughts would expose him to ridicule or criticism, he responds as little as possible. The formal test is a valid sample of verbal performance in situations resembling the present school. A low score, however, does not show a lack of "verbal ability." The big question is: What ability does the child show when at ease?

In an individual test the tester notes the extent to which impulsiveness, overcaution, resistance, and other expressions of personality enter into an ability score. The teacher who gives a group test does not observe individual style, and may fail to realize that the performance is an expression of the person as a whole. Even a reading or arithmetic test is influenced by the person's self-confidence and by the extent to which he accepts the ideal of doing his best.

PRODUCTION DEFICIENCIES   The person who might be intellectually capable of carrying out a task, and willing to try, will do it badly if he chooses a bad technique. Moely et al. (1969) apply the term *production deficiency* to poor scores that are traceable primarily to an inappropriate style.

If we ask children to memorize word pairs, the ones who form meaningful connections between paired words will remember more pairs. It is not hard for a schoolchild to make up a sentence connecting, say, *tree* and *bed*. Many children who do badly on the paired-associates task improve their scores after the sentence-building technique is suggested. The advice, which changes the task from meaningless to meaningful, "raises ability" in only a superficial sense; the passive style is what changes.

Production deficiency arises in part simply from misunderstanding of the task, or failure to realize what the observer will pay attention to. This difficulty may be overcome by adequate instructions. For example, advising the person that the penalty for a wrong answer is not severe, that he should offer his best answer to every item, will overcome some deficiencies. Similarly, if the person tracing a path through a maze is told that the neatness of his line does not matter, but that he should avoid crossing over any of the walls, he will come nearer to earning his best score. In assessing ability, there is no advantage in leaving a task ambiguous.

## A psychological examiner's report

A Puerto Rican 3-year-old in New York City was tested (in Spanish) by a psychologist who wrote the following report for the file (Hertzig et al., 1968, p. 39). Under some circumstances (for example, an older child failing to make progress in reading), the report would include results of more tests and would be more diagnostic.

> The child smiled and answered the examiner's greeting when the latter arrived at her home to take her to the office for testing. She contentedly said good-bye to her grandmother. Later she entered the office and the playroom matter-of-factly, with a brisk step.
>
> During testing she was aware of environmental sounds and had to be reminded frequently to return to the task demands. Although she was pleasant, she required encouragement because she often resisted items and expressed a desire to be finished with the test. She had a short attention span and was not absorbed in the test. Throughout, she persisted in her interest in toys and in her desire to stop the testing.
>
> She appeared to have some difficulty in understanding instructions. At times she anticipated them, but more often she did not listen. She often appeared to be asking for help as she looked at the examiner's face for a cue to whether or not she was answering correctly. Her speech is immature with respect to diction—she leaves out the initial syllables of many words.
>
> On the Revised Stanford-Binet, Form L, Spanish-language version, she achieved a mental age of 2 years 11 months and an IQ of 90. . . . [As harder tasks were reached,] she consistently rejected tasks and expressed the desire not to do any more. She is functioning within the average range of intelligence. Her vocabulary score is consistent with her mental age. She was prevented from passing certain items by her failure to listen to instructions before making answers.
>
> In summary, she is an attractive 3-year-old functioning within the average range of intelligence, as measured by her performance on the Revised Stanford-Binet, Form L; her orientation seems to be primarily toward people rather than tasks.

Not all production deficiencies are easily removed. As I said earlier, the test-taker is unlikely to extend himself unless he believes that success is within his reach. Production deficiencies that express personality rather than technique are not mere errors of measurement. A person who applies an inappropriate style to a test when he knows the recommended technique will, very likely, adopt the same style in his schoolwork, and hence the low score implies lack of readiness.

## MEASURING SCHOLASTIC APTITUDE

If one wants to know how well a third-grader will do in a two-week unit introducing the metric system, and where he will have trouble, the most direct indication would be given by a test covering the ideas and skills the lessons will call upon. One might check up on reading, ability to count and add, ability to use a ruler marked in inches, and understanding of weight and volume. Such detailed assessment of readiness is carried out by informal techniques as a teacher embarks upon a new unit. A broader perspective is needed in making plans for a year or more. A survey test of achievement in the basic school subjects predicts how rapidly a group is likely to proceed, and how individuals are likely to rank within the group. Achievement tests, then, can give a satisfactory estimate of group or individual readiness for most kinds of instruction.

Other tests used to assess probable success can conveniently be referred to as *scholastic aptitude tests*. Some of these tests are no more than composite measures of reading comprehension, arithmetic reasoning, and perhaps English usage. Some present tasks having little to do with schooling—mazes, for example. It is a mistake to think of "aptitude tests" or "intelligence tests" as measuring something unique; as we shall see, the tests that present novel problems rank most children about the same as achievement tests do. The two kinds of test have similar relationships to home background, to subsequent success, and even to parents' ability.

The name "intelligence" is especially misleading because these tests cannot assess the intellectual power a person "was born with." Originally, "intelligence" meant little more to psychologists than "effective performance in tasks requiring control through concepts and mental images"; in fact, Binet's research reports that led to the first significant test were published under the title "Attention and Adaptation." Some of the meanings that have come to be associated with the term "intelligence" are insupportable. Some people want to think of an inherited "potential" or "capacity," mystical as those notions are.

The very idea of "capacity" as an upper limit to performance is false. There is a limit to the difficulty of the problems a person is able to solve, given his life history. But some other treatment (a different prenatal diet for his mother? training in symbolic logic at age 7? anxiety-relieving drugs?) surely could have raised his performance. So long as the way is open to invent better conditions of development, no one knows the limit of human potentialities.

Tests measure the intellectual skills a person now has and uses—nothing more. Whenever he tries to learn or to understand something, he can put certain of these skills to use: breaking wholes into parts, making careful comparisons, putting what he observes into words, holding an idea in mind, and so on. Most of these skills develop without direct teaching, out of the person's total experience. A person who commands these intellectual tools can of course do better schoolwork than one who lacks them.

Measuring intellectual skills one at a time is not very practical. A task calls upon several skills at once (p. 694). Moreover, abilities go together. Superior ability to learn meaningful material is associated with superior comprehension of ideas and superior reasoning. Superiority in vocabulary is associated with superiority at jigsaw puzzles. A person who does better than average in one school subject has a high probability of doing better than average in other subjects. The correlation between performances on two intellectual tasks will be far from perfect, but the various skills do go together and hence it is profitable to think of a single, comprehensive scholastic aptitude.

McClelland (1973, p. 9), among others, dissents from this position. Testing efforts should develop a detailed profile of specific competences, he says. As one example, he speaks of abilities required by the millman in the lumber industry: ability to measure angles, to sharpen tools, and to identify sizes and types of fasteners by using gauges and charts. Such microanalysis is useful in monitoring instruction (p. 685) and in deciding whether the trainee is ready to move onto the job. Such data (collected before training) are not likely to yield a prediction of success different from that given by a general ability test. The person who has been learning from the culture in the past is the one who will take the specifics of a new task in stride. Hence one broad sample of present accomplishments predicts as well as another. It is in *diagnosis* that the specifics become important.

"Intelligence" is not a thing, it is a style of work. To say that one person is "more intelligent" than another means that he acts more intelligently, more of the time. "Efficiency" is a word of the same type. We cannot locate the efficiency of a factory in any one part of the operation. Rather, the purchasing division, the people who maintain the machines, and the operators, inspectors, and shippers do their tasks with few errors and little lost time; efficiency is an index of how well the system functions as a whole. After Binet had observed excellent and inferior intellectual performance of children, he summed up the difference in this famous three-part description of intelligence:

> the tendency to take and maintain a definite direction;
> the capacity to make adaptations for the purpose of attaining a desired end;
> the power of auto-criticism. (Translation by Terman, 1916, p. 45.)

The first point has to do with accepting a task and keeping one's mind on it. The second point contrasts intelligent behavior with acting out of habit, with little analysis of the immediate situation. The third emphasizes that better performers prevent errors before they occur or catch them promptly when they are made.

**16** Does the maze task, in which one must trace the correct path through a confusing layout, test all three of Binet's elements? Does the maze task assess *scholastic* aptitude?

**17** Does Binet's definition distinguish intellect from personality?

**18** Can any of Binet's three elements be developed through education?

**19** In the past generation, mankind has extended human life expectancy into the 80's, the human range of observation to the dark side of the moon, and the speed of calculation by a factor of millions. Could one speak of human "capacity" for long life? For distant observation? For speed in calculating?

# Tasks used by Wechsler to assess mental abilities

## VERBAL SCALE

*Information*

**How many nickels make a dime?**
**Who wrote** ***Paradise Lost*?**

*Similarities*

**In what way are an** ***hour*** **and a** ***week*** **alike?**

*Arithmetic*

**Sam had three pieces of candy, and Joe gave him four more.**
**How many pieces of candy did Sam have all together?**

*Vocabulary*

**What does** ***bicycle*** **mean?**
**What does** ***obliterate*** **mean?**

*Comprehension* [Understanding of everyday affairs]

**What should you do if you see someone forget his book when he leaves his seat in a restaurant?**

*Digit Span*

**Say back to examiner: 4–7–1–5–3.**
**Say these numbers backward: 8–3–2–7.**

## PERFORMANCE SCALE

*Picture Completion*

**Find the missing part.** [For example, buttonholes in a coat]

*Picture Arrangement*

**Arrange in sensible order to tell a story.** [Three to five pictures]

*Block Design*

**Copy the pattern.** [Arranging cubes; see picture, next page]

*Object Assembly*

**Put the pieces together.** [For example, eight pieces that make up a face]

*Coding*

**Fill in the symbols rapidly.** [Nine numerals and symbols]

*Mazes*

**Trace, with few or no errors, the path through the maze.**

SOURCE: Certain of the items used by courtesy of the publisher, The Psychological Corporation.

## Tests Given Individually

The Wechsler scales are used more often than any other individual test; virtually everything we say about them applies also to the older Stanford-Binet Scale, save that the Binet does not offer separate Verbal and Performance IQs. Individual tests figure in much of the best research on intellectual development. Individual tests are used primarily in the intensive study of those who are having difficulty in adjustment, in school or elsewhere. As a greater variety of tasks can be used, there is more chance to enlist the interest of the subject and more chance to observe the nature of difficulties. The individual test is almost as important as an opportunity for observation by a skilled clinician as it is for the score it yields.

The Wechsler scales (WPPSI for ages 4–6½, WISC-R for ages 6–16, WAIS for ages 16 and up) are organized into subtests, each with a different task. Half the tasks are *performance tests,* in which responses call for little verbal expression. The illustrative items in the box are simulated to resemble those actually in the test.

The subject can earn a high score on the Verbal Scale by calling on information familiar to most persons who have participated fully in the culture, by discriminating what is most relevant, and by expressing thoughts clearly and accurately. You might think that some responses require sheer recall of associations, but Estes (1974) has pointed out that even simple tests require complex intellectual activities. A good answer on a vocabulary item requires the person

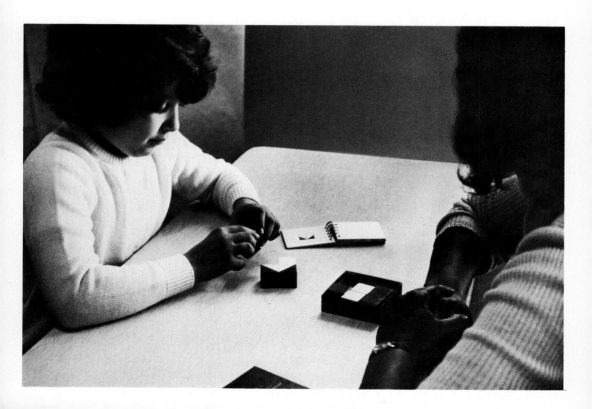

# What response deserves credit?

Rules for scoring psychological tests are worked out with great care to ensure that all examiners apply almost precisely the same standard, and to make sure that there is a real difference between the responses that get credit and those that do not.

   Below are reproduced the instructions for scoring a portion of a test for preschool children. The child is asked to copy first a circle, then a vertical line. As you can see, many of the responses given full credit are "incorrect," but they appear to show that the child has grasped the essential point. Scoring decisions are backed up by research; the test developer had to look at other behavior of the children who gave responses like C to Task 1 before deciding that that clearly "wrong" response was superior to responses I, J, K, and L.

1. ◯

CRITERIA:
- The drawing is a *curved* figure, even if heart-shaped [**B**], apple-shaped [**D**], etc. It may be a circle that wraps around itself [**F**], or one where the starting and/or finishing points lie outside the circle [**C** and **E**]. Do *not* credit a circle which contains scribbled lines [**I**].
- The circle is at least ¾ closed. (**G** barely passes this criterion, whereas **K** fails.)

Score 1 if *both* of the above criteria are met.
Score 0 if only one (or neither) of the above criteria is met.

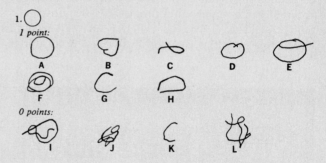

2. |

CRITERIA:
- The line is approximately vertical (i.e., it varies from the vertical by not more than 30 degrees), but it may be slightly curved or broken. (**C** varies about 30 degrees from the vertical and barely passes. **B** is as broken, and **D** is as curved, as a line may be in order to pass this criterion.)
- The line measures at least ¼ inch and is no longer than twice the length of the examiner's sample.

Score 1 if *both* of the above criteria are met.
Score 0 if only one (or neither) of the above criteria is met.

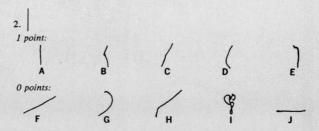

SOURCE: Manual for the McCarthy Scales of Children's Abilities (McCarthy, 1975, pp. 98–99). Copyright © 1970, 1972 by The Psychological Corporation. Reproduced by permission.

to recall associations. But he must also bring out the features of meaning that distinguish the word from others: for example, a *festival* is not just a holiday. The individual must, Estes notes, have in his mind a standard for acceptable answers, and must judge his provisional tries against the standard before he commits himself out loud.

> For a child who has grown up in a more or less average home environment with numerous opportunities and occasions to inquire concerning the meaning of words and to have these explained . . . this requirement is [not troublesome]. . . . A child who has not had these opportunities will lack the basis for corrective feedback of his production. (Estes, 1974, p. 746.)

Thus the precision of thought in the home, and the standards taught there, can have as much effect as the parents' vocabulary itself (p. 494).

Even the Coding subtest, which correlates relatively low with other mental tests, requires more than rote recall. The successful performer, says Estes, breaks the string of numbers into "chunks" of perhaps three numbers each, and then stores the sequence of chunks in his memory. On recall, he has to reconstruct the sequence. The person who merely relies on a kind of phonographic memory, without reorganizing the materials for temporary storage, will not be able to handle long strings or the task of saying the string backward.

The most interesting of the performance tests is Block Design. It calls for a high level of analysis and intellectually regulated performance, yet it does not draw upon school learning or verbal expression. Such tasks are particularly helpful in assessing children who have verbal handicaps. The performance tasks are more diverse in their psychological demands than the verbal tasks, but there is considerable overlap among them, and comparatively little overlap with the verbal tasks (Kaufman, 1975).

---

**20** Binet, whose pioneer work created the first useful general mental test, thought that the principal characteristic that distinguishes the bright person from the one who has merely mastered his school lessons is "judgment." Can judgment be regarded as an intellectual capacity, independent of motivation?

**21** A woman occasionally recalls that in school she did not do as well as she could have on tests in arithmetic and mathematical reasoning, working carelessly or leaving the test unfinished. Her reason, she says, was that the group would have been hostile toward any girl who showed herself to be brilliant in this "masculine" subject. What are the implications of this story for junior-high-school counselors and teachers? Do the tests have any use in such cases?

**22** "The individual test is almost as important as an opportunity for observation as it is for the score it yields." Illustrate this by reference to the box (p. 273). Do you think the clinician gave a fair appraisal of the Puerto Rican girl?

---

## Group Tests

A group test is limited to items that can be administered by reading simple directions and answered by a mark on paper. Except for a few tests designed for the early grades, group tests are in a multiple-choice form that can be scored mechanically. Objective, high-speed scoring is especially important in testing for college admissions, where thousands of scores must be compiled.

The Scholastic Aptitude Test (SAT) of the College Entrance Examination Board is representative. It has separately scored verbal and quantitative sections. The verbal items call for judicious use of vocabulary. Items* such as the following will, it is hoped, favor the intellectually competent student over the one who has merely crammed his head with uncommon words.

---

**Find the word that is most clearly opposite in meaning:**

**COMPOSURE:**

   (a) analysis   (b) alertness   (c) contrast
   (d) agitation   (e) destruction

---

**Find pairs similar or parallel in nature:**

**CRUTCH : LOCOMOTION**

   (a) paddle : canoe   (b) hero : worship   (c) horse : carriage
   (d) spectacles : vision   (e) statement : contention

---

Correct answers: d, d.

In another type of verbal item, the student selects the best of several interpretations for a paragraph from college text material.

The quantitative section calls for mathematical reasoning (box). Students with two years of high-school mathematics will have had experience with the mathematical principles required to solve the problems; the task is to use well the principles they know. The information given has to be assembled in just the right way to get the correct answer.

It can be seen that the SAT is very nearly a work sample of the interpretation and problem solving required in college, leaving out knowledge of specific subject matter. A person who does poorly on these tests is likely to have similar difficulty with college assignments.

Scholastic aptitude tests for lower grades are sometimes much like the SAT. They measure developed abilities (for example, reasoning with fractions, word usage) that can be turned directly to use in comprehending tomorrow's lesson. Sometimes the tasks are varied, ranging from school-like items to "non-

---

* From *About the SAT*, College Entrance Examination Board. Reprinted by permission of the Educational Testing Service, the copyright owner.

## Quantitative aptitude—more than mathematical achievement?

The Scholastic Aptitude Test of the College Entrance Examination Board is intended to measure ability to think quantitatively. The illustrative items shown below are from the mathematical section of the text; they do not directly echo high-school lessons in mathematics.

If 16 × 16 × 16 = 8 × 8 × P, then P =
  (A) 4   (B) 8   (C) 32   (D) 48   (E) 64

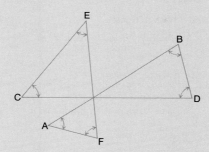

In the triangles above, if AB, CD, and EF are line segments, what is the sum of the measures of the marked angles?

  (A) 180°   (B) 360°   (C) 540°   (D) 720°
  (E) It cannot be determined from the information given.

*Directions:* Each question in this section consists of two quantities; one in Column A and one in Column B. You are to compare the two quantities and on the answer sheet blacken space

  A if the quantity in Column A is the greater;
  B if the quantity in Column B is the greater;
  C if the two quantities are equal;
  D if the relationship cannot be determined from
     the information given.

|  | *Column A* | *Column B* |
|---|---|---|
|  | $5x = 0$ | |
| 1. | 1 | x |
|  | $k^2 = 4$ and $j^2 = 9$ | |
| 2. | k | j |

**Correct answers: E, B, A, D.**

SOURCE: *About the SAT,* College Entrance Examination Board. Reprinted by permission of the Educational Testing Service, the copyright owner.

verbal" tasks independent of past schooling. The Cognitive Abilities Test (CAT; Thorndike & Hagen, 1971) is representative of those used at school ages. One group of tasks provides a Verbal score; the subtests assess vocabulary knowledge, choice of words to complete sentences, and verbal reasoning. The relevance of information as well as reasoning is evident in these items for use around Grade V:

---

**COMPLETE:**

I find it hard to decide _____ to go or not.

    A. whether  B. how  C. but  D. when  E. if

---

**WHICH GOES WITH THESE?**

maple      elm      beech      walnut

    A. oak  B. wood  C. palm  D. fir  E. tree

---

The Quantitative section has items that require reasoning about numerical relations.

---

**Which is larger: 10 dimes or 15 nickels?**

---

**Which number should come next?**

2    2    3    3    4    —

    A. 3  B. 4  C. 5  D. 6  E. 7

---

The Nonverbal section (Fig. 7.3) makes little use of schooling or of verbal understanding. Success depends on ability to reorganize the stimuli conceptually, checking one's thinking with care. A test of this sort, requiring controlled manipulation of ideas, undoubtedly measures intellectual development. In order to emphasize the pattern of abilities, the CAT does not report a total score or IQ. The three parts are, however, influenced by an underlying common factor (Thorndike & Hagen, 1974).

---

 **23** Comment on the following statement: "Success on the so-called nonverbal task usually requires a verbal-encoding process." (Compare Estes, 1974.)

---

## FIGURE 7.3

**Specimen items from the Nonverbal section of the Cognitive Abilities Test**

Complete instructions for each test, read aloud by the teacher, are elaborate and include practice items.

*Figure Classification*

**How are the figures at the left alike? Which drawing on the right belongs with them?**

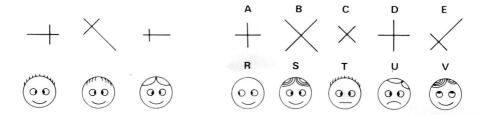

*Figure Analogies*

**The first two drawings are related in some way. Find one on the right that goes with the third drawing in the same way.**

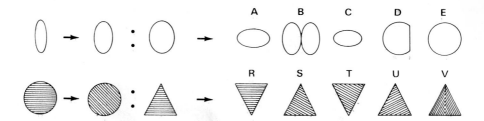

*Figure Synthesis*

**Which of the shaded shapes can you make using the two black pieces?**

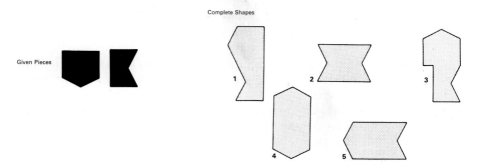

# THE VARIETIES OF MENTAL ABILITY

Most discussion of mental ability speaks of the IQ or of "scholastic aptitude"; that is, it looks on ability as a *general,* all-round competence. A typical composite measure does identify persons likely to succeed in most kinds of instruction. But more specific abilities are also significant. The would-be architect, for example, has to do considerable mathematical work. In engineering drawing, he must reason about shapes and structures. And he calls upon artistic and creative abilities. Hence superior general academic ability is not enough to make a superior architect.

This reference to plural abilities may seem to contradict the earlier statement that mental abilities hang together. But it is true both that (a) most students who do well in one subject do better than the average in other subjects, and that (b) each student does better in some kinds of work than in others. When verbal and numerical abilities, for example, are measured separately, they correlate 0.40–0.70, a moderate relation that supports both Statement a and Statement b.

The pattern of performances has little educational significance until age 14 or later, except to the clinical diagnostician. (He may be asked to assess possible brain dysfunction or sensory defect in a child of age 4. The profile of subtest scores on the Wechsler Preschool Scale gives clues to the clinician, and he can add information from more specialized tests.)

## Ability to Learn

Psychologists have long debated whether the commonplace scholastic aptitude test really measures "ability to learn." Early testers thought this obvious. Test scores have a strong relation to subsequent success in school; and a person with a larger vocabulary, a greater ability to express himself, and a habit of checking his own work for errors will do better in schoolwork. But some of this correlation arises because the person who has learned more in the past has a head start toward the goals of this year's learning. What happens in learning new matter, where everyone starts from scratch?

The weight of evidence now comes down strongly in support of the view that those who do well on mental tests or tests of past achievement are—on the average—superior at meaningful learning. It was once thought, for example, that programmed instruction—which leads the person by very small steps from the most elementary ideas to complex conclusions—would work as well for dull students as for bright ones. Since this system of instruction has infinite "patience" and limited objectives, it is true that with sufficient time everyone can learn the material. The time needed to master it, however, does correlate with ability. When the instructional time is limited, the amount acquired from lessons (programmed or not) usually correlates with tested ability (Cronbach & Snow, 1977). The children who do well on ability tests seem to have just a small average advantage on any one learning task. One small advantage after another is not to be dismissed as trivial, however; advantages probably add up to a considerable superiority in school learning. Each extra bit of success supplies some extra advantage on the next lessons dealing with the same topic.

Strictly rote learning does not correlate consistently with performance on conceptual skills, with knowledge, or with broad measures of aptitude. On the basis of this finding, Jensen (1969) once suggested that the school ought to use rote methods to teach reading and arithmetic to children who are average or better at rote learning, and not so strong in conventional aptitudes. Present evidence does suggest that 6-year-olds of MA 5 are likely to respond to rote instruction about as well as those of MA 7. Rote teaching of words or number combinations does, in a sense, "overcome the handicap" of the Low-MA pupils—but that may not be sufficient to justify Jensen's recommendation. One wonders whether rote instruction over a long period brings the Low-MAs further than they would have come if taught meaningfully. The school beginner with good rote ability no doubt can profit from *some* rote instruction, and in the process can gain confidence and satisfaction that will have long-term benefits. But not much that really counts educationally can be taught by rote, and hence rote-learning ability does not count for much in school.

---

**24** Which of the following can be taught by rote in the elementary school?
   a. How different groups in the community vary in their life style.
   b. How communications and transportation have made the world smaller.
   c. The main facts about the voyage of Columbus.
   d. The locations of the states on a map of the United States.

---

## Fluid Ability

A test such as the Nonverbal section of the CAT (Fig. 7.3) or Block Design in the Wechsler scales (p. 276) is sometimes said to measure *fluid ability*. The contrasting term is *crystallized ability* (Cattell, 1971). The usual mental test mixes tasks calling for adaptation and problem solving—"fluid" thinking—with tasks calling for intellectual performances that rest heavily on previous training (such as vocabulary and arithmetic computation)—"crystallized" responses. Score differences on Block Design, Mazes, Hidden Figures, and Figure Classification—all unfamiliar, previously unpracticed—depend primarily on adaptive abilities. Any 10-year-old in the United States probably possesses all the knowledge needed

## Sex differences in aptitudes?

Boys and girls in Western cultures do not differ much on ability measures. This is partly because psychologists have tried to select test content that would give neither sex an advantage, and partly because opportunities for development are much the same until the school-leaving age.

The one important early difference is that boys are more likely to fail in beginning reading than girls. Since readiness tests at the start of Grade I show little sex difference, the difference in performance could be motivational in origin (see p. 176). The failure in reading, until overcome, seriously affects readiness for later learning.

On tests that require reasoning without requiring reading, the two sexes do equally well. This is seen, for example, in raw-score averages for an abstract-reasoning test in a national sample of 15-year-olds: 8.35 for boys and 8.31 for girls (Shaycoft et al., 1963, pp. 111–13). A raw-score difference is hard to evaluate, so I have converted the differences below, shown in tests of specialized abilities and achievements, to a ten-point standard score scale and have estimated the percentage of girls who exceeded the boys' average.

| | |
|---|---|
| Mechanical reasoning | 8 (17%) |
| Spatial (three dimensions) | 2 (40%) |
| Mathematics | 1 (46%) |
| Abstract reasoning | 0 (50%) |
| Vocabulary | −1 (55%) |
| Reading | −1 (56%) |
| Clerical checking | −2 (57%) |
| English achievement | −4 (68%) |

Only the difference in mechanical reasoning is large. Differences on information tests of various sorts (hunting, home economics, and so on) were equally large. Sex differences in ability have other patterns in cultures where the sex roles are unlike ours.

to use those abilities. Many test tasks call on both crystallized and fluid abilities. A nonverbal test usually emphasizes fluid ability more than does a verbal test of scholastic aptitude.

The CAT Verbal score correlates about 0.80 with an achievement test in one of the basic subjects given at the same time, but the Nonverbal IQ correlates only about 0.60 with the achievement measure (Thorndike & Hagen, 1971). Since unreliability holds correlations below the theoretical limit of 1.00, this means that the Verbal IQ reflects the same individual differences the achievement battery does. Allowing for error of measurement gives correlations about 20 points higher. It appears that a number of students who have only average achievement are outstanding in the flexible, critical skills the Nonverbal test calls upon. Though fluid ability is not an especially good predictor, it is worth the educator's attention.

The person who stands considerably higher in fluid ability than he does in crystallized ability evidently has not polished his tool skills as much as he has developed flexible use of his intellect. Adaptive problem solving is acquired incidentally, as collateral learning; the crystallized abilities are built up chiefly through deliberate practice in school. Since schoolwork relies daily on crystallized abilities, a poor command of them leads to a relatively bleak prediction (but see p. 294).

The person who scores much higher on crystallized ability than on fluid ability evidently has been mastering those things directly taught, but does not cope well with intellectual surprises. Defensive motivation (p. 642) is one possible explanation. Sometimes the superior performance was produced by intensive instruction that hammered in responses without developing flexible understanding.

The person whose standing in crystallized ability is lower than his standing in fluid ability has often been labeled an underachiever. This would be sound enough if the fluid ability score indicated a fixed potential and the crystallized ability were evidence of the use made of that potential. But fluid ability is itself an achievement. The difference is not that one ability is achieved and the other not, but that one is achieved mostly through direct practice and the other is the residue of indirect learning from varied experiences—that is, a product of transfer.

---

**25** For sixth-graders, would the ability required by each of the tasks below be classed as fluid or crystallized?
   a. Count to 100 by sevens.
   b. Arrange these words to make a sentence:
      *to   was   crop   there   rain   enough   give   good   a*
   c. We want to make a booklet with ten stories. Each story takes two sheets of paper. We want to put one blank sheet between stories. How many sheets do we need for the booklet?
   d. On this map, find the shortest path by water from Buffalo to Galveston.

**26** Does the classification of a task as fluid or crystallized vary with the population tested?

**27** Is it sound to identify the Wechsler Verbal and Performance IQs with crystallized and fluid abilities, respectively?

**28** Frieda Painter contends that the British schools fail to develop the proficiency of very bright children. Her evidence (reported in the *Times* of London, June 16, 1976, p. 3) is the achievement of children whose Stanford-Binet IQs were 140 or higher, giving them mental ages around 14 even though their chronological ages were 8–10. On tests of mathematics and written English, they averaged only as high as representative 11½-year-olds. If the gifted were being fully developed, Mrs. Painter argues, the achievement scores would match those of 14-year-olds. This amounts to a statement that general ability tests and achievement would have a correlation of 1.00 if schools were fully efficient. How reasonable is that demand?

**29** Would it be socially desirable to have a perfect correlation among fluid and crystallized abilities? (Assume that this could be produced by some new educational policies, without changing the mean and the s.d. of any ability.)

## Abilities With Vocational Significance

Specialized abilities come into play when a person begins to narrow his range of vocational choices or to choose a field of study. Tests have been devised for a remarkably large number of specialized abilities. The person applying tests, however, is interested only in the subdivisions of ability that have direct implications for decisions.

The kind of test battery used in vocational guidance includes tests for several abilities; the whole set is standardized on the same reference group. The profile of scores displays comparative strengths and weaknesses. Vocational aptitude test profiles most commonly report scores on verbal, numerical, spatial, and mechanical reasoning, and "clerical" abilities. One such battery, the Differential Aptitude Tests, is primarily for Grades VIII–XII. It requires about

**FIGURE 7.4**

**Items from six subtests of the Differential Aptitude Tests**

No items are shown from the Language Usage and Spelling subtests.

*Verbal Reasoning*

**Pick out a pair of words to fill the blanks so that the sentence will be true and sensible.**

...... is to foot as hat is to ......

A   toe —— head
B   ankle —— head
C   stocking —— band
D   stocking —— head
E   toe —— band

*Numerical Ability*

**Pick out the correct answer.**

Multiply

2.40
25

A   40.00
B   60.00
C   1000
D   6000
N   none of these

## Mechanical Reasoning

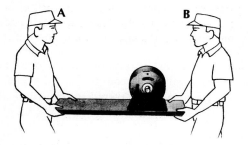

Which man has the heavier load?
(If equal, mark C.)

## Abstract Reasoning

**Pick out the picture which would be fifth in the series.**

 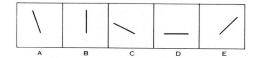

## Space Relations

**Which figure can be made from the pattern shown?**

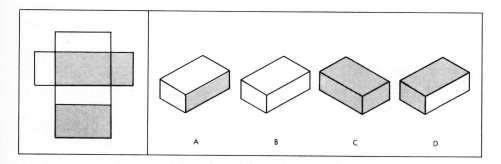

## Clerical Speed and Accuracy

**Underline . . . the symbol which is just like the underlined symbol at left.**

| AB AC AD AE AF | AC AE AF AB AD |
| A7 7A B7 7B AB | 7B B7 AB 7A A7 |
| Aa Ba bA BA bB | As bA bB Ba BA |

SOURCE: Items copyright 1972 by the Psychological Corporation. Reproduced by permission.

four-and-a-half hours of testing. In addition to the subtests illustrated (Fig. 7.4), scores are obtained on spelling and language usage (important for commercial and office work). The functions of the subtests illustrated are as follows:

- Verbal reasoning requires a well-developed vocabulary and ability to understand relations among concepts.

- Numerical ability examines facility in arithmetic operations. (Tests usually emphasize analysis rather than sheer computational speed. The specimen DAT item, you will note, can be answered intuitively, without calculation.)

- Mechanical reasoning tests ask how machinery operates and how physical principles can be applied. (The tests can be passed on the basis of everyday experience, although training in shop or science tends to improve the score. A test of this sort is distinguished from tests of shop knowledge and from tests of manipulative skill.)

- Abstract reasoning is comparable to the Nonverbal section of the CAT. It measures ability to trace relationships independent of reading and expressive language.

- Spatial tests require ability to think about geometric forms and relationships. (Spatial abilities are required in some mathematics courses, in engineering, engineering drawing, sheet metal work, and dressmaking.)

- Clerical perception calls for rapid detection of errors. It does not require judgment, but it does require careful, rapid work of a routine nature. (This ability predicts success in simple office jobs, but it is only one of the aptitudes pertinent in more responsible work such as bookkeeping and stenography.)

# PREDICTING SUCCESS IN SCHOOL AND WORK

For selecting among applicants for training, for deciding whether a student is prepared for an advanced course, or for advising a student about his vocational prospects, the aptitude test ought to measure readiness for the tasks ahead. How well a test predicts is investigated by a correlational study. A test is given to trainees entering a training program. When they finish the training, their accomplishment is measured. The two sets of scores are correlated. If accomplishment is strongly related to the aptitude score, the test is shown to be a relevant predictor.

# Prediction of Achievement

The Orleans-Hanna test is a special instrument for predicting achievement in algebra. The test items resemble work in algebra, but are designed so that the student who has not studied algebra can comprehend what is wanted. Whether to admit a ninth-grader to algebra is a serious decision. Completion of the course is an important first step in the college-preparatory program, but the failure rate is fairly high among unscreened students. The Orleans-Hanna test was given to students in nine schools in the spring of one year. Other information from tests and school records was collected, and the eighth-grade teacher was asked to forecast what mark the student would make if he enrolled in algebra. The follow-up study is confined to students who were admitted to algebra and who completed the course—about a third of the original eighth-grade sample. For them, teachers' marks (midyear and end-of-year) were collected, and an end-of-year standardized test was given. These three measures are said to be *criteria* of success in algebra.

A pattern of results like those in Table 7.2 is commonly found in academic prediction. The criteria correlate only 0.60; they are not interchangeable indica-

TABLE 7.2

Correlations of success in algebra with four kinds of predictive information

| Variable | Correlations with predictors* | | | | Correlations with criteria* | |
|---|---|---|---|---|---|---|
| | APT (1) | IQ (2) | Mark (3) | TP (4) | Mark (5) | Test (6) |
| PREDICTORS | | | | | | |
| 1. Algebra prognosis test | | .82 | .57 | .50 | .62 | .80 |
| 2. Measure from group mental test | .82 | | .49 | .40 | .55 | .70 |
| 3. Most recent report card grade in mathematics | .57 | .49 | | .72 | .50 | .49 |
| 4. Eighth-grade teacher's prediction of algebra mark | .50 | .40 | .72 | | .53 | .46 |
| END-OF-YEAR CRITERIA | | | | | | |
| 5. Algebra mark | .62 | .55 | .50 | .53 | | .60 |
| 6. Algebra test | .80 | .70 | .49 | .46 | .60 | |

SOURCE: After Hanna et al. (1969).
N = 310.
*Numbers in parentheses correspond to those of variables.

tors of the same thing. Such correlations are pulled down by variation of marking standards and by any tendency of teachers to give credit for dutiful completion of assignments as well as for accomplishment. The achievement test is probably the sounder criterion.

Note also the correlations among predictors. The two ability tests ranked students similarly; and the two measures that reflect the eighth-grade teacher's evaluation tended to agree. But many students who did well on the tests were rated average by the teacher. The tests predicted the results of the final algebra test much better than teachers' forecasts did.

The correlations of 0.70 and 0.80 show excellent prediction—better, indeed, than is usually found. These results, taken at face value, seem to justify using the Orleans-Hanna test in advising the eighth-grader about his chances for success in algebra. But perhaps the special test is unnecessary. The Orleans-Hanna test predicted somethat better than the IQ, but in other research (for example, Sabers & Feldt, 1968), a special aptitude test for algebra did not predict better than a comprehensive measure of educational development to date.

Ordinarily, specialized aptitude tests for the more academic school subjects are not needed. A comprehensive measure such as the Iowa Tests of Basic Skills (p. 261) is more convenient than a special test because it is relevant to many decisions.

Progress in a foreign language does seem to depend on special aptitudes (Carroll & Sapon, 1959, 1967) in addition to general verbal-intellectual abilities. Specialized tests are also useful in vocational courses.

Three kinds of predictor are ordinarily available to the educator: aptitude tests, achievement tests, and a cumulative average of past grades or teachers' reports. The correlations of these with success in the next year or so of schoolwork are usually in the range 0.40–0.50. Prediction can be improved perhaps to 0.70—if two or three types of information are combined. The correlation also goes up when the accuracy of the criteria is improved. The three kinds of predictors have roughly the same degree of predictive power.

If the previous grade average predicts as well as the test, then why give a test? If a broad achievement test predicts at least as well as the scholastic aptitude test, what is the use of aptitude tests? Tests have the virtue of impartiality, whereas marks reflect ability to please the teacher as well as knowledge (p. 698). Tests are especially useful in comparing applicants who have been taught by different teachers, since standards vary. The scholastic aptitude test has a possible advantage over the achievement test in such comparisons, since it is not directly related to the content of lessons and so may permit a sounder comparison of persons who have followed different programs. When the achievement test measures general verbal-mathematical competence rather than knowledge of history or trigonometry or pre-med physiology, it is as appropriate as an "aptitude" test.

PREDICTION OVER SEVERAL YEARS  In long-range prediction the story is much the same. An achievement test in Grade V predicts achievement in Grade XI a bit better than the general ability test does. Hundreds of students in many districts were tested in Grade V and again in Grade XI; Table 7.3 presents the correlations obtained among boys. The correlations are higher than one finds in a single school.

SCAT is a verbal-numerical aptitude test, whereas STEP is an achievement measure. Look first at the correlations within Grade V (left side of table). Patterning is nearly absent. The verbal, reading, social studies, and science tests all hang together (intercorrelations 0.80 to 0.85). The math and quantitative tests correlate only 0.75; their correlations with verbal tests are that high.

The predictive correlations (right side of table) ranged from 0.56 to 0.72. The composite of all tests correlated 0.85 over six years. Evidently, standings were remarkably stable. The aptitude tests were *not* better predictors than the achievement tests; Reading, for example, correlated about 0.03 higher than Verbal. Was achievement in Grade XI best predicted by achievement in the *same* subject at Grade V? Yes, but the tendency was so weak that it might as well be forgotten. Reading V predicted Reading XI with a correlation of 0.72; other achievement scores predicted just a trifle less well. Verbal achievements in Grade V predicted Math XI about as well as Math V and Quant. V did. This is powerful evidence that mental abilities develop along a broad front. The shape of an ability profile prior to age 14 is not at all stable (see p. 312).

For purposes of selection and prediction, then, the school can rely on past records, supplemented by a test of intellectual skills. This may be an "achievement test," an "aptitude test," or a "readiness test." The test of fluid ability does not predict well. Its proper function is not to "predict" so much as to

## TABLE 7.3

### Prediction from achievement and general ability over six years

| Tests in Grade V | Correlations with other Grade V measures at same time | | | | | | Long-term correlations with Grade XI measures | | | |
|---|---|---|---|---|---|---|---|---|---|---|
| | Verbal | Reading | S.S. | Quant. | Math | Sci. | Reading | S.S. | Math | Sci. |
| SCAT Verbal | | .82 | .84 | .71 | .72 | .80 | .69 | .70 | .58 | .62 |
| STEP Reading | .82 | | .84 | .74 | .81 | .85 | .72 | .70 | .62 | .65 |
| STEP Social Studies | .84 | .84 | | .72 | .75 | .82 | .69 | .70 | .59 | .60 |
| SCAT Quantitative | .71 | .74 | .72 | | .75 | .71 | .63 | .59 | .64 | .56 |
| STEP Math | .72 | .81 | .75 | .75 | | .78 | .67 | .64 | .66 | .61 |
| STEP Science | .80 | .85 | .82 | .71 | .78 | | .68 | .67 | .61 | .67 |

SOURCE: Data from Thomas Hilton (personal communication); see also Hilton et al. (1971).

shake up predictions. If a 10-year-old has done badly in his schoolwork and yet has a nonverbal IQ of 100 or better, it is a sound prediction that he will continue to do badly in schoolwork. The fact that he performed certain intellectual tasks at a normal level in the fluid test ought to cause the school to question its approach to him. If encouragement, remedial help, or tasks that appeal to him can build up his attitudes or skills, the boy can be lifted out of his groove. The teacher would like to offer such help to every weak student, but it is the one with this gap between educational performance and general abilities who is the priority target for the teacher's attention.

---

**30** In Table 7.2, consider the correlations of the four predictors with end-of-year marks. The pattern differs from that for the end-of-year test. How might the difference be explained?

**31** The correlation of aptitude with outcome is generally higher when a group ranges widely in aptitude. Apply this principle to interpret the following facts:
   a. The algebra students (Table 7.2) were a select group; eighth-graders with poor records were advised not to enroll in algebra.
   b. The correlations where many schools were combined (Table 7.3) are larger than those found in a single school.
   c. During the years when it was given a preliminary tryout, a medical aptitude test predicted class standings. When the test was used to select medical school entrants, its correlation with standings was much lower.

---

## Aptitude and Academic Decisions

Norms for a mental test are intended to describe the distribution for all children of a given age in the nation. These norms do not describe the distribution in a community or in a class. An IQ of 90 is near the 45th percentile nationally. In a poor community this score is likely to be about average. An IQ of 90 may be in the bottom 10 per cent, however, in a high school serving mostly professional families. Dropouts are much more common toward the lower end of the ability range, especially at the legal age for leaving school.

College students are a selected group, though college attendance is determined by many factors other than ability. An able girl is less likely to go to college than an average boy from the same graduating class, and more likely to drop out after a year or two than a male student of equal ability. Family attitude, financial resources, and the student's self-concept are important determiners. Consider the reasonably able group—those around the 80th percentile in ability. For example, in 1960, among high-school graduates in the top ten per cent of the family-income distribution, 90 per cent of boys and 90 per cent of girls entered college. In the median income bracket, the percentages were 80 and 70, and in the next lower bracket, 75 and 57 (Flanagan et al., 1967, p. 11–20).

No one ability level defines the college-capable student, especially with today's wide range of colleges and programs. A student of IQ 95 can complete four years of college if he selects a suitable institution and curriculum, if he is motivated, and if he gets help in overcoming emotional problems or deficiencies in his basic skills. Indeed one out of every 30 Ph.D.'s was recorded by his high school as having an IQ below 100 (L. Harmon, 1961). Cantoni (1954) tells of a boy with an IQ of 93 (according to repeated tests in Grade IX) who ultimately became a lawyer. This boy showed evident signs of maladjustment, which no doubt impaired both his test score and his schoolwork. Encouragement from a counselor helped him toward a more positive attitude in school; an intermission for military service also contributed to his maturity. Such exceptional cases warn against taking the mental test or academic record as a final verdict on a student's promise. But these cases *are* exceptions. Considering any large number of students, the risk of failure in college (or dropout) increases with each step down the IQ scale.

A reasonable rule for interpreting scholastic aptitude scores of students with a normal background is: Every student above standard score 60 (84th percentile) in general ability should think seriously about going to college; no student below standard score 50 (50th percentile) should plan on a four-year college course unless the counselor has evidence that his score is held down by specific handicaps that remedial help can remove. This rule is deliberately left inexact; it recognizes that neither a favorable nor an unfavorable prediction can be made in the middle range, that final decisions must rest on many facts other than the test score, and that education can be continued in other ways than a four-year college course.

When a student belongs to an ethnic minority, the adviser has to weigh evidence with more than the usual care. Statistically speaking, scholastic aptitude tests predict college marks of black students as they do for whites; in most schools, the expectation of success that goes with a certain aptitude score is the same for blacks and whites (Linn, 1973). But colleges differ in their readiness to make special provision for minority students, the students differ in their degree of motivation, and in some cases the counselor will have evidence that casts doubt on the validity of a low aptitude score.

TIMING OF DECISIONS    Decisions about educational plans are not to be made at any single moment. Over many years, the student and his parents should form a realistic picture of his probable performance, and should set their eyes on a suitable educational goal. Grade IV is none too early to begin the systematic identification and encouragement of talent. Otherwise, an able student can coast through the grades without realizing his own competence; indeed, he may seriously underrate himself. About Grade VII, the work becomes harder and a serious effort is required. The stiffer demands and more systematic assignments

## What can Karla expect of herself?

Karla, a senior in high school, came to the counselor in distress because she was failing in a shorthand course; her plan had been to attend secretarial school and then work in an office. The school had no recent test information (and we are not told what her high-school marks and teachers' reports indicated about her). The school had given a general mental test in Grade X and Karla's IQ was 120. The junior high school had given the DAT battery in Grade VIII, and the profile shown below was recorded.

Making the somewhat risky assumption that Karla's profile in Grade XII is consistent with that in Grade VIII, make a judgment as to the reason for Karla's difficulties and as to what might be a sound plan for her career education. (Karla's story is continued on p. 298).

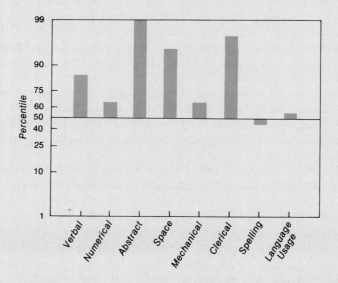

SOURCE: G. K. Bennett, H. G. Seashore, & A. G. Wesman, *Counseling from Profiles* (New York: The Psychological Corporation, 1977).

of the junior high come up just at the age when sports, dating, and a part-time job put in competing bids for time and interest. By Grade IX, the student will have established a consistent record as a superior performer or as an academically weak student. The school routes one student into academic subjects and encourages him to plan for college, or encourages another to prepare for a job at the end of high school.

This abrupt decision at the start of high school is false to the facts of development, even though past records do predict future records in the majority of cases. Motivations change during high school. Roughly a third of the boys who in Grade IX say they will not go to college reverse that decision by age 18.* And nearly a third of those who planned on college in Grade IX decide not to go (Cooley & Lohnes, 1968, Ch. 4, p. 50). Some of these changes reflect the discovery of new interests, thanks to the diversified high-school program or to out-of-school activities. Some reflect a more realistic sense of the demands of the vocational world.

Thus Flanagan (1966) found that 21 per cent of ninth-grade boys listed engineering as their preferred career, but by Grade XII only 8 per cent still planned to be engineers. The percentage planning to be engineering aides and skilled workers went up. Early in high school at least half of the boys had unrealistic career plans, Flanagan says.

By the time students leave high school, the school has given them signals (right or wrong) as to their prospects, and they have made up their minds whether to seek further schooling. Jencks (1972, p. 184) suggests that the best available follow-up report is one made in Wisconsin, where occupational plans at the time of high-school graduation were compared with actual occupations seven years later. The *average* shortfall was quite small—about two points on a standard score scale, or, as Jencks says, about equal to the difference between "chemical and industrial engineers or between municipal and private policemen." Equally significant is the fact that the correlation of aspiration with outcome was only 0.48. This means that many individuals finished far above or far below the level they planned on.

The school does a disservice when it makes the ninth-grade decision a watershed in the student's life. There is good reason to start certain students on the algebra-chemistry-physics sequence as early as possible, and good reason to start others on a solid sequence of shop courses. But by age 16 or 18, some students in the shop program are ready intellectually and emotionally for tougher courses in math and science. The high school or community college that makes these courses available when the student is ready removes an artificial barrier. The current policy of colleges—to admit anyone who shows adequate general educational development, rather than to make specific courses such as chemistry a prerequisite to admission—also smooths the path for late bloomers. The "open" universities of the 1970s seek to extend college-level instruction to persons of any age, often through correspondence or broadcast media. As these projects take root, they will increase the chances of self-development for the person who could not postpone his entry into a paying job at age 18, and of the person who had little interest in academic work during high school. It is inappropriate that schools should try to complete their role in socialization before the person "goes out into the world."

---

*The emphasis on male career development in this section reflects two things. Far more data were accumulated on males (simply because more of them stayed in the labor force). Second, career patterns for women are changing so rapidly in the 1970s that the limited data on women's career histories in previous decades probably do not apply to today's female students.

For guidance purposes, especially in the high-school years, schools make considerable use of batteries of aptitude tests. One such battery, the DAT, was described above (p. 288).

On page 296 you saw the profile of Karla. Here is the story told by her counselor:

> Karla was a very bright girl whose intellectual abilities indicated that she should consider pursuing her studies after high school. Her father, a mailman, and her mother, a housewife and former secretary, had never attended college and felt that Karla's "best hope" for future economic security was to attend secretarial school for a short time after graduation and obtain employment in this field. Karla was not too happy at this prospect, but since it was what her parents wanted and since most of her friends were planning on entering the job market after high school, she seemed resigned to it. Her lack of enthusiasm for secretarial work was reflected in her coursework, however, and Karla came in to see the counselor because she was in danger of failing shorthand.

In conferences with the counselor, Karla was soon off the subject of shorthand, discussing her great enjoyment of her English classes and the fact that she "loved to write." Her family and friends had discouraged that interest. She quoted her father: "No one is ever going to pay you for sitting around reading books, Karla. You've got to learn a skill." The profile shows that Karla had considerable ability; the Verbal score and the Abstract Reasoning score are in agreement with the reported IQ of 120. At least in Grade VIII, Karla had not developed her abilities evenly. She was outstanding in nonverbal adaptive performance, but her verbal reasoning lagged behind her nonverbal reasoning and her crystallized abilities (Numerical, Spelling, and Language Usage) were only at an average level. Average scores in these are sufficient for learning of office skills, so the counselor is right to emphasize the motivational reasons for Karla's failure in shorthand.

In my opinion, the counselor ought to have given a fresh test to update the profile and an achievement battery to identify defective skills. If the new record told the same story as the one from Grade VIII, the counselor might work with Karla's teachers to develop a crash program to rebuild her command of fundamentals in language and mathematics. Her performance in those is at a level acceptable in an average student, but the level is so far below Karla's general ability that it has to be considered a handicap in her case. The counselor might also have considered with Karla whether she had any interests that could capitalize on her remarkably high nonverbal competence.

The counselor chose to pursue the issue of motivation. The counselor met with Karla's parents after she began to understand Karla, and held several sessions in which Karla's record and test profile were carefully interpreted. Karla regained her confidence, and the parents began to realize that they had underrated her. Karla decided to go to a junior college, which admitted her even though her high-school program had not met all the admission requirements. A community fund provided financial aid. Karla's plan, at last report, is to transfer to a state college and work toward a bachelor's degree in English. Teaching is mentioned as one possible career.

Interest patterns have as much to do with persistence in a line of study and with occupational choice as abilities do. In fact, at the college level, those who complete different courses of study differ more in interest profiles than in ability profiles (J. W. French, 1961). Stable interest patterns begin to emerge among boys as early as Grade V. The basic distinction, Cooley and Lohnes (1968) suggest, is between interest in people and interest in things. The orientation toward people embraces interest in communications, in cultural activities, in face-to-face relations, and, later, in business contacts. The orientation toward things includes mechanical, technical, and scientific interests. This contrast is much too simple to account for the multidimensionality of adult interests, but it does lay a base for choices among courses and outside activities during adolescence. Cooley (1963) classified boys as having interests potentially leading to science careers. Two-thirds of the boys held the same classification in Grade IX

as in Grade V. In another sample (Cooley & Lohnes, 1968, Ch. 4, pp. 49 and 50), those classified as "interested in things" in Grade IX were far more likely than the others to enter college training in science, engineering, and medicine. The interest patterns did not predict which ones in the noncollege group would go into technical careers, however.

ACADEMIC ABILITIES AND VOCATIONAL SUCCESS    Scholastic abilities have significance for occupational guidance as well as for academic success. Where a person eventually settles—in professional, skilled, or unskilled work—is appreciably related to his general ability. One of the many pieces of evidence comes from a study of young candidates for flight training tested by the Air Force in 1943. About 10,000 of these men were questioned ten years after they had been discharged, to determine what occupation they had settled in (Thorndike & Hagen, 1959). The largest occupational groups were distributed as follows in relation to the 1943 test-score levels:

> Highest level: engineers, physicians, scientists
>
> Second level: accountants, dentists, managers, lawyers
>
> Third level (roughly, IQ 95–105): carpenters, clerical workers, farmers, wholesale salesmen
>
> Fourth level: bus and truck drivers, machine operators, mechanics

Men grouped by high-school record would sort out in a similar manner.

These group averages do not tell the whole story. Every group had a wide range; one quarter or more of the accountants, for example, came from the top level, and another quarter fell below IQ 100. The wide range within an occupation demonstrates that IQ does not alone determine one's status. To put it in another way: men of IQ 120 are found in every occupational level from semi-skilled laborer to professional.

With regard to the profile of abilities, the Air Force follow-up gave the results in Fig. 7.5. "General reasoning" in this tabulation includes both verbal and mathematical reasoning; the numerical score is primarily a measure of speed in computation. The perceptual-spatial score includes spatial reasoning and speed in interpreting visual signals. It is evident that these men who have survived training and the initial years of practice in an occupation typically do have a pattern of abilities suited to that work.

Test scores have surprisingly little relation to professional success among men who complete the same amount of education. The students with higher test scores in high school will tend to have better adult incomes. But among those who complete law school, neither the high-school tests nor the tests for law-school admission predict income. In the Thorndike-Hagen study, the correlation, for men within the same occupation, between Air Force test scores and later income was invariably close to zero. Adolescents whose test scores differ by ten standard-score points will wind up five standard-score points apart on the occupational scale, on the average. But the difference will be only one or

## FIGURE 7.5

## Men in the same occupation tend to have similar abilities

The heavy line indicates the average score among all men tested.

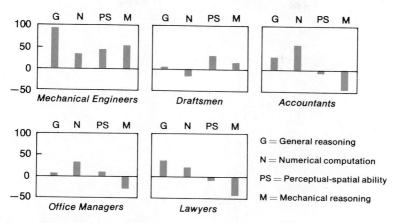

SOURCE: Data from Thorndike & Hagen (1959).

two points for two young people who complete the same amount of education. If two boys—one of IQ 110 and one of IQ 120—go on to finish engineering school, they have similar economic prospects. Or, more accurately, their comparative life chances depend on things the IQ and the college grade average do not measure (Jencks, 1972, p. 186).

Further light on the relation of ability test scores to job performance is provided by Ghiselli's compilation (1966) on lower-level occupations. Tests to select workers are legitimate only if they actually predict success. Therefore, an employer tests the tests, comparing the test score at hiring with later evidence on the worker's success. Sometimes the criterion is a record of success in the training program for the job. (Did the person finish the training? How long did it take? How well did he do on the test at the end?) Sometimes the criterion is a record of performance on the job. (How much work does he turn out? What is its quality? How does his supervisor rate him?) Ghiselli found a consistent pattern over a great number of blue-collar jobs. Tests of general ability correlate—on the average—0.42 with end-of-training criteria, yet they correlate only 0.23 with on-the-job measures (Ghiselli, 1966, p. 121). Specialized tests of mechanical abilities, however, often correlate 0.40 or better with on-the-job criteria (for jobs having a mechanical reasoning component). A similar statement holds true for spatial and perceptual abilities. General ability tests do predict on-the-job performance in many (but not all) white-collar jobs.

*"After all, Mr. Jackson, we do require our students
to have some degree of aptitude."*

These observations raise a fundamental question: Should young people be screened out of an occupation because of limitations in their *scholastic* aptitude? If limited ability to read and to follow verbal-symbolic instruction causes one to fail in training to repair TV sets, applicants who have interest and talent for the job itself are being denied an opportunity. If, on the other hand, there is a genuine verbal-symbolic component on the job, the verbal tests and the verbal element in the training are screening out people who would be inept on the job. It comes down to this: Do we really believe that the verbal element in the training is relevant to the job?

For lawyers, the answer is probably yes. For TV repairing, no. The educational community realized—at a late date—that doctors do not need Latin, so high-school Latin is no longer an obstacle that keeps some persons out of medical school. The community ought to be suspicious when a verbal test is used to select police officers. Even if it does predict their scores on a written examination at the end of training, the burden of proof is on the city manager who says that verbal ability makes the difference between good and poor police work. If that is not the case, a less verbal training program and a less verbal final examination ought to be designed.

**32** Practicing physicians make almost no use of algebra or higher mathematics. Is it reasonable to require that persons interested in medical school survive a program that starts with algebra in Grade IX?

**33** In certain developing countries, nearly all the young people must go into work on farms or as unskilled laborers. The 15 per cent of the adolescents who respond best to schooling are held in school, and approximately the top 5 per cent are encouraged to train for professional and managerial roles. The next 5 per cent are prepared for white-collar jobs, and the remainder are prepared for skilled trades. The country cannot afford now to extend secondary education to a larger segment of the population. The schools are asked to identify the most talented young people and prepare them to contribute as much as they can to the developing economy, considering the slots available for trained workers. The result is that positions such as mechanic are primarily filled with people whose scholastic rather than mechanical aptitude is near the top. What are the merits and defects of this policy? (Assume that the correlations between abilities in a developing country are like those found in advanced countries.)

**34** At what point in a school career would it be most valuable to administer and interpret a battery such as the Differential Aptitude Tests (p. 288)? Consider the case of Karla in your discussion.

**35** McClelland (1973) notes that the chances of professional success are as great for the student earning a C average in (for example) law school as they are for the A student. He then suggests that it is improper to rule prospective C students out of law school when competition for places is strong. The argument rests in part on the assumption that C students who finish law school are no different from the C students who fail to finish. How reasonable is this assumption?

**36** McClelland (his pp. 2 and 3) argues as follows against giving preference in admissions to those who are likely to succeed in school:

> . . . one would think that the purpose of education is precisely to improve the performance of those who are not doing very well . . . . high-scoring students might be poor bets because they would be less likely to show improvement in performance. To be sure, the teachers want students who will do well in their courses, but should society allow the teachers to determine who deserves to be educated, particularly when the performance of interest to teachers bears so little relation to any other type of life performance?

What do you think?

**37** How can a teacher encourage a fifth-grader to think of himself as academically able without arousing jealousy in the class and without giving him false impressions of his ability?

**38** Is it legitimate for a teacher or counselor to discourage the ambition of an eighth-grader who has poor marks and poor test scores, yet plans to be an engineer?

**39** What careers might Karla have considered, late in high school, that would fit especially well with her aptitude profile? Now that she is an English major, do the strong points in the profile suggest anything about possible career lines?

READING LIST

Anne Anastasi, "Clinical Testing," in *Psychological Testing,* 4th ed. (New York: Macmillan, 1976), pp. 464–90.

> This well-established text covers all topics in this chapter. The chapter on clinical testing goes further, describing the diagnostic procedures such as the school psychologist uses in studying exceptional children. The section on "learning disabilities" may be of special interest.

Lee J. Cronbach, "Ability Profiles in Guidance," in *Essentials of Psychological Testing,* 3rd ed. (New York: Harper & Row, 1970), pp. 353–83.

> Describes the Differential Aptitude Tests and similar batteries, and summarizes information on their validity for vocational prediction. Points out the uncertainties in predictions made for guidance purposes and suggests how to help counselless use of information intelligently in making plans.

John W. Gardner, "The Identification of Talent," Chapter 5 in *Excellence* (New York: Harper, 1961), pp. 46–53.

> The idea that the school is the "sorting agent" for society was introduced in my Chapter 2. Gardner summarizes the reasons for placing greater reliance on tests than on teachers' judgment, and comments on why tests used in this way are unpopular. He points out major cautions in the use of tests to select talent.

John L. Horn, "Intelligence—Why It Grows, Why It Declines," in *Human Intelligence,* ed. J. McV. Hunt (New Brunswick, N.J.: transaction books, 1972), pp. 53–74.

> Introduces a variety of mental test items and explains why each kind of task is useful in tapping a different aspect of mental functioning. It also discusses changes in ability patterns with age.

Richard L. Venezky, *Testing in Reading: Assessment and Instructional Decision-Making* (Urbana, Ill.: National Council of Teachers of English, 1974).

> Offers ten canons to guide the teacher and administrator in deciding how much effort to spend in assessment and how to make good use of results. Although the content refers to tests and instructional practices in reading, the canons apply to all school subjects.

George Weber, "College Admission Tests," in *Uses and Abuses of Standardized Testing in the Schools,* Occasional Paper No. 22, Council for Basic Education (Washington, D.C., 1974), pp. 22–28.

> Describes the role admission tests play in distributing opportunity more widely, and evaluates criticisms of them.

# NATURE
# AND ORIGINS
# OF GENERAL
# ABILITIES

The preceding chapter was primarily a description of tests and their internal characteristics. Chapter 8 will discuss the psychology of abilities—where they come from and how they function. Evidence on the inheritance of ability and on the influence of the home environment will help explain why students differ. The chapter summarizes and interprets some of the differences in the average scores of social-class and ethnic groups, and comes to grips with the issue of test bias. Alternative policies for responding to individual differences in school will be the chief topic of Chapter 9. As was said at the start of Chapter 7, it is necessary to rely heavily on evidence from general mental tests, but when similar studies are made with achievement tests, the conclusions remain essentially the same. Hence the conclusions to be presented are significant both for those educators who use general mental tests and for those who oppose their use.

## STABILITY AND CHANGE OF INDIVIDUAL DIFFERENCES

Many teachers (and some psychologists) have assumed that standings in mental ability do not change. Standings remain fairly stable over the years (p. 293), but the IQ is not "constant." Neither is any other index of ability.

## Correlations As Summaries of Change in Standing

Most reports on stability take the form of correlations. The earlier discussion of correlations (p. 133) is expanded here. Figure 8.1 shows scores of the same persons on two tests that present different tasks on two occasions. Both tests are scaled to make 50 the average and 10 points the standard deviation (p. 117).

Just what does a correlation of 0.80 mean, in terms of changes in standing from one test to another? Suppose there are 12 persons with scores of 50 (average for the norm group) on Test A. When one of them takes Test B, his standing will be higher or lower depending on his growth in the interim, on his

FIGURE 8.1

Shifts in standing corresponding to two correlations between tests

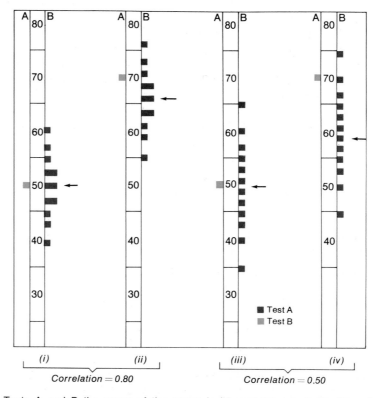

For Tests A and B the mean of the group is 50 and the s.d. is 10. The chart shows the spreads, on Test B, of the subgroups having a mean score of 50 and of 70 on Test A. Arrows show the means on Test B.

possession of abilities that one task requires but that no task in the other test requires, and on errors of measurement. The small squares in Column i show how the scores of the 12 persons are likely to spread on Test B. When the correlation is 0.80, about one third of such a group shifts more than 6 points (on a scale where the s.d. is 10). For this group the average remains at 50, as the arrow shows.

Column ii shows the change in the scores of persons who start at a standard score of 70 (98th percentile). They too spread on Test B. Moreover, most of them drift toward the mean. This fits with everyday experience: "You can't win 'em all." Those who score highest on Test B *are* likely to have been above average on Test A, but not many of them will come from the very top rank.

This probability that persons at the extreme on one measurement will shift toward the average on another is referred to as *regression*. It was originally noticed in the tendency of sons of tall men to be shorter than their fathers; the sons "regress toward the average." (See also p. 323.)

Columns iii and iv show how much change occurs when the correlation is 0.50. In Column iii, about half the persons shift as much as 6 points.

When two equivalent standardized tests of mental ability or achievement are given a few days apart, the correlation (reliability) is around 0.90. Scores change a bit simply because of error of measurement, the person's mood, and so on. (The correlation will usually be higher than 0.90 if the test is very long; it will be lower if the group has a comparatively narrow range; and it will usually be lower if the group is young.) Take the Iowa Tests of Basic Skills as an example. When fourth-graders are tested on the work-study-skills section (p. 261), two forms being given a week or so apart, the correlation is 0.85. On the entire test (five sections), the correlation is 0.96. Such high reliability is found only in long tests.

## Correlations over Time

When the interval between tests is long, standings change more. Follow-up studies show these retest correlations over time:

| Interval between tests | Iowa Total Score | Work-Study Skills | Reading |
|---|---|---|---|
| About one week | 0.96 | 0.85 | 0.85 |
| One year | 0.91 | 0.84 | 0.83 |
| Two years | 0.91 | 0.84 | 0.81 |
| Three years | 0.89 | 0.79 | 0.78 |

(Coefficients for students first tested in Grades III, IV, and V are averaged here. The coefficients come from the test manual.) Similar correlations are found for scholastic aptitude tests. (See also p. 293.) Changes are larger, however, for subjects younger than 7.

Evidently, individual differences in basic skills are highly stable; the student who is ill prepared for Grade III has a high probability of being ill prepared for Grade VI. Schools make it possible for each student to build on what he brings to class. Much can be done to develop the skills the weak student lacks, but the strong student is meanwhile advancing to higher levels.

A change of 10 points in the standard score (or 15 points on the IQ scale) would probably be large enough to change the school's evaluation of a student; in many contexts it amounts to a change from B level to C level, or vice versa. According to Fig. 8.1, when the correlation is as high as 0.80, changes of 10 standard score points are uncommon. Those who change markedly usually have scored in the top or bottom ten per cent on the first test. When an observed score changes by 10 standard score points and $r = 0.80$, about half of

**TABLE 8.1**

**Relation of IQ change to schooling**

| | Mean IQ ten years later | | |
| IQ at age 8 | Men completing primary school only | Men with secondary schooling or more | All men |
| --- | --- | --- | --- |
| 80–89  (123)* | 92 (113) | 101 (10) | 93 |
| 110–119  (92) | 108  (39) | 118 (53) | 114 |

SOURCE: Data from Husén, 1951.
*Number of men is shown in parentheses.

the change reflects true change in the person; the rest reflects error of measurement. So the true scores of the great majority of students are remarkably stable over time.

Consistent with the reported long-term correlations is a Swedish study (Husén, 1951). IQs obtained for boys in the elementary schools were compared with scores on tests given ten years later, when, as young men, they entered the Army. Since Sweden had universal military service, the scores are representative of males in the age group. In the period of this study, more than half of all Swedish males left school in early adolescence. On the average, according to Table 8.1, persons who received more schooling increased in IQ. Husén's results at other IQ levels exhibit the same trends (except that those educated men who started above 125 tended not to gain). More schooling raised the IQ to some extent by improving vocabulary, problem solving, and so on.

## Consistency in Individual Records

Despite the statistical stability indicated by the correlations over time, important changes occur in some individuals. Figure 8.2 charts standard scores of five girls who took mental tests periodically. The five cases were selected to show the variety of records; records of boys are similarly varied.

As the jumble of lines at the left end of the chart indicates, performance before age 4 is extremely unstable. A score is often 10–15 points from the score recorded three months earlier. This reflects the day-to-day responsiveness of the young child as well as spurts and lags in early growth. Early tests have almost no relation to school-age tests. Tests in infancy measure motor coordinations and attention patterns, not the intellectual, analytic abilities tested in later years. Language abilities are tested at ages 2–4, but differences are not stable.

## FIGURE 8.2

The course of IQs for five individuals from childhood into adulthood

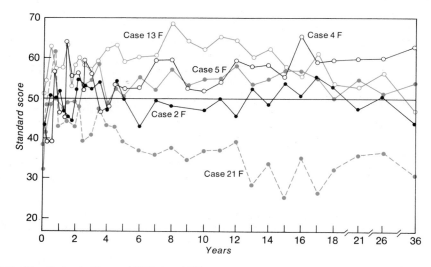

SOURCE: After Bayley, in Mussen (1970), I, p. 1175.

After Grade I, the person usually retains his or her relative place in the group. But important changes in rank do occur. Obviously, long-term plans should never rest on a single test, particularly a test given some years earlier.

A test given at the beginning of a child's school career has to be regarded with special caution. The child is likely not to be a good "test-taker" (pp. 272 and 702). He has not yet been taught to pay attention to directions, to check his answers, or to express his ideas clearly in words. Only after a child understands the rules of the game and is at ease with the tester does a test score become a stable indicator.

## Stability of Profiles

Subdivisions of general ability or language ability can be measured from age 3 onward, and such information has some short-run diagnostic value. But the peaks and valleys of a child's aptitude profile have no long-term meaning. If, for example, a child's numerical ability is below his general performance in Grade I, that deficiency is as likely as not to change to a superiority (L. Tyler, 1958). In later years the *marked.* peaks and valleys in the profile (for example, Verbal, high; Numerical, low) have some long-term stability. But changes in profiles are common among both boys and girls between Grades X and XII (Droege, 1967). This finding reinforces the recommendation that guidance should include a periodic review of performance, aptitudes, and interests.

1 Wechsler's Coding subtest requires one to write various symbols alongside the digits 0 to 9 as fast as one can. (See p. 276.) Bayley's longitudinal study (in Mussen, 1970, I, p. 1185) traced average scores on this test at various ages. Raw scores rose from age 16 to 18 to 21, then dropped from age 21 to 26 to 36. The scores at age 36 averaged close to those at age 17. Can you suggest an explanation for this drop-off? Averages on nearly all other subtests improved from age 18 to age 26 or later. (See p. 341.)

2 If correlations of scores on work-study skills are as high as 0.84 over a two-year interval, is there any justification for giving such a test early in *each* school year?

3 Could the school adopt instructional policies that would make standings on the Iowa test (p. 261) much less stable than they now are? If so, would this be socially desirable?

# HERITABILITY OF TEST PERFORMANCE

The essential concepts, facts, and conclusions about heritability are worth your attention chiefly because of the controversy about them; it is my view, however, that the facts on inheritance have little or no bearing on present-day educational policies.

Abilities, being developed out of experience, are strongly influenced by the conditions of development. Abilities are strongly influenced by the genes. These two statements are not inconsistent, as the following shows.

## How Heritability is Defined and Assessed

*Heritability,* a statistical concept, comes from genetics—more specifically, from animal breeders. Breeders of cattle want to increase milk yield or resistance to a certain disease. So they want to know how much they can influence the trait by selective breeding. To answer this, they mate cows and bulls of a certain kind and rear the offspring under uniform conditions of pasture, climate, and so on.

The cows in the second generation, at maturity, differ in their milk production or susceptibility to disease. How much of that variation is traceable to heredity?

The proportion, symbolized by $h^2$, is calculated in various ways: from the resemblance between parent and offspring, between half-siblings, and so on. The proportion can range from .00 to 1.00. The heritability for milk production is about 0.30; small though this number may appear to be, it gives planned breeding great economic importance.

In this ideal experiment, any environmental influence that is not uniform for all cows is essentially random. Interpretation is unambiguous, and the information is of both practical and theoretical value. Other points to note:

- The heritability coefficient applies to the particular kind of cow; in another breed it could have a different value. Although $h^2$ could be calculated from a mixed group—say, from cattle representative of all those in Wyoming—it would not be illuminating.

- The coefficient applies to the particular environment. If the cows were reared on poorer pasturage, milk yield would go down, and the coefficient might change. Because of heredity-environment interaction, the cows who produced best on the poor pasture might not be of the strain that did best on a rich pasture. (The word *interaction* has the same sense here as in the person-situation interaction of Domino—see p. 141.)

- Even if a very high coefficient of heritability appeared in this strictly designed experiment, it would be absurd to say that environment, therefore, has no influence on milk production.

Research on the heritability of human traits does shed light on development. When a disease is shown to be heritable, genetic counseling can reduce the number of children born with that disease. It is equally important to discover that certain abnormalities are *not* heritable, since parents who have had one child with a nonheritable disorder can be reassured that subsequent children will probably be normal. Research on human heritability is hard to conduct because one cannot mate humans at will and cannot standardize the environment. The question is posed as before: Within a certain population, what percentage of the variation in the trait that interests us can be attributed to inheritance? But the answer has to be reached indirectly.

Most of the research has been on American and English white families. Since mating is neither controlled nor random, an allowance has to be made for the tendency of women to marry men from their own social group, who may be more like them genetically. The environments in which the offspring are raised vary considerably, and there is no adequate way to assess these variations. Perhaps certain genes are more frequent among college-educated parents, but such parents also more frequently provide a highly verbal environment. If their children turn out to be superior on certain tests, the effect could be credited to heredity, or environment, or their interaction. Indirect statistical reasoning can do no more than set broad limits on heritability estimates for humans.

Here are estimates of $h^2$ for various human characteristics:

| | |
|---|---|
| Number of fingerprint ridges | 0.98 or less (Huntley, 1966, p. 214) |
| Eye color | 0.96 or higher (Jensen, 1973, p. 300) |
| Height | 0.81 (Dobzhansky, 1973, p. 18) |
| Weight | 0.78 (Dobzhansky, 1973, p. 18) |

For certain disorders carried by relatively simple genetic mechanisms, heritability can be established by tracing the family histories of sufferers. And, as with sickle cell anemia and Tay-Sachs disease, the evidence establishes that the damaging genes are more prevalent in one ethnic group (blacks and Jews, respectively, for these disorders). Most psychological characteristics are influenced by many many genes acting in concert, and the direct method of tracing inheritance does not apply.

One can analyze heritability within a black population as well as within a white one (Loehlin et al., 1975). But such studies say nothing about the extent to which differences *between* races are associated with genetic differences. Some writers have argued that black–white differences in average test performance reflect differences in the distributions of genes. And others have argued that the difference between blacks and whites attributable to the genes is zero, on the average. Neither of these positions is well supported; neither one has been disproved. It is possible—in view of the environmental handicaps blacks have suffered—that, if reared in the same environment, black children would outscore whites on the average. Let us set aside the question of genetic race differences related to the development of ability, which is surely unanswerable at the present time, and try to get clear what the within-race studies mean.

## Findings from Mental Tests

That heredity has much to do with ability was suspected from the fact that some families produce eminent persons generation after generation. This is uncertain evidence, however, since a distinguished family can provide many advantages for its children. The best evidence comes from twins. One-egg—monozygotic (MZ)—twins receive precisely the same genes. When they are reared in the same home, their experiences also have much in common. There are lesser degrees of similarity among less closely related persons; this adds to the picture. Two-egg—dizygotic (DZ)—twins, or brother and sister, or parent and child, have just 50 per cent of their genes in common.

The correlation of test scores for MZ twins reared together is about as high as the correlation of two tests on the same person. The correlation for DZ twins is generally around 0.50, equal to the correlation between brother and sister.

The more closely persons are related, the more alike their IQs tend to be (Erlenmyer-Kimling & Jarvik, 1963). True, but there is also an effect from environment: unrelated persons from different homes, paired arbitrarily, are less alike than unrelated persons who grew up together.

A second line of evidence comes from the comparison of relatives reared together and relatives reared separately. Raising MZ twins in different environments lowers the resemblance in ability—but not by much. These studies are weak evidence. Few cases of separated twins can be found, and it may be that the homes in which the twins were placed were not very different. Table 8.2 presents some data from one of the better studies. The small differences within

**TABLE 8.2**

**Resemblance among identical twins reared separately**

| Pair number | Sex | Age at separation | Age at testing | In years of schooling | In estimated educational advantages* | In estimated social advantages* | In estimated physical advantages* | Twin difference in IQ |
|---|---|---|---|---|---|---|---|---|
| | | | | | Environmental differences | | | |
| 11 | F | 18 mo. | 35 | 14 | 37 | 25 | 22 | 24 |
| 2 | F | 18 mo. | 27 | 10 | 32 | 14 | 9 | 12 |
| 18 | M | 1 yr. | 27 | 4 | 28 | 31 | 11 | 19 |
| 4 | F | 5 mo. | 29 | 4 | 22 | 15 | 23 | 17 |
| 12 | F | 18 mo. | 29 | 5 | 19 | 13 | 36 | 7 |
| 1 | F | 18 mo. | 19 | 1 | 15 | 27 | 19 | 12 |
| 17 | M | 2 yr. | 14 | 0 | 15 | 15 | 15 | 10 |
| 8 | F | 3 mo. | 15 | 1 | 14 | 32 | 13 | 15 |
| 3 | M | 2 mo. | 23 | 1 | 12 | 15 | 12 | −2 |
| 14 | F | 6 mo. | 39 | 0 | 12 | 15 | 9 | −1 |
| 5 | F | 14 mo. | 38 | 1 | 11 | 26 | 23 | 4 |
| 13 | M | 1 mo. | 19 | 0 | 11 | 13 | 9 | 1 |
| 10 | F | 1 yr. | 12 | 1 | 10 | 15 | 16 | 5 |
| 15 | M | 1 yr. | 26 | 2 | 9 | 7 | 8 | 1 |
| 7 | M | 1 mo. | 13 | 0 | 9 | 27 | 9 | −1 |
| 19 | F | 6 yr. | 41 | 0 | 9 | 14 | 22 | −9 |
| 16 | F | 2 yr. | 11 | 0 | 8 | 12 | 14 | 2 |
| 6 | F | 3 yr. | 59 | 0 | 7 | 10 | 22 | 8 |
| 9 | M | 1 mo. | 19 | 0 | 7 | 14 | 10 | 6 |
| 20 | F | 1 mo. | 19 | 0 | 2 | ? | ? | −3 |

SOURCE: After Anastasi (1958), p. 299. For all save one twin pair, the data are taken from Newman et al. (1937).
*Ratings are on a scale of 50 points; the higher the rating, the greater the estimated environmental difference between the twins. A negative difference in IQ indicates that the less advantaged twin scored higher.

twin pairs do support the view that genes affect ability. But the large differences in IQ in those pairs whose environments differed greatly support the environmentalist.

A third line of investigation considers the resemblance of children to foster parents. Those findings come out on the hereditarian side. The correlation of an adopted child's test score with the average score of his true parents is 0.58 (a combined estimate from several studies). The correlation with the ability of the foster parents is only 0.19 (Munsinger, 1975).

Though objections can be raised to the quality of some of the data and the assumptions that go into estimates, there is a consistent indication that heredity has an influence. Any other conclusion would violate common sense, since development has a biological base. Anatomical and biochemical differences can surely be expected to have behavioral consequences. Research on animals shows solid evidence for the inheritance of physical qualities that influence learning.

Animal research also turns up interactions. If you pick rats who learn standard mazes in comparatively few trials and crossbreed them, in half a dozen generations you can separate out a strain of "maze-bright" rats. Cooper and Zubek (1958) had both maze-bright and maze-dull strains to work with, but instead of merely demonstrating the hereditary difference, they raised the young in three kinds of cages. In a barren, uniform environment, the genes produced no performance difference on a maze test at age two months. In an environment that encouraged perceptual activity and manipulation of objects the strains also came out about even. It was in the moderately rich environment that the bright strain outstripped the dull strain (Table 8.3).

Authors give different values for the coefficient of heritability for human ability. (They differ in how they treat genetic dominance, how much allowance they make for assortative mating, and how they allow for the probable correlation

TABLE 8.3

Mean errors in maze performance of two strains of rats reared in comparatively rich and in poor environments

|  | Restricted environment | Normal environment | Enriched environment |
|---|---|---|---|
| Maze-bright strain | 169.7 | 117.0 | 111.2 |
| Maze-dull strain | 169.5 | 164.0 | 119.7 |
| Advantage of bright strain | −0.2 | 47.0 | 8.5 |

SOURCE: Data from Cooper & Zubek (1958).

of heredity and environment.) Many of them have put the value of $h^2$ for achievement or ability around 0.80, but their assumptions and evidence are debated. An authoritative recent review (Loehlin et al., 1975, p. 233) warns against taking numerical values of coefficients seriously, in view of the problems of estimation, but offers this conclusion:

> Within populations of European origin, both the genotype and the environment demonstrably influence IQ, the former tending under present conditions to account for more of the individual variation in IQ than does the latter.

CAN HERITABLE QUALITIES BE CHANGED? A high coefficient—even, say, one of 0.80—does not mean that ability is predetermined. A coefficient of 0.78 for weight was given a few paragraphs back. But weight changes with nutrition, and when people are better fed, the average weight in the nation goes up. The heritability estimate for performance on a broad measure of subject-matter achievement is about equal to that for intelligence tests. A person who applies the same formulas and assumptions to both kinds of data will get the same heritability coefficient for both. But it is obvious that the average level of school attainment in the population has been advancing from generation to generation.

A coefficient of heritability is only an historical fact. It tells what the balance was (between the influence of inherited differences and the influence of environmental differences) in the generation and in the place where the study was made. If environments are rather uniform, or are distributed so that those who have a superior inheritance are given better opportunities, $h^2$ will be high. If environments are quite diverse, and especially if they are distributed so that those with an inferior inheritance are given the better opportunities, $h^2$ will drop. The fact that heritability of ability is substantial says only that the differences in individual opportunity and environment among white American homes and schools in the past two generations have not been large enough to be the *chief* influence on standings in ability. Even Jensen, who puts great emphasis on the hereditary component, estimates (1973, p. 164) that environmental effects on IQ are sometimes as large as 15 points (in either direction). No informed scholar believes today that inheritance fixes the IQ in advance.

Mental ability has indeed been going up in the United States. When the publishers of the Stanford-Binet needed new norms in 1971, they tested a representative sample at ages 2 and 18 (R. Thorndike, 1973, 1975). In comparing this sample the norm group tested around 1936, it became evident that today's children perform better during the preschool years and in adolescence. There was essentially no difference between the two generations at ages 7–10. According to a follow-up study, preschoolers whose average in 1971 was ahead of the old norm for that age had fallen back toward the norm by the time they were three years older. "Sesame Street" and other recent cultural opportunities have accelerated the development of young children in this generation (Thorndike, 1975). For other evidence on the rise in ability, see Loehlin et al. (1975, pp. 134ff.), and, regarding American adults, Schaie and Labouvie-Vief (1974).

**4** Which of these statements is plausible as an explanation of the rise in IQs from 1936 to 1971?

    a. Selective mating raised the genetic level of the population in this period.

    b. Today's child has a richer verbal environment prior to age 6 than children in the earlier generation.

    c. Today, young people are not so likely to drop out of high school before finishing.

    d. The elementary school has improved its techniques since the 1930s.

**5** Comment on this playful passage from *Flowers for Algernon* (Keyes, 1960). A patient in a mental hospital says:

> I'm not sure what an IQ is. Dr. Nemur said it was something that measured how intelligent you were—like a scale in the drugstore weighs pounds. But Dr. Strauss had a big argument with him and said an IQ didn't weigh intelligence at all. He said an IQ showed how much intelligence you could get, like the numbers on the outside of a measuring cup. You still had to fill the cup up with stuff.

**6** Is regression greater with a correlation of 0.80 or with a correlation of 0.50?

**7** Suggest some biological mechanisms by which physiological characteristics could influence how much the child learns during his first six months; during the second year of life.

**8** Suggest some possible causes of the interaction demonstrated by Cooper and Zubek (Table 8.3). Might there be some environment that would cause the "maze-dull" rats to outperform the "brights"?

**9** In the following quotation, Deutsch and Deutsch (1974, p. 5) describe the views of "extreme" hereditarians and environmentalists.

> Clearly, educational practice and theory can be the football between protagonists in this field. The hereditarians would set goals for a child based on his genealogy, and until the achievement of some ideal of uniformly excellent genes in the entire population, the numbers of individuals would decrease at successive educational levels. The environmentalists would, on the other hand, set goals to be achieved by all, and would attempt to carry all individuals to the highest levels offered. Education would be likely to start very early and continue very late. Reasons for failure would be sought.

Are these the only social policies consistent (respectively) with belief in high and low values of $h^2$ for abilities? (Note that the Russians are committed to environmentalism, and yet have a strongly selective system of higher education. Their selection is based on course examinations.)

# DEVELOPMENTAL INFLUENCES

## How Environment Affects Ability

Achievement is affected by environment. The food the child gets, the conversations addressed to him in the home, and the emotional support that follows his early trials and failures all leave a mark on his intellectual development. Later, his peer group and his teachers make a difference. Consistent opportunities to use a type of reasoning or discrimination, with appropriate reward, enhance that ability (box).

Conversely, restricted experience retards development. It is repeatedly found that rural children, blacks, and children from remote regions in Appalachia earn, on the average, lower scores than white children in the suburbs. (Though these facts are important, differences *within* groups are much larger than those *between* groups. Many poor children earn high scores on mental tests.)

The effect of restricted environment becomes worse the longer a person remains within that environment. L. Wheeler (1932, 1942) tested children in Tennessee mountain hamlets. In 1930, the 6-year-olds were close to the national norm, their average IQ being 95. But the average dropped steadily with age, the average IQ at age 12 being 80. In a second study a decade later, after roads had opened the area to permit consolidated schools, and after industrial employment had improved the standard of living, the decline with age was much smaller; the mean IQ at age 12 was 90.

## A tale of the South Pacific

Samoans earned exceptionally high scores on a Navy test of aptitude for learning radio code, which calls for memory of rhythmic patterns. Ford (1957) explained the result as follows:

> The basic elements of Samoan music are percussive rhythm instruments, principally sticks, hollowed logs, rolled-up bundles of matting, and empty biscuit tins. Any group of Samoans engaged in group dancing will employ several of these rhythm instruments producing a total effect of very complex rhythmic patterns, against the background of which dancing and singing are performed. Consequently, from childhood the Samoan is accustomed to highly varied and rapid systems of rhythmic beats similar to those found in radio transmission. So proficient do the Samoans become as radio operators that on the Naval circuits between Samoa and Hawaii, which are in use to this day, it was customary to employ Samoans at the Hawaiian end because of the difficulty in obtaining any other kind of personnel who could receive messages sent from Samoa, so great was the rapidity of the Samoan operators in Pago. Since nearly everything in Samoa is done rhythmically, it is not at all surprising that the Samoan radio operators are among the finest transmitters of [code] messages in the world.

It oversimplifies to say that good environments or poor environments account for differences in ability. This explanation would imply a steady rise in standing for some children (good environment) and a steady decline for others. But individual retest records are of many shapes. As you saw in Fig. 8.2, there are some steep declines, some up-and-down patterns, some records that run level for many years and then march upward. Perhaps hereditary patterns of physiological development control this timing of mental growth to some degree. The few pairs of identical twins who were retested repeatedly showed sufficiently similar mental growth curves to support this speculation (Sontag et al., 1958, p. 122).

Some increases or declines reflect radical changes in the child's emotional relations with his world, as in the case of Danny (Lowell, 1941). Danny's mother, having to work, left him in the care of aging grandparents who were irritable and easily disturbed. Therefore, Danny was restricted and discouraged

when he sought to satisfy his curiosity through questions and exploratory play. A nervous disorder was an additional complication. At age 5, Danny was one s.d. below average in mental ability. His mother, suddenly realizing how he was chained down intellectually and emotionally, moved away from the grandparents. Over the next several years Danny received proper medical care, superior schooling, and much greater attention, affection, and encouragement. His scores showed a steady, gradual rise, until he was 2 s.d. above average at the age of 12.

Parental attitudes and techniques affect intellectual development. It will be recalled (p. 214) that children from "democratic" homes tend to be more curious and competitive when they enter school. It is also found that exceptional increases in ability from age 6 to age 10 are strongly associated with the

**FIGURE 8.3**

Relation of IQ at ages 14 to 18 to mother's behavior when the child was under age 3

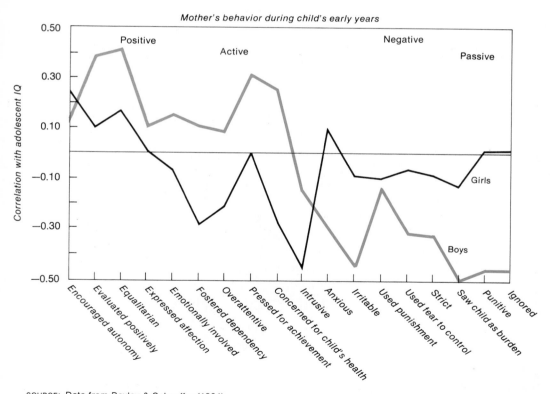

SOURCE: Data from Bayley & Schaeffer (1964).

## Like mother, like child?

The phenomenon of *regression toward the mean* shows up in every relationship, because psychological and social phenomena are only roughly correlated. Hess and Shipman (1967) tested black mothers in several social classes and their 4-year-old children. The averages of IQs did show a trend with social class:

|  | *Mother's IQ* | *Child's IQ* |
|---|---|---|
| Upper middle | 109 | 109 |
| Upper lower | 92 | 99 |
| Lower lower | 82 | 96 |
| On relief | 82 | 94 |

There is a parent-child correlation, but the socially significant point is this: The mothers who, on average, did badly on the test tasks produced children who, on the average, performed in the normal range.

Regression toward the mean is also found above the average: Parents who do well tend to have children somewhat less able than themselves. It did not turn out that way in this study, however.

child's personality at age 6. The one who will gain tends to be aggressive and competitive, and is more likely to initiate his own activities. The independent child is emotionally free to gain more from his environment (Sontag et al., 1958, pp. 116, 126–29).

The effect of the home atmosphere is traced by observing the parent-child interaction and then testing the child at successive ages. A large sample is difficult to follow, and therefore only scattered evidence is available (Baldwin et al., 1949, Bayley & Schaefer, 1964; Honzik, 1967; McCall, Applebaum & Hogarty, 1973). The studies agree in finding autonomy, democracy in the home, and a positive emotional tone beneficial; but each study adds important details. Figure 8.3 displays some of the Bayley-Schaefer evidence. What the mother does in the first three years has a strong relation to the boy's midadolescent IQ. Maternal style seems to have less effect on the girl's characteristics.

The boys who developed intellectual strength had been subject in early years to encouragement *and* strong pressures. The boy reared by a hostile mother typically showed inferior intellectual performance from age 4 onward. It is the solicitous, overattentive mother who seems to damage the girl's long-run intellectual development.

## Comparisons Among Cultural Groups

Virtually every study of mental-test performance finds differences between social-class groups in cognitive tests. Whether social class is defined in terms of

## Black Africans: How do they compare with Westerners?

Test comparisons usually show that persons from Western nations do better, on the average, than persons from developing countries. And within developed countries the black population is often reported to average lower than the white population.

Perspective on these facts is given by Bakare's study in Nigeria (in Cronbach & Drenth, 1972, pp. 355ff.). He gave schoolchildren in the city of Lagos the task of drawing a man, "the best man you can." This is a task that depends little on language but does serve as an index of general ability. Part of Bakare's sample consisted of children of Americans and Europeans working in Lagos. The average scores of the children, classified by parental occupation, were as follows:

| Parents | Grade I | Grades II–III | Grades IV–V |
|---|---|---|---|
| Americans and Europeans Professional-managerial families | 22.0 | 30.5 | 36.5 |
| Nigerians Professional-managerial families | 20.0 | 30.7 | 35.7 |
| Lower-level occupations | 9.6 | 10.9 | 15.4 |

At the professional level the ethnic difference disappeared. The great majority of Nigerians, of course, are still in lower-level occupations, and no doubt a national average for Nigerians would be much lower than that for Americans. But when social class and education are held constant, members of different cultures are likely to do about equally well.

income or education or neighborhood, the difference appears. It appears in developing countries as well as in Western countries and Japan. In the United States, the correlation of scholastic aptitude with father's education or occupation is about 0.30 (Jencks, 1972). The difference is important for society, but the large spread within groups is equally significant. Thus, although the group average for children of blue-collar workers is below the national norm, such children still account for about 40 per cent of the upper end of the aptitude distribution—and about 53 per cent of the lower end (Flanagan et al., 1964, pp. 5–55; see also p. 73). These results refer to test performance, not to ability in some abstract sense. Production deficiencies (see p. 272) are common, particularly among children from lower-class homes.

Within any nation, persons reared and schooled in different traditions have different experiences. Even more dramatic are the differences in culture between, say, Eskimos and Bushmen and suburban Californians. Psychologists have often compared test results of groups that use different symbol systems, place more or less emphasis on written language, and make different demands on the growing child. What was once a rather academic question has come into the spotlight of public debate, as ethnic minorities have found a political voice and now challenge the fairness of the school system. The readers of this book have heard the American disputes (if not the facts); but the arguments are universal—Malay versus Chinese in Kuala Lumpur, English versus Pakistani in London, tribe versus tribe in many an African country.

Generalization is fantastically difficult. Reuning reports (see Cronbach & Drenth, 1972, pp. 171–81) on the Bushmen. Various bands, all leading the same nomadic, hunting, skin-of-their-teeth existence, differ from each other in average score on tests carefully devised to be suitable for Bushmen. Reuning attributes the superior mental alertness of one band to the vivacious spirit of a single young woman who keeps the group more active socially than most. In the same source (pp. 183–95), on the other hand, is an equally credible report of uniformity from Ord. Groups scattered over the length and breadth of New Guinea, from remote mountain to farm village, and with distinct genetic and cultural backgrounds, Ord says, show about the same average test score. (This on tests that do not require reading or verbal response, and after subjects were familiarized with the tests.) It is not uncommon to find a cultural group inferior on one set of tests and superior on another. The Westerner is proud of his group's greater success in, for example, the maze test, compared to that of "primitive" groups. But the psychologists who study isolated non-Western cultures are fond of asking how long the Westerner could survive in the Kalahari desert. Could he, for example, find an arrow that has missed its antelope? (Arrows are precious in a desert.)

Returning to the American scene, what about ethnic differences on the common variety of scholastic aptitude tests? Children from the mainstream culture do have appreciably higher means than children from minorities other than Orientals and Jews. But the majority and minority groups span much the same range. The average differences show up in achievement as much as in IQ. In Grades K–VI of a California school district, the mean black–white difference (expressed relative to the s.d., as with sex data earlier) was 14 on Verbal and Nonverbal IQ; 15–16 on Paragraph Meaning, Arithmetic Applications, and so on; and 10–11 on Spelling and Computation (Jensen, 1973, p. 110). Evidently, the difference is smaller when the test emphasizes crystallized abilities.

Black-white differences are to a large degree a reflection of social-class differences (C. Deutsch, 1973). When comparisons are made of blacks and whites of similar socioeconomic level, the averages differ much less than overall averages. This is true also for other ethnic comparisons. Moreover, social-class differences among black children are small up to age 3, suggesting that, in families below the poverty line, *early* development is as rapid as in middle-class homes (F. Palmer, 1970). If so, the poorer standing of lower-class children at school ages is probably attributable to experiences at age 3 and later.

Studies among the Venda in South Africa, among Malays and Chinese in Malaysia, and (box) in Nigeria (Grant, Harrell, and Bakare in Cronbach & Drenth, 1972) support the view that group differences in performance on sym-

bol-laden tasks reflect social class and education, not ethnic differences or differences between city living and rural living. (See also Scribner & Cole, 1973.)

Superiority on a particular test can appear when a culture emphasizes some specialized talent, as in the case of the American sex difference in mechanical reasoning (p. 286) and of the Samoan aptitude for radio code (box, p. 320). Also, a culture can suppress general mental development when it insists on passive imitation and dependency among children (LeVine, in Mussen, 1970, I, pp. 580–81).

**10**  Do two children growing up in the same family have the same environment?

**11**  In Chapter 6 (p. 214) and in the preceding section, it was reported that the maternal style that has beneficial consequences for a boy tends to have detrimental consequences for a girl. Are such findings probably a reflection of the American culture at the time, and subject to change in another generation? Do they suggest that a mother should deliberately provide different kinds and amounts of stimulation in rearing a boy and a girl?

**12**  What practices should preschool teachers adopt in order to make the environment optimal for intellectual growth?

13 Instruction in sixth grade can place comparatively heavy demands on crystallized abilities or on fluid abilities. What teaching procedures would have each effect?

14 It appears from Jensen's evidence that an emphasis on crystallized abilities would tend to reduce the average difference in accomplishment of black and of white students. What are the arguments for and against such an emphasis in the classroom?

---

# THE COURSE OF INTELLECTUAL DEVELOPMENT

Chapter 5 pointed out the cumulative, active nature of personal development, and showed that physical and intellectual activities contribute to all facets of development. We have seen too that homes have different effects by providing different kinds of stimulation and feedback. But we have not yet examined in any detail how intellectual performance changes. What processes enter into effective performance at various ages? How does the child master these processes?

It is convenient to speak of "stages" or "phases" in intellectual development, but the changes are more gradual than those words suggest. Logic does not hatch out at age 11 like a butterfly from a cocoon, even though psychologists speak of "the beginning of formal operational thought" at age 11. Nor is any other transition abrupt.

Thinking back to Binet's definition (p. 275), we note that "to take and maintain a direction" has motivational as well as intellectual components. The child has to be willing to try; with each added experience of payoff following a bit of effort, his willingness to try is strengthened. To set his own direction, he has to visualize goals. The rather simple goals of early childhood—for example, making a "train" out of a few blocks—are picked up by observing models. With increasing age the child is able to think of more original goals. And he learns to point his efforts toward a goal a day off, then a month off. To *maintain* direction, he must resolve a large task into intermediate tasks and give himself an instruction for each step of the journey.

The third element, "self-criticism," likewise has both emotional and intellectual components. Emotional readiness to review one's impulses obviously grows out of relations with authority in early childhood. The intellectual component includes knowing how to recognize a good performance and knowing the difference between functional criticism and niggling perfectionism. (Recall Estes' remarks on vocabulary, p. 279.) The second of Binet's elements—"analysis and adaptation"—is the center of Piaget's theory, to which we now turn.

Although Piaget is a highly original thinker, his work is a direct outgrowth of Binet's. Piaget started out in Binet's laboratory, testing the reasoning of schoolchildren. Both men were interested in *why* children make mistakes and in how children control their responses so as to reach excellent performance. In his own research, Piaget watched individual children, month-by-month—and even day-by-day, in infancy—to see how more mature mental operations come into being. Piaget's interpretations have had great influence on developmental psychologists in all countries, particularly since 1960. During this same recent period an experimental cognitive psychology was being formulated almost independently, mostly in British and American laboratories. These theorists describe "information processing" in a language different from Piaget's, but the concepts are close to those of the developmental psychologist. Here we stick to Piagetian language; in Chapters 10–13 you will encounter other terminology.

## Construction of Schemata

Piaget's observations make a convincing case that mental "structures" are developed out of the child's physical actions. As Piaget puts it, the child gradually assembles a "construction of reality" in his mind, and uses that to interpret new events. He creates for himself the very idea that his ball is the same ball each time it rolls behind an object and reappears. The idea is a residue of dozens of experiences with disappearance and reappearance. As a person gains control of physical actions he also stores up an image or *schema*. For example, you can imagine the act of tracing a circle on the blackboard; your mental schema is the residue of dozens of physical performances. You interpret a novel situation by mapping it into an appropriate schema from your store. Thus, if someone places × on the blackboard and asks you to draw a circle with the × at the center, you will mentally run through the drawing action and will "see" that you must start your chalkmark a foot or so to one side of the ×, and must regulate your swing in order to keep the circle the same distance from the × in all directions.

Psychologists use the Greek word *schema* (plural, *schemata*) to describe the little-understood process of storing up concepts or images. A schema is not just a label or a definition; it is "a cognitive structure which has reference to a class of similar action structures" (Flavell, 1963, pp. 52–53). Schemata are surely not "photographic" records; your schema for a circle is in part a record of the muscular sensations that go with the act (see p. 405). Schemata may be partly verbal or abstract, as in the concept of maintaining equal distance from the center to get a true circle. As you can see, the schema of "circle" is far more than the formal definition found in a geometry book.

When you use a schema to interpret an event, you "assimilate" the event to what you know. You "take in" the event or object and operate on it mentally. When you say, "A round patch two inches across will just cover that

*"That was the easy part, Joey. Now the trick
is gettin' it back IN!"*

hole," you have assimilated the irregular-shaped hole to your concept of "circle" and planned an effective repair (p. 398). When your attempt to use an existing schema—your attempt at *assimilation*—does not work out, you "accommodate." *Accommodation* is Piaget's term for the process of modifying your schema or building a new one. A child's concept of "circle" develops gradually. At about age 3, the child is willing to accept any closed curve with a single inner space as a circle. (Recall the "successful" attempts to copy a circle on p. 278.) Later, perhaps as a result of hundreds of experiences of trying to fit objects into holes, he is far more attentive to precise shapes. His concept of circle evolves. He also learns, as he handles circular objects, that circles do not look the same from every angle. In time he comes to interpret the figure shown here as a round-topped can.

Many basic concepts are acquired through reversible actions. As you tilt a disk, its image is round, then elliptical, then round. The child sees this hundreds of times as he plays with round objects. Hence he forms a concept of the

## When inside is out

Schemata make it possible to "grasp" a verbal statement or a visual impression. Thus it is easy to visualize a strip of leather whose ends connect to form a belt or shallow cylinder, which, of course, has an inside and an outside. (Note how many concepts were used in that sentence, all referring to schemata I expect you to have in your head.)

Suppose one end of the strip is turned over before the ends are fastened to each other. This creates a surface for which few people possess a schema. This "Möbius strip," illustrated here, resembles the belt or cylinder, yet it has no outside and no inside. If such strips become important to you, perhaps in the course of mathematical research, you will handle the strips, turn them about, and gradually build up a new schema.

shape of an object, a concept independent of the sensory impression of the moment. His schema acquires a dynamic element. Knowing the shape of an object, he can visualize it from various angles; he can turn it in his mind. And, seeing a new object from an odd angle, he can visualize the head-on "shape." This is useful, for example, in assembling a cutout puzzle; schemata enable him to test possible moves before he makes them. Schemata for shapes are put to more serious use in sewing, carpentry, and problems in physics.

Psychologists do not look on schemata as innate properties of the nervous system. They develop out of experience. This view is bolstered by reports from studies of primitive cultures whose technology makes little use of straight lines (Segall et al., 1966).

Accommodation plays a large part in the evolution of ideas. Newton started with a simple schema: "Objects fall toward the earth." This was consistent with an endless series of human experiences. But when he substituted the schema "objects moving toward each other," he had a more powerful intellectual tool. Most of us have physical experience that makes the "falling" concept highly meaningful, whereas "mutual attraction" is abstract and not fully internalized. As with the Möbius strip (box), we have to believe it; but we do not feel it in our bones.

It is easiest to illustrate the ideas of Piaget with geometric concepts, but his argument is general. Ideas about number, about the force that must have existed to produce an observed change, about musical harmony, even about social relations—all are developed in a similar manner, according to Piaget's theory. To take a social example: The essence of fair play is reversibility. "If I were in the place of the other person, would I be satisfied?" The concept is built up through physical experience: actually sharing out cookies, for example. The adult can encourage experiences that will revise the primitive egocentric view: "You fill plates for everybody; then everyone takes a plate, and you get the last one." The trick is to set a rule that makes the child visualize alternatives.

The process of developing a schema, then, has these elements:

- The person is repeatedly in situations that exemplify or embody the concept.

- The person acts on the objects and observes changes. He often acts in a back-and-forth manner, changing arrangement A to B and back to A again.

- The person begins to anticipate what will happen in such actions, and reality confirms (or disconfirms) his expectation.

- The set of confirmed prediction rules is stored as a schema.

- When assimilation fails and some expectation is not confirmed, the person carries out further manipulations or transformations until familiarity generates a new schema.

The number of schemata a child develops is almost endless, but Piaget has singled out a few of special interest. Somewhere around ages 6 to 8, the child develops conservation principles with respect to number, weight, quantity, and shape. With regard to quantity or volume, for example, he knows that when you pour the orange juice from a fat glass to a skinny one, the amount remains the same. When he knows, he *really* knows. The 5-year-old is likely to say that the tall skinny glass contains more juice because the level is higher. The 8-year-old can imagine reversing the pouring operation and getting back the original amount in the fat glass. Having an operation in mind that ties down the

concept of an unchanging amount, he now is less dependent on perception. A mature schema enables him to correct the false interpretation based on the visual impression. When the child enters what Piaget calls the stage of "concrete operational thought," knowledge overrules perception. Let us now look at Piaget's system stage by stage.

## Stages Toward Mature Intellectual Control: Piagetian Theory

Intellectual activities become more controlled as children grow older. Every stage of intellectual growth depends on its predecessors and leads up to the learning that follows. Educational plans must take into account what earlier schooling can do or must leave undone. For teachers in higher grades, there is an additional reason to understand the early stages. Many reports speak as if children at age 8 think differently from those at age 5. This is only partly true. A person never leaves the early stages behind. The stranger the situation—Möbius again—the more one must drop back to primitive performance and work his way toward understanding.

Piaget's observations are summarized in the following list of stages. (See also Table 8.4.)

| | |
|---|---|
| First two years | Acquiring sensorimotor control |
| Age 2– | Extracting concepts from experience |
| Age 4– | Intuitive judgments |
| Age 7– | Mastering concrete operations (control through perceptual anticipation of consequences) |
| Age 11– | Progress toward formal operations (control through logical deduction of possibilities and consequences) |

This time schedule suggests approximately when a type of performance begins to be prominent. The point of emergence varies with the concept, the method of instruction, the cultural group studied, and so on. The typical American student is still have difficulty with certain concrete operations at age 12, when he is beginning to reason formally. The last step is not taken by everyone. Kuhn et al. (unpublished; see Kohlberg, 1973) report that the percentage of persons displaying formal reasoning on one Piagetian task is 45 at ages 10–15, and does not rise above 65 in age brackets ranging up to age 50.

SENSORIMOTOR CONTROL    The child initially brings perception and motor response under control by observation and by trial and error. During the first two years there is, presumably, little thoughtful regulation of response. Starting with a visual image that is presumably no more than a disorganized jumble of sensations, the infant creates an organization. "Fields" of color and pattern that move

**TABLE 8.4**

**Stages in the mastery of operations**

| Age level* | Designation | Principal features |
|---|---|---|
| 0–2 | Acquiring sensorimotor control | Extensive trial-and-error movements develop bodily control and eye-hand coordination. The perceptual field is organized into objects. |
| 2– | Extracting concepts from experience | Words heard are associated with objects. Concepts are formed for recurring experiences. |
| 4– | Intuitive judgments ("preoperational") | Direct perceptual comparisons are accurate. Associated concepts are confused. Complex situations are reacted to as unanalyzable wholes; conclusions are based on superficial impressions. |
| 7– | Concrete operational thought | Comparisons requiring that information be held in mind are accurate, if the information is presented concretely. Operations can be imagined and results anticipated. Adjustment by reversal leads to an exact result. Associated concepts (for example, height and width) are distinguished; one can be changed while the other stays fixed. |
| 11– | Formal operational thought | Operations among symbols or abstract ideas can be carried out in the mind. A complete array of logical possibilities can be systematically considered. Relations involving more than one variable can be comprehended. Accurate comparisons and deductions can be made from information not concretely presented. |

*See cautionary note in text.

together he comes to distinguish as objects: his mother, his nursing bottle, his stuffed tiger. He organizes the field by "constructing" objects out of sensory impressions (Piaget, 1954).

The infant practices a thousand times the arm movement toward a dangling object. He is motivated, so far as we can tell, by the sheer satisfaction of producing the result he foresees. He repeats a babbling pattern—apparently satisfied just by the accomplishment—until he can make the sound when he thinks of it. Only then can he imitate what he hears and learn his family's language.

EXTRACTING CONCEPTS FROM EXPERIENCE    The child must achieve concepts for himself; they cannot be handed to him. The child has to form for himself even the idea of sameness or identity.

Particularly at ages 2–4, vague relational concepts—bigger, older, more numerous, and so on—are extracted or constructed from experience. Such concepts can be formed without verbal instruction, through frequent association of a consequence with some aspect of the stimuli. A child can form the concept of ledges, high stools, and so on as things he might fall from, even though he is given no name for the idea. He may in time make up his own word for such a concept.

He also learns by hearing relation words associated with consequences. His mother says "Too much water; you'll spill it," and "Mary can stay up because she is older." The child cannot be told directly what the relational word means. He must extract the idea of quality—"too much," "older"—from the contexts in which it appears.

INTUITIVE JUDGMENTS    The child at ages 4 to 7, having inexact language for relations, applies concepts impressionistically. Many small pieces of chocolate he thinks are more than one unbroken piece. His judgments are not controlled by abstract concepts of unchangeable shape, volume, and so on, so he fails the conservation tests.

The child's concepts do not yet permit him to think ahead. Piaget (1950, p. 37) cites the experiment of his colleague Rey, who hands out a piece of paper with a three-inch square in the middle and asks the child to draw the largest and smallest squares he can on the page. The 8-year-old (who has advanced beyond the intuitive stage) properly draws a tiny square in the center and a large one crowding the edge. For him, increase in size is an "operation"; he foresees what will happen when the enlarging operation is applied repeatedly. The 6-year-old (who has not mastered the operation) draws just inside and outside the standard, and then makes other squares, moving inward and outward, approaching the goal a little at a time. He shows no anticipation of the final result. He cannot "carry" the idea of "square" through the series without drawing intermediate steps.

At this stage the child makes excellent *perceptual* judgments. He can compare two servings of cake by placing one alongside the other, or two handfuls of candy by pairing off the pieces. Asked to make a bead chain to match one he is given—red, yellow, blue, yellow, blue, and so on—he does it well *if* he can lay his chain alongside the model so as to obtain perceptual feedback (Fig. 8.4). His judgments are performed directly on sensory experience; he does not hold the information in mind or rearrange it mentally. He cannot think of two aspects of an object at once, nor imagine how it would look from a different angle.

# FIGURE 8.4

## Progression in use of the concept of *order*

The child is told to arrange, on the rod he holds, a sequence of beads exactly like that of the model.

PREOPERATIONAL THOUGHT (ABOUT AGES 4–5)

a.

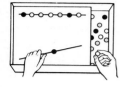

Child adds one bead at a time, putting copy alongside model to check, regulating by touch or short eye movements.

b.

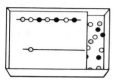

Rod is fixed by tester in offset position. Child adds one bead at a time, regulating by back-and-forth eye movements.

c.

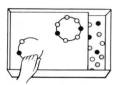

Child breaks circle into parts. Tends to lose his place and reverse direction. Has no concept of "between."

d.

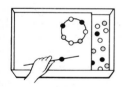

Response is mediated by image of the circle "opened out," transforming the task to one resembling that in *b*.

OPERATIONAL THOUGHT (ABOUT AGES 6–7)

Child is told to make a chain with the order reversed. He must extract the order, neglecting appearance. The performance is regulated by verbal mediators such as "next to" and "between."

e.

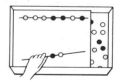

Child is told to make a chain with the order reversed from a given starting point.

f.

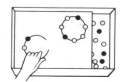

Starting point is given. Child mediates response by naming colors in order while working on each section.

g.

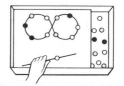

SOURCE: Data from Piaget & Inhelder (1956).

## "Minus times minus equals . . ."

Piaget's insistence on developing operational concepts through action is well illustrated here:

> . . . everyone knows the difficulty that secondary students (and even university students!) have in understanding the algebraic rule of signs—"minus times minus equals plus." This rule of signs is discovered in action by children of seven or eight, already under different qualitative forms. When a thin iron rod transversing three beads, ABC, is turned around a small screen (with the movements of the rod being visible, but not those of the beads), the child understands that the order ABC changes to CBA. He then understands that as soon as two turns around are completed the order becomes ABC again, that three rotations becomes CBA, etc. In this way he discovers, without knowing it, the rule of composition that states that two inversions of direction cancel each other. In other words, "Minus times minus equals plus." But when he reaches fifteen to sixteen years of age, he will not understand the algebraic computations, of which he will learn the existence, unless they appear to him as a continuation of actions of this type! (Piaget, 1973, pp. 104–05.)

The child at this age can rarely break a complex impression into perceptual segments or describe relations correctly in words. Consequently, relations over a distance are hard for him to compare. When the bead model is moved away from his rod (*b* in Fig. 8.4), perceptual point-to-point comparison becomes difficult. Looking back and forth, he loses his place. He lacks the verbal control that would fix the order in his mind. He gradually becomes able to encode information verbally and to transform it (*c* and *d* in Fig. 8.4). The active transformation and reinterpretation of the world that establishes concepts is helpful in most learning. Other chapters will have much to say about the role of mental transformation, or *recoding,* in learning and thinking.

CONCRETE OPERATIONS    Bruner (1960, p. 35) has observed:

> An operation is a type of action: it can be carried out rather directly by the manipulation of objects, or internally. . . . Roughly, an [internalized] operation is a means of getting data about the real world into the mind and there transforming them so that they can be organized and used selectively in the solution of problems.

Operations *in thought* make overt physical trial-and-error operations unnecessary.

Somewhere around age 7, the child begins to see each common relational concept as implying a continuous operation that is reversible (growth and shrinkage, adding to and taking away from, rotating to the left and to the right, and so on). Reversibility is the key to precise adjustment. Two quantities can be made the same by up-and-down corrections, as Alice in Wonderland adjusted her height by nibbling the left- and right-hand mushrooms in turn.

Suppose the child is asked to aim a marble from a pivoting tube so it will bounce off a cushion and strike a target each time. The child who works intuitively shoots from haphazardly chosen positions; he has difficulty in zeroing in on the exact solution. The older child, making controlled back-and-forth adjustments, gets organized information. He relates the marble's path to the angle of aim. Thinking replaces overt trial (Piaget & Inhelder, 1956).

According to this theory, a concept is fundamentally an imagined action. The infant's turning a toy about in his hands prepares him to rotate an object in imagination and envision the consequences. Only command of this operation leads one to ask, "What does the other side of the moon look like?" An operation links experiences and makes one aware of gaps.

Just such a discovery was expressed by my daughter, youngest of three, as she extended her 5-year-old idea of "older" to see that it means nothing without a "younger" element. During that year's Christmas vacation, the oldest daughter was home from college, full of plans for marriage. The younger girls were impressed by her "graduation" from the family, and by Number Two's moving into the place of Big Sister. Came the day when Number Three left her dolls, sought out her mother, and half in question and half in distress exclaimed: "When *I* grow up and am a Big Sister—why—*I won't be!*" One can almost see her lining up the procession in her mind and working her way up to the front, only to find when she gets there that no one is behind her.

### Concrete operational thought

*"But Mommy . . . what do they do when the basement is full of steps?"*

Drawing by Richard Kluga

In concrete operational thought, a person reasons successfully about things that are or have been concretely present before him. Distinctions between related properties (for example, *weight* and *density*) are a necessary preliminary to operational thought about them (Ervin & Foster, 1960; Bruner et al., 1966). A person who cannot distinguish true distance from "distance as it appears from this angle" cannot think accurately about distances. The learner who connects each concept with its unique operation can separate concepts and attend to one at a time (Elkind, 1961b). In art and history, as well as in scientific areas, one deals with relations of properties and facts. Keeping two facts or purposes in view becomes possible at the concrete operational stage.

Operational thought about a concept is frequently shown by the child's use of a conservation principle: breaking a piece of candy into several pieces does not change its amount; changing the shape of plasticene does not change its weight; looking at a mountain from a new angle does not change distances on its slopes. The concept of conservation is fundamental to disciplined thought: in geometry, maintenance of shape as triangles are moved; in engineering, conservation of properties of materials; in history, the search for facts independent of the observer's viewpoint. Use of a conservation concept to regulate thought comes slowly. The child judges familiar materials accurately long before he can pass a similar conservation test with unfamiliar objects (Lester & Klein, 1973).

FORMAL OPERATIONS    A 14-year-old shoots a marble from a tube toward the cushioned edge of a billiard table three times. His remarks show logic at work (Inhelder & Piaget, 1958, p. 11).

> "The more the target approaches the plunger, the more the plunger must also approach the target. . . . If there were a line here [perpendicular to the cushion], the ball would come back exactly the same way" (i.e., would make equal angles on both sides). Questioned on whether his law always works, he replies, "It depends on the cushion too, . . . it has to be completely horizontal. But if the cushion were oblique, you would have to trace a perpendicular to the cushion and you would still have to take the same distant [angle] from the plunger [to the cushion and] up to the target."

This adolescent is using formal operational thought. He is reasoning accurately about a possibility present only in his imagination.

The early adolescent begins to make logical inferences and to cast his experience into rigorous verbal principles. He becomes better at ignoring the perceptions and prejudices that becloud logical arguments (p. 183). The transition from concrete to formal operations is illustrated by the child who is asked to draw a big rectangle in the same shape as a smaller rectangle. Aids such as rulers are provided (Piaget & Inhelder, 1956, p. 370). The 5-year-old child cannot preserve the shape; he increases length and lets height come out as it will. A few years later, he will mark off the length twice and the height twice—a concrete operation. Intermediate, fractional enlargements are still beyond him.

His next advance is to make a trial enlargement and judge impressionistically whether the shape is right. Once he can judge, he can attain the right shape by reversible adjustments. Ultimately, he becomes able to abstract the ratio *Length 1 : Length 2.* Now he has a formal operational concept of proportion. He can accurately and straightforwardly enlarge the rectangle by any amount.

Formal operations enable one to consider all the possibilities, in or out of experience. All the combinations can be identified. The adolescent is asked to observe a horizontal rod before and after weights are hooked to the end. Some rods (thinner, or longer, or less rigid) bend more than others. With command of formal thought, he is able to check off possible combinations and identify the regularities so he can make sound predictions about additional rods.

> Since, unlike the concrete-level child, he does not have to limit his consideration to a single relationship at a time, he can then proceed to the consideration of other variables which might determine it. He "feeds" his information into a general mechanism [for comparing and combining statements] . . . which assimilates the facts in the form of propositions and arranges them according to all possible combinations. . . . He can move around among these possibilities [to select an explanation] . . . : for example, that length alone does not determine flexibility so that another factor was involved for the short rod that bent. . . . The adolescent both discriminates between parts (variables or specific events . . .) and generalizes to an over-all explanation of the results and to [predictions about] other potential situations. (Parsons & Milgram, in Inhelder & Piaget, 1958, p. xviii.)

DISCUSSION   To speak of mental "growth" as a continuous process resembling growth in height is an oversimplification. It also oversimplifies to map "stages" onto the age scale. Each stage prepares for the next, but there are no sharp transitions. Although concepts emerge in sequence, it is quite possible to have command of one operational concept while using another intuitively, or to apply the concept at one moment and not at another.

There is no discontinuity between stages. As we saw in Fig. 8.4, progress is gradual; one learns to use his concepts, operations, and sensorimotor controls more expertly, and extends their reach. A child playing checkers may be able to think three moves ahead in some plays, one move ahead in others, and not at all when—to his confusion—he finds himself challenged at two points simultaneously.

Intellectual processing advances one step at a time through the intuitive recognition of vague properties; the isolation of one relational concept from another; the ability to perform the action mentally with anticipation, reversal, and conservation; and, finally, to the representation of the operation in a formal symbolic system. Understanding of any single effect or relation starts from very hazy impressions, often logically inconsistent or factually incorrect. One masters a concept only through operating with it in a variety of situations. When a concept becomes "operational," one can treat it imaginatively. A person forms, for example, an internal scale of historical time along which he can run, in his imagination. Then he can think of social conditions as smoothly changing, rather than as static or abruptly changing. The operation replaces the impressionistic leap from data to conclusions with a series of small, reversible steps, each of which the person can judge in turn to be reasonable or unreasonable.

The progress exhibited is primarily a gain in rigor of control. The child gains control of a movement. Then he gains control of an image of a movement: on seeing a triangular block, he can judge whether or not the block, if transported and turned, will fit into a puzzle. This is a provisional try with feedback just as much as if the response were made muscularly. Control though anticipation speeds up the trial and makes overt error infrequent. At a later stage, the student will be able to measure sizes and angles formally, so as to predict the fit of pieces far too complex for a perceptual judgment. Thought becomes increasingly regulated or disciplined (Binet's self-criticism).

Mental discipline is seen to consist not of a vague mental power but of ability to apply specific operations in transforming information. It is not "being bright" that prevents an error in copying a bead chain; it is being able to keep one's place and sense of direction. The correlation between ability to use number concepts operationally and mental age on the Wechsler scale is only 0.40 in school beginners (Elkind, 1961a). Being "bright" does not guarantee that one has attended to the specific properties of numbers. The number scale, the coordinate plane, parallelism, and so on are specific instruments of mathematical thought, not aspects of undifferentiated "mental growth." Biological science has its operational concepts: growth, metabolism, evolutionary development. Similar concepts underlie successful reasoning in geography, economics, and social science. The ideas that seem to matter are very broad concepts, not specifics about the Corn Laws or the parts of a leaf. Mental development comes through practice in which success with a less-controlled, impressionistic response builds up conceptual mediators. These have the power to regulate response in confusing circumstances and in circumstances where a radical transformation of information is required. Extensive experience apparently is needed to make a concept truly operational.

## Ability in Adulthood

The intellectual processes described by Piaget appear in adult thought. When first trying to understand something new (say, the game of *Go* or the theory of musical harmony), even the adult must work his way from perceptual comparison to intuition to operational thought. He cannot think abstractly without a base of experience. If something in his present repertoire of operational concepts seems to apply, however, he can begin operational thought at once, at least as a provisional try. The theory of crystal structure, for instance, can be studied in a formal way by a person who has mastered the formal structure of solid geometry, because the latter rests on an adequate base of intuitive familiarity. Analysis of novel material is greatly facilitated by earlier mastery of a pertinent formal theory.

One of the most dramatic reversals of a once-accepted psychological conclusion is the evidence on trends in average test score with age. When mental tests were first applied to large samples, in World War I, it was reported that "the average adult has the mind of a 13-year-old." This could be believed, since the test performance called upon verbal and mathematical skills that, in adolescents, were still fresh. Eventually it was realized that a *cross-sectional* study comparing 40-year-olds in 1920 with 13-year-olds in 1920 showed little about the course of mental growth. When education is expanding, older adults in any decade are less educated than younger adults. A fair picture of the trend during a lifetime can be obtained by testing the same persons repeatedly over 30 years or more—a *longitudinal* study. A way to get pertinent data more quickly is the *overlapping longitudinal* study: persons representative of various ages are tested, and each group is retested a few years later.

Recent findings with overlapping samples (for example, Schaie & Labouvie-Vief, 1974) dispel the old belief that the mind somehow becomes less flexible after adolescence. Vocabulary remains steady during a person's working years, and number skills are also maintained. Success with unfamiliar problems perhaps peaks before age 60, but the subsequent decline is slow. (The peak age depends somewhat on the reasoning test used.) Decline is more rapid after age 60, perhaps due to loss of interest in test taking, or, in some persons, to physiological deterioration.

The findings argue that, if adequately motivated, people in middle life and even those near retirement can learn as much from instruction as young people. We hear much today of plans to put schooling on a part-time basis and extend it to later ages. This would give the adolescent time to play a larger role in the community, and give the older person a greater opportunity to acquire training as he comes to want it. Such plans could meet the demand of adolescents for "relevant" activity, and could serve the older person who finds his interests broadening or his skills becoming obsolete. The findings strongly encourage such plans, because they imply that so far as ability is concerned youth is *not* the golden age for learning.

---

**15** In one of Piaget's tests the child sees dolls of three colors (A, B, and C) tied onto a wire. The experimenter pulls the wire into a tunnel (made from a box) so that the dolls are hidden. The child is asked which doll will come out first when the wire is pulled further in the same direction, or is pulled backward. Explain these results (Piaget, 1950, p. 135).
  a. Three-year-olds correctly give the answer for the forward order of the dolls.
  b. Three-year-olds cannot give the answer when the wire is pulled backward, but 5-year-olds can.

c. When the box with the dolls inside is turned through 180° (reversed), 7-year-olds can predict which doll will come out first, but younger children cannot.

d. Having made several trials in which A or C comes out first, the 5-year-old is likely to predict B as the answer to a new question, because "B is due to have a turn."

16 In the test with the three dolls, where does an "operation" enter? Is anything "conserved" during the operation?

17 For Piaget a concept is an imagined action, as this quotation illustrates:

> To perceive a chair, said Pierre Janet, is to see an object on which one may sit; and to perceive a house, says von Weiszäcker even more emphatically, is not to look upon an image which enters you through your eye, but on the contrary to recognize a solid into which you may enter! (Piaget & Inhelder, 1959, p. 21.)

a. Show that an adult's concept of a hen's egg is a collection of "imagined actions."

18 Consider whether the bead-chain performances in Fig. 8.4 can be described in terms of each of these concepts. If so, illustrate the application of the term.
a. assimilation
b. accommodation
c. schema
d. operations in thought

19 Identify three of Wechsler's subtests that require use of operational thought, and three that require little or no use of operational thought.

20 A person studying genetics learns about Mendel's experiments with round and wrinkled peas, about dominant and recessive traits, and about the role of genes and of DNA. Can any part of this learning be described as mastery of "operations" in Piaget's sense?

21 Modern economics is based on a formal theory that allows accurate reasoning about changes that can occur in the system. Does Piaget's theory imply that teaching of economics should be delayed until the person has become competent in formal operational thought?

22 To study how individual patterns of motivation develop, an investigator proposes to study twins, finding out at what ages and in what circumstances members of a twin pair develop dissimilar values and interests. Describe how data would be collected for a cross-sectional study, for a longitudinal study, and for an overlapping longitudinal study. Which of these procedures would you recommend?

# POSSIBLE BIAS FROM TESTS OR FAILURE TO TEST

Impressed by the stability of ability tests and their correlation with later school performance, educators have often reasoned as follows:

> One cannot learn unless given tasks for which one is ready.

> Low-scoring students lack readiness for the regular school curriculum.

> Therefore, low scorers should be given little verbal work and little work requiring abstract thinking.

This reasoning is of a piece with the belief in "waiting for maturation" (p. 164). It also fits with the "child-nurse" view (p. 52), which, in its commitment to keep the child happy, keeps demands as light as possible. Thus, some high schools routinely assign students with subaverage mental test scores to vocational training. In elementary social studies, while the others are using the library to prepare reports, the test-poor student is set to cutting out pictures for a scrapbook. This makes it certain that he will learn little.

Critics of testing assert that letting the teacher know the child's IQ biases decisions. Much is expected of the high scorer, and he learns much; little is expected of the low scorer, and his failures are accepted rather than overcome.

There are three questions to consider:

> Should the teacher be guided by his perception of the student?

> Do tests of readiness introduce bias into the teaching situation?

> Are general mental tests more damaging than other readiness or aptitude tests?

As for the first question, this book has insisted on the importance of perceiving the student as an individual. The teacher interprets events in the classroom before deciding what to do next. He will interpret rightly or wrongly what the student does, but interpret he must. The teacher who does not fit the work to the student's apparent intellectual and emotional readiness is reduced to trying to treat everyone alike. Expecting everyone to reach the same standard at the same time can only shortchange one fraction of the class while keeping another fraction under intolerable pressure.

None of us makes trustworthy judgments of persons we meet for the first time. Sex, race, and manners that reflect background influence impressions. It was just because teachers failed to recognize talent evenhandedly that mental tests were invented. As Gardner (1961) puts it, "The tests couldn't see whether the youngster was in rags or in tweeds, and they couldn't hear the accents of the slum." Even in 1969, teachers questioned by Goodwin and Sanders considered the social class of the school beginner's family a good indicator of his

## Do tests work magic?

Serious policy issues underlie controversies about testing. How early should differentiation of education begin? What role should objective information play? The public debate on these has been clouded by the publicity given to flimsy evidence on the presence or absence of biases in tests.

Much newspaper space was given to an experiment reported under the title *Pygmalion in the Classroom* (Rosenthal & Jacobsen, 1968). In November, each teacher in the study was given the names of a few "magic children" who had done well on a mental test. This false report was made up for experimental purposes; names listed had been picked at random. According to the report, these randomly chosen children made greater intellectual gains than their classmates by the time of a retest in May. The argument is that the teacher believed in their excellence and did more to teach them—a self-fulfilling prophecy.

The Rosenthal-Jacobsen result is not to be believed. The study was riddled with procedural and logical faults (Elashoff & Snow, 1971). Indeed, so little did the list of names capture the teacher's attention that, at the end of the year, the teacher could not even recall which children were on the list. Other studies (for example, Fleming & Antonen, 1971; Dusek & O'Connell, 1973) lead us to think that teachers are not unduly influenced by favorable or unfavorable test reports—at least, not to the point of causing high scorers to make progress beyond what their aptitude itself promised.

The lesson in the *Pygmalion* hullabaloo is that misunderstanding flourishes when a conclusion that agrees with the popular biases of the moment catches the attention of the mass media (Cronbach, 1975b).

probable school success. In setting expectations, these teachers would evidently pay more attention to social class than to ability tests. (See Brophy & Good, 1974, pp. 7–13, for this and several similar studies.) Nonetheless, offering an objective appraisal of what the student can do—over the whole spectrum of relevant abilities—ought to offset some of the teacher's biases and help him to pitch instructional tasks nearer the right level.

The point of objective testing—whether of IQ or achievement—is partly to reduce casual errors, partly to prevent *thoughtless* discrimination. To see what happens when tests are not taken seriously, look at a shocking report (Rist, 1970) on the treatment of black children in a ghetto kindergarten. The teacher (herself black) grouped the pupils around three tables, and, as Rist saw it, the assignment to tables was based on such cues as physical appearance, body odor, a background questionnaire filled out by the mother, and dialect. The division was made after eight days of school, with no direct evidence of ability in hand. Once placed in a group, almost every child who stayed in the school was kept with that same group, at least through the second grade. The teacher *made* fast learners out of Group 1. These children—cleaner, from less poor homes, with high-school-educated parents—were the ones who led the Pledge of Allegiance, recorded attendance, received the bulk of the teacher's time, were in the center of every discussion.

> The Friday after Hallowe'en, the teacher informed the class that she would allow time for all the students to come to the front of the class and tell of their experiences. She, in reality, called on six students, five of whom sat at Table 1 and the sixth at Table 2. . . . During one observational period of an hour in May, not a single act of communication was directed towards any child at either Table 2 or 3 except for twice commanding "sit down."

The teacher wrote on the segment of blackboard beside Table 1; the children at Table 3 were unable to see what she wrote. The discrimination practiced by the teacher had the effects on morale one might anticipate. Table 1 children scorned the lower groups, and these either withdrew into sullen silence or quarreled with each other.

Going on to the first grade, those children who had been at Table 1 were assigned to the fast-reading Table A, the others to slower groups B and C. The second-grade teacher named her groups: Tigers, Cardinals, and Clowns(!). Sure enough, no one became a Tiger who had not been at Table A in Grade 1 and at Table 1 before that. The first-grade classification was based on somewhat objective information: only the Table 1 children had completed enough of the readiness lessons to be ready for a regular reading program. But instead of continually encouraging progress by individuals and making periodic reassignments, the teacher held each group to its predestined path. Thus, no Table B child who began to show rapid progress was allowed to shift to Table A books until he had read all the books on the list for Table B.

We do not know what tests would have shown if they had been given to these children when schooling began. At the end of kindergarten, IQs were recorded (but it appears that no teacher made use of them). At that point, even after a year of discriminatory treatment, several children in Groups 2 and 3 scored as high as children in Group 1. If the initial grouping had been based on ability fairly measured, the insensitive kindergarten teacher would still have damaged the educational chances of two thirds of her class. But tests, if they were taken seriously, could perhaps have reduced the teacher's social-class bias.

In the nation as a whole, school practice has been liberalized by the recognition that the IQ range among black children stretches well up into the distribution usual for college graduates, and that a large fraction of the children of factory workers are entirely capable of mastering academic work. Teachers are now trained to resist stereotypes about poor neighborhoods and to foster each talent the tests detect. Reports such as Rist's, however, warn that the training has not always succeeded.

Misuses of readiness tests will do harm. The principal misuse is to make an irreversible judgment, assigning a child to a category from which he is not allowed to escape. This was indefensible in the kindergarten Rist studied and it

Español | English
Buenos días. | Good morning
Buenos tardes. | Good afternoon
Buenas noches. | Good night
Me llamo Juan. | My name is John
¿Cómo estás tú? | How are you?
Estoy malo. | I am sick
Estoy bien. | I am well

would have been inexcusable even if the initial judgment were based on thorough and objective measurement of readiness. A diagnostic approach permits the teacher to do something for the child's readiness; a simple predictive approach only sorts out the promising ones for favored treatment. Predicting what kind or pace of work the student can be expected to handle in the next year is a sensible starting point. Working on specific weaknesses may well make any long-range prediction invalid. Judgments about readiness should be updated as week-by-week progress brings in new information.

The charge that general mental tests are more biased than other tests has both true and false elements. The truth is that they are more often misused. Too many educators still think of the IQ as a fixed report of an inherited capacity, and perhaps as a mark of natural merit. If they were to think of it as an overall estimate of present level of intellectual performance they would be on safe ground. But that overall estimate is of limited use, since far more than a single score is needed to diagnose readiness.

The false aspect of the charge is in the belief that mental tests predict less success for the poor student or the student of minority background than he will actually have. The facts do not support that charge (p. 295). It is true—recall our comments on production deficiency (p. 272) and on motivation (p. 222)—that lower-class children have ability their test scores do not show. It is true that children whose native language is not English would usually do better if tested in the native language. It is true (p. 325) that blacks average closer to whites in using crystallized abilities than in using fluid abilities. These same limitations— in motivation, in techniques of learning, in use of English, in fluid adaptation— are limitations in school also. Hence the low test score does indicate substandard readiness for ordinary schooling, just as it does for a middle-class white student.

On the other hand, when a student of minority background earns the same score as a student from a mainstream background, this does not mean that the two are just alike. As the president of the Educational Testing Service has remarked (W. W. Turnbull, in Sawuda, 1975, p. ix): "Scores of a minority student, on a college-aptitude test . . . tell you nothing about the odds against which he or she has had to struggle in developing those particular abilities. . . ."

The problem always comes back to that of adapting schooling. Slowing the pace is just one of many adaptations. Teaching a good part of the program in the student's native language is a sensible adaptation. One of Labov's suggestions is to add a young black male to the junior-high-school teaching team, to interact with the students in a culturally familiar style. A low test score is a warning that a student will encounter trouble if he is expected to take the regular school situation in stride. It is not a prediction that nothing can be done for him.

---

**23** Legislatures and school authorities have adopted various policies regarding the use of mental tests in schools. What is to be said for and against each of these policies? (Consider Grades III–VI and Grades IX–XII.)

    a. Group mental tests may be administered only by a qualified psychologist, and the scores obtained should not be disclosed to teachers. Teachers should be provided with scores only on achievement tests.

    b. Group mental tests may be used and the scores may be reported to teachers, provided the tests yield scores for two or more abilities.

    c. Tests of both fluid and crystallized abilities may be used so long as no IQ is calculated.

**24** "Many [mental test items] contain obviously middle-class social and cultural biases (e.g., 'why do we have books?')" (J. Ryan, 1972, p. 47). On what grounds might the test-developer argue that this question is a proper one?

**25** In the light of what has now been said, how do you react to the dispute regarding Gary Brock (p. 160)?

---

 READING LIST

Theodosius Dobzhansky, "Diversity of Individuals, Equality of Persons," in *Genetic Diversity and Human Equality* (New York: Basic Books, 1973), pp. 3–50.

> A distinguished geneticist explains the fundamentals of genetic reasoning and seeks to overcome the usual misunderstandings about the inherited component of ability. He goes on to argue that a society can open opportunity far more widely if it recognizes the options that genetic diversity permits.

Christopher Jencks, "The Heredity-Environment Controversy," in *Inequality* (New York: Basic Books, 1972), pp. 64–84.

> Jencks summarizes the principal sources of evidence on both within-race and between-race differences, and indicates why findings on heritability have little meaning for policies to reduce inequality.

Jane L. Mercer, "Psychological Assessment and the Rights of Children," in *Issues in the Classification of Children,* vol. 1, ed. Nicholas Hobbs (San Francisco: Jossey-Bass, 1975), pp. 130–58.

> Mercer shows how failure to interpret test scores against the person's socioeconomic background, and alongside information on the person's adaptive functioning in the community, leads to false and unjust classifications. She advocates "pluralistic multicultural assessment."

Jean Piaget, *To Understand Is to Invent* (New York: Grossman, 1973), 148 pp.

> In these two papers written for UNESCO, Piaget makes a special effort to present his ideas simply. He ranges over numerous aspects of educational policy and classroom procedure, relating his advice to observations made in his laboratory.

Julian C. Stanley, "Predicting College Success of the Educationally Disadvantaged," *Science* 171 (1971), 640–47.

Stanley argues for screening out of demanding college programs students with poor school records and poor test performance. He supports his position with a review of research.

Lewis M. Terman, "The Discovery and Encouragement of Exceptional Talent," *American Psychologist* 9 (1954), 221–30.

In this article, the developer of the Stanford revision of the Binet scale reviewed a lifetime of research on the significance of tested mental ability for later achievement.

# INDIVIDUAL DIFFERENCES AND SCHOOL PRACTICE

Every school system has some policy for organizing students into instructional groups. The attempt may be to put similar students into the same working group, in the hope that all will be ready for the same lessons and can proceed at the same rate. Though no group can be truly uniform in readiness, it is sensible, for example, to require successful completion of a basic chemistry course of those entering the study of organic chemistry. And it makes sense to teach long division only after students have a good command of simple division. Whether schools should form "tracks" of high and low ability or establish "compensatory" programs for those with less readiness are more complicated questions. This chapter examines the logic of devices for taking differences in readiness into account, and considers evidence on their effectiveness. I shall conclude that the school should adapt the program so that the student gets the lessons he is ready for, and that the program also ought to strive to increase readiness. Insofar as exercises such as $6)\overline{46}$ pave the way for learning to solve $16)\overline{460}$, teaching obviously contributes to readiness. Remedial and therapeutic programs also improve readiness when they develop skills or remove emotional blocks. The controversial issue is whether some modified form of schooling or some supplement to the traditional program can accelerate *general* intellectual development. This echoes the controversy over maturation (p. 163). An effective large-scale procedure to increase general readiness would greatly increase the life chances of the children who now lag in readiness. Since these children tend to be from poor neighborhoods and often belong to ethnic minorities, success in raising their general aptitude for schooling would do much to spread social opportunity.

# CAN MENTAL DEVELOPMENT BE ACCELERATED?

Three strategies might assist the child who lags in readiness:

- Give intensive training, with adequate diagnosis and remediation, in the fundamental skills related to language and number.

- Give specific training in such broad concepts as "conservation of number," identified in the research of Piaget and his followers (p. 331).

- Provide some kind of broad stimulation and experience with problem solving in order to improve the child's work attitudes, analytic skills, and conceptual resources.

The first two can be thought of as *training* methods, the last as *enrichment*. Enrichment methods try to provide a varied and encouraging environment but do not set out to teach particular responses. In the more sharply focused training methods, the student is taught particular significant responses; for example, the preschool child is taught to count.

Little controversy arises regarding targeted training. Most defects in subskills, once pinned down by diagnosis, can be overcome by carefully targeted remedial exercises. Overcoming such defects may or may not bring the student "up to the average," and he may progress slowly. But the lessons are unquestionably helpful. The only criticism of such efforts is that they are incomplete. Training on operational thought is more controversial (p. 367). Piaget's research suggests that operational thought is attained very gradually through a combination of maturation and varied interaction with the environment; if so, crash programs are unlikely to speed up the process. Piaget's followers point out that children taught to give the right response on a particular task often have not really improved their thinking. Some psychologists, however, believe that suitable training can have broad effects.

Most of the debate on acceleration has focused on efforts to enrich the child's experience so as to accelerate the development of broad skills of problem solving and learning. The IQ is the most obvious way to assess these, being independent of whatever particular lessons have been taught. Consequently, the debate has centered on whether the IQ is fixed or can be raised; in particular, on whether preschool instruction can raise it. No single index is an adequate basis for evaluating a program, but the IQ has figured large in the controversies over compensatory education. There is more research on the IQ than on any other measure (and more misunderstanding of the results). Since the analytic skills, work attitudes, and conceptual resources that earn a good IQ do facilitate learning in school, a genuine, lasting rise in such abilities would promise improved school performance in subsequent years.

We saw in the last chapter that ability is constructed through the child's use of his environment. Even though inheritance does enable some persons to use opportunities better and so to accumulate a significant lead, what a person can do at a particular age is not fixed by his genes. Nor is his rank in his age group predetermined. With so much evidence that environment does matter, how can there be debate about raising ability? Misuse of the idea of "capacity" or "potential" (see p. 274) is one source of dispute. Insofar as a test forecasts how far one will go in school and how good a record one will make, the test implies a *lower* limit to potential. The test does say, "This child has the potential to go this far"—that is, "He will probably succeed to this point." Despite their margin for error, such predictions have a good deal of validity, in schools as they are typically organized. If we find some way to boost the student's readiness, however, or invent a program that fits him better than that of the traditional school, he can go further. The prediction becomes invalid. No one can say what any person's potential is in an environment optimum for him.

Although in theory a richer environment can accelerate mental development, undirected stimulation does not prove to be very effective. Pessimism regarding enrichment dates back to a flurry of experiments in the 1930s on the effects of nursery schools. The findings disappointed enthusiasts for early education. The rather well-to-do children who attended nursery schools in those days showed, on the average, no great improvement in test score. They developed at about the same rate as the control groups (Whipple, 1940). Other discouraging evidence came from work with the mentally retarded. Occasionally, a child far below normal is reeducated with some degree of success. Itard's pupil, the "wild child" of Aveyron (depicted in a recent movie), is a classic example of a child coming from a severely restricted environment (Lane, 1976). Retarded children who have grown up under ordinary home conditions generally do not benefit much from special treatment, however. (See Kirk's study on the next page.)

Preschools to benefit urban children were given Federal support in the 1960s. For political reasons, the programs were launched hurriedly, without careful pilot work. The programs did benefit the health of the children and the sense of political efficacy of families and communities (Zigler, 1975). But studies on their intellectual effects, reported between 1966 and 1970, were about as discouraging as the earlier studies with well-to-do children and with the retarded. We shall look at some of the evidence and at some problems of obtaining sound evidence. We shall see some hopeful findings amid the gloom, mostly from training programs that set out to remedy specific defects in readiness rather than to promote broad functioning.

At present there is no across-the-board "cure" for inadequate intellectual development. The theory of intellectual development argues that ability is built up steadily through thousands upon thousands of transactions with the environment. It is reasonable to hope that some structuring of the environment will make the transactions more profitable and so accelerate growth. One can cling to this hope without claiming great virtues for the compensatory programs in use today.

## An Experiment with the Mentally Handicapped

Kirk (1958) developed an instructional program for institutionalized children in the hope of raising their ability. His study was cited even in 1975 (by the significant Hobbs report, p. 378) as an especially clear example of what intervention can do. The children, about 4½ years old at the start of the study, had IQs between 45 and 80. One group spent six hours per day in a preschool that provided group experience, opportunity to draw, to tell stories, and so on. The child was tutored in those abilities that seemed especially weak, but the program was more one of enrichment than of training. After one to three years of such instruction the children entered Grade I. The most important finding (Table 9.1) comes from the follow-up test given after the children had had one year in school. There was an evident and lasting effect, at least for some. Six of Kirk's 15 preschool children and none of the 12 untrained controls had progressed enough to leave the institution. A similar special program had much less effect on the child whose rearing environment was in the normal range.

Kirk also provided preschool experience for retarded children living at home, comparing their development with that of similar but untrained children. The results (Table 9.2) showed that the special training produced marked gains during the preschool period. But the children who had been left in their normal environment with no special treatment made up much of the difference during the first school year. The experimental group had only a short-lived advantage. In Grade I, their achievement was superior to that of the control group only in art and writing. (Here the creative experience of the preschool presumably helped.) Even short-term improvement was uncommon among children with

**TABLE 9.1**

**Effect of preschool on institutionalized children**

| | Change in Stanford-Binet IQ from initial test | | Percentage of group with IQ above 85 on follow-up test |
|---|---|---|---|
| | at end of preschool | after one year of school | |
| Children given preschool experience | +11.0 | +10.2 | 27 |
| Children given no supplementary experience | −7.2 | −6.5 | 0 |

SOURCE: Data from Kirk (1958), p. 185.

**TABLE 9.2**

**Effect of preschool on children living at home**

| | Change in Stanford-Binet IQ from initial test | | Percentage of group with IQ above 85 on follow-up test |
|---|---|---|---|
| | at end of preschool | after one year of school | |
| Children given preschool experience | +11.2 | +11.7 | 60 |
| Children given no supplementary experience | −0.6 | −6.9 | 58 |

SOURCE: Data from Kirk (1958), p. 178.

physical impairment of brain functioning and among children whose parents were restrictive and uninterested in their development. Among the untrained children also, first-grade progress was poorest among those from "psychosocially inadequate" homes.

Kirk's finding brings up an important methodological point: The evaluator ought to look for lasting results. Special experience often raises scores on a test given at the end of the instruction; a month later the advantage may have vanished. In the Brownell-Moser study (p. 122), you will recall, children taught the

## Why simple analyses of intervention effects are misleading

Results of preschool experiments are easily misinterpreted. Teachers and administrators feel at home with statements about gains between pretest and posttest: Whichever method produces large average gains appears to be the best. This inference is sound enough when groups started even (but if so, it is simpler to compare the posttest averages directly). When the groups were not equal at the start, to compare their average gains is misleading. There are two reasons:

- Gains of persons in the high and low ranges of a scale are not logically comparable. An example will show this. Eric has been bowling for five years and his average is a creditable 140. He joins a league and, in a year, brings his average to 180. He is picking up spares and gets a good many strikes. Joe is a novice and not adept at sports. Casual play has brought his average to 90. He signs up for a course in bowling and at the end averages 130. He now picks up 7 to 9 pins with his first ball and makes about half of his spares. So Joe and Eric both have gained 40 pins. It is meaningless to ask who gained the most. Literally as well as figuratively, Joe and Eric are not in the same league. Count number of strikes, and Eric gained most; count total number of pins knocked down, and Joe gained most. Any change in the scoring rule changes the picture.

- The group that starts lower can be expected to make a larger average gain, simply by chance. If a group selected for compensatory education (having poor initial scores), gains more than an average group given no special treatment, this means nothing. To see why, return to Fig. 8.1 (p. 308). There we saw that a group scoring 70 on Form A would average 66 on Form B, under the assumptions of Panel ii. Similarly, a group scoring 30 on Form A would average 34 on Form B. The respective gains, then, were $-4$ and $+4$. This *regression effect* works to enhance the apparent gains of those who scored low on the first test.

Results become clear when groups have been assigned to treatments at random. Then (if everyone stays to the end) the posttest averages tell the story. But it is not easy to arrange for some children of a neighborhood to be helped while ignoring a randomly selected group of controls.

Education is evaluated mostly by quasi experiments in which the experimental group is compared with some group that just happened not to get the treatment. These controls may be children whose parents did not enroll them in the compensatory program, or children in a community that did not establish one, or a national "norm group" whose training no one knows about. The important point is this: If the groups were not assigned at random, they may have differed at the outset, and any comparison of end-results is of uncertain meaning. The available statistical techniques cannot give unbiased results, and usually it is impossible to tell whether the bias works for or against the experimental treatment (Cronbach et al., 1976). Decisions have to be made from the facts policy-makers can afford to collect, so quasi experiments are worthwhile. But their ambiguity accounts for a large part of the contention about whether "compensatory education has failed."

equal-additions technique of subtraction performed, on an immediate test, as well as those using the borrowing technique, but dropped behind on a delayed test.

On a follow-up test, the group receiving no special stimulation often catches up with the experimental group. Superiority on an immediate test has little social importance if normal experience will develop the same skills in the control group during the next few months. The major evaluation of Head Start (Westinghouse, 1969), for example, reported end-of-training gains in intellectual performance, but these did not hold up at the end of the year in Grade I. (Recall also the Hilgard study, p. 164.) Developing intellectual skills faster in the experimental group is important only if the next phase of schooling will capitalize on this momentum. If the children do not go on developing at a good rate, the intervention has no ultimate payoff.

Gains in test scores may be illusory in another respect. The baseline is established by a pretest given when the experimental children enter preschool. Neither the experimental nor the control child is accustomed to performing tasks at a stranger's bidding. The child's performance is likely to rise several points when he is given a few days to become accustomed to the tester and his games. The gain in production—due to adaptation to the situation, not to coaching or intellectual growth—typically averages about 6 IQ points (Cronbach, 1970, p. 263). Many an "optimistic" report from a compensatory program claims a gain no larger than this; perhaps the whole effect of the experience is to improve test taking.

---

 **1** Is it ethical to provide compensatory treatment for a random fraction of children in a neighborhood and not others, in order to make a valid evaluation of the program?

---

## Evidence on Compensatory Education

A person who wishes to emphasize the negative side can report data where compensatory efforts seemed to have no lasting effect. A person who "believes in" the programs can point to successes (Zigler, 1975). The record is mixed, and both human sympathies and psychological interests prompt one to emphasize the positive side. Here only a fragment of the evidence on compensatory programs can be reviewed. For reasons that will become clear, I start with some paragraphs reprinted verbatim from the 1963 edition of this book, published when the compensatory education movement was just getting underway.

> HIGHER HORIZONS: ENRICHMENT IN THE JUNIOR HIGH SCHOOL.   Fundamental change in attitude toward education, achievement, and one's own worth is rare after the elementary grades. Great interest therefore attaches to the pioneer-

ing experiment of a New York City junior high school, where the student body is largely Negro and Puerto Rican, and where prior to the experiment few graduates did well in high school or went to college. Beginning in 1954, these "culturally deprived" children were subjected to an invigorated program of counseling and remedial instruction. Parent education was carried out simultaneously. Perhaps most important, pupils took field trips to entertainments, museums, colleges, and the larger world whose excitement had never penetrated their tenement neighborhood. Nonverbal mental tests were used to guide the counseling and remedial efforts. As a formal study, the experiment was loosely controlled and incompletely evaluated (Wrightstone, 1960).

Many of the results, however, were so dramatic that the only question left to answer is just what the limits of the approach may be; that it works appears to be beyond question (Morse, 1960, pp. 41ff.; Mayer, 1961, p. 124). There are stories of children who gained 40 points in IQ (remedial reading is a large part of the story) and carried off college scholarships. On the average, the IQs rose about seven points, and the average gains in reading were one and a half times the normal rate. Since progress in arithmetic was no better than the usual rate, that part of the program is being changed (an example of the importance of careful investigation, even in a program that justifies enthusiasm). All reports on pupil motivation and parent interest in their education are favorable. It remains to be seen what these pupils will do after high school to participate in New York's cultural resources and opportunities for achievement.

The glowing account in the preceding paragraphs reflects the temper of the times in which the great compensatory programs were launched. The Morse and Mayer books were addressed to the general public, and propagandized for the educational innovations of those years.

Updating the report here will demonstrate some realities of educational research and innovation. The educational literature is filled with enthusiastic reports, and these are picked up by the popular press. After a time, the innovation is likely to drop from sight, with no public explanation as to why it was abandoned.

By 1963, the New York program had been extended to a larger group of schools, had been thoroughly evaluated, and was on the way out. The evaluation report (Wrightstone et al., 1964) remains in library archives, perhaps just because it was sobering rather than dramatic. It was never written up for professional journals, nor was it publicly discussed by the national journalists who had been quick to publicize the first flush of apparent success.

The New York City schools, encouraged by Wrightstone's pilot study, launched the extension under the banner "Higher Horizons" in 1959. Third-grade classes from 52 elementary schools and seventh-grade classes from 13 junior high schools entered a three-year enrichment program. The activities were like those described in the quoted paragraph. The experimental junior high classes were compared with a control group in traditional schools having similar initial ability and family background. Table 9.3 presents the chief findings. In this mass of evidence, there is scarcely a hint of benefit from Higher Horizons. Teacher opinions were moderately favorable, chiefly because the program broadened students' cultural interests and identified talents other than academic ones. With regard to academic benefits, the teachers' ratings were lukewarm. (The data for elementary schools led to much the same conclusions, though the experimental group did a little better in arithmetic than the controls.)

I present all this detail because it demonstrates the need for a solid, impartial evaluation of innovations. If the New York evaluation had rested solely on personal judgments by teachers and principals, the report would have been favorable. Principals gave the program an endorsement and 87 per cent of the teachers wanted to see the program continued. (A third, however, wanted it modified.) In fact, the program was not doing what was intended during the years 1959 to 1963.

Higher Horizons was not truly a large-scale version of the initial program for which success was claimed. In going to a large scale it was necessary to decentralize; in the end, inadequate planning was one of the teachers' most frequent criticisms. The original program tried to serve the abler segment of the poor community, but the large program tried to serve the whole range. Expenditures were cut from the original program's $80 per student per year in junior high to $61.

Critics of school expenditures can condemn the program as having given the public nothing for the added dollars spent. The person who is sympathetic, but still sensitive to evidence, is likely to point out how hard it is to enlarge a program. When a small program directed by an enthusiastic, freshly recruited staff pays off, the larger version may not have the same vigor.

**TABLE 9.3**

**Mean scores of junior-high-school students in a compensatory program and in a standard program**

| | Higher Horizons group | Control group | Interpretation |
|---|---|---|---|
| IQ* | 91.1 | 91.7 | No benefit; difference favoring controls can be regarded as a chance occurrence. |
| Reading comprehension (grade-level score) | | | |
|   Students with IQ below 85 | 5.4 | 5.3 | No benefit; analysis with a different type of control group did suggest a small net benefit. |
|   Students with IQ 85 and higher | 9.0 | 9.0 | Same as directly above. |
| Arithmetic computation (raw score) | 14.8 | 14.8 | No benefit. |
| Class conduct (rated on 80-point scale) | 61.0 | 62.3 | No benefit; classes ranged widely. |
| Attitude toward school (self-rating, 200-point scale) | 168 | 172 | No benefit; differences in other samples were smaller, and mixed in direction. Teacher ratings likewise showed a negligible difference. |
| Percentage with good attendance | 89.3 | 88.4 | No benefit; this slight difference between schools was present before experiment started. |
| Percentage choosing academic course in high school | 56 | 58 | No benefit. |
| Job aspiration (50-point scale) | 36.3 | 37.2 | No benefit. |

SOURCE: Data from Wrightstone et al. (1964).

* Measured after one year of the program. Other results are based on data after two or three years. Where year-by-year findings are available, they support the conclusions in the table.

Evaluators who report disappointing data are sometimes accused of working against the poor and the minorities. To throw out a compensatory program that accomplishes nothing, however, is in their interests; it keeps them from being victimized by educational patent medicine. To decide, after considering evaluations of inadequately designed or supported programs, that *no* program can significantly improve the educability of the poor child—that *would* be a tragic error.

RESULTS IN EARLY CHILDHOOD   We turn now to more recent evaluations. The American Institutes for Research (AIR; Wargo et al., 1972) took on the assignment of summing up the evaluation reports streaming to Washington on government "Title I" programs, under which local school districts were given funds to help poor children of school age. District reports were assembled at the state level and sent to Washington. AIR did not find synthesis easy, as programs took many forms and measured the effects in various ways. AIR concluded that, considering all the data together, the Title I funds had not enabled the poor children to come up to the average. This summation is confirmed in a review by one of the original planners of Head Start. Bronfenbrenner (1974c) says: "Although there were some modest achievements, by and large the results were disappointing. The effects were at best short-lived and small. . . ."

Looking at data from one community at a time, the AIR reviewers saw hits and misses. Results were good in some places, negligible in others. Policymakers (and psychologists) like to generalize: the program works or fails. It is foolish, however, to judge "compensatory education"; one cannot draw a conclusion that generalizes about schools that are doing different things. The AIR report went on to ask the right question: What characteristics distinguish the local programs that showed good results?

Typically, the more effective program in the early grades:

    had clearly stated objectives or plans;

    had planned carefully and had trained its teachers in the methods the project would use;

    employed small-group or individual instruction;

    carried out instruction directly relevant to the outcomes measured;

    had instruction of high intensity;

    cultivated active involvement of parents.

Effective preschool programs also had these characteristics (S. White et al., 1973, vol. II, p. 109; Bronfenbrenner, 1974a).

Not many surprises. Perhaps we are only being told that haphazard, ill-directed compensatory education does not work. The suggestion that structured programs pay off leaves a question open. Training programs (definite goals pointed toward specific outcomes) can be counted on to produce impressive short-term results on tests that match the lessons. Until it is shown that the effects persist and transfer into broader readiness, structured training has not been proved to be an ideal form of compensatory education.

It would be easy to cite success stories of isolated compensatory programs. (For a near-exhaustive catalog, see S. White et al., 1973, and Bronfenbrenner, 1974a.) Some of the positive reports are no doubt invalid, contaminated by the biases of subjective evidence, small samples, and inadequate experimental design. Some no doubt describe programs that truly are beneficial, because of the personal skills of those who pioneered them; these programs will be hard to propagate to new settings. The third category of success story is the important one: genuine effects, reached by principles and materials that new groups of teachers can put to use.

Today no one can judge which of the positive reports belong in this third category. The judgment can only be made following toughminded evaluations, after a certain program has been installed for two or three years in a range of communities. Why two or three years? Because the first year is likely to be unrepresentative. The teachers are just learning how to use the new opportunities. And, on the other hand, the initial excitement of the shakedown period may give results (sometimes called the "Hawthorne effect") that cannot be maintained when the glamor wears off. Even when the weight of evidence shows a certain kind of compensatory instruction to be beneficial, the next school to adopt the program ought to monitor its results. There is many a slip.

## Points of View in Compensatory Education

The state of the art in early education is well represented by the Maccoby-Zellner (1970) compilation of information on the compensatory program called Follow Through (whose major evaluation is soon to appear). The Follow Through developers have made optimistic assumptions. According to Maccoby and Zellner (pp. 23ff.), they agree that:

- Education must begin from the child's level. It is necessary to inventory what the individual child can and cannot do, and tailor activities to fit.

- Teaching should be individualized.

- If a child is not learning, the fault lies in what the teacher is doing—not in the child. With some exceptions (true mental deficiency), the child from a poor, minority home can be expected to learn all the essentials of a standard curriculum: "It is a cornerstone assumption of the compensatory education movement that as a whole such children are educable, but that the circumstances of their lives are such that they often do not acquire some of the skills and motivations that underlie success in school."

- A program cannot succeed if the intended learning outcomes are not clearly identified.

- Schooling ought to be enjoyable. There should be no fear, no punishment, no sense of being a failure. (This is not to say that the child should never confront a task at which his initial tries will be unsuccessful.)

Under these assumptions, undifferentiated enrichment is not adequate.

Alongside these shared views are differences. A particular program may adopt any of the following approaches (or some blend of them):

- *Behavior modification*   Specific acts are to be made habitual by systematic reinforcement.

- *Cognitive-developmental*   Normal progress toward more complex mental structures is to be facilitated by activities that call for continual problem solving.

- *Competence motivation*   The child is to pursue his own goals. Intellectual curiosity is stimulated by providing a range of experiences and materials. The activities are "oriented toward self-actualization," to quote Maccoby and Zellner (pp. 25–26).

- *Sociopolitical*   Some of the programs reflect the pressure for the return of power to local communities and for greater respect for minority clienteles. Any pedagogical tactic consistent with the learner's self-respect is acceptable. The first requirement is that the school work closely with the community.

The first three styles have obvious affiliations with behavioristic, cognitive-developmental, and humanistic psychology.

Associated with the sociopolitical emphasis is an insistence on the term *cultural difference* to replace *cultural deprivation* or *disadvantage* or *deficit*. *Difference* is a more palatable word, but cultural norms that interfere with the aspirations of the members of the culture are deficits, not merely differences. (See also pp. 53 and 220.)

## FIGURE 9.1

## A "matrix game"

This matrix is part of the Matrix Games procedure developed by Lassar Gotkin for early education.

SOURCE: Gotkin (1967). Reproduced by permission of New Century Education Corporation.

ACCELERATION IN A PIAGETIAN FRAMEWORK   Some provocative observations on attempts to speed up mental development have been inspired by Piaget's description of intellectual processes. Simply placing the child in an enriched environment does not improve performance much. Highly structured lessons on the names of numerals, the distinction between *under* and *over,* and so on do increase the child's response repertoire, but such lessons do not come to grips with deficiencies in problem solving and self-regulation. Piaget has been inclined to think that the child must work his own way from intuitive to operational thought (p. 328) and that his development is paced by his neural maturation. That would seem to deny the possibility of significant acceleration (but in Green, 1971, p. 212, Piaget comments that Elkind's remarks [box, p. 166] are too pessimistic). Many psychologists in the United States have tried to invent lessons that will move the child to higher stages of development—the Gotkin matrix games, for example. Maccoby and Zellner (1970, p. 13) describe how children are shown pictures like those in Fig. 9.1 and

directed (or direct one another) to "put a blue circle on two boys drinking milk." The cognitive requirements increase in complexity as the children gain facility with the task. For example, sequencing may be introduced by instructing the child: "*First* put a blue circle on two boys drinking milk, *then* put a red X on one girl putting on her hat." Or the teacher might cover up one of the squares and ask the children to figure out what her "secret" picture is.

Controlled, short-term experiments on Piagetian kinds of reasoning have reported both success and failure. There have been enough successes to suggest that operational thought about a concept can indeed be taught (Goldschmid, 1971; Brainerd, 1973). One has to teach one operation at a time, and has to devise a method that will root the concept deeply, so that it regulates the child's response to new situations. Piaget's theory is that the child develops a *schema* (p. 327) by using it in diverse contexts, reshaping or extending it when his interpretation is contradicted. Simply telling the child that volume or number is conserved (p. 331) will not plant an operational concept. The more successful experiments have taught indirectly, confronting the child with concrete situations in which his perceptual interpretations are contradicted when tested. As he confronts flaws in his impressionistic interpretations, he builds more rigorous concepts and uses them.

Just one session of individual training in rudimentary measurement operations enabled Bearison (1969) to teach the concept of conservation of quantity to kindergartners. Three-fourths of his subjects passed conservation tests seven months after the training sessions, whereas among untrained children of comparable age only a third passed. In the training the children compared quantities of fluid that they poured into small jars of differing diameters. Each judgment the child made was then checked by transferring the fluid to vials of equal size and counting the vials. The successive steps in Bearison's little curriculum required increasing reliance on reasoning.

Short-term accelerative efforts can push children only a short distance, as Elkind et al. (1962) demonstrated. Making the most of a picture has to be learned. Where conflicting interpretations are possible or where one can see the parts without perceiving an integrated whole, the young child often overlooks some of what is shown. For training, Elkind et al. used ambiguous pictures such as the one at right. If the hidden duck was difficult for the child to find, the child was given as much help as he needed. Some children required nothing more than encouragement. Some had to have most of the figure blocked off before they could detect the hidden duck. While training helped many children at age 6, the training was much more

From the Picture Ambiguity Test.
Reproduced by permission of David Elkind
and the University of Chicago Press.

## Coached responses are no sign of insight

Kamii and Derman set out to find out how 6-year-olds thought about buoyancy after they had been carefully taught the verbal rule that an object sinks "if it is heavier than a piece of water of the same size."

Carl had separated the objects he expected to float from those he expected to sink. Comes the test of maturity of thought:

Examiner: (Picking up a large paper clip,) Why do you think this will float?
Child: Because it is lighter than a piece of water the same size.
Examiner: Okay. Shall we try it? You put it in and see if it will float. . . . Oops! So we've got to put it in with the things that sink. (Then, picking up a small piece of soap,) Why do you think this will float?
Child: Because it is lighter than a piece of water the same size.
Examiner: Okay, you try it. . . . What happened?
Child: It sank.
Examiner: But you told me it was lighter than a piece of water the same size.
Child: But it sank.
Examiner: Okay, then, how come?
Child: It is heavier than a piece of water the same size.
Examiner: Now, let's try the things that you think are going to sink.
Child: (Tries the block.) It floated!
Examiner: It's heavy, and it still floated?
Child: Yes. (Tries the big candle. It floats.) How come everything in the sinking pile floats? (Picks up a big ball bearing, and says) This one will sink. . . . It did.
Examiner: How come you were so sure that one would sink?
Child: Because it is heavy. . . . (Puts large green bar of soap in the water.)
Examiner: How come it sank?
Child: Because it is heavier than a piece of water the same size.
Examiner: (Picking up the bar of Ivory soap) Will this one sink?
Child: Yes. (Tries it.)
Examiner: How come this one didn't sink?
Child: Because it is lighter than a piece of water the same size.

Kamii and Derman conclude: "The imposition of rules can prevent children from thinking and discovering."

SOURCE: Kamii & Derman (1971), pp. 143–44.

effective a year or two later. Children who required large amounts of help during the training had little permanent benefit to show for it. Evidently it is the child who is almost ready to climb to a higher level of performance who is most helped by coaching.

These studies seem to suggest that teaching makes a difference only if the teacher goes to work at the particular "teachable moment" when transition has already started. Turiel (in Travers, 1973, p. 746; see also p. 811) suggests in-

# Does teaching a verbal rule about buoyancy lead to sound reasoning?

Here, Maccoby and Zellner (1970, p. 49) give detailed information on Kamii's observations (box opposite).

> . . . children would recite the rule correctly when asked to *explain* why [an object] had sunk or floated. When the large, heavy ball bearing was put into mercury and it floated, the children were surprised, but said that this occurred because it was lighter than a piece of *mercury* the same size. Thus, they were able to generalize the rule to a new medium.
>
> But when asked to *predict* whether a piece of soap would float if it were put into mercury, they thought it would sink—thus revealing that they had not mastered the seriation aspects of the problem. Dr. Kamii presented the children with a number of objects—a paper clip, pieces of soap of various sizes, a metal plate, ball bearings of various sizes, a needle, and candles of two sizes. She then asked the children to put them into two piles—the things that would float in water and the things that would not. They classified objects according to a number of sometimes inconsistent principles, just as a group of untrained children their own age would normally do. . . . They said a paper clip would sink because it had little hooks on it that would pull it down into the water. They said the needle would sink because it was thin, or would float because it was lightweight. They did not pick up the needle and say, "Well, this is so small, a piece of water this size wouldn't weigh very much." The small candle would float because it was small; the large candle would sink because it was large and therefore "heavy." In other words, when asked to *predict* about floating or sinking, they did not make use of their rule and they reasoned "pre-operationally."
>
> Engelmann argued that this occurred because the children had no knowledge about the materials things were made of. . . . [H]ow would they know that the big candle was made of the same material as the small one? The proper test, Engelmann insisted, would involve cutting a candle into two unequal pieces, putting one portion into water, and asking the child to predict what the other portion would do. When the test was performed in this way, the children passed it. . . . [D]uring the Kamii prediction test, the children never asked for the information they needed. They never asked . . . whether candle wax weighs more or less than water—they simply regressed to a less mature mode of thought. (Italics added. Paragraphing altered.)

stead that the child is always in transition from one substage to a higher one, and that teaching can help him, provided that the analysis he is taught to use is just a little ahead of his present level. Thus, any one fixed method of teaching more advanced thinking will be right for just a few children and over the heads of others. But with proper adjustment of method, every child can be helped.

The behaviorists have tried direct teaching of operational concepts. Siegfried Engelmann (in Green, 1971), who favors highly structured curricula, introduced lessons on specific gravity to children of age 6. His approach was verbal and didactic: "Children, some things float in water, some don't. How can you tell which will float? An object will float in water if it is lighter than a piece of water of the same size." Engelmann claimed that the children had full command of the concept after a few brief lessons. Constance Kamii challenged this claim and tested a few children who had finished Engelmann's lessons. Her tests (box) showed that the children used the concept less effectively in novel circumstances than in circumstances similar to those in the training. However, some transferable learning had occurred (Kamii & Derman, in Green, 1971).

A fair interpretation may be this: Any lesson or experience-with-reflection moves the child a short distance toward mastery of a concept. Whether the lesson is consolidated and remembered will depend on whether the child continues to use it and to extend its use. There will be a fairly long period during which the concept flickers in and out of the child's awareness; hence, unless provision is made for continued experiences to strengthen the concept, the ini-

## Cultural deficit comes to Simplicia: a parable

In cultures that have had little contact with the technological world, straight lines are a small part of perceptual experience. Upright timbers, straight roads, and squared-off building lots are unknown in Simplicia. Simplician children fail at perceptual tasks that are easy for the Western child. When the child draws a map of his village, he identifies localities as he experiences them, strung out along a path of indefinite shape; he places sites in a realistic order, but distance and direction are loosely represented. Is this a difference or a deficit? So long as the culture remains static, the fact that Simplicians perform badly on Western tests of "spatial reasoning" is only a difference. They are not handicapped in their daily adaptations. They do not have to reason about rectilinear objects and drawings.

Suppose, now, that a firm from Modernia comes to install a railroad, to bring ore to the coast from Simplicia's back valleys. The socially aware Modernians want Simplicians to share in their enterprise, and are prepared to give technical training so that Simplicians can be hired as surveyors and mechanics, and can work up into management. The training is doomed to failure; what was a difference before the Modernians came is now a deficit. It prevents the Simplicians from sharing fully in the emerging culture.

Within a short time there will be a two-class system in Simplicia, with the Modernians dominating the development of the culture and the Simplicians increasingly discontented as they carry on with the economic and cultural activities of former years. The only bright note is that the next generation, seeing engineering objects on every hand, can grow up without the cultural deficit of their parents and join the mainstream. The alternative future for the Simplicias of this world is to wall them off as "ethnological parks," unexploited, out of contact with the larger world, and sharing none of its standard of living (see R. Adams, 1975).

tial lessons will have little permanent value. Consolidation should proceed more rapidly in a school where every day the child has to analyze, predict, and verify than in a school where the activity is less intellectual. Challenging the child to make predictions about floating must—according to Piaget's own theory—bring the concept to maturity faster than leaving the child to notice the principle some day while in his bath.

2  A psychologist who read the section (pp. 364–69) on acceleration based on Piagetian ideas commented as follows:

> Teaching Piagetian concepts is a waste of time, and the issue as to whether we can teach the concepts is much ado about nothing. Teaching the specific concepts is like treating the symptoms of an illness rather than finding the cause. A child's overall mental organization, based on his everyday interactions with the environment, will determine how he approaches each new problem. Piaget has chosen certain concepts to study, but these are illustrative rather than an exhaustive list of what the child should understand.

What reply do you think Engelmann would make? In your opinion, how large an emphasis should the curriculum in early education put on Piagetian concepts?

3  The Follow Through developers agree on five assumptions (p. 362). Are these truisms that no one could doubt? Or is there an alternative position that reasonable persons might believe (or have believed)?

4  The Modernian Corporation (box) announced that it would take into its training program any Modernian who scored 62 or over on the Spatio test, since persons with that score usually succeeded in the training and on the job. They said that, to give Simplicians every chance, they would take in any Simplician who scored 50 or over, even though few of these were likely to finish the course successfully. The average score among the young men of Simplicia was 35 at the time. Is the use of this test culturally fair or a discriminatory practice? What about 15 years later, when the average young Simplician scores 48?

5  Gains of a few points in test performance are usual soon after a child's first exposure to a school setting. (When he takes a "pretest," he is in a strange situation and probably does not score as high as he could if he were at ease and worked efficiently.) Any such change is credited to the compensatory program in the usual pretest-posttest comparison. Is that change evidence of an educational benefit conferred? Or should it be dismissed as evidence only of "test-wiseness"?

# SCHOOL ORGANIZATION TO ACCOMMODATE DEVELOPMENTAL DIFFERENCES

## Age Placement of Educative Experiences

Schools have to organize learners and lessons, and they are continually trying to devise plans that will make management easier. Traditionally, the school has been *age graded.* One age has been considered normal for entering school and settling down to the serious work of learning to read. Another age has been considered normal for ending schooling and taking up full-time employment. The young—even in college—have been sorted according to age or seniority, and each branch of learning has entered the curriculum at a certain age. Reading was assigned to age 6, the world of careers to early adolescence, psychology to the second year of college. Belief in age-grading can be traced as far back as Aristotle: "A young man is not a proper hearer of lectures on political science; for he is inexperienced in the actions that occur in life, . . ."

The organization of the school, with distinct units beginning at certain ages, reflects assumptions about the mental abilities, interests, and social characteristics of those years. The very idea that childhood and youth is the period for education, and that one should work straight through to his highest degree, defines the student as a person who has not yet taken his place in society. Consequently, the educational arrangements are likely to treat the student as less mature than he is (Panel on Youth, 1974).

Organizational plans that violate the facts of development are continually under challenge. Some challenges to the old age-grading simply match roles to ages on another schedule. Thus, after studies of child development identified some of the distinctive concerns of the early adolescent, the junior high school was established (p. 182). The one-teacher classroom was maintained through Grade VI; beyond that grade, each subject was taught by a different teacher. Seventh-graders and eighth-graders could enter a ceramics class or a typing class together. The 13-year-olds could work on the tasks of social adjustment without being intimidated by the savoir-faire of 16-year-olds, as they would be in a six-year high school. The junior high offered a varied program in which the adolescent could explore his interests and talents, and so come better prepared to the momentous decision at the start of high school—whether to head for college or toward a post-high-school job.

Today, physical and psychological features typical of adolescence appear prior to age 12. The old rationale no longer holds, so a "middle school" and other alternatives to the junior high school are being tried. Elementary schools now have richer programs so that exploration of varied interests begins earlier. And the high school is more ready to allow the explorations to continue, instead of forcing the ninth-grader to place all his chips on one big decision.

## Bonjour, mes enfants. Bienvenus à l'école!

Montreal is a bilingual city, and to participate fully in its business and cultural life a resident must have nearly as much command of French as he would need in Paris. Parents of English extraction hope that their children will grow up and remain in Montreal, and therefore want them to be educated bilingually. The experimenters (Lambert & Tucker, 1972) set up not a bilingual program but a school where French was the only language from the first day of kindergarten. This was the child's first exposure to French.

When French had to be used for every communication with the teacher, rudimentary skill was picked up rapidly. Before long, the children were using French as much as English in their conversations with each other. Lessons in reading and other subjects began later and were conducted entirely in French, with French texts. Only in Grade IV did instruction in English start: lessons on English vocabulary, spelling, and grammar, confined to specific periods of the week.

Judging by test results at the end of Grade VI, the experiment was a complete success (W. E. Lambert, in Cronbach & Drenth, 1972, and personal communication). The experimental children were not a select group; on the contrary, they were probably representative of the lower middle class. On the achievement tests used in the Montreal school program for children from *French*-speaking homes, taught in French, the experimental children attained average scores. And when given the achievement tests used in the English-language schools of Montreal, they responded to questions in English as well as the children who had used English throughout their schooling. Some educators fear that bilingualism will cause confusion. In these children it did not.

The timing of an educational experience is sometimes an echo of intellectual and educational history. Classical languages entered the American curriculum as a vocational subject for ministers, lawyers, and scholars. Later, language study was supposed to sharpen the intellect of the advanced student; languages, including modern languages, were therefore located in the secondary school, reserved for the minority going on to college. Yet a second language can be learned by preschool children—and by students of low IQ—when the method of instruction does not call for reading, writing, or grammatical analysis. We have already encountered Penfield's statement (p. 167) that languages need to be acquired before age 9 if perfect speech is to develop. Awakened to the fact that delaying language instruction had no justification, schools added languages to the elementary curriculum.

Just how radical a challenge to traditional organization can be is suggested by an experiment in Montreal (box). There, instruction was given entirely in French, to children coming from homes where they had heard nothing but English. It is noteworthy that when they entered school, these children possessed none of the skills that make up readiness for traditional instruction in French; they did not know the alphabet, they knew nothing about grammar, they had not learned to make phonetic discriminations. But the method used in the kindergarten was the method by which the infant picks up the language from a French-speaking parent. With the method properly chosen, the children had quite sufficient "foreign language aptitude." In any subject, what constitutes readiness depends on the form the instruction takes.

In mathematics, also, educators have questioned the assignment of particular topics to a particular age, to be taught in a particular order. Introductory courses traditionally deal with the most ancient content; the newest branch of a subject must fall in at the end of the line. The principles of set theory were available a century ago, but as recently as 1940 they were rarely encountered prior to the graduate school. This placement was challenged by mathematicians who believe that set theory provides a system of ideas more helpful in understanding mathematics than such time-honored content as the solution of right triangles and the "mixture" problems of arithmetic. (How many students will become surveyors or grocers?) Today the traditional engineering mathematics for freshmen has been replaced in many colleges by a course based largely on set theory. Basic concepts about sets are brought in successfully as early as Grade I.

Recent curriculum movements have brought ideas into the elementary curriculum that were formerly reserved for high school, and have brought "college" material into the high school. Once it was thought that the elementary school should teach just information, plus technical skills in calculation, writing, and so on. Contemporary programs assume instead that critical thinking, creative expression, and skills of independent investigation should be fostered from the early years. Most psychologists have come to believe that readiness is created through experience and is not something that simply unfolds according to Nature's timetable. Typical is the influential statement of Jerome Bruner (1960, pp. 12, 33):

> We begin with the hypothesis that any subject can be taught effectively in some intellectually honest form to any child at any stage of development. . . . Experience over the past decade points to the fact that our schools may be wasting precious years by postponing the teaching of many important subjects on the ground that they are too difficult. . . . The basic ideas that lie at the heart of all science and mathematics and the basic themes that give form to life and literature are as simple as they are powerful. To be in command of these basic ideas, to use them effectively, requires a continual deepening of one's understanding . . . that comes from learning to use them in progressively more complex forms. It is only when such basic ideas are put in formalized terms as equations or elaborated verbal concepts that they are out of reach of the young child. . . . Fourth-grade children can play absorbing games governed by the principles of topology and set theory, even discovering new "moves" or theorems.

The influence of psychologists during the past 40 years was often on the side of postponing instruction. Studies of the maturation of neural processes suggested that growth could not be accelerated. (Recall Elkind's statement, box, p. 166.) The correspondence between mental age and success in school implied that students fail if asked to do work "beyond their ability." Failure was known to produce loss of confidence, emotional interference with thinking and a high dropout rate. Tests were used to decide who was ready to enter school, as in the case of Gary Brock (box, p. 160). Investigators concerned with reading failures reported that the student was likely to fail if his mental age was below 6½; consequently, prereading instruction replaced the primer as the first semester's work for most children. Investigators identified topics in arithmetic that students found difficult and moved the topics to a later grade. These studies were sound, and their lessons are not to be neglected. It is not good for a child to encounter frequent failure, and the timetable of mental development is not easily changed.

But a significant fact is overlooked by those who wait for readiness to develop. Readiness is not readiness for a subject or a topic; it is readiness for a certain learning experience. As Gates said (1937), "The age for learning to read under one program or with the method employed by one teacher may be entirely different from that required under other circumstances." Figure 9.2 displays some of his supporting data. The four schools for which data are shown taught reading differently. Schools A, B, and C had good teachers; in A and B, special materials including easy supplementary books and diagnostic aids were used. School D had poorly qualified teachers and a poor selection of materials; the teachers seldom worked with individual children. If we say that "readiness" is present if 75 per cent of pupils succeed in reading, then a mental age of 5 is sufficient in schools A and B, a mental age of 6 in C, and a mental age of 6½ in D.

The teaching of fractions, according to some, should be delayed until Grade IV or later; but H. E. Moser (1947) found that if teachers continually explain the meanings of the fractions and of the operations, even second-graders have little difficulty. Current attempts to place intellectual content earlier in the

FIGURE 9.2

Combined effects of mental age and teaching method on reading accomplishment

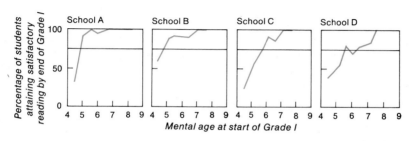

SOURCE: Data from Raguse (1931) and Gates (1937).

curriculum assume that methods can be adapted to the concepts, thought processes, and attention span of the younger child.

Whereas some educational innovations reshuffle age placements, others challenge the whole idea of age placement. This is most evident in the "open" universities, which invite the adult to study whenever in his life he feels the urge. Such a university requires an untraditional organization, so that the adult can enter the program without giving up his occupational and family responsibilities.

No basic idea or skill belongs exclusively to one year of life. A basic idea such as inheritance of traits can be considered many times during a student's schooling, taking on new significance or depth in each new context. A study of his own family tree gives inheritance personal meaning for the fourth-grader. The high-school senior deals with the idea quite differently when experimenting with fruit flies or discussing the population explosion.

The real problem is not when a particular subject is to be taught, but when certain types of understanding or performance can be developed by the best methods of teaching. It makes sense to break up biology or economics so as to introduce some concepts years earlier than others. Students do not learn to type at an employable level until high school, but primary children can begin to type and this beginning helps them in all language learning (B. D. Wood & Freeman, 1932; R. C. Atkinson, 1974).

---

 **6** As a child learns his native tongue, is he rewarded or punished when his sentences are partially wrong in structure? Is the ability to form sentences acquired intuitively or formally?

7 What answer could Bruner give to Aristotle's remark (p. 370) on the teaching of political science? Are their views in conflict?

8 If we find that several important scientific ideas can be understood in Grade II, on what basis should the ones for study at that level be selected?

9 Many adults need to know how to choose annuities and similar investments wisely. They could learn in high school or alternatively in an adult education program. What would be psychologically the best time to learn this? Take into account readiness, the opportunity for learning through practice, and forgetting.

## Ability Grouping

It makes no sense to assign children to learning experiences solely on the basis of age. Some young people have made their vocational decisions, sound or unsound, before they reach junior high school, and some have no concern about vocation until age 20. Comparable differences in development are found for any other interest. Interest in the opposite sex emerges rather suddenly, but the age when it emerges may be 11 or it may be 18.

Among students who have been in school for the same number of years, abilities range widely. As shown in Fig. 9.3, which is based on national norms in reading, the lower third of the student population in Grade VI occupies

### FIGURE 9.3

Range of upper, middle, and lowest thirds of classes in reading at the beginning of a school year

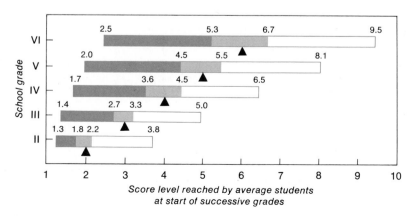

*Score level reached by average students at start of successive grades*

SOURCE: Adapted from Guy L. Bond and Miles A. Tinker, *Reading Difficulties: Their Diagnosis and Correction,* 3rd ed., © 1973, p. 51. Adapted by permission of Prentice-Hall, Inc., Englewood Cliffs, New Jersey.

about the same range of proficiency as the upper two-thirds of Grade III. Students with the same reading score in these two grades are far from alike, however, as the emotional development and motivation of the sixth-graders who read poorly probably has been set back by their years of frustration.

Grouping by a combination of test score *and* age seems like an obvious way to cope with the range of ability. Fourth-graders may be allocated to different classes according to total ability and achievement scores, or a single class may be subdivided into permanent working groups. Ability grouping of this type does not create a class with uniform readiness. Because different aspects of readiness are only moderately correlated, *students homogeneous in one or two respects differ in other dimensions almost as much as unselected students.* Suppose every student is selected to be above average in mental ability; differences in reading and arithmetic ability remain and require adaptive teaching. Figure 9.4 shows the typical relation between abilities. The group of superior readers (right side of chart), homogeneous in reading ability, varies from superior to poor in arithmetic. In the lower section of the chart, where no one is superior in arithmetic, quite a few are superior in reading. As more abilities—art, spelling, oral communication, committee work—are considered, it is quickly seen that the "homogeneous" group is a collection of unique individuals. They vary in abilities almost as much as those in the original pool from which they were chosen. Furthermore, the personality differences that require the teacher to restrain one, inspire a second, and give emotional support to a third will be found no matter how select the students are in ability.

Grouping does function at the higher levels of schooling. If a college class must cover several hundred pages of reading a week, the average 18-year-old will not survive. Selection procedures shunt the poor readers into less demand-

FIGURE 9.4

Range of one ability within groups sectioned on another ability

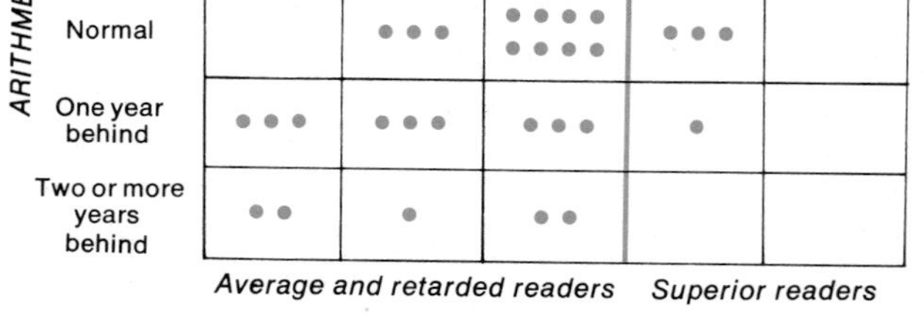

|  | Two or more years behind | One year behind | Normal | One year advanced | Two or more years advanced |
|---|---|---|---|---|---|
| Two or more years advanced |  |  | • • | • | • • |
| One year advanced |  | • | • • • | • • • | • • • |
| Normal |  | • • • | • • • • / • • • • | • • • |  |
| One year behind | • • • | • • • | • • • | • |  |
| Two or more years behind | • • | • | • • |  |  |

*Average and retarded readers     Superior readers*

ing colleges or into course sections that demand less reading. Prerequisites for a course operate similarly to enable the teacher of an advanced course to draw upon concepts from basic courses. The teacher of calculus will be glad to know that all his students have passed a course in trigonometry. Still, some of them have not used the ideas for two years or more. And others learned the computational routines for solving triangles without grasping the abstract concept of trig functions that the calculus teacher proposes to use. The procrustean device of a placement test to sort some students into the calculus course and some into a review section will reduce the spread, but important differences in readiness will remain within each class.

Many experiments, some on a large scale, have compared schools that sort students into "lanes" or "streams" or "tracks" with schools that make each class a cross-section of the student body. These studies rarely report any great advantage for the students who were grouped.

The major American survey of results on this problem (Findley & Bryan, 1971) concluded that abler students do make somewhat more progress when grouped. Dahllöf (1971) examined Swedish data alongside some of the best American data and put the conclusions in a different light. As he sees it, the main difference between grouped and nongrouped classes is less in the psychological qualities of the classroom than in the amount of ground covered when everyone in a class is to move through the same lessons. The teacher "steers" to keep the lessons within the reach of those just below the average of the group. Under such a regime, the ablest students waste time, whereas in a fast class, they would move on to advanced units. Few of the experimental comparisons give students in high-ability classes credit for the extra ground such classes cover. The comparison is nearly always made on a test of what has been worked on by both groups. The students in the high group do not get a chance to show all they have learned.

Average and below-average students are likely to achieve somewhat less in ability-grouped classes than in wide-range classes. Perhaps the weaker students benefit from the stimulating tone of the balanced group, or perhaps from the pressure of lessons that move along faster. It is commonly said that forming a section of low-ability students makes them feel inferior. The evidence does not support this; in fact, one occasionally finds higher average self-concepts in a low-ability group than among similarly weak students in homogeneous classes (Drews, 1963). It is easy to understand that the pressure on the weak student, who has to keep up with abler classmates, hurts the self-concept more than assignment to a section where the pressure is reduced.

As we saw in Rist's study (p. 344), assignments to ability tracks tend to be rigid. Even if the school conscientiously shifts the child to a faster or slower class as new evidence on his progress comes in, such transfers are awkward. After three years, a fast group is likely to have moved so far beyond the middle group that "promoting" even the ablest student from that group carries an appreciable risk. Not only does he have to adapt to a faster pace, but he finds that his new classmates are making proficient use of ideas he never reached in the slow section.

GROUPING WITHIN CLASSROOMS   Since the philosophical objections to day-long, year-long ability grouping are not offset by any evidence of practical advantages, schools have organized more flexibly. A common practice today is to regroup students within a class for each subject as the day proceeds. The teacher may identify four levels of reading ability and meet each group separately, guiding them through appropriate books. The teacher cannot be in four places at once, but by developing units that learners can work through on their own or with the help of a teacher-aide, the teacher can provide 45 minutes of work in reading each day for each level while spending only about an hour (total) in his own direct reading instruction. Mrs. Whittier (p. 97), used this technique. Flexible grouping can profitably be carried further, as we shall see (p. 382).

## Providing for Students with Low General Ability

Practices for dealing with students who have exceptionally low readiness for conventional schooling have evolved slowly (Mercer & Richardson, in Hobbs, 1975b, vol. 2). There has been a steady movement away from the attempt to place some children in a special category labeled "retarded," "educable retarded," or the like. One tiny group of children who suffer from genetic misfortunes, brain injuries, and other physical defects cannot lead a normal life in the community. They will typically have IQs below 50 despite the most painstaking efforts of a qualified tester. Children in this group almost never come into the school population. Therefore, our concern in this section is with the group whose IQ scores are between 50 and 80 or 85 on an individual mental test administered in the language they know best. Such children will lag behind their age group on other tests of knowledge and problem solving, and they will almost certainly have difficulty keeping up with the usual school program.

The most common practice in recent decades has been to establish special classes for the so-called "retarded," the label being intended to suggest that if the classwork is presented at a properly slow pace, the child can ultimately learn the same skills and concepts of the normal curriculum. The difference is not merely one of rate of development and learning, however. The 9-year-old with MA 6 (IQ 67) is not like the typical 6-year-old. He earns just as many points on a mental test, but he earns more of his points by recalling information and fewer by adaptive thinking. He approaches problems less analytically and concentrates less. He does not, then, get from the curriculum the same insights and problem-solving skills that a younger child with the same MA does, even when instruction proceeds slowly.

In the adult world, the person of relatively low IQ performs much like the average member of the community: he holds a job and manages his affairs without special help. Adults with present IQs in the range 75–85 are predominantly self-supporting. Even among adults whose childhood IQs were around 60, 65 per cent are fully self-supporting (Baller, Charles, & Miller, 1967; Mercer, in Hobbs, 1975b, vol. 1). The approach that has done most to help the retardate take a place in society has been routine training in vocational and prevocational skills. As the British expert Lionel Penrose has said:

> The most important work carried out in the field of training defectives is unspectacular. It is not highly technical but requires unlimited patience, good will and common sense. The reward is to be expected not so much in scholastic improvement . . . as in his personal adjustment to social life. Occupations are found for [retardates] of all grades so that they can take part as fully and usefully as possible in human affairs (1963, p. 282).

The fact that these persons function adequately in the community as adults reminds us that the low childhood IQ is a sign of limited *scholastic* aptitude. Wherever the world allows an adult to follow familiar routines, developed through specific training or long experience, one with low academic abilities does well enough. What limits his response to instruction is the demand it often makes for abstraction, adaptive problem solving, and self-direction.

Translating a low test score—even on the best of mental tests—into the label "mentally retarded" is much too broad an interpretation. Schools have not been adequately critical in their use of test information. Children with abilities in the normal range have often been assigned to special classes when their poor showing reflected a language difficulty, unwillingness to cooperate with the tester, or emotional disturbance. The schools are far more inclined to classify a child as mentally retarded than other agencies, and it is charged that schools apply the label disproportionately often to children of minority groups (Mercer, in Hobbs, 1975b, vol. 1).

Special classes for children with low readiness make it possible for them to proceed gradually, relying on concrete materials in place of words and symbols wherever possible. The teacher, having had special training, is expected to make better diagnoses of inadequacies than the teacher in the regular classroom.

The device of special classes has been misused, however. A child assigned to special classes is likely to spend the rest of his school career there; neither instruction nor administration have been geared to remove him from the "special" category. Some classes slip into a caretaking pattern and abandon any attempt to set out "work" for the child. That is *not* special education. It has even been said that teachers use the label "learning disability" as an excuse for not teaching the child. Some programs settle for minimal vocational training instead of bringing the student in contact with the broad sweep of knowledge and the arts.

Segregating him for the entire school day has been criticized as inevitably limiting the student's social development. The child of limited general ability can fit into many of the activities of the regular classroom, when the class members range appreciably in age and are continually being reassembled into working groups for various activities. In such a setting, however, the child of low ability is often rejected by the others. Keeping him in the wide-range group, then, does not guarantee a normal social experience.

In theory, the small classes and specially trained teachers usual in "special education" should improve learning. Evaluations do not support this expectation (Sparks & Blackman, 1965). From the evaluation studies, G. O. Johnson (1962) concluded that "the mentally handicapped children enrolled in special classes achieve, academically, significantly *less* than similar children who remain in the regular grades. . . . The results related to personal and social development are not in complete agreement. . . . any advantage over the regular class groups . . . [is] slight and not particularly meaningful. . . . The mentally handicapped children *are* more accepted by their mentally handicapped peers in a special class" (p. 66; italics added). This is not evidence that special classes cannot work; it does show that the programs that have typically been offered in special classes have had no great benefit. Johnson's recommendation for the special class is what one would recommend for any class: Learning activities should be meaningful; children should have a purpose for engaging in them; "realistic stress should be introduced"; but the demands should be at a level where, exerting some effort, the children can achieve them.

A national commission (Project on the Classification of Exceptional Children; see Hobbs, 1975a, 1975b) has argued against classifying children under *any* label. This applies not only to labels such as "slow learner" but also to "hyperactive," "delinquent," "schizophrenic," "dyslexic," "learning disability," and even "ortho-

## The blind lead the blind

... many teachers in public schools who work with the visually handicapped but are used to dealing with sighted children are quite satisfied with minimal scholastic performance from their blind pupils. They tend to view a whole category of children as incompetent to achieve on a high academic level because of their "handicap." The term *handicap* attached to these children, coupled with such observable behavior as slowness or timidity in mobility and poor motor coordination, leads to lowered expectations and to the general impression that these children are handicapped in scholastic aptitude. In addition to permissiveness and overprotectiveness, there frequently exists an undue amount of sympathy, which can be psychologically devastating.

SOURCE: Goldstein et al., in Hobbs (1975b), vol. 2, pp. 24–25.

pedically handicapped." The labels, it is said, block thinking, exaggerate differences, and lose sight of individuality. The group recommends as a substitute the development of a profile of the child's strengths and weaknesses in school tasks and daily living, and a profile of the supports and limitations in his home and neighborhood. This would enable the school or social agency to identify the kinds of special services the child should have, and so the kinds of personnel and activities to be provided in the district. The services contemplated range far beyond slow-paced and diagnosis-based teaching. Mention is made, for example, of camping programs, residential schools, special diets, guidance to the child's parents, and neighborhood family-activity centers.

In this proposal two features should be noted. The child's readiness for school is assessed as a part of his total adaptive functioning, rather than as a narrow concern by school personnel for his life in school. Second, the proposal suggests ecological intervention (Bronfenbrenner, 1974b). Compensatory instruction plus treatment that promotes adjustment to school may have little effect if the child spends his time outside the school in an unstimulating and emotionally unhealthy environment. Proposals for improving the child's out-of-school life are still far from definite, but they are rapidly replacing the forlorn hope that the schools and daycare centers will by themselves resolve all social problems of child development.

According to the Hobbs proposal, some children needing special services will live most of the school day in the regular classroom, perhaps being removed to a special group for a brief period. Some will spend most of the day in a specialized, protective, perhaps quasi-tutorial environment. The Hobbs group neither advocates nor dismisses the use of special classes. It advocates giving the child the special services he needs in settings as near to normal—as little restrictive—as the school can manage. The low-ability child should participate in whichever of the regular school activities he can cope with. If it is decided that he can best be served by assigning him entirely to a special class, his progress should be monitored, and he should be returned to the regular classroom as soon as his progress allows.

10 The Hobbs group was asked to concern itself with children who are at a special disadvantage, not just with those of low academic ability. Do the recommendations summarized above appear to be appropriate for blind children (box)?

11 Do the recommendations of the Hobbs group suggest a sensible policy for dealing with children who are exceptionally superior (in academic performance or some other abilities)?

12 Do the recommendations of the Hobbs group apply particularly to "exceptional" children, or would the same policies be ideal for every student?

## Diversifying Assignments and Activities

Opinion today is opposed to keeping children of a special kind in a program of their own for the entire school day, whenever this can be avoided. This statement applies to grouping according to interests, talents, and, of course, sex—as well as to grouping according to handicaps. With or without homogeneous grouping, any assemblage of children or adults ranges widely in interests, developed skills, abilities to learn, and personal styles. Uniform treatment of the group is a compromise that fits no individuals well. The teacher or team of teachers has to manage a class by ingenious combinations of large-group, small-group, and tutorial work or individual projects.

NONGRADED CLASSROOMS    So long as every child in a classroom was regarded as "following the second-grade curriculum," with everyone working on the same daily lesson, misfits were inevitable. Schools came to question not only the attempt to hold class members to the same rate of progress but also the idea of year-long organization of classes. Numerous forms of reorganization have been tried, and even more numerous names have been applied. Many of the innovative plans are referred to as "open education"—but be wary of labels. One school, becoming "open," settles for an architectural arrangement that throws several classes and teachers into one room where instruction proceeds formally within ability groups. Another settles for a plan in which each student works at his own rate through formally ordered lessons. A third, in an attempt to foster self-satisfaction, shifts to a permissive and possibly anarchic mode. Open education can be purposeful, flexible, and exciting; but the label promises nothing. (See p. 654.)

Many innovative plans start with what is often called a "nongraded" organization. Instead of being "assigned to Grade II," the pupil is placed with children having roughly his degree of academic proficiency, some of whom have recently left kindergarten and some of whom have already had two years in the program. Grouping within such a class takes account of the diagnostic information on each child. There are likely to be many levels of (for example) reading activity within a classroom. The student is shifted to a higher group within the class as soon as his progress warrants. The groups are not "a year apart," so the child who is moved up will not find that the faster group is far beyond him. In such a plan students can be shifted at any time during the year. A student who repairs some fundamental inadequacy may make several successive shifts upward. In a plan of this sort, the age range within a "class" using the same space may be three or more years. The social pressure to progress as fast as the average child of the same age is greatly reduced, and exceptionally able children can be moved up to work that challenges them.

Whereas ability grouping within the year-long class has shown little value in (possibly inadequate) experimental tests, nongraded plans have a good record. Pavan (1973) located 16 comparisons of nongraded and graded plans. In half the studies, achievement and adjustment averaged higher in the schools where flexible grouping had been used. Nongrading was especially good for maintaining healthy self-concepts and favorable attitudes toward school in poor achievers. (It did not eliminate poor achievement.) In only one study did the traditional organization show better results. The fact that the two techniques came out even in nearly half the comparisons again indicates that a single administrative change will not necessarily improve instruction.

## Adapting instruction to emotional differences

Schools usually offer bloodless lessons and purely token consequences, but many learners—children, adolescents, and adults—are truly aroused only by problems that stir their emotions. Bruno Bettelheim (1966) argues that lessons can properly include material that is exciting and even violent. He refers to Sylvia Ashton-Warner's description of Maori children (1958). In her words,

> Rangi, who lives on love and kisses and thrashings and fights and fear of the police and who took four months to learn [to read] *come, look,* and *and* takes four minutes to learn: *butcher-knife; gaol; police; sing; cry; kiss; Daddy; Mummie; Rangi; haka* (a native word); *fight.*

Bettelheim worked with emotionally overwrought children in a special school. They, like Rangi, learn to read and spell quickly when the words are close to their hearts: *fire, knife, scream, yell, orange juice, hot dog.* The primer's pallid stories of a boy who lives in a green house and finds a blue cap are not compelling to children whose heads teem with fears and fantasies. Bettelheim makes the additional point (by no means incidental) that bringing violence into the open for honest discussion acknowledges the long-standing importance of violence in Western culture. Discussion helps youngsters to acknowledge and control their impulses.

INDIVIDUALIZED ASSIGNMENTS  Many educational psychologists (for example, Bloom, 1976) presume that any child can learn anything if he is allowed to proceed at his own pace with excellently designed instruction. This idea was put forward in a more cautious form by J. B. Carroll (1963); he was thinking particularly of the success in teaching foreign languages by intensive, "total-immersion" methods. These methods, using diversified teaching techniques including taped drills, conversations during everyday activities, and printed exercises, do bring even the less capable students forward. Some take longer than others to "finish the course"—that is, to reach functional proficiency—but all of them learn. The Montreal experiment (box, p. 371), is one bit of evidence supporting Carroll's position. The argument applies to cumulative mastery of well-defined skills. Intensive training for intellectual and emotional understanding—for example, of human cultures—is hard to envision. The devices for scheduling instruction to fit the individual's pace have therefore been primarily confined to the teaching of skills or factual lessons.

Some techniques have mechanized the diagnostic process, making it possible to prescribe for individuals at modest cost. A curriculum can be reduced to elementary subskills, for each of which a test is prepared. When the student has completed several lessons on, say, locating the decimal point in a division problem, he is tested on the subskill. If mastery is inadequate, the teacher arranges for more exercises and another test. A grand roadmap can show what elements the student is to have at his command before he proceeds to relatively complex division tasks (p. 535). As Bloom (1971) has said, this technique is suited for subject-matter that is "closed"—that is, in which there is a single definite right answer to each question, and no creativity or personal interpretation is wanted. The technique is easy to apply to phonics, harder to apply to paragraph comprehension. As for higher levels of reading, humanists would surely object if anyone suggested that reading poetry equals the sum of recognition of rhyme, recognition of metaphor, and so on, and nothing more.

Superficially similar to this so-called "mastery" procedure is a plan using "modules." A module can be a series of lessons on a subskill or it can be a project of wider scope. For example, there might be a module in which the student—as one of several activities—collects information at the supermarket and calculates the per-ounce or per-serving price of foods packaged in different sizes. He thus practices the skills of division in an interesting context but he does not focus wholly on division. A module may call for pooled efforts of a small group. The classroom that uses modules is typically arranged into activity "centers" that attract the student into new lines of work (Fig. 9.5). The student has considerable freedom in choice of modules (though he is guided by the teacher on the basis of test information); he can complete the work at his own rate. Often, teacher and student enter into a "contract" in which the student commits himself to a delivery date.

**FIGURE 9.5**

**Partial view of classroom designed to encourage individual and small-group work**

SOURCE: *Change for Children: Ideas and Activities for Individualizing Learning,* by Sandra Kaplan, Jo Ann Kaplan, Sheila Madsen, and Bette Taylor (p. 25). Copyright © 1973 by Goodyear Publishing Co. Reprinted by permission.

RESPONSE-SENSITIVE INSTRUCTION   In most systems of matching lessons to students, decisions are made at long intervals. The decision in choosing between the academic and vocational paths through high school typically holds for four years. Assignment to a nongraded classroom holds for several months. Assignment to the ten-o'clock reading group holds for at least a few weeks. Prescription by a weekly test seems highly flexible, but even it is coarse adaptation, compared to what R. C. Atkinson calls "response-sensitive" instruction. This is not a new idea. Deciding what to tell or ask the learner next, after hearing his response, is good Socratic technique for the one-on-one teacher. In computer-aided instruction modern technology offers a mechanical Socrates; handling groups of students, it can choose a next question for each individual by rule. Such a system relies on a library of exercises (and sometimes explanations) that the computer can call on. Fairly complicated rules govern what it displays to the individual at a given moment. For example: "If the student answered eight out of ten questions on this subskill correctly, shift to a new subskill now. Also, schedule a review for his next session. If he got fewer than eight correct, did he make serious mistakes or borderline mistakes? If borderline, give him five more exercises. If serious, schedule him for a review explanation before his next exercise." The most efficient rule is determined by tryout. I shall have more to say about the principles that influence the rules in Chapter 12.

For now, the point is that this kind of microadaptation—in which instructional choices may be made 30 times in a 15-minute session—puts into mass production what was previously the cherished skill of the master teacher. The simulation of the master teacher is imperfect, but the computer never tires, and it can attend to thousands of students at once. But it replaces human teachers only in functions that truly can be reduced to rules.

LARGE-GROUP PROJECTS   Often the teacher can devise a group activity within which every student works at his own level. The student then has the self-respect and interest that comes from contributing to a group project, without the frustration of a too-difficult task or the tedium of work that is too easy. Within the main unit each student can work on a subdivision that arouses his interest. If he has a special weakness, he can be directed into a task that will remedy it; if a talent, into a task that will develop it. Instead of reading from the same source as every other student, he reads what he is able to read.

In a sixth-grade unit on railroads, some youngsters may be making a map of early American railroads while others are drawing people in the costume of 1890 meeting a train. The first group will need less creative skill than the second. Both groups will have to do library work to get the necessary information, and the harder investigations can be allotted to the more capable students. For all the teacher's efforts to "de-sex" the activity, boys will be more concerned about the train in the mural, and girls with the costumes. Both could be developing artistic skill. Students take various social roles. Terry is the chairman of a committee; Margo is secretary; Jill arranges a visit to the long-abandoned local

depot; Frank serves as classroom librarian. Mark, who lacks persistence, gets the task of collecting records on old railway routes for use by the map-making team; their constant "Have you got the information for this section yet?" keeps him aware of his responsibility until he completes it. Claude is a good worker and skilled at lettering, but he tends to work by himself. In addition to working on the map, he is asked to assist the others to improve their lettering on the charts and graphs of railroad services they are making.

Diversified activities require ingenuity. The teacher cannot plan a lesson and use it year after year, nor can he purchase his plans and materials from a school supply house. Even if next year's class takes up the same topic, the unique social structure and interests of that group call for somewhat different emphasis, organization, and source materials. Differentiated activities make teaching·easier in some ways, since they result in greater interest and fewer problems of discipline. The fact that each student is working on material he can master makes helping him far less of an uphill job.

**13** What would happen under a graded and a nongraded three-year primary plan

    a. to a girl who is very bright and learns the fundamentals of reading after two months of school?

    b. to a girl of average general ability who has special difficulty in reading throughout the first year?

**14** Can differentiated assignments be used in a college class?

**15** How might a high-school civics class be organized to allow for differences in interests and abilities?

**16** What parts of the content of Chapter 8 of this book are "closed," enabling the teacher to check off when a student has mastered the subskills? Which objectives are difficult to reduce to elements that can be checked off by a formal test?

## READING LIST

Urie Bronfenbrenner, "Is Early Education Effective?" *Teachers College Record* 76 (1974), 279–303.

> Surveys studies of educational intervention during the first six years of life. The plans investigated range from schooling, through schooling with parental involvement, to programs that transfer the very young child from the home to a presumably superior environment for the entire day. Bronfenbrenner emphasizes the positive results, but he also demonstrates that results vary considerably from program to program.

Herbert Goldstein et al., "Schools," in *Issues in the Classification of Children,* ed. Nicholas Hobbs (San Francisco: Jossey-Bass, 1975), vol. 2, pp. 4–61.

> Reviews the practices of the schools in dealing with children of low ability, identifies some of the social forces that perpetuate unsatisfactory systems, and recommends new approaches to classification and treatment.

Arthur R. Jensen, "The Culturally Disadvantaged: Psychological and Educational Aspects," *Educational Research* 10 (1967), 4–20.

A review of psychological evidence indicating that a limiting environment can damage readiness for school and arguing for a serious investment in compensatory education. There is no fundamental inconsistency between this paper and Jensen's later (and better-known) writings, where he criticizes the ineffectiveness of nearly all the large-scale compensatory programs of the 1960s.

Ray C. Rist, "Student Social Class and Teacher Expectations: The Self-Fulfilling Prophecy in Ghetto Education," *Harvard Educational Review* 40 (1970), 411–51.

How three successive teachers guaranteed the educational failure of the children initially assigned to the lowest track in a three-track primary system. Rist offers the controversial hypothesis that many of the discriminatory practices may have been half-consciously designed to foster the upward mobility of the favored students. (Both the teachers and the students were black; the study can be read as an account of social-class bias within the black community.)

Julian C. Stanley, "Intellectual Precocity," in *Mathematical Talent: Discovery, Description, and Development,* ed. J. Stanley et al. (Baltimore: Johns Hopkins University Press, 1974), pp. 1–22.

Stanley argues for specialized and intensive education for students who demonstrate unusual intellectual performance. He describes cases of mathematically exceptional boys who were moved directly into the University at age 13, skipping high-school work. The essay also describes the history of interest in the exceptionally able during the past century, and points to many successful life histories of persons whose schooling was accelerated.

# PART THREE

## Fundamental
## Learning Processes

# 10

# SKILLS

Skilled performance is shown whenever a person runs through a complex series of well-practiced actions to accomplish a familiar task. A man rises from bed, dresses, shaves, walks downstairs, feeds himself, and drives to his office. Each of these acts is a highly developed skill. Even so simple an act as rising from bed consists of carefully selected movements. If the man had not learned them, he would be reduced to clumsy trial and error, but thanks to experience he can perform rapidly and accurately without giving the act his full attention. This chapter concentrates on psychomotor skills. These are the main concern of some teachers and a central responsibility for others (box, p. 394). But even a teacher of philosophy will find the concepts of this chapter useful, since much complex behavior develops as skills do.

For our purposes, a skill is best defined as a performance that—once learned—can be carried out rather accurately with little or no conscious attention to the component acts. Eating is an example that fits my definition. You can carry on a discussion of United States foreign policy while "skillfully" eating a hamburger. Skills shade into problem solving: eating spaghetti takes your mind off the conversation a bit.

Concern here is chiefly with sequences of response that occur in *continuous* skills—speaking, typing, running. Some change of emphasis is needed in discussing *discrete* skills—archery, or titration—where sequences are short and pre-

## Skills to be taught

Most examples in this chapter are homely ones, such as driving an automobile. The range of skills developed in education is far wider. This list suggests some kinds of objectives to which concepts of this chapter directly apply. The concepts also bear on discrimination, associative learning, and speech (Chapters 11 and 12).

| | |
|---|---|
| *Early education* | Buttoning, carrying a tune, handling a crayon, climbing, catching a ball |
| *Science and medicine* | Taking measurements, focusing a microscope, preparing slides, finding a familiar micro-organism in the microscope field, tying sutures, testing pH of a sample |
| *Language* | Using an index, reading unknown words such as *Yoruba* and *cyclopentadecanone* |
| *Vocational training* | Assembly work, inspecting factory output, taking a micrometer reading, operating a machine (including calculators), weaving |
| *Arts* | Kneading clay to consistency, connecting two points with a straight line (freehand or otherwise), sketching a tree in a landscape |

**TABLE 10.1**

**Fourfold classification of skills**

|  | Continuous skill | Discrete skill |
|---|---|---|
| Closed skill | Operating a disk-cutter (p. 403)<br><br>Dealing cards in a bridge game | Performing a jackknife dive from a fixed height<br><br>Separating an egg |
| Open skill | Skating in a crowd<br><br>Cursive writing | Swatting a fly<br><br>Braking a car |

cision is what counts. It is also useful at times to contrast closed skills and open skills. In the former, the situation confronting the performer is essentially the same on all occasions; in the latter the situation changes—perhaps while the act is in progress.

In learning a skill, the first step is to interpret cues from the situation. The learner recognizes a goal and selects a trial response. The process of learning is the usual one (p. 86), except that, with extended practice, a well-defined response pattern is shaped and polished. Many principles of psychomotor learning apply also to performance where the motor element is of only minor importance—in surveying, for example. In planning a course in surveying, the educator will carry out many of the acts this chapter discusses: task analysis, identification of parts and wholes, demonstration and explanation, monitoring, and so on. Most of the concepts listed at the beginning of this chapter are also highly pertinent to improving intellectual performances. In fact, one important message of this chapter is that the learning of a skill *is* largely intellectual. In learning a skill one relies on attention, memory, interpretation, and even deliberate problem solving. Only after the intellectual work has set the pattern for the task does excellence of execution come into its own. Even then, novel conditions can call for additional intellectual analysis.

1  Is frying an egg a skill, as defined above?

2  Is reading a bar graph such a skill?

3  Classify the following skills as open or closed, continuous or discrete.
   a. Putting in golf
   b. Shooting a pistol at a target
   c. Doing simultaneous (oral) translation

# MARKS OF EXPERTNESS

A person in an unfamiliar situation must find out what to do. His actions are likely to be hesitant, with many pauses to examine consequences. In a familiar situation, actions are direct and usually successful. Only when a person encounters difficulty will he be indecisive. On a well-known road, a driver sails along. He shifts gears, gives the car extra gas on a hill, and takes curves without interrupting his conversation with his companion. His handling of the car and his pathfinding performance (for he is selecting his path moment by moment) illustrate mature skills.

One person is said to be more skilled than another when he reaches his goal with fewer pauses to make choices or to correct errors. We can describe skilled performance by such words as *automatic* and *smooth*. Any skilled performance, even writing the letter *a,* is a complex, integrated series of hundreds of nerve-muscle coordinations.

## Immediate Response Replaces Awkward Trial

INFORMATION PROCESSING IN EARLY AND LATE PERFORMANCE     The change from conscious step-by-step direction to an automatic performance is in large part due to the dropping out of *mediating responses* (mediating = "in the middle"). When the beginner takes up a new piano selection, his chain of stimulus-response associations runs like this:

1. Sight of note produces thought: "That stands for B-flat."

2. Thought of note produces image of B-flat position on keyboard: "Of the three black keys, the one farthest to the right."

3. Sight of keyboard and hand, matched against the image, produces thought: "B-flat is next to the little finger."

4. Player directs self to move little finger up and to the right.

5. Player strikes B-flat key with little finger.

Each of the mediating responses is a thought directing the performer one step along the way. The beginner's performance, broken into steps, is clumsy. With practice, the separate mediating responses become unnecessary. After the beginner practices piano for a while, the thought "B-flat" leads without a pause (*immediately*) to movement of the proper finger. Later, the sight of the note becomes a sufficient stimulus for the movement. Stimulus substitution has occurred. Once the stimulus needed to produce the act was the spelled-out verbal direction from the teacher; a bit later the sign "B-flat" caused the performer himself to give the verbal direction, in unspoken words. Ultimately, the words become unnecessary.

Mediation translates the concrete into a code or label; that is, it changes sensed reality into symbols that refer to stored verbal knowledge. And, at the conclusion of thought, mediation provides a verbal order directing action (symbol to reality). Psychologists speak of these processes as encoding, information processing, and decoding. Between stimulus and response, then, are five stages:

1. Intake: Stimuli set off nervous impulses.

2. Encoding: Stimulus information recognized, translated into concepts. (Black key is labeled "B-flat.") This is what Piaget calls *assimilation* (p. 329), mapping the new into what has already been learned. Chapter 11 will examine encoding processes.

3. Information processing: Associations and thought are used to derive from the information a symbolically stated prescription for action. ("Strike with middle finger.")

4. Decoding: The symbolic order is turned into nervous impulses directing muscles to act on the physical situation (finger movement at the piano).

5. Output: Nervous impulses cause the muscles to act on the external world.

## Decoding

In a thoroughly practiced skill, the step from sensory information to action is taken *immediately*, without symbolic interpretation.

COGNITIVE, ASSOCIATIVE, AND AUTONOMOUS PHASES   Fitts and Posner (1967) speak of three phases in acquiring a skill:

1. A cognitive phase. In this, the person is getting in mind just what is to be done. Progress comes through deliberate interpretation—sorting out cues, planning, recognizing alternative techniques. Verbal mediation usually plays a large role (J. Adams, 1971; Boucher, 1974). One learns what to attend to and how it may be encoded.

2. An intermediate associative phase. Provisional actions are made and the results observed. Actions are compared grossly to the model formed in Phase 1. The most satisfactory actions are tied together in a new complex response.

3. An "autonomous" stage. When this stage is reached, the sequence seems to run by itself, with little direct attention and correction. The person can complete the act while his mind is on other matters. As the response moves into this stage, the directing program is perfected, and fractional responses are harmonized in a patterned motion sequence. The performer gives no time to mediating responses until, under some exceptional circumstance, the program breaks down.

The word *program*, used repeatedly in this chapter, is borrowed from everyday usage. The program of a ceremony is a list of things to be done in order: musical selection, invocation, flag salute, speech of welcome, and so on. The term becomes a metaphor in speaking of automatic machines. The dishwashing machine has a simple program to follow. Its timing and regulating mechanism "instructs" it to rinse for, say, 45 seconds, close the drain, tip the soap receptacle, add water until a certain level is reached, spray the soapy water over the dishes for eight minutes, and so on until it turns off a signal light, ending the cycle. A slightly more elaborate program is required for a clothes washer, which can be set for different fabrics, each switch setting altering the timing of events.

The job of the human being's directing program is to assemble actions. Here is an example:

Suppose, for example, an individual learning to drive an automobile has already mastered the part-skills of driving backwards, of turning the steering wheel to direct the motion of the car, and of driving (forwards or backwards) at minimal speed. What does such a person need yet to learn in order to turn the car around on a straight two-lane street? Evidently, he needs to learn a procedure in which these part-skills are combined in a suitable order, so that by making two or three backward and forward motions, combined with suitable turning, the car is headed in the other direction. This procedure is the executive subroutine. It is obviously an intellectual kind of process which "tells" the driver what to do next. Thus the internal process is not in itself "motor" at all. (Gagné & Briggs, 1974, p. 67.)

An "unconscious" neuromuscular program regulates strongly patterned motions. Recall Penfield's remarks about the programs that regulate speaking (p. 167). For more on such programs, see box, p. 406.

Though programming is an essential feature of skill, the skilled performer need not know about the program. Often he is unaware of the movements he is making and of the cues he responds to. The child's speech is an obvious example. Conscious analysis of the program—as distinct from attention to the movements—sometimes helps the learner to improve, sometimes creates confusion.

It *is* important for the teacher to have clearly in mind what acts form an effective program. Knowing the actions to be performed and the cues that guide them is the teacher's first step toward designing training activities. (See p. 413.)

**4**  Which of the following performances would be called skills?
   a. A person signs a check.
   b. A person subtracts $2.40 from $15.00 without error or difficulty.
   c. A quarterback notices that an opponent is out of position and calls a successful play through that spot.
   d. A quarterback throws passes that consistently "lead" the runner by just the right amount, though the direction, distance, and wind conditions change from occasion to occasion.
   e. A child on his third trip to a small zoo names all the animals correctly.

**5**  Show that a sequence of decisions or actions is involved in each of the following skilled performances.
   a. A cook makes pancakes.
   b. A child sings the familiar "Yankee Doodle."
   c. A student translates into English: *Der Hund sieht das Fleisch.*

**6**  Can each of the following acts be described as the execution of a program? If so, which of the three Fitts-Posner stages has the performance reached?
   a. You approach a familiar door, remove your keys from your pocket, pick out the right one, and let yourself in.
   b. You look up a word—say, *vermiform*—in the dictionary.
   c. You run downstairs.
   d. You use a calculator to find 6 per cent of 172.54.

**7**  What mediating responses that are present in early typewriting drop out with practice?

## Subtle Cues Are Used

An action is guided by cues from the situation. The cues may be seen, heard, or felt. A relevant cue is any stimulus from outside or from within the body that can help a person to recognize a situation or to direct an action. The person who sits at a typewriter for the first time will guide his response almost entirely by sight cues. The letter on the key says to him, "Strike here and you will print the letter you want." The trained typist, however, guides his action by muscular cues. At each instant he can sense where his fingers are, relative to the keyboard, and how he must move them to strike the desired letter (Fig. 10.1; see also West, 1967).

As a person acquires experience, more and more cues become useful in selecting the right response. A beginner depends upon the most obvious cues. Later, many additional cues guide him. He finds that one particular reach on the piano keyboard (yielding a muscular cue) is equivalent to a movement regulated by a visual cue, from the seen position of the note A to the seen position of B-flat. The boy starting to play a horn can judge whether or not his action is right only by the tone that comes out. Soon he finds that the right action *feels* different from the wrong. His lips feel right in one position, wrong in another, and if he uses this wrong position the wrong tone comes out. Lip-muscle cues are now as significant as the sound cues. The muscle cues are more useful, because they are available before he blows and they permit him to correct his action without first sounding a false note.

**FIGURE 10.1**

**Performance with and without visual cues in relation to skill of typist**

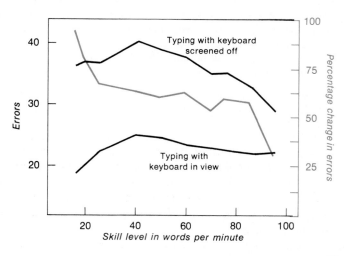

SOURCE: After West (1966).

The performer usually is confronted with dozens, if not hundreds, of stimuli. Some are fundamental cues, which one must notice to respond at all successfully; others are secondary, helpful in regulating the response; and still others are irrelevant. For the shortstop, the swing of the bat and the initial motion of the ball are fundamental cues that send him into action. The spin on the ball and the conditions of the infield are of no help to the beginner, but they help the expert to anticipate the hop of the ball. The position of the umpire, the roar of the crowd, and a million other stimuli are to be ignored.

The expert gives more of his attention to the secondary regulating cues. A toddler put upon a stage would have to give his full attention to the rim of the platform and to his muscular sensations to avoid toppling off. A 10-year-old presenting a talk needs to give no attention to standing and balancing; however, *he* will have to think very hard about what he is trying to say. Getting words in the right order and remembering a series of ideas will take concentration. A more experienced speaker, master of what he is trying to say, can arrange the words with little conscious consideration of alternatives, and his postural reactions need no conscious direction. He is free to watch the expressions and reactions of his audience and to alter his speaking adaptively.

**8**  In rifle marksmanship, are any cues pertinent other than the visual cues from the target?

**9**  Which of the following statements could be illustrated in attaching a two-prong plug to an electric cord?
    a. The expert makes use of cues that the beginner ignores.
    b. The expert makes more precise judgments than the beginner.
    c. Many aspects of the situation are ignored by the expert.

**10**  Suppose that building a campfire is a skill important enough to be the subject of a training program. What cues are fundamental, what cues secondary? Is the best procedure simply to have the learner build campfires under natural conditions?

## Mistakes Are Caught Before They Happen

A skilled act may look like a single motion, but it is not. If we could put behavior under a microscope—something like this can be done by recording electrically the actions of separate muscles—we would see that the smooth motion is a chain of impulses. Each impulse checks, redirects, or augments the preceding action. Even in so simple an act as throwing a dart, no two performances are identical.

Especially in a continuous skill, trials and corrections take place in mid-act. A person steering a car does not—indeed, cannot—point the car down the road and hold it straight. He aims it more or less well, and then judges whether he is drifting to the right or the left. As soon as he senses the drift, he turns the wheel to correct it. Usually he corrects too far, and soon must move the wheel back. Thus, the path is a zigzag, never a straight line.

The expert comes closer to the ideal path than does the novice, and his corrections are made without thought. But his action consists of repeated sensing and correcting—a feedback process. The driver's action has certain consequences. Knowledge of these consequences is fed back to the driver in visual and other cues. If he is dissatisfied, he takes a further action; soon *its* consequences in turn are fed back.

Feedback is easily observed in mirror drawing because initial performance is primitive. The subject is asked to trace a path, looking not at his hand but at its reflection in a mirror. The reflected hand seems to move away when the real hand is pulled closer. The person who has not practiced with the mirror produces a jagged, zigzag line quite unlike regular drawing (Fig. 10.2). He is like the man blundering across a strange room in the dark, who starts in the direction that seems best, comes up short when he brushes an obstacle, turns on a new tack, cracks his shin, turns again, and so on. Feedback in the drawing experiment keeps the person near his proper path, but errors and too-strong corrections slow the performance. Just as the horn player gets an early warning, and so cuts off the sour note before he blows, the person before the mirror becomes sensitive to early warnings. As soon as the tracing begins to wander from the correct path, he changes course; his lines become smoother. In time, much of the visual guidance is replaced by muscular guidance. Often the expert does not even wait for a muscular signal; he can become aware that he has given his muscle an incorrect order and countermand it before it takes effect (Higgins & Angel, 1970; see also box, p. 406).

**FIGURE 10.2**

Trial and correction in mirror drawing

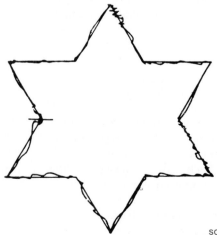

SOURCE: After Dearborn (1910).

## FIGURE 10.3

Records of machine operation
by a trainee with increasing
amounts of practice

After 9 hours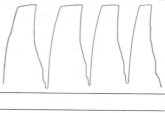

After 45 hours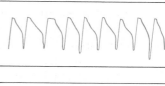

After 141 hours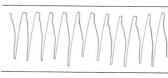

After 239 hours

SOURCE: After Lindahl (1945). Copyright 1945
by the American Psychological Association.
Reprinted by permission.

In a nonmotor performance also, the proficient person is likely to catch his mistake before it "comes out." There is an anecdote about a teacher of bridge who, after watching Charles Goren and his partner win a national championship, sniffed, "He's not so wonderful. He didn't do a single thing that I wouldn't have done." Goren's comment was, "But . . . would she have done everything we did for 36 straight hands?" The player who commits the fewest overt errors is the one who wins.

Improvement during practice is shown by Fig. 10.3. These records show the learning of an industrial skill. The worker presses a foot treadle that drives a cutter, which in turn slices disks from the end of a rod. He is supposed to come down smoothly, follow through after the cut, and return to position for the next cut. Jerky action breaks cutting wheels and produces jagged disks, which have to be discarded. The performance records were made by fastening a recorder to the treadle. A steep line shows a rapid movement. In each strike we see the starting pause at top, the rightward slant of the cutting stroke, the follow-through, and the upward return. Even in the final record, each stroke is a bit different. If you look closely, you can see the tiny wobbles that indicate sensing and correcting.

How important feedback is for continuous skills is shown by experiments in which the feedback is disturbed. In one investigation (W. Smith et al., 1960), the subject's hand was shielded so that he could not watch it as he wrote (or traced a path). Instead, he was allowed to watch his hand on a TV screen. In the important experimental condition, the TV image was electronically delayed one-half second. Having to watch the screen for cues had only a small effect. But delay of feedback disrupted the performance: the time necessary to write a word increased three- to tenfold and writing became illegible (Fig. 10.4).

Internal feedback (knowledge of the act itself) shades over into "knowledge of results" (from outside). The feedback from touch and other senses that tells the archer whether the bowstring is taut helps him judge when to release the arrow. Knowledge of the end result—that his arrow hit the target, or was six inches too high—affects his next shot. The skilled performer rarely has to wait for the result to know how he is doing; the skilled archer can judge, at the instant he looses the arrow, whether it is likely to be on target.

Psychological writings confuse internal feedback regarding the act with results observed by the performer and with reports of results "fed back" by an experimenter or teacher—as in the important but ambiguous conclusion of Bilodeau and Bilodeau (1961):

> . . . feedback or knowledge of results . . . [is] the strongest, most important variable controlling performance and learning [of motor skill]. . . . It has been shown repeatedly that there is no improvement without knowledge of results, progressive improvement with it, and deterioration after its withdrawal.

## FIGURE 10.4

### Delaying feedback disrupts coordination

"S" and "F" indicate start and finish of trace, respectively.

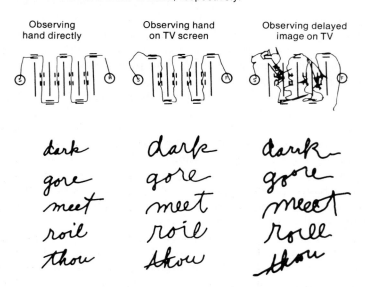

SOURCE: Smith et al. (1960). From *Science*. Copyright 1960 by the American Association for the Advancement of Science. Reprinted by permission.

**Expert**

© 1975 United Feature Syndicate, Inc.

In the laboratory, it is possible to cut off direct knowledge of results by placing the target where the subject cannot see it. Then the experimenter controls external feedback. In few real-life skills can the learner be deprived of the opportunity to observe his own results. Only reports from others can be "withdrawn." The Fitts-Posner model (p. 398) suggests that information on results counts heavily in the second phase, and that internal feedback matters most when a skill matures.

STORING AND USING A TEMPLATE  As information comes in, the feedback mechanism compares it against an image of what ought to be coming in. To evaluate, the person has to know what a proper response feels like at each stage of the act. The cues generated by action are matched against the ideal in mind for that moment (J. Adams, 1968). Moreover, the images for submovements are linked (see below) to make up an image, or template, of whole passages of action. For the learner, the "template" is not a schema; it is more like an aspiration. The expert's template and the schema he has under command are nearly identical (Schmidt, 1975b).

The whole point of the Suzuki method of training very young children to play the violin (box) is to embed a model of excellent performance against which they can match their own tries. The expert serving as model communicates a visual, auditory, and rhythmic image. In training for most skills, Posner and Keele (in Travers, 1973, p. 824) suggest, much time could be saved if the beginner were to develop a correct image at the outset. Posner and Keele would

## Learning to make music: songbirds

The song of the bird is an intricate motor performance. In the following passage, Posner and Keele (in Travers, 1973, pp. 823 and 824) explain how the bird acquires the song of its species.

> Considerable insight into the acquisition of motor programs has come from recent studies of bird song development. . . . Some birds, such as European chaffinches, white-crowned sparrows and Oregon juncos, exhibit flexibility in song development. Although they cannot learn the songs of other species, there are different dialects that develop out of a rudimentary song common to the species. Marler has shown that if young birds are raised in isolation never hearing an adult song, then an appropriate song does not develop as the young bird learns to sing. On the other hand, if isolated juvenile birds are exposed for only a few weeks in the summer to the adult song and then do not hear it again, the appropriate song is developed the following spring. The acquisition of a motor program appears to require storage in memory of a standard or model of the final skill.
>
> In subsequent studies Konishi (1965) deafened young birds at different stages of development. If the young birds exposed to an adult song in the field were deafened, the appropriate song failed to materialize even though a model was presumably stored. When deafening was delayed until after the song had been established, however, the appropriate song persisted. Auditory feedback was no longer needed. And . . . Nottebohm (1970) has shown that when portions of a well-developed song are eliminated by [surgical] de-innervation of some muscles involved in song production, other portions of the song persist even though both auditory feedback and kinesthetic feedback are disrupted.

SOURCE: Both boxes from Michael I. Posner & Steven W. Keele, "Skill Learning," in *Second Handbook of Research on Teaching*, R. M. W. Travers, ed. (Chicago: Rand McNally, 1973). Copyright 1973, American Educational Research Association, Washington, D.C.

have the beginner spend considerable time closely observing expert performers, live or on film loops. When kinesthetic elements are critical, they suggest "putting the learner through the motions" by mechanically guiding his limbs. The purpose "would not be to build a motor program but to build a template to which feedback resulting from execution of a motor program can be compared." For the learner who has reached the associative stage, mental practice (p. 426) also serves this purpose.

**11** With all but the most elaborate hairstyles, people can groom their hair without using a mirror. What internal feedback or information about results do they rely on?

**12** Chemistry students set up apparatus to generate hydrogen when acid is poured onto zinc. The instructions are clearly given in the laboratory manual, and the students work individually at their benches as the instructor circulates. When do the students receive feedback or knowledge of results?

**13** Compare Suzuki's training method (p. 407) with the way in which a child learns to speak the language of his parents.

## Learning to make music: tiny violinists

In Japan the tiniest children are taught to play tunes on the violin. At a demonstration of the Suzuki method one may see dozens of 4-year-olds playing, in unison, pieces of moderate difficulty. Posner and Keele (in Travers, 1973, p. 824) here compare Suzuki's method of developing the young performers' neural programs with the way birds learn to sing.

In Japan more than 20 years ago Suzuki devised a teaching method for violin playing that bears a striking resemblance to bird song acquisition (Pronko, 1969).

The Suzuki technique calls for the playing of a single selection of great, high fidelity music to babies only a few months old. The same piece of music is played repeatedly for perhaps several months until the baby recognizes it as evidenced by the music's soothing effect. At that point another piece is selected. Further selections are gradually added to the growing child's repertoire until the age of three or four years, when he is sent to music school. The young child most certainly is not taught how to read music at that age. Rather, he learns by ear. The sounds that he produces on the instrument are presumably matched to auditory templates stored in memory since the time of infancy, and corrections in the pattern of movements are made. As the skill is acquired, students develop excellent playing abilities on other music. It is only at the age of five or six years that the child begins to read music.

According to reports, the Suzuki method produces extremely capable and occasionally internationally known musicians. Of course it is impossible to separate a motivational from a memory template explanation of success of the method.

## Movements Are Linked Up

In a continuous skill especially, it is the mark of the expert that he makes use of signals well in advance of the action. His movements are tied into long sequences. As the beginner depends on cues closer to the time of the action, his responses are less integrated (F. Bartlett, 1958, pp. 15–16).

The expert develops an individualized program. Good tennis players, when making a forehand drive, time muscle contractions accurately and consistently, but each has his own "signature," his particular coordination pattern (Slater-Hammel, 1949).

In a well-coordinated movement, each subordinate act occurs at just the right time. Its force is in correct proportion to the force of the other movements. Even putting a period after a sentence calls for many muscles pulling against each other to move the pen straight to the paper. The superior pianist keeps his eyes on the printed music well ahead of his fingers. Seeing what is coming, he can be in position for it. He sees and comprehends a whole phrase at a time, and plays it expressively as a phrase rather than note by note. In continuous action, the muscles used in the later parts of the action are poised and ready to act as soon as the right amount of time has elapsed.

The timing and the regulation of the force of subskills also are controlled by a program. Think of how you pick up a pencil from the desk. The eye locates the pencil, directs the hand into position so that the fingers come down an inch or two from the point. The thumb comes down opposite the first two fingers. You grasp the pencil between thumb and fingers, then between the two fingers, and without thought turn the pencil past the thumb into writing position. You have performed this act thousands of times without being aware of what you did. Even my description is incomplete. Did you notice that your thumb had its own part to play while the two fingers were rotating the pencil? The same executive program handles a slender pencil or a half-inch marking pencil. The fingers close until the pressure (feedback from sense organs in the finger) seems right for lifting the pencil, each pencil requiring a different finger position.

Psychologists do not have a good understanding of how these programs work. An active question in current research is whether the timing of movements is regulated by some sort of "timer in the head," or whether a muscle sensation from one act triggers the next (J. Adams, 1971; Christina, 1971; B. Jones, 1974). The evidence that birds continue to sing when deprived of muscular feedback (box, p. 406) does suggest that muscular cues are needed more during the learning stage than after the response sequence is thoroughly established.

Pacing is controlled in part by external events. From time to time, unexpected cues call forth an adaptive action that lasts for several seconds. The performer plans as he goes. The skater judges where he will turn and then modifies his approach when movements of other skaters cut him off. The cue-response-feedback sequence goes on steadily. The continuous skill is not a truly unbroken flow. The action is a sequence of acts—corrected and redirected perhaps as often as twice per second (Poulton, 1966).

Discrete skills, with short bursts of action, are in some ways easier to teach. The sequence can be demonstrated more readily. After a trial there can be a pause to examine results and criticize the action.

---

**14** List the signals to which an automatic pinsetter in a bowling alley responds, and the sequence of actions it performs. How does this differ from what a human pinsetter would do?

**15** The definition of a skill as programmed behavior says nothing about the correctness of the technique, the speed of the performance, or the quality of the product. Why?

**16** "When an expert typist types the words *died*, *hidden*, *did*, and *board*, the act of striking *d* is different each time." What does this statement mean?

---

## Performance Holds Up Under Difficult Conditions

Performers who earn equal scores are not necessarily equally expert. To decide who is the most skilled, one would have to know who performs the most consistently when conditions fluctuate. Some aircraft pilots who do well under normal conditions lose much of their skill when fatigued or ill. Also, errors increase when complicated acts are performed simultaneously. Smooth response sequences disintegrate; early warnings are overlooked and the person falls back on jerky last-second corrections. The truly best pilots are those who maintain well-coordinated, well-regulated performance under adverse conditions. Among the stresses that upset the person who is only half-expert are fatigue, illness, emotional pressure, and a confusing external situation (F. Bartlett, 1948).

The expert, as I have already remarked, can make use of a wide variety of cues, and his actions are tied into long sequences. This gives him several advantages:

- The expert can perform when discrimination becomes difficult. Some of the usual cues may be missing (for example, when driving in a snowstorm). Distractions or stress cause signals to be missed. The expert can get by with fewer, fainter cues. His responses, "locked in place" as a sequence, do not depend solely on cues at the instant of action; he can continue smoothly past a temporary interference.

- The expert is able to anticipate a hazard. He knows what to expect and takes advantage of cues when they first become available. By making an earlier adjustment (for example, slowing a vehicle before it comes to a slick place), he avoids what would create an emergency for the novice.

*(text continues, p. 412)*

# The Woodchoppers' Ball

A fable by a psychologist, the late Harry M. Johnson of Tulane University:

Once upon a time there lived in the Great North Woods two lumbermen. One was a Swede and one was a Finn, and both of them were experts with the axe. All the Swedes in the Great North Woods thought that the Swede was the greatest axeman in the world. All of the Finns in the Great North Woods thought that the Finn was the greatest axeman in the world. Nobody else in the Great North Woods, if there *was* anyone else in the Great North Woods, really mattered.

Naturally, this division of opinion led to arguments. Frequently, especially on weekends, these arguments led to fights. Since none of these seemed to settle the point, someone, more intelligent than the rest, suggested that a contest be staged. It was further suggested that the contest be followed by a party with a dance and that the entire affair be called the Woodchoppers' Ball.

Elaborate plans for the Woodchoppers' Ball were made. A huge hall with a stage was engaged. A judge was chosen who happened to be half Swede and half Finn and was trusted by everyone. A band was hired to play for the dance. And loads and loads of wood were brought for the use of the contestants.

Meanwhile, all over the Great North Woods, wagers were made on the outcome of the contest. People who had money bet money. People who had principles, or who simply didn't have money, put up all sorts of personal possessions or agreed to do things that were dangerous or ridiculous or difficult or tedious if their protagonist lost. As the time of the Woodchoppers' Ball approached, feeling was running very high.

When the great day came, the Judge got up on the platform and called the meeting to order, "Ladies and Gentlemen," he shouted in a very loud voice. "This here is a contest to decide which of these two men is the better man with an axe. This is not a contest of luck, and it is not a contest of popularity. It is a contest of skill. We are here tonight to decide which of these two men is the most skillful axeman in the world."

"That being the case," he went on, maintaining his remarkable volume, "my assistants and I have spared no effort to keep things fair. These chopping blocks you see before you are standard in size and shape and absolutely identical. On either side of the stage, and carefully guarded, you will see two tremendous piles of wood which have been perfectly matched, stick by individual stick. And the lights for the positions of the two contestants are as nearly identical as we can make them. We will now flip a coin to see who gets the east end of the stage and who gets the west end, and then the contest can get under way."

The coin was flipped, positions were taken, and the contestants were ready to begin. Each contestant was given ten cords of wood, specifications which the men must meet in chopping the wood were carefully explained, and the Judge raised the starting gun. The crowd went quiet, waiting for the signal to begin.

When the Judge fired the starting gun, the Swede and the Finn began to chop and the audience began to yell. The more the men chopped, the more the people shouted, especially since it became increasingly evident that the finish would be very close. In fact, as nearly as anyone in the audience could tell, the two men struck their last blows at exactly the same time, and the crowd hushed tensely, waiting for the Judge's decision. There was considerable delay while the Judge consulted with the people who had planned the party, but finally he bravely stepped forward to the edge of the platform, and announced, "Ladies and Gentlemen: I hereby declare the contest you have just witnessed to have ended in a draw!"

The first reaction to this was a moan of disappointment, but, as the full import of the decision sank in, this swiftly gave way to manifestations of indignation. The

410

murmur of the crowd grew louder, and several angry remarks were shouted. The Judge raised his hands for silence. "We knew you'd feel this way," he said loudly, "so me and the committee has decided to do something about it." His judgemanship, leadership, and diplomacy were much better than his grammar. After all, English was a third language. "We have plenty of wood, and skill ain't all speed. We're going to test the *accuracy* of these two men and decide who the skillful one is that way."

So, the axemen competed in splitting matches and they competed in splitting straws. They competed in hitting pencil marks and they competed in hitting bird shot. In short, they competed in about every test of accuracy the Judge could devise. But anything the Swede could do the Finn could do likewise, and anything the Finn could do, the Swede could do as well. In accuracy, it gradually became clear, the Swede and the Finn were as evenly matched as they were in speed.

Finally, an old man with a long white beard whispered something lengthy in the Judge's ear, and the Judge made the following announcement: "Ladies and Gentlemen," he said, although by this time nobody was either. "Since this ain't gettin nowhere, I'd like to ask your opinion of a suggestion that's just been made. These men are obviously equal in speed and they're just as equal in accuracy. But there's still a side to chopping wood that we haven't tested. The more skill an axeman has, the less effort he'll use to get the job done. These two men are of an age and of a size. We propose that they be given all the wood they want and both chop until one of them drops. If that's agreeable to the contestants and agreeable to the audience we'll test their skill by that." The two heroes glanced at each other grimly and nodded their heads. The crowd shouted its approval.

But they didn't know what they had let themselves in for. At the end of an hour, the men were still chopping, and keeping up the required cords per hour. At the end of two hours, they were chopping yet, and many of the spectators had found entertainment of their own. To make a long story short, some time later, ninety-nine per cent of the crowd was mightily surprised by a loud thud and a louder silence which signified that both contestants had dropped to the floor.

This third tie, showing the Swede and the Finn to be equal in "form" as well as in speed and accuracy, was almost too much. The contest had just about lost an audience. But the old man with the beard stepped up to the Judge once more. This time he didn't consult so long, but he gestured quite a bit. When the judge stepped forward this time he had a proposal that, as it turned out, let the gamblers settle their bets and the dancing begin. "We've compared these men in speed, we've compared them in accuracy, and we've compared them in what you might call smoothness. But in all this, they've worked on standard chopping blocks and they've used their own axes. Now, let's see how adaptable they are. They will now be asked to chop wood of various heights. They'll chop under various conditions and they'll chop with various axes."

At this suggestion, the Finn grew pale and gripped his axe. However, he gamely entered this strange new kind of battle. But the truth was quickly out. The Swede could chop any wood under any conditions that the Judge saw fit to impose. Moreover, he chopped on any block and he chopped with any axe. Without his own axe and block, the Finlander was an ordinary man. In terms of adaptability, the Swede was easily superior, and nobody argued, although half of them were sad, when the Judge declared the Swede the Most Skillful Woodchopper in the World.

And so the story is ended. But one word remains to be said. The writer hastens to take this opportunity to assure the fair-minded reader that the outcome of this contest is unrelated to the writer's nationality.

Reprinted with permission of author and publisher from *Perceptual and Motor Skills* (1961).

- The expert has deeper knowledge. Failure to achieve a result forces the performer to "shift down," giving attention to mediating responses. When the expert does pause to analyze, he recalls correct mediating responses. The less expert performer may be uncertain which mediating response is correct.

- Whereas stress upsets the nonexpert performer, it often brings the expert to his peak. The higher tension of a public performance elicits more nearly perfect responses from the experienced performer than does a rehearsal, just because he comes nearer to giving 100 per cent of his energy and attention.

Paradoxically, the expert is more upset by delayed feedback than is the average performer. In singing, for example, delaying the sounds (through earphones) so that the singer hears them late, causes well-trained singers to break down and often to refuse to sing. Their performance is highly regulated; they use immediate information to hold their tones under tight control. The inexpert singer is satisfied merely to approximate correct tone; he can ignore the confusing feedback and still meet *his* standards. The expert, with higher standards, is bothered by the irregularity (K. U. Smith, 1966, p. 441).

Learning is never complete or perfect. Even if the person achieves a perfect score in, say, the basketball free throw, he very likely has not perfected his skill as highly as some better player. The difference will show when both perform under emotional pressure, or when fatigue builds up at the end of a tournament. A person who scores 100 per cent by one standard usually has much room for improvement by some other standard. When a skill is "closed" (as the free throw is), so that the requirement of the task is identical from one setting to another, the task can in a sense be "mastered." In more typical skills, there is no known limit to improvement.

**17** Teachers are often urged to bring students to "mastery." Can a performance standard that represents mastery of driving a car be defined? Or is improvement so much "a matter of degree" that it is arbitrary to divide persons into masters and nonmasters?

**18** Is it strictly true that the free-throw task is identical in all settings? If two high-school players pass a "mastery test"—say, ten of ten test shots correct in the home gym—might they nevertheless differ in expertness?

**19** Good performance under stress is a sign of expertness. How might one use this idea
  a. to measure the proficiency of truck drivers at the end of an army training course?
  b. to measure proficiency in speaking a foreign language?

# ANALYZING TASKS AND MODIFYING THEM FOR INSTRUCTION

Teaching requires considerably more than turning the learner loose to practice. Particularly in teaching of a skill, where the criterion of excellence is well defined, task analysis paves the way for organizing lessons. Here I can dicuss task analysis only in a general way, with concrete examples related to familiar skills. An actual analysis may collect detailed and objective information on how the task is performed, perhaps by a time-and-motion study or a recording device like Lindahl's (p. 403; see also p. 474). Also, the analysis may probe deeply into the foundation of knowledge underlying a particular skill. Thus, analysis of a language skill is improved when the teacher knows psycholinguistics, and it is useful for the French teacher to know just what movements in the throat produce a French *r* sound. In training swimmers for competition, the coach needs to know a good bit about respiration before he can judge how often the swimmer should take in air, and how deeply. The track coach may even turn to engineering studies of the forces in the vaulting pole to help his jumpers reach their peak.

The psychological questions whose answers can guide the selection of tasks are these:

- How is a good performer defined? (What magnitude of error is to be considered acceptable at the end of training? What frequency of error? What rate of performance?)

- What cues does the situation offer that are capable of regulating the performance? Which of these do expert performers use? What problems arise in discriminating and interpreting external cues—among beginners and among experienced performers? What internal cues do experts use? What problems arise in discriminating them?

- What is the hierarchy of subskills to be acquired? (Compare Fig. 2.4, p. 62).

- What are the segments or subroutines into which the experienced performer subdivides the task? What part-actions can be carried out independently without distorting them? In mature performance, how closely are parts linked?

- With respect to any one recurrent movement, what force, direction, and speed produce a good result?

To add some flesh to the questions, consider a fraction of the answer Mr. Wells (p. 100) might have given if applying them to typewriting.

To state a standard is, in a sense, to set a behavioral objective. Mr. Wells might define good performance as the ability, at the end of three months, to type steadily from simple meaningful copy, making no more than five errors per hundred words on the average and without jamming of keys. Speed might be left open, on the assumption that the smooth, steady typist will pick up speed later in the year. What standard is set partly determines how training will proceed: emphasis on steadiness leads to one kind of practice; emphasis on speed, to another.

With regard to cues, Mr. Wells would note the importance of the distance and direction from the "home keys" as cues to guide the reach for, say, the letter *p*. Implication: Beginners ought to start all movements from the home position. Second, Mr. Wells would note that the letter on each key is a potential cue the touch typist does not use. Implication: Students should learn to rely on touch cues and not sight. Mr. Wells, you will recall, allowed students to work for a few days in a hunt-and-peck fashion; this had a motivational value and perhaps gave them a start toward a template for their later blind movements (see p. 420).

With regard to segmenting the typing task, the obvious candidates are letters, words, phrases, sentences, paragraphs, and so on. But in fact the expert typist works with a string of words that do not necessarily correspond to a thought unit or phrase. If, while the typist is moving along at speed, you snatch his copy away from him, he will type three or more words before he runs out of mediating orders. Photographic analysis shows the typist's eyes running well ahead of his fingers. He holds the orders in a temporary memory (p. 449).

The skilled typist, then, scans continuous copy and encodes a stretch of it into short-term memory; his directing program identifies a "bundle of strokes" that forms a well-learned motor unit and issues an "Execute!" command to the muscles. Implication: The student cannot become a mature typist if he practices only single words, one at a time. He should practice the larger task of continuous processing. That does not necessarily mean he should practice only from pages of copy once he has the basic strokes. Flashing a phrase of copy on a screen for a fraction of a second is a valuable supplement (Winger, 1951; H. Palmer, 1955). This prevents a read-a-letter-type-the-letter-read-another-letter sequence of response. By forcing the student to grasp a whole phrase at once, this exercise encourages longer sequences of encoding and decoding.

These examples, along with the ones in Chapter 3, indicate the nature of task analysis, even though the story is incomplete. When a truly peak performance is desired, the analyst may not be content to find out what experts do; he may try to devise a more efficient program. Credit for sports performances that break world records goes in part to the coaches who devise new ways of organizing the action. Something like this was done for typing by the late August Dvorak (Dvorak et al., 1936). Dvorak, a psychologist, found that the keyboard layout impedes fast, smooth action and leads to unnecessary fatigue. The important letter *a* is assigned to the weakest of all the fingers. Some fingers are given far more to do than others. Some common words—*from*, for example—require awkward sequences of motion. Dvorak and his coworkers laid out a new keyboard (Fig. 10.5) in which the strokes for frequent combinations such as *er* and *fr* alternated from left hand to right hand,

## FIGURE 10.5

Dvorak keyboard arrangement

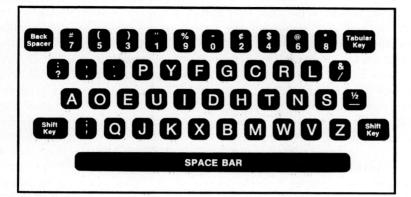

SOURCE: Dvorak et al. (1936), p. 145.

so that one hand could be moving into position while the other is striking. Typists can learn faster and reach a higher level if they use the Dvorak keyboard, but the market did not accept Dvorak's invention.

Practice exercises may or may not start with the full, natural, on-the-job task. Most likely, the teacher will simplify it. Desirable modifications for classroom tryout will be suggested by the teacher's task analysis. Some modifications are as obvious as breaking the response sequence into segments to be practiced separately. One can enlarge equipment so as to make discrimination easier (such as a slide rule that is several feet rather than ten inches long). Also useful is equipment that permits focusing on part of the task (such as a dummy piano keyboard for practicing fingering). And one can isolate the skill from its usual context (as in use of the batting-practice "cannon" that fires balls over a home plate in a bare gymnasium). Any one of these tricks, and many others, may have a place in developing a particular skill. Hence the final question in organizing the curriculum has to do with arranging the right sequence and progression of exercises or practice situations.

**20** Apply the task-analysis questions to one of the following:
    a. Using a carpenter's plane to smooth a board
    b. Making a pie crust

**21** Riding a bicycle is ordinarily learned by practicing the whole act on the usual equipment. Even so, the task is altered somewhat for the usual learner (trainer wheels, practicing away from traffic). Suggest other ways in which the task is or might be subdivided for practice, or artificially modified.

## Reducing the Complex Situation

Whether early practice should be on the complete, final skill or on somewhat artificial segments of the task is a decision teachers have to make over and over. If the task is to be segmented, the question remains of just how finely it is profitable to subdivide.

The teacher, for example, may wish to develop skill in using the library, which—like typing or bicycling—is an assembly of many skills, not all of which are tightly linked. The teacher has a choice. The practice may take place in connection with larger projects, such as a class discussion on the United Nations, or through formal exercises in library skills. Each approach has advantages; the choice depends on the complexity of the skill, the extent to which the context determines the correct response, the value of the projects in their own right, and the maturity of the learner.

Using a response in a significant context is often advantageous. A player learning to catch flies during an actual ballgame must take into account new wind and sun conditions in each game. Fifty flies in two dozen games are more varied than 50 flies hit to him in the same practice session.

But practice incidental to a larger activity may be too scattered and too little thought about, and the conditions too varied, for successful learning. If the student "practices" only once the use of the dictionary key to pronunciation, he probably will not remember what to do when, weeks later, pronunciation is pertinent to another report. Using the library, he may be rewarded in the end by completing his report to the class on time. But unless he or the librarian pauses to evaluate the library work, he may not realize how he wasted time or what resources he neglected. Without this reflection on the performance, the practice leads to less improvement than it might.

Practice on a motor performance can be organized so that the person tries from the start to carry out a complicated action as a whole, difficult though that may be. Or the learner can start with parts or elements. The evidence strongly supports moving to larger units or "wholes" as rapidly as possible (Naylor, 1962; G. Briggs & Naylor, 1962).

In writing a word, the person will frequently shape a letter differently or alter his timing, depending on what letter comes next. Only practice on the complete word gives practice in the connecting stroke between letters as an integral part of writing both letters together. The letter is not a true segment in handwriting; the word is. (The timing and pattern one employs in writing *the* is not affected by the word that precedes or follows it.) Any sequence of interpretation and trial that retains its "shape" when preceded and followed by a pause is a true segment and makes a good unit for practice.

Wholes or even natural segments can be too complex for efficient practice (Naylor & Briggs, 1963). Or, to put it differently, what constitutes a unit for the experienced person may be so difficult for the novice that he inevitably breaks up the action.

Wholes are put within reach of the beginner by what Oxendine (1968) calls *progression levels.* Gymnastic routines, a dancing pattern, diving (box) and

## Progress by easy stages

Oxendine (1968, pp. 90 and 91) describes how a difficult task can be approached by stages. The learner finds satisfaction in accomplishing the stage even though he is a long way from his end-goal of performing the complete skill. To quote Oxendine:

> An example of the use of progression levels can be illustrated in the teaching of springboard diving. The child who has no experience and perhaps some fear of plunging into the water cannot be easily coaxed into taking a running approach dive off the board. Rather, he may start by sitting on the side of the pool with his feet in the water. From this position he is asked to put his arms and hands in front of his body, tilt his head forward and downward, and lean forward until he falls into the water. This act is rewarded verbally and practiced a number of times until the child feels comfortable entering the water that way. In the second progression step, the child kneels at the pool's edge and falls forward into the water. Again, this act is reinforced and practiced until the learner feels confident in this technique. Next, the child stoops, or crouches, and later stands at the side of the pool to make his entry. At this point he should not be afraid to enter the water from a standing position at the side of the pool.
>
> He must now be taught to dive rather than merely fall into the water. Beginning work in diving can also be done from the side of the pool. The child is taught to dive, i.e., bend his knees and push off during his headfirst fall into the water. Later he is taught to increase the dive or push-off, while practically eliminating the forward fall of his body. After the child has learned to dive properly from the side of the pool, he is asked to walk onto the low diving board. While standing at the end, the child gets the feel of the board by bouncing slightly. He is then encouraged to dive off the end of the board in the same way he dived from the side of the pool. Much verbal reinforcement is needed to make the child feel comfortable and exhibit good form in the springboard dive. After some success has been accomplished in the standing springboard dive, attention can then be devoted to the approach. The student can be taught the four step approach on the deck rather than on the springboard. After the steps, hurdle, and two-foot take-off have been practiced until the student has them well learned, he can be taken back to the board to combine the approach and the forward dive. Then practice can continue for refinement of form on the standard forward dive and, later, for the different types of dives.

SOURCE: Joseph B. Oxendine, *Psychology of Motor Learning*, © 1968, pp. 90 and 91. Reprinted by permission of Prentice-Hall, Inc., Englewood Cliffs, New Jersey.

other performances are so tricky that the learner who sets out to perform the whole task is sure to fail many, many times before he acquires the knack. Motivation can be maintained by defining a series of tasks, not segments but limited wholes. Each is a step on the way to the final goal. In mastering these successive approximations the learner gains satisfaction and acquires patterns that, reshaped at each step, fit into the final whole.

---

**22** What is the advantage, if any, of formal exercises (as distinct from practice in the course of a project) for teaching the following?
   a. Proper capitalization of titles
   b. Outlining of a composition or talk
   c. Focusing of a microscope

**23** Can the tennis serve be taught by a "progression levels" technique? What would the coach using this technique do that he would not do if teaching the act "as a whole"? How would progression levels differ from a hierarchical plan (p. 62)?

**24** Would it be reasonable to divide the running of low hurdles for practice by having the runner master one hurdle as a "part"?

---

## Realism

The first rule in training for a skill is: Make available the cues that are later to be used in applying the skill. This may seem obvious, but all too often lessons have omitted crucial cues. For example, an inadequately skilled second-language teacher speaks to the class without grouping her words into phrases as a native speaker would. The student driver applying the brakes in a stationary car gets none of the feel that regulates braking on the highway.

Appropriate realism is illustrated in the design of simulators. Psychologists and engineers have developed expensive apparatus to train airplane pilots. The expense is justified by the alternative: to risk real airplanes, pilots, and instructors in training exercises. A simulator can reproduce all the cues, visual and muscular, that an aircraft pilot making a real instrument landing would experience. He can make an error and become familiar with the early-warning cues that follow—at no risk whatsoever.

The cues that direct significant action should be realistically reproduced; irrelevant aspects of the situation need not be. Thus the radar screen of a simulator for air-traffic control should carry, along with the spot for each airplane, the specks of interference that appear during normal operations; otherwise, the operator will not learn to locate a faint target through interference. The brightness-control knobs should resemble operational equipment in shape and location, since the operator will form the habit of feeling for a certain knob without

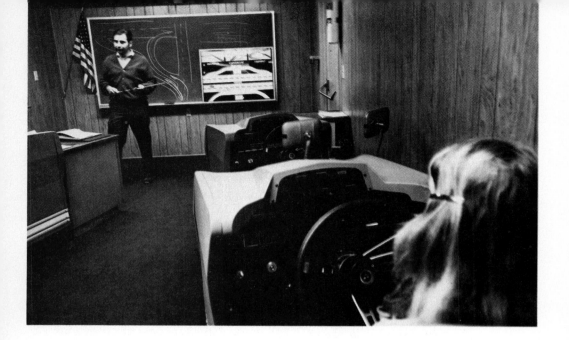

looking. There is no virtue in realism for realism's sake, however. One can learn to keep his bearings as well from a rowboat as from the bridge of an ocean liner (see also p. 510).

What should be simulated if classroom training were to replace a part of the road training of drivers? What would be the merit of showing a motion picture of a road, as seen through the windshield, and giving the student a steering wheel and brakes so that he could respond? This device might be of some use in teaching the quick response (for example, when a child suddenly appears beside the road). It is of no use in teaching motor skills, however, because the essential visual and motion cues are lacking.

If a task is changed in some fundamental way when it is made easier, practice loses much of its value. It "simplifies" the handwriting task to have a beginner trace well-formed letters through a tissue overlay, but he is no longer calling to mind an image of the correct shape and no longer directing his muscles to produce it. He is responding to cues that are absent in free writing (p. 115). Manuscript writing, on the other hand, *is* a reasonable simplification to prepare for cursive writing. The perceptual cues, the template for a good response, and the motions used in writing

$$\text{bed}$$

all resemble those present in the more elaborately organized skill:

$$\textit{bed}$$

"Simplification" can make the task more difficult. Some teachers, believing that mature typists do not use visual cues, require students to type strictly by touch from early periods. West (1966) concludes that this only increases the rate of error.

Usually, the best sequence for training is to begin with easy discriminations that help the learner to identify major cues, and then to move gradually toward more subtle discriminations (Schmidt, 1975a, p. 65). In a paced task, for example, it may be desirable to perform for a time at a low speed to consolidate the interpretation, before practicing at speeds where information comes too fast for full attention (D. H. Lawrence & W. Goodwin, 1954).

**25** For students learning to fill out and to interpret bank checks, which of the following is important to reproduce in the teaching situation?
   a. The space provided for the amount in both numerical and verbal form
   b. The phrase "Pay to the order of"
   c. The number identifying the bank (in magnetic ink, for processing the check by machine)

**26** It has been shown that in learning to type, the student should practice striking the key with a quick movement even though a slower, more controlled movement would permit hitting the key more squarely. What cues does the student use in each kind of practice?

## Variety

Should practice materials and conditions be uniform so that the person will learn an instantaneous, fixed response? Or should the materials be varied so that one is constantly judging and adapting? Most drill procedures are designed to promote automatic response to uniform or highly regular stimuli.

Psychologists have sometimes suggested that even in the teaching of open skills, the learner should face precisely the same situation until his responses become mechanical. It has been suggested, for example, that all arithmetic problems requiring a given operation (say, subtracting cost price from selling price) be worded in the same way. This tactic, however, teaches only a limited skill.

It is much better for the student to practice reflectively in the greatest variety of situations he can cope with (Schmidt, 1975b). Variation requires him to isolate the essential elements and respond to them. Even from the beginning, for example, the student learning French should hear the taped sentences of several speakers so that he comes to disregard the irrelevant aspects of personal intonation and rhythm. Thus he learns to pluck the same pattern out of different aural surrounds. No one recommends helter-skelter variation that leaves the learner continually off balance. He should attain a reasonable degree of success before the next complication is piled on. Often it is beneficial to alter one element of the situation at a time.

## Aids to Interpretation

The teacher sets out the practice situation with an eye to the nature of the task and the learner's characteristics. The learner interprets the situation, perhaps consciously comparing alternative actions or perhaps sensing roughly what he is to do and making a stab at it. If the teacher can prove his interpretation, this raises the probability that his try will produce satisfactory results. Hence, as Posner and Keele advise (p. 405), it is generally valuable to supplement training by providing a model. Sometimes verbal advice is enough to set the performer on the right track.

Demonstration or verbal explanation tells the learner which of the responses already under his control he should employ and what cues he should react to. One college archery class was told how to stand, how to hold the bow, and how to release the arrow; these aspects of the performance were inspected by the teacher. This instruction was valuable. After 18 periods, the group given this guidance was hitting on 65 per cent of its shots, compared to 45 per cent in a group that relied on unaided trial and error (Davies, 1945). The demonstration group paid more attention to correct form. According to the investigator, the group given no demonstration "concentrated mostly on aim throughout the entire experiment. They thought about form only when they were not being as successful as they thought they should be, and their concentration upon aim had not helped them. The students did not seem to realize the necessity for perfecting the parts of the technique in order to raise their scores." Manahan (1972) tried to make discovery more effective by directing attention to form, asking the student to plan and evaluate his own technique. Even so, students given a demonstration did much better, because the members of the discovery group settled on clumsy techniques. Motion pictures, which can enlarge and slow action, are a superior way to demonstrate certain skills (Vander Meer, 1945; T. Anderson, 1942).

Welford (1972, p. 305) notes the danger that the learner will hit upon a bad technique, and goes on to recommend what is sometimes called "error-free" practice.

> The art of training seems to be to let the trainee make his decisions about what to do, but to design the training procedure in such a way as to ensure that these decisions are always correct, especially in the early stages. An elegant example of how effective this can be is a laboratory experiment by von Wright (1957), who required subjects to learn a kind of maze by following along a track with a stylus.

He found that learning was appreciably faster if, for the first four trials, the wrong turnings were omitted. This enabled subjects to follow along the path without any possibility of taking a wrong turn. Their performance was, however, essentially passive in that they never had to make choices between one direction and another. For a further group, therefore, the wrong turnings were left in, but clearly marked at their entrances so that, although subjects had to decide which way to go, they could always do so correctly. This group learnt much faster than either of the others.

Both guidance procedures formed "templates," but marking the choice points called more of the relevant stimuli to attention.

A demonstration is effective to the extent that the learner really sees what is going on. This requires not only that he pay attention, but that he analyze the action and somehow construct within his own mind a scenario he can act out when it is his turn. This was dramatized by an experiment with a complex jigsaw puzzle. Fifth-graders were shown, individually, how to assemble it, and then each one practiced until he could assembly it without error. Table 10.2

**TABLE 10.2**

**Effect of alternative demonstration procedures on performance**

| Group | What child did as he watched | Verbal explanation by demonstrator | Time required to do easy puzzle | Time required to do hard puzzle |
|---|---|---|---|---|
| 1 | Counted to 100 by 2's | None | 5.7 | 25* |
| 2 | Said what demonstrator was doing | None | 3.1 | 22 |
| 3 | Kept silent | Incomplete description | 3.5 | 16 |
| 4 | Kept silent | Full description | 3.2 | 14 |
| 5 | Said what demonstrator was doing | None except to correct child's errors | 2.2 | 12 |

SOURCE: Study by Louise Thompson, summarized by May (1946).
*Only 3 pupils out of 25 could finish the puzzle under these conditions.

outlines the experiment. Some children merely looked on silently. Others were asked to describe aloud what the demonstrator was doing, which demanded their close attention. Some children were asked to count aloud during the demonstration, and thus were prevented from describing the actions of the demonstrator to themselves. The demonstrator helped some learners by telling them what she was doing or by correcting the child's misstatement. Those making up Group 5, who expressed what they saw in words and were corrected, learned fastest. They observed most closely and saw best what was happening.

It is often beneficial to point out the critical features of a performance, so that the learner will see the significant things that the demonstrator is doing (Bandura et al., 1966; F. Sheffield & N. Maccoby, 1961). It is all too easy to keep one's eyes on the swing of the bat, and ignore the pivoting of the batter's foot. Young children, particularly dependent ones, are likely to be as faithful in reproducing the details that do not matter as they are in capturing the essentials (Ross, 1966). Give a verbal description prior to the demonstration, to organize the learner's perception, and he will depart in sensible ways from the model, adapting the pattern as circumstances change (Poliakova, 1958).

Selecting cues for attention calls for skill in observing. The learner cannot and should not "see everything." As L. Locke (1972, p. 380) says:

> The most common problem encountered by the learner is not stuffing his control system with information for mindless processing, but deciding [consciously] what to notice, what the various signals mean, and what to do about them.

Skill in observing a demonstration is itself acquired; the person *learns* to profit more from models. Cox (1933) provided evidence of the value of explanation and of specially designed exercises for teaching vocational skills. The task of assembling an electric lamp was broken into subtasks. Each group of subjects practiced one of the subskills and improved in it; but they did not improve on subtasks not practiced. For example, practice on wiring did not improve skill in fitting wooden wedges into place at the top of the lamp. In a second experiment, subjects went through:

Exercises on arrangement of parts on workbench, manner of holding parts, and so on

"Eye observation exercises" on what to observe; noticing spatial relationships

"Finger observation exercises" to notice muscular sensations accompanying actions

Exercises in control of attention and effort

Practice in applying the various exercises to the task

The observation exercises promoted the conscious analysis of cues. In the experiment, all these exercises were applied to just the subskills of container assembly; no other subskill was practiced. Yet at the end of this training *all* of the subskills had improved substantially. General techniques of efficient work had been acquired.

Learning among a group of Congolese tribesmen demonstrates the same principles even more strikingly. It was hoped that these men could master industrial tasks such as mechanical assembling. Three teaching methods were tried: demonstration, demonstration plus verbal instructions, and a third, unusual method. In the third method the verbal instructions were given to the men, who had to memorize them; when they had the instructions fully in mind, each one dictated the steps to the instructor, and *he* carried out the mechanical operations. This method, ensuring that the trainee had fixed the guiding information in mind, enabled him to perform the task well on his first trial with the equipment. The conventional forms of demonstration did little to reduce first-trial errors. The same result was found with Belgian boys. The investigator (Ghilain, 1960) goes on to say:

> The best results continued to be obtained with memorization even with the best [ablest] subjects, and this occurred despite the discredit that the teaching profession has heaped on memorization. It is however necessary to take the precaution of providing a text to be memorized which is somewhat under the maximum memorizing capacity of the subject. Then, too, the psychologist should take the precaution to very carefully prepare the text to be memorized.

Although demonstration has a clear value, there is also a case for learning by discovery. In trial-and-error learning, the learner does come to sense the correct pattern through his own eyes and muscles. Despite the Posner-Keele suggestion that the learner's limbs be mechanically guided (p. 406), an instructor can tell a person little or nothing that will bring an untrained set of muscles under control. Nor does the performer know precisely what adjustments he makes when he does attain a desired result. How do *you* make the sounds for *t* and *d*? Although you have spoken English for many years, you probably are unaware that a vibration in the vocal cords is required at the start of the sound of *d*, and that otherwise the actions are the same. A teacher can do little to help the individual student discover the basic movement patterns of the hands, the tongue, and the other motor organs. At best, the teacher can give some slight direction to the process of discovery, and, of course, can show how to monitor responses.

---

**27** In Table 10.2, why did Group 5 do better than Group 2 on the easy puzzle?

**28** Why did Group 2 fall behind Group 4 on the hard puzzle?

**29** Would demonstration or unguided practice be more helpful in learning to whip cream? What cues must be differentiated for skilled performance?

---

# MAKING PRACTICE EFFECTIVE

The term *practice* refers to any repeated attempts to perform a task. Practice may be systematic, or incidental to other school activities. It may be routine and repetitious, or every trial may be an adventure. But in either case, practice is a series of ever-changing provisional tries. Spaeth (1972, p. 352) speaks of "repetition without repetition," adding that practice "does not consist of repeating a single solution to a motor problem, but rather consists of repeating the process of solving the problem by techniques which are changed and perfected" from trial to trial.

## The Function of Active Practice

The beginner can learn to read the signals produced in his own body only through carrying out movements, feeling them, and recognizing which ones signal blunders. So also with external cues. The learner is told how his car must be positioned so he can back into a parking space parallel to the curb. But until he has tried to park many times, he judges his position wrongly and fails in the maneuver. The judgments that a craftsman makes of the stages of the product, the coordinations in fine assembly work, and the rhythmic movements of the dancer are polished through practice and only through practice.

As one gains experience in a situation one's response tends to stabilize. True, but practice is no guarantee of desirable learning. The response acquired may be awkward, inefficient, even totally unsuccessful. What actions are learned and at what level of mastery depends on the situation, the explanation given the learner, the method of monitoring or evaluation, and other factors.

Practice periods have to be properly located in relation to explanations. The person who practices before he knows the correct general pattern of the task is likely to practice wrong actions. If given extensive explanation before he knows the task firsthand, he will understand little of it. An interplay among explanation, practice, and further explanation is called for.

A small amount of overt practice suffices if the explanation can be very clear and the cues obvious. More is needed when a response is hard to explain or demonstrate. A skill that requires delicate discrimination or exact timing needs much practice.

For closed skills the external cues are pretty much fixed. For example, the musician who wants to play a piano sonata is probably wise to devote considerable time to studying the written music before he begins physical practice. Activity, bringing in response-produced muscular cues, complicates matters at a time when the player needs to give his full attention to getting the music in mind and to thinking out the fingering for hard passages.

An interpretation, once firmly grasped, directs a patterned motor performance. Coordination of movements then is polished by physical practice.

MENTAL PRACTICE   "Mental practice" can substitute for physical practice, refining the person's internal image beyond the point to which demonstrations carry it. For example, the basketball player can *imagine* that he is shooting baskets from the foul line. Mental practice strengthens the internal image of the action sequence and its timing. Tasks where stimulus materials have to be interpreted—for example, sorting mail into bins according to destination—are particularly suited to mental practice. When the motor element is much less important than the symbolic associations (as, for example, in solving mazes), overt motor practice may be a comparatively poor way to learn (p. 465; but see box, p. 114). In kinesthetic-motor tasks, it is advisable to intermix mental and physical practice (Richardson, 1967; Oxendine, 1968).

## Monitoring

Important as feedback is, the advice to "give plenty of feedback" misses the point. It is the *perceived* consequence of a trial that determines whether an interpretation is retained or altered (Bilodeau & Bilodeau, 1961). The learner will rely chiefly on the "natural" feedback provided by the situation, since that is normally present on every trial. This feedback will be augmented by information from the teacher: "Not enough backswing" or "This shaft you milled is out of tolerance."

The learner tends to judge his success by his product: how many words he types correctly, how far he drives the golf ball, how long it takes him to adjust his microscope. When he thinks he is gaining he rarely worries about form. The teacher should remind him to judge progress in terms of technique. Lindahl's tracings of disk-cutting performance (Figs. 10.2 and 10.6 and pp. 403 and 430) had teaching value because they signaled errors in technique. The workers became interested in making a good tracing instead of trying to see how fast they could cut. As their patterns became better, they broke fewer cutting wheels, spoiled fewer disks, and attained a higher rate of output (Lindahl, 1945). Recording exactly what the learner did is more important in a closed skill than in an open skill (Del Rey, 1972).

Rules of scoring define the task for the learner, telling him what "good performance" means. Lindahl changed the scoring rule, as it were, from disks per hour to length of stroke beyond rod being cut, evenness of strokes, and so on.

Too often, scoring systems focus all attention on the outcome rather than on the technique and style of performance; hence scores need to be balanced by providing some form of process-oriented feedback. If, in a sport like bowling, one were to provide the player with information on his speed of delivery,

his attention would go into adjusting his speed. If the report were to focus on his control instead, he would concentrate on improving control. Most significantly, when one of two aspects is stressed in evaluating performance, the aspect not evaluated is likely to decline (Malina, 1969). The teacher should see that all the dimensions of the performance are given suitable emphasis in his critique—not all at once, but in balance!

Learners are likely to judge themselves unrealistically. Martha, learning to type, fixed an incorrect technique because she was not corrected at the right time. She moved her right hand about while she typed, striking with any convenient finger. An expert could have told Martha at the outset that this was inefficient, but Martha, pleased because her errors were decreasing, established a faulty habit. Students practice faulty procedures because they do not comprehend what is suggested, do not realize its importance, or are unable to recognize that they are not following the procedure.

If the learner knows the marks of good form, he can judge himself to some extent. DeBacy (1970), for example, showed that college women were likely to overrate the quality of their golf swings when comparing their performance to models seen on videotape. When they also saw themselves on the videotape, their self-ratings became more realistic. "Seeing oneself" is no sure cure. Even after watching a videotape of his performance, the student bowler overrates himself on such points of technique as "The first step of your approach should be shortest of all" (Robb & Teeple, 1969). The same problem arises in speech (box, p. 491). Just as one must learn to attend fully to a demonstration, one must learn to perceive what one does.

Knowledge of results comes promptly in using a saw or separating an egg-yolk. But consider the student potter. He applies a glaze and does not find out until the kiln is cool the next day that the glaze baked badly, apparently because he made the coating too thick. Delayed feedback does work, assuming that the potter recalls what he did. But for such recall an action probably has to be one describable in words. The performer cannot store up muscular feelings on a certain trial for later recall. Delayed reports may serve adequately for discrete skills. It may even make sense to provide knowledge of results after a block of trials rather than on each trial. The archer who corrects his aim after each shot may be more erratic than one who gets off half a dozen shots and then inspects the pattern at the target. But unless the teacher especially wants the potter to "see for himself," the teacher had better tell him to wipe off that thick coat of glaze and try again. That way, learning can move ahead faster. In most laboratory studies that force a performer to rely wholly on reports from others, learning does not suffer when the report of scores is delayed. I recommend that the teacher's critiques and report of scores be prompt, unless there is a positive reason for delay—even though in some research delay has not been found harmful (J. Adams, 1971; Schmidt; 1975a, pp. 91–93; see also p. 619).

Monitoring can be overdone. Detailed coaching can, as Locke (p. 423) said, overload the learner. Moreover, pointing out his every departure from ideal form leads him to think, "I can't ever do anything well enough to please this instructor." Attention should be called to consistent and significant faults at a stage when the learner is likely to be able to remedy them.

---

**30** Would it be desirable to have learners take turns monitoring each other?

**31** In frying an egg, what consequences besides the way the egg tastes confirm (or disconfirm) the provisional try?

**32** Under what conditions is videotape recording likely to be useful in the classroom teaching of skills? (Disregard questions of cost.)

---

# Recommendations for the teaching of skills

No general prescription for the teaching of skills can be given. There are open and closed skills, discrete and continuous skills, skills that are largely new and skills that merely recombine acts within the learner's command. With the warning, then, that they do not apply everywhere, let me bring together the chief recommendations for the teacher that were introduced in the preceding pages:

- Confront the learner with the cues that he will respond to in using the skill. Additional cues to aid discrimination in early practice can be beneficial; false cues cannot.

- Simplify the task at the start of practice. The simplification should not violate the pattern of the task as a whole.

- Provide occasion for adapting responses to different purposes and different contexts.

- Analyze the task to determine the best pattern of response. Demonstrate it or give a clear verbal prescription. Direct attention to important cues. The timing of explanations and demonstrations has to be worked out for each task; explanation usually has the greatest value early in training.

- Monitor to make certain that the basic form of response is correctly practiced.

- Teach the student to judge his own performance, especially its form.

## The Practice Schedule

How should practice be scheduled? One hour per day? Ten minutes per week? Unfortunately, the research that has been done on this topic has little bearing on educational schedules. Comparisons of "massed" versus "distributed" practice have often been made, but in very short training programs. Only an occasional study has educational relevance.

College women had nine practice sessions in which to learn billiards. Three groups had nine uniformly spaced practice sessions with intervals of 1, 2, or 7 days. The best results—initially and on a one-year followup—were obtained by those in a fourth group that had increasing intervals—for example, sessions on January 1, 2, 3, 5, 8, 13, and 21 and February 3 and 24 (J. Harmon & A. Miller, 1950; Oxendine, 1968).

With a longer interval, weaknesses or confusions are more likely to reveal themselves. A technique or interpretation that is shaky is more likely to be identified after a forgetting period.

Long practice sessions lead to fatigue and boredom. Consider a boy who is trying to purse his lips properly for blowing a horn. For ten minutes he obtains good tones. Then his lips tire and he makes errors. This reduces his confidence and interest. If he tries to force the horn into tone by pressing his lips harder, he may get the right effect in the wrong way.

Short, widely spaced practices are generally recommended, subject to the following cautions:

- Within a school year, extending the intervals between practices reduces the total amount of practice.

- Intervals can become so long that forgetting is excessive. Practice sessions are probably too far apart if the average student is unable to regain his normal level fairly early in each session.

- A practice period is too short if it does not extend well beyond the warmup period. The time needed to loosen muscles, recapture interpretations, re-establish timing, and so on varies with the skill.

- If the skill is a continuous one, the practice period should be long enough to allow practice on the whole sequence. In general, longer periods and shorter intervals between practices are advisable for beginners.

# MEASURES OF PERFORMANCE DURING TRAINING AND LATER

## Training Records

A learning curve is a plot of scores made on successive occasions. The learning curve, properly interpreted, can give the learner a sense of progress. Curves help the teacher detect who is in a rut or losing ground. The cumulative records of the behaviorists (p. 21) perform the same functions. In the behaviorist's use of the technique, however, the aim is often to increase the frequency of a response the person already possesses rather than to improve a response.

How might the improvement in disk-cutting recorded in Fig. 10.3 (p. 403) be summarized in a score? The number of acceptable disks cut per hour would not describe change in the performance itself. Looking at the movement tracings, we can see improvement in speed (strokes per minute), smoothness (number of visible jerks per stroke), and overthrow (length of stroke beyond rod being cut). Speed should rise with practice; jerkiness and overthrow should decline. A count of the number of complete strokes per line gives the following results:

**FIGURE 10.6**

**Learning curves for three aspects of disk cutting**

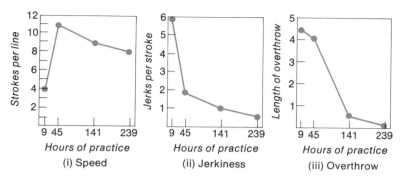

*Curves are based on the performance records shown in Fig. 10.3.*

SOURCE: Lindahl (1945).

| Hours of practice | 9 | 45 | 141 | 239 |
|---|---|---|---|---|
| Strokes | 4 | 11 | 9 | 8 |

These numbers, plotted, form Panel i of Fig. 10.6. Evidently this man acquired speed early in training. In fact, to improve in disk-cutting he had to reduce his speed. Now consider smoothness and overthrow:

| Hours of practice | 9 | 45 | 141 | 239 |
|---|---|---|---|---|
| Smoothness (jerks per stroke) | 6 | 1.8 | 0.9 | 0.6 |
| Length of overthrow (arbitrary units) | 4.5 | 4.1 | 0.7 | 0.1 |

Smoothness (Panel ii) shows rapid early improvement. There was little improvement after 100 hours because jerks had nearly disappeared, save for the one at the top of the return stroke. This subskill could be mastered later; perhaps at 1,000 hours all jerks would be gone. The overthrow curve dropped markedly between 50 and 150 hours. After that, progress was slower.

The following principles are supported by many additional studies:

Parts of a skill develop at different rates or at different points in training. (Speed and smoothness developed early; overthrow took longer to bring under control.)

While one part of a skill is showing little improvement, the person may be mastering another important element.

The speed of performance may increase while the form remains poor or deteriorates. (The speed was too high at 45 hours; better control of overthrow was achieved at the expense of speed.)

## FIGURE 10.7

### Learning curves during three years of typing practice

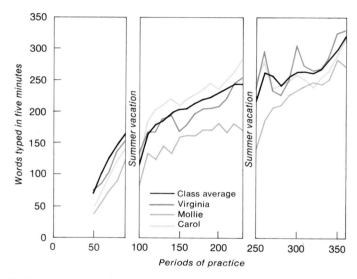

SOURCE: Sandiford (1928), p. 208; original study by W. G. Edwards.

Individual learning curves are characteristically irregular, reflecting transient shifts in interest, energy, rhythm, and so on. The teacher and the learner should not place much weight on a single striking success or a brief slump. The peak of each fluctuation shows what the person can do when all conditions are favorable, but the athlete is unrealistic if he is discontented with 14-foot pole vaults after he has once made 15 feet. If he is distressed by what is really an admirable average, he may worry himself into a serious slump. He may start experimenting with his already excellent technique and thereby spoil it.

Performance early in training is not a dependable predictor of ultimate proficiency in a psychomotor skill. The learner who catches on quickly, either because he transfers related past experience or because he has superior intellectual ability, gets off to a head start. These initial intellectual differences are likely to count for rather little in the end, especially in a motor skill. Those slower to understand a complex situation often overtake the early star performers. Differences later on depend on coordination and speed.

Individual progress in typing over three years of steady practice is illustrated in Fig. 10.7. Virginia remained fairly close to the class average throughout. Carol was below average during the first year, but when school resumed the next fall she showed fast progress. During the second year, she sailed ahead of the class, only to remain on a plateau in the third year, which permitted the rest of the class to overtake and pass her. We cannot be sure what caused these changes. Greater maturity in the second year may have helped Carol; loss of interest or faulty technique may have caused her third-year stagnation. Mollie learned typing slowly. Her progress was relatively poor from the start, and she made little gain in the second year. In the third year, she hit a rapid stride. She ended the year only forty strokes behind the average, although she had been seventy strokes behind at the end of the second year. In view of her steady

climb, there is no reason to think that Mollie has neared her limit; with further practice on the job she has a good chance of attaining average speed.

Especially in tasks where progress is gradual and in tasks where day-to-day scores are likely to fluctuate, the long-term record gives perspective. The technique is only useful where the same measure is pertinent in successive weeks and months, as is the case in typing. Even so, there is a risk that too much weight will be placed on the particular index chosen for plotting. In typing, the chart of words per minute is a composite embracing many subskills. The shape of the person's learning curve depends on what aspect of performance is measured (Fig. 10.6). In a subject where the student moves forward to new tasks—for example, through lessons on the various grammatical forms in French—the simple quantitative learning curve does not make sense (p. 719).

**33** How might the record shown at 239 hours (Fig. 10.6) improve with much more practice?

**34** What part-skills in multiplication might conceivably be measured separately?

**35** After two years of typing practice, students' scores on speed tests were only a few words per minute faster than at the end of the first year. Is this a fair basis for concluding that they learned little in the second year?

## Retention and Transfer

How well skills are retained over an interval of no practice is suggested by the three typing curves of Fig. 10.7. During the summer following the first year of training, the typing speed of each of the young women dropped substantially; after ten hours of renewed practice, each woman had regained her end-of-year speed. This occurred again following the second year.

In an experimental study, college women were taught various athletic skills, including a lacrosse throw and balancing on a bongo board. They practiced the skills for ten days; then, during the next 12 months, they had no opportunity to try the skills again. On the retention tests, the average score was 94 per cent of the level originally attained; many of the women did better than they had originally. Three days of renewed practice was sufficient to restore whatever skill had been lost (Purdy & Lockhart, 1962).

Continuous skills are complex linkages of responses. Each segment of the act is, in the course of extended practice, built into a program; then many cues can guide a particular response. Consequently, when some of the connections "fade out" during a long period of nonuse, plenty of them remain to hold the structure together. To be sure, one may "lose" the details of a segment in the middle of a complex act—for example, the knack of fingering a particular passage in a piano selection. But, as Gagné remarks (1970, p. 133), "Once a forgotten link is restored [by renewed practice], the entire chain may reappear in its totality."

Some writers suggest that discrete skills are less well retained (Irion, 1969, p. 18). Every golfer has experienced the frustration of being way off in his putting after long absence from the game. Comparatively few cues are available to guide the instant and precise correction such a short action sequence requires. Another consideration is the emphasis placed on precision in evaluating performance in discrete or short-sequence skills. Coordination is itself the mark of excellence in the continuous skills; most discrete skills are scored in terms of some external result, such as closeness to the bull's-eye. A person distressed by his score may fail to realize how much of the *act* he has retained.

The obvious way to measure the permanence of learning—but not the best way—is to test after an interval. The boy who learned to swim last summer swims successfully on the first day of the new season; that is evidence enough that most of his learning stayed with him. But poor performance on the delayed test is not proof that all is lost. The gringo who carried out tourist-level conversations in the native language the last time he visited Mexico is sure to flounder through the first day or two of his next visit, but soon his skills will be reinstated.

The best way to investigate the permanence of learning of a skill is to give the person a chance to practice after a long interruption, noting how long he needs to restore his skill. This is the "savings" method, so named because it asks how much practice time the earlier training saved in comparison to the time required by a learner starting from scratch.

Positive transfer is to be expected; the discriminations and cue-response sequences for one skill are usually helpful in others. The young person who can ride a bicycle learns to slow down when he observes children at the edge of the street, to correct steering on the basis of visual feedback, to estimate how soon a car in a side street will reach the intersection he is approaching. When he begins to drive an automobile, all these interpretations will be helpful. The timing of actions will have to be altered, but the old timing does not interfere for long. Comparable facilitation is expected in learning a second language. Ability to listen to another person and to imitate what he says is developed at about age 1, in thousands of trials. It is brought forward to the service of second-language learning. Likewise, knowing what sound to make when seeing the letter *t* in English is an aid to learning French.

Despite what was said earlier (p. 420), facilitation from a difficult task to an easy task is sometimes greater than from easy to difficult. This happens when the harder task requires accurate attention to detail (and yet is something

## Savings in learning as evidence of transfer

Savings in relearning are a good index of retention. Savings in learning a new task are evidence of transfer. Suppose the person learns Skill A, and after some interval, long or short, is trained on Skill B. His training time on Skill B is compared with that of a person who had no training on Skill A. Consider these hypothetical findings:

Trials to learn A                 40
Trials to learn B after A     25
Trials to learn B without A   50

Savings: 25 trials (50 per cent)

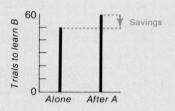

Skill A evidently has transfer value; it facilitates the learning of Skill B. Interference (negative transfer) has occurred if the findings look like this:

Trials to learn A                 40
Trials to learn B after A     60
Trials to learn B without A   50

Savings: −10 trials (−20 per cent)

the learner can master). Once this task is in hand, a similar but less demanding task is quickly conquered. The person who first masters the easier, less precise performance may be quite unprepared for the close tolerances of the second task (Welford, 1968, pp. 310–12). This is a theoretical point, not a general argument for hard task first. Most often, moving from a less precise to a more precise task is sound pedagogy—a progression in Oxendine's sense (p. 417).

Interference is to be expected when old cue-response sequences are not entirely appropriate. Pei (1960, p. 87) picks up the example of transfer from English speech to French:

> The written notation may be the same, but the spoken sounds for the most part diverge, sometimes slightly, sometimes to an astounding degree.... Any French grammar, for instance, will warn us to pronounce the written symbol *u* in French with rounded lips, not like the *u* of "union" or "cut"; but comparatively few French grammars will warn us to pronounce French *t* with the tip of the tongue touching the back of the upper teeth, not the upper gums, as we do in English.... It is precisely by these trifling differences that a native speaker can be distinguished from a foreigner who has learned the language....

When the cue is received, the person makes the response learned in the past; that is, he transfers the response. If the response is made provisionally, with a lively sense of doubt, the person is more likely to perceive differences between the sound he makes and the sound produced by the French speaker. The learner who observes consequences less carefully considers his response confirmed. It sounds nearly right and others understand him. In any particular transfer situation, facilitation and interference are both likely to occur. (See also p. 457).

Serious interference with learning occurs when the new task requires a change in some part of the original response that is not under voluntary, verbally mediated control. A response under voluntary control, on the other hand, is easily altered. A person makes some early errors by carrying forward an old interpretation, but he rather quickly overcomes them. The child who has learned to sight-read tunes in the key of C will make some errors when he begins to read in F, where the note on the third line of the staff (B) must be flatted. But he learns to discriminate, and to respond with B or B-flat according to the key of the selection. Learning the extra discrimination is easier than learning to read in the key of F without prior experience with the simple key of C. Interference with learning is small, compared to the facilitation from earlier practice.

When the player feels at home in the key of F, he sometimes plays a B unflatted because he is careless and fails to make a discrimination that he is perfectly capable of making. This is *habit* interference. In motor performance, habit interference occurs more often than interference with learning.

"Careless errors" occur when an old, thoroughly learned habit intrudes into a less familiar situation. Habit interference is especially likely under conditions of stress or fatigue. Smode et al. (1959, p. 12) tell of an airline copilot who had just been trained on a four-engine plane after long two-engine experience:

> On becoming airborne on a night take-off, the command for "wheels up" was given and the copilot reached for the handle to retract the gear. However, on the four-engine craft, the landing gear handle position was different from that on the two-engine aircraft; also, the flap lever on the four-engine aircraft was positioned similarly to the landing gear handle on the two-engine craft. The copilot, who stated that he was fatigued at the time, activated the flap lever for the wheels up command.... [Instantly, however,] he "felt" a sensation on the lever different from that expected from pulling the landing gear lever. He immediately [corrected his error].

The copilot failed to make the correct initial discrimination, but he saved himself because he was alert enough to attend to the feedback. Habit interference is reduced by more thorough training on both the old *and* the new responses. This strengthens both sets of cue-response connections and develops the ability to discriminate between the situations. *Overlearning*—practice well beyond the point where the skill becomes complete and smooth—is highly desirable to reduce interference (p. 467).

**36** Interference indicates that a response has been transferred to a new situation. In what sense is this transfer "negative"?

**37** What facilitation or interference would be expected in these situations?
- a. An adolescent who has learned to use a hand saw uses a table-mounted power saw.
- b. A person who has learned to use a table-mounted power saw uses a portable power saw.

**38** If learning of skills is "permanent," how do you account for the big-league pitcher who wins twenty games one year and loses his first seven starts the next season?

## READING LIST

G. J. K. Alderson, D. J. Sully, and H. C. Sully, "An Operational Analysis of a One-Handed Catching Task Using High Speed Photography," *Journal of Motor Behavior* 6 (1974), 217–26.

> Shows how precise analysis (with timing down to one-thousandth of a second) identifies subunits in a motor skill and indicates what cues the learner relies on.

Lawrence F. Locke, "Implications for Physical Education," *Research Quarterly* 43 (1972), 364–86.

> In this concluding paper of a series summarizing research on skill learning, Locke speaks of teaching. According to modern theories, both teaching and learning of sports skills are to a large degree intellectual. What matters is the learner's understanding of the goal and the task. The message should be relevant far beyond sports, to teachers of music, industrial arts, foreign language, and so on.

Mark A. May, "The Psychology of Learning from Demonstration Films," *Journal of Educational Psychology* 37 (1946), 1–12.

> May's suggestions for using films in teaching skills will help teachers obtain benefit from these aids, but they will also help in any explanation or demonstration. Compare May's suggestions with the customary use of films in the classroom, as you have experienced it.

George A. Miller, Eugene Galanter, and Karl H. Pribram, "Motor Skills and Habits," in *Plans and the Structure of Behavior* (New York: Holt-Dryden, 1960), pp. 81–94.

> This volume, which discusses how people plan and regulate their behavior, has had considerable influence on thinking in physical education as well as in psychology. It supplements statements in this text about programs and about feedback, and clarifies the limitations of verbal tutelage in teaching skills. In addition to the section cited (Chapter 6), Chapters 2, 10, and 12 are especially relevant to educators.

Joseph B. Oxendine, "Mental Practice," in *Psychology of Motor Learning* (New York: Appleton-Century-Crofts, 1968), pp. 222–40.

> Describes experiments in which mental practice was used to promote various motor skills. Describes techniques the performer can use to improve his own skill by thinking about his actions.

A. T. Welford, "Acquisition of Skill," in *Fundamentals of Skill* (London: Methuen, 1968), pp. 286–316.

> A leading investigator of skill learning summarizes general principles and the related research. Such topics as understanding the task, feedback, and whole–part learning he covers in more detail than does this chapter.

# 11

# PERCEIVING AND REMEMBERING

The next three chapters are concerned with intellectual skills—dividing numbers, for example, or interpreting a wiring diagram—and with systematic knowledge such as is acquired from the study of history or zoology. This chapter takes up comparatively elementary forms of associative learning. Many of the processes seen in the learning of motor skills (Chapter 10) reappear in associative learning.

## LEARNING TO LEARN

One lesson can facilitate learning of the next (p. 435). Partly this occurs through carry-over of particular interpretations and responses, but this is a less significant kind of transfer than broadly improved ability to learn. Cox (p. 423) showed that a person given training in attending can take better advantage of subsequent demonstrations, for example. Other learning-to-learn takes place while the person is acquiring lesson-specific discriminations and associations; this is collateral learning (p. 39)—a by-product of the lessons. Discrimination is, quite simply, the noting of similarities and differences. Is there a spin on the

## Discrimination

"Good heavens, Emma! I thought this was you."

tennis ball coming toward me? Is my A string in tune with the piano's A? Do those clouds signify that I should carry a raincoat? One must discriminate to answer such questions.

To investigate discrimination, the psychologist arranges a task that presents the person with no difficulty except that of making the right distinction. One common laboratory setup uses a tray with two shallow pans. Each pan has a cover, and a reward, such as a raisin, is hidden in one of the pans. There are two objects, one atop each cover. In the simplest of tasks, the objects would be radically different—a silver thimble and a wooden spool, for example. To investigate the subtler process of color discrimination, the objects might be a red cube and a red-orange cube. It is possible to vary the objects from trial to trial, keeping (say) the color as the cue that identifies the correct choice each time.*

---

\* The laboratory psychologist calls the task where *many* features vary a concept-attainment task, rather than a discrimination task; but we can ignore the distinction.

In the experiment where the red cube is "correct," the tray is set before the subject time after time, with the red cube sometimes to the right and sometimes to the left. The subject who looks beneath the red cube will get the reward every time. If he looks beneath the red-orange cube, he finds nothing. As soon as he has looked into the pan (and taken the reward if it is there), the tray is withdrawn to prepare for another trial.

If the contrast between the objects is apparent to the subject and the reward appealing, he ought to perform perfectly on the second trial and every trial thereafter. Young children and animals are not that efficient; quite a few trials may be needed before they eliminate all errors.

A famous observation on monkeys, subsequently duplicated with children, was made by Harlow. Harlow presented a pair of visually distinct objects; the monkey had as many trials with that pair of objects as he needed to reach error-free performance. After a monkey had done hundreds of such problems, each with a new pair of objects, he was highly efficient in using first-trial information (Fig. 11.1). To say that Harlow's monkeys became more intelligent claims too much, but they did learn to cope with an intellectual demand.

## FIGURE 11.1

### Use of information by experienced and novice learners

The lower curve is an average for monkeys working on their first eight discrimination problems. The upper curve is an average after they had experience with 200 problems. On the first trial, only a chance score of 50 per cent is to be expected.

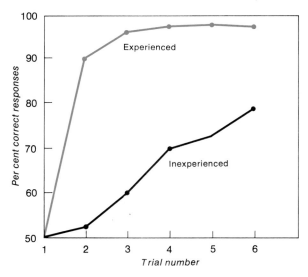

SOURCE: Adapted from Harlow (1949). Copyright 1949 by the American Psychological Association. Reprinted by permission.

Children learn to learn much as Harlow's monkeys did. In one experiment, very dull children (age 10, MA near 4) found certain discriminations hopelessly difficult; but with experience on easier tasks they learned to take advantage of shape cues. Here—and in Table 11.1—are the details. These severely retarded children had little success in discriminating between patterns painted on square tiles. Even after 500 trials with feedback, those in Group 1 were unable to pick the right tile consistently. Choosing between cutout forms is easier; evidently, the feel of the objects gives a better cue. Group 2 started with that task. As soon as the child was choosing the correct cutout four times out of five, he was asked to make the same choice when presented with the two patterns painted on square tiles. Children in Group 2 did far better at that task than those in Group 1. Group 3 was pretrained on cutout figures, again to a four-out-of-five standard. When shifted to flat patterns, the Group 3 child was given a *fresh* problem. Even so, Group 3 far outperformed Group 1. Trials on the first, manageable problem taught Groups 2 and 3 to attend to shape and color and to hold the information long enough to take advantage of feedback.

Gaining command of the discrimination task is more than a laboratory trick for these children. A next step might well be for teachers to use the setup to teach them to discriminate which of two dot patterns has more dots, or to distinguish letter shapes (as in Williams's experiment, p. 110).

What happens in this learning to learn? Partly, the subject learns the rules of the psychologist's game. He learns (as, for example, in the case of the red and red-orange cubes) that position is not related to the reward. He catches on to the fact that the reward is not placed at random, that something gives away its position. But what is the cue? To determine this he learns a technique:

## TABLE 11.1

Improved ability to discriminate printed shapes after practice on an easier discrimination

| Group | Initial discrimination task | Second discrimination task | Percentage succeeding on second task |
|-------|------------------------------|------------------------------|--------------------------------------|
| 1 | (No first task) | Black ■ and yellow ⊤ painted on tiles | 20 (after 500 trials) |
| 2 | Cutout black ■ and cutout yellow ⊤ | Painted black ■ and yellow ⊤, as above | 70 (after 250 trials)* |
| 3 | Cutout red ✚ and green | Painted black ■ and yellow ⊤, as above | 50 (after 250 trials)* |

SOURCE: Data from House & Zeaman (1960).
* Includes trials on both the first and second tasks.

444

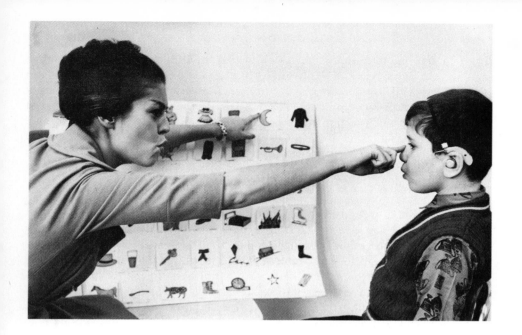

1. He asks himself, What is one difference between the objects (cubes)?
2. He holds one such difference in short-term memory as he makes his try.
3. He chooses one of the two objects as his provisional try.
4. He attends to the consequence. If his try is rewarded, he enters in his long-term memory the characteristic that identifies the object chosen. If his try is wrong, he enters a rule: "Do not use that characteristic as a basis for choice in the future."

Similar learning to learn takes place under regular school conditions. The first-grader learns, for example, that the correct response to a word in his primer depends strictly on the configuration of letters, not on the size of the print or the position on the page. He learns not only to make a try at reading it off, but also to attend to the feedback the teacher provides, and to store for future use the information gained. Comparing unschooled children with Liberian Kpelle children of the same age who had school experience, Scribner and Cole (1973) found the schooled children superior at novel tasks requiring efficient handling of information. School experience, then, makes students more efficient in detecting and recalling regularities.

Perceiving, transforming (recoding), and storing in memory are intimately related. We shall therefore shift back and forth between them. At this point we turn to memory, returning to discrimination later in the chapter.

Fixing information or verbal associations in mind is a skill. Therefore, the student can improve his ability in verbal learning by identifying good technique and adopting it. Woodrow, as far back as 1927, produced evidence that one can train this skill. He first tested the ability of college students to remember various kinds of material. He then trained one group of poor memorizers to use four learning techniques: active self-testing, rhythm and grouping, meaning, and secondary associations. This group practiced the new methods for a short while. A second group "exercised" their memories, memorizing material but being shown no new techniques. A third group of students (controls) received neither training nor practice in memorizing. On the final day, students studied (for example) English equivalents of 30 Turkish words for six minutes, and then took a test. The group trained in techniques of studying gained in ability to translate Turkish words (Table 11.2) and to remember historical dates and connected prose.

Woodrow's experiment was historically important because it contradicted the view that ability to learn is a matter of inborn intelligence only. Woodrow's result supported the idea of targeted training for inefficient learners. Previous investigators, starting with William James, had shown that "exercising the memory" did not lead to improvement. The conclusion that engaging in mental activity has no effect on ability is too strong, however. In the right kind of activity, a person discovers techniques for himself, especially when a type of learning is new to him. Young children make large gains. The older and more experienced the learner—hence the more set in his ways—the less likely he is to discover improved techniques without help (Goulet, 1970).

Gains in technique are remarkably long-lasting, according to the few studies that have been made by follow-up tests (box; see also p. 436). The right-left-left-left-right . . . succession of responses for a particular maze is just one of hundreds of possibilities; it has no meaning or pattern to distinguish it from the alternatives. No wonder, then, that the response sequence does not come to mind when the person encounters the maze months later. Quick *re*learning, however, gives evidence that something was retained. The fact that the students learned a new maze just as easily as they relearned the first one implies that the first experience improved, more or less permanently, their technique of learning. Such findings imply that improved learning ability for a certain kind of task may be one of the most important outcomes of a period of instruction.

## TABLE 11.2

### Improvement in memorization with training in technique

| Group | Score on pretest | Final score | Change |
|---|---|---|---|
| Students receiving no training | 16.2 | 16.1 | −0.1 |
| Students receiving only practice in memorizing | 14.6 | 15.1 | +0.5 |
| Students taught new methods | 13.6 | 21.1 | +7.5 |

SOURCE: Adapted from Woodrow (1927).

## Remembering how to learn

One kind of maze consists of a series of T-shapes connected like this:

In Husband's experiment (1947) these patterns were engraved on a surface, and the student learned by tracing with his finger, backtracking when he reached a dead end. Students learned one of these mazes and then came back at a later date to try what they thought was a new maze. Actually, half the students were given a new maze and the other half were given the original one. Any recall of the earlier path should have helped the latter group.

The time required to master the second maze well enough to trace the path without error is shown in the figure. (All the times are shown as percentages of the initial learning times.) It appears that the specific associations did last, but they accounted for far less of the savings after six months than the transferrable learning skills did. The group learning a new maze after six months actually showed about as much saving in learning time as the group that had been introduced to mazes just a week before learning a new one. (The groups were small, hence the increase over the period from one week to six months can be disregarded.)

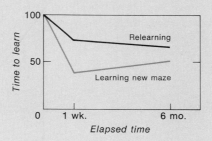

---

**1** In the House-Zeaman experiment, is it likely that any collateral learning occurred that would help the children in tasks other than visual discrimination?

**2** In each of the following kinds of instruction, is learning to learn possible? If so, just what responses are learned?
    a. Students learn to recognize leaves of trees by studying mounted specimens.
    b. Students view films on the exploration and settlement of the American West.

Most research on memory uses picture–word pairs or simple verbal material. Sometimes pairs of "meaningless" syllables are presented—*FIP::DAK*. Later, one member of the pair is presented, and the person is asked to recall the other member. The simple associations of memory research have their counterparts in school: "George III"::"American Revolution" or "Napoleon"::"Bonaparte" or "Test for hydrogen ion?"::"Litmus turns pink." Even in learning *FIP::DAK* there is thinking, not just "rote" learning. Many learners transform the syllables into images. FIP may become "flip" and DAK may become "deck"—simple, then, to visualize a Frisbee being flipped across a deck. It is a good bet that just this one image will enable you to bring out the response *DAK* to the stimulus *FIP* a few days from now.

Three stages can be distinguished in the process of filing information for later reference (R. C. Atkinson & K. Wescourt, 1975; Shiffrin, 1975).

- Taking information into the sensory register (the first step) is passive. Energy hits the eye or ear. The optic nerve or the auditory nerve carries an electrical signal to the brain. The sensory register assembles at most a few seconds' worth of signal, which is then interpreted. For example, the viewer recognizes a face; the listener detects a string of words in an acoustic signal.

- The discriminated, interpreted signal is held for a bit in short-term memory (STM), also called "the short-term store." The greeter in a reception line manages to hold in mind the name of the guest being introduced. That name vanishes from his mind when he turns his attention to the next guest. STM does not hold much, and it does not hold it for long—not without deliberate rehearsal.

- Some of what enters STM is transferred to long-term memory (LTM), very likely being reorganized in the process. The person exerts considerable control over what is stored and how it is arranged for filing.

STM and LTM are of importance here; I shall say no more about sensory processes. You should not think of STM and LTM as different "parts of the brain"; more nearly, the terms provide a convenient language for summarizing results from immediate and delayed tests of retrieval (Postman, 1975). Some writers speak of intermediate memory processes in addition.

Psychologists assume that once a verbal association, meaning, or schematic image of a visual display is sent into LTM it is held in storage more or less permanently. When you want an item from that store, whether you recall it depends on your ability to locate it, to "retrieve" it. For items that have often been used, retrieval may be simply a matter of bringing an intact image or verbal chain back to the surface. More often, the person brings back partial associ-

## Still another memory?

Greeno (in Gregg, 1974, pp. 23–24) holds that the learner does not just soak up information; he actively constructs conceptual relationships. The constructing takes place in an "intermediate memory" that makes semantic interpretations. The resulting ideas or beliefs (as distinct from words as such) go to LTM. When working at interpretation, the intermediate memory holds material for minutes, or even for several hours:

> Much classroom evaluation involves knowledge stored in intermediate memory which does not become transferred in detail to permanent semantic memory. When a professor prepares a lecture, he generally reviews material or prepares notes by referring to articles and books. That is, material stored in long-term semantic memory is usually not sufficient; structures must be generated in intermediate memory to ensure that the desired information will be included and presented intelligibly. Similar preparations are standard practice for businessmen before they present complex information at meetings, and for attorneys before they present arguments at court.

ations and meanings that enable him to reconstruct an approximation of the original information. Remembering, then, is mostly problem-solving!

To illustrate this reconstruction process, let me ask you something you have had ample opportunity to learn: Which number on the telephone dial is paired with the letter *N*? You are not likely to "know" this, but you do know that *A* is paired with *2* and that three letters go with each number. With just a trifle more information—including the alphabet, which is readily pulled out of LTM—you can work out the number that goes with *N*. That is, you can construct the response you never had occasion to commit to memory.

(By the way, what syllable goes with *DAK*? Do you recall? Did just the response come to mind? Or the Frisbee image and then the response?)

## Short-Term Storage

Short-term storage is the gatekeeper—an important role in performance and in learning. Sight-reading music, for example, a player holds notes in STM; if he is a reasonably skilled performer, his eyes run some measures beyond what his fingers are playing. Similarly, a reader comprehends the end of a paragraph because he has woven the words just decoded into a short-term record of the ideas picked up earlier in the paragraph.

The first concern of the teacher is to get the key information into STM. The student never notices all that is present in an auditory or visual display—a microscope slide, for example. All the data reach the sensory register, but only a few items or aspects are perceived. Experience or a teacher's guidance enables the student to pick out the elements worth carrying into STM. The short-term store cannot retain a detailed image; it can retain a schematic visual representation or a verbal label. The photographic or phonographic sensory record has to be encoded to enter STM.

The child in school may be asked to hold a stimulus in mind that he cannot encode well. A letter is printed on the left-hand page of the kindergartner's workbook, for example. He is asked to draw a line, connecting it with whichever shape on the opposite page it matches. In the workbook the letters are far apart, so the child has to try to hold the visual impression in mind while he scans the second page. This is too difficult. The teacher would be wise to remove the burden on the child's memory by using movable forms, which can be laid alongside the figure on the page; even then, the task of perceptual comparison is not easy for a kindergartner (p. 116). Later, when the child has learned to name the letter, he can hold the name in STM; he will remember *that* well enough to do the matching. He can go on to more complicated tasks such as letter bingo (photo), which presses him to use his naming skill and so sharpen it.

The short-term store seems to retain only a limited amount of information, and that very briefly. Look up two telephone numbers—and the first will escape your mind while you read the second. You can hold only a limited number of items in STM—perhaps five to nine. The digits of the telephone number are probably coded one by one, but often an item is a "chunk" made up of several elements. A chunk is an idea or image that stands independent of the other items—for example, one entry in a list. The chunk may be complex (for example, "George Washington Carver") so long as it is familiar. In a letter-string experiment, *TCA* takes the space of three chunks but *cat* is just one chunk. And

## How big is a chunk?

Present common one-syllable nouns at a slow, steady rate. You will find that most adults can say back six or seven of them in a row. Herbert Simon (1974, p. 483) set himself a harder assignment:

> . . . I tried to recall after one reading the following list of words: Lincoln, milky, criminal, differential, address, way, lawyer, calculus, Gettysburg.

Shut your eyes! How many can *you* recall?
Now, back to Simon's story:

> I had no success whatsoever. I should not have expected success, for the list exceeded my span of six or seven words. Then I rearranged the list a bit, as follows:
>
> Lincoln's Gettysburg Address
>
> Milky Way
>
> Criminal lawyer
>
> Differential calculus
>
> I had no difficulty at all. . . .

to a computer specialist, 100110101 is just the binary form of 565—three chunks, not nine (G. Miller, 1956; Simon, 1974).

STM seems not to improve with age (Belmont & Butterfield, 1969). This will not surprise the adult who has played the game "Concentration" with a 6-year-old and worked hard to keep up. The adult has an advantage where his experience enables him to recognize patterns that can be stored as chunks; but Concentration is patternless.

What is one chunk for the teacher may be a dozen for the student. The algebra teacher is so familiar with $(a^2 - b^2) = (a - b)(a + b)$ that the whole formula is a single unit for him. The beginner in algebra recognizes no chunk larger than $b^2$ or $a + b$. One way to lighten the load on STM is to write key points or details on the blackboard. Then the student can think about one fraction of the information without losing the rest.

Making successive tries in a task, the student cannot remember all the responses he has tried. Reducing the load on memory will help him master the task. For example, he will be much quicker to sort out the correct path through a maze if allowed to keep a record of his turns. The notation for chess moves (P–K4, for example) has this same function of freezing a bit of experience so that the learner can study it at his leisure. Memory support is most needed, of course, when the patterns are unfamiliar. The chess expert needs no written record when attack and response conform to the old Ruy Lopez opening; when the game begins to take a shape of its own, even the expert needs a record—if he is to replay the game and learn from it.

Some items enter STM just once and, if not lost, pass directly and finally to LTM. That is not what happens when one is *trying* to learn. The intentional learner inspects material several times, and, in the process, reorganization and consolidation occur. The material usually is restructured: rhythm is imposed on a number string, a picture is invented to link a pair of syllables, related facts are brought together in a cluster. You can observe how you yourself have chunked items at the time you learned them. Say the alphabet backward rapidly, and note where you pause. You will find that you bring little bundles of letters—*LMNOP*, or *GH*—to the working surface of the mind and "read them off" in the required order. A pause indicates where one bundle is finished and a new one is brought forward. (See box, p. 479, for another example.)

Gordon Bower speaks of the short-term store as a "mental scratch pad." A learner constructs images or meanings, some of which he decides to store. When retrieving, he brings traces up to the pad for rearrangement—as with the alphabet. William James offered an even more striking metaphor when he spoke of bringing ideas "before the footlights of consciousness." The working memory is a puppet stage; you can shift the players about and regroup them.

## Long-Term Storage

"Long-term" memory, says the psychologist, is operating whenever a person lets an item drop from the active surface of his thought and then comes back to it. According to present psychological evidence, memory traces lasting for years are no different in kind from those formed yesterday. Two superficially contradictory statements can be made:

> Perhaps no association that enters the long-term store is ever forgotten;

> The longer the elapsed time since the last recall of an item, the harder it is to bring it to mind.

Memory traces—at least some of them—can be thought of as permanent (Tulving, 1974). Some physical change takes place when an association is stored. A computer, storing information, encodes it in a series of dots and spaces, and records the dots electromagnetically on a tape or disk. In the brain, the same sort of recording may occur through chemical change in a molecule of a brain cell. Those who argue that the records never vanish can point to the many instances in which an ancient memory comes clearly to mind. I can give two examples from my recent experience. Each time I used a new bicycle lock, the numbers 28–0–18 came to my mind, though the new lock had a quite different combination. The numbers from memory, I feel sure, belong to a lock I used more than 20 years ago—I cannot recall where. The new lock, physically like the old, provides a sufficient cue to bring the well-learned numbers out of storage.

Some items one makes no effort to store are nonetheless recorded permanently, as my second anecdote illustrates. Recently I heard on the radio a bit

## Long-term storage

"We've already done this room. I remember that fire extinguisher."

Drawing by B. Tobey; © 1953 The New Yorker Magazine, Inc.

from an obscure operetta that I had heard just once, decades ago. The music at once brought back the name *(The Chimes of Normandy).* Moreover, it brought back a vague image of the leading singer, a hometown adult I never saw before or since, and his name. Formal evidence of permanent storage exists: direct electrical stimulation of the brain surface can elicit vivid accounts of forgotten scenes far in the past (Penfield & Roberts, 1959). Many psychologists think of the memory trace as a Sleeping Beauty, ready to spring youthfully to life at the first magic call from the right stimulus. Efficient retrieval, then, makes the difference between "a good memory" and a poor one.

Material in LTM is evidently stored systematically, not heaped up with the most recent traces on top. The bundles are sometimes arbitrary—*LMNOP*—but meanings usually dictate the organization. Specific ideas are generally subordinated to broad categories. The Collins-Quillian tree sketch (box) is an idealization. Structures are not truly so orderly. Categories overlap (warm countries, Latin countries, . . .) and there are cross-linkages. For more elaborate presentations of the theory, see Collins and Loftus (1975) and Meyer and Schvanefeldt (1976). Whatever the specifics of the filing system, recollections are organized in terms of beliefs, concepts, and relations, not as a chronologically ordered tape of experience.

Did Madame Curie come before or after Florence Nightingale? When you try to answer, the long-term store supplies material you acquired at different times in different contexts. This is possible because your storage is organized. You bring the material up to the forefront of consciousness; then you look for facts that you can compare, to ultimately reach the answer (Linton, 1975).

## The mental filing cabinet

In the mental filing system, Collins and Quillian (1969; in Gregg, 1972) suggest, something true generally of birds is filed with the concept *bird.* This is the kind of network of associations they envision:

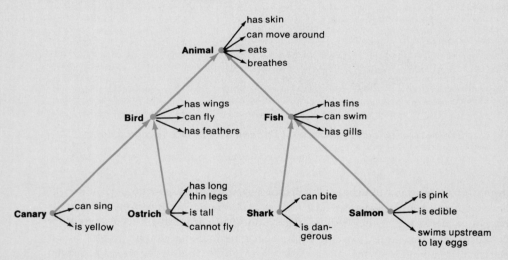

SOURCE: Collins & Quillian (1969).

As evidence to support this hypothesis, they have measured how long it takes to judge a sentence as true (or false). Here are some of the true sentences and the average times for judging them (in seconds):

1.00 *A canary is a canary.* (0)
1.17 *A canary is a bird.* (1)
1.24 *A canary is an animal.* (2)
1.30 *A canary can sing.* (1)
1.47 *A canary has skin.* (3)

The number in parentheses indicates how many links have to be brought from storage to verify the sentence or to contradict it. According to the figure, there are three links in the last sentence: canary to bird to animal to skin. (The time to verify "A canary is an animal" appears to be out of line. The explanation is that links between large categories come to mind more quickly than links to properties.)

**3** Students use short-term memory in taking lecture notes. What facts about STM are significant for the lecturer who wants his students to make a good record of certain ideas?

**4** Which of the following bits of information is hard to bring to mind? Does the difficulty depend solely on time elapsed since last recall?

    a. The name of your fourth-grade teacher

    b. The names of the countries of South America

    c. The events of Alice's last few minutes in Wonderland, before she woke up at home

## Forgetting and Relearning

HOW MUCH IS FORGOTTEN? If a person fails to make a response he formerly was able to make, we say that he has forgotten it. We apply the term also to a loss of speed and precision (for example, in adding) and to inconsistency in performance ("I keep forgetting to speak slowly.").

Lapses in memory, like lapses in skill, are a matter of degree. You forget elements in a complex response, not everything at once. Is it cumin or oregano in your father's chili recipe? Bone meal or superphosphate, for his rose bed? In recalling the need for some exotic spice and some source of phosphate, and in recalling the likely alternatives, you remember more than you forget. Even when you do not recall the response, you may recall enough to work out the response rapidly. The American back in Paris after a considerable absence will not recall just how to get from the Opéra to Boul' Mich'—but he will find his way by successive approximations that waste little time. Within a few days, he will recapture his orientation; in any once-familiar part of the city he can choose his path unerringly.

Our everyday ideas about forgetting rest on a simple performance test. Can you prepare the chili without looking up the recipe? Right off, can you name the tallest mountain in North America? A test of recall asks you to respond correctly, without warm-up. Much research on retention stops with such a measure, but a relearning measure is more adequate.

In Chapter 10, we saw that a "lost" skill is regained rapidly when practice is renewed. Our man in Paris similarly regained his command of its geography. Savings in relearning give the best indication of what a person retained from his French course or from his study of contract law. When and if contracts come up in the person's later study or work, he will not have to retrieve his original knowledge instantly. Almost always, he has some opportunity for review.

Investigators most often measure recall because it is so impractical to measure savings in relearning. In considering the findings below about the extent to which lessons are recalled, bear in mind that a measure of savings would give evidence of greater retention.

Husband's findings on maze learning (box, p. 447) are like those often found in the laboratory. The correct responses in a maze are not distinct from the competing responses; with such tasks, retrieval is difficult or impossible after much time has passed. Husband's students, during the months of no practice, showed a steep initial decline in their knowledge of the maze, and then a leveling off. Similar declines are reported for word pairs and other associations.

Remarkably few controlled studies have measured the retention of school learning. Tyler's data on recall in college zoology (Table 11.3) are suggestive, but they require cautious interpretation. The baseline measures were part of

### TABLE 11.3

Performance on tasks in zoology at the end of instruction and one year later

| Task | Average score at start of course | Average score at end of course | Average score on retest one year later | Percentage of gain retained |
|---|---|---|---|---|
| Naming structures of animals in diagrams | 22 | 62 | 31 | 23 |
| Identifying technical terms | 20 | 83 | 67 | 74 |
| Relating structure to function in type forms | 13 | 39 | 34 | 79 |
| Applying general principles to unfamiliar situations | 35 | 65 | 65 | 100 |
| Interpreting experimental results | 30 | 57 | 64 | 125 |

SOURCE: Adapted from R. W. Tyler (1934).

the students' end-of-course examination; the repeat test a year later was solely for research purposes. The students had surely reviewed for the end-of-course test and were more strongly motivated for it. Moreover, they may have had a chance to practice some of the skills and not others during the intervening year. Taken at face value, the data fit with Husband's finding: more general techniques and insights are easier to call up than unsystematic associations.

Controlled studies of learning from text material support the same conclusion. Ideas that are comprehended and interrelated are comparatively easy to recall later. More arbitrary associations are poorly recalled—unless, like the combination for my bicycle lock, they are practiced hundreds of times.

Pictures are easy to remember and easy to associate with verbal responses. In one study, students looked at more than 2,500 photographs, each one being presented just once for ten seconds, the sessions being spread over several days. The test called for recognition, not recall. On the test day, the students were shown one of the original pictures paired with a picture they had not seen, and had to say which one they had seen. Scores were remarkably high, in the neighborhood of 85–95 per cent (Haber, 1970). Drawings and color photographs serve much better than words as cues for simple associative learning (F. W. Wicker, 1970). The evidence on this advantage of pictures suggests that schools ought to use more pictorial stimuli than they do, at least in those subjects where the person will apply his knowledge to events before his eyes.

Ability to store associations is not *directly* related to general mental ability. When everyone understands the items under study equally well, brighter persons do not remember more than average persons (Hagen, 1975; Schonfield & Robertson, 1966). Better initial understanding and organization of ideas means better retrieval, of course, and intellectual ability counts in that. The person with a better supply of concepts and better techniques of analysis can make better sense of the material.

INTERFERENCE    Forgetting is explained in part by conflicting responses. The person confuses similar stimuli or is unable to choose among the "reasonable" responses that come to mind. The more confusions there are, the worse the person does on a test.

R. C. Anderson and D. L. Myrow (1971) demonstrated interference by having high-school students study two lessons. One experiment centered around a text on the primitive Himootians. Two days after studying that lesson the experimental (E) subjects studied a text on a second tribe. Control (C) subjects, as their second lesson, studied a text on drug addiction—unlikely to be confused with the first lesson. A week later all students were tested on knowledge of the Himootians.

The Himootian male, said the lesson, has to become competent in work before he can marry; the male in the second tribe has to perform a feat of daring. This discrepancy is expected to cause interference. Second, both tribes make beer from squash; this concordance ought to facilitate retention of the fact. Third, there were "neutral" topics in the Himootian passage that did not enter the second lesson.

## FIGURE 11.2

### Retention of text content after studying similar, unrelated, or conflicting material

For the experimental group, Category 1 content in the first lesson was similar to that in the second lesson; Category 3 content in the first lesson was contrary to that in the second lesson.

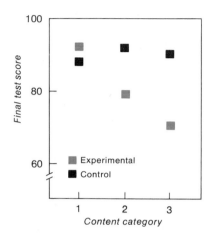

SOURCE: Adapted from R. C. Anderson & D. L. Myrow (1971), p. 87. Copyright 1971 by the American Psychological Association. Reprinted by permission.

Figure 11.2 shows the scores by type of item. The score on the final test is expressed as a percentage of the score earned on a test given immediately after the first text had been read. (This calculation allows for the fact that some items were easy to learn initially.) Having no interference, the C's retained the concrete Himootian content. On items where interference was possible for E's, they did only about half as well as the C's. On topics echoed in the E's second text, they did better than the C's.

The curriculum asks the student to learn different answers to very similar questions (Bower, 1974). Learning to classify animal species, for example, using the same attributes in different combinations, is a confusing task because the combinations are hard to discriminate. In history, too, confusing combinations abound:

> "When A was King and B was his General, War C was fought. But when A was King and D was the General, War E was fought. Confusion would surely reign when the student sorts out in memory which king went with which general and which pair got involved in which war." (Bower, p. 7)

Bower had students study a fact-laden biography. The experimental group then studied a biography of a second person; the new biography followed the same outline but changed many of the facts (occupation of father, for example). A control group studied a passage on an entirely separate topic. The confusion showed up as predicted, the experimental group losing about a third of the facts they knew originally. Most of their errors were "intrusions" of associations from the second biography.

The teacher may mistakenly believe that interference has been overcome when the student consistently makes the correct response at the end of a lesson. Even though this response is *now* stronger than competing responses (which arise from past lessons or from misinterpretations), it may not remain stronger. If the new response is not solidly implanted, with plentiful interconnections to other responses, it can easily be pushed out by a strong-rooted competitor. Details are especially subject to interference, and most of them disappear rapidly; broad ideas are far better retained.

The key to reducing interference is solid, meaningful initial learning. Original learning is better and retention is better if:

The stimulus or situation is clearly discriminated from alternative stimuli.

The appropriate response is clearly discriminated from its alternatives.

The correct linkup can be made to seem more reasonable than the alternative linkages.

All the techniques discussed in the section that begins on page 469 improve retention as well as initial learning.

5 Foreign-language vocabulary could be taught by associating each word with a picture of an object or action. Is this a good idea?

6 What has been forgotten when a teacher "forgets to speak slowly"?

7 Could economics or history teachers reduce interference by presenting content in the form of word-picture associations?

8 Students recall only 19 per cent of the factual content of a high-school chemistry course five years later (Sterrett & Davis, 1954). There are similar findings in other subjects. Does this imply that it is pointless to teach the high-school student numerous associations so that he can call on them during his adult years?

9 Tyler's test on interpreting experiments was more or less similar to that of Burmester shown on p. 726. Instead of being "forgotten," the skill tested by Tyler improved during the year following the zoology course. Suggest an explanation.

## Reconstruction

## Reconstructing a Response from Memory

In a motor skill, the performer constructs his response as he goes, holding mistakes in check by continual monitoring. The act of recall can be described similarly.

Sketch a map of western Europe, showing the outlines of countries from Denmark around to Spain. As you start, you probably have only the haziest of images. You remember Denmark as north and east of Spain. Perhaps you recall the location of a couple of other countries. You fit them together. Having, say, Spain and France in position along an ill-defined coastline running north from Gibraltar, you ponder the gap to the north. European countries ... Germany, Holland, Switzerland, Sweden. Holland has to be in here—Hans Brinker, dikes, North Sea. Does Holland touch Denmark, or does Germany come between? After you decide on an order of countries, you try to firm up the coastline. You may remember to jut Spain into the Atlantic, and may forget entirely the Norman peninsula. Perhaps you trace the coast of Holland straight to the east with no downward slant, misled by "North Sea" into thinking that all the dikes face north. You produce the map more by reconstruction than by recall—and this would be true even if you tried to portray the locality you know best. Any map from memory is certain to be imperfect. In retrieval, as in initial learning, the process is one of provisional try and correction.

Your response was organized. The names of countries blocked it out. You knew that Europe is a continuous land mass; this interpretation required that you make countries touch. Within a country there was organization also; if your recall was good, you had Normandy, the Biscay coast, and the Channel coast as subunits; you might know enough to give each of these some finer delineation.

As Collins and Quillian (box, p. 454) point out, much organization in memory is hierarchical. In this example, rivers and peninsulas were subordinate to countries, and countries were subordinate to the continent. Historical knowledge is organized into blocks of time. Some of your ideas about plants may be organized within broad botanical categories, some within regional categories, some within functional categories (herbs, say, or annuals). The rubrics in which you store knowledge correspond to the interpretations you made when acquiring your experience. Categories that help organize bits of information at the time of instruction make the information easier to retrieve. The halogens, the Romantic composers, the –ir verbs—such organizing concepts provide file drawers for storage, and ready handles for retrieval.

Reconstructions depart from the original in various ways. The changes tend to make the material more regular or orderly than the original. Details, qualifications, and exceptions tend to be lost, and a strong pattern seen in the original material is likely to dominate the reconstruction. Think of the shape of Nebraska on a map. Unless you live in or near Nebraska, you probably recall a rectangle, forgetting that Wyoming takes a bite out of the southwest and that a river rounds the opposite corner. This process of "improving" the structure of the original is illustrated in Fig. 11.3, from the famous research on reconstruction processes of the English psychologist F. C. Bartlett. Bartlett also found that the person who tells a story rebuilds it as he recalls it. Any element of the original that seems not to make good sense, or that is peripheral to the main story line, is suppressed or revised until the recalled story is well unified.

## FIGURE 11.3

### Simplification and organization in reproduction

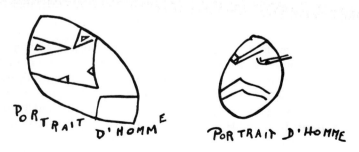

SOURCE: Bartlett (1932), p. 178. Reprinted by permission of Cambridge University Press.

Sometimes details, instead of being lost, are exaggerated; when the person brings one to mind, he gives it more significance than it originally had. Thus, if he thinks to put the "Hook of Holland" into his map of western Europe, he may make it a prominent feature whereas it would be tiny if in proper scale.

Once the person has reconstructed a lesson from memory, the reconstruction itself goes into his store. He is likely to remember inaccurate aspects of the reconstruction better than the original lesson unless his trial reconstruction is corrected. In some investigations, students study a passage, write out what they recall a week later, and then reread the original. A week later they again write from memory and again reread. After a few repetitions the student has developed a statement of his own, with its own emphasis and its own selection of specific content. Elements of content or interpretation not present in the original appear. The passage he writes is much the same from week to week; when he rereads the original passage, he fails to notice how it differs from his version (Kay, 1955; Howe, 1970). This is like what occurs in motor performance. The golfer develops a backswing that differs from that of the model, and he is unlikely to perceive the difference. The teacher can profitably monitor the student's reproduction of information for the same reason that the golf coach monitors the backswing.

---

**10** Sometimes, as in reciting a poem, one wants the reproduction to match the text exactly. Does reconstruction enter the learning process in that case? What must the learner do to avoid altering the text?

**11** The learner "improves" the structure of material he studies. Does this help or hinder a high-school student in his study of an article on a chemical discovery or a historical period?

---

# ACQUIRING VERBAL ASSOCIATIONS

Most learning in school is verbal and consists of linking one concept or name with another. Associative learning is not "rote" learning, as we have seen. Even when nothing more than a pair of arbitrary syllables is presented, the person creates a meaning to connect the pair. Nor is associative learning strictly verbal. Pictorial images are used to make word strings memorable, and verbal chains are used to connect a nonverbal response to an object or event perceived visually.

The intent to remember is important. To be sure, some fraction of the things one observes in passing go into LTM when there is no effort to store them. This is referred to as *incidental learning.* But most of what enters STM escapes, leaving no residue. A student has to work at learning, to store up a significant fraction of the information he encounters during instruction. Active trial is required. The trials may be systematic, as when the student turns through cards with German words on one side and checks his recall of the meaning against the translation on the reverse side. The trials may be casual, as when members of a class learn each other's names; it is the names you respond to often, or use often, that you learn first.

**12** What part do verbal associations play in the following performances?
    a. Tuning an automobile engine
    b. Selecting paint colors for a poster
    c. Finding the third angle of a triangle, given the size of the other two in degrees

ENGAGEMENT    The more actively the learner engages the material, the better he learns it. The youngster who builds a radio set learns more about circuits and transistors than the one who studies a text. The one who discusses the character of Macbeth learns more than one who only watches the action unfold. The

one who speaks French with his classmates, however haltingly, develops fluency faster than the one who only looks at words in a textbook. In every action or remark or reflection on the content, the learner makes an active interpretation and tests his understanding. Out of confirmation comes assurance. Out of contradiction comes correction.

The school sometimes fails to encourage plentiful practice. The lecture method, for instance, makes no provision for overt trial—and very little provision for thought. Likewise, students usually study a text just by reading it over and over. But trying to answer questions put to oneself (self-recitation) produces greater mastery than trying to absorb by reading or listening.

Gates asked one group of students to memorize numerous statements by reading them over and over. Others were told to use a certain portion of the time for active trials, saying back to themselves what they had read. Table 11.4 shows that on this material it was profitable to spend over half the time in reciting. If the material is hard to comprehend, more time has to go into examining the text. With material whose elements are easily perceived—English equivalents of French words, for example—the self-testing can profitably occupy virtually all of the study time.

Engagement may take many forms: rehearsal, looking for meaningful connections, visualizing what is described, thinking of examples, and the like. Di Vesta and Gray (1972) had college students listen to a short talk on an unfamiliar topic, processing the material in various ways: taking notes, reviewing mentally without notes, and taking a test just after the lecture. The student was told to use none, one, two, or all these techniques. At the end of the study period, the student wrote down everything he could recall. Those who had engaged in more study activities recalled more ideas. Each activity seemed to add about equally to recall.

It is unsafe to generalize. Experiments on the value of note-taking—with or without opportunity to review the notes—are amazingly inconsistent (Howe,

TABLE 11.4

Effect on recall of trials during study

| Percentage of study time used in reciting | Average score on test of recall | | |
| --- | --- | --- | --- |
| | Grade III | Grade V | Grade VIII |
| 0 | 4.8 | 7.2 | 9.6 |
| 20 | 5.8 | 8.2 | 11.6 |
| 40 | 8.2 | 10.5 | 15.3 |
| 60 | 9.4 | 12.3 | 15.8 |
| 80 | 8.9 | 10.8 | 15.5 |
| 90 | 8.7 | 11.6 | 14.5 |

SOURCE: Gates (1917).

1972, pp. 60–66). What mode of engagement works best depends on the material, the student's maturity, and how he plans to use the content.

Students trying to learn from a text often do not work with full efficiency. One way to heighten their alertness is to supply test-like questions during their study. These direct attention and arouse motivation. (The procedure can backfire if the students focus so narrowly on the topics of the questions that they neglect other contents—see p. 600.) Boker (1974) supplied students with 20 questions, two for each 250-word section of an assignment. Some students read the questions on a section at its beginning; others encountered the question at the end of the section to which it applied.

A week after studying, the average scores on the questions were as follows:

| | |
|---|---|
| Control group (no questions) | 12.5 |
| Group seeing these questions before reading | 13.8 |
| Group seeing these questions after reading | 15.2 |

Questions placed at the end did the most good. How did the questions influence retention of *other* content of the same sections? Here are the averages on questions not presented during the study period:

| | |
|---|---|
| Control group | 11.5 |
| Group seeing other questions before reading | 10.9 |
| Group seeing other questions after reading | 13.9 |

The group facing questions after reading the text remembered more, even about topics those questions did not touch on.

Such a result has been found by others also (Carroll, 1971). Moreover, questions requiring reflection and interpretation have a greater effect than the simple factual questions Boker used (G. H. Watts & R. C. Anderson, 1971; Rickards & Di Vesta, 1974). No ironclad law can be laid down, however. In some studies, questions before reading prove helpful; in some studies, questions at the end do not pay off. It depends on the content and the students. For the teacher, the proper conclusion is: Questions attached to the text are a technique worth trying.

ANALYSIS AS A SUBSTITUTE FOR OVERT TRIAL   Analysis can substitute for overt trial in associative learning, just as "mental" practice can be profitable in motor learning. Rosenbaum (1967) had some children feel their way through a grooved maze, while others tried to learn by watching them. In order to encourage storage of verbal rules—which are more precise than an image—Rosenbaum numbered the branches at each choice point. The child could learn the path by fixing the right series of numbers in mind. During the practice trials, a light went on as soon as the performer entered the right alley—an immediate confirming signal. There were three groups of subjects. One group of active performers (Group 1) simply did their best to locate the right path on trial after trial. They could use the numbers but they did not have to. Performers in Group 2 were directed to say aloud the number of the branch chosen as soon as the light signaled it as correct. They thus brought the label back into STM. Group 2 outdid Group 1.

The observers (Group 3) did best of all on the final test—which was their first actual performance. The observer had merely watched a member of Group 2 on every trial and listened to what he said. The performer in Group 2 had to do several things—hazard a choice, place the stylus, watch for the light, recover from an error. This probably distracted him, whereas the observer was free to concentrate on rehearsing the critical verbal information. Bruner et al. (1959) report a similar finding. When a task can be performed accurately if one just gives the right verbal orders to oneself, overt practice is generally an inefficient way to learn (but see p. 512).

The zoology student would be expected to learn more anatomy by watching a film of a dissection than by trying to think and dissect at the same time. Either way, it is important that he encode the experience verbally. Perhaps he should watch a film once while the sound track describes what is seen, and then watch it again supplying his own commentary. (Recall Thompson's study, Table 10.2; see also p. 510 on learning from visual presentations.)

Overt practice during study of history, arithmetic, and so on has two chief values. It guarantees attention and engagement; and it brings responses into the open, where they can be judged. In the past decade, however, psychologists have been surprised to discover that "covert" practice often works just as well. The programmed-instruction movement was one of the "big ideas" of education in the 1960s. An offshoot of Skinner's behavioristic research, it was based on three principles:

> Master one micro-objective after another, advancing in easy steps through carefully organized content.
>
> Make many overt responses; usually one per sentence of explanation.
>
> Find out at once that the response is correct or incorrect.

These ideas are useful in planning instruction, but they are not universal rules for effective learning. (We shall see [p. 544] that the person can learn when he organizes material for himself, and that it sometimes is better not to correct each response as it is made [p. 619].)

Our concern at the moment is with the "overt-response" principle. Students who fill in the response blanks in programmed text—overt response—have been compared with others who simply study the same sentences with all the "responses" printed in. Differences between such groups are not large and do not run consistently in either direction. The explanation is that the student can actively think about the filled-in text, his responses being "covert." Engagement can be as great in this mental practice as in "overt" practice.

The trial-and-confirmation principle is valid whether the trial is overt or covert. Truly overt response has its greatest value under the following conditions (Levie & Dickie, in Travers, 1973, p. 876):

> Where the task calls for forming a new response or for choosing between responses that are quite similar (as in pronouncing words in a foreign language).

> Where the response is executed sequentially, and one response provides cues for the next. (Especially true of motor skills, and of chained responses in speech.)

> Where the material is hard to grasp, so that many corrections are required.

> Where there is much to be studied, so that motivation is likely to fade before completion.

> Where the learner lacks interest or confidence, so that external encouragement is needed.

OVERLEARNING AND REVIEW  Most students are satisfied with their study when they stop making errors. If their practice or study ends there, they may find it hard to recall the material after time has passed. If they have additional occasions to deal with the same information, they will learn it so thoroughly that it always comes quickly to mind. Consider the alphabet. As a child you chanted the alphabet, recited it, used it a thousand ways in schoolwork. When the alphabet is called for, you rattle it off easily, for it has been "overlearned." Crystallized knowledge (p. 285) is laid down firmly when a person continues to use a response repeatedly, with confirmation.

Judd and Glaser (1969) see two phases in the learning of verbal associations: first, the responses are "acquired"—that is, matched to their stimuli; second, the connections are made more direct and automatic, and tied to other parts of the mental network. It is during the overlearning period, after surface mastery has been attained, that quickness, sureness, and permanence of association are improved.

Nearly all the research on overlearning of intellectual associations has used syllable pairs or mazes. In one study, college students learned a maze; on the average, it took 4.6 trials to reach an errorless run. Students who stopped practicing as soon as they got the path correct required 3.6 trials (average) to relearn the maze four days later. Those who practiced four or five extra times on the first occasion needed only 2.3 trials to recapture their learning. The extra trials strengthened the associations (Krueger, 1930).

Even when the person seemingly has mastered a lesson, as judged by test performance, he can improve with further practice. Among those who "know the answer" to a question, there are degrees of expertness. As with a motor skill, the difference between the expert and the modestly trained person is the greater ability of the expert to respond promptly and soundly under adverse conditions (p. 190). The person who has not thoroughly mastered an association (recognizing a cedar waxwing, for instance) has more trouble than the expert when discrimination becomes difficult (for example, in poor light). Also, weak associations are more subject to interference. The person who half-learns to name one bird later learns names for other birds; the responses compete. Extensive practice—overlearning—makes interference less likely.

When an association is stored and then not used, retrieval becomes more difficult. Whether the decline is severe or slight depends on the thoroughness and meaningfulness of the original learning. The way to keep associations alive and ready for quick recall, obviously, is to reduce the period of disuse. Sometimes a school lesson is used in the work of each succeeding week, though not at the focus of attention. That use strengthens the learning. Sometimes a topic is considered for two or three weeks and then set aside. The history lessons may discuss the French and Spanish explorers of the North American continent and then pick up the story of the English colonies. In the succeeding months the students have no occasion to think of LaSalle and Coronado; the conditions are ideal for losing touch with the material.

Where it is inefficient to make lessons cumulative, reviews are required to keep the knowledge alive. The review, like the original learning, should be more a matter of active trial than of passive rereading or listening. Retrieval (or relearning) is more rapid when the interval of disuse has been short. This seems to argue for scheduling fairly frequent reviews of material that is not in regular use, insofar as time can be spared from new learning.

**13** In which of the following would overt response appear to be important?
  a. A high-school student wants to understand Morse code so that he can listen in on short-wave transmissions of plain language messages.
  b. A soldier is being trained to take down Morse messages that are coded as meaningless groups of five letters, not words.
  c. A high-school student has a part in a play to memorize.
  d. A geometry student must prove a number of theorems about parallel lines.

**14** Judd and Glaser speak of two phases of associative learning. Compare their concept with the Fitts-Posner stages of motor learning (p. 398).

**15** After David Starr Jordan, a zoologist, had been president of Stanford University for a time, he complained about the effect of his new duties on his career. "Everytime I learn the name of a student," he said, "I forget the name of a fish." Do you think he did lose some of his knowledge? Explain your answer in terms of principles in this chapter.

**16** Questions before reading and questions placed at the end evidently have different effects on how the student processes what he reads. What effects on attention and other processes do you expect each type of question to have?

**17** Physicians in training study many facts on physiology. They no doubt overlearn the most fundamental ideas, but details are too numerous for overlearning. Would it be advisable for them to take systematic refresher courses on such basic sciences throughout their careers?

**18** In which of the following kinds of learning would observation—with verbal encoding—probably be superior to direct trial?
a. Learning the names of strangers at a reception. (Compare the greeter with the wallflower within earshot of the greeter.)
b. Learning to conjugate *être*
c. Fixing in mind the provisions of the Bill of Rights

## Organizing Content for Storage

Retrieval and reconstruction depend on the connections of stimulus and response to other items in memory. Therefore it is advantageous to build up a strong organization at the time the material is learned. Content that has been consciously grouped into categories or arranged in a network is more rapidly learned and resists interference (Tulving, 1974).

The principle applies to learning from a text or from a lecture. The student who perceives only separate items has a forbidding number of elements to riffle through when the time for retrieval comes. The student who pays attention to the outline of topics retrieves the answer to a test question more quickly because he can concentrate his search in the relevant sector. The teacher or textbook writer assists study when he makes the outline of ideas evident. A good pedagogical device is to display the lecture outline before the talk begins; section headings in a text serve similarly.

A class discussion rarely sticks to a systematic order of topics, but the teacher can provide a structure when summing up. If the writer or teacher does not lay out the structure, the student ought to formulate one during the first review of his notes.

A student can "make sense out of" most associations he has to learn in school. He could simply memorize the date at which Stravinsky introduced his most innovative music. But if he knows more about the evolution of orchestral music, he will know that Stravinsky capitalized on a century of development of instruments and of orchestral color. Moreover, Stravinsky came at a time when sculptors, painters, and architects were deliberately violating traditional rules of

*(text continues on p. 472)*

## Awareness of connections holds scattered information in place

A memory experiment presented 51 words to be recalled after four minutes of study (Wittrock & Carter, 1975). In each of six conditions, a hierarchical display was used to present the word list. The diagram shows part of a "proper" hierarchy, an arrangement that makes sense. In the scrambled condition these same words appeared in other locations. The words were placed haphazardly, with some of the more specific words in the "main heading" boxes. The third version used miscellaneous words picked hit-or-miss from the dictionary; these did not fall naturally into categories. These three presentations were crossed with two response conditions (table).

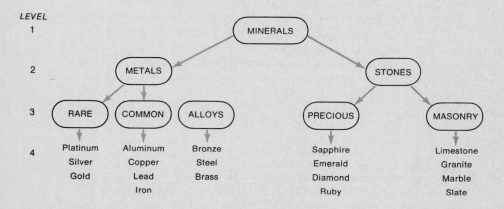

SOURCE: Bower et al. (1969).

Half the students were told to copy the lists during the four-minute study period. Among the copiers, those who worked with organized material had a great superiority on the test of recall that followed.

The second half of the students were directed to look for connections. They were to shift the words into a sensible structure and then to copy it. With every type of list, this active analysis greatly increased the amount learned. Having an organized list was not important when students were finding connections themselves.

The mean number of words recalled on the test was as follows:

|  | Unrelated list | Scrambled hierarchy | Proper hierarchy |
|---|---|---|---|
| Copying | 6 | 11 | 17 |
| Analyzing and copying | 13 | 21 | 22 |

composition. It was no accident that the *Sacre du printemps* was introduced in 1913; Stravinsky's piece was an expression of the times. It is not profitable to trace out such a long explanation if only a single date is to be learned; but into this kind of intellectual map, dozens of composers and artistic innovations can be fitted. Once the learner sees how one event contributed to another, it is nearly impossible for him to reconstruct their dates in a wrong order (Linton, 1975).

You will recall the Brownell-Moser finding (p. 122) that subtraction rules, taught meaningfully, were better retained than rules learned only by rehearsal and application. Similar meaningful teaching of fractions to second-graders proved highly advantageous (H. Moser, 1947). The teacher showed the children how the several concepts and procedures fitted together. Performance actually improved in the weeks after instruction on fractions ended. The students had found fractions so much fun that they made up problems for themselves, "playing" with fractions and so learning more and more. The children understood what they were doing, were successful rather than baffled, and so learned to enjoy manipulating fractions.

The quality of the student's errors often shows whether he is analyzing for meaning (Clinchy & Rosenthal, in Lesser, 1971). An answer may be far off the mark and still good if it shows that the student is using sound principles. When Alice writes *squrrl*, this "error" shows that she understands the spelling-sound relations of English. When Beth gives *strign* for *string*, a teacher suspects a serious problem; she has not learned to test spelling by pronouncing what she has written.

When the associations have no logical structure (box, p. 472) or where the structure is hard to fix in mind, mnemonic devices are useful. A passport number—G216566—is hard to remember. Code it into an optimistic sentence: "Going, in a silver plane safely flying," and the right numbers are easily retrieved. The steps in converting a compass heading to a true heading are not arbitrary but they are hard to keep straight: "Start with Compass, apply Deviation, get Magnetic course, and apply Variation to get True course." The time-tested mnemonic of student navigators, Stephens (1961) tells us, is Can Dead Men Vote Twice? For the reverse, the true-into-compass conversion, students have little trouble remembering that True Virgins Make Dull Company.

**19** Here is a mnemonic for the value of $\pi$ (pi): "See, I have a rhyme assisting my feeble brain its tasks ofttimes resisting." Does this really make the learning easier, or is learning the rhyme as much work as rehearsing the digit string? Should the mnemonic be given to students when they start to use $\pi$?

One evening we were entertaining a visiting colleague, a social psychologist of broad interests, and our discussion turned to Plans. "But exactly what is a Plan?" he asked. "How can you say that *memorizing* depends on Plans?"

"We'll show you," we replied. "Here is a Plan that you can use for memorizing. Remember first that:

> one is a bun,
> two is a shoe,
> three is a tree,
> four is a door,
> five is a hive,
> six are sticks,
> seven is heaven,
> eight is a gate,
> nine is a line, and
> ten is a hen."

"You know, even though it is only ten-thirty here, my watch says one-thirty. I'm really tired, and I'm sure I'll ruin your experiment."

"Don't worry, we have no real stake in it." We tightened our grip on his lapel. "Just relax and remember the rhyme. Now you have part of the Plan. The second part works like this: when we tell you a word, you must form a ludicrous or bizarre association with the first word in your list, and so on with the ten words we recite to you."

"Really, you know, it'll never work. I'm awfully tired," he replied.

"Have no fear," we answered, "just remember the rhyme and then form the association. Here are the words:

1. ashtray,
2. firewood,
3. picture,
4. cigarette,
5. table,
6. matchbook,
7. glass,
8. lamp,
9. shoe,
10. phonograph."

The words were read one at a time, and after reading the word, we waited until he announced that he had the association. It took about five seconds on the average to form the connection. After the seventh word he said that he was sure the first six were already forgotten. But we persevered.

After one trial through the list, we waited a minute or two so that he could collect himself and ask any questions that came to mind. Then we said, "What is number eight?"

He stared blankly, and then a smile crossed his face, "I'll be damned," he said. "It's 'lamp.'"

"And what number is cigarette?"

He laughed outright now, and then gave the correct answer.

"And there is no strain," he said, "absolutely no sweat."

We proceeded to demonstrate that he could in fact name every word correctly, and then asked, "Do you think that memorizing consists of piling up increments of response strength that accumulate as the words are repeated?" The question was lost in his amazement.

SOURCE: *Plans and the Structure of Behavior* by George A. Miller, Eugene Galanter, and Karl H. Pribram. Copyright © 1960 by Holt, Rinehart and Winston, Inc. Reprinted by permission of Holt, Rinehart and Winston.

## Discrimination

We return now to the perceptual processes by which one interprets the situation before him. A person has developed a repertoire of discriminations and concepts he can bring to bear. When he recognizes a situation as representing a certain concept, he can bring to bear his associations regarding that concept. Verbal associations are of little use unless one knows when to use them. The garden book, for example, says that chlorosis in plants is a condition in which leaves turn yellow because of a deficiency of iron. To make use of this knowledge, the gardener has to discriminate the chlorotic leaves from leaves that are naturally yellow or have dried up. Likewise, he must know that "iron" refers to iron in its ionic combining form, not to metallic iron.

As was said at the start of the chapter, to discriminate is to recognize similarities and differences. In the simplest experiments, the elements to be compared are fixed (the cross and circle of the House-Zeaman experiment, for example). Outside the laboratory, however, objects or figures of the same kind vary. A physician, for example, must learn to classify tracings of electrical currents from the heart muscles to recognize three types of disorders. The "characteristic" features of the three disorders are seen at the top of Fig. 11.4; they are readily distinguished. Actual tracings, however, are diverse, and the patterns can occur in combination. Try your skill at recognizing the four patterns in the

**FIGURE 11.4**

Four ideal patterns used in teaching recognition of heart disease, and four tracings of actual heart action

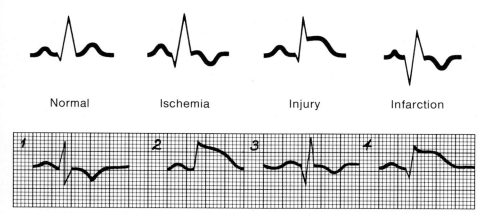

Normal          Ischemia          Injury          Infarction

SOURCE: The ideal patterns are from Tobias (1968), the tracings from Mechner (1965).

## The sounds keen ears miss

Sonarmen interpret underwater sounds picked up from a distance by a submarine's listening gear. Some sounds are almost unmistakable: the high-pitched hiss from a bed of shrimp, the crunch-crunch-crunch-crunch of a freighter's slow propeller. But some are deceptive. The four beats of a freighter's blades, if not recognized as a group, sound like four complete turns of a warship's screws. The distinguishing feature is the accent—sometimes only a slight one—that marks off the repetitive four-beat pattern of the freighter. Instructors have to help students find the beat by telling them what to listen for, then by "beating the time" visually.

At a time when I was developing training exercises for sonarmen, experienced men coming back from the fleet told us that they could discriminate whether a distant ship was coming closer or opening the range. If new sonarmen could be trained to make such reports they would be of considerable help to the captain. Our first step was a kind of blindfold test on some of the men who claimed to detect direction. Aboard a sub, the captain would pick a target through his periscope, give the sonarman its bearing, and ask him to report its heading. We did find a couple of men who were able to judge the heading most of the time.

What distinguishing features were they using? They tried to tell us in words—something about a "crackle." The rest of us could not hear it. High-fidelity records of the same ship going and coming sounded alike to us. Passing the sound through filters and tracing the energy pattern for high-pitched sounds and low-pitched sounds gave us a physical analysis. Sure enough, when the ship was approaching, there were very brief, intense spikes of energy in the high-frequency tracings.* These spikes we could detect—yes, as "crackles"—when we were listening closely *and* could see on the tracing just where the delicate sound was going to appear.

That became the basis for the training technique. We prepared drills in which the listener had to say "coming" or "going" in a trial-and-correction mode. But we also produced demonstration records with examples of the crackle. As such a record was played, the instructor displayed a photographic blowup of the visual tracing. The instructor's pointer enabled the men to match sound cue to picture. Even this much aid did not make the learning easy. The man still had to pick out the spike of sound for himself, and extensive drills were required before he could do it.

---

* The spikes could not be heard from astern of the ship because the bubbles in the ship's wake diffused the energy of the sound.

lifelike tracings shown in the lower row. The correct answers appear at the end of the chapter.

To discriminate, the learner has to pick out "distinctive features" that mark a particular object or kind of object (E. J. Gibson, 1969). The distinctive feature of ischemia, for example, is the inversion in the last wave of the tracing, combined with the absence of a major downward spike. A cue such as that enables the physician to recognize the presence of ischemia no matter what configuration it is imbedded in. Distinctive features often enable you to recognize or classify an object you could not describe fully or draw adequately. (What are the distinctive features of the appearance of George Washington?)

After much practice in discriminating a particular figure, the person may develop an image far more complete and unified than the isolated features he initially relied on. Probably as a schoolchild you first thought of the sign 𝄞 (treble clef) as "something like an S" or "something like a dollar sign." Even that crude an analysis enables you to distinguish it from the 𝄢 (bass clef). After you encountered the treble clef sign repeatedly, you stored up an image, or template, which enables you to recall what the sign looks like and to write it more or less exactly. Similarly, you have a template stored for the figure "circle" that enables you to judge, without measurement, whether an object is appreciably out of round.

Selection of distinctive features, and formation of a template, are most easily illustrated with visual examples, but the other senses function similarly. You learn distinctive features of clarinet and sax, of tweeds and velvets, of dill and nutmeg. More abstract concepts develop similarly. Sedimentary rocks, baroque concertos, and torts—concepts in geology, music, and law—are names that mark off one set of instances from others that are superficially similar. The crucial cues must be recognized in each new instance.

Some discriminations are rather easy, but important differences may be hard to detect (box). You will recall that Williams's preschool children (p. 110) had great difficulty in recognizing a letter-like form. Focusing children's attention by requiring them to copy the forms did not teach the discriminations. Practice at matching the forms did improve discrimination.

Students will not necessarily hit on the most useful distinctive features unless they are properly challenged, as R. O. Nelson and K. S. Wein (1974) demonstrated. They had children match letters. Some letter-pairs are highly confusable, whereas others cause little trouble. Some children (LC group) were trained with low-confusion alternatives (say, match M to one of these: Q L M). The average child needed three practice sessions before he could make all the matches without error. The other children (HC) were given such challenging tasks as matching M to the right element in M N W. The HCs required six sessions (on average) to earn perfect scores. On a final test with both hard and easy items, the HCs did appreciably better. The nature of the errors deserves notice. When M was mismatched on the test, was it mismatched with a high-confusion (HC) letter or a low-confusion (LC) letter? The error counts were as follows:

Group trained with HC alternatives: 3.8 HC errors, 0.3 LC errors.

Group trained with LC alternatives: 8.8 HC errors, 0.1 LC errors.

Each kind of training reduced both kinds of errors, but the HC training paid off best. HC errors are numerous, hence more important to reduce.

A challenge in another medium is illustrated in the photo. Students making pots while blindfolded came to realize how many useful cues their fingertips and muscles could pick up (Mueller, 1975). Without being forced into difficult discriminations, they would not have realized the significance of nonvisual cues.

**20** In the House-Zeaman experiment, children benefited from comparatively easy training. In the Nelson-Wein experiment, comparatively hard tasks gave best results. Are the results truly contradictory, or can you fit them into a general explanation?

**21** In the Nelson-Wein experiment, the LC group received fewer training sessions. What do you think would have happened if the three LC sessions had been followed by three additional LC sessions for "overlearning"? What if the three LC sessions had been followed by three HC sessions?

**22** In high-school geometry, what are the distinctive features of each of these?
  a. A perpendicular
  b. A diagonal

**23** Is it possible for a student to rely on a wrong feature in the instances in Question 23? Do distinctive features correspond to the elements in a verbal definition?

## Perceiving Patterns

Interpretation of a situation is not merely a process of recognizing, one by one, the objects in it. On the contrary, the skilled interpreter discriminates configurations or patterns—a chunking process. He leaves close examination until later and neglects some elements altogether. When you watch a football play unfold you do not perceive 22 men and track their movements. You are aware of two opposing groups; you are aware of the offensive backs as a subgroup, and become aware that a shift piles power toward the right. You note the handoff from quarterback to someone else, and watch a defender cut into the charging pack and bring down the ball carrier. Not more than three or four individuals caught your attention. You saw swarms and thrusts of opposing power. A perceptual whole is not a sum of parts; it is a unified pattern.

A person imposes order wherever he can, identifying familiar, orderly patterns. More than that, he imposes the pattern even where it fits poorly. Perception is a continual matching of a complex reality to patterns or templates previously learned. Nothing is perceived in exact detail, as a camera plate would register the image. Our minds always turn to the simplest pattern that will summarize the main cues we notice.

Structuring is a source of error in initial intake of information, just as it was in the delayed recall of Bartlett's subjects (p. 461). The pattern imposed may neglect vital details, it may distort relations, and it may freeze interpretation prematurely. One observes only as carefully as immediate goals require. A student learns that North and South America are in the Western Hemisphere, that Miami is on the Atlantic Ocean, and Valparaiso, Chile, on the Pacific. Through his years of encounters with maps and globes, he is unlikely to recognize—until somebody lures him into a bet on the matter—that Miami is west of Valparaiso. He thinks of the continents as arranged on a north-south line, and ignores the general easterly slant as one goes south because he has never needed to examine that relation.

Treacherous though it can be, patterning generally produces a net gain. A patterned perception that is not entirely valid will take in more information than one gets when attempting to do without patterns.

Ability to find structure amid complexity is a mark of the expert, to be added to our list from Chapter 10. The advantage of the chess expert (box) is not a greater mental capacity but an ability to organize. He holds more in mind at once. The several chunks, suspended in his thought at the same time, give him a sense of the balance of forces, the weak points, and the strong points. The beginner notices numerous elements and few combinations; he is unable to think about the battle in the large.

In any complex display the experienced person looks for the chief sections, the dominant elements, the lines of force or linkage. His display space can hold only so much, and he is skillful in neglecting the elements that matter least. Figure 11.5 shows the circuit diagram for an audio amplifier; a thicket of details bewilders the untrained eye. A person who tries to decode all the elements ( ⌇⌇⌇ is a resistor, for example) can do so quickly enough, but he learns no more about the circuit than he would if he saw all the pieces loose on the bench, before assembly. The more experienced eye is likely to note first that the left third seems to constitute a unit. Its function must be distinct—yes, "bass" and "treble" labels tell us that this subunit is the tone control. The two

**FIGURE 11.5**

Schematic wiring diagram of an audio amplifier

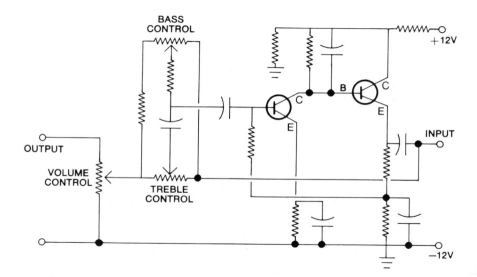

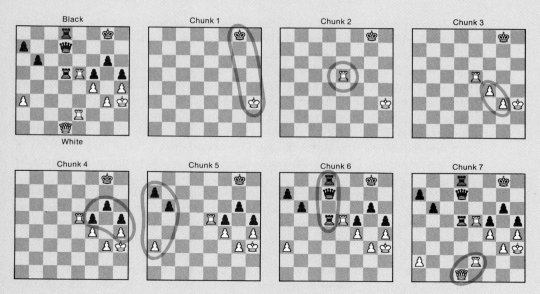

SOURCE: Chess layout from Reinfeld (1945); remaining figures adapted from Chase (1972), pp. 221 and 235.

A chess master studied the diagram at the upper left for five seconds. Then, from memory, he placed pieces on a board to duplicate what he had seen (Chase & Simon, in Chase, 1972, pp. 215–81). When a few pieces were set down in quick succession, the investigators assumed that those pieces had been stored in memory as a "chunk." The pauses as he laid out the pattern suggested that he had formed seven chunks. The master was far more successful at recall than weaker players. His ability to remember was traced back to his ability to form larger chunks and to reproduce them before STM went blank.

The master's superior memory apparently is to be credited to his "vocabulary" of familiar patterns. He was given successive trials at reproducing a middle-game position like the one shown at the upper left; his average performance on such tasks is labeled "real boards" in the chart. Second, the master was given several trials at learning a board with pieces scattered at random. A player with little chess experience tried the same tasks. As the chart shows, whether the display "made sense" did not affect the beginner's success. The master's performance was poor, however, when the pattern violated his experience.

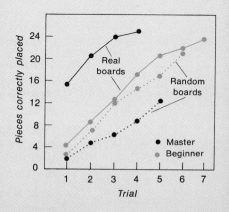

479

heavy circles indicate transistors; the right-hand section, then, is a two-stage amplifier. With this overall pattern in mind, the person can move to smaller elements, perhaps noting next the three resistors with arrows that are the "moving parts" of the control system.

Ability to resolve a complex display into a structure arises from familiarity with many variations of a particular kind of display (wiring diagrams, for example). This is the same process of extracting concepts from experience that was discussed in Chapter 8 (p. 334). The experienced person develops a stock of concepts that identify units and configurations (tone control and direction of flow, for example). Teachers of course teach many of these organizing concepts explicitly.

How large a structure should students try to deal with? Is it profitable to comprehend the parts before looking at the whole? The whole is often too much to grasp; even the master has to think of a chess game in terms of phases and episodes. Parts often lose their meaning if examined out of context: what looks like an even exchange of pawns at the left of the board may be injudicious if it adds to the burden of a bishop at the far right. The best general maxim is "Wholes before parts, the largest wholes the person can comprehend." From a psychological point of view, a functional whole is something that can be understood by itself. A movement in a symphony is, in that sense, a whole; only a highly sophisticated listener thinks about relations across movement boundaries. The New Deal—like any other segment of history—is linked to movements of previous decades or even centuries. But in the student's first attempt to comprehend it, a superficial summary of the 1920s provides as much orientation as he can use.

---

**24** Illustrate the concept of a "vocabulary" of structures, or patterns, in each of these contexts:
  a. A chart shows the lineage of English kings appearing in Shakespeare's works.
  b. An anthropologist observes the culture of a village.
  c. A critic listens to an unfamiliar violin concerto.

**25** The scientist tries to report exactly what he sees. In observing, say, a butterfly emerging from a cocoon, can he record all the elementary facts? To what extent is patterning likely to distort or omit information?

**26** What principles seemed to determine what the chess master (box) grouped into the same chunk? How much attention did he pay to the tactical situation? (For example, White's queen is threatened, and one of White's castles is attacking a Black castle).

**27** Why did the master recall a random chess board less well than the beginner?

---

## Concept attainment

FRED BASSET by Alex Graham, © Associated Newspapers Group Ltd. 1975,
Dist. Field Newspaper Syndicate, 1975

## Verbal Concepts

Verbal concepts play a key role in perception, remembering, and thinking.
Cues for which a person lacks verbal labels are comparatively hard to use
(Klausmeier et al., 1974).

Unfortunately, concepts misrepresent reality, exaggerating similarities and
differences just as perceptual patterns do. Thus, we may try to reason exactly
with words that are inexact representations of events. A foreign policy is sure
to go wrong, for example, if it looks on "developing countries" as just about
alike. When the government finances an agricultural experiment station, that is
called "government spending"; when a corporation that sells hybrid corn finances a field station, that is called "a capital investment." When such labels
create artificial differences or paste a stereotyped interpretation on unlike
events, unsound conclusions follow.

Each concept is created by the individual from his own experience. Misun-
derstandings arise when two persons match the same word to different concepts. What is your understanding of the range of numbers included in the
meaning of *several?* More than three? Five to nine? Where does *few* end and *several* begin? People differ in their understanding of *several,* and this impedes
communication. In particular, it causes trouble in instruction, when the student's meaning for a term does not coincide with that of the teacher or textbook writer.

A concept is at first impressionistic, associated with some cues that are
truly pertinent and some that are not sound bases for discrimination. Most of
our everyday, nontechnical concepts are left in this primitive stage. A *lake* is a
body of water—6-year-olds know that. But how big does the body have to be
before the term can properly be applied? How big may it get before we must
call it something else? Here is a vast body with no inlet or outlet; can we call it

a *lake* even if the map calls it Salton Sea? How about Devil's Lake, which has no stream flowing in or out but is said to be filled by an underground river? What shall we call a *lake*?

In one sense, a person has attained a concept when he can discriminate the situations to which it *does* apply from all the rest. The learner has to identify a kind of distinctive feature—perhaps an abstract one rather than one that can be directly perceived. Discrimination is only a part of concept development, but it is a critical part. Most often, a word is first encountered in a specific context. The student learns to match it with that exemplar, and then gradually stretches it when he finds it being used for other objects or phenomena.

The child hears that Sacramento is the capital of his state, that Washington is the capital of the nation. As Eskridge's data show (Table 11.5), initial mean-

### TABLE 11.5

Refinement of concepts with increasing experience

| | Percentage of students who choose each alternative | | | |
| --- | --- | --- | --- | --- |
| | Grade IV | Grade V | Grade VI | Grade VII |
| The *capital* of a country means | | | | |
| 1. The chief seaport of the country | 2 | 1 | 0 | 2 |
| 2. The city which is nearest the middle of the country | 7 | 12 | 13 | 4 |
| 3. The largest city of the country | 28 | 12 | 16 | 7 |
| 4. **The city where most of the government work is done** | **42** | **64** | **62** | **86** |
| "I don't know," omitted, or other answer written in | 21 | 11 | 8 | 1 |
| If people have *communication* with each other, that means | | | | |
| 1. They write letters to each other | 6 | 4 | 3 | 1 |
| 2. They telephone each other | 8 | 4 | 6 | 3 |
| 3. They talk with each other | 38 | 29 | 31 | 17 |
| 4. **They have some way of exchanging information** | **13** | **17** | **46** | **70** |
| "I don't know," omitted, or other answer written in | 35 | 46 | 14 | 9 |

SOURCE: After Eskridge (1939), pp. 52 and 58.

ings are likely to be rough approximations. A person develops only as precise a meaning as he must—which is just what was said earlier about perception. When misconceptions lead to trial responses that fail, concepts are sharpened. It was not until Grade VII that the children who had settled on too narrow a meaning for *communication* got into instructive difficulty. Initial meanings may focus on a feature irrelevant to the concept. Asked to say what *west coast* means, Eskridge's fourth-graders said, "The west coast of Norway is rocky and hilly. *Natives* are "a black race of people that live in Africa."

Fuzzy concepts are disastrous in technical subjects, since technical principles become untrue if words are used loosely. Most applications of principles require exact interpretations of terms: *friction, denominator, participle, freedom of speech,* and so on. To take advantage of a verbal principle, one must first discriminate: "Does this term apply here or doesn't it?" To multiply fractions, the student is told to multiply the numerators and the denominators. But in $1^3/_4 \times {}^2/_5$, what are the numerators? To many students, the distinctive feature of the *numerator* is that it is "the number on top." Ergo, the numerators are 3 and 2—and the answer is wrong.

Is a verbal concept going to be important to the student? Then he ought to see its range of application quite early. Presenting fractions in one standard form, for example, makes it comparatively easy to learn appropriate responses. But this approach leads to difficulty later if the student encodes his ideas about numerators around features that appear only in the standard form.

Often, a verbal definition is not enough to communicate the concept. Comprehending the definition may itself be difficult. Definitions are succinct and are designed to help the person whose concept is almost correct rather than the novice (Olson, 1970). Learning proceeds better when the definition is simplified to suit the learner's maturity. Presenting the definition along with varied exemplars and nonexemplars is much more effective than presenting just a definition *or* exemplars (Feldman & Klausmeier, 1974; Klausmeier & Feldman, 1975). A single example is rarely sufficient. Diverse exemplars and nonexemplars are required to bring out the distinctive features. After any important concept is introduced, the teacher ought to present a further mixture of exemplars and nonexemplars for the student to classify, so as to check whether discrimination is adequate.

Many fundamental concepts, including Piagetian schemata (p. 328), have to be extracted from long experience. Right versus left is one of those concepts that the person must feel inside himself, and so is the physical, invariant shape or color of an object, as distinct from the object's transient appearance.

Acquiring a concept is more than discriminating where to apply a label. Around the label, a system of meanings and beliefs develops. When a person recognizes that one of his concepts fits the object or scene before him, the associations linked to the concept in his mind permit him to state a great variety of interpretations and expectations. Take the fact that rubber is elastic. A child who mentions a few uses of rubber, such as rubber bands, shows minimal comprehension. He shows greater comprehension when he thinks of using rub-

## "Discrimination is happy and not happy"

A social concept such as "racial discrimination" can be defined in words, but only living with the concept generates a full-blooded meaning. The definition in the title was written by a third-grader after his class had been living under discriminatory rules for two days.

Teacher Jane Elliott designed the activity for a school in an Iowa town where few blacks lived (W. Peters, 1971). News events arising from the civil rights struggle had been discussed by the children without much understanding. "Suppose," Mrs. Elliott then suggested, "that we make the rule for today that blue-eyed people are inferior. We can see what discrimination is like. Then tomorrow we can try it with the brown eyes inferior." A simple game; the class agreed. Mrs. Elliott started the first day with deadpan statements to the effect that Brown Eyes are smarter and more dependable. Cleaner too. Given that, rules were agreed on: row leaders are to be Brown Eyes, Brown Eyes sit up front, Blue Eyes are to wear blue-paper collars, Brown Eyes enter the lunch room first and may have second helpings, and so on.

As the day progressed, both children and teacher kept up the game. When a Brown Eye did something wrong, the criticism included a reference to eye color.

ber for tasks where he has not previously seen it used. (Perhaps a piece of old inner tube makes a spring for a door.) The chemistry student can go on to explain that rubber stretches because its very long molecules can pull out and coil up again. With still deeper understanding, the chemist goes on to explain why the molecule is a coil. There is no end to improving one's understanding. The meanings of a concept—intellectual and emotional—grow as the student lives with the concept (box).

**28** For Piaget, a concept is "an imagined action" (p. 342). Can this idea be applied to the concept of *west coast?* of *mammal?*

**29** In teaching a concept, instances and a verbal rule *combined* generally have advantages over either one alone (M. D. Merrill & R. C. Boutwell, 1973, p. 119). Under what circumstances would the combination not be needed?

The smug girl in the photo is Brown Eye Susan Ginder. Mrs. Elliott has just re-proved a Blue Eye who forgot his glasses: "Susan has brown eyes. She didn't forget her glasses." By lunch time, the Brown Eyes clearly believed that they were superior, and the Blue Eyes lined up for lunch behind them with a hangdog shuffle.

Next day the story was reversed, the Blue Eyes being given all the privileges. The tensions remained the same. The Brown Eyes quickly forgot yesterday's advantages as they found that today they could do nothing right. John Bentine, in the second photo, has just been hauled out of a playground scuffle. Yes, he admits, I hit Russell. "Hit him in the gut. Russell called me names." What name? "Brown Eyes."

The activity ended with a round-up discussion on the following day, and with the writing of compositions on discrimination. Ted Perzynski's composition ended:

> I do not like discrimination. It makes me sad. I would not like to be angry all my life.

**30** Into what categories is reading matter commonly divided in high-school English courses? Do these categories influence pupils' attitudes?

**31** Choose one of the following pairs of terms and show that a continuous variable would describe the underlying phenomenon better. (Example: *level of business activity,* a continuous variable, is more accurate than the categories *prosperity–depression.*)

    inherited–acquired   prose–poetry   stable–neurotic

**32** To reduce the fraction $\frac{6}{8}$, some teachers would speak of "canceling." Others would teach to "divide both numerator and denominator by two." When the student encounters

$$\frac{6x + 2}{2}$$

which concept is most helpful?

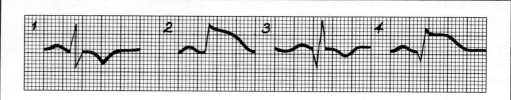

Classification of traces in Figure 11.4:

Trace 1 shows ischemia;
Traces 2 and 4, injury;
Trace 3 shows infarction.

 READING LIST

Eleanor J. Gibson, "The Ontogeny of Reading," *American Psychologist* 25 (1970), 136–43. Also in Rosenblith (1973).

> The perceptual problems the young child faces in reading are discussea. Gibson's experiments indicate how children learn to break up words and recognize letter combinations. She concludes that the child can acquire a "set to look for structures," which assists him in learning to read.

Ulric Neisser and John A. Hupcey, "A Sherlockian Experiment," *Cognition* 3 (1975), 307–12.

> Members of the Baker Street Underground, devotees of Holmes, were asked to identify stories from which test sentences came. Only sentences that were concrete in reference and central to the plot were identified with the right story. The usual path of retrieval was that the sentence suggested an incident in which it might have occurred, the incident suggested the story line, and then the title could be recalled.

Donald A. Norman and David E. Rumelhart, "Memory and Knowledge," in *Explorations in Cognition,* Norman and Rumelhart, eds. (San Francisco: Freeman, 1975), pp. 3–32.

> An introductory presentation of frontier thinking of experimental psychologists. Among the topics covered are structures in memory, errors in reproduction of visual experience from memory, and comprehension of language.

William D. Rohwer, Jr., "Prime Time for Learning: Early Childhood or Adolescence?" *Harvard Educational Review* 41 (1971), 316–41.

> Reports an investigation that contrasts several procedures for memorizing, each consistent with a different theoretical view of learning. The larger message of the article is this dramatic hypothesis: Western culture is wrong to make mastery of verbal lessons a developmental task at age 6.

Asahel D. Woodruff, "How Music Concepts Are Developed," *Music Educators Journal* 56 (1970), 51–54. Reprinted in Clarizio (1974).

> Woodruff emphasizes the importance of nonverbal experience, including affective response, in the formation of concepts, and suggests the kinds of instruction that will promote growth in concepts. Ideas and feelings about music are used as examples.

# 12

# THE STUDENT'S COMMUNICATIONS, AND THE SCHOOL'S

The school communicates to the student in many ways: through printed materials, through the words of the adults in the classroom, through audiovisual presentations, and through practice exercises. The first section of the chapter considers how language develops outside the school, and the skills and shortcomings the child brings to school; then it examines ways to improve language skills. Language is the principal medium of exchange between the student and the school. Writing and speaking are skills, having much psychological resemblance to the motor skills treated in Chapter 10. When a person produces a verbal statement, he has in mind a template or image of the sequence he wishes to produce; most of the time, he executes the sequence as easily as he descends a flight of stairs. What a reader or listener does is less observable than speaking or writing, but the excellent reader likewise exhibits the characteristics of expert performance discussed in Chapter 10. Most of the curriculum communicates verbal principles that the student is to understand, fix in mind, and apply. The middle section of the chapter considers how to make communications effective—not only verbal presentations but also audiovisual presentations and direct experience. Practice exercises too are communications and the last section of the chapter considers what makes exercises effective. Instruction by computer receives particular attention because it so well illustrates the attempt to apply psychological concepts in designing instruction.

---

**1** Which "marks of the expert" (pp. 346ff) apply to each of the following?
    a. Directing a stranger across the campus to the university library
    b. Following a recipe for making a new spaghetti sauce
    c. Sight-reading a Beethoven sonata
    d. A sixth-grader reading *The Call of the Wild*

---

# THE DEVELOPMENT OF LANGUAGE SKILL

Language skill grows rapidly during the preschool years. Subtle discriminations and elaborate rules for response patterns are mastered at that time. Proficiency appears remarkably early. Even in the first months, an infant makes fine distinctions; he can respond differently to the stop consonants /b/ and /p/ (Eimas et al., 1971). The infant covers the full range of sounds in adult languages as he babbles, and he rapidly gains control of whichever sounds the persons around him use.

By age 3 the child is producing sentences of some length and complexity. Preschool children can produce astonishingly complex constructions, and logical ones at that (O'Donnell et al., 1967). One preschooler gave the following title to a drawing just completed:

> Once upon a time at the Oakland International Airport a dog named Cricket who rides a motorcycle was on the airplane.

From the earliest stages of speech the child does more than simply repeat what he hears (Cazden, 1972b, pp. 1–6). He forms rules for generating one linguistic construction after another. He observes a model, just as one observes someone performing a motor skill; then he perceives a pattern and assembles his own template for producing a similarly patterned response. The child learns that "What are you eating?" takes the answer "I am eating X." Several experiences of that sort give him a template for answering questions, says Cazden, so that when asked "What are you doing?" he responds "I am doing dancing." Only gradually does he come to realize that ". . . doing?" calls for a different template: "I am X-ing."

Trial-and-correction takes place, but since the child hears the very signal he intended to produce, he is not quick to catch an error. Nor can an adult easily correct him (box). The child uses his idiosyncratic pattern to his own satisfaction; that confirms it as a valid response. Why should he give it up, merely because someone once in a while objects to it? When at a later age the child is "on top of the game," he will more readily perceive discrepancies in syntax just as he ultimately learns to correct his drawing of a square until it really is square.

Children develop orderly, systematic conceptions of languages, but these conceptions may not match the ones adults have. The teacher "knows" what sound a word contains; but then the teacher is conditioned by years of spelling the word. What the child senses in the sound may be astonishingly different. Thus, Read (in Cazden, 1972a, p. 63, and Read, 1971) asked kindergartners to select pictures whose names had the same first sound as, for example, *truck*. Quite a few of them chose a picture of a chair, along with pictures for *tree* and *truck*. Equally surprising is their matching of *jacks* to *dragon*—but where to draw a boundary between the initial sounds of these words is largely a matter of convention. To the adult, the /dr/ of *dragon* and the /j/ of *jacks* are separate species, but if you observe how your tongue produces them, you will notice what close cousins they are. Concepts and categories oversimplify (p. 477).

## Shortcomings in Language Skill

Two kinds of difficulty with language show up when the child reaches the schoolroom. This section is concerned with one of them: immaturity in language skill—that is, inexpertness. The next section looks at cultural differences

## Learners fail to hear distinctions in speech

Here is a transcript of a psychologist trying to "correct" her daughter's speech:

| | |
|---|---|
| CHILD | Nobody don't like me. |
| MOTHER | No, say "Nobody likes me." |
| CHILD | Nobody don't like me. |
| MOTHER | No, say "Nobody likes me." |
| CHILD | Nobody don't like me. |
| MOTHER | No, say "Nobody likes me." |
| CHILD | Nobody don't like me. |
| MOTHER | No, say "Nobody likes me." |
| CHILD | Nobody don't like me. |
| MOTHER | No, say "Nobody likes me." |
| . . . . [four more repetitions] | |
| MOTHER | No. Now listen carefully; say "Nobody likes me." |
| CHILD | Oh! Nobody don't likes me! |

SOURCE: McNeill (1966), p. 69.

491

in dialect and language style. These cause difficulties in communication between persons even when each one *is* expert in his own variant of the language.

Language presents a complex stimulus. Small details of word order, word form, or emphasis can radically change the meaning. Hence persons who "know the language," be they adults or children, can fail to get the full meaning from messages or fail to communicate completely and unambiguously. A person grows continuously toward ability to handle more complex sentences and more abstract content. Perhaps more fundamental to readiness for school than this growing skill is an *attitude* of respect for detail in language. This should be formed at an early age.

At each age, some children are deficient in language development. The child who is less articulate uses less varied vocabulary than the proficient child; his sentences are simpler and more stereotyped in form. He thus communicates less specific information and fewer of his unique perceptions. Apparently, he does not rely on language to manipulate and reorder his world to the extent the language-proficient child does. Conversely, he is less accustomed to pay close attention to the language he hears. This means that the child with an immature approach to language is less prepared—intellectually and emotionally—to take in the verbal interchange that is the way of life in the typical classroom. And he is less prepared to put his ideas before the others, which would contribute to his own learning.

The common shortcomings are not so much matters of ability as matters of style. The immature child, responding to the teacher's questions, seems to make little effort to shape his words into responsive, informative communications. Some main shortcomings are these (DeLawter & East, 1966):

> Failure to clarify the question asked. The child says something in response that does not bear on the question. The child fails to ask for a restatement of a question that is unclear.

> Poor organization, poor subordination. The child starts to "free-associate" instead of pausing to select what he says. He runs unrelated ideas together in the same sentence, without pause.

> Unsupported conclusions; lack of critical thinking; failure to separate fact from opinion. Asked, "How do you know John and his father are good friends?" the child replies, " 'Cause that's his son."

> Indefinite descriptions. The listener is left unable to visualize what the child is talking about. In a discussion of bicycles, the child, asked what a "skinny wheel" is, replies: "It's a big bike—handbrakes on it. Some of 'em have handbrakes, some have footbrakes. I like handbrakes; you don't have to put your feet back."

Some of these difficulties may reflect lack of relevant concepts or skills, but they seem mostly to reflect misdirection of effort. Superficial attention, unreflective response, failure to hear one's words "through the ears" of one's audience—such faults are less disabilities than failures to use ability. Children who do not extend themselves in ordinary speech prove capable of elaborate speech in certain settings (pp. 272 and 498).

Failure to produce sentences with definite meanings is perhaps the most pervasive shortcoming in language, among adults as well as schoolchildren. "How's it going?" has a social use, and so do other rather empty phrases. Classroom communications, however, do a poor job when the meaning is thin:

> "Where is Ireland on the map?"
> "It's up there near England."

The listener who does not know where to locate Ireland has been given no help, and the teacher cannot be sure that the speaker really could find Ireland. When communication is his aim, a skilled speaker produces a sentence that has one and only one meaning. Whether a person holds to this standard is mostly a matter of self-evaluation, of being able to distinguish a definite sentence from a fuzzy one. One who cannot make this judgment will not be able to edit the sentences he writes; nor will he realize all that is said in the sentences he reads and hears. Also, since he uses words imprecisely, he describes objects and events inexactly to himself. In his learning of school subjects, then, he uses verbal interpretations less effectively than others do.

How well a child can put information into his speech is sometimes tested with the experimental setup in Fig. 12.1. It is easy for a 5-year-old to tell his

## FIGURE 12.1

### Apparatus for testing skill in communication

The speaker takes a block from the dispenser, describes the figure that appears on it, and mounts it on the stacking peg. The two patterns shown at the right are among the many novel figures used. The speaker is asked to describe the figure so well that the listener, looking at the assortment of blocks before him, can select the block that matches the speaker's.

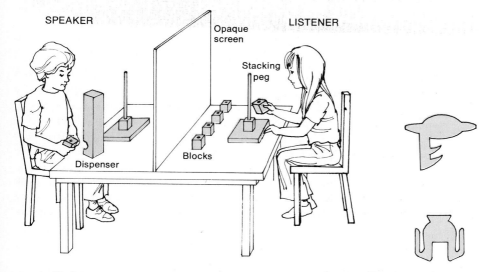

SOURCE: Glucksberg et al. (1966). The patterns were first published by Krauss & Weinheimer.

partner what blocks to choose when each block carries a picture of a familiar animal, but blocks marked with nonsense forms put the child's skills to a severe test. In this task, the children with comparatively mature language are of course more successful in guiding their partners. They produce longer messages and they give more detail. As listeners, they try harder to pick up details in the message and make use of them.

So far, research has provided no clear picture as to why some children develop more effective communication than others (Glucksberg, Krauss, & Higgins, 1975). Performance improves only slowly with age. Not until the junior-high-school years does proficiency in sending messages reach the adult level, though listening proficiency is good in the early grades. In some studies, communication skill has correlated with measures of general mental ability and/or with social class, but the relationships are so weak and inconsistent as to suggest that some special ability or attitude is at work (Higgins, 1976).

Communication is most effective when the speaker can put himself in the listener's place and realize what will be fully clear to *that* listener. It seems likely that the deficient communicator fails at just this self-evaluative step, either because of inability to hear through the other's ears or failure to try to do so.

The home is critical in the development of proficient use of language by the young child. Mothers, in particular, influence the child through the model of communication they set and through the extent to which they press the child to be exact in his requests and remarks. Everyday affairs in the home offer a pattern for reasoning. Among well-to-do families, Bearison and Cassell (1975) distinguished two styles. One emphasized formal rules and rigid definitions of right and wrong conduct. In the other style the parent repeatedly led the child to try to imagine how others would be affected by a decision and how they would feel; his action was to be chosen accordingly. Six-year-olds whose mothers adopted this second, socially-oriented style were far more effective in conveying messages. Their experience in seeing the other person's viewpoint presumably made the difference.

Many reports on communication deficiencies have emphasized social-class differences. Such differences do appear (Higgins, 1976), but once again I must emphasize that members of a cultural community vary widely and that, with respect to any performance, social-class groups overlap. The home training of young children does appear to be critical in building readiness for school, and good training is more likely to be found in middle-class homes. But quite a number of middle-class children will show a poor style of communication.

Some mothers are far more precise in their language than others. Hess and Shipman (1967; Hess et al., 1968) compared black mothers ranging from the upper middle class to the poverty level. The mother was to teach her 4-year-old how to sort toys by color or how to create a simple picture with the Etch-a-Sketch toy. Some mothers gave the child a rather full orientation to the task, gave fairly specific instructions, checked how well he understood, introduced some hint of reward for good performance, and showed the child how to moni-

# Pronouns set a puzzle for the listener

To demonstrate the imprecision that is characteristic of poor communicators, P. R. Hawkins (1969) showed 5-year-old children the pictures shown here and recorded what they said. Then he sorted out the better and poorer communications and constructed these syntheses:

---

(A) **Three boys are playing football and one boy kicks the ball—and it goes through the window—the ball breaks the window—and the boys are looking at it—and a man comes out and shouts at them—because they've broken the window—so they run away—and then that lady looks out of her window—and she tells the boys off.**
    **No. of nouns: 13 No. of pronouns: 6**

---

(B) **They're playing football—and he kicks it and it goes through there—it breaks the window and they're looking at it—and he comes out and shouts at them—because they've broken it—so they run away—and then she looks out and she tells them off.**
    **No. of nouns: 2 No. of pronouns: 14**

---

SOURCE: Hawkins (1969), p. 127.

Story A has only six pronouns; every pronoun has a clear reference save the second "it" (ball? window?). Story B has 14 pronouns and only two nouns; "he" and "it" shift meaning as new characters and new objects appear. The speaker who uses the B style has not set himself the task of conveying a message. He tells all the news, but his story makes sense only to a listener who is looking at the picture and so can interpret "they" and "he" and "she."

tor himself. At age 6, the child whose mother had been using this style tended to show superior reading readiness. Children whose mothers used fewer words and did less to clarify the task were less advanced at age 6. The careful style of teaching was most frequent among middle-class mothers, infrequent at lower class levels.

Differences appear at age 2. Shantz and Wilson (1972) put 2-year-olds through a nonverbal task much like Harlow's (p. 443). The children, of course, found it difficult to locate the hidden cookie. Then the experimenters tried to make the task very easy. They pointed to one of the odd-looking objects providing the cue and said something like "This is a valve. The cookie is under the valve." This did bring the task within the reach of infants whose mothers were college-educated; but children of less-educated mothers took almost no advantage of the verbal guidance. Even when they reach first grade, some children still need to learn the *value* of language. Games based on devices such as that seen in Fig. 12.1 are one means to that end.

A "universalistic" standard judges a message through the ears of a neutral, representative hearer, who has to learn everything from the words of the message itself. A universalistic message is complete in itself. The school, with its commitment to transmission of knowledge that is independent of the observer, wants the student's language to meet a universalistic standard. The child may have learned, however, a style that assumes that he and the listener see eye to eye; that makes it natural to use pronouns freely, as in Story B of the box. Bernstein (1970) argues that the lower-class home actively fosters the style of Story B; in that home, sharing of feelings and perspectives is important to family solidarity. Gesture and tone, rather than explicit wording, are to carry much of the burden of communication. Bernstein refers to this as a "restricted code," since it impedes communication with strangers. Labov (1970), among others, objects to this characterization. Language in the lower-class home is capable of rich and detailed communication, he says, even though it is not in the style of the dominant community.

Value judgments aside, the child whose home has not taught him to speak in objective terms does find it difficult to meet the expectations of the typical school. Bernstein (1970, p. 157) comments that "the child is not at home in the educational world" if the stories and examples of the school

> are not triggers on curiosity and explorations in his family and community. If the teacher has to say continuously, "Say it again, darling, I didn't understand you," then in the end the child may say nothing. If the culture of the teacher is to become part of the consciousness of the child, then the culture of the child must first be in the consciousness of the teacher.

Similarly, Cazden (1972a, p. 161) counsels that, in reading,

> comprehension and not pronunciation must be the critical test. One result of dialect differences in pronunciation is a set of homonyms that are different from the teacher's and may be more numerous than hers. If one has pronounced *during* and

*doing* the same way all one's life, learning to read the two words and associate differential meaning with differential spelling is no different from what every English speaker does with *sun* and *son.*

---

**2** How could a fourth-grade teacher organize an instructional game, employing the arrangement in Fig. 12.1 or something similar? What kind and amount of feedback or monitoring would be advisable?

**3** Chapanis (1975) has studied two-way communication of older persons, using a variation on the scheme of Fig. 12.1: A has a map of Washington, D.C. on which his supposed residence is marked. B has a list of names and addresses of physicians, but no map. As if at the end of a telephone line, B is to help A locate the physician who lives nearest his home.

Devise another task of this kind that would have teaching value for high-school students whose communication is not precise.

**4** What does Bernstein mean when he says "The culture of the child must be in the consciousness of the teacher"?

---

## Cultural Variations in Language

Differences arising in the home deserve to be classified as shortcomings when they limit communication and hinder the child in understanding the universalistic ideal of the school. Many language variations that handicap the student would not hinder him if the school were better prepared to accept cultural variations. This section takes up the tough question of evaluating dialects and departures from standard English.

FUNCTION VERSUS PRESTIGE   The common language of educated parents approximates the "good grammar" the school has traditionally tried to teach. The student who possesses this language has an easier time in school and is treated with more respect in the community, even though not all of the forms that go into good language are critical for communication. "It's me" and "Who am I talking to?" violate grammatical convention, but no one will misunderstand. They are errors only to the scholastic ear.

Linguists who have studied the natural variations of language report that every language that diffuses widely develops variants, and that each variant of a sophisticated language communicates about as well as every other. Condemning the speech of outlanders has always been a form of vanity, of refusing to recognize the worth of alien groups. Pride in one's own traditions is natural—but there is no warrant for deterring others from having pride in their traditions. It is one thing to press a student to clarify his remarks so that his message gets across; it is quite another to press him to imitate the speech forms of whatever societal group the teacher represents. At one time, jobs as news broadcasters were open only to persons who spoke an educated "Middle Atlantic" dialect. Now, pressures to recognize cultural diversity have brought soft Spanish accents and regional drawls into the newsroom. If the users of the elite dialect have to listen a bit harder sometimes, that inconvenience is offset by the number of listeners who find a particular non-elite speaker easier to follow.

Adult speech samples show that language form is largely a matter of cultural style. Adults in New York City had to read a list of words, then to read a passage aloud for meaning. They were also observed when being careful to express something and in casual conversation with acquaintances. Figure 12.2 indicates how often they gave full value to the sound *th*, rather than a hard sound: "ting" for *thing*, "duh" for *the*, "troo" for *through*. Middle-class speakers rarely used the nonstandard form. Persons of lower status generally used the less "elegant" forms when they were speaking connected prose (or reading it). But when they read word lists they pronounced *th* much as the middle class did. Members of the middle class monitored their own *casual* speech, and lower-class speakers did not. This same tendency of lower-class speech to vary with the demands implied by the situation was seen in a study of fourth- to sixth-graders (Table 12.1). Students of lower-class origin gave a more-than-minimal response only when the form of a question required it. Any question that could be answered in just one word was likely to get such a minimal an-

FIGURE 12.2

Proportion of speech that uses standard forms in each social class

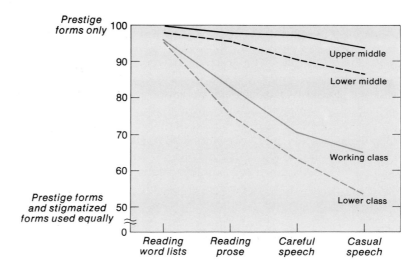

SOURCE: Adapted from Labov (1966), p. 169.

**TABLE 12.1**

Willingness of middle-class and lower-class children to amplify responses

| | Percentage of elaborated responses | |
| --- | --- | --- |
| Type of question | Middle-class | Lower-class |
| Open question ("How do you play Kick the Can?") | 79 | 81 |
| Simple question ("Do you play baseball?") | 50 | 31 |
| Request for the name of something | 30 | 21 |

SOURCE: Data from F. Williams & R. C. Naremore (1969).

swer from the lower-class child. Insofar as fuller responses to classroom questions offer clearer evidence of knowledge, a teacher tends to see a child with such a production deficiency as less able than he is.

What the teacher expects of a student may be unduly influenced by the child's speech (F. Williams, 1972). Such effects were demonstrated when Seligman et al. supplied teachers with files on third-graders. For each child the file held a speech sample, a photograph, and a written composition. Teachers were asked to rate the ability and personality of each child. Each "child" was an artificial composite; files had been prepared by making up balanced combinations of "good" and "poor" specimens. Thus, one file held a tape of standard speech, a bit of good writing and an attractive photo; in another file good speech was put with poor writing and an unappealing picture. There were eight files in all. The attractiveness of the photos did not influence the teachers' ratings. Speech had a marked influence, far greater than that of writing (Fig. 12.3, p. 500).

It does not improve *communication* to teach someone to say "these" instead of "dese" and to avoid "I'm not going nowhere." The reason for equipping the student with the culturally dominant speech pattern is to help him escape unfair treatment. Indeed, black parents are emphatic in wanting their children to acquire standard English (Cazden et al., 1972, pp. 73ff.). "When one teaches a variety of language to children for whom it is not a normal variety," says Hymes (in Cazden et al., 1972, p. xxxi), "one is engaged, not in [promoting] logic, or reasoning, or cognitive growth, but in social change."

LANGUAGE OF BLACK STUDENTS A child of foreign-born parents who comes to school speaking little English is at a great disadvantage. That is why American law requires that the school teach in the minority languages where practicable. It is harder to reach agreement on the significance of the dialects referred to as Black English.

## FIGURE 12.3

## Ratings of students by teachers using information from a file

Each point represents the average rating of four files on a 1-to-7 scale. To provide balance, the four files with good speech samples, for example, contained two attractive and two unattractive photographs, and two good and two poor compositions.

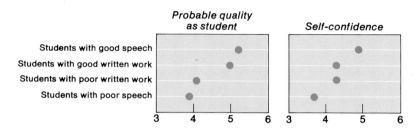

SOURCE: Data from Seligman et al. (1972).

This is not the place to examine the rules of Black English or its function in strengthening group identity. Our concern is with response to schooling. Lower-class children, I have said, have somewhat restricted language development. Do lower-class blacks have, in addition, a kind of "foreign language" problem when they come to school? The evidence is that race is not much related to accuracy of communication, when comparisons are made within the same social class (Higgins, 1976).

Many of the differences between "Black" English and "standard" English have to do with pronunciation. There are differences in grammatical structures also, but these are surface differences (box).

Labov (1967, pp. 163–64) made the following comment on the common reaction of the teacher to a black child's speech. A boy reading *He passed by both of them* says something like "He pass by bof a' dem." For precision, the linguist codes the speech in a phonetic alphabet: hi pæs baˡ bof ə dɛm.

> The teacher [says Labov] may wish to correct this bad reading, perhaps by saying, "No, it isn't [hi pæs baˡ bof ə dɛm], it's [hi pæst baˡ boθ əv ðɛm]." One difficulty is that these two utterances may sound the same to many children—both the reader and those listening—and they may be utterly confused by the correction. Others may be able to hear the difference, but have no idea of the significance of the extra [t] and the interdental forms of *th–*. The ... boy ... may have performed his reading task correctly, and understood the *–ed* suffix just as it was intended. In that case, the teacher's correction is completely beside the point.
>
> We have two distinct cases to consider. In one case, the deviation in reading may be only a difference in pronunciation on the part of a child who has a different set of homonyms from the teacher. Here, correction might be quite unnecessary. In the second case, we may be dealing with a boy who has no concept of *–ed* as a past tense marker, who considers the *–ed* a meaningless set of silent letters. Obviously the correct teaching strategy would [treat] ... these two cases ... quite differently.

## Respecting the child's language

Dialects are adequate languages, according to Elsa Bartlett (in Cazden, 1972b, pp. 62ff.). There is not one shred of evidence, she says, that the language of the school is the only sound vehicle for accurate thought. Bartlett complains that teachers' manuals often take such an indefensible position as this:

> [Standard English] grammar . . . is the form of English used in conveying information to students and it is expected to be reproduced in their own writings and communication process. It is not just a matter of their having a different vocabulary due to different life experiences, but also of their not having the same *flexibility in manipulating words grammatically*. For example, "When he arrived, we were having breakfast" becomes in one nonstandard form, "When he arrive, we have breakfast." The *ed* ending, indicating the past tense, is omitted on the verb *arrive*. Without this . . ., *the meaning is ambiguous*. There is a *lack of clarity* in timing of the event. When the context is unambiguous, this is an adequately functional form, but in school the context is more difficult to grasp. . . . The student is *handicapped in his ability to communicate and to receive communications*.
>
> *Without an adequate grasp of language, it is impossible to cope with abstract ideas. For this reason, children must be encouraged to develop their language. It enables them to think.* (Bartlett's italics)

Bartlett denies that standard English enables children to have better ideas.

> [The manual says that] the nonstandard sentence is ambiguous. Ambiguous to whom? Not, certainly, to speakers of the nonstandard dialect who are perfectly aware of the rules in their dialect for rendering tenses. . . .
>
> Just because a time relationship in nonstandard dialect is rendered differently than it is in standard dialect is no reason for supposing that the time relationship is not rendered at all.
>
> This leads us to another misconception: that nonstandard dialects . . . are, in some way, less flexible than standard dialect. . . . Some educators . . . seem to . . . match a nonstandard dialect against standard English and—when a difference occurs—they seem to assume that the difference indicates a deficiency in the nonstandard forms. That is, they treat the points of difference as if they were errors or "lacks" in the nonstandard dialect. As a result, they can arrive at a point where it seems reasonable to describe a dialect as not "having" a past perfect tense or a copulative or whatever. Of course, such a description is completely absurd. Nonstandard dialects simply follow different rules.
>
> If dialect-training is to be undertaken, the teacher must deal with the child's existing dialect as well as the new one. Children, like everyone else, are likely to assume that if language change is required, then the existing language must be considered in some way deficient. And this, in turn may lead children either to feel ashamed of their own home dialect or angrily reject the new one. . . .
>
> It is possible to imagine [teaching that] . . . treats both dialects with respect and, in addition, treats each dialect as the intact system which, in fact, it is. Such programs would develop children's awareness of languages and dialects as alternative coding systems. . . .
>
> Activities could include some of the following: listening to tapes of the same story told in each dialect; listening to tapes of stories in which each character spoke a different dialect; providing dialogue for puppets, each of which speaks a different dialect; role playing situations in which the characters speak with different dialects; translating the same message from one dialect to another; inventing a simple "dialect" or coding system. At the very least, this kind of approach . . . would help children maintain respect for their home dialect while learning to communicate in a second dialect. . . . (pp. 63–64.)

SOURCE: Bartlett, in Cazden (1972b). Copyright © 1972, National Association for the Education of Young Children, 1834 Connecticut Avenue, N.W., Washington, D.C. 20009. Reprinted by permission.

**TABLE 12.2**

Ability of fourth-graders to imitate and comprehend details of standard speech

| | Percentage of correct responses | |
| --- | :---: | :---: |
| | *Imitation* | *Comprehension* |
| Middle-class | | |
| Suburban whites | 89 | 76 |
| Lower-class | | |
| Urban whites | 68 | 64 |
| Rural whites | 72 | 68 |
| Urban blacks | 66 | 66 |

SOURCE: Data from V. C. Hall et al. (1973).

The black child generally has adequate ability to comprehend what is said to him in standard English. White and black children of the same social class are equal in ability to comprehend the teacher's speech and equal in remembering the substance of what they hear or read. Table 12.2 reports one of many studies. After hearing a sentence in standard dialect, the fourth-grader was to repeat it exactly. Then, to test comprehension, the student chose the one of three pictures whose meaning matched the sentence. The chief difference was related to social class and not race. (In Grade I, blacks did have greater trouble than whites in imitating sounds.)

Black dialect, according to other research, gives more trouble to both black and white children than the same content does when spoken in standard English. Sometimes Black English seems to cause more trouble for black children than for whites (V. Hall & R. Turner, 1974); but perhaps the investigators did not control social class (see also W. Hall & R. Freedle, 1973; Nolen, 1972; L. Quay, 1971).

---

**5** The following statements are called "myths" by Cazden et al. (in Cazden et al., 1972, pp. 90ff.) For each statement, indicate why some persons might believe it and why the belief is open to challenge.
   a. Some languages are better than others for abstract thinking.
   b. Some dialects represent bad language usage.
   c. People who speak a nonstandard dialect are stupid.
   d. Learning a nonstandard dialect is not learning a language.

**6** Labov offers two interpretations for the speech of the boy who omitted *–ed* in reading "He passed." How can the teacher decide which interpretation is correct for this student?

---

# IMPROVING COMPREHENSION AND EXPRESSION

## Comprehension

To comprehend is to grasp the idea behind a sentence or a paragraph, not simply to attach a meaning to each word in turn. The message is linked up with meanings (expectations) already in long-term storage. To comprehend "John is coming to dinner" may be to note a change of guest ("John, not Sven"), an added guest ("John as well as Sven"), a change of time, or a change of plan.

Words carry some of the meaning, but the way the words are assembled (structure) also matters. With regard to the sentence, linguists emphasize its "deep structure" (Cazden, 1972a; Fodor et al., 1974). Surface structure is the ordinary phrasing that breaks a sentence into units. "John is coming to dinner." "Mary is hoping to go." These have the same surface structure. The deep structure, however, refers to the operational connections between the objects (or concepts or actions) mentioned. Logically, "coming to dinner" is the same as "will move to the place where dinner is located." The phrase "hoping to go" makes no sense if translated (in parallel fashion) into "will hope to the place where go is located." Its deep structure is something like: "has a hope that she will go." One deep structure can be molded into many sentences: "John is the one who is coming. . .", "John is coming to *dinner*", and so on. The variations alter the emphasis, indicating just what aspect of the hearer's record in memory has to be updated—but each one tells the same story.

To comprehend a sentence, the reader or listener identifies a reasonable deep structure. Since the grammatical classes of the words and their order give no sure guide to the deep structure, he can at best choose a structure that makes good sense in its context. Active trial and correction go on in listening and reading (usually rapidly).

Sentences in arithmetic also have deep structure. When reference is made to sets of size 3, 5, and 8, their whole-part relationship forms the deep structure. It can be expressed in a variety of sentences—for example, $5 + 3 = 8$, $8 = 3 + 5$, $8 - 5 = 3$.

The sentences $8 - 5 = ?$ and $5 + ? = 8$ are no more than further linguistic variants. A child who understands that a number is a count of a set of objects can readily understand that these two questions are the same. When words are used to express this structure, still more transformations become possible. The sentence $8 - 5 = 3$ appears in arithmetic books in all these alternative forms:

> Five is subtracted from eight. The difference is three.
> Five less than eight is three.
> Eight decreased by five is three.
> The difference of eight and five is three.
> Three is five less than eight.
> Eight minus five is three.

Three is five shorter than eight.
Eight, take away five, is three.
Remove five from eight, three are left.   (Cazden, 1972a, p. 26.)

Reducing the linguistic variation would, in a sense, make for easier comprehension. A textbook writer might adopt one of the eight sentence forms for every example of subtraction, and urge the teacher to use that same form and to require students to use it. Such standardization of language forms is pedagogically unsound. The student learns to respond to the recurrent surface structure without digging down to the mathematical idea. The uniform expression gives him an easy way to communicate with *this* textbook and the persons in *this* class, but he is not taught to comprehend what the rest of the world says about subtraction.

The student should learn to reduce verbal forms to the basic pattern of the objects described. The skill of comprehension is not to attach a new meaning to each surface structure but to extract, from whatever form the speaker used, an idea about a relation. It is ideas around which long-term memory is organized, not sentence forms.

Teachers ought to ask students to practice forming sentences that convey the same idea in different ways. That leads them to recognize basic messages in what they read. They develop a concept of conservation—conservation of an idea, similar to the conservation of shape a child builds up by rotating an object to see its many images (p. 329).

A fundamental test of comprehension is to ask students to put a sentence or paragraph or essay into their own words. But paraphrase is not full evidence of comprehension. It is not hard to paraphrase sentences made up of meaningless words ("When frightened by the gramlix, the ondostob could only wengle."). We know that the student comprehends the link between idea and real world when he draws an example or counterexample out of his own experience. He comprehends a narrative if he can suggest what will happen next or how the characters felt.

Prose is often a well-developed argument leading to a conclusion. This may be true of a third-grader's picture story on rainbows as well as of a judicial opinion. In a tight argument, there is a deep structure to be comprehended. Just as words may be ordered in many ways to convey the same meaning, so there are a large number of ways to spell out an argument. The student who comprehends is able to sort out the essential from the nonessential, to reorder, and to see how changing one sentence in an explanation of rainbows ("Red light is bent more.") would change other sentences. Kamii and Derman (p. 366) challenged the preschool child's comprehension of a sentence about buoyancy by asking the child to fit it to events he had never had a chance to observe.

The teacher encourages deeper comprehension by challenging students and by teaching them to challenge themselves. The student is often satisfied that he "has read the assignment" when he has merely looked over each sentence in turn. The student should learn to process the whole more actively—"What message did the author think most important?" "What was his bias?" "Could a reasonable person point to exceptions?" and so on. Then he is more likely to connect the content with what is already stored in his mind and to detect ideas that run contrary to his established beliefs.

7  Mattick (in Cazden, 1972b, p. 109) warns that children often seem to understand a sentence when in fact they are relying on supplementary cues. As an example, she refers to the preschooler who relies on the teacher's gestures and eye movements to interpret "under the easel," "behind you," and the like. Should teachers suppress such nonlanguage cues?

8  In a "shadowing" test, a string of words is heard against a noisy background that blots out some of the detail. Eight-year-olds are much more able to say back meaningful sentences than arbitrary but grammatical word strings; for 5-year-olds, the greater meaning makes no difference. Says McNeill (in Mussen, 1970, I., p. 1122), "It apparently makes little difference whether one says to a 5-year-old child *wild Indians shoot running buffaloes* or *wild elevators shoot ticking restaurants*." What processing abilities, acquired between 5 and 8, might explain the 8-year-old's greater expertness in aural comprehension?

## Stimulating the urge to communicate

When the subject is close to his heart, the student's speech rises to its best level. Preschool children were turned loose with simple cameras, and the snapshots they made were used as subjects for conversation in school. There were two groups of pictures. Some had been taken at the school, during the period when an adult was showing the child how to use the camera. The child was following directions when he made this set, whereas the pictures made at home showed scenes of his own choice.

When the children talked about the scenes from home, they were more fluent and produced longer, more complex sentences. Adult probing was needed to keep the conversation going. Cazden (1972a, p. 207) gives these examples (from a study by Strandberg and Griffith) of the two kinds of conversation, the first picture referred to being one taken under adult direction:

> That's a horse. You can ride it. I don't know any more about it. It's brown, black and red. I don't know my story about the horse.

> There's a picture of my tree that I climb in. There's—there's where it grows at, and there's where I climb up—and sit up there—down there and that's where I look out at. First I get on this one and then I get on that other one. And then I put my foot under that big branch that are strong. And then I pull my face up and then I get ahold of a branch up at that place—and then I look around.

## The Student's Communications

We want the student to be fluent, definite, and clear. The first requisite for fluency is having something to talk about, preferably something the speaker cares about and has confident knowledge of. The best opportunities to develop expressive language arise in activities where the child has an *urge* to communicate. In the photo above, we see a child dictating a story to a teacher aide; the box suggests another form of stimulation.

Lucid speaking and writing is to a considerable degree a matter of style ("typical behavior") rather than ability. The style in turn depends on what students have learned to regard as appropriate. Psychologists studying child language emphasize the importance of invitations to elaborate (Smothergill et al., 1971). The child who elaborates gets more experience in full communication. When the fourth-grade teacher usually accepts a two-word answer and goes on without a pause to his own next remark or question, students take the hint. They keep their replies succinct, and so never reveal the richness of their insight—or the subtlety of their misconception. The teacher encourages elaboration by a question that keeps a story going, or by a remark that paraphrases what the child said and "hangs in the air" at the end as if there were more to be said. As we saw in Table 12.1, the teacher elicits more from the child simply by framing questions for which no one-word answer will serve.

The teacher is a model; also, the teacher points out models for the student to emulate. The model, however, may not be accepted. Posting on the corkboard the composition the A+ student wrote leaves the average student feeling that he can never produce anything the teacher will find worthy. Posting a clear paragraph written by an average student conveys a message of hope—particularly if the teacher signals what it is a model of. ("Good start. The first few words tell the reader just what your topic is.")

Models sometimes convey nonfunctional standards. Many students think that long words and long sentences are a mark of maturity. The truly skilled writer, however, falls back upon them only when simpler words and shorter sentences cannot contain his ideas. Again, we come back to the teacher's values; does the teacher display models of elaborate writing? or of readable writing (p. 514)?

The more of the intended audience a communication gets across to, the better it is. That is a test the student can learn to apply to his own expressions. In doing so, he starts to learn the thousand subskills that improve expression. One of several ways of encouraging this is to have the student put away what he has written for three days, and then try to read it "cold," perhaps aloud. A mature oral reader can phrase well-written prose smoothly at first sight, unless the vocabulary is strange.

---

**9** A parlor game of "Gossip" can be adapted as a teaching device. The first student writes a message. Student 2 reads what Student 1 wrote, then from memory writes the message as accurately as he can. Student 3 reads what Student 2 wrote, and, in turn, tries to reproduce it. The team earns a good score if the message can go through, say, five links without distortion. What can students learn from playing this game and observing the distortions that occur in some passages?

**10** Mellon (1969) was able to bring about substantial improvement in quality and complexity of expression of seventh-graders by teaching them—through example and practice—to combine sentences. To put two clauses into a single sentence requires attention to relationships among the thought units, and produces a more continuous, more elaborate message. Is this kind of teaching entirely consistent with the suggestions in the preceding section?

---

# INSTRUCTIONAL COMMUNICATIONS

## Experience As the Base for Meaning

Language is a device for helping the person to recall his past experiences and develop new meanings for them, or to extend them into a vision of new possibilities. The teacher cannot expect to communicate if he talks about things that have no connection with the student's experience. A sea chantey is "a rhythmic song, sung in chorus by a ship's crew"—but this is a pallid image to the student who has never heard one. He still wouldn't recognize a chantey. A rainbow, a banana, or a baby defies description; its characteristics become known only through encounters with the real thing. Many concepts deal with relations or abstractions (heredity, kilowatt, a billion dollars) and the teacher cannot point directly to an example. But he can connect them with familiar experience ("A kilowatt would run ten light bulbs like this.").

Images of concrete objects and events are a necessary background for comprehending an abstract relation. Whenever an activity puts the student into intimate contact with real objects, he amasses experiences that can clarify theoretical concepts and principles. The adolescents who make radios acquire images of objects and operations associated with electricity. They know what an added resistor does; they have seen lights dim and have felt wires grow warm. Consequently, they find physics easier to grasp. The class that sets out to persuade the city council to change its bicycle ordinance gains a picture of realities of which the formal chart of government structure is only a reminder.

The child with a garden watches it closely every day and builds up intimacy with soil and insects and rainfall. He knows from digging that water is stored beneath dry topsoil. This illumines facts in his geography that otherwise would have little significance. After the child has waited impatiently for the soil to dry so he can plant a spring garden, reading that the growing season begins two months later in Russia sets meanings rolling in his head. He can draw implications from the facts: how much Russians can produce, why they do not grow slow-maturing corn, why a few weeks of bad weather cause serious concern in Russia.

Experience can provide links that bind facts into systems. Then one fact helps the student recapture others. One might teach "100 addition facts," and then have students memorize "100 subtraction facts." But if the process of addition is made sufficiently meaningful, the student visualizes $8 + 5 = 13$ as an operation, as a union of sets, or as two steps along the number scale. This fact he can use to transform $13 - 5 = \square$ into $\square + 5 = 13$. Activities with plastic disks or the like will help the student form an image such as this:

Here, the "easier" facts $8 + 2 = 10$ and $5 = 2 + 3$ locked $8 + 5 = 13$ in place. In a second or so, the student can check operationally the fact he pulls out of memory. When he thinks in this way, one set of 100 facts serves for both addition and subtraction. Each of the 100 facts can be checked; he can easily identify what response is right when interference does occur.

One does not want the student to fall back on the component operations in every problem. It is lack of confidence that causes some persons to use primitive techniques even after years of experience. The reason for laying down a base of meaningful operations is to provide the student a low gear for use when the going is difficult.

INDICATORS OF MEANINGFUL LEARNING   Learning that could be meaningful is too often left as an arbitrary association. One example is the Pledge of Allegiance. This ritual is supposed to instill loyalty to American ideals. But how little do students comprehend the ideals. Students are quite prepared to recite gibberish if no one checks for meaning, as is shown when they try to *write* the pledge:

> I pledge the legions to the flag, of the United States and to the legions for which it stands, one nation individual with liberty and justice for all.
> I plague the legion to the flag of the United States of America and to the republic for Richlan stand's one nation in indivisible with librty and jesta straw. (From A. Moser & B. David, 1936.)

Memorization without comprehension is especially likely when students are responding to an unvarying stimulus. If the goal is to give an instant answer when the teacher says "Define *parallelogram*," the student will drill himself to rattle off, "A parallelogram is a quadrilateral whose opposite sides are equal and parallel." His try will be confirmed by approval. Yet he may not realize that a square is a parallelogram or that ◻ is not. Exercises that can be answered by sheer recall encourage reiteration without comprehension. If an association is potentially meaningful, as are most of the "facts" taught in school, tests and recitations should call for some display of understanding.

At least superficial understanding is shown when the learner gives examples of a principle, answers a question using the information, or restates an idea in his own words. These responses show that the principle is connected in his mind with real objects or with other principles. The best evidence is application in a new situation or explanation of an unfamiliar phenomenon (p. 484).

AUDIO-VISUAL DISPLAYS   Sometimes concepts to be learned cannot be described verbally and cannot be introduced concretely into the student's life. The Arctic is too far away, the migration of birds covers too much territory, the French Revolution is long past, the marketing of wheat is a complex flow of events. Visual aids bring these to the classroom in a form the student can comprehend. A well-planned motion picture can give an experience as vivid as if the student had lived through the event. Because photography can take close-up views and long views, can retard motion or telescope time, the camera shows some relations *more* clearly than direct observation. Dramatic sound recordings also bring events to life.

On film or on television, a run-of-the-camera travelogue or laboratory demonstration has less impact than a carefully edited presentation in which segments are repeated, shown from different angles, organized to point out similarities and contrasts, and clarified by supplementary diagrams, summaries of main points, and other expository devices. Clarity, not technical brilliance, is what counts. An animated motion picture made from crude sketches is likely to teach as much as a superbly polished color film costing ten times as much to produce (Barrington, 1971).

A richly varied concrete or pictorial experience by no means develops all the meanings it could, unless the teacher makes these meanings explicit. The teacher, by directing attention, greatly influences what students take from an experience.

## Test your memory!

Some psychologists investigate memory of connected prose instead of nonsense syllables. The passage below (which is *not* meant to be well written) was used in some experiments to be described later. To get some feeling for the task, read the story *just once* and try to fix it in mind. Then, in your own words, jot down as many of the statements as you can. (The investigators had subjects listen to the story instead of reading it.)

> If the balloons popped the sound wouldn't be able to carry since everything would be too far away from the correct floor. A closed window would also prevent the sound from carrying, since most buildings tend to be well insulated. Since the whole operation depends on a steady flow of electricity, a break in the middle of the wire would also cause problems. Of course, the fellow could shout, but the human voice is not loud enough to carry that far. An additional problem is that a string could break on the instrument. Then there could be no accompaniment to the message. It is clear that the best situation would involve less distance. Then there would be fewer potential problems. With face to face contact, the least number of things could go wrong.

What the investigators learned from this study is described on p. 524.

SOURCE: J. D. Bransford & M. K. Johnson, in Chase (1972), pp. 392–93.

May and Lumsdaine (1958, pp. 165ff.) showed a simple film on the rotation of the earth, in which many photographs and drawings of a globe representing the earth were supposed to make various ideas clear. Fifth-graders learned certain items fairly well. "The axis is an imaginary line" went from 16 per cent knowledge on a pretest to 56 per cent knowledge on a posttest. But other items—"What fraction of the earth's surface is in daylight at any one time?"—showed no gains even though in the picture each fact seemed to be clear. The well-learned items were generally the ones put into words on the sound track. Verbal encoding gave the student something he could store correctly; the pictorial image gave depth to the meaning.

There is a bit of a paradox here. The research on learning from pictures demonstrates that verbal encoding is the key to exact recall. The research on learning from verbal stimuli demonstrates that pictorial imagery is of great value (pp. 457 and 516). These can be reconciled by seeing the two forms of storage as supplementary; pictorial perceptions are usually more integrated, more continuous, and more elaborate, while verbal representations are more definite. (Compare your vision of a rainbow with the ROY G. BIV mnemonic for the colors—Red, Orange, and so on.)

What is dramatically presented is likely to be well learned. In the teaching film investigated by May and Lumsdaine, a boy and a girl carry a globe around a lamp as a means of explaining why there are seasons.

> During the first part of the demonstration the globe is at the December position in relation to the lamp—the North Pole tilted away from the sun. When the boy carried the globe to the opposite (June) side of the table, he made two mistakes. First,

he goes the wrong way around the table and, second, he holds the globe so that the North Pole is always tilted away from the sun. The father corrects these mistakes and emphasizes the counterclockwise revolution of the earth in its orbit. He also stresses the point that the North Pole of the earth's axis is always pointed toward the North Star. In moving the globe to the spring and fall position, the girl starts to make the same mistakes, but corrects them. Mention is made of this fact.

The gains on these items were exceptionally large. On a test item, "The earth's axis is always pointed toward the North Star," 37 per cent were correct before seeing the film and 80 per cent afterward.

The teaching value of audio-visual devices lies not in the gadgetry but in the student's thought and feelings. Students may fail to take a useful message away from visual material that is potentially instructive. Venn (1946; see also Wesley, 1962) showed a well-edited film on the nervous system to college psychology students individually. He questioned each one to see how much could be recalled immediately afterward. The students had grasped only a fraction of the content. A second showing taught almost as many additional ideas as the first run. On one run, the viewer literally does not see all that is shown. Some of what he does see has no meaning until after the structure of the whole presentation has become clear. This occurs in reading, which is why we advise students to *study* texts rather than to read them once over lightly. But the idea of *studying* visual aids is strange to teachers and students.

FROM VERBAL PRINCIPLES TO ACTION    Theory can influence action in concrete situations—but often it does not. Studying the relevant theory does not in itself make one a better performer. For example, Colville (1957) had one group practice certain billiard shots. Another group spent part of its time in practice, but only after studying the relevant physical principles of reflection and momentum. The group taught theory did not shoot better. Another study (Hendrickson & Schroeder, 1941) had students shoot at underwater targets. An explanation about the refraction of light had little value.

The explanations in these studies offered relevant abstract principles without connecting them to a verbal prescription for action. Students did not understand the deep structure well enough to derive a helpful rule for themselves. Teaching a verbal rule for action would have bridged the gap between the theoretical knowledge and its use. The difficulty is that discussed in Piaget's theory (p. 331). Over a period of adaptive practice guided by a rule, a concept such as reflection or refraction becomes a reversible, flexible concept. Primitive, impressionistic solutions work well only so long as conditions remain fairly simple. When complications set in or surface impressions become misleading, then a verbal formulation that can regulate performance is especially needed (pp. 437 and 546).

Systematic verbal knowledge is an efficient way to summarize experience, not a substitute for it. To act on a concrete situation on the basis of verbal knowledge, one must translate physical cues into a schema—"seeing" the angle of reflection on the billiard table, for instance. Moreover, one must be able to derive from a general principle a prescription telling what action to take and then be able to translate the words into acts. Sometimes the steps in applying verbal knowledge are obvious. But ordinarily the teacher who would make a verbal principle useful to the student must give direct attention to the steps of encoding and decoding. ("How can you decide when you have the right aiming point?") Often—as Piaget's research suggests—considerable concrete experience should precede the verbal rule. The impressionistic trial and error makes it easier to comprehend the rule.

When and if students have adequate operational concepts, abstract instruction is effective. Let us look at details of one study (Thune & Ericksen, 1960; see also p. 546). Students were given brief training in operating a calculator. First there was a 20-minute familiarization exercise with a Friden calculator, in which they pushed the buttons and read off numbers. The next 20 minutes were a waiting interval for Group I, the control group. During that time Group II (concrete training) did addition, subtraction, and multiplication problems directly on the Friden machine; the tasks progressed in a sensible instructional sequence. Members of Group III (abstract training) were taught the principles of using *any* calculator, but did no calculations. They worked with a schematic diagram that had labeled registers and controls, and answered multiple-choice questions. Questions were arranged so that the student could reason out each answer from the information given. He reasoned out what acts to call for, in what sequence. That is, he went from principles to a verbal rule for action, but the rule was a general one applying to any calculator.

Three tests were given. Test A called for seven calculations on the Friden machine. Test B consisted of an equally difficult test on the Friden the next day. Following Test B the student was given 20 minutes of familiarization with a Marchant machine; its controls are arranged differently from the Friden but it works on the same principles. Test C required calculations on the Marchant. As Fig. 12.4 shows, the group directly trained on Friden calculations had difficulty on the strange machine. Still, their Friden training made them better at the

**FIGURE 12.4**

**Abstract training has advantages for transfer**

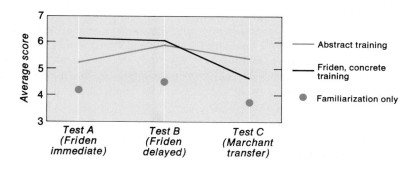

SOURCE: After Thune & Ericksen (1960).

transfer task than the controls. The abstractly trained group was slow on Test A and their scores suffered, but they learned on the job. (So did the controls.) The transfer test shows that abstract training produced versatility.

Concrete experience is needed so that the person can make sense of verbal explanations and imagine the operations they relate to. Much concrete experience may be required if the learner has had little prior experience—with musical harmony, for example. Very little new experience is required if the person has an adequate base—as when an American cook is told how to use a wok. Performance can be sharpened quite adequately by demonstration and concrete practice, if the task will always be much the same. The more the person will have to cope with changing situations, the more he can profit from abstractions.

**11** The principal who found that students could not write the Pledge of Allegiance asked teachers to present lessons on it. When the students wrote it from memory a week later, errors were few and were limited to punctuation and spelling. "This," says the principal's report, "is evidence enough that the Pledge is now more than a meaningless formality." Criticize this conclusion.

**12** Just as there are effective techniques of studying a printed text, there are techniques for gaining more from an instructional film or videotape. List some of them. What can the teacher do, in presenting a film, to make it easier for students to grasp what it teaches?

**13** Ausubel and Robinson (1969) see well-organized presentations of knowledge as one of the principal functions of pedagogy. While they consider "concrete props" useful in the elementary grades, they continue as follows:

> Beginning in the junior-high-school period, students can acquire most new concepts and can learn most new propositions by *directly* grasping relationships between abstractions. . . . They need no longer depend upon . . . concrete empirical props, and hence are able to bypass completely the limited type of understanding inherent in such dependence. . . . It is unnecessary to *routinely* introduce concrete props . . . to enhance *intuitive* understanding of abstract propositions. (p. 99.)

This implies that general-science and physics teachers can present a topic such as optics abstractly and symbolically. Most of them, however, set up demonstrations or laboratory tasks so students can observe how lenses reshape light beams. What merit is there in the Ausubel-Robinson argument? In what way does it overstate?

## Readable Writing

As has been said, comprehension rests on the base of experience the student has built up through hands-on experience or through observation. But comprehension also depends on the language of text and teacher. This section will

## Reducing the reader's burden

Selection I was written by an anthropologist for a magazine whose readers are mostly well-educated adults. Rudolf Flesch (1943) prepared Selection II to put the ideas within the reach of average seventh-graders, contending that the simplification loses none of the message. Flesch sees no virtue in the more complex form of the original, even for an educated audience.

### I

Anthropologists have long recognized that the spread of customs from one group of people to another—"diffusion" in anthropological terminology—accounts for at least nine tenths of the culture of any group. On its face, this would seem to assign any kind of economic determinism an insignificant role. An analysis of this problem, however, in the light of what is known of culture change among primitive peoples, both before and after they have experienced acculturation resulting from contact with European cultures, exposes its considerable complexity. Under certain conditions, subsistence patterns—that is the activities concerned with acquiring food, clothing, shelter and other things indispensable to existence—have imposed very narrow limits on possible variations of social and economic organization. Under other conditions, it is evident that considerable latitude is possible in the socioeconomic structure.

### II

At least nine tenths of the culture of any group of people goes back to customs spread from another group. Scientists have known this for a long time. So it seems there is not much to the theory that our habits and ideas are shaped by the way we make our living. But it is not as simple as that. We know a lot about how primitive people change their customs. We know how they do that before they get in touch with European ways, and we know how they do it afterwards. In some cases there is very little they can change in the way they live and work together. It is all tied up with what they have to do to get food, clothing, shelter and what else they need. Under other conditions, we can see that the people have much leeway in the setup of their group life and work.

concentrate on written presentations, but the same ideas apply to oral presentations.

Instructional materials ought to be "readable," in the sense that on the first read-through the student will pick up the main message. He ought to be able to put each major clause or each whole sentence into his short-term memory—not as words but as concepts and relations. This first reading will not usually bring full comprehension. He reaches that by seeing connections between sentences and paragraphs, and by connecting those to ideas in his store. But the first task of the writer is to make it easy to take the message off the page.

Readable writing may not be much like literary writing, and it certainly will not resemble the writing of academic and technical journals. Technical writing addresses a limited, qualified, highly motivated audience. It attempts to say much, very exactly, in little space, so that the reader has to reconstruct the argument for himself. Literary writing relies on indirection—the nuance of word choice, the covert message cued by a change of rhythm, the evaluation of a character that is hinted at but never stated. The educational writer should use whatever literary devices will add interest and richness of feeling, and should use technical devices to add precision. But he should bring his message to the surface, allowing himself such nonliterary devices as bold type for key points and numbered steps in an argument.

The pedagogical writer has to have a clear sense of the message the student is to take from the page (and of the relation of the message to that of the chapter). The point is not to "cover ground." Exposing the student to an idea is not teaching; the exposure must be thorough enough that he comprehends and retains the important part of the presentation. Texts often present information too densely. Language is a distilled extract of the speaker's thought, and beginners find a concentrated dose too strong for them. The criterion is not how much is packed into the chapter, but how much the typical student reader takes out of it and repackages for future use.

Readable writing relies on simple words, on comparatively short sentences, on connecting links that help the reader see where he is going, and on topic sentences or previews that help pull the main message out from the background of detail and example. This recommendation is not in conflict with the usual standards of clear writing; any teacher or educational writer would do well to absorb the wisdom, for example, of *The Elements of Style,* a writer's guidebook by Strunk and White (1972).

Wording that makes material easy to visualize makes it easier to remember. Concrete examples, adjectives that lend color to an otherwise formal statement, analogies, drawings—all these can contribute to a vivid, and hence a more retrievable, mental image (Kirchner, 1969; R. Anderson, 1974; R. E. Johnson, 1974).

The teacher or writer should not use vocabulary more complex than the material requires. Technical words must, of course, be introduced (in history, for example, *abolition* and *amendment*); but teachers and texts often use uncommon words that are not essential. "Upon the accession of Queen Victoria" has no advantage over "When Victoria became Queen." Using concrete words, readily visualized, in place of abstract words helps in reading and in remembering (McGinitie, 1970, p. 119). Abstract or technical words are appropriate when they communicate to the student a more exact meaning than simpler words. When technical terms are used, their meaning should be developed carefully. A word the student understands only vaguely makes communication inexact, no matter how precise the meaning is for the writer and *his* peers.

Simple sentences make reading easier. Long sentences with many clauses make a passage hard for the learner even though it may be instantly clear to someone familiar with the topic. Compare Flesch's version of a paragraph with the original (box). One version is highly readable, the other suited only to superior adolescents and adults. When a writer uses a style more elaborate than his message requires, he confuses at least some readers. (Tortuous sentences in a lecture or discussion cause less trouble than awkward writing. The ear forgives many sins against syntax.)

It is all too easy to write elegantly instead of coming to the point. Chapanis (1965) gives this example from industry:

> Warning: The batteries in the AN / MSQ–55 could be a lethal source of electrical power under certain conditions.

One worker, who understood about readability, added a more instructive bit of text:

> Look out! This can kill you!

A reader learns to pass over specific word forms and fix on the deep structure. The person often stores an image of the scene described even if, to make up a coherent picture of the scene, he must add to the original words (Bransford & Franks, 1961). In rearranging and embellishing, the student can easily distort. The teacher is wise to set out events and rules in a form that requires little transformation. A 4-year-old can obey "Make it so the red block is on top of the blue block"—if the blocks are on the table. But if he has the *blue* block in his hand, he will put that block on top because it is salient to him. Adding the restatement "Remember, red on top of blue" makes the communication more primitive, but it works. The result to be attained is described in a form that sticks in mind (Bem, 1970). Much the same thing is to be said about comprehension of verbal problems. Compare

---

**How many stamps did Dave start out with if he found 2 stamps and ended up with 6 stamps?**

---

**If Dave ended up with 6 stamps and he found 2 stamps, how many stamps did he start out with?**

---

The first, "natural" order—which matched the sequence of events—was much easier for third-graders to handle (Rosenthal & Resnick, 1974).

REDUNDANCY    It is inadvisable to avoid repetition in an instructional passage. To repeat what is important, in different words or from different angles, makes a message unmistakable. Without repetition, the reader who overlooks or misconstrues some element in the message misses his only opportunity. Rereading is of no help when the difficulty is miscomprehension.

A message is said to be redundant if the content can be reconstructed when a portion is lost. The archexample is the SOS message from the sinking ship: nothing but "SOS 30° 17′ N 46° 35′ W" over and over. When the signal fades and is masked by static, the distant rescuer still gets the message. Redundancy carries the signal through the noise. See how you can reconstruct a message when parts are obscured:

■t w■ll t■k■ ■ff■rt t■ r■■d th■s, b■t y■■ c■n m■n■ge ■v■n s■.

Your knowledge of likely letter combinations and phrasing carry you to a sense of the whole, from which any still-obscure part can be deduced. Similarly, you _____ probably read this _____ even though it has _____ in place of

# Mutilation as a test of redundancy

Selection II is from a psychology textbook (E. R. Hilgard and R. C. Atkinson, 1975, p. 346). There is a great deal of redundancy—much of the first line is repeated in the seventh, for example. Selection I is a rewriting that removes most of the original redundancy, reducing the passage by more than half. How much readability was lost in the reduction?

I have applied the cloze technique, removing every third "content" word. Prepositions and other connectives were left intact, but one third of the verbs and modifiers and nouns that carried the message were removed. Can you fill in the blanks with words that restore the original message? (The answers appear on page 540).

## I

A polygraph—commonly _____ a "lie detector"— _____ the reliability of statements. _____ measures physiological _____ of intense emotion.

The _____ records the base _____ while the subject is _____. Yes-or-no questions _____, with recovery pauses between. A _____ stronger than that on _____ questions suggests a _____.

An innocent emotional _____ may appear to be a _____. Not every _____ responds emotionally. And _____ strong reactions to _____ questions will mask _____ responses.

## II

Physiological changes _____ intense emotions are the _____ for use of the polygraph, _____ known as the "lie _____," in checking the reliability of an _____ statements. The term _____ detector is actually _____. The polygraph does not _____ lies; it _____ measures some of the _____ accompaniments of emotion. . . .

The _____ procedure in operating a _____ is to first _____ a recording while the subject is relaxed; this _____ serves as a base _____ for evaluating subsequent _____. The examiner then _____ a series of carefully _____ questions that are answered _____ or "no." "Critical _____" are interspersed among "neutral _____," and sufficient time is _____ between questions (usually a _____) for the measures to return to _____. Presumably, the subject's _____ is revealed by heightened _____ responses to the critical _____.

some _____. (There is some ambiguity; the first blank could contain "can" or "will" or "have".)

This last example illustrates a way of testing one aspect of comprehensibility. The so-called "cloze" technique consists of eliminating some fraction of the words from a page—every fifth word serves well—and asking representative readers to guess the original words. Redundant writing allows the reader to overcome the interference the blanks cause.

Similarly, redundancy provides a margin of safety for the reader who has the complete text but fails to comprehend a bit here and there. Good text material is redundant—enough so that the reasonably diligent reader will miss nothing that matters. The student who misunderstands a point can catch his error when the thought is echoed in succeeding sentences. Direct repetition is rather ineffective. It is better to restate the idea, or to elaborate by means of examples.

Readers and listeners do remember more from redundant passages (Aquino, 1969; R. J. Browne & O. R. Anderson, 1974). Admittedly, a speaker or writer who repeats himself may be called uninteresting. But the main goal of the teacher is enlightenment, not entertainment (Cantril & Allport, 1935).

E. B. Coleman (in E. Rothkopf & P. Johnson, 1971, pp. 155–204), having obtained cloze results for 36 passages, analyzed them to find which aspects of the writing made for difficulty. The following aspects are among the most troublesome:

- Uncommon words to carry content. Rare "function words" such as *notwithstanding* or *whereas* cause no difficulty, but uncommon "content" words do.

- Longer words.

- Many clauses per sentence. Complex construction packs information more densely. Undergraduates require greater time to grasp sentences with several clauses when sentence length is held constant (Fig. 12.5). But long sentences of simple construction also are hard to read.

- Many prepositions. Prepositions tend to appear in elaborate constructions.

- Nouns that do not describe concrete objects. Examples: *side, image, chore, depth.*

Although readable writing is appealing, motivated students can get the sense out of a passage that is hard to read. They will dig out the meaning and learn it if they have sufficient time and if they want to do well. One experiment

## FIGURE 12.5

### Effects of sentence complexity on speed of storage

By pressing a light switch, the student exposed the sentence for 1 second; he repeated this until he could hold the content in mind. Examples of sentences used:

**Compute the mean, square it, and add 2.** (three clauses)
**Square the odd number in the first row.** (one clause)

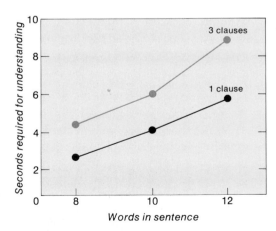

SOURCE: Adapted by permission of the publisher from Edmund B. Coleman, "Developing a Technology of Written Instruction: Some Determiners of the Complexity of Prose," in E. Z. Rothkopf & P. E. Johnson, editors, *Verbal Learning Research and the Technology of Written Instruction* (New York: Teachers College Press, © 1971 by Teachers College, Columbia University), p. 199.

compared ten 1,500-word passages on the same topic; all selections shared a common core on which an examination was written. Each passage was studied by a different group. The average score on the test was correlated with the characteristics of the text material, with these results (Rothkopf, 1972, p. 319):

| | |
|---|---|
| "Readability" of text | 0.30 |
| Average sentence length | 0.03 |
| Average word length | −0.50 |
| Number of technical terms | −0.45 |

Readability made only a modest difference in learning. Diligent rereading evidently could cope with long sentences.

---

**14** Rothkopf reported a correlation of −0.71 between the test score on a passage and the amount of incidental information it contained. (Information that was not part of the common core, and therefore did not appear on the test, was classed as incidental.) The correlation indicates that the more extra ground a passage covered, the less well the students knew the core. Does this evidence justify advising writers of text material to confine the content to the minimum essentials that form the common denominator of texts in the subject?

**15** Redundancy reduces the amount of material a professor can "pack into" a series of lectures. What determines the ideal balance between coverage and redundancy?

**16** How redundant is each of the following passages? Depending on your answer, rewrite the passage to decrease or increase its redundancy.

> A possible point of departure in analyzing the nature of mental processes in relation to the products of thought is through investigations of problem-solving. Problems can be selected for which only a limited number of solutions are appropriate, although the methods by which the solutions are reached cannot be so easily limited. It is possible to select problems such that some can be solved quickly and simply by the subject, while others tax the subject's mental resources to the utmost. (Bloom and Broder, 1950.)

> Allergic disorders constitute a number of reactions occurring in different organs of the body. Eczema, asthma, hay fever, hives, and swellings of the lips and eyelids are the most common manifestations of allergy. There is no general agreement as to what causes allergic reactions, although, with the development of psychosomatic medicine, increasing attention has been paid to psychological factors. (Fouracre, 1960, p. 1002.)

**17** In Selection I of the box on p. 518, which of Coleman's signs of troublesome writing appear?

---

## Organizing the Instructional Message

The person hearing or reading a complex communication about unfamiliar material cannot store the incoming pieces of the message efficiently unless he perceives the general direction the argument is taking. Without that overall conception, he has to store sentences one at a time, with consequent distortion and rapid loss. If properly oriented to the communication at the outset, he calls upon his background of relevant images and uses them to interpret the new communication. It is well, then, to begin an instructional communication with some kind of initial orientation.

Directing a stranger to his crosstown destination, it is wise to sketch the overall direction and main segments of the trip before getting down to the brass tacks of "Go to the first stoplight and turn left." The diagrammatic introduction to the process of learning in Chapter 3 was an organizer, a tree on which the reader can hang the topics in later chapters. A lecturer helps hearers keep their bearings by writing an outline on the blackboard, or by starting with "The main message I want to get across today is: . . ."

Being able to organize elements into familiar chunks or sensible structures greatly increases the amount remembered, as was seen repeatedly in our examination of perception and memory. Presenting broad statements and general concepts prior to specifics makes it easier to grasp the structure of a paragraph or essay (Greeno, in Gregg, 1974; box, p. 524).

Surprisingly, it is not necessarily beneficial to organize the message in a text (Cronbach & Snow, 1977). Experimenters have made up "scrambled" texts, with the ideas in haphazard order. Students learning from these often do as well in the end as students given the same material in a sensible order. Duller students probably need organization more often than bright students. The able students, who actively rearrange the materials and succeed in making good sense of them, seem to gain from that intensive effort (Gagné, 1973, p. 13). The inconsistencies do not contradict the general principle that comprehension should be encouraged in every possible way; the inconsistency arises because no one tactic for doing this is best under all circumstances.

The student brings his own belief system when he enters the classroom, and this provides a structure into which he can fit some messages and not others. Majasan asked college students about their views on human nature and on psychological investigation as they entered their first psychology course. He also obtained their instructors' views; Instructor 3 was comparatively humanistic, Instructor 10 strongly behavioristic, and Instructor 5 in between. Scores at the left end of the scale in Fig. 12.6 reflect a humanistic conception of psychology, and scores at the right end, a behavioristic orientation. The curves show the trend of student achievement relative to viewpoint. In these and other classes, the students who did best were the ones who shared the instructor's outlook from the outset. They seemingly were better able to comprehend his message.

A continuous internal structure is especially important in presentations for the elementary school. The child finds it difficult to arrange a meaningful whole

## FIGURE 12.6

**Learning as a function of the match between beliefs of student and instructor**

The arrow indicates the instructor's beliefs.

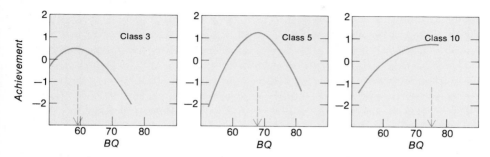

SOURCE: Data from Majasan (1972); for further details see Cronbach (1975b). Copyright 1975 by the American Psychological Association. Reprinted by permission.

from an experience cluttered with detail (Wohlwill, 1960). Plot continuity in stories is necessary for him; an adult can keep subplots in order. A continuous, dominant melody is helpful in music a child is to appreciate; an adult can take in more complex counterpoint. In explanations and descriptions for the child, one should give the main ideas in a straightforward way, keeping details and anecdotes clearly subordinate.

When the nature of any detail is determined by the whole—and this is true for machines, scientific theories, literature, and history—then understanding of the part must wait on comprehension of the whole. Before presenting details, it is wise to give a general overview so that each part will be more meaningful.

The organization that seems to be most useful generally is the *whole-then-part* approach. If a class is studying a play, the first step is to gain a sense of the whole, the main plot line (D. E. Palmer, 1949). The teacher might give a summary, or the students might read the play superficially to identify the main action. Having the overall plot in mind, students then can see each act as a unit and look for its basic events. The first act can now be read to comprehend *its* main contributions to the plot or to character revelation. When the pattern of the act is clear, it is time to place attention on particular speeches or single lines. In fact, without the larger setting, students would find interpretation of these details difficult. The progress from gross structure to detail equips students for whatever activity is appropriate: learning lines, staging the play, analyzing the dramatist's technique, or working out paintings to express the ideas. This approach is far different from reading the play line by line, requiring understanding of each word in order. Only when literature is very simple for the reader can he read for both the whole sense and the line-by-line meaning at the same time.

The "whole" must not be larger than the students can comprehend. The proper whole is to be judged by the readiness of the students as well as by the

## The urban serenade

To demonstrate the role interpretation plays in remembering, J. D. Bransford and M. K. Johnson (in Chase, 1972, pp. 392–407) had college students listen to the story on p. 511. The students were asked to remember as much as they could. These students (Group 1 in the table) could not make sense of the paragraph and remembered little of it. They recalled 3.6 ideas on the average (out of 14 possible). Group 2 was shown this picture before they listened to the paragraph; with the image in mind, they made sense of the paragraph. Recall was much improved.

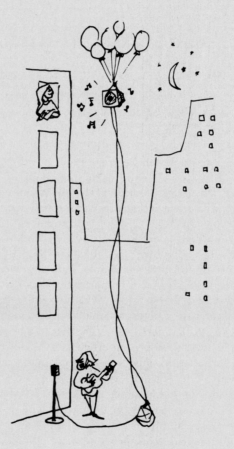

SOURCE: Chase, ed., *Visual Information Processing* (New York: Academic Press, 1972), p. 396.

Group 3 did not see the picture. It did not help that they were told in advance that the paragraph was to deal with "possible breakdowns in communication during a serenade." Groups 4 and 5 were given a key to the puzzle immediately *after* they heard the paragraph; that was of no help.

| Group | Recall score |
|---|---|
| 1. No context for interpretation | 3.6 |
| 2. Context before listening: Picture | 8.0 |
| 3. Context before listening: Topic | 3.9 |
| 4. Context after listening: Picture | 3.6 |
| 5. Context after listening: Topic | 3.6 |

subject-matter. The character of local and state governments can be seen most logically within the total framework of government services and powers. But the students would be hopelessly confused if such a comprehensive picture were his first introduction to government. If the third grade is to understand meteors, the teacher should describe the sun with the earth revolving around it, and the meteor swarms through which the earth passes. This is the minimum "whole" necessary to get a correct picture of the "part," the meteor coming into the earth's atmosphere and blazing up for a moment. This framework is sketchy: the moon and the other planets are omitted, and little is said about the universe beyond the solar system. But enough is presented to clarify where meteors come from, why we can't see them steadily, and why they recur in yearly cycles. The explanation would fail unless students could comprehend the earth moving around the sun, and some pains would have to be taken with this notion that seems to defy common sense.

---

**18** Does "the whole give meaning to the parts" when
    a. a student is memorizing a poem of many stanzas?
    b. a student is learning the functions of the parts of a plant?
    c. a student is learning the principal parts of an irregular verb?

**19** What "whole" might be appropriate if a high-school class is studying the publication of a newspaper? if a third grade is studying it?

**20** Fourth-graders are to learn about Egypt from a map. Which of the principles of communication in this chapter can be applied in designing and using the map or maps?

**21** Interpret the results of the Bransford-Johnson experiment (box).

---

# EXERCISES TO TEACH PRINCIPLES AND PROCEDURES

A principle is a statement that connects two or more concepts, telling what to *expect* under certain circumstances. A procedural rule is generally based on a principle, but it tells what to *do*. The principle might be: When, driving down a hill, you shift into a lower gear, the momentum of the car has to turn over the engine more times per minute. The rule might be: To reduce your speed while going down a steep hill, shift to a lower gear. The driver in training should be able to grasp the principle, infer the rule, and turn it into an action when the time comes; failure then is unlikely. The difference between principle and rule appears to be small, but it is important (p. 512).

## Exercise

Drills and exercises make up a large part of the learner's work at every level, from basic school subjects to industrial training. These drills are communication devices, intended to get a message from the culture's store into the student's. Exercises require the student to recall and apply this knowledge, perhaps in a varying context. Properly designed and properly monitored, exercises ensure that the meaning the student has developed in *his* mind matches the meaning intended. He can go from rule to action to handle common situations, and from principle to adapted rule to action in order to handle less familiar ones.

Exercises are an occasion for interpretation of situations, for provisional tries, and for confirmation or correction. Nothing new here; the question is, what can be said about organizing such activities?

Sometimes educational reformers (box) seem to advocate turning the child in school loose to live, instead of setting tasks for him. It is one thing to decry unimaginative drills, spooned into the child in relentless doses; it is quite another to deplore planned curricula. Any activity the child engages in is purposeful. Children acquire language "spontaneously" because they are using it daily to serve their own ends. But the goals that arise spontaneously as students pursue their present interests are limited in range. A sound curriculum consists of invitations to work toward goals some of which the student might never consider otherwise. The curriculum also consists of opportunities to make sufficient trials to consolidate the responses that lead to the child's goals. Exercises are efficient to teach subskills of reading; they supplement the everyday uses of reading—such as reading the names of classmates. The everyday uses are what make concentrated work worthwhile.

I prefer to speak of sequences of exercises rather than drills, and I distinguish *exercises* from *problems* (Cronbach, 1948). In an exercise, the teacher sets forth the process (the successive steps or rules) that will guarantee the right answer. The same situation is turned into a problem when the teacher does not specify the procedure, either because of the openness of the task or because he wants the student to find his own method. A problem is a situation where the person does not know what sequence of responses will bring him to the desired result.

English usage, for example, may be taught with page after page of exercises. The correct matching of singular and plural forms to *every, all,* and such words is demonstrated at the top of the page, and a rule is stated. The student

## Is it a mistake to plan lessons?

John Holt (1967, pp. 56–57) is critical of instructional plans that derive from systematic task analysis. In this argument, he starts by quoting a teacher whose experimental techniques he admires:

> Bill Hull once said to me, "If we taught children to speak, they'd never learn." I thought at first he was joking. By now I realize that it was a very important truth. Suppose we decided that we had to "teach" children to speak. How would we go about it? First, some committee of experts would analyze speech and break it down into a number of separate "speech skills." We would probably say that, since speech is made up of sounds, a child must be taught to make all the sounds of his language before he can be taught to speak the language itself. Doubtless we would list these sounds, easiest and commonest ones first, harder and rarer ones next. Then we would begin to teach infants these sounds, working our way down the list. Perhaps, in order not to "confuse" the child—"confuse" is an evil word to many educators—we would not let the child hear much ordinary speech but would only expose him to the sounds we were trying to teach. . . .
>
> Everything would be planned with nothing left to chance; there would be plenty of drill, review, and tests. . . .
>
> Suppose we tried to do this; what would happen? What would happen, quite simply, is that most children, before they got very far, would become baffled, discouraged, humiliated, and fearful, and would quit trying to do what we asked them. If, outside of our classes, they lived a normal infant's life, many of them would probably ignore our "teaching" and learn to speak on their own. If not, if our control of their lives was complete (the dream of too many educators), they would take refuge in deliberate failure and silence, as so many of them do when the subject is reading.

is set to filling blanks in sentences to which the rule applies: Everybody should trust _____ own instincts. A contrasting technique engages students with (for example) the problem of producing a newspaper. Again, they try their English usage and confirm or correct it. The task takes a new shape each day, with new subproblems. No directly apt model can be provided. No one response is practiced repeatedly. The learner's satisfaction comes from completing the job and from readers' reactions, more than from what the teacher says.

The problem approach is an inductive one; the learner gets some amount of experience out of which he develops insight and—it is hoped—comes to formulate a general principle. Exercises employ an expository procedure: the teacher communicates the principle or procedure, and then the student applies it to illustrative situations. Whether experience-before-rule or rule-before-experience is the best sequence is a much debated issue. I shall postpone discussion of inductive teaching and teaching by problems to Chapter 13.

In this section on expository instruction, instead of discussing typical exercise sheets prepared by teachers or textbook writers—which as a student you have seen by the hundred—I take up computer-aided instruction. Computer presentation allows an unusual degree of control over sequence and timing, and therefore the designer of exercises is able to apply the relevant psychology in an unusually precise manner.

---

**22**  When the teacher sets a task for the student, what determines whether the task is a problem or an exercise for that student?

**23**  Taking the square root of a number on a calculator that does not have a "square root" key can be done by using trial divisors. To get the square root of $x$, one divides $x$ by some arbitrary number $A_1$ to get a quotient $B_1$. Then the average of $A_1$ and $B_1$ becomes the next divisor $A_2$. And so on. When $A$ and $B$ finally approach equality, the task is finished. Only a few cycles are required if a good first guess is made. How could this procedure be introduced to students in the experience-before-rule sequence? in the rule-before-experience sequence?

**24**  In the study of Mayer et al. (p. 281), one group received neither concepts nor formulas. For them, were the computational tasks "problems" or "exercises"? What about the group that received both kinds of preparation? Interpret the results for these groups.

**25**  Do you think confusion in instruction (box, p. 521) is evil?

---

## Standardized Instructional Procedures

An instructional procedure can be called *standardized* when it is the same for everyone, or where any variation is regulated by well-defined rules. Standardized materials are usually edited with care and then used year after year. The chief arguments for using standardized materials are these:

- Ready for use, they free the teacher's time so he can lead other activities. Standardized procedures and more spontaneous activities can be used side by side.

- They capitalize on technology. A printed map in several colors can be more precise and more vivid than one a teacher can prepare.

- It is feasible to "road test" materials that will be much used. Thus, a map can be pretested to discover what items of information students overlook or find confusing; the instructional designer can add exercises that draw attention to those points, or he can eliminate the troublesome detail.

COMPUTER-AIDED INSTRUCTION   The highest development of instructional technology is computer-aided instruction (CAI). The presentation to the student follows a program. As was said in the discussion of the development of speech and other skilled performances, a program is a planned sequence of events. Programmed instruction is a planned sequence of explanations and tasks, together with a feedback system and perhaps a branching system for modifying the instruction to fit the learner (p. 531).

Standardized instruction can employ a fixed sequence of exercises. Every student faces the same questions and receives the same hints. (But students still process the material differently and have different experiences.) Completely fixed procedures serve for only a limited kind of training. It is often better to assemble for each learner his own sequence of activities. As we shall see, standardized instruction, though prearranged, can literally be individualized.

Unless the desirable response at each point has been identified in advance, there can be no standardized procedure for telling the learner that he is doing well, or for detecting his errors and guiding him back onto the track. Thus, it is usually necessary to state micro-objectives in behavioral form (p. 59). More than one response may be counted as acceptable. Suppose that the student's task is to write harmony to fit a melodic line. The computer can be programmed to accept any chord consistent with certain general rules. Then each student can create his own harmonic line, and yet all can be judged correct.

Instructional computers, though expensive and experimental, are already in wide use (Bunderson & Faust, 1976). Large-scale use will bring costs to a practicable level. It will become increasingly important for educators to judge when, where, and how to employ computers. Research on computer-assisted instruction is important to educators not using computers because it sheds light on possibilities of improving printed materials and teacher-directed practice.

The computer, connected with student stations—perhaps by long-distance telephone—can converse with a hundred or more students at the same time. The student's terminal is likely to be an electric typewriter, which prints questions and accepts answers. Headphones may be added, especially for instruction in language. There may be a picture tube on which are shown letters or diagrams, or perhaps slides. The student answers questions by pushing buttons, or typing an answer, or pointing with a wired stylus to a spot on the picture tube. Both the hardware and the software—the apparatus and the programs—vary in complexity and flexibility from one CAI installation to another. (One flexible system used to teach difficult college-level materials is described by S. Smith & B. Sherwood, 1976.)

The important features of CAI are these:

- The program is fixed. A planned sequence of displays and rules for judging responses is loaded onto a tape. Once stored, the displays can be delivered in an identical manner to every student, wherever he is. Any improvement in the program can affect hundreds of thousands of students. This prospective payoff warrants extended pilot work, first to identify spots where learning does not proceed smoothly and then to test revisions.

- Explanations are carefully sequenced, and exercises progress in difficulty. Some instruction (box, p. 534) is paced so gradually that the student is likely to make few errors.

- The student responds actively during the whole of his time at the station. In an ordinary class, the teacher addresses the student personally

## Branching uses practice time efficiently

In a study of CAI, preadolescents were taught spelling as straightforward associative learning. Each student had his own list of 48 words to learn; a pretest had selected these as words he could not spell.

The standard procedure (S) was applied to 24 words; these words were presented in random order, eight in any one session. The student heard the word through headphones, then typed it. The computer judged his spelling and then printed the correct spelling.

A branched procedure (B in the figure) was applied to 24 other words. The computer kept track of successes. After the student had had one or more tries on every word, the computer chose for each trial a word that the student had had trouble with. He had only one or two trials on the easiest words, and several extra trials on the words he found difficult.

As the chart shows, scores on the B list were poorer every day than scores on the S list, because the B list was stripped of the easier items. When all 48 words were presented as a posttest, however, errors on S words were twice as frequent as errors on B words. On a test a few days later, the B scores remained higher than the S scores.

only once or twice in a class period. With CAI, he can be addressed a hundred times in a much shorter period, each time with a question requiring a response. When he gets stuck on an exercise in an ordinary class, he can do nothing save signal for help—and sit idle until the teacher gets around to him. A "Help!" message to the computer brings an immediate hint or explanation.

- The response is objectively and instantly judged. A right answer is promptly rewarded by a signal. When the student completes a whole set of exercises, he may receive a message of commendation. (One of the Stanford programs for teaching young children transmits over the headphones a warm message: "Betsy! You passed the unit on *a* sounds!"— with a crowd roar worthy of a touchdown in the background. See p. 107.)

- The computer detects each error instantly. The program may call no attention to the error, simply presenting the question again later. Most often, the error is signaled—by a statement of what went wrong, a printout of the intended answer, or a request to try again.

- The program can be "branched" to fit the student. Compared with exercises in printed form, the greatest advantage of the computer is its capacity to adapt. The student begins with exercises thought to be appro-

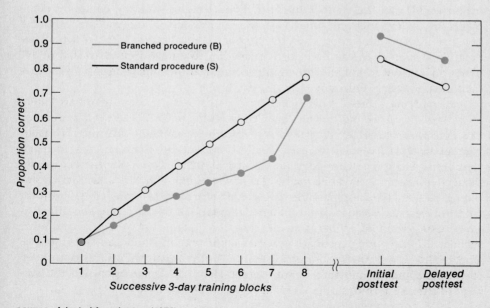

SOURCE: Adapted from Lorton (1972) and Atkinson & Paulson (1972). Copyright 1972 by the American Psychological Association. Reproduced by permission.

priate for his experience, but within a few minutes the computer has obtained evidence that this level is too advanced or too easy. The difficulty level of exercises is shifted up or down until the student is encountering the amount of difficulty that, experience has shown, facilitates learning. The computer stores information on performance; when the student signs on for another session on a later day, the lesson starts at the right level for him. When the content has been outlined as a hierarchy, the computer will identify a strand of content where the student is especially weak. It chooses exercises to develop that competence and ignores the content that the student already has command of. The computer can keep track of the spelling words the child failed on, and sprinkle in as many reviews as needed to bring each specific word up to par (box, p. 530).

- The total amount of instruction can be adjusted. Students who take longer to master fundamentals can be given more time on the machine each day or kept on the program for more days, while the rapid learners are freed to pursue their own projects.

These technical capabilities are used flexibly. To foster self-evaluation, for example, it is easy enough to inform the student that he will get no feedback for a period, or that only at the end will his errors be reviewed.

Computers are used for instruction ranging from teaching the shapes of letters to teaching physicians about patient care. In the latter application, the student physician is given the history and current chart of a hypothetical patient, and can order a specific treatment. If he calls for a laboratory test, he gets back a report. Meanwhile, the patient's condition has been changing (as it normally would) and the chart is updated. From time to time the computer comments, as an experienced supervisor would. Physicians and medical students say that the communcation "has the feel of" clinical work with an actual patient. (The simulation can be realistic indeed; if too much time is wasted in exploration without treatment, for example, the examinee may be told: "The patient died. End of problem.")

In applying principles, as in other kinds of performance, errors are likely to be specific, reflecting misinformation or faulty technique. When a monitor can detect the character of errors and inform the student, learning is faster. Hammond (1971) wished to teach medical students to combine cues to make sound diagnoses. The cues have only a probabilistic relation to the disease; no distinctive feature is invariably present. In the Hammond task, a student combining cues in the best possible manner would reach a score of 92 per cent (short of perfect, because of the inherent limitations of the diagnostic information). One group of students made repeated judgments in a trial-and-error manner. Right / wrong feedback was not sufficient, and they did not improve. The feedback left them confused because—with imperfect information—even their sound judgments were wrong on occasion. The error signal led the student to alter his working rule when he should not have.

Students told the principles for making sound judgments—and also given trials with right / wrong feedback—progressed slowly and leveled off with scores of 60–70 per cent. The verbal principles gave only limited help, as judgment and not mechanical calculation was needed. A third group of students received the same explanations and made trials, but they received a different kind of feedback: after each series of trials, the computer summarized and reported the *direction* of their departures from sound judgment (for example, too much weight on cue B, too little on A). With this kind of coaching, members of the third group quickly approached the highest possible score.

**26** Fifth-graders are to develop map-reading skills.
  a. How would instruction by computer proceed?
  b. What activities in the classroom would be useful to supplement the instruction by computer?
  c. To what extent can a teacher preparing all his own lesson materials (and accumulating them from year to year) include the valuable features of instruction by computer?

**27** Which features of standardized instruction are present in a language laboratory? Which are absent?

**28** If, in developing this textbook, I had set out to perfect it through pilot studies, what would it have been useful to investigate?

**29** Does the elementary school have any intellectual objectives for which standardized instructional materials could not be developed?

## Sequencing of Subskills

LEARNING HIERARCHIES   Chapter 2 (p. 62) introduced the idea of organizing objectives into hierarchies—that is, into tree-like systems of part-skills that go into a complex task. The tennis serve provided an example. The experiment of Mayer et al. (box, p. 28) used such a progression of subskills to teach students to calculate with binomial probabilities. Mayer et al. had a strong belief that conceptual training would be a helpful preliminary. They arranged a 2 × 2 factorial experiment in which some students had conceptual training and computational training, some had one, and some had none. All four groups then worked on questions that could be answered using the formulas. These tasks were "problems" for the concepts-only group, "exercises" for the formulas-only group. On a test like the practice tasks, the concept-trained group did as well as the formula-trained students. Evidently, these mature students made the bridge to application for themselves. When story problems (unfamiliar to both groups) were encountered, the formulas-only group was at a loss. Other studies also show that experience in analyzing problems is needed to carry students into flexible application (pp. 558–75).

Introducing ideas gradually makes it possible to teach a principle that would be hard to teach directly. For first-grade science, Keislar and McNeil (1961) developed a series of 13 lessons, each with 30 to 40 items combining explanation and response; three items from the twelfth lesson are shown here. The pictures show molecules. The child learned the code in an early lesson: a short "tail" indicates a molecule that is moving slowly.

The instruction was presented by machine. The child saw the picture, heard the recorded statement and the question, pushed a button to show his choice of answers, and then (if right) heard the approving message or (if wrong) a repetition of the question.

To evaluate the instruction, some students were asked in an interview to explain a phenomenon they had not studied, but to which the principle of molecular attraction applies. Two-thirds of the children could pass this transfer test after studying the program.

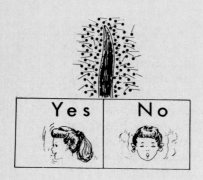

6. Which picture shows how the water vapor molecules would look after hitting something cold?

Yes, the water vapor molecules are attracted to each other when they are slowed down by something cold.

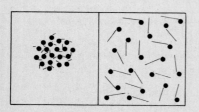

7. Here is a tiny blade of grass that is cooled when the sun goes down. Will the water vapor molecules go faster near the blade of grass?

Good for you! Because the grass is cool, the molecules will slow down near the blade of grass.

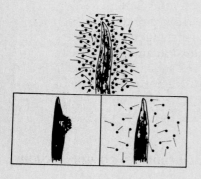

8. Here is a tiny blade of grass. The sun is setting and so the water vapor molecules near the blade of grass are slowing down. What happens to the water vapor when the molecules slow down? Which picture shows?

That's right! If water vapor slows down enough, the molecules will come together or condense.

Hierarchical analysis does not just develop a formal logical outline. Several logical ways to approach any body of content can be found. Among the sequences that can serve a sophisticated learner, some are far superior for teaching the neophyte. The hierarchy derives only in part from the logic behind the subject-matter. The logic indicates, for example, that the student will not be able to apply the binomial theorem (p. 28) unless he understands what the symbol $p$ represents and knows how to determine its value from the pertinent numerical information. The logical hierarchy offers a starting point, a way of rejecting hopelessly bad plans and of discovering possible paths into the material. The logic does not dictate precisely how instruction should proceed. It might be sound to teach the solution of complete but simple problems *before* teaching the student to determine $p$ from complex data.

The hierarchical organization enables the instructor to introduce complexities gradually (box). To cast content in programmed form, the writer breaks it into short paragraphs or sentences, each posing a question. The program writer usually attempts to make the progression so gradual that the student moves ahead with few or no errors. The student turns to the writer's answer as soon as he has given his own, and thus any error he makes is corrected promptly.

An instructional sequence generally has to be divided into blocks or units. The topical outline selected should of course be consistent with the best available theories of the subject-matter. Given their similarities in anatomy and physiology, it makes more sense to consider insects together in one unit than to jump from butterfly to earthworm to horse. But if instruction is concerned with a functional topic, such as ecological balance, it would not be so wise to separate the insects from the other relevant organisms. One wants to lead the student through a series of passages or bodies of thought, each of which he can grasp, and which as a set provide a sound structure to which he can add later.

In preparing sequences of instructional material, many psychologists suggest that the analysis work backward from the final objective to locate prerequisites. The argument is that the learner must have prerequisites under reasonably good control before he can make good provisional tries on the larger task.

Suppose, for example, that the end-objective of a unit in Grade VII is "to recognize that all animals have specialized organs for each of these functions: respiration, digestion, and reproduction." What accomplishment or understanding comes prior to this? There are various plausible answers, but one prerequisite is to understand the concepts in the sentence. If the student can recognize these three types of organs in dissimilar animals, he should not find it hard to grasp the general statement. The planner might think of splitting the instruction, proposing to teach about respiration in many animals before taking up a second function. But it probably is wiser to look at the several organs in one animal and sort out their functions. Matching of organ to function—perhaps in dogs—can enter the sequence of the instruction early. The content can be well organized and is not so confusing as working across different orders of animals. To go on to identify comparable organs in half a dozen mammals establishes the first-order generalization that these specialized organs exist over a large class of animals. When the students go on to a less obvious class—reptiles, say—they can use all the concepts from the study of mammals except details of the structure of the organs.

Gagné has diagrammed learning hierarchies for processes in language, science, and mathematics, the attempt being to identify prerequisites that must be recalled when undertaking the task at the next step up the ladder. In a 1973 paper, he made various comments clarifying his point of view. Here, I paraphrase and comment on his statements.

- Skills—motor or intellectual—can readily be ordered in hierarchies for teaching. When he speaks of a skill, Gagné seems to refer to closed subject-matter where definite rules or procedures are to be taught. Not much associative knowledge can be so strictly arranged, however. Indeed, research on memory suggests that if the content itself has a hierarchical structure, one should teach from the apex down, not from the base up. Likewise, problem solving cannot be reduced to a systematic ladder of component responses.

- So far, each hierarchy has been developed for one skill at a time. The appropriate way to arrange such lesson-sequences into a curriculum (in elementary mathematics, for example) has not yet been investigated thoroughly. I foresee a difficulty in using a comprehensive hierarchy. Probably one could organize a year of foreign-language lessons into a tree structure. But the curriculum would be lifeless if—to prevent "difficulty"—students were not allowed to engage in rewarding communication until they had mastered all the subskills. (Do I sound like Holt?)

- A sequence of instruction should be designed to ensure that subordinate skills are successively mastered, says Gagné. I prefer not to distinguish what is "mastered" from what is partially learned. Command of a response is a matter of degree even among experts. The student has to command the subordinate response well enough that it is not a stumbling block when he moves to *simple* tasks at the next level. I would not have the tennis-player "master" the forehand drive before he engages in an actual game; but being able to hit back most of the slow balls that come near him is a reasonable prerequisite. The same idea of limited mastery applies in moving beyond counting to addition, or beyond an exercise in subordination of ideas to outlining a composition. A modest control of subtasks puts within reach a task the student sees as more purposeful. When he moves ahead, practice on the subskills does not stop.

- The hierarchies Gagné presents are incomplete, he says. The hierarchy lists the "intellectual skills" needed but it does not describe motivational prerequisites and verbal information. Teachers using the notion of hierarchy ought to keep an eye on information prerequisites. Note also that a Gagné hierarchy emphasizes what is positively to be taught, ignoring responses that have to be overcome. The hierarchy is written as if the student comes to the skill with a blank slate, but students often bring in perceptual errors, inappropriate habits, and so on (Case, 1974). An example is the 5-year-old's difficulty in distinguishing height from quantity of liquid in a conservation task. Overcoming a wrong interpretation may require more than merely communicating the right one.

Evidence to support the use of hierarchies is of two kinds. First, students who have trouble with a subskill have considerable trouble with the tasks above it in the hierarchy. This is logically obvious; if this were not true of a supposedly hierarchical set of exercises, that would be evidence that the set is badly constructed. The other evidence comes from comparative experiments. Students following less systematic lessons are compared with students given hierarchical lessons—the latter group being held at work on each subskill until they show adequate command of it. Gagné (1973) cites several findings in various grades and subjects, reporting that the hierarchical lessons used in this manner produce superior results. Just what this proves is uncertain. Branched instruction, which keeps the student at work on whatever difficulties are diagnosed, is known to be beneficial. The experiments have not contrasted branching within a hierarchical plan with branching in some other organization of lessons.

**30**  How does a Gagné hierarchy differ from an ordered sequence of tasks such as Piaget describes? Use the bead chain (p. 333) as example.

**31**  How would a learning hierarchy for scanning poetry and classifying the meter—as iambic (da dá), dactylic (dá da da), and so on—differ from the logical outline of content for an article in a school encyclopedia?

**32**  Can a learning hierarchy be developed for the following? If so, illustrate subskills at two or three levels.
   a. Learning to judge livestock as a show judge would
   b. Understanding the periodic table of chemical elements
   c. Reading the stock market report in the daily newspaper
   d. Learning to score in bowling

**33**  Outline a hierarchical plan and a nonhierarchical plan for teaching children to read melodies in the key of C and to play them on a xylophone. How would branching be used in each plan?

## External Control of Sequence and Pacing

In standardized instruction, particularly in learning at a computer terminal, the stimuli presented to the student are controlled by the pretested plan. The student may be given some latitude; for example, he may be allowed to request a review on Gresham's Law. But most of the time the computer decides what subtopic to take up next and how fast to move. Control can be equally external in Socratic teaching, or at the dissecting table where the student physician learns anatomy.

Certain humanistic or progressive writers favor giving the student considerable freedom to choose what he will study, at what pace, and toward what level of excellence. (Holt is one such writer.) The student does have an important role to play in setting classroom goals and in evaluating himself (Chapters 14–16). Such responsibility develops self-direction and social skills, quite apart from its effect on competence in subject-matter. Unfortunately, when instruction is comparatively standardized, achievement is not likely to be improved by giving students a choice regarding pace, type of exercise, and sequence.

Three reports on CAI will serve as illustrative evidence. M. D. Fisher et al. (1975) allowed elementary-school children to choose the difficulty of computer-presented exercises in arithmetic. Every 15 minutes the Experimental (E) child stated whether he would like his next batch of exercises to be at a higher level, at a lower level, or at the same level of difficulty as those he had just completed. The experiment extended over three weeks. The E's paid attention to the teletypewriter and the exercises far more steadily than the Control (C) children, who had no choice. At the end, the E's saw success in arithmetic as depending more on their effort than on outside factors; their sense of efficacy, then, exceeded that of the C's. So far, so good. This favorable evidence was more than offset by the finding that the C children had completed more problems per unit time and that they had become somewhat more competent than the E's.

Figure 12.7 presents an experiment (Atkinson, 1972) in the same research program as the Lorton study (box, p. 530). College students were to learn English equivalents of German words. In the standard procedure (S), the German words were presented for trial about equally often, in continually changing order. If the student could not answer or made an error, the correct answer was supplied. The branched procedure (B) was "response-sensitive" (p. 386). Here, as in the Lorton study, a word handled correctly dropped out, so that the learner spent more time on whatever he found difficult. In the learner-controlled procedure (LC), the learner himself called up the words he wished to review; he was advised to spend time on items not yet mastered.

During the practice sessions, LC students called up somewhat easier words than the computer chose for B students. According to the final test over all the words, given one week after study ended, the B schedule taught much more than the self-regulated LC schedule, which in turn was superior to the nonadaptive S procedure.

A third example is a year-long course in fifth-grade geography that used sequenced packages of books, filmstrips, and worksheets, plus exercises and problems (V. Campbell, in Rothkopf & Johnson, 1971, pp. 257–73). One group followed a fixed sequence of activities within each unit; the student in a second group was given the file of materials for the unit, and he proceeded in his own way.

## FIGURE 12.7

### Effect of allowing learners to select items for practice

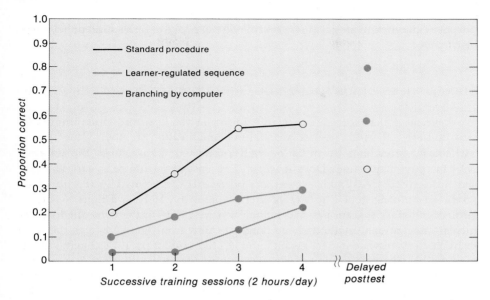

SOURCE: Adapted from R. C. Atkinson & J. Paulson (1972) and R. C. Atkinson (1972). Copyright 1972 by the American Psychological Association. Reprinted by permission.

Such differences in achievement as appeared favored the predetermined sequence. As for motivation, students in the controlled group more often took work home; on the other hand, liking for geography increased most in the self-directed group. Campbell suggests that choice among *topics* for study is a better arena for self-direction than choice among activities or exercises.

It is a bit of a leap from programmed instruction in elementary grades to the regular college classroom, but the same issue of control or freedom arises there. The recurrent finding is that some students respond well to instructor-directed course procedures, and some do much better when given considerable freedom to choose their own topics and schedule. Domino (p. 141) found that more conforming students did best when given little responsibility, and more independent students did best when the instructor encouraged self-direction.

Other studies (McKeachie, 1974; Cronbach & Snow, 1977, Chap. 13) reach roughly similar conclusions. Each study deals with a different course, with a different set of personality traits, and with students of a different age, so results do not coincide neatly. The trend of the results can be summed up by saying that those with a more constructive motivation—greater autonomy and security—react better to freedom. Those who are more defensive are thrown off balance when given responsibility, either for planning their work or for drawing their own conclusions.

Much current research is going beyond the simple question of whether control by the learner is advantageous. It begins to appear that giving the learner greater control affects *what* is learned, rather than simply how much (Mayer, 1976). If that is so, certain kinds of learner control will prove to be advantageous for certain purposes, but maximizing learner control will not prove to be a sound policy for all instruction.

## Effectiveness of Instruction by Computer

We have seen that some parts of the rationale for CAI and programmed instruction are not valid, at least not without qualification (p. 466). Other parts—particularly branching—seem to be well supported. That leaves the educator with the payoff question: Does it work? The answer is that ten years of intensive work with CAI and a longer period with programmed instruction have produced no consistent evidence of their superiority. Here and there a particular instructional program has had notable success, but—in the controlled experiments—conventional methods have taught as much on the average as the more technological methods. McKeachie and Kulik (1975, p. 177), having documented this with relation to college instruction, add:

> Few familiar with CAI would take the present negative results to be the final conclusion. New programs are being developed, and basic research on learning is progressing. Very likely CAI is in its Wright Brothers era, with its jet age in the future.

**34** Review Holt's remarks (box, p. 527). Is his criticism of designed instruction a fair comment in the light of what this chapter has said about exercises?

**35** Return to the principles on which programmed instruction was originally grounded (p. 466). Which ones are consistent with current research?

---

Key to completions for selections on p. 518.

**I.** mislabeled/ checks// It/ accompaniments// operator/ line/ relaxed// follow/ response/ neutral/ lie// reaction/ lie// liar// deliberately/ neutral/ critical

**II.** accompanying/ basis/ commonly/ detector/ individual's// *lie*/ incorrect// detect/ simply/ physiological// standard/ polygraph/ take/ recording/ line/ responses// asks/ worded/ "yes"// questions/ questions/ allowed/ minute/ normal// guilt/ physiological/ questions

W. Howard Levie and Kenneth E. Dickie, "The Analysis and Application of Media," in *Second Handbook of Research on Teaching,* ed. R. M. W. Travers (Chicago: Rand McNally, 1973).

> A thorough, readable review of the research on audio-visual presentations. Pictures are viewed as a kind of language; the problems of effective communication and comprehension are similar to those in verbal instruction.

W. H. MacGinitie, "Language Comprehension in Education," in *Psychology of the Educational Process,* ed. J. R. Davitz and S. Ball (New York: McGraw-Hill, 1970), pp. 101–56.

> Reviews the main findings on factors affecting readability and on the barriers to comprehension.

E. Z. Rothkopf, "Experiments on Mathemagenic Behavior and the Technology of Written Instruction," in *Verbal Learning Research and the Technology of Written Instruction,* ed. E. Z. Rothkopf & P. E. Johnson (New York: Teachers College Press, 1971), pp. 284–303.

> "Mathemagenic" refers to generation of knowledge, specifically to the acts of the student trying to learn the content of a text. Rothkopf here experiments with adjunct questions and other aspects of instructional design.

Dan I. Slobin, "Seven Questions About Language Development," in *New Horizons in Psychology 2,* ed. P. C. Dodwell (Baltimore: Penguin, 1972), pp. 197–215.

> A survey of research on language in the young child, covering these questions among others: What does the child mean to say? How does the child organize language? What does the child pay attention to in listening?

Arthur Whimbey, with Linda Shaw Whimbey, "Advanced Reading Comprehension: A Primary Expression of Intelligence," in *Intelligence Can Be Taught* (New York: Dutton, 1975), pp. 70–103.

> The Whimbeys argue that comprehension is a skill to be directly taught and describe simple diagnostic and remedial procedures.

■ The student may understand a relation better if he discovers it for himself. Students asked to discover should receive enough help to make successful discovery likely.

■ In thinking, one oscillates between intuitive pattern-seeking and systematic verification of hunches.

■ Students often fail at problem solving because they do not use their abilities; this is a motivational failure. Schooling sometimes teaches students *not* to be intellectually self-reliant.

□ Likewise, some students who can reason accurately are much poorer at free-wheeling visualization of fresh possibilities. Possibly their ability is inhibited by fear of criticism.

■ Teaching logical principles and analytic skills can improve thinking, particularly in adolescence.

■ In some instruction, teacher and students attack a problem for which no one knows the answer. It may be a scientific investigation, a mathematical game with new rules, a social inquiry, or an artistic effort. In such work students learn how knowledge is created and gain pride in their own powers.

■ Learning cumulates; attitudes and broad concepts acquired in one context aid the person in later situations. The amount of transfer depends on the nature of the teaching.

**CONCEPTS**

*expository teaching*
*inductive teaching*
*guided discovery*
*problem solving*
*reasoning*
*intuitive thinking*
*convergent /*
  *divergent processes*

*formal-symbolic processes*
*style in problem solving*
*flexibility*
*cognitive restructuring*
*Venn diagram*
*inquiry by students*
*cumulative learning*
*transfer*

# 13

# PROBLEM SOLVING

Once more we turn to large questions of intellectual development; this chapter is concerned chiefly with how a student becomes an expert at solving problems "in his head."

In its first section, this chapter is a continuation of Chapter 12. The final section of that chapter discussed how the teacher or a series of exercises directly communicates a rule to the student. As an alternative, the teacher can withhold his knowledge, arranging for the student to discover the rule as he solves problem after problem by his own crude methods. That is the inductive approach, which the first part of this chapter evaluates.

The central section of the chapter compares expert and inexpert problem-solvers, and suggests what can be done to improve reasoning and creativity. The final section returns to learning *by* problem solving. When students solve problems on their own, they develop insight into the structure of knowledge in various subjects.

# TEACHING SPECIFIC PRINCIPLES: THE INDUCTIVE APPROACH

Should the textbook and teacher lay out the principles to be learned? Or should the student "discover" the relations for himself? (See Shulman, in Travers, 1973, pp. 1111ff.) This question contrasts expository* teaching with learning by induction. In expository teaching, the rule is set out and the student applies it to examples. In the inductive approach, the student works through specific cases by trial and error. He ultimately formulates the general rule. When a definite principle or a preferred procedure is to be learned, standardized instructional materials—even programmed lessons—can be used to guide the inductive process. The end of the chapter takes up a more complex kind of problem-centered instruction.

In the inductive method, the student is given many problems to work through. He is to infer the underlying rule. He might, for instance, discover the properties of magnets by carrying out experiments as directed and reaching the principle that opposite poles attract. Is lesson content taught in that way better understood, better remembered, better applied? The argument for inductive learning takes many forms and has diverse psychological roots. One argument is that finding things out can be fun. Another is that such experience promotes autonomy. The third and more fundamental argument is that the student understands better a principle he has himself extracted from experience. This last claim in particular needs to be examined.

Setting the student to figure out a general rule without guidance is rarely the best way to teach. The student may be blocked in his effort to reach solutions; then no good comes of his effort. Or he may reach an inexact or incorrect conclusion. At best, induction takes a long time. But inductive sequences are not to be dismissed, since a verbal formulation given prematurely is of little help. Schemata are built up inductively. In discrimination learning, features often cannot be fully described in words, and then learning has to proceed by trial and error. My discussion of experience as the base for meaning (p. 508) also illustrated informal inductive learning.

The evidence does favor using *guided* induction at selected places in the curriculum. The student should be given considerable help in amassing relevant experience and organizing it so that he will reach a conclusion.

Consider a simple example. Kindergartners can be taught to associate sounds with printed words. In theory, they can detect regularities and then decode new words. They detect these regularities only when the pattern is easy to perceive. Suppose the training series is *hat, pan, get, ran, sun, dad, man,* . . . . If the child is trained to read these words, he is unlikely to detect *-an* as a pattern;

---

*Some educational psychologists use the term "deductive."

the first time he sees *tan* he cannot read it. In contrast, a grouped training series—*pan, ran, man,...*—brings the regularity to his attention (Silberman, 1964).

Working out the rules of congruence of triangles is too sprawling a task for junior-high-school students. A subquestion is a reasonable place to start: "How many different shapes of triangles can we make with these three sticks?" The teacher had better add (to make the problem clear): "Do not count triangles as different if you can rotate one to fit over the other." As the student generates one triangle after another, he soon learns that just two classes of triangles can be made with his three sticks, one being the mirror image of the other. This is a principle he can put into words.

English grammar can be handed down as a cut-and-dried formality from some scholar's workroom, or it can be developed inductively. Formal grammar is only an attempt to capture on paper the living patterns that most people in the community—children included—are already using. Like slow-motion films of a jackknife dive, grammatical analysis can show the student what he is doing and contrast it with the patterns others use. Students are able to detect structure for themselves even in early grades. Thus, the fourth-grade teacher may write one sentence on the blackboard, and ask the class to think up sentences that match it word for word. Soon the blackboard reads:

| The | man | ate | his | lunch. |
|-----|-----|-----|-----|--------|
| A | boy | stole | Mike's | bike. |
| The | cat | climbed | the | tree. |
| My | father | smokes | a | pipe. |
| The | wind | blew | Sally's | hair. |

Students catch the pattern, without any names for "parts of speech." The sentences they add do match the others. Now the teacher suggests a game. Read left to right, picking any word from each column, for example: "A man blew Mike's pipe." Every trial produces an interpretable remark, sometimes one to laugh over. Next a question: "Will any other order work?" And so on. Students begin to see remarks about form as a report on speech patterns they xave been using, not as a pointless rule. With this introduction, they begin to ask about rules, to function as junior linguists (Bruner, in Shulman & Keislar, 1966).

Inductive trials orient the student to the subject-matter. They create a matrix of experience. Once the pattern in that experience is perceived, it can be recorded in a tight summary statement—an important finishing step. You could set out inductively to understand a word such as *abstruse,* trying to infer its meaning from numerous sentences in which it appears. After you reach a tentative meaning, you would try to make sense of further sentences. But you probably learn the word less efficiently this way than you would if you looked up a definition and used it along with the examples. Examining sentences without help, you can guess several meanings for *abstruse*—all of which make sense. Even at best, induction leads only to a loosely formulated meaning. A firm definition sets sharper bounds on the meaning than a hundred extra examples can, once the first several sentences have given you a feel for the word.

Unless the student who is learning inductively carries on to the point of stating a verbal conclusion, he retains only a vague impression. His verbal statement is itself a provisional try, subject to correction. Teachers will expect more adequate statements in the higher grades, of course, and will demand greater precision there.

Students are often wrong in their attempts at summary; recall the example of *numerator,* p. 543. Similarly, the geometry student may arrive at a half-truth: "Two sides and an angle determine the shape of a triangle." The teacher's monitoring is required to make sure that the student's rough generalization becomes a soundly framed conclusion. The student can, at best, formulate a conclusion that covers his own experience. A statement that is logically adequate to sum up simple instances may become a stumbling block in advanced lessons, unless the teacher rewords it. The teacher will want the student to take away a sound statement of the principle. The function of the inductive effort was to prepare him to comprehend that statement.

In any course, induction can develop only a fraction of what is to be taught. It makes sense to have a home economics class prepare a number of cakes experimentally, altering the order in which ingredients are added and the amount of

## It is fun to detect regularities

Intellectual activity is play, even for students of low ability, when patterns are not too hard to detect. Robert Davis has described his experience with seventh-graders of low IQ and impoverished background. He set them the task of finding pairs of whole numbers to satisfy this equation (and others like it):

$$(\square \times 3) + 2 = \triangle$$

> We passed out graph paper and suggested that suitable pairs of whole numbers be [plotted with $\square$ and $\triangle$ as] . . . coordinates. Very nearly all of the students made the obvious discovery that there is a simple linear pattern. . . . A considerable number of them actually applied this discovery, by extrapolating according to the pattern, then checking to see if their new points gave numbers that satisifed the equation. . . .
>
> Some . . . spent several days working with various linear equations. . . . This . . . seemed to fascinate children far beyond their normal degree of involvement with school (R. B. Davis, in Shulman & Keislar, 1966, p. 115).

beating. If these variables do make a difference, the experimental results will dramatize the importance of correct technique. If not, the results will teach that bakers need not be slavish to directions. This is a useful orientation. The teacher can profitably supplement it with exposition; for example, the teacher can display enlarged photographs of cakes mixed in various ways. Hands-on experience has prepared the class to comprehend them. (See also p. 572.)

Psychologists have made many experimental tests of inductive learning. Two classes work on the same bit of content, one inductively and one by exposition-and-trial. The research to date (Shulman & Keislar, 1966; Ausubel & Robinson, 1969) is limited in scope and inconclusive. The studies have been brief and many have used artificial materials. More serious, evidence on long-term retention and application has not been collected. One might expect induction to be especially helpful over the long haul. A principle can easily become obscure or confused in the student's mind during months of disuse; if he worked it out for himself originally, he should be better able to reconstruct it. But evidence for or against this proposition is lacking.

To contrast expository and inductive work in the classroom poses too simple a question (Cronbach, in Shulman & Keislar, 1966; Shulman, in Travers, 1973). Inductive activity is not an all-purpose instructional method. The designer of lessons should regard the inductive approach as a technique of teaching that he is to shape through his own tryouts, to serve particular purposes within his course of study. The research has often investigated procedures in which induction was not guided appropriately. The research has not come to grips with the problem of combining inductive and expository modes in a curriculum sequence.

The Babikian study, though limited, is representative of the better experiments. Babikian (1971; see also Cronbach and Snow, 1976, pp. 314ff.) taught Archimedes' principle of buoyancy to eighth-graders in five class sessions. In the

## FIGURE 13.1

### Knowledge of buoyancy in groups taught by two methods

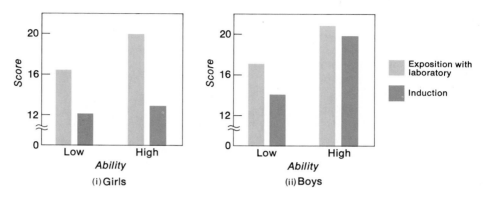

The test was a mixture of recall and application items.

SOURCE: Data from Babikian (1970).

expository-laboratory method, the teacher presented the ideas and the students followed laboratory directions to confirm them. In Babikian's inductive procedure, the students were given instructions for finding the principles by using the laboratory equipment. Each student worked independently; the teacher helped with the procedures but supplied none of the theory. All lesson plans included the same concepts, exercises, and review questions—hence discovery was to some degree guided.

For analysis, Babikian divided the students by sex and IQ level.* On a test at the end of the week, the inductive approach produced poor results except among the brighter half of the boys (Fig. 13.1). The test had several parts, and—except among able boys—expository teaching produced higher scores on most parts of the test: multiple-choice questions, numerical application of formulas, and recall of the verbal principles. Results were quite different, however, on a transfer test where the student had to predict sinking or floating of objects in novel situations (Fig. 13.2). Transfer from inductive experience was good, surprisingly good in view of the group's poor performance on more direct verbal questions. Those who had worked inductively made excellent use of what they knew, but too many of them had had difficulty in reaching a sound verbal conclusion. If Babikian's teachers had given more help, the inductive approach probably would have worked a good deal better. You cannot "learn by discovery" if you fail to discover.

---

*Babikian also had a third ("expository-verbal") treatment group, in which teaching was entirely verbal save for blackboard drawings. The teacher's explanation preceded seatwork with exercises. The averages in this group were not greatly different from those in the expository-laboratory group.

## FIGURE 13.2

**Ability to reach correct conclusions about buoyancy in new situations**

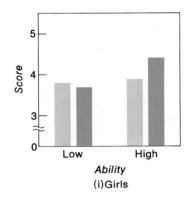

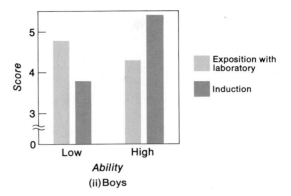

(i) Girls

(ii) Boys

SOURCE: Data from Babikian (1970).

1 What more would have been learned in Babikian's study if he had examined transfer only in those students in the inductive group who succeeded in arriving at the verbal principle?

2 How do you explain the sex difference seen in Figs. 13.1 and 13.2? Would you expect a similar difference if students had been taught several other topics by the same procedures before taking up the study of buoyancy?

3 In which school subjects does the content make inductive activities possible?

4 Are there educational objectives that can be reached only through inductive activities?

# THINKING AS A SKILL

Thinking goes on in school and out. The school wants the student to think about each unit of subject-matter, so as to understand how the ideas fit together and how they are established to be true. More than that, however, the school ought to want to improve the student's thinking. One aspect of learning to learn is learning to think: learning to generalize, learning to formulate and test propositions experimentally, learning to follow the logic of someone else's argument, learning to assemble and test logical arguments.

Many educational theorists of former times thought of intellectual ability—problem solving by mental analysis—as a kind of undefined "power" or "faculty." Some spoke of an inborn power; others have been positive that the power would develop as a by-product of *any* intellectually demanding curriculum. Today, psychologists accept neither of these views. They see problem solving as much like other performance—as a complex combination of interpretation, trial, and confirmation. It differs from other performance in that the "action" takes place mostly inside the person's head. Like any other competence, problem solving can be directly taught, with the aid of supervised and guided provisional tries. As research identifies the processes that enter problem solving, it also identifies ways in which thinking can go astray; instructional methods are devised to forestall these errors.

*Problem solving* is a broad term, applicable to almost all adaptive behavior (pp. 45 and 85). *Thinking* and *reasoning* are more limited. We usually speak of *thinking* when the person does much of the work in his head, testing provisional tries against verbal principles or trying to identify alternatives and compare them in his imagination. Some writers use *reasoning* as a synonym for thinking, but I restrict the term to the production of a publicly verified argument, so strong that everyone must accept the solution as valid. *Reasoning,* then, is developing an explicit communication that proves to others that your conclusion is correct and sufficient. (It need not be necessarily the *only* sound solution.) To convince a stubborn, rational skeptic is one of the most difficult intellectual tasks. Only a verbal or symbolic argument can be airtight; preparing this argument is the kind of problem solving I refer to as reasoning.

Psychological experiments (and Piagetian case studies) investigate problem solving and reasoning in limited, controlled situations. Just as skill is investigated by arranging conditions that tax the performer, the psychologist who investigates reasoning sets up tasks that put everyday experience into conflict with logic. By stating a premise that goes against the grain of experience ("Some rabbits are hawks") the investigator finds out whether the subject can apply logic in confusing circumstances. The problems presented in experiments on instruction in problem solving are usually closer to practical life: locating a malfunction in an electronic apparatus, diagnosing a patient from a fever chart and other data, and so on. Even so, the task is made comparatively abstract and artificial, in order to limit complexity and to make sure the problem is novel to everyone.

---

**5** How early in life does each of these occur: problem solving? thinking? successful reasoning?

**6** Do adults have occasion to use reasoning (in my restricted sense of the term) outside their employment?

---

# Imagery and Symbolic Thought as Complementary Processes

Consider this problem:

> **All dice are alike in the configuration of their spots. Spots on opposite faces add up to 7. What number is on the bottom of Die A?**

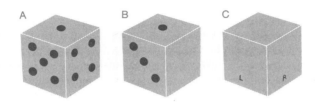

That is a problem rather than an exercise, since you have to create a procedure for solution. You have to encode the picture and the verbal rule into some form that allows direct comparison. Most people would convert both to numbers: "1 and ☐ add up to 7." Next, a somewhat harder problem:

> **What number of spots must appear on the blank face of Die B?**

(Find the answer before you read further.)

Very likely you "wasted" some time at the outset, perhaps making a guess and then realizing that you had to verify it before you could claim success. Perhaps you started by elimination: The answer cannot be 4, as then two faces of B would match the picture of A, but the third would not—violating the rule about uniform configuration. Better to see what is known for sure: 6 on the bottom, 4 at the back. So only 2 and 5 remain as possible answers. "Aha!" Die A has a 1–4–5 corner; so B has one also—1 at top, 4 at back, 5 on the blank face. But how prove that the 5-spot is visible? Could there not be a 1–4–5 corner at the back? To settle this, a reasoner notes that 1–4–5 proceeds clockwise around the front corner of A. In B, the back corner reads 1–☐–4 clockwise; the right-hand corner reads 1–4–☐ clockwise. To get the same configuration as in A requires 1–4–⑤. Hence 5 is visible. (Possibly, of course, you found some other way to prove that 5 and not 2 is the answer.)

My scenario included provisional tries, hypothesis testing, divergent thinking, insightful recognition of a pattern (1–4–5), use of an abstract concept ("clockwise") to chunk a display for easy checking, and some of the imaginative rotation of mental images that Piaget describes. The process was not straightforward; groping and false starts are usual in problem solving. Emotional factors can enter too. The person who impulsively gives his answer and fails to double-check will not be consistently successful. The successful problem solver holds up—"inhibits"—commitment to a response until he has checked to rule out other possibilities.

Now, a third problem:

---

**The three faces of Die C that you see do not carry the 1 or 4 or 5 spots; what could the spots be? That is obvious. Now put them in the proper places.**

---

(Complete the task before you read on.)

There are six alternatives for arranging 2, 3, and 6. A good tactic here is to start with an arbitrary guess. What if 6 is on top? Then 2 and 3 are on the sides. Is 2 at R or L? Perhaps you can visualize the back bottom corner of Die A, where 6, 2, and 3 appear. Their configuration is hard to check in an image. Checking is easier if you try to visualize the corner of B. Face 6 is on the bottom, 2 hidden at left—so the lower left corner of B is 2–3–6. It is easy to "see" that the order is clockwise. In Die C the clockwise order is R–L–6; you must put 2 at R. No uncertainty, no guesswork; the answer is locked in place. (Would the same order be found if you had tried 2 on top?)

The foregoing examples exhibit a characteristic mixture of intuitive and formal-symbolic processes. (The latter are formal operations in Piaget's sense; for present purposes, I shall include concrete operations within the intuitive category, though Chapter 8 used the term more narrowly.) The image of the die was transformed impressionistically, with the rule of shape conservation in mind. To ensure greater precision, elements were encoded in discrete symbols. This made it possible to identify the range of possibilities and check them off one by one.

Imaging is a fluid, inexact process, and symbolic processes check on it to prevent errors. You could easily be wrong in visualizing how Die A looks from the back bottom corner. Once you recognize that the same corner is nearer the front in B, you have the easier task of visualizing Die B from an angle. Still, it is easy to go wrong in rotating Die B mentally to bring 6 to the top. The label "clockwise," however, cannot slip out of shape while being carried to Die C. Discrete symbols or labels are sharply distinguishable and easily held in working memory (if not too numerous).

The die problem shows how abstract reasoning checks on imagery. It does not show the equally important fact that intuitive operations check on abstract operations, but this you have experienced in other contexts. For example, you have long known that only by making rough estimates in your head can you keep calculations with decimals from going wildly astray once in a while.

Solutions by means of images are based on ordinary experience; often they hinder thinking about the extraordinary. Formal abstractions are able to range far beyond experience and even into the impossible. Philosophical, mathematical, and scientific problems are solved by setting aside intuitive notions and relying on formal reasoning. An example is the physicist's conclusion that the "solid" table top is mostly empty space, occupied by widely spaced, tiny particles. The limitation of abstract thinking is that it has to use simplified representations. Aerodynamic theory can suggest efficient designs for aircraft, but

"Want to know something, Dad?"

Drawing by Alain; © 1953 The New Yorker Magazine, Inc.

mock-ups have to be tested in a wind tunnel to cross-check any proposed design. Air turbulence is too complex for the theory to capture fully.

Problem solving, then, goes well when one can imagine concrete possibilities *and* can analyze abstract representations formally. The excellent thinker knows which to rely on for particular kinds of problems and subproblems.

**7** Illustrate a problem that an automobile driver would solve
   a. primarily by imagining concrete representations.
   b. primarily by formal, abstract analysis.

**8** In writing science fiction, how much use is made of formal, symbolic thinking?

## Divergent and Convergent Processes

Problem solving has two phases: finding trial responses, and choosing one of them as adequate. The problem-solver constructs one provisional interpretation or plan after another. He tests each interpretion in turn—and rejects most of them. He narrows down the field of candidate solutions and finally makes a commitment to just one.

The first phase, the process of recalling, recognizing, or inventing alternative solutions, is commonly referred to as *divergent* thinking (Guilford & Hoepfner, 1971). The person considers a variety of paths to his goal. He is more likely to include the best path if his thoughts range widely—that is, if the

### Creators set their own standards

Education fails to improve on the productive thinking of children, and it may even cause a decline in ability over the years (see p. 563). So Edward de Bono (1972) asserts. He places high value on the divergent phase of discovery. The school seeks to transmit knowledge; "teachers are keenly aware that the only valid criterion of success is for the pupils' output to match the teacher's input" (his p. 9). To demonstrate the fluency and enthusiasm with which children organize their experience into original combinations, he asks them to design a machine for walking a dog, or a bicycle specially suited to postmen, or the like.

The drawings here are among those made by schoolchildren asked how to stop dogs and cats from fighting. In the first solution the cat is disguised as a dog, and the dog is made up to look like a cat. From behind his disguise the cat

paths that he considers diverge. The second phase, the process of reducing the array of possibilities until one answer is chosen, is *convergent.* The person may alternate between the phases. Indeed, one mark of the expert is the ability to return to the divergent phase and suggest fresh possibilities after all the original suggestions had to be rejected (pp. 588ff.).

Convergence may be strictly a mental process, or it may consist of physical trial of a proposed solution. Instead of testing the *solution* physically, one may test the *interpretation.* Suspecting that the patient has disease X, the physician does not test empirically by treating him for X until he recovers or dies. Rather, he looks for supporting indicators of disease X by examining blood samples or by injecting a drug that produces a visible skin reaction in disease X patients.

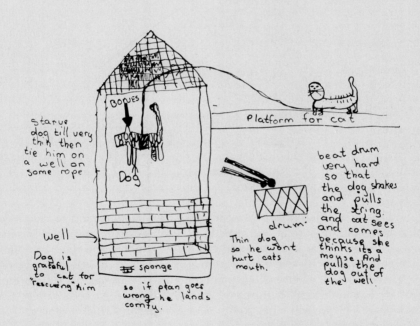

looks out, sees another cat, and acts in a friendly way; likewise, the dog responds positively to what seems to be a dog. What better start for a friendship?

The dog-in-the-well is an elaborate construction, with built-in safety features. The diagram is self-explanatory—but perhaps it is not obvious that, once the thin dog is in place in the well, you start the action by beating on the drum. Here the dog loves the cat in the end; the artist seems not to have worried about the cat's disappointment.

SOURCE: "Cat and Dog"—Fig. 15 (p. 29) and Fig. 24 (p. 38) in *Children Solve Problems,* by Edward de Bono. Copyright © 1972 by The Cognitive Trust. By permission of Harper & Row, publishers.

In most problems, a great deal of the testing is done mentally. The facts are weighed against each other and against the analyst's knowledge. For example, a certain diagnosis that fits the symptoms is set aside because the physician knows that the disease is rare. A person sees several moves ahead, envisions the consequences to be expected at each point *if* he is on the right track (Simon, in Gregg, 1972). Solving a problem, then, often amounts to laying out a plan and a series of expectations; the confirmation process goes on for some time.

In some problem solving, the convergent phase proceeds quickly. An item costs 38 cents; you pull a handful of coins from your pocket to pay for it: dime, two quarters, two pennies, nickel. The payment won't come out even, so you offer the two quarters and let the clerk make the change. You invent one adequate solution and settle for it; who cares if there are alternatives? At the other extreme, verifying a scientific theory goes on for decades. Indeed, the argument never is so complete as to defend a theory against new evidence.

In a process of discovery, both convergence and divergence are required. One has to perceive possibilities, but he also has to satisfy himself that the one he settles on fits the facts at hand. He may or may not be correct in his conclusion or solution. Columbus, you recall, did not think he had discovered America; to the best of his knowledge, he had discovered the route to India. The discovery phase ends in personal subjective satisfaction with the solution or interpretation.

Creative work in the arts can be seen as essentially the same as discovery. The same process of suggesting diverse solutions and of choosing among them goes on. The rare psychological studies that have been made of artistic and musical composition (Patrick, 1934; Reitman, 1965—and Heidi, of course) find the artist engaged in much the same activities as appear in more formal problem solving.

The chief difference is that the artist has no obligation to convince others that his solution is right. An artistic creation is complete when it satisfies its maker. Others may like it or not, but they cannot argue that it is "incorrect." The point was nicely made by a schoolgirl. A visitor looked at the work on her easel and asked, "What is your picture about?" "I'm making a picture of God." The visitor protested: "But, honey, you can't do *that*! Nobody knows what God looks like." "They will when *I* get through," said the artist serenely.

---

**9** Is there a necessary connection between intuitive and divergent processes? between formal and convergent processes?

**10** After a person has found a solution that satisfies him, finding an argument that will convince others is, in a sense, a new problem. Illustrate that reasoning has both divergent and convergent phases.

**11** Is "discovery" in any way different from "provisional try and confirmation"?

---

The excellent thinker does not "do everything right." He temporarily overlooks relevant information. He makes logical slips. He tries ideas that do not work. He finds himself at a dead end. Such human failings of experts are well exhibited in Watson's *The Double Helix*, an account of how DNA researchers fumbled their way to the Nobel Prize. Expertness lies in diligent, perhaps quick, recovery. The expert catches his errors more often than the novice and has both the determination and the ingenuity to find new leads.

Success or failure in solving problems depends on three things: motivation and style; cognitive reorganization; techniques for and concepts about problem solving. These aspects are not distinct; efficiency, you should remember (p. 275), consists in bringing each aspect of a performance into play in the right way at the right time. This interlocking character may be seen in the fact that intense motivation can reduce flexibility in reorganizing. This is so crucial a difficulty that reorganization will be taken up under the first as well as the second heading below.

## Motivation and Style

Whether a person commits himself to a problem in the first place depends largely on motivation. Many people, in school and out, fail at problems because they do not put forth their best effort. Problem solving is stressful. Everyone enjoys a certain amount of stress, so long as he hopes for success (pp. 198 and 607). With great stress or little hope, there is a tendency to give up or to settle for less than the best possible solution. On the other hand, the incentives may be too small to warrant effort. (You would have been foolish to stand at the counter debating whether two quarters was a better payment than dime + quarter + nickel.)

The term *style* refers to typical behavior—an aspect of personality. A person who is strongly motivated may adopt a self-defeating style. For example, some anxious persons "lose their heads" when under pressure, and abandon all effort to plan. They try over and over the response that failed, or turn to thoughtless trial and error (Suedfeld et al., 1967). Interests, confidence, and self-acceptance all influence a person's approach to problems (see pp. 603ff.).

There are various ways in which a person may fail to work at his best:

- He makes too little effort to comprehend what the problem is. He neglects or misunderstands some of the information given, or is unclear about the goal. Though competent to follow the directions, he plunges in too fast, grasping at bits and pieces and impulsively constructing solutions (Bloom & Broder, 1950). Holt (1964, p. 9) speaks of a girl who—

because of anxiety—could not bring herself to attend closely to reading and spelling tasks: "She closes her eyes and makes a dash for it, like someone running past a graveyard on a dark night."

- He rejects the task. The mathematics student, encountering difficulty with a homework problem, may assert that the answer in the back of the book is a misprint—cover for an inglorious retreat. It is especially common for students to reject a demand for formal reasoning. Asked to judge the strictly logical character of an argument, to set all intuitions aside, students often ignore the directive. They respond in common-sense terms rather than with logical analysis (Henle, 1962). For many of them, abstract thought is an alien language, and is rejected emotionally.

- He chokes off his divergent thinking, perhaps because he wants to proceed methodically and hence safely. Or perhaps, to maintain his acceptance in his group, he does not try to defend his own thoughts. Torrance points out (1963, pp. 72–88) that teacher and classmates often are critical when children think for themselves, discouraging independent thought.

- He fails to test hypotheses diligently. A person wants his hypothesis to survive, which biases the confirmation process. Given information in successive trials with feedback, the typical student tends to overlook, even at the college level, any results contrary to his forecast (Shulman & Elstein, 1975). When the "trials" are experiments he himself sets up, the student does not try to check out all the alternatives to his hypothesis. On the contrary, he sets up experiments that he expects to support his views (box). By such devices, he reaches a sense of confirmation prematurely. One further source of inefficiency is that people fail to keep track systematically of the hypotheses tried.

- He lets sentiments enter what should be a coldly neutral reasoning process. The student asked to judge the logical validity of syllogisms is fairly good at detecting a logical fallacy when the conclusion of the false syllogism contradicts his beliefs. When the conclusion is a statement he endorses, he is likely not to detect the logical error (Bolton, 1972, p. 142).

FLEXIBILITY AS A LEARNED STYLE    Much of problem solving consists of changing a strange pattern into a more familiar one. Sometimes perception is quick and solution easy. We are concerned here with the person's ability to *re*structure after his first interpretation of a situation proves inadequate.

Max Wertheimer asked various people to find the area of a parallelogram. Areas, of course, are understood in square units, and there is no direct way to fit squares to the sharp-angled figure. The insightful person restructures the figure into a shape to which his basic notion of square units can apply. One 5-year-old came straight to the point. Once she understood what was wanted, her response was "This is *no good here*"—pointing to the WZ part of the figure—"and *no good here*"—pointing to XY. "May I have the scissors? What is bad here is just

# Half-hearted experimenters

---

I have a rule in mind that defines a class of numbers. *2 4 6* is one member of the class. You suggest sets of three numbers, and I'll tell you whether or not each set belongs to the class. That way you can discover my rule.

---

College students facing this problem seemed to fix on a hypothesis instantly, even though there are a million classes into which the set *2 4 6* could fit (Wason, 1968). If the student's first hypothesis was "even numbers," he would test by offering something like *10 16 20* as an exemplar. Yes, Wason would say. (*His* rule in this case was "Increasing numbers.") The student continued to offer similar sets: *8 12 18, 36 100 222, . . . .* Each time Wason said yes, and now the student was sure of his even-number rule.

The student usually said "I've got it!" and stated his rule without making the crucial test: offering up a *negative* instance for sacrifice. If he offered *11 1 5* and was told no, that would give significant support to his even-number rule. If he tried *1 5 11*, the hypothesis would be shattered. Students avoided combinations that they expected to draw no as an answer. Yet in formulating a principle or concept one knows next to nothing until he knows where it does *not* apply. The following is a representative set of hypotheses and rules offered by a college student in response to Wason's *2 4 6* problem. The signs in parentheses show whether Wason said yes ( + ) or no (—) after the hypothesis had been stated.

Information supplied by the experimenter is in color.

| Instances | | Hypotheses |
|---|---|---|
| 8 10 12 | ( + ) | Two added each time. |
| 14 16 18 | ( + ) | Even numbers in order of magnitude. |
| 20 22 24 | ( + ) | Same reason. |
| 1  3  5 | ( + ) | Two added to preceding number. |

Announcement: *The rule is that by starting with any number two is added each time to form the next number.* (Incorrect)

| 2  6 10 | ( + ) | The middle is the arithmetic mean of the other two. |
| 1 50 99 | ( + ) | Same reason. |

Announcement: *The rule is that the middle number is the arithmetic mean of the other two.* (Incorrect)

| 3 10 17 | ( + ) | Same number, seven, added each time. |
| 0  3  6 | ( + ) | Three added each time. |

Announcement: *The rule is that the difference between two numbers next to each other is the same.* (Incorrect)

| 12  8  4 | ( — ) | The same number is subtracted each time to form the next number. |

Announcement: *The rule is adding a number, always the same one, to form the next number.* (Incorrect)

| 1  4  9 | ( + ) | Any three numbers in order of magnitude. |

Announcement: *The rule is any three numbers in order of magnitude.* (Correct: 17 min.)

SOURCE: Wason & Johnson-Laird (1972), p. 209.

what is needed here. It fits." (Wertheimer, 1959, pp. 47–48). She sliced the figure down the middle and reassembled it as a rectangle.

On any task calling for fluid ability, performance suffers if one clings to the initial perception. Binet (p. 275) talked about taking and maintaining a mental set; restructuring, however, calls for *giving up* a mental set or perceived pattern, and that too is a part of problem solving. Flexibility—freedom to give up one's first interpretation and to generate multiple alternatives—is in large part stylistic or motivational.

Wertheimer and his student Luchins have argued that expository teaching encourages a rigid style. A class of older students had been taught to reason about the parallelogram in the usual formal manner, by drawing in two perpendiculars, one from Z to the baseline and one down from Y. The class "knew" that the parallelogram was the same in area as the rectangle produced by the perpendiculars: "Area equals base times altitude." The students thought they really understood the rule and the example. But Wertheimer presented them with parallelogram EFGH; a new configuration. Dropping perpendiculars produced a rectangle, but matching triangles had not been cut off, and the eye was not satisfied that the areas of rectangle and parallelogram were the same. Most students were perplexed, but a few did find ways to make the rectangle-parallelogram match apparent to the eye. One solution follows as soon as one realizes that he has used too narrow a concept—that it is not necessary for a "base" to be horizontal.

Restructuring calls for divergent thinking, and that is not tested in the usual multiple-choice form of ability test. A question intended to appraise excellence in divergence has no "right" answer; there are many plausible answers, perhaps an unlimited number. "What," the tester may inquire, "are some unusual ways to use tin cans?" Or, "Tell me all the things you think this drawing could be." Children responding to the figure below—from Wallach and Kogan (1965)—reach out for such interpretations as "two haystacks on a flying carpet"—once they have become sufficiently accustomed to the game to turn their imaginations loose.

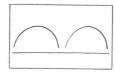

Restructuring plays a fundamental role in creative work. Copernicus broke up a centuries-old perception of the solar system, demoting Earth from the

Water-jar problems demand only simple arithmetic, but the student has to use the number system flexibly. Luchins (1942), a student of Wertheimer, had classes work through a series of problems. A fairly easy one runs like this:

> If you have a 7-quart jar and a 4-quart jar, how can you get exactly 10 quarts of water?

Solve it before you read on.

To describe solutions succinctly here, I use a code. For this problem, $7 = A$, $4 = B$. The solution is: Fill $A$. Fill $B$ from $A$. Empty $B$. Pour the 3 quarts remaining in $A$ into $B$. Fill $A$ again. ($10 = 14 - 4 = 2A - B$.)

The teacher led the class through a hard problem:

> Get exactly 100 quarts, when Jar $A$ holds 21 quarts, $B$ 127, and $C$ 3.

The answer: Fill $B$; pour from it into $A$ and $C$; empty $C$ and pour from $B$ into $C$ again. ($B - A - 2C = 127 - 21 - 6 = 100$.) Next, members of the class worked silently on other problems with the same structure. The numbers changed, but the rule I have coded as $B - A - 2C$ worked for everyone. Now came these problems:

| $A = 23$ | $B = 49$ | $C = 3$ | Get 20 quarts |
|---|---|---|---|
| $A = 28$ | $B = 76$ | $C = 3$ | Get 25 quarts |

On the last one, the solution rule $B - A - 2C$ will not work. Even though there is a simple solution, as many as 80 per cent of the class fail—in college groups as well as among 12-year-olds. On the next-to-last problem, most students say $B - A - 2C$, missing the simple elegant solution. (Did you find it?)

Luchins reported that the students he tested had been taught *not* to think about arithmetic. Each day the teacher had demonstrated how to solve that day's exercises; students succeeded on all the exercises if they followed the model given. Indeed, the students complained that Luchins's problems were unfair: "If you wanted us to use an $A - C$ rule, you should have shown us that way." Blind imitation was at its height in tense, competitive classrooms, and in classrooms where the teacher stressed obedience.

starring role and replacing it with the sun. Stoppard turned *Hamlet* inside out in a similar manner; in *Rosencrantz and Guildenstern are Dead,* he put those characters at center stage and moved King, Queen, Ophelia, and even Hamlet into the supporting cast. Picasso was a restructurer, and so was the unsung genius who first cut a bar of soap into flakes. The student must go through much the same process in constructing solutions for problems.

Students who succeed in learning a procedure the teacher demonstrates may acquire only a brittle knowledge. If they cannot bend and adapt the procedure, they cannot cope with situations that depart from the lessons (box). We have seen other evidence in the studies of Mayer et al. and Babikian (pp. 28 and 547). Rigidity is fostered by a teacher who organizes all exercises the same way, demonstrates one procedure, and insists that the student follow that set series of steps. If students do not encounter varied configurations they will not recognize where their knowledge is useful, and they will not develop necessary self-reliance. Students become more adaptive if they work with diverse problems and must search for a line of attack each time. Schroder and Rotter (1952) showed just that. They trained one group with problems that required different attacks, whereas a control group had tasks that could be handled by a single method. The control group got through the exercises rapidly, but had trouble on a transfer test. When the method they had practiced failed to yield a solution, they did not know how to proceed. The students with varied experience were prepared to search for ways of reorganizing the material, and they succeeded on the novel problem. Flexibility is to a large degree a matter of attitude.

Does the person who is facile at producing divergent interpretations also do well in evaluating them? In some studies, scores on divergent and convergent ability have correlated as high as two scores on convergent ability do, but in others the divergent-convergent correlation is close to zero. The result seems to depend on the testing and scoring technique, and on the group studied. Though the processes are distinct, intellectually adept persons are superior in both of them. Some writers have referred to divergent tasks as "tests of creativity." That is a mistake; both divergent flow of ideas and convergent criticism are needed for genuine creativity.

Investigators have studied persons with various combinations of convergent and divergent abilities. One study is summarized in Table 13.1. The all-round students in Cell A are adaptive, whereas those in Cells B and C are intellectually one-sided.

Getzels and Jackson (1960) asked adolescents to interpret pictures. Here is a typically reasonable, controlled, unimaginative answer from a B-type student:

> Mr. Smith is on his way home from a successful business trip. He is very happy and he is thinking about his wonderful family and how glad he will be to see them again. He can picture it, about an hour from now, his plane landing at the airport and Mrs. Smith and their three children all there welcoming him home again.

Here is the gaudy, unique (and hostile!) response of a C-type student:

> This man is flying back from Reno where he has just won a divorce from his wife. He couldn't stand to live with her anymore, he told the judge, because she wore so much cold cream on her face at night that her head would skid across the pillow and hit him in the head. He is now contemplating a new skid-proof face cream.

This divergent response is not necessarily praiseworthy, but it does show a willingness to take chances with wild ideas. Such wild ideas are rich raw material from which convergent evaluation may or may not extract a commendable product.

**TABLE 13.1**

**Personality patterns associated with high and low ability scores**

| | | Divergent ability | |
|---|---|---|---|
| | | *Low* | *High* |
| Convergent ability | High | **B** Inclined to excessive striving / Emotionally constricted | **A** Rational / Conscientious / Delighted in own powers |
| | Low | **D** Boys: Resigned or Hyperactive / Girls: Resigned in academic matters | **C** Rebellious / Badly adjusted socially / Boys: Artistic / Girls: Responsive to games |

SOURCE: Descriptions by Wallach & Kogan (1965).

Wallach and Kogan (1965) provide thumbnail sketches of children in each of the four cells. The patterns of thinking reflect patterns of personality and in turn contribute to (or hinder) adjustment. Table 13.1 is my summary of their sketches of four boys and four girls of each type. Florence and Harry, two C-types, are described in the boxes. Both have personal problems, but their coping styles differ. The adjectives in Table 13.1 only hint at the complexity of the individual. The Wallach-Kogan typology is not supported by much evidence; take it as an hypothesis.

Among students with good convergent ability, a large number show up badly in a divergent task. There are causes at the group level and at the individual level. Torrance (1970), like Luchins and de Bono, concludes that divergence is discouraged by most schools, especially around Grade IV.

In about Grade IV, teachers begin to say "Think before you speak." This one-sided emphasis on convergence inhibits students. A deliberate effort should be made throughout the years of schooling, according to Torrance, to set up activities where fluency, diversity, and novelty are rewarded, and where there is no stress on the quality of ideas as they emerge (box). A person cannot get far with convergent thinking until he has a good supply of tentative ideas to choose among. Divergence and convergence are separate performances, each with its own criterion of excellence; the student should learn to recognize both as worthwhile kinds of achievement.

**Harry— a C-type boy**

[Harry] is described by his teachers as a "learning problem" child. They report that he seems bright, but that his aptitude and achievement scores do not show this. Difficulty with word reversals is noted in his earlier record. In general, teachers have described Harry as unable to control and channel his thoughts long enough to concentrate on a piece of academic work, and as frequently escaping into daydreams and fantasies. "Short attention span" is a term that has often been used in discussing him. On the other hand, Harry also is described as acutely perceptive, capable of sophisticated humor, and highly imaginative in artistic areas. Various tensions exist in his family situation.

Harry's difficulty in working on academic topics seems to stem from an inability to exert control over the variety of impulses which stir within him. When he feels delight, happiness, anger, violence, sadness, these are quite directly recorded on his face and in his actions. Feelings of violence, for example, are vented through humor, fantasy, and a kind of ritualistic play in which he pretends violence but does not carry it out in reality—such as pretending to hit another boy over the head. Harry's art ability recently has been accorded recognition by the art teacher, and this recognition has noticeably caused Harry to swell with pride. Such a channel of support may help him to overcome the aura of failure and rejection which pervades so much of his school life. The humor which he is able to muster in facing his current academic problems is well exemplified by a desire which he recently expressed for "a full education but no school."

**Florence— a C-type girl**

Flo . . . seems to prefer an infantile state to one of growing up and becoming an active participant in school. She is old for her grade; yet she appears to the casual observer to be one of the youngest looking and acting children in the class.

The girl's school history provides a listing of one severe emotional difficulty after another. In kindergarten she evidenced excessive nervousness by chewing and biting things. She was extremely shy and always played alone. In subsequent grades she developed an attitude of strong hostility toward her classmates, so that she continued to be left alone. Teachers report that she can control her hostility if she must do so in order to gain something that she really wants; otherwise, her negative attitude toward others dominates her behavior and leads to social ostracism. She continues to be very shy, but will, on the other hand, characteristically become quite dependent on whoever sits closest to her. This dependence on her seat-mate results in her being easily led into mischief, and perhaps affords her social support in aggression toward others. At the least, it functions to keep her attention focused upon nonacademic activities.

Flo does little or no school work. When forced to consider an academic topic, her reaction is one of complete listlessness. She seems quite unable to concentrate her thinking for sufficiently long to carry any school task through to completion.

In striking contrast to this approach to academic tasks was her behavior with the experimenters. In the game-playing situation, Flo was active and expansive, high in productivity and uniqueness, sensitive to affective states, and skilled in visualizing. It may well be that this strong difference in behavior stemmed in part from the warmth extended to her by the experimenters, and in part from the lack of explicit demands placed upon her by the experimental procedures. She loved coming to the games and was quite eager to converse with the experimenters at great length. In terms of the foregoing characteristics, and in terms of integration, coherency, and concentration of attention as well, her behavior in the experimental situations was dramatically different from her customary mode of conduct in school.

SOURCE: *Modes of Thinking in Young Children* by Michael A. Wallach and Nathan Kogan. Copyright © 1965 by Holt, Rinehart and Winston, Inc. Reprinted by permission of Holt, Rinehart and Winston.

An individual who has good intellectual resources but is poor at divergent tasks is to be suspected of an emotional block. A student does not come up with a wild idea if he fears the reaction of others. The creative person comes up with many ideas that others reject; divergent thinking, indeed, is intended to come up with ideas that will be discarded. The person who is secure—either in his relations with others or in his enjoyment of his own ideas—can accept as a part of the game the dozen "failures" that have to be discarded. The person who needs continual success to keep his sense of worth afloat is not comfortable with such risks. Anything the teacher can do to reduce discomfort will help the student to use both kinds of thinking ability.

## Practice in divergence

The following Associated Press dispatch describes a social studies activity that encouraged diversity.

# 4th graders slide right into oil issue

FINDLAY, Ohio (AP) — Fourth grade students in this community where Marathon Oil Co. is located have ideas to solve the national energy dilemma. Here is a sampling:

—"Find out if oil has another name besides petroleum and look for it under that name."

—"Everyone that visits a foreign country with a lot of oil, bring back a quart of oil with them."

—"Change jobs so that everybody is working at the place closest to their homes."

—"Pull out all the kinks in the road so we don't have to drive so far."

—"Put a plastic bag over the pipe in the back of the car and catch the stuff that comes out so it can be used again."

—"Keep a dog in the car that is trained to bark if the car goes faster than 50."

—"Help around filling stations so they can have more time to go out and drill for oil."

—"Learn how to change water into oil."

**12** What sort of feedback can encourage divergent interpretation? When the student offers a wild suggestion, what consequences appropriately confirm or contradict his expectations?

**13** After the divergent phase of the class discussion on oil (box), how could evaluation of ideas proceed without causing any student to feel threatened by criticism?

**14** Several faults in problem solving are listed in this section. Restate each in positive terms to describe the corresponding motivation or style of the mature problem-solver.

**15** The subject in Wason's experiment repeatedly gave the same hypothesis in different words. How can you account for this "stubborn" persistence?

**16** Luchins regarded the "rigid" behavior of students in his water-jar experiment (box, p. 566) as showing inefficient problem solving. Norman (1975, p. 539) takes a different position:

> I believe it to illustrate . . . the efficient use of strategies. I suspect that the development of a new strategy [solution rule] . . . requires a good deal more effort than the following of a previously determined strategy. If this is true then it is more efficient for a subject to use a known strategy, no matter how clumsy it might be, than to attempt to invent a new one. A measure of efficiency must include a measure of the amount of mental effort involved.

Do Norman's and Luchins's interpretations lead to conflicting suggestions for the educator?

**17** Would it be advisable to measure ability to produce divergent interpretations as a part of assessing readiness? If so, at what level of schooling or in what subjects?

## Cognitive Restructuring

Our consideration of restructuring now shifts to processes of attention, coding, and transformation.

Given a problem to solve, even motivated persons often have difficulty in keeping their eyes on the right problem (Hayes & Simon, in Gregg, 1974). A person overlooks a crucial fact or misunderstands a rule, and sometimes tries to take irrelevant elements into account. Try this problem:

> **On the next page is a square containing nine dots. Find a way to connect all the dots using just four straight lines, not lifting your pencil from the page in making the lines.**

You probably have trouble finding a plan that will work. The square frame is not part of the problem, but many people try to keep the pencil within the square, which makes the problem impossible to solve. Now that I have helped you define the problem, the solution should come quickly.

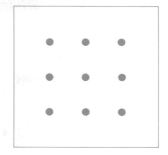

It is not easy to distinguish the relevant from the irrelevant, as is shown in the following story. In experiments in a certain laboratory, a standard injection of hexobarbital had always put mice to sleep for 35 minutes. In a new series of tests, mice of the same kind were miraculously back on their feet just 16 minutes after injection of the drug. The investigators found no evidence of change in the drug, the technique, or the strain of mice. Then they realized that this was the first assay of hexobarbital since the laboratory was refurbished. Could that somehow have changed the effect? Painstaking detective work revealed that replacing the maple shavings formerly used as bedding with pine shavings had caused a change in metabolism. When maple shavings were put down in the new cages the drug again took 35 minutes to wear off (Vesell, 1967). Just as you ruled the square into the dot problem, the physiologists for a time ruled the bedding out of their problem.

It helps to know about the subject-matter of a problem. Asked to find on a street map the shortest route to a new destination in Berkeley, the person who has driven through Berkeley many times can do so much faster than a person in Berkeley for the first time. Experience assists in chunking, it permits one to form valuable images, and it suggests possibilities and probabilities.

But experience can misdirect. Specific physical disorders are associated with specific organisms, according to the view that prevailed when—around 1900—scientists set out to prevent beriberi. So team after team of investigators tried to isolate the "beriberi germ." The germ theory misdirected attention just as did the square in the nine-dot puzzle. The true story emerged only when an army doctor in the Philippines noticed that beriberi was more common in certain encampments, and matched this to a difference in diets (R. Williams, 1961). Restructuring, again.

Failure to separate the formal problem from the context given by experience accounts for many failures in logic. Everyone is accustomed to translating verbal statements into real-world images. In a logical task, however, he is told to forget the reality and attend only to the sentence and its deep structure.

---

**Some owls are hunters.**
**No hunters are rabbits.**
**Therefore, no owls are rabbits.**

---

The temptation to call the reasoning valid is very strong, just because the conclusion is valid. The person who forms visual images will be misled. He sees owls searching and pouncing, he sees rabbits hiding—the two actors cannot be the same, he concludes.

In logical reasoning, one must at times close his mind to images and meanings and concentrate on the symbols. This skill is learned by practice in distinguishing sound syllogisms from unsound ones. Some of the practice syllogisms will have false premises ("All owls are rabbits.").

Since college students find abstract reasoning troublesome, it is not strange that children in the early grades should be ill at ease in making logical judgments. This is a test item for children:

---

**The chip in my hand is blue and it is not blue.**
**True? false? or can't you tell?**

---

The chip is hidden in a closed fist, and most children say "I can't tell." The ability to look for meanings in language *apart from* events develops late. It is acquired alongside other techniques of formal operational thought (Osherson & Markman, 1975).

To derive implications, one transforms the symbols given. Surface structure is changed to deep structure (D. M. Johnson, 1972, Chap. 6). Abstract statements are often misread: "Some blengs are nops" may seem to say "Some *but not all* blengs are nops"—but the three added words alter the meaning.

Venn diagrams such as those shown here assist in logical recoding. They also perform a chunking function that makes it easy to compare propositions. The diagram at left applies to "All blengs are nops." (The *?*, which does not usually appear, reminds us that logically we do not know if any nop is outside the set of blengs.) "Some blengs are nops" is correctly diagrammed at the right.

Putting material into abstract form does not eliminate errors, but it changes the nature of the errors (Wason & Johnson-Laird, 1972, Chap. 11; see also Table 13.2). Symbolic forms such as Venn diagrams are useful checking devices, but only after one is thoroughly familiar with them.

Insufficient command of schemata for making transformations is a source of trouble even for adults. Gavurin (1967) used anagrams to demonstrate this. He tested college students and found them able to make a word out of letters on scattered tiles. When the tiles were glued to the work surface, though, some of them failed. Evidently they needed the memory support that a physical rearrangement of the tiles provided. These students were less capable at spatial visualization (p. 286) than students who could solve glued-in-place anagrams. In

**TABLE 13.2**
Readiness of adults to accept invalid conclusions

| Symbolic form of propositions | Concrete form of propositions | Proportion accepting conclusion | |
|---|---|---|---|
| | | Symbolic | Concrete |
| Premise:<br>All X are Y. | All the men belonging to the Athletic Club belong this club. | | |
| Conclusion 1:<br>All Y are X. | All the men belonging to this club belong to the Athletic Club. | 25 | 4 |
| Conclusion 2:<br>Some Y are not X. | Some men belonging to this club do not belong to the Athletic Club. | 14 | 21 |

SOURCE: Data from Wilkins (1928).

syllogisms and other problems also, the person who cannot label information efficiently needs memory support before he can get on with problem solving.

Dividing a task into subtasks is a particularly important kind of restructuring (Reed & Abramson, 1976). Psychologists have used the Tower of Hanoi, shown here, to study the subdivision process. The conical stack of disks on Peg

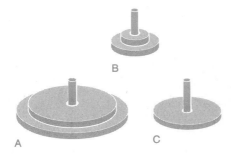

A is to be transferred to C. One disk is moved at a time, and it can never be placed atop a smaller disk. The task has a logical structure:

> To shift five disks from A to C, one must first set up a cone of four disks on B. (With these out of the way, the bottom disk at A can be moved to C. Then the problem is: Move four disks from B to C.)
>
> To get four at B, one must first put a cone of three disks on C.
>
> The previous stage is a two-disk cone on B.
>
> So the first requirement is to move the smallest disk to C.

As dozens of moves are required, trial and error can go hopelessly wrong. The analysis, however, shows that at any moment one is building up a one-disk cone on C, then a two-disk cone on B, and so on. The player can ignore the two largest disks while building the three-disk cone on C; that makes a comparatively easy subtask. Then one moves Disk 4 and shifts the three-disk cone over to it—the same easy task again.

High-school students working without guidance succeed in shifting a four-disk cone. They lose their place, however, when given five or more disks at the start. If given an explanation of the substages, the student is able to focus on the simpler part and keep his place (R. Gagné & E. Smith, 1962).

A good solver of problems, of course, does not have to be taught the structure; he locates intermediate goals or segments of a task for himself. Egan and Greeno (in Gregg, 1974) encouraged high-school students to figure out a *general* procedure for the tower problem while solving the four-disk version. Students who had been so challenged did much better on five- and six-disk problems than students without experience, or students who had been told vaguely to "try to profit" from the four-disk experience. Analysis cut the problem down to size.

CONCEPTS AND TECHNIQUES   The capable problem-solver commands a large repertoire of specific concepts for problem solving, and many specific codes and techniques. Few fit any one problem, but the person who has a large repertoire and makes clever use of it is ready to tackle almost any problem. Among such codes or labels illustrated earlier are Venn diagrams for syllogisms (p. 568), "clockwise" for the die problem (p. 551), and, for the bead-chain problems, "order" and "between" (p. 333). Logical principles help to regulate thought; for example:

The converse of a true proposition may not be true.

A sufficient condition is not a necessary condition.

These are general ideas; and like other principles, the learner has to apply them in concrete contexts before he really understands them.

Among the teachable techniques that can help in collecting and organizing information are these:

- Setting out all possible solutions in a systematic way, then proceeding by elimination. The tree structure is particularly useful in keeping track of combinations (see p. 572). Hierarchical structures seem to exist in memory (p. 454), and some psychologists believe that assembling possibilities into hierarchies is a major part of successful inductive problem solving (Egan & Greeno, in Gregg, 1974). Thinking of a tree structure for the tower problem makes one conscious of choice-points (first move to B? or to C?) and brings the structure of the game to the surface.

- Experimenting with extreme cases. In Wason's problem (box, p. 559), for instance, one might find out if the range of the numerals is important by trying 4 4 4 (−) and 1 500 9000 (+).

- Working backward from the desired end-state. That is how one comes to realize that the proper first move in the tower game is to C and not to B, when there are five disks.

**18** There are various solution rules for the tower problem. Would it be helpful to teach any of the following rules? How early in the person's work on the task?
  a. The sequence is 1 2 1 3 1 4 1 2 1 3 . . . .
  b. Never move the same disk twice in succession.
  c. Move odd-numbered disks counterclockwise and even-numbered disks clockwise.

**19** Here is a problem for you:

7 4 3 9 5 3 4 1 9 4 7 6 1 9 5 2 0
**In this row, every digit save one appears. What digit is missing?**

Did you find the missing digit? Why did you accept (or reject) the problem? If I had presented a whole page of numbers, would you have accepted the task of finding the missing digit? What does this indicate about why a person rejects some problems and not others?

**20** Demonstrate that a structure of subgoals is needed in
  a. designing the floor-plan for a two-bedroom house.
  b. writing a book review.
  c. figuring out why an automobile will not start.

# INSTRUCTION IN PROBLEM SOLVING

Equipping the person with knowledge or with techniques of analysis contributes to his success in problem solving. Also, stimulating autonomy (pp. 196 and 577) promotes effectiveness. So problem solving can be improved. To speak of improving problem solving, however, brings us back to the idea of improving mental ability; and we saw in Chapters 8 and 9 that most efforts in that direction have not produced demonstrable, lasting results. The contradiction appears less marked when we realize how broad are the resources that enter into effective problem solving, and how slowly they accumulate. Instruction intended to overcome one kind of inefficiency or to teach one technique can produce significant but limited gains. It is too much to expect that any limited school experience will provide the repertoire and the range of styles necessary to cope with all the problems—real or artificial—that may arise. This cautious appraisal does

## FIGURE 13.3

### The leak-detection problem (set by Duncan) and the decision tree

The boxes across the top represent stages in purifying acid. If the quality-control sample drawn off at *q.c.* shows excess water, samples are tested at earlier points. The numerals in the boxes are probabilities; water is more likely at Stage 5 than at any other point. The numerals below the boxes are costs of taking samples; samples at *b* and *c* are most costly. The decision tree consists of branching rules that on the average will be efficient with these numerical values.

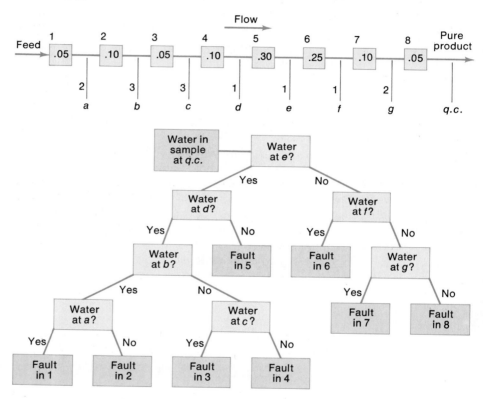

SOURCE: K. Duncan (1971), p. 441. Reprinted by permission of Cambridge University Press.

not boil down to advice that the school should abandon the effort to improve problem solving and reasoning. Rather, the advice is to make this a conscious and continuous aim in all subjects and in all years of schooling.

K. Duncan (1971) trained 16-year-olds to cope with a complex problem. The information on retention and transfer from his training closely resembles that of Husband (p. 447) on maze learning, which is a kind of problem solving; Duncan worked with industrial trainees who had to understand a certain production system. An acid being purified passes through eight processes, represented by the boxes at the top of Fig. 13.3. If water leaks into the acid, that is detected when a quality-control sample is drawn off at *q.c.* To locate just where the leak occurred, one draws off samples at points *a* to *g*. It costs something to draw a sample—three units at *b*, in this example, one at *d*, and so on. The probability of a leak varies—0.30 at Box 5 and only 0.05 at Box 8. The leak is to be found while keeping down the cost for samples. The decision tree lays out an economical sequence of tests; for a person who knows the decision tree, finding the leak at a properly low cost is only an exercise.

By a lengthy process, Duncan built up the needed concepts for his trainees. Then he showed the trainee the decision tree and taught him to use it. On Trial 1, the instructor arbitrarily chose Box 4—let us say—as the location of the leak. The student called for a sample. If he sampled at *f*, for example, the instructor said yes (excess water). If he sampled at *a*, he was told no. Drawing further samples, he could zero in on the leak. At a later date, as a test, the student was asked to locate leaks in the system. The costs and probabilities were as before, but he was not supplied with a tree. Next, he was asked to locate leaks with new numerical values for the costs and probabilities. To that transfer task, a new decision tree applied, and the trainee was left to work it out for himself. The tests were given six days after training for some, and after two months or six months for others.

Duncan separated students of high and low ability in his analysis. Ability was defined by the person's score on the ten trials completed before the decision tree was introduced into the training. By the end of training, the low-ability trainees learned enough to far outperform an untrained control group in locating leaks within the system they studied (Fig. 13.4). But on a *transfer*

## FIGURE 13.4

### Retention and transfer of a problem-solving skill

The score represents "excess cost"; the most efficient solution receives a score of zero, so a "low" score is desirable. The asterisk indicates the performance of a control group; they did about equally well on both tasks. Duncan did not report separate averages for high- and low-ability segments of the control group.

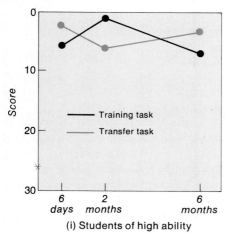

(i) Students of high ability

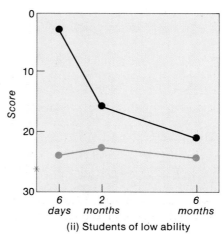

(ii) Students of low ability

SOURCE: Adapted from K. Duncan (1971), p. 445. Reprinted by permission of Cambridge University Press.

test—even an early one—they did no better than the untrained persons. As time passed, the low-ability trainees lost most of what they knew about the training task. Their learning, then, was specific and transient. The story is entirely different in the high-ability group. Able trainees did fully as well on the transfer task as on the one they had practiced. They had learned the *technique* of locating faults economically. Their ability to analyze was just as strong six months after training as it was when they had just been trained. (See also Duncan & Gray, 1975.)

Before the tree was introduced, the trainees of high ability were well oriented to the task and had discovered some approximate rules of procedure. They, then, were ready for Duncan's explanation. (Duncan did not prove that men of low ability cannot be trained. He might have devised a procedure better suited to orient the low-aptitude men, before trying to teach the tree structure.)

Duncan's problem requires formal operational thought—recognizing the full range of possible actions and choosing among them. According to Piaget, formal thought becomes possible in adolescence; but not all adolescents and adults think systematically, and none of them does so on all types of problems (Elkind, 1975).

Formal analysis can be taught in early adolescence, with better results after age 13 than at earlier ages (Barrett, 1975; Siegler & Liebert, 1975). Siegler and Liebert rigged an electric train so that it would move only when each of four switches was properly set; the student was to discover the setting. With four switches there were 16 combinations; the subject had to use trial and error, but if he planned carefully he would avoid duplication and would miss no possibilities. The

## FIGURE 13.5

### Effects of teaching a logical schema

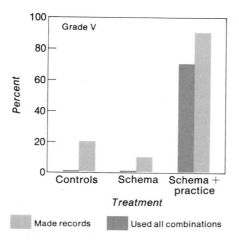
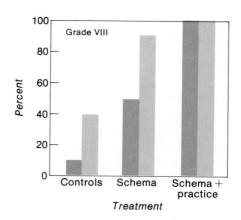

SOURCE: Data from Siegler & Liebert (1975).

## Lessons in productive thinking—do they work?

One series of lessons for the upper elementary grades (Covington et al., 1974) carries the student through a series of adventures in which Lila and Jim, helped by their Uncle John, resolve mysteries. In the Deserted House story, Jim is frightened by flickering ghostly figures as he looks into the old Parker mansion one night. Telling Uncle John about it, Jim recalls details such as a low humming noise. The students "think along" as Jim and Uncle John search for a unifying explanation—which turns out to be a movie projector. (How it came to be there is a puzzle for a later lesson.) The students also solve problems on their own and—most important—discuss how to be effective in solving problems.

Wardrop et al., (1969) found that four weeks of work (on the first unit of the course) did improve average scores on many thinking processes. Teacher style had an important influence. Before the experiment, an observer had classified teachers as "facilitative" or "nonfacilitative." Facilitative teachers, in their lessons outside the experiment, allowed free discussion, accepted unusual ideas, and pressed students to think for themselves. Classes of the facilitative teachers did somewhat better at the start of the experiment than other classes, and the four weeks of training did not improve their scores. As teachers were required by the experimental course to foster student thinking and discussion, those who were usually "nonfacilitative" had to adopt a new style. *Their* classes gained considerably from the novel instruction, in the new style.

SOURCE: *The Productive Thinking Program*, Basic Lesson 12, p. 10.

---

experimenter in fact controlled the train by a hidden switch. He did not fix the "right" combination in advance; rather, he kept track of the combinations the student tried. When and if the student had finally tried every one of the combinations, the last one tried was treated as the correct answer for that student. That is, the student got no reward for trying 15 different combinations, but as soon as he tried a sixteenth, he was rewarded by motion of the train. A student who checked possibilities systematically could solve the problem with few wasted trials.

Some students were given no preparation, some were trained in a logical schema for identifying all possibilities, and some were taught the schema and given practice in applying it. The schema was a tree diagram much like Duncan's. There were four levels of branching, and each path identified a different combination of four factors—16 possibilities in all. The Schema-plus-Practice group studied this abstract schema *and* applied it to two problems having nothing to do with the train. When they were given the train problem they were not told that the schema applied to it. The experimenter did say: "You might like to keep a record of which choices you have tried." As Fig. 13.5 shows, the untrained Controls tended not to keep records. When a Control did keep a record it seemed not to help him. The Schema-plus-Practice group kept records and made good use of them. Schema training without practice in application did not increase efficiency of fifth-graders. It was only partially successful with eighth-graders.

**21** Duncan showed the tree diagram but did not teach rules for constructing the diagram to fit a new problem. Could he have taught this explicitly? Would it have been advantageous?

**22** Suggest a teaching approach that might have brought the leak-finding problem within the reach of the low-ability students.

**23** "Teaching logic," said William James, "never made a man reason rightly." Is this consistent with the analysis and evidence in this chapter?

# ADVENTUROUS INQUIRY:
# LEARNING TO CREATE KNOWLEDGE

Direct investigation of natural phenomena by students is of limited value in teaching particular principles (p. 547). Its function is more general: to show the student where knowledge comes from, and to equip him to discover and test for himself. As Glaser (in Shulman & Keislar, 1966) puts it, the point is not "learning by discovery" but "learning to discover." The student who has formed his own generalization about goldfish, Indian tribes, or the use of *who* and *whom* has become less dependent on authority. He has a new sense of his own intellectual power and a clearer view of the nature of knowledge. He expects other generalizations in the field to make sense, and also begins to understand the limitations of knowledge derived from evidence such as he used. Each adventure in constructing knowledge can be expected to make all work in the subject seem more valuable and more intelligible.

The person who reaches advanced levels in a field of study or application must recast information from others into a form that he understands and reconstruct principles half-forgotten. As he reaches advanced problems for which there are no set formulas, he must invent a method of attack. Students who have once discovered a principle are much less bewildered when they must think for themselves in the next situation. Their superiority lies in specific concepts and techniques (cutting up the irregular figure to form familiar shapes), and also in self-reliance.

In every field of study, *some* of the teaching should be by methods that require the student to work out principles for himself. Such problem solving should be spaced throughout the curriculum. An attitude toward history or art or physics is not established at any one point in life. There is a place for discovery in the child's earliest learning in the field, and also in the training of the graduate student. Rediscovering what the teacher already knows has some value, but the impact on the student is more significant when teacher and class work together on a problem for which even the teacher has no solution.

Inquiries may be simple, as when the fourth-graders record the price of sugar of different brands, in different packages, from different stores. The teacher knows at the outset that variation will be found, and can guess at the trends that will appear. The teacher can communicate those hunches and can encourage class members to put forward hunches of their own; then everyone starts the inquiry on an even footing. It is more fun to practice arithmetic in such a context, but that is not the point of the activity. Planning is required so that accurate and representative information will be collected. The information has to be organized so that conclusions can be drawn. At the end come attempts at explanation. This may lead to a further inquiry—into, say, the cost to the merchant of the various packages. Because new relationships are being turned up, the inquiry is an adventure into the unknown. The students are not simulating the processes of inquiry in the adult world. They are engaging in them, in a context they understand.

Such activities, spread over the years and over the various school subjects, teach many things. The student comes to realize that knowledge has not been laid down for all time; he becomes aware that, both in everyday affairs and in

academic subjects, there is new knowledge to be developed. Second, he learns that the power to create knowledge is not restricted to a handful of geniuses. The student sees that it is in *his or her power* to create patterns and discover regularities in the world. Third, the student comes to know criteria for testing ideas: agreement among samples in social research, for example, or measured growth rate in an experiment on plants. Thus, the student comes to understand the nature of knowledge, as well as the content of textbooks. This will be made clearer by the examples that follow.

## Curricular Examples

SCIENCE AND APPLIED SCIENCE  In the chemistry laboratory, the student mixes two compounds and observes the "blue-green precipitate" the text mentioned. He learns something, but not much. If he has not been told what to expect, he learns more. He faces the scientist's problem of describing an observation (Boeck, 1951). Not having been told an answer in advance, he is open-minded. He may not see the precipitate as green at all, which provokes discussion of how to develop a precise language for observations. This leads him into scientific thinking; a routine confirmation of the textbook's statements does not.

Indeed, if trust in the book is taught, the science course is generating an unscientific attitude. Scientific knowledge is transient; theories accepted today will be partly obsolete in a decade or two. Many lower-level science courses convey an incorrect image of science (Schwab, 1960):

> The traditional course has tended to treat only the outcomes, the conclusions, of inquiry, divorced from the data which support them and the conceptual frames which define—and limit—their validity. The result has been to convey a false image of science as knowledge literally true, permanent—even complete. . . . We tend to provide a structure which admits of no loose ends. We minimize doubts and qualifications. . . .
>
> The student is led to treat conclusions as inalterable truths. When, five or ten years later, this conviction proves false, he retreats from clarity to confusion and from confusion to generalized suspicion of scientific competence and authority. . . . We need to imbue our courses and our exposition with the color of science and inquiry to give the student an effective glimpse of the vicissitudes of research.

The need for problem-oriented teaching is equally great in applied science. To teach students in home economics to formulate a recipe, rather than to follow recipes, is to teach an entirely different subject. How long should a pork roast be cooked? The recipe book specifies a certain number of minutes per pound. An experiment will lead in the end to much the same conclusion, but the class will, in the process, come to realize that a value judgment entered the final figure, and that the cooking time that pleases the majority will not please every taste. The class learns that the book can at best give a rule of thumb, and that the art of cooking rises above obedience to authority.

SOCIAL STUDIES   Social processes and history can be taught by putting challenges to the class. "What would happen if . . ." recasts abstract concepts, long-dead events, and immutable facts into a moving, meaningful system of forces. "What does the public think about (say) the police?" can be the start of a field project. The student learns about the diversity of political views and about investigation (about sampling and interviewer bias, for example). "What was it really like in those days?" sends students to diaries, newspapers, and letters from an earlier generation—possibly located in family storerooms or in document collections published for school use.

Geography traditionally includes such matters as mapping, regional characteristics, and the physical properties of the earth—not exciting topics for high-school students. The High School Geography Project (J. Barth et al., 1974) set out to change that. Many of its topics are contemporary, and its approach challenging. One unit—"The Geography of Cities"—starts with a map of physical features of a region, before settlement. Students identify reasonable sites for settlement and for transportation routes. They consider the likely occupational makeup of communities close to the forest, or at the communication center, and so on. Having formed some ideas about geographical causes, students next try to account for the existing features seen in maps and photos of New Orleans. They go on to relate, for example, data on proximity to railroad and number of shade trees in various neighborhoods to property value, income, educational level, and so on. Throughout the course the student thinks about development over time, about cause and effect, about needs and resources. He learns a way of thinking about social geography that applies to any time and place.

MATHEMATICS   From arithmetic up to calculus, the course content usually has consisted of procedures, definitions, and established propositions. That is not mathematics. True mathematics is a game of teasing out what is implied by a set of made-up rules. In a sense, the best mathematician is one who thinks of interesting rules to start from. The first step is curiosity. Galileo began on the path to fame when he sought regularity in the paths of cannonballs. The creative mathematician, puzzling over a problem, applies reversible operations in much the manner of the child adjusting the proportions of a rectangle to match a specimen. The mathematician's elegant formal model comes only after much exploratory activity. Proof is a still later step—not unimportant, but pointless until he has an insight that deserves formal derivation. Galileo required 30 years to move from an impressionistic and incorrect understanding of acceleration to a satisfactory formula (Hanson, 1958, p. 42).

A "proven" conclusion is not necessarily true. It is merely a result that fits with a set of assumptions, assumptions that the mathematician changes at will. True mathematics is more nearly a game than a study of what is true. To learn about probability, for example, is to learn moves in a game invented by some clever people, long ago.

## Looking for a strategy

Teachers use mathematical games to develop foresight and to teach students to formulate accurate statements.

The most elementary games depend on chance rather than judgment. Kohl (1974, p. 119) gives an example played on a board like that shown here. (The fish plays first, and others follow in the usual order.) A spinner determines how many squares the player is to move; if he lands on certain squares he takes a bonus move or a penalty (indicated by the numbers). Before using a board with numbers Kohl uses one with verbal labels—a penalty square on the desert, for example, says "No water or oasis—go back 2." As Kohl says, the game "is an easy way to introduce the concept of negative numbers. For most youngsters the idea of moving backward is clear, while the idea of numbers less than zero can seem mystical."

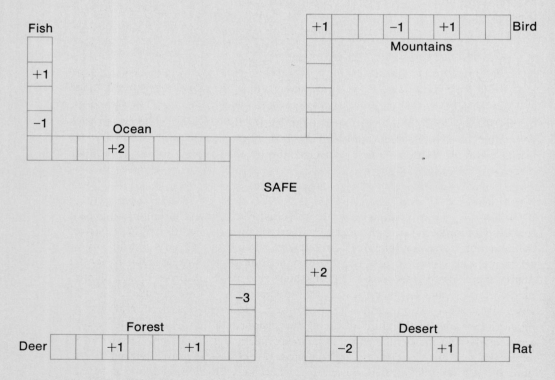

SOURCE: Adapted from Kohl (1974).

After the students have gained a bit of experience, the question arises, which player has the best starting position? A larger question can lead to days of experimentation: How should bonuses and penalties be placed on the pathways to give the four starting positions an equal chance of winning?

In mathematical games, children can find good moves impressionistically, years before they can work out a systematic analysis. Indeed, with a little guidance, even kindergartners can make up games (Kohl, 1974; box). Building familiarity with mathematical ideas through concrete activities has three virtues: it provides a base for understanding later instruction, it conveys a sound understanding of what mathematics is like, and it makes the subject fun.

ART   When the teacher of art appreciation distinguishes Renaissance painters from those who went before, he distracts the student from the essential continuity of artistic evolution. Neat categories tend to block one from later observing the similarities between "modern" art and some "classical" art. The student can be led to form his own concepts, however. Bettelheim (1942) provided high-school students with postcard prints of many paintings of all periods and styles. The student was asked to sort them into sets of similar pictures. Each student had his own way of sorting. This called forth a discussion of various ways of thinking about art (subject, treatment, color, technique). Moreover, when the group settled down to study one kind of painting, they saw it in relation to the total field, isolated only for convenience.

All production in art is a process of adventurous inquiry (Fig. 13.6). Those who are not artists themselves may fail to appreciate that art is a process of deliberate problem solving. In any medium, the artist has some idea of the effect he wants to achieve, and has to search out and evaluate alternative ways of getting there.

## The Teacher's Role

The teacher's activities in helping students inquire are much like those in other teaching, save that the teacher does much less guiding and demonstrating. The teacher chooses—or helps students choose—a problem that is within the yntellectual resources of the class (considering time, ability, equipment needed, and so on). The teacher helps the group define the task. The teacher can play a role much like the one the students play; it would be reasonable, for example, in the cost-of-sugar problem (p. 577), for the teacher to lead one team to stores across town while all-child groups go to the nearby stores. Sometimes this provides the teacher an occasion to demonstrate technique unobtrusively, and sometimes it demonstrates that the adult has no special magic. The teacher will encourage student awareness of procedures and critiera: Did we do all we could to make sure no errors got into the cost data? Have we enough evidence to be sure of each sentence in the report?

At some point, there should be discussion of the nature of knowledge in general—of how science, mathematics, and history differ, for example. The actual inquiries provide a background for overarching concepts that can never be reached through cookbook laboratory work and study of texts.

## FIGURE 13.6

### Achieving a three-dimensional horse

These drawings were made by a child (Heidi) within the single month when she was 8½. The comments are those of a psychologist, Sylvia Fein. (See also pp. 131 and 176.) Fein's notes open with a reference to Heidi's immediately preceding "experiments," as a result of which she changed the rider from a kind of gingerbread cutout to a figure facing the horse's head, with one arm clearly on the far side of the rider's body. This learning transferred, but the similar transformation of the horse required a fresh series of provisional tries.

Stimulated by her experiments with the rider's arms, Heidi will now apply them to the legs of the horse. She wants to make clear that the horse has two legs on one side of his body and two legs on the other. In spite of her excitement and the multiple possibilities her mind pours out, she proceeds in a cool workmanlike fashion by first creating a clear example of how she handled the legs before the new idea occurred to her. She is consciously approaching the problem of showing a third dimension, without ever having heard the word, and it now confronts her with the complexity of overlapping.

*This is the horse before the changes.*

**24** Reference is made above to criteria for testing ideas. What "criteria" apply to each of the following? Note that "criteria" does not mean "arguments"; it means bases for comparing and settling arguments.
   a. The plan for a vegetable garden
   b. An outline for an essay on ragtime music
   c. A proposal to require that every community resident give ten days each year of unpaid public service
   d. Suggestions for a mural on "The First Thanksgiving"

**25** Recall Kagan's statement (p. 183) that ability to entertain false-to-fact propositions emerges in adolessence, and the Siegler-Liebert finding on systematic analysis (p. 574). Does this research imply that inquiry into far-out possibilities should be reserved for Grades VIII and above?

**26** Schwab seems to refer to confusion in the student's mind as bad; Holt (p. 527) objected to the educator's attempts to minimize confusion. One could argue that "adventurous inquiry" in the classroom generates confusion when it teaches that intellectual matters are rarely settled, that rules reflect judgment rather than truth. How would Schwab or Holt respond to this argument?

The next horse is similar, but the breast line crosses the leading front leg. She presses harder on the pencil as she overlaps, to emphasize the change.

Next she applies her discovery to the hind legs, extending the belly line across the leading leg.

Now with confidence and sure of control, Heidi returns the legs to the walking position. She rounds muzzle and hoofs, slightly tapers the legs, and in her finest draftsmanship she embellishes with studded bridle, breastband and saddle.

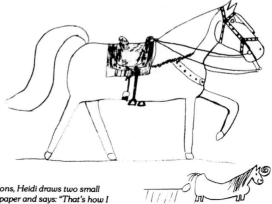

To affirm her new spatial revelations, Heidi draws two small horses in the lower corner of the paper and says: "That's how I used to draw horses."

A few days later the new horse is smartly walking, an easy fluid curve barely lifting the leading leg from the ground. The other front leg dramatically slants backward, almost touching the leading hind leg. The tail swings away from the body. Rigidities Heidi imposed upon the structure of the horse while working her ideas have gone. This is another beginning.

SOURCE: *Heidi's Horse,* text by Sylvia Fein, drawings by Heidi Scheuber (Pleasant Hill, Calif.: Exelrod Press, 1976), pp. 88–91.

# PROMOTING CUMULATIVE LEARNING

Learning is cumulative, to a far greater extent than the student realizes. Education sometimes seems to be nothing but a kaleidoscope of episodes, so much is attention focused on this day's lecture, this night's assignment, and this week's test. Education seems all the more episodic because so much of last week's lecture and last year's course is forgotten. But it is the skills and attitudes that go into problem solving, into information finding, and into new learning that are the permanent and valuable residue from education. This collateral learning is made possible by the lessons.

The collateral value of schooling is made clear by studies that compare persons with much and little schooling—among older children, adolescents, and adults in various countries. The schooled individuals, on the average, react "more intellectually" to new situations (Scribner & Cole, 1973):

They take in more.

They organize scattered information.

They extract general rules from a series of experiences.

They are more ready to accept arbitrary assumptions in a logical problem.

They carry forward insights from one problem to another.

They are able to describe their provisional tries in words (and so they know *what* interpretation is being contradicted when they fail).

Curricula have sometimes been too much concerned with the topics considered and too little concerned with the broad structure of knowledge and the techniques of information processing to be used. The lessons bear down on specifics to the neglect of what is more general. When I started out as a teacher of high-school chemistry before World War II, I thought I should "meet student needs" by covering topics in chemistry related to their future lives. So I emphasized applications of chemistry: in making soap, in refining petroleum, in producing a great variety of alloys, and so on. The link to immediate "needs" went so far, I recall, as to encourage one of the teenagers to report to the class on the use of sulfur in treating acne. The teaching had its values; it should have communicated respect for the utility of chemistry to the world. But my course made only minimal mention of atomic structure, which did not seem "relevant." The general student, I thought, was not going to solve problems where understanding of electrons and atoms would matter; and the science specialists could pursue the matter in college. The release of atomic energy in 1942 changed all that. Since then, few scientific matters have been of wider public concern than atomic and nuclear power, civilian and military. Broad and fundamental ideas have this property of appearing over and over as themes in new contexts.

Learning has transferred when the person copes with a new situation with the aid of concepts or techniques or attitudes. Whenever the person shows better thinking or quicker learning, there has been transfer. We saw transfer in Piaget's description of intellectual development, in studies of learning to learn, and in studies of problem solving. Many kinds of learning can transfer:

- Programs of motor response. Learning to move in time with music helps one to learn any new dance. The more movement patterns brought under control, the easier it is to pick up a new routine.

- Specific facts or associations. A single fact may clarify many situations. The student learns that *pre* means before, as in *preview, predict,* and *prepare.* He can transfer this response to *preheat.* (But he may also apply it to *pre-eminent,* where it interferes with interpretation unless he keeps on testing his hypotheses.)

- Broad concepts and generalizations. A gardener learns to cope with diverse insects by classifying them. "Use malathion to spray aphids" is a prescription with a narrow application; "Use malathion on sucking insects" is broader, permitting him to combat an unfamiliar insect. To give another example: A teacher helps a student to analyze a tax proposal in terms of general concepts: its effect on economic growth, its fairness to each type of citizen, and the efficiency with which it can be collected. Having been alerted to these concepts—in addition to "How will it affect my pocketbook?"—the student is better able to think through all problems of taxation.

- General techniques of analysis. The skills of communicating, studying, and problem solving fall in this category. The student will learn to look for the topic sentences in paragraphs, or for the major and minor themes in a symphony. Skillfully taught, he will generalize this into a technique of seeking the central structure in any work of art. Faulty techniques— for example, copying extensively from a text while studying—are just as easily retained and transferred.

- Attitudes toward subjects or situations. Correcting a mechanical malfunction by trial and error, testing each part in turn, is inefficient. A worker who believes that time is saved by stopping to think about the symptoms of malfunction will do better. In effect, a change in attitude can raise "mechanical aptitude." Similarly, students learn that foreign language makes connected sense and need not be puzzled out one word at a time.

Cumulative learning can have bad results. A person can develop a philosophy about nature and about knowledge that makes him intellectually active or passive. Studies of "modernity" and "sense of efficacy" suggest that some indi-

## What school subjects are of most worth?

A recurrent issue in educational policy is whether certain subjects have greater value in developing the intellectual powers than others—quite apart from the usefulness of the specific content of the lessons. Claims for such values were advanced, early in this century, to uphold the place in the high-school curriculum of the classical studies—Euclidean geometry, Latin, and the like.

E. L. Thorndike (1924), the founder of American educational psychology, attacked the claim by showing that students in these courses did not improve in the problem solving and reasoning required by a general mental test. Thorndike went on to make this famous statement:

> The chief reason why good thinkers seem superficially to have been made such by having taken certain school studies, is that good thinkers have taken such studies, becoming better by the inherent tendency of the good to gain more than the poor from any study. When the good thinkers studied Greek and Latin, these studies seemed to make good thinking. Now that the good thinkers study Physics and Trigonometry, these seem to make good thinkers. If the abler pupils should all study Physical Education and Dramatic Art, these subjects would seem to make good thinkers. These were, indeed, a large fraction of the program of studies for the best thinkers the world has produced, the Athenian Greeks.

viduals and some cultures are more than ready than others to respond enthusiastically to new ideas. Majasan's evidence (p. 524) suggests that a person who takes a behavioristic view of man finds it hard to learn from a humanist, and vice versa. Similarly, according to Robin Horton (see Scribner & Cole, 1973), students in Nigeria come to school believing that the world is disorderly, uncontrollable, and inexplicable. Even when they reach college, they find unbelievable the fundamental assumption of regularity on which post-Newtonian science depends. Then they cannot truly assimilate their science lessons.

The foregoing remarks recapitulate comments scattered over many preceding chapters. This is a good place for review, since we have come to the end of the chapters that emphasize intellectual development. (In the remaining parts, motivation and attitudes are central.) To round off this portion, I review some of the prominent suggestions for promoting transferrable learning. Similar ideas have entered in several contexts; this review provides some integration. The review is necessarily selective, and leaves out important recommendations.

- Make new concepts and principles meaningful. First, provide an appropriate base of experience. Second, orient the student by providing a structure into which details can fit, or leading him from simple examples to complex ones. Third, check his provisional interpretations. Monitor as the student applies rules to new situations or formulates rules. And provide feedback of the kind that helps him correct his errors.

- Confront the student with varied, realistic situations. Variety in the configurations the person creates with his manipulations is needed in forming schemata. In motor skill and in discrimination, it is necessary for him to recognize recurrent cues and to ignore irrelevant context. In applying principles, it is again necessary to locate relevant elements—the *numerator*, for instance—within ever-new configurations. If the student works on varied problems or exercises he is unlikely to fix rigid, non-adaptive responses.

- Set up problems so that the student must actively restructure. Again, this is consistent with Piaget's thinking about the child's development. The student ought to break up configurations to test hypotheses and learn to take disconfirmations in stride—and sometimes to figure out the sense of the subject-matter for himself. Too much demonstration and guidance is detrimental. Recall that in both the Wertheimer and Luchins incidents students had learned not to think; it was unfair to ask that they go beyond the lessons, they said. Confronting open problems, the student comes to realize that human knowledge is still growing, and that he can discover problems worthy of thought.

- Provide memory support. The working space of the mind is limited. Trying to juggle too much, students will fail at intellectual tasks they could otherwise handle. The load on memory is reduced by identifying subgoals, by using notes or physical models to keep facts in view, and by rearranging materials to make the central structure evident.

- Teach general codes. These assist in chunking so that more can be kept in view. Venn diagrams, decision trees, and broad concepts such as cause-and-effect are examples.

- Teach students to use precise wording wherever exact control of a response is needed.

- Teach techniques of problem solving. Make students conscious of the techniques they are using. Students can understand the function of suspending criticism for the sake of divergent perception, of deliberately trying to disprove one's own rule, of looking closely at the requirements of a problem, and so on. Moreover, they can profit from specific techniques for devising possible solutions and for checking them.

Some educational theorists have suggested that only the superior, college-bound student should be taught to think for himself. For anyone else, the argument goes, basic literacy and vocational skills taught chiefly through sequenced exercises are the proper goal. I contend that everyone should improve his ability to analyze situations. This ability develops gradually over the years, and is not the special province of isolated, advanced courses in geometry, economics, philosophy, and so on. If the young child is encouraged to look always to adult models for the answers and is discouraged from putting forth ideas of his own, his progress toward intellectual autonomy will be choked off. Manipulation of centimeter rods in Grade I will not itself equip him to think mathematically; but it lays groundwork that later meaningful teaching can build on. The same is true in language, science, social studies, and art. At each school age, the student—whether average or superior—should be gaining in intellectual power by acquiring concepts, techniques, and self-confidence.

27 Hand calculators are now available to every student in some classes even in Grade I.
   a. Does this aid make it possible to teach concepts from statistics and economics earlier than has been traditional?
   b. What possibilities for problem solving does this aid open up? (You need not confine your answer to the curriculum in arithmetic.)

28 In the light of what is known today, do you think that some school subjects promote intellectual development more than others? Is a mental test a reasonable way to collect evidence on this issue?

29 Gladwin (1970, Chap. 6) argues that persons in many cultures, including American minority cultures, perform difficult tasks by following concrete, traditional modes of analysis. Their traditions place no value on finding innovative solutions, and they are likely to fail when a school curriculum presses them to carry out self-directed discovery or verification. Established rules and their application, then, should constitute the curriculum for such groups. Evaluate Gladwin's position.

30 What general responses might fourth-graders acquire from a study of Holland? If the prominent minorities in their community are Mexicans and Armenians, what greater transfer value would a study unit on Mexico or Armenia have?

31 Is the research on transfer consistent with the following opinon?

   Laboratory work and shopwork engender a habit of observation, a knowledge of the difference between accuracy and vagueness, and an insight into nature's complexity and into the inadequacy of all verbal accounts of real phenomena. . . . They confer precision; because, if you are *doing* a thing, you must do it definitely right or definitely wrong. They confer honesty; for . . . it becomes impossible to dissimulate your vagueness or ignorance by ambiguity.

Frank Barron, "The Psychology of Creativity," in *New Directions in Psychology,* ed. Barron et al. (New York: Holt, Rinehart and Winston), 1965, pp. 1–134.

> After describing techniques used in research on creativity, Barron discusses the studies made of creative mathematicians, writers, scientists, and artists. Finally, he suggests what schools can do to foster creative powers.

Jerome S. Bruner, "The Growth of Mind," *American Psychologist* 20 (1965), 1007–17. Also in Rosenblith (1973).

> Bruner illustrates classroom practices that help a preadolescent to recognize general principles of human life and to form a problem-seeking attitude. He advocates study of concrete cases (for example, of Eskimo life), with the teacher drawing challenges out of the discussion instead of giving answers.

Gary A. Davis, *Psychology of Problem Solving: Theory and Practice* (New York: Basic Books, 1973).

> A simplified account of ideas about problem solving advanced by various psychologists. Describes several classroom programs for increasing skill of children and adults in invention and discovery. Cites the pertinent evaluations.

M. J. A. Howe, "Questions and Answers in School Learning," in *Understanding School Learning* (New York: Harper & Row, 1972), pp. 179–202.

> Howe illustrates how teachers pose questions that cause students to restructure the subject-matter and so to perceive it more clearly. He discusses how student errors may be interpreted by the teacher and used constructively.

D. M. Johnson, "Deductive Reasoning As Problem Solving," in *A Systematic Introduction to the Psychology of Thinking* (New York: Harper & Row, 1972), pp. 229–71.

> A summary of the research findings on formal reasoning.

E. Paul Torrance, "Examples and Rationales of Test Tasks for Assessing Creative Abilities," *Journal of Creative Behavior* 2 (1968), 165–78. Also in Torrance and White (1975).

> A dozen tasks that can be used either as formal tests or as classroom exercises are described. The scoring emphasizes divergent thinking and originality rather than the convergent processes usually tested in school.

# PART FOUR
## Planning, Motivation, and Evaluation

■ Action is directed by goals—immediate or distant—inherent in the task or merely associated with it. Motivation is sustained when the person accepts a long-range goal with intrinsic appeal.

■ When the consequences of a response match the person's expectation, he is likely to use that response on future occasions. Aspirations are influenced by past success and failure, and by the social context.

☐ Schools vary in their motivational climates; the group spirit encourages certain activities and provides little motivational support for others.

■ Reinforcing events arranged by a teacher or experimenter serve as signals by which the learner judges the adequacy of his response. In most circumstances, prompt, frequent, information-rich signals serve best.

☐ Candy or prizes provide information plus payoff. Payoff is not needed when the person has other motives for learning, and it can have undesirable effects.

■ Systems of rewards and record keeping can maintain typical behavior at a desirable level. Acts to be discouraged should be ignored; alternative acts should be rewarded when they occur.

■ The school promotes adaptive response after failure by selecting appropriate tasks, making goals attainable, and reducing emotional penalties for poor performance

*level of aspiration*  
*realistic goals*  
*group standards*  
*school atmosphere*  
*reinforcing event*  
*aversive event*  
*contingent reinforcement*  
*reinforcement as signal*  
*reinforcement as payoff*

*intrinsic motivation*  
*maintaining a habit*  
*token economy*  
*extinction*  
*adaptive response*  
*goal substitution*  
*defensive motivation*  
*optimum arousal*

# 14

# PURPOSES AND CONSEQUENCES

The teacher's eternal question, "How can I motivate students?" becomes, on examination, a series of other questions. "What sorts of goals do students work toward?" "What causes a student to select one goal rather than another?" "How can the teacher influence students to choose appropriate goals?" These questions all deal with purposes. A second series of questions deals with consequences: "What effect does punishment have?" "Should competition be encouraged?" and so on. This chapter opens the discussion; Chapter 15, on the teacher as classroom leader, goes on to discuss specific motivating procedures.

Goals of instruction are, from one point of view, imposed by the adult community. From another point of view, they are chosen by the learners as they encounter the instructional program. The two sets of goals can be brought into harmony; indeed, they must be, if the school is to succeed.

A learning activity can bring satisfaction in three ways: through pleasure in the course of the activity, pleasure in completing the task, or pleasure in making progress toward a distant personal goal. The task itself, or the social interchange that accompanies it, may provide joy enough to motivate sustained involvement. There is additional satisfaction to be found in completing an assignment or reaching a certain standard of accomplishment. Another kind of short-term satisfaction is offered by artificial incentives—grades, payments for performance, and so on. It is the promise of long-term satisfaction that sustains effort when the work is dull and progress difficult. The learner who sees his efforts as helping him with a developmental task or helping him to fulfill an ambition persists despite obstacles.

The ideal learning activity will appeal in all three ways, but any of the three appeals can adequately motivate a learning effort. The maturity of the learners, their group spirit and their individual personalities, the material to be taught, and the style the teacher finds comfortable will all influence the teacher's choice among appeals.

All activity is directed toward goals. As a person interprets a situation, he recognizes desirable things that can happen to him or desirable states that he can bring about. His immediate goal is a set of anticipated consequences, consequences he thinks his responses are likely to bring about. The actual consequences of his act confirm or contradict his expectation. His feeling of success or failure depends on how he evaluates his action. Although an act has many consequences, his feeling about his try depends on what consequences he notices. Often, when two students act similarly and reach the same result, one retains his interpretation on the next trial, whereas the other alters his. The difference lies in what consequences they noted and in how these compared to what they had hoped for.

Grace, in sewing class, chooses a dress pattern and a neat cotton print to make it from. She chooses this pattern because she believes that she will be able to do the sewing it requires. A more intricate pattern, she fears, would prove unmanageable. She chooses this print rather than another because she thinks that she and her friends will like the result. She places some values ahead of others: perhaps she chooses the print because it is similar to what her friends wear and will make her feel more "in the group" even though she herself admires a solid color. As Grace completes the dress, she will experience confirmations and contradictions of her expectations. Her success will confirm her estimate of her capacity. Her friends express interest in her dress, as she had hoped. But the pleats are hard to iron, and she will begin to wish that she had chosen a straight skirt; next time she probably will. Grace overlooks some further consequences. Trimming in red gives a less striking effect than trimming in blue would have. Her mother, impressed by the achievement, begins to treat Grace more as a grownup. Consequences overlooked do not modify future interpretations. One part of teaching is making students more sensitive to consequences.

 **1** According to the theoretical statement of Chapter 3, is a goal best described as a desired consequence, an intended consequence, or an expected consequence?

## Multiple Goals

It is easy to regard each act as directed to one specific goal. The boy makes a kite "because he wants a kite." But goals usually are complex and multiple. The kite-maker may be concerned with getting his parents' praise for being usefully occupied. The very making of the kite can be socially rewarding, if the maker shares the work with friends. When the boy gets to use his father's tools in this work, the permission proves that his maturity is recognized. Elements of pride or self-respect make the effort worthwhile. He may carry his work into unnecessary refinements in order to use more tools. Many motives enter kite making.

The performer does not wait for the end of his work to judge how he is doing. Any complicated activity involves continual checking to see if the process is going forward according to expectation. The navigator of a plane, having set a course, continues to make celestial observations or to listen to the radio range beacon for confirmation. Feedback about intermediate consequences alters plans in mid-act. An important step in teaching, then, is to define intermediate goals. Thus, one tells a future farmer how to judge whether pigs are feeding properly long before their weights report their growth.

**2** A teenage girl selects lunch in the school cafeteria. What goals may she have beyond the desire for food whose taste she likes?

**3** What goals are present in a committee preparing a classroom exhibit of rocks?

**4** What cues help an actor on stage judge whether he is performing well?

## Remote Goals

For the older person, most of today's tasks are connected with goals well off in the future. The college student goes to the library to read two articles. This is, in part, a matter of putting in enough study time to clear his conscience. Another goal is being able to report to the instructor tomorrow that he has completed 50 pages of reading. The pages he reads may contribute to a paper he has to deliver at the end of the term. The hour in the library has still more remote consequences. His work on this course determines his eligibility for the basketball team. Even further in the future are job ambitions: good grades will perhaps help him find a good job, and the knowledge acquired from his reading may help him perform the job.

A person's goals are arranged in a plan that sets out where he expects to be at a certain time. He has a fairly definite picture of the consequences he expects in the next few minutes, less exact expectations for the next hour or next day, and a few unclear visions that reach months or years into the future.

An older person can learn to make a correct response even if the perceptible consequence is long delayed, so long as the correct response is readily discriminated. Mowrer (1960, p. 383) explains this as follows:

> Human beings, with their remarkable skill in symbolic manipulation, can easily keep, or re-establish, the "connection" between two events (action and reward or action and punishment), even though these events are considerably separated in time. For example, if a subject "knows" that a given response is responsible for a given (delayed) effect, he might say to himself, immediately upon completion of the response: "Although there will be a delay now, before I get the reward, I nevertheless *know* I have done the right thing, so all I have to do is wait."

The ability to foresee consequences thus appears to depend upon the ability to use words and thoughts effectively. A young child's response is unlikely to change unless a rather obvious consequence follows the act immediately. The first-grader, asked to assemble an unfamiliar object, works on scattered bits of the task with little idea of where he is going and of how the part fits into the whole. Hence he lacks persistence. The fifth-grader takes a global view, perceiving each act as a part of the larger whole. Thus, actions become more meaningful, and each step is well motivated (Shalemon, 1959; Kuvshinov, 1959). Only with the achievement of formal operational thought, in adolescence, can one trace out possible consequences of an action in imagination and so develop a high degree of foresight. Foresight depends on knowledge that enables one to predict, and on alertness to possible consequences. One function of education is to convey what others have learned about consequences. Understanding of remote consequences is developed in social studies, literature, science, and philosophy.

REMOTE VERSUS IMMEDIATE GOALS IN THE CLASSROOM   The goals proposed to the student should fit his maturity. Plans of very young children must be quickly fulfilled, before their appeal fades. "This will help you when you grow up" is a pallid advertisement compared with the immediate enjoyment of a comic strip and a baseball game. But some remote goals appeal even to the young. Boys try earnestly to become strong, though it takes a long while to put on muscles. "When I grow up and become a mother" is a conscious plan for the 6-year-old girl, which helps shape her interests and her self-concept. Perhaps the efforts of some modern parents to equalize their roles will make "When I become a father" just as significant for their 6-year-old son.

With success in short-range plans, the person gains confidence in his ability and enough interest to sustain a longer activity. The teacher who helps chil-

## Delay of gratification

*"Think I'll take all the money I've been saving toward a fur coat and go buy a chocolate sundae!"*

"Bobby Sox" by Marty Links. © 1975 United Feature Syndicate, Inc.

dren plan toward short-term goals assists them to develop foresight. Near goals can be reached before tedium sets in. If all the goals are distant, there are discouraging stretches where the only promise of satisfaction lies far ahead. A child can get a glimmer of ambition to become a concert musician, but he is more likely to sit down at the piano because he thinks he can play a piece from beginning to end *now*. The small landmarks—playing "Three Blind Mice" by ear, sight-reading "Jingle Bells" and having it sound almost right, overcoming the hurdle of a one-sharp signature in "America"—divide the long pathway into challenging, satisfaction-giving segments. As a person succeeds in attaining one goal, he becomes readier to dedicate himself to a slightly more remote goal.

Remote goals become useful for motivation only when the path to achieving them becomes visible. Realizing what steps are to be taken reduces a vast ambition to specific activities one can confidently tackle. As Wright (1948) has said:

A goal can be only a point at a distance, with a void in between. Then, all the child can do is dream about it. On the other hand, a goal can be an extended region of activity the finish line of which is tied in closely with steps on the way, so that these steps become parts of the larger goal-structure. John wants to "play in the band." An adult at school has helped to set up this goal, but lets it go at that and, except for tall imagining, so does John. Henry, after exchanging ideas with his teacher, wants to "mow lawns or deliver papers to earn money to spend on a cornet to blow thirty minutes everyday so he can play in the band." He can act with some degree of effectiveness because there is a path to follow. Henry's teacher has helped to arrange a situation in which a "goal with a path leading to it" are defined. Situations like this increase the freedom of children to satisfy their needs.

The planning process in the schoolroom makes the student aware of the many sorts of satisfaction and improvement an activity can lead to. It specifies end goals, which direct the activity, and intermediate or process goals (box).

Definite targets have more influence on behavior than vague ones. When drivers of logging trucks were urged to "do their best" to bring their trucks to a full load before driving to the mill, their average load was about 60 per cent of the legal limit. When they were told to aim for 94 per cent as a goal, their loads rose steadily, reaching 90 per cent in three months and holding at or above that level thereafter. Some of the drivers invented ways to modify their trucks so they could better judge if they were up to standard. The change was accomplished merely by defining the target, without extra reward or threat (Latham & Baldes, 1975). E. Locke (1968) compiled evidence on the same point from dozens of laboratory studies. When the person *accepts* a definite, observable, difficult-to-reach goal—whether he sets it himself (p. 611) or is assigned it—he turns out more work than when told, "Do your best."

## A plan comes first

The poster reproduced here is used in the elementary schoolroom that is organized around centers for art, music, science, math, and so on. The child is encouraged to present a lesson to a small group after he or she completes an inquiry or a series of exercises. The planning guide will improve the teaching the child does, and it will also teach planning.

SOURCE: *Change for Children: Ideas and Activities for Individualizing Learning,* by Sandra Kaplan, Jo Ann Kaplan, Sheila Madsen, and Bette Taylor (p. 25). Copyright © 1973 by Goodyear Publishing Co. Reprinted by permission.

### HOW TO TEACH A LESSON AT YOUR CENTER

Answer these questions before you teach.

1. What do I want to teach?
2. How will I spark interest for my lesson?
3. What materials will I need to use?
4. What will my teaching steps be?
5. What will students do or make after the lesson?
6. How will I evaluate my lesson?

The goal-setting process itself can generate a commitment that fosters learning. Gaa (1973) arranged for a first- or second-grader to select goals (from a checklist) in individual consultation with a teacher's aide—goals that he would try to reach during the next week. At the end of the week the teacher rated him on all the goals. Thus, the pupil knew whether he had reached the targets he chose. The children Gaa assigned to a control group also discussed the goals in individual conferences, but they did not themselves set the goals. Over the period of the experiment, goal-setters progressed further in reading than the controls. In the final week of the experiment, all children had a chance to set goals; the ones with experience in goalsetting set more realistic, more attainable goals. (See also p. 606.)

LESSON OBJECTIVES AS GUIDES TO THE LEARNER    Stating educational objectives contributes to the teacher's thinking, as we saw in Chapter 2. Stating objectives can help the student also. Recognizing what he is expected to learn, he allocates study time more efficiently and monitors his progress. Objectives can be brought into focus in various ways. Objectives can emerge from group planning. A comprehensive list of specific, behaviorist-style objectives for each lesson or each unit can be printed out. Or a collection of test questions can serve as a self-test and study guide.

Announcing specific micro-objectives in advance of study has both virtues and faults (Duchastel & Merrill, 1973). It gives the student a sure sense of where the teacher wants him to go and enables him to judge reasonably well when he has accomplished his task. Unfortunately, it can curtail his learning. The following study (M. Duchastel and B. Brown, 1974) illustrates what can go wrong.

# Higher-order quizzes; higher-order learning

An eight-week experiment in Grade VIII history classes was conducted by McKenzie (1972). The teachers taught in their usual manner, not knowing which student was assigned to each treatment group. The experimental variable was the form of item used in weekly quizzes on the text.

The quiz sheets handed the Knowledge group (randomly selected within the class) had them recall scattered facts from the chapter and discuss each one briefly. For example:

> **The first city on Manhattan Island was built by the**
> **(a) Dutch   (b) English   (c) French   (d) Spanish**
> **Why?**

In the Inference group (within the same class), each question asked for an interpretation the text did not give about some fact. Thus, when the textbook stated that the Boston Port Bill closed the port of Boston, the inference question was:

> **The Boston Port Bill most directly affected the business of**
> **(a) farmers   (b) merchants   (c) laborers   (d) planters**
> **Why?**

When the student turned in his quiz paper for week 2, he got to look over his corrected paper from week 1 for a few minutes. There was no class discussion of the quizzes, and students in one group had no chance to see the quiz the other group took. Such delayed feedback was continued throughout the experiment.

In the eighth week, students were told to prepare for a review test over five chapters. The two experimental groups did equally well on a factual test. But the students in the Inference group did better on nearly every item in an inference test similar to that used during instruction.

Students required to go beyond the text in their weekly quizzes learned to think about the meaning of the facts their text presented.

College students studied several consecutive units. For each unit a list of objectives was provided along with the text material. The posttest was matched closely to the objectives, so that the student encountered no surprises. Students learned, then, to rely on the objectives. Following this conditioning period came a short experiment. The students were allowed 30 minutes to study an article on mushrooms. Specific objectives (essentially, test items) were prepared—for example, "Give two examples of plants which form a cooperative symbiosis with fungi." One group of students was handed 12 objectives for the article; another group, given no list, was simply told to learn what was in the article. The posttest included items on these 12 objectives and on 12 other points in the text. The two groups did equally well. But look at the breakdown of average scores.

On the 12 items identified in the list of objectives:

7.4 correct among students targeted onto those topics

5.1 correct among students studying without a guided list

On 12 items not in the list of objectives:

3.2 correct among students using the list to guide their study

5.6 correct among students studying without a list of objectives

The teacher apparently is wise to provide a list of objectives when he will be satisfied to have students master those specific points and nothing else. Specifying objectives can choke off incidental learning, however.

Tests or questions at the end of study likewise define for the student what he should attend to in the future (pp. 465 and 686; box). If test coverage is not comprehensive, it promotes learning of one aspect of the course and promotes neglect of another.

**5** Illustrate multiple goals, intermediate goals, and remote goals that might be present when
 a. fifth-graders write a letter to the town newspaper to advertise their school carnival.
 b. an adolescent assembles a radio transmitter from a kit.
 c. a high-school student reads a Spanish assignment in *Don Quixote.*

# HOW ASPIRATIONS ARE SET

Whether a response will be repeated on later occasions, or abandoned, depends on how well its consequences measure up to the person's expectation.

A person has an expectation when he attempts something. If he attains the expected results, he is, in one sense of the word, satisfied. If he does less well than he expected, he experiences some degree of failure. A student may do as well as the teacher expected and receive a favorable comment, yet be annoyed because he aimed higher. Another accepts a poor performance as inevitable. Thus, the one who "fails" objectively is confirmed in his original expectation, and the one who "succeeds" in the teacher's eyes is not.

The standard a person expects to reach in a particular performance is referred to as his level of "aspiration." One's expectation or aspiration has three aspects: what characteristics of the performance he considers desirable, how

well he expects to perform in each of these respects, and how important each of the characteristics is to him. Consider Ruth, giving an oral report on mining to her science class. What characteristics does she consider desirable in an oral report? She probably asks herself such questions as these:

Was I ready on time?

How did the teacher react?

Did I get through without forgetting what I wanted to say?

Did the other students appear to be interested?

A report that comes up to these standards might not satisfy Ruth if she had also asked:

Will the others remember the ideas I presented?

Did I use my voice in a pleasing and effective way?

Did I select the most important ideas for presentation?

## The Influence of Success and Failure

The level one aspires to grows out of experience. As a typist, Roger has tested himself repeatedly. On his next test he anticipates a score near his previous average. If he betters it a little, fine; but he will not expect to double his rate immediately. Roger expects to do well in any sport he undertakes. He considers himself moderately competent in using tools and expects to complete simple repairs, but does not expect a high order of craftmanship of himself. Roger expects to be criticized by teachers—so much so that he shrugs off the advice when a new teacher urges him to study harder.

Confirmation, I have said, encourages one to repeat an interpretation. This is not the same statement as, "What is rewarded will be repeated; the response that is unrewarded will be dropped." The bowler is not likely to change his technique when he fails to make a strike. Whether he reconsiders his interpretation depends on his expectation. If he thinks his best ball will get him about three strikes per game, he probably will continue in the same way despite the fact that he averages seven "punishments" for every three "rewards." Three strikes per game are a confirmation, if not much of a success.

Jucknat (1938) asked a child to tell how rapidly he thought he would do the next puzzle in a series. This was done repeatedly. Some children started with an insoluble puzzle, others with an easy one. As Fig. 14.1 shows, most of the successful group raised their aspiration on the next trial, confident that they could do the next puzzle even faster. Failing children rarely raised their aspiration. How the person feels about his success affects his motivation. Some of those who succeeded were excited about their success, and their next aim was

## FIGURE 14.1

### Aspiration follows success

The children in the three failure groups had been asked to solve a maze that was insoluble.

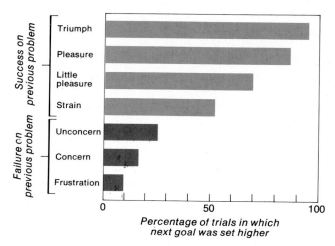

SOURCE: After Jucknat (1938).

high. Those who succeeded after a struggle were hesitant to raise their sights. Among the failures, those most annoyed by the experience were least willing to try for a higher goal the next time. Fear of failure came to outweigh hope for success.

The student's whole history of success has a cumulative effect on his self-concept and his expectation. In a classic study, Pauline Sears (1940) compared fourth- to sixth-graders having good school records with others who had been rather unsuccessful. She gave simple word tests (for example, finding synonyms for well-known words like *cap*). After each trial, she told the student his time in seconds. Being unfamiliar with time scores, he could not judge whether his time was good or not. Then she asked what score he was going to try for on the next test. She particularly wanted to determine whether or not students would set reasonable goals—goals near to or slightly better than their last performance. The same procedure was followed with an easy addition test. Figure 14.2 shows the results. More of the children successful in past schoolwork set realistic but optimistic goals.

The effect of repeated failures is hard to predict. Students who had done badly in school set unreasonable goals in Sears's study. Some, cautious, set a goal much below what they had already achieved. If adult pressure had been absent, many of them would have abandoned the task. Others with records of failure—and a low sense of efficacy—set goals so far above their performance as to be unreachable (de Charms, 1976). It is as if they said, "My attainments aren't much, but at least my *goals* are worthy of praise. And failing to reach a lofty goal hardly counts as a failure."

A person with a history of success may still back off if he expects a new task to give him difficulty, and vice versa. Teachers increase motivation just by building expectations of success. It is possible to persuade a student that he can do a task well—even if his record to date is poor. Groups so encouraged participate more actively and learn more than untreated controls (Brophy & Good, 1974, pp. 65–69). To develop enjoyment of an activity, there is no better tactic than to give a feeling of continually rising accomplishment. This can be done by arranging tasks the student can handle and making sure that he recognizes even small progress.

Some children and adults have a generalized attitude of defeat. Such indiscriminate self-depreciation is common among children of the poor. Many of them come to school believing that they cannot amount to much, and trouble with schoolwork drives home the message. Defeatism is a conspicuous symptom among those who drop out of school at the earliest allowable age (p. 803).

A defeated person is likely to depreciate the success he has. When you tell a person with a poor self-concept that he is doing great work, he may not believe

**FIGURE 14.2**

Goals set by preadolescent achievers and nonachievers

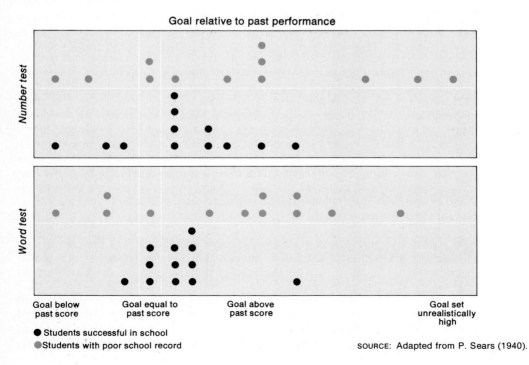

Goal relative to past performance

SOURCE: Adapted from P. Sears (1940).

In a certain elementary school, it was observed that children were setting unrealistically high goals for themselves and being frustrated as a consequence. Psychologists helped the teachers develop a procedure that would encourage the children to set realistic goals for themselves in spelling. de Charms (1976, pp. 72–73) describes the method and results:

> In these sixth grade classrooms the teachers used a spelling book that presented twenty new words each week to the children. The Spelling Game was built around these books. On Monday the children took a pretest on the words for that week. Tuesday and Wednesday were devoted to practice in any way that the teacher or workbook suggested. Thursday was the day for the game. By Thursday the teacher had checked the Monday papers and had marked correct and incorrect words and kept the list herself. The children began by choosing two teams as in a traditional spelling bee. When they were ready, the teacher called on the first member of team A.
>
> "John, what would you like to try, an easy word, a moderately hard word, or a hard word? If you spell the easy word correctly your team will receive 1 point. Correct spelling of the moderately hard word gives 2 points. Hard words result in 3 points. Incorrect spelling of any word results in no points and I will spell it for you."
>
> John was faced with setting a goal and unbeknownst to him the difficulty of the words were scaled according to his own ability. The teacher had in front of her his spelling paper from Monday. An easy word was one he spelled correctly on Monday; a moderately hard word one he spelled incorrectly on Monday but had a chance to study; and, a hard word was from a future list tailored to his ability. John's teammates were allowed to consult with him on setting his goal, thus giving group support.
>
> We decided not to tell the children the method of selection of words to see if they did, in fact, have more success with moderately difficult words and tend to choose them more often as time passed. The teachers were initially concerned that the children would think it unfair to change standards for each child, but their fears were quieted, as the children heartily approved. As the children said, even the worst speller could get two points for his team if he studied the words he missed. The teachers also wondered if the children would start looking at future spelling lists and apparently some did. In the context of the game this might be considered cheating, but hardly something to be discouraged.
>
> With the children, the Spelling Game was clearly the most popular of the four units. The project staff collected data on it for five weeks, but all classrooms continued to use it for at least five more weeks and some used it until near the end of the year, from February to May.
>
> Many of the teachers considered this the most successful unit: "It taught them how to set a moderate goal. They learned immediately the dangers of setting one that's too high and also they learned that there is no satisfaction in setting one that's too low. . . . Also this was something easy to transfer to areas other than just the spelling game."
>
> During the Spelling Game the teachers recorded the type of words each child chose. From these data we were able to demonstrate that the number of moderately hard words chosen increased progressively over a five-week period while the number of hard and easy words chosen decreased. . . . Apparently we had succeeded in encouraging the children to select their goals more carefully and realistically.

SOURCE: R. de Charms, *Enhancing Motivation: Change in the Classroom* (New York: Irvington, 1976), pp. 72–73. Reprinted by permission.

your encouraging words; a cooler, more factual report elicits better effort. Moreover, he is likely to be suspicious of the praise: "You can't put me on!" (Aronson & Carlsmith, 1962; Andrews, 1967; M. Deutsch & L. Solomon, 1959). When external feedback is lacking or unclear—as is the case in much schoolwork—low-achieving boys judge their work to be considerably lower in quality than it really is (Katz, 1967). (Katz was working with blacks at about age 12. He found no similar relationship among girls.)

As Baron (1966) put it, a person forms an idea as to what level of success or encouragement is "appropriate" for him. If the feedback places him near to or moderately above what he has been accustomed to in that context, he finds it credible. When he scores far outside his normal range, in either direction, he does not know what to make of the strange event. Objective feedback from events themselves has greater credibility than the praise of a teacher.

THE APPETITE FOR CHALLENGE    This is not to say that motivation rises when all schoolwork is "easy." People like challenges. Day and Berlyne (in Lesser, 1971, p. 329) report that students rate as most interesting the textbook that is a bit *beyond* their usual level of comprehension (see also p. 609). Other evidence, however (p. 558), reminds us that in school there are those who seek safety rather than challenge.

Persons with strong need to achieve or a strong sense of efficacy like challenges (J. Atkinson & N. Feather, 1966; Karabenick, 1972; D. McClelland & R.

Watson, 1973). We interpret nAch as a measure of the motive to seek success; it has to be considered along with the motive to avoid failure (as determined by an anxiety questionnaire). These two motives are not simple opposites. A person can be strong in one and weak in the other; in Fig. 14.3 these two patterns are both counted as intermediates. That figure displays a representative finding. College men were put to work on tedious, not particularly difficult arithmetic. In the "contingent" condition, they were told that they had to pass each short test in order to go ahead to another. If they failed they would have to sit idly until the end of the hour—a modest punishment. The second group knew they would take all the tests regardless of how they scored; for this group poor quality had no consequence. The figure charts the number of problems done correctly on the first 25-item test. (Number attempted showed a similar trend.) Personality made little difference when achievement "did not count." Under pressure, men with inhibiting motivation (low nAch and high need to avoid failure) fell off. Men with the opposite, constructive pattern surged ahead.

The secure performer finds fun in accomplishing something the hard way. A nice example comes from an experiment in which an 8-year-old girl was asked to guess whether a big or a little kangaroo would turn up next in a pile of picture cards. There were about three big kangaroos for every little one; she divided her guesses in about that proportion. Toward the end of the series she confided to the tester: "I know how to be right most often. I only need to guess the big kangaroo all the time. But that wouldn't be any fun" (Solley & Murphy, 1960, p. 159). She was willing to settle for this lower rate while trying to beat the odds through good guesses.

## FIGURE 14.3

### Intellectual work with and without pressure to achieve

Constructive motivation is a combination of high nAch with low anxiety; defensive motivation is a combination of low nAch with high anxiety.

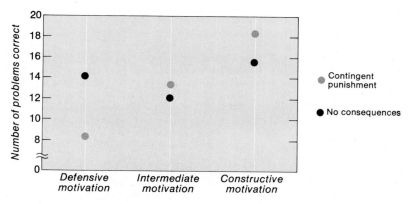

SOURCE: Data from Raynor & Rubin (1974), p. 185.

## Fear of success in women

Apparently, many able girls and women anticipate unpleasant consequences should they strive and succeed. Striving in a competitive situation is an aggressive act, out of keeping with the role into which women have traditionally been socialized.

Horner (1968) presented cues such as the following:

---

**After first-term grades are out, Joan finds herself at the top of her class.**

---

The respondent was to write a brief story explaining what led up to this and how others would react. Most college women in Horner's sample gave stories in which the woman's fear of success was implied. Men (responding to the same sentence with "John" in place of "Joan") introduced fear themes in fewer than half their stories.

Fear themes appeared in the stories of 54 per cent of the junior-high-school girls Harvey (1975) tested. Here is what one girl wrote:

> Last week, after the first term grades were given out, Joan found herself at the top of her class in school. She was very surprised but also happy as she knows her friends will be pleased.
>
> She attained these marks by faithfully studying for the exams each night for a month. She didn't tell anyone about this. Before she had been just an average student. The other students, however, feel she has achieved this mark by cheating. They are all very jealous.
>
> They plan to go to the principal and demand her marks to be lowered.

In a task that called for diligent application of ideas from their home economics course, adolescent girls who wrote positive stories about achievement for Harvey outperformed, in a 6-to-1 ratio, those who wrote fear-of-success stories. Among Horner's college women, those who wrote fear stories did much better in noncompetitive tasks than in competitive tasks; the minority who showed little fear did their best when in competition. (See also p. 643.)

A controlled study tells a little more about students who seek challenge. Gewirtz (1959) set out puzzles to solve, letting the child decide whether his next puzzle would be of the same type as the one he had just worked on. The children who wanted to move on to a different type after success were the ones with high ability and strong achievement needs. Near-duplicates of tasks already mastered did not satisfy them.

The clearest maxim for the teacher is, "Keep tasks within reach." Reaching does require effort. To maintain self-confidence, the learner should be able to complete most of his undertakings. But no harm is done if he tries for some goals that he has small chance of reaching. Reaching an unlikely goal once in five tries can strengthen willingness to try and readiness to take the risks of divergent thinking. It is important that the one success be gratifying and that the learner understand that his misses are not to his discredit. The reformer, the inventor, the politician, the athlete, the artist, the teacher—all of them must try many times to be rewarded with one triumph. Experience in school can teach one to accept the "failures" that are the inevitable price of daring.

**6** A teacher says, "I always grade pupils severely during the first marking period of the semester. Then, when I give higher marks during the second period, they feel successful and are encouraged." Comment.

**7** Miss Nagle says, "I never make promises to my second-graders about things we are going to do until I am certain that we will be able to do them." Miss Tompkins says, "I don't think that is so important. They get a lot of pleasure from anticipating things, and they can understand that it is often necessary to change plans. I tell them about pleasant things I have planned, even if they won't always work out." Which of them do you side with?

**8** A "4-10" split on the bowling alley confronts the bowler with two pins on the opposite sides of the lane. Picking up one pin is not hard. Trying to nick the 4 pin so that it slides across and knocks down the 10 usually fails; often one misses both pins. Gloria almost always goes for both pins; why does she choose near-certain failure?

## Group Standards

Goals depend on standards set by one's group. The person who values his group membership will strive for the attainments that go with that membership status. Goal setting is influenced by the example of others with whom he identifies. Festinger (1942) gave an information test to college sophomores. Each one was allowed to compare the score he reached with a table of norms, and then had to estimate what score he would make on a second, similar test. To carry out the experimental plan, Festinger falsified the "norms." He told some of the students that they had scored below the undergraduate average. They usually said they would do a little better on the next trial. Other sophomores, told that they had fallen below the high-school average, announced a much higher goal for the next trial. If told that he fell slightly below the graduate norm, the sophomore raised his expectation hardly at all. Goals are set at the level demanded for self-respect.

GROUP DECISIONS The teacher wishing to increase student effort faces a problem like that of the industrial manager who wants more production. The worker usually produces less than he could, and those who do set a fast pace are under group pressure to slow down. Allowing workers to participate in setting work goals often leads to higher production. Whyte (1955) tells of a factory where young women complained bitterly about the speed of the moving belt that set the pace at which they were to paint toys. The pace had been carefully set within the normal ability of workers. The women, paid on a piecework basis, lost money when they did not keep up the pace. In response to the complaints, the workers were allowed to adjust the belt speed themselves, changing

## Making the peer group a positive force

Some elementary schools have been able deliberately to bring a new group standard into being. Schmuck (adapted from Lesser, 1971, pp. 521–22) recommends the following process:

> The elementary teacher who discovers antilearning, antischool student norms in the classroom peer group can take a course of action that has proven successful in several instances. It involves a rotating student steering committee that lends leadership to the development of group norms about classroom behavior and which evaluates the operation of the classroom weekly. The following steps can be taken to implement such a project: Sociometric questions are developed and administered so that the most popular and influential peers represent the membership of the initial steering committee. A five- or six-person steering committee of highly popular and influential boys and girls is appointed. This group meets with the teacher once every week to discuss problems in the classroom and to initiate ideas about appropriate classroom rules and regulations. A tentative set of rules for classroom behavior, a kind of class constitution, is developed and presented to the entire class for their evaluation and vote of confidence. A new steering committee is appointed by the initial committee and is asked to serve for a prescribed period of time, perhaps three weeks. This committee, in turn, appoints another committee and this process continues until all members of the group have served. A certain time of the week is set aside to review the class's behavior during the week, to revise rules that are no longer applicable, and to create new rules as needed. The steering committee takes charge of this meeting and is responsible for its agenda and for keeping order in the group.
>
> In classrooms where this approach has been tried, significant gains have been made in the level of initiative and responsibility taken by the students for the operation of the classroom. Antischool, antilearning reactions have decreased and the teacher has been able to decrease his control functions. Some students tend initially to be overly strict in the formulation of rules, but groups usually are able to control their most extreme and deviate members. Classroom norms can be changed when the teacher arranges ways in which the students, through group action, can develop and formalize their own rules and regulations.

It is much more difficult for educators to modify group standards among adolescents, Schmuck says. Teenagers fear social rejection and are slow to move away from the prevailing standards. The first step in group change has to come within a few students. A minority who shift to a nonstandard position may eventually attract enough others to establish a new norm. (This echoes what was said about value shifts at pp. 194ff.)

**TABLE 14.1**

**Features of Massachusetts classrooms most often reported by students**

| Statement | Percentage of agreement |
|---|---|
| *Statements that most students say are true of their school:* | |
| Teachers will raise a student's grade if they think that the student has worked hard. | 85 |
| In this school students ask other students to visit them at home. | 85 |
| In this school students usually have to line up before going into the classroom. | 82 |
| Social studies is not a very important subject in this school. | 82 |
| Most of the teachers are very hard workers and they think that the students should be hard workers too. | 81 |
| *Statements that most students say are false:* | |
| In many classes, students sit in any seat they choose. | 15 |
| Bells ring during the day to tell students what work to do next. | 16 |
| Most teachers do not try to get students interested in what's going on in the United States. | 18 |
| Students get good grades without spending much time studying. | 19 |
| Most of the teachers do not care about problems that the students are having. | 19 |

SOURCE: Adapted from Sadker, Sadker, & Cooper (1972), p. 292.

it from time to time during the day if they wished. The complaints disappeared, and the women pushed the speed up to an average higher than the engineers had set. Group goal setting is not likely to raise the goal, of course, unless the worker sees the higher production as contributing to something he cares about.

Establishing a group consensus was effective in changing housewives' meal planning (Lewin, 1958). In a time of meat shortage it was necessary to persuade them to serve liver, heart, and other meats they did not ordinarily use. Exhortations and factual lectures had no effect on the meals the women served. A large factor seemed to be their pride in "setting a good table"—which meant providing the roasts and steaks that were scarce and costly. The women felt they were failing as providers if they served the more available but less elegant cuts. When a group of housewives discussed meal planning and reached a *group* decision to use more liver and heart, the individual women actually did feed these meats to their families. The ideal of being a good cook was redefined by the group; members had a new basis for judging whether they were successful.

A group decision about a goal can be expected to lead to superior performance when three conditions are met: the individuals care about holding the approval of the group; the goal truly serves their own interest in a way they can understand; and the group is genuinely free to raise or lower the goal (J. R. P. French et al., 1960). Consulting the group is a waste of time otherwise.

THE SCHOOL ATMOSPHERE    Every school has its own atmosphere, derived from its traditions, its admission policies, the attitudes communicated by the faculty and the community, and the group spirit. Research on school (and class) climates is conducted by having students check, on a questionnaire, items that describe their situation as they see it. A report of a study of elementary schools in Massachusetts is illustrative (Sinclair & Sadker, 1973; Sadker, Sadker, & Cooper, 1972). In 54 randomly selected schools, all the fifth- and sixth-graders responded to 80 statements. The practices reported by the great majority of students (Table 14.1) are traditional.

Figure 14.4 summarizes the responses in terms of clusters of items, seven related items constituting each scale. The profile of means adds to our image of typical schools. Sense of community or belonging (lack of alienation) is strong, but the emotional tone (morale) is most often in the neutral range.

School 1 was identified by Sinclair and Sadker as having a desirable atmosphere.* School 2 was picked as having a less desirable pattern. The profiles give a good deal of information, though not as much as the report of a sensitive observer. For all its good qualities, School 1 is no better than the average school

* Scores nearer 100 would be welcome, but close agreement among students is not to be expected when items refer to emotional responses.

FIGURE 14.4

**Profiles of two elementary schools based on student descriptions**

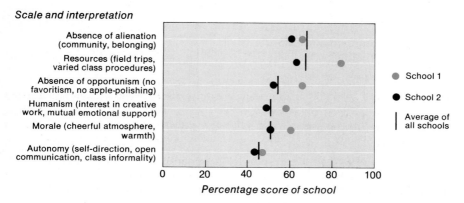

SOURCE: Data from Sinclair & Sadker (1973) and Sadker, Sadker, & Cooper (1972).

with respect to autonomy and lack of alienation. School 2 seems to have average autonomy and morale, but has more alienation than most schools.

At high-school and college levels, there is institutional variation in the stimulation offered to students (more tennis courts or more visiting scientific lecturers?), in the faculty-student relations, and in the activities that command respect. In one school, political interests mark a person as the campus bore; in another, as one of the moving spirits. The student who falls in with the ruling enthusiasms gets many subtle reinforcements. To some extent, each college has its own "personality." The reputation is self-perpetuating, inasmuch as the college-bound student looks for the school that is most compatible with his or her personal aims and styles.

The students and faculty combine to produce a distinctive set of pressures. The atmosphere encourages certain values and provides opportunities for certain types of learning. To change the campus atmosphere is not easy, but the faculty can encourage the minority of students who are ready to move in some educationally desirable direction.

Coleman (1961a, 1961b; Schmuck, in Lesser, 1971) traced some of the effects of high-school atmosphere on morale and performance (Table 14.2). In nine public schools in northern Illinois, he asked such questions as "What does it take to get in with the leading crowd in this school?" In every school, personality and good reputation were among the qualities most frequently mentioned. For boys, athletics was considered important. But there were striking variations. In Green Junction, a school of 500 in a community of 5,000, athletics was mentioned as important by 27 per cent of the boys; in the superficially similar Maple Grove, 14 per cent mentioned athletics. In these schools, just over 10 per cent mentioned grades as socially important.

Only at Midcity were grades more important than athletics. The social importance of a good school record was less in smaller communities. (It is not safe to generalize from Midcity to all urban high schools, nor from a 1961 report to the present.)

The social importance of grades influenced effort. The average mental ability of boys earning grades of A and A– is expected to be high where the brightest boys are taking their schoolwork seriously and teachers grade on performance. This was indeed the case; grades correlated most strongly with ability at Midcity, Elmtown, and Marketville.

From these findings, alongside rather similar results for girls, Coleman concluded gloomily that

the adolescent subcultures in these schools exert a rather strong deterrent to academic achievement. . . . Those who are seen as the "intellectuals," and who come to think of themselves in this way, are not really those of highest intelligence, but are only the ones who are willing to work hard at a relatively unrewarded activity.

To check on self-respect and morale, Coleman presented this item:

| If I could trade, I would be someone different from myself. | Agree | Disagree |
| --- | --- | --- |

## TABLE 14.2

Effects of peer attitudes on academic effort

| School | Community population | Enrollment | Percentage of boys mentioning grades as important[1] | Percentage of boys studying at home[2] | Mean ability of boys earning A's[3] |
|---|---|---|---|---|---|
| Midcity | 100,000 | 1,935 | 19 | 40 | 63 |
| Millburg | 25,000 | 1,383 | 14 | 28 | 62 |
| Executive Heights | 17,000 | 1,862 | 10 | 42 | 60 |
| Newlawn | 9,000 | 1,053 | 7 | 10 | 58 |
| Elmtown | 7,000 | 513 | 12 | 39 | 63 |
| Maple Grove | 6,000 | 421 | 12 | 26 | 60 |
| Green Junction | 5,000 | 538 | 11 | 15 | 62 |
| Marketville | 4,000 | 364 | 16 | 34 | 65 |
| Farmdale | 1,000 | 169 | 6 | 0 | 56 |

SOURCE: Data from Coleman (1961b), pp. 70, 263, 267, and personal communication.

[1] In indicating what is required to be in the leading crowd.
[2] Boys studying two hours or more per night; data in this column based solely on boys whose fathers attended college.
[3] Standard score, relative to the school average of 50.

A student agreeing with this statement is clearly expressing dissatisfaction with his role and prospects in life, as well as with his present performance. The students outstanding in something the peer community cared about proved to be considerably happier than the good scholars. In those schools where grades were unimportant for social acceptance, the high-achieving boys were no happier than the average boys, and the high-achieving girls were distinctly unhappy with themselves. Likewise, athletic distinction or popularity with the opposite sex contributed much less to self-satisfaction in the school where that trait was not rated high by the group.

9   In Executive Heights, the qualities boys considered necessary for being in the leading crowd were as follows: personality, mentioned by over 20 per cent; athletics, good looks, popularity with girls, and good reputation, 10–19 per cent; good grades, car ownership, and money, less than 10 per cent. How do you suppose their fathers would answer if asked what is needed to be in the leading adult crowd?

10  In what ways can teachers legitimately influence the opportunities a student has to be a leader in the school?

11  What is the effect on the educational process of a climate that demands deference and order?

12  Show how group standards would cause a bowler to be content with an average of 150 whereas the same bowler in a different group would be discontented.

13  Could group decision making be used in determining the number of books to be read by high-school English students during a semester?

14  Could group decision making be used in determining when an assignment is to be completed?

15  Why might each of the following practices not work out as intended?
   a. A junior-high-school teacher wants all his students to find art pleasurable and interesting, and therefore praises all their work and gives no grade but A.
   b. A teacher tries to obtain greater effort by telling students that unless they improve they will all have trouble with the statewide test to be given a month hence.
   c. A teacher systematically tries to point out the faults of students who seem complacent and to provide steady praise for those who have had poor records. He intends each student to set the highest goals he can reach.

# REINFORCEMENT IN THE COURSE OF NEW LEARNING

A behaviorist is concerned with the direct, observable effect of consequences. A pleasant consequence the behaviorist refers to as a "reinforcer." In my less behaviorist view, a reinforcer is something the learner takes as a sign that he has reached, or is progressing toward, one of *his own* goals. (Compare Bindra, 1974.) Instead of speaking of disconfirmation, the behaviorist speaks of an annoying consequence, an "aversive event"—one that turns the person away from the path he last used.

A reinforcing event has two aspects. First, contingent reinforcement is a signal. It tells the learner that his interpretation was sound *or* that he should react differently on another trial. Second, it is a payoff. Whether contingent or noncontingent, it gives direct pleasure or displeasure, and as such is a source of motivation. Generally speaking, a person acts in ways that lead to pleasure. Most rewards are symbolic. A pat on the back, a smile, the words "Good job," even a bonus in one's pay envelope—these function mostly as symbols of approval.

Reinforcement during learning influences what one learns, and how rapidly. This is true whether we are considering the acquisition of knowledge and skill or the acquisition of a habit. Reinforcement also plays a significant part after a habit is learned. Knowledge or skill is likely to be maintained by the natural consequences of its use. Habits too are maintained by natural consequences. But reinforcements provided by others play a large part in maintaining them; and altering the contingencies of reinforcement is a most powerful way to extinguish one habit and replace it by another.

## Categories of Reinforcement

A bit of candy or a pleasant word following a response is a reinforcer. Small plastic tokens can have the same emotional significance, once a child understands that a pile of tokens can be turned in for a toy or a privilege.

In the classroom, the aversive event following a wrong response may be giving up tokens from one's pile or just hearing the word *Wrong*. The experimenter in the laboratory can keep a loud buzzer going *until* the subject makes the desired response; turning off that aversive stimulus then is a positive, reinforcing event.

On any one trial the experimenter or the teacher has three alternatives: arrange a positive consequence, arrange a negative one, or provide none at all. He can intermix positive and zero reinforcement—for example, over a series of trials. On the "nonreinforced" trial the learner is given no feedback from the person who set the task. (Does that mean that he receives no reinforcement at all?)

The categories fit natural settings only loosely. In the laboratory, the experimenter can rig a task so that without the reinforcer the learner has nothing to guide him. (For example, the learner may have to shoot at a target he cannot see.) Outside the laboratory, self-reinforcement can operate: the performer judges himself, though not always correctly. Another complication is that many real-life consequences are hard to classify as positive or aversive. Is it pleasant or aversive for the Socratic teacher to follow up a correct response with a further, deeper question? What is "aversive" depends on the person and the situation.

Contingent and noncontingent reinforcement are important to distinguish. Laboratory reinforcements are usually contingent on the response: only the response the experimenter wants brings the reward. Contingent reward may be steady or probabilistic, the reward following every correct response or following one correct response out of three.

Unfortunately, classroom reinforcement is often noncontingent. A teacher who makes a general principle of being supportive is likely to say "Good" without regard to whether the speaker has truly contributed to the discussion. Such noncontingent reinforcement is haphazard. Reinforcement theory can state laws for contingent reinforcement. Noncontingent reinforcement has unpredictable effects; at best it can increase effort, but it cannot direct it.

Vicarious reinforcement occurs. In vicarious reinforcement, the subject sees another person receive contingent reinforcement (Bandura, 1971; see also p.

465). This can modify his behavior as much as if he himself received the reinforcing signal. Thus, in the classroom, the teacher's encouragement of a halfbaked idea from one student opens the way for others to put tentative ideas into the discussion.

The section that follows considers reinforcers as signals, which is their primary role in new learning. Then we examine whether much is gained by adding payoff (for example, by giving candy for right answers). Punishment for wrong answers is scarcely mentioned in this section; the later section on maintenance and extinction of habits goes into more detail about aversive consequences.

**16** Would it be correct to say that most aversive consequences arranged in classrooms are symbolic?

**17** Under what circumstances would "nonreinforcement" be aversive?

**18** A college teacher tries to keep a uniform tone in his comments on students' short essays: a word of acceptance, plus a remark to the effect "Perhaps you should think more about . . ." to stimulate growth. Is this reinforcement contingent or noncontingent? What effects do you expect it to have?

## Informative Feedback

One cannot learn without knowing when he has made a sound response. The beginning reader has trouble remembering which letter to call "bee" and which "dee." He needs an external signal to help him discriminate. When better at reading, he is less dependent. He can catch his own errors because what he reads does not make sense. Reinforcing signals from a teacher are not required after the person becomes competent and willing to judge his own work.

Every trial can be followed by an explicit signal. Such right/wrong indications are built into many kinds of drill. The signal may be simply a display of the correct answer, against which the student judges the answer he gave. Laboratory studies find little difference between positive and negative signals when the two carry equally specific information (Travers et al., 1964). In a choice task with two alternatives, for example, an experimenter who says right after every correct response is conveying the same information as the one who says wrong after every incorrect response. (But see p. 626.)

Reinforcing signals have their greatest effect when they are linked to particular responses. A false interpretation is corrected promptly if the first error triggers a warning. If the student multiplies a pageful of decimals, turns the paper in, and gets it back next day with his errors marked in red, he can profit. But if his answers were evaluated as he finished each problem, he would have corrected his faulty interpretation early in the practice session. He would then have been practicing correct responses rather than errors. In some circumstances the teacher will be wise to observe several trials and then to direct attention to a *consistent* error. Where performance is variable, trial-by-trial feedback overloads the performer with trivial reports. (See also pp. 428 and 532.)

The more information in the signal the better, as a general rule. Compare the following reports:

> Your arrow missed the target.
>
> The arrow flew three feet above the bull's-eye and a little to the left.
>
> You probably caused the miss by shifting your weight as you released the arrow.

All are negative signals, but the messages are not the same.

Essays written in high school and college are too often returned with a grade but with no comments to serve as directive signals. Insofar as time permits, the comments by the teacher ought to be appreciative in the full sense of the word—drawing the student's attention to the techniques that contributed to his success, helping him recognize how he can achieve a better product another time. Information-rich signals reshape behavior instead of merely encouraging or discouraging it.

Giving a reinforcing signal after every provisional try is appropriate in some circumstances, disruptive in others. Especially, discrimination learning calls for regular signals (as in the "bee" versus "dee" example). These help the learner sort out the critical cues. But the French teacher would be most unwise to try to signal after every try at the *u* sound. Interrupting the sentence to tell the student how well he made the *u* sound would interfere with his thought, his speech rhythm, and his confidence. There is a place for trial-by-trial signals in an occasional isolated drill on the *u* sound. Even in such drills, it may be best to record the student's speech on a tape and have him listen to and judge his response before the teacher does, and again after. This moves him more rapidly toward self-sufficiency.

## Effect of Pleasant Consequences on Effort

"Knowledge of results" is indispensable. About "payoff," there is disagreement. Does the child who receives bits of candy (in addition to a signal) when he answers correctly learn faster? If so, does a larger reward help?

The answer seems to hinge on the extent to which the student is interested in the task itself. When the student is emotionally engaged, he attends to emo-

## The right form of praise

The late Haim Ginott (1972) makes a valuable distinction between the teacher's praise of the student's work and the teacher's praise of the student or some aspect of his character. Ginott warns against use of the latter (his p. 45):

> If we met Picasso, we would not say to him, "You are a great painter. You are doing a fine job." We would not dare to set ourselves up as judges. We might say, "Thank you, Mr. Picasso, for your paintings. They have enriched my life." Children deserve similar courtesy. They too need praise that appreciates, not praise that compares or condescends.
>
> Evaluative praise is often experienced as a threat. It brings discomfort, not delight; fear, not joy. Children often squirm under the stress of judgmental praise, and they become defensive and evasive. . . .
>
> Ben threw a dart at a target and hit the bull's-eye. His gym teacher said, "You are great. You have a perfect eye. You are a marksman." Ben walked away from the game. The teacher was surprised. He had intended to encourage him, but the praise apparently discouraged him. . . .
>
> After the praise, Ben thought: "This teacher will expect my every dart to hit the bull's-eye. I am not a marksman. . . . I'd better quit while I'm ahead.". . . .
>
> *Conclusion:* Productive praise describes a child's efforts and accomplishments and our feelings about *them*. [Italics added.] It does not evaluate personality or judge character. The cardinal rule in praising is: Describe without evaluating. Report—don't judge. Leave the evaluation of the child to him.

tionally neutral signs of progress. Nothing is added by intensifying the payoff. If the activity is not rewarding in itself and not a source of pride, extra payoff may serve to keep the student at work.

WHO RESPONDS TO REWARDS? Personal differences can be discussed with the aid of a scale of evolution of motives. (This scale, from Havighurst, foreshadows his ideas about character that will appear in Chapter 18. See also Zigler, 1970.) In order of their development the motives are:

1. Physiological needs or appetites

2. Desire for concrete rewards (toys, money, tokens)

3. Desire for approval from others

4. Self-approval on the basis of conscientious conformity to standards

5. Self-management (commitment, security) in the light of one's own aspirations

This last echoes the notion of motivation for competence (Chapter 5), and Maslow's well-known concept of self-actualization. With mature motivation, a person invests in a task an effort coordinate with its place in his life economy, considering its long-run consequences; at the lowest levels, effort depends on immediate gratifications. All these motives appear in some form before age 6, but the balance shifts as emotional maturity increases.

The balance for the typical schoolchild from a middle-class home is already far up on Havighurst's scale. Payoff—as distinct from informative feedback—does not mean much to him. He is already likely to be interested in the task, to value symbolic rewards, and to see the payoff as trivial. Added payoff can even do harm (see p. 607 and box, p. 627). As to whether tangible rewards improve the learning of lower-class children, the evidence is inconsistent (C. Schultz & R. Sherman, 1976). The hypothesis that the teacher will find lower-class children responsive to tangible payoff is supported by anecdotes, but not by solid research under long-run schoolroom conditions. One preschool teacher, for example, tried by encouragement and praise to get a black, poor child to talk more frequently, with no effect. When the teacher switched to saying that the child was doing so well that he would soon earn this or that concrete reward, the child became more talkative. Approval was not, by itself, a significant payoff (Reynolds & Risley, 1968).

By adolescence, social rewards seem to work effectively with all groups (Havighurst, 1970). Black adolescents who read very poorly were the subjects in one experiment (Clark & Walberg, 1968). In addition to keeping an accurate tally of progress (as in the Willis experiment on p. 622), the teachers were directed to make sure that every student received some praise during each class hour. This plan worked. The greater the amount of praise, the more the reading test scores increased. As the study was brief, it appears that the change was in the student's willingness to try hard, rather than a spurt in proficiency. Perhaps, over time, effort would be sustained and would add to proficiency; but noncontingent praise cannot guide improvement.

Beyond the payoff necessary to get a student to engage himself seriously, increases in reward seem to do no good. That is why symbolic rewards are often sufficient. Offering a large payoff may work out badly; the person narrows his attention to what is strictly relevant to getting the reward. Given the hint, "This week's test will be on verb forms," the student rehearses the responses to be rewarded to the neglect of other responses that are equally part of the week's lessons. Working for the reward, he attends to only a fraction of the information in the material (R. Atkinson & D. Wickens, 1971; Quartermain & Scott, 1951; see also box, p. 600). As a further example, note what happened when children were offered a two-dollar prize for "the best story." Some classes were told that, while the story should be original and interesting, the prize would be given for excellence of format, grammar, and so on. Other classes were told that the prize would go to the most original and interesting story. Sure enough, both the number of technical errors and the level of interest and originality went up in the second class (Torrance, 1965, p. 137).

Payoff affects attention, effort, and performance, but does not directly "strengthen a connection" between stimulus and response (Glaser, 1971, especially pp. 3–7 and 124–28). This is a subtle point, since common sense says that a response, when rewarded, will be retained. But suppose we instruct a child to point to *b* when confronted with a *b–d* or *d–b* display, and reward that response. His ability to point to *d*, a response we are not rewarding, will be strengthened equally. Confirmation strengthens the *interpretation* that led to the response; another time, the same interpretation may call up a response that is different, but correct in the new situation.

Pleasant after-effects may not be needed but they tend to work out well. Providing unpleasant after-effects, however, tends to work out badly. Strong punishment makes the setting for learning unpleasant. The learner will withdraw from it if he can, or reduce the number of tries he makes.

THE VALUE OF OBJECTIVE RECORD KEEPING    Supportive comments most often convey a general message: "You're doing fine. Keep up the effort." Such nonspecific reinforcement does tend to increase effort and level of participation (Spear, 1970; Spear & Spear, 1972; Dusek & Dietrich, 1973). An objective record of progress may do more than generalized emotional support to improve behavior.

For example, three elementary-school children being given remedial instruction in reading were exposed to two conditions: one of general support and one where objective self-charting was added (J. Willis, 1974). During the baseline period of general support, the tutor praised each successful reading of a sentence. Any error he corrected in a neutral tone. (The child did not see the tutor's count of correct and incorrect readings.) In the period with more formal reinforcement, the child was handed a green chip after each sentence read correctly, a red chip otherwise. After each day's session, the child charted the number of chips of each kind. During this second period, the tutor continued his emotional support and commented on the progress the chart showed. As can be seen in Fig. 14.5, all three children improved, reading more and more accurately. General emotional support kept them at the job, but keeping score emphasized doing the job right. Keeping score had appreciable motivating value; there was no other payoff.

Whereas Willis started with encouragement and added a contingent informative reinforcer, Spear (1970) reversed this, providing a neutral reinforcing signal and then adding approval or disapproval. Children worked individually at simple rote learning. The experimenter presented a pair of drawings, having arbitrarily identified one member of the pair as "correct." The child pressed a button to indicate his choice. This was a guess at first. On a later repetition of a pair, a correct response indicated recall. After each response, a light signaled which choice was correct. The child the experimenter assigned to receive "praise" heard encouraging remarks from time to time, regardless of the response he had made (noncontingent). To the child in a second group, the experimenter said "You're not too good at this," or the like. A third group (controls) heard nothing from the experimenter. Among first-graders, the praised children did learn the list faster than the others. Among fifth-graders the reverse was the case; the control children learned fastest. For them, the light provided adequate knowledge of results and adequate encouragement. There was practically no difference between the praised and criticized groups in Grade V. Either praise or disparagement slowed down their learning. The

## FIGURE 14.5

### Rate and accuracy of reading with and without specific contingent reinforcement

Condition I: General emotional support only; Condition II: General emotional support supplemented by tokens marking correct and incorrect sentences.

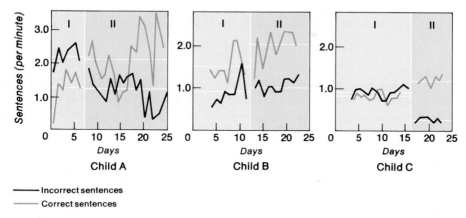

——— Incorrect sentences

——— Correct sentences

SOURCE: Adapted from Willis (1974).

widespread belief that support fosters learning was not valid among these fifth-graders on this task.

INTRINSIC VERSUS EXTRINSIC MOTIVATION    A distinction is sometimes made between "intrinsic" and "extrinsic" motivation, often with the hint that only the bad teacher relies on extrinsic motivation. There can be no dispute about the value of intrinsic motivation (high on Havighurst's scale). When the learner rationally chooses to perform a task, the natural consequences of his efforts provide adequate regulatory signals. His progress supplies an adequate reward. Extra payoff adds nothing.

At times, the teacher has to develop a response whose intrinsic payoff is slight, at least until the student later becomes able to put a number of piecemeal responses to work in an intrinsically rewarding context. For example, a 10-year-old boy may have intrinsic motivation for writing at some level of legibility, but he is not likely to be enchanted by the task of making all his letters uniform and attractive. Yet he will be better off in the long run if he learns a neat handwriting rather than a sloppy one. This will only happen if the teacher starts him on his way by pointing out the difference between a well-shaped letter *a* and a haphazard one, and provides some payoffs to remind him of the ideal.

Extrinsic reinforcement can be overused. First, to rely exclusively on gold stars and other tokens is to fail to keep the student mindful of the larger purposes and pleasures toward which his learning is directed. Second, as extrinsic rewards rest on evaluations made by an authority figure, they actively discourage the student from developing and applying his own distinctive standards of taste. Third, insofar as added payoff raises the level of tension it may impair performance. There is an optimum level of tension for a particular task (p. 643).

# MAINTAINING HABITS AND EXTINGUISHING THEM

Once the person has acquired a response, he may or may not use it. The prospect of reward has much to do with whether the person *will* do what he *can* do. Many of the techniques of behavior modification rely on contingent rewards to increase the frequency of desirable actions. Sometimes this is no more than a control device to reduce misbehavior here and now. When the reinforcement serves as a reminder to help the person change his behavior in a way he himself desires, however, the improved behavior may be maintained when external reinforcement is no longer supplied.

## The Token Economy

Systematic reinforcement is a common technique for getting the student to work at his best. In some classrooms, most control is maintained by a "token economy." Here is a sketch of the technique (see also p. 22) and the point of view behind it from B. F. Skinner (1970), the psychologist chiefly responsible for today's interest in reinforcement procedures.

> To induce members of a classroom community to behave well with respect to each other, additional reinforcers may be needed.
> The main problem is to make these reinforcers contingent on the desired behavior. They are often not available on the spur of the moment. The teacher cannot conveniently reinforce a child when he sits quietly by sending him off on a field trip, or when he stops fighting by handing him an ice cream cone. A "generalized reinforcer" is needed—something which is exchangeable for reinforcing things. Money shows the archetypal pattern. We pay people even though at the time they receive our money they are not hungry for the food they will buy with it or in the mood for the film they will use it to go to see. Credit points or tokens can be used as money in the classroom. They are relatively independent of the deprivations which make them reinforcing and of the circumstances under which the things they are exchanged for will be consumed.
> In one procedure the behavior of the students is sampled from time to time. A student is chosen with some such mechanical system as spinning a dial or drawing a name from a bowl, and his behavior is sampled for, say, 20 or 30 seconds. He is then told that he has been observed and that he has or has not received a

token or credit. A day or two of this is often enough to make a great change: the room grows quiet as the students go to work. Sampling can then become less frequent. Eventually, as the students begin to be reinforced in other ways when they find themselves working more effectively in a quiet room, they will construct their own social contingencies, which may eventually replace those arranged by the teacher.

Skinner speaks of tokens that can be exchanged for toys or other tangible rewards. The payoff in the classroom is more often some privilege, such as an extension of recess time or getting to hear the teacher's aide read a story. The rewards may be made contingent on the behavior of the entire group rather than on that of individuals; for example, if the entire class is at work during the interval sampled, the class earns credit toward such a reward as early dismissal (Greenwood et al., 1974). Sometimes this group payoff works better than keeping score on individuals, and it is much easier to manage.

Whereas there has been much research on maintaining classroom effort and attentiveness by rewards, there has been almost none on the effect of explaining to the student why he should engage in the desired conduct. That tactic can work very well. Taffel et al. (1974) found that telling a second-grader why he should work on arithmetic produced better work than giving praise. The findings on leadership reported in the next chapter are consistent with this. (See also Staub, 1972).

---

 **19** An old line of the teacher is: "If you finish the exercises on this unit before the others do, you may go to the library." How is this practice like the "token economy"? Are there any psychological differences?

---

## Discouraging An Act That is Not Desired

PENALTIES AS A CONTROL TECHNIQUE   Punishing a certain response makes it less frequent. But does punishment eliminate the response, or only suppress it until the threat is gone? The finding from the laboratory is that mere nonreinforcement is more certain to eliminate responses than ordinary levels of punishment. Traumatic levels of punishment, such as strong electric shocks, can permanently suppress a response, but milder levels have rather unpredictable effects (R. Solomon, 1964). All the evidence—human and animal—seems to imply that punishment has its chief effect in suppressing a response in the immediate situation where the punishment is expected. When mild punishment is accompanied by a rationale—a simple explanation of why the act is wrong—deterrence over a long period is more likely than with penalty alone (Parke, 1974, p. 113; see also p. 809). If, in addition to suppressing an inappropriate act, the teacher reinforces a desirable substitute act, the change is more likely to be lasting. In procedures where the learner keeps records of his own acts and "reinforces himself," the intellectual commitment to a new standard of conduct may be more significant than the reinforcement itself (Sherwood & Gray, 1974; see also p. 748).

Whether a payoff rule is *called* a penalty for misbehavior or a reward for good behavior can make a difference. Costantini and Hoving (1973) demonstrated this by asking children to inhibit a response. (See also Brackbill & O'Hara, 1958.) One task was to walk slowly along a six-foot board, the slower the better. In the reward condition, the child earned a marble for every 10 seconds his walk lasted (up to 120 seconds). A large clock showed him how well he was doing. The child in the punishment condition was supplied 12 marbles at the start, and penalized one marble for every 10 seconds his walk fell short of 120 seconds. Thus, both groups performed under an essentially identical rule for the concrete payoff. Figure 14.6 shows the average times in the two groups. The children were apparently under greater psychological pressure when the rule was expressed as a threat of penalty. These results are for 8-year-olds; findings for 6-year-olds were much the same. In another study, saying "Right" to a good guess produced quick learning among lower-class boys on a dull guessing task, and saying "Wrong" after every bad guess produced slow learning. The two techniques were equal in their effect on middle-class boys (Rosenhan, 1966).

Generalizations cannot safely be made regarding reward and punishment. Payoff effects vary, depending on the subjects, the task, and so on. The teacher would be wise to try different reinforcement patterns and observe their effects in his situation.

FIGURE 14.6

Self-control when the same payoff is stated as a bonus and as a penalty

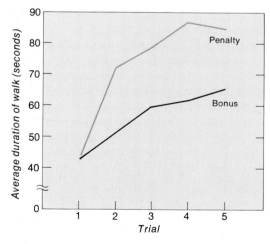

SOURCE: Data from Costantini & Hoving (1973).

## Turning play into work

There is a paradoxical kind of extinction in which cutting off the reward drops the response far below the original baseline. Perhaps the first hint of this paradox came in a study by Gately (reported by Harlow, 1953). Monkeys were given a chance to work on mechanical puzzles. One group of monkeys received no special reinforcement; *they* continued to explore and manipulate the puzzle after they had taken it apart. In an experimental group, the monkey was given a food reward as soon as he solved a problem. The rewarded monkey never touched the pieces after getting the reward. Receipt of the reward became a signal for withdrawing attention from the puzzle.

Studies by Lepper and his associates show a similar effect in preschool classrooms; others have reported the effect in older persons, including adults. In one study (Lepper et al., 1973), the 4-year-old was taken to the experimental room, provided with large sheets of white paper and colored magic markers, and told that he could draw pictures. The subject in the experimental group was shown a "good-player" award (a badge with red ribbon, gold star, and place for the child's name) which each child could earn if he drew well. The control subject was not told of the award in advance, but half of the controls *were* given the award at the end of the session. Any child who got an award filled in his name and mounted it on the experimenter's honor roll; hence the badges were not displayed in the classroom. Two weeks later, the magic markers and papers were set out on a table in the main playroom; observers checked how long each child used them. The average percentages of time the children spent in this activity were as follows:

| | |
|---|---|
| Children who received reward but had not been "working for it" (rewarded controls) | 18 per cent |
| Controls who did not hear of reward and got none | 17 per cent |
| Children who knew of reward in advance and earned it | 9 per cent |

A second study (Greene & Lepper, 1974) confirmed that having worked for the extrinsic reward made children less interested in the activity itself. Lepper argues that the promise of extrinsic reinforcement turns play into work if an activity is attractive in itself. Work is something one does only for a payoff.

In the second study, the quality of drawings during the initial experimental session was scored. Those working for the award turned out somewhat more drawings, but of poorer average quality.

---

EXTINCTION    If a person is working for a reward, and for no other reason, he can be expected to drop the response when it is no longer rewarded. Responses can be "extinguished" by cutting off the reinforcement abruptly. If, during the reinforcement period, the response was rewarded every time it was made, a few unrewarded trials are sufficient to discourage the response. The extinguished response is not "forgotten"; rather, it is put into storage, for use when and if there is again a promise of payoff.

## Attention seeking and the tactics of indifference

Reinforcement theory warns the teacher against reacting in any way to an undesirable act; even a scolding has a perversely reinforcing value for the attention-getter. The behaviorists Haring and Phillips (1972, pp. 170ff.) advise the teacher to ignore completely and consistently whatever response is to be eliminated.

They offer this example. Townsend, a 4½-year-old in Head Start, was aggressive toward everyone and uncontrollable. Teachers were instructed to turn their backs on Townsend when he assaulted another child (but to help the other child to safety!). They were to leave the room whenever Townsend chose to have a tantrum. After describing how well a few days of these procedures worked, Haring and Phillips go on to say:

> During this period of withdrawal of adult attention for the two classes of maladaptive behaviors, Townsend began dumping his lunch on the floor and then smearing it around with his feet or hands. The teachers handled the situation the first few days by getting sponges and towels for Townsend and instructing him to clean up the mess. However, a teacher always participated in the cleanup. The food-dumping and smearing continued day after day with the teachers obviously not realizing that their insistence on the cleanup and their assistance in the task were maintaining the food-dumping at a steady rate of one plate and one glass per day. The teachers were, therefore, instructed to ignore the entire episode and to give their undivided attention to the other children who were attending to the meal. Songs were to be sung if necessary to override peer comments calling attention to Townsend's behavior. On the first session of extinction Townsend himself called attention to the episode repeatedly: "Hey, looka I done." "I make a mess." "Get a sponge, we gotta scrub." The teachers failed to "see" or "hear" any of this. Instead, they sang a bit more lustily, calmly finished lunch with the children, and helped them get ready for outdoors. When Townsend came over to the wrap area, he was matter-of-factly helped with his clothing, with no acknowledgment of his continuing suggestions that "We gotta clean up a big mess." On the following day he again dumped his plate; teachers followed the procedure of the previous day. That session marked the end of the food-dumping except for one isolated episode two and a half months later, which the teachers again ignored.

The typical behaviorist experiment on effects of reward carries the person through three phases: a "baseline" period, when his rate of response is observed without comment or reward; then a period in which the desired responses are rewarded more or less steadily; and then, an extinction period in which there is again no reward. The response rate usually then settles back to the baseline.

Teachers who want to eliminate misconduct are advised to make sure that the student is not receiving positive reinforcement when he misbehaves (box). The psychologist assumes that if the act occurs regularly it is being encouraged in some way—perhaps just by the attention it receives. Hence it will vanish only if the reward disappears. Krumboltz and Krumboltz (1972, p. 160) offer this example of simple extinction:

> Ginger would not wait her turn to share ideas in the third grade classroom but would interrupt whoever was talking whenever she thought of something to say. The teacher discussed with the class the rules for sharing ideas, and the class agreed on a "courtesy rule" of raising hands and waiting turns before sharing ideas during class discussion. Even though she had taken part in establishing the new courtesy rule, in the next class discussion Ginger again broke the rule.
>
> The class then agreed that they simply would not listen to anyone who broke the courtesy rule. When Ginger interrupted, the teacher and the class would try not to look at her or give any indication that they heard but would continue to devote their attention to the person who had permission to speak. After being ignored three times in a row, Ginger stopped interrupting, raised her hand, and waited her turn to speak.

Any reaction to Ginger's interruption—even an impatient request that she wait her turn—might serve to reinforce her misbehavior.

**Resistance to extinction**

*"When I said you were allowed one phone call,
I did not mean __another__ obscene one."*

Drawing by Chas. Addams; © 1974 The New Yorker Magazine, Inc.

## Captain Ross makes aversive tactics work

This chapter warns against making it punishing for the student to try, and there is substantial evidence of the detrimental effects of harsh teachers. Is it possible to reconcile anecdotes such as the following with psychological findings on motivation and reinforcement?

Gann (1961, esp. pp. 53ff.) was an airline copilot, being trained by his captain for the pilot's responsibilities. No doubt Captain Ross was an excellent pilot and made an equally precise and resourceful pilot out of Gann. Yet here is a partial description of Ross in the flight cabin:

> As the weeks turned into months, he became continually harder and less forgiving. . . . Ross never relented in his instruction, which had the quality of ceaseless pounding, so that frequently at the end of a flight my brain seemed to hang limp between my ears, twisted and bruised. My percentage of mistakes fell away rapidly, a condition which caused those few remaining to stand out even more sharply. Punishment was always quick and sure. An acid tongue-lashing, at which Ross was wonderfully adept, would be followed by a hard blow on my shoulder or whatever other part of my anatomy was convenient. The free-swinging blow served as a sort of punctuation mark to his verbal acrimony. . . .
>
> Ross's demand for perfection remained a match for the remarkable stiffness of his shirts. He was not satisfied with the allowable fifty feet of difference between chosen cruising altitude and that actually flown. . . . A variation of even twenty feet either above or below brought forth a searing admonition to sit up and fly right. Rough air was no excuse.
>
> He teased, bullied, inspired, threatened, and connived until by the full heat of summer it came to pass that I could occasionally please him.

HOW AVERSIVE TECHNIQUES BACKFIRE   The teacher is generally advised not to add aversive stimulation. Consistent punishment can be expected to suppress unwanted responses during the time students are under the teacher's eye. Punishment, however, will not teach them to regulate their own conduct so that the teacher's pressure can be removed (p. 662). Kounin and Gump (1958, 1961) studied various control techniques in the kindergarten. The child was most likely to do what the teacher wanted when the teacher indicated positively what response was wanted. Roughness and bad temper in handling misbehavior disturbed the whole class, not just the child criticized. The pupils' minds were taken off their work and tension rose.

Threats, sharp scoldings, and continual vigilance build up pressures. Children become aggressive; also less insightful about the reasons for good conduct. Punishment arouses resistance to the teacher and dislike for the activity; this effect carries forward after the threat of punishment has been removed.

Aversive techniques do not always succeed even in short-run suppression of unwanted acts. Madsen et al. (1968) made observations over a month during which there were two "baseline" periods. On baseline days, the teacher did nothing about the fact that one or another child was standing when he should have been seated. Later, the teacher shifted to an aversive technique, speaking sharply to any child who was out of his seat. While this no doubt had a momentary effect on the child addressed, the net amount of standing increased (Fig. 14.7). (Greater tension? Gratification in receiving attention?) Madsen et al. then raised an additional question. Should not the teacher supplement nonreinforcement by encouraging the correct response? In the final ten days of the month the teacher was told to ignore standing, but to make a point of praising the group when all were in their seats. Sure enough, praise worked.

Something beyond management by reinforcement was going on in this class: the children were being made aware of an ideal. This paves the way for self-monitoring, so that the desired conduct will ultimately be maintained without systematic external reinforcement. This is what makes positive reinforcement a valuable temporary device. As noted earlier, the person accustomed to steady positive reinforcement is likely to discard the response as soon as reinforcement is cut off. Tapering off reinforcement permits a transition from exter-

## FIGURE 14.7

Deterioration of behavior under aversive conditions and improvement with positive technique

Condition I: Teacher ignores acts of standing; Condition II: Teacher says "Sit down" whenever a child stands; Condition III: Teacher periodically gives praise for sitting properly.

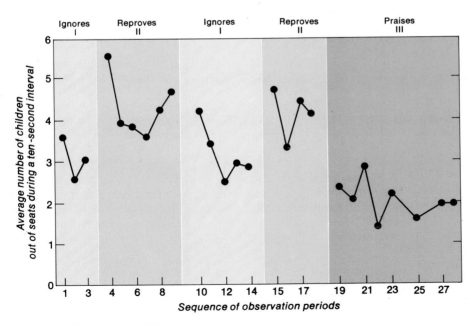

SOURCE: After Madsen et al. (1968).

*"And now listen to what 'Consumer Reports' has to say about your Model 1211 Electric Train: 'Extremely noisy, poor rail grip on curves at even moderate speeds, offers only fair protection against shock, and displays an utter lack of historical accuracy in re-creating B. & O. circa 1890.'"*

Drawing by Dedini; © 1974 The New Yorker Magazine, Inc.

nal control to self-regulation. The teacher may need to praise children fairly often at the outset, to keep them mindful of the ideal, but soon he will be able to skip a day, then a week. When self-reinforcement proves to be insufficient, occasional positive remarks by the teacher reinstate awareness of the ideal.

**20** A teacher of algebra considers it important that students complete each day's homework exercises prior to the class discussion. What kinds of reinforcement are available to the teacher? What "reinforcer" would you recommend? Would you apply it every day, or intermittently?

**21** Krumboltz and Krumboltz (1972, p. 232), after warning that punishment is a risky technique, offer this cautious encouragement: "To stop a child from acting in a particular way, you may arrange for him to terminate a mild aversive situation immediately by improving his behavior." Illustrate what is meant by "terminate a mild aversive situation." Just how does this differ from the usual concept of punishing an undesirable act?

22 Roger is told by the teacher that if he does not finish his spelling lesson for the day, he will not be allowed to sit in on the special math session, which he enjoys greatly. For several days now Roger has failed to complete spelling, and has had to work on it during the math session. His spelling has fallen even further behind and he has begun to behave in a disruptive manner. Analyze the reinforcement contingencies in this situation.

23 How sound is the statement that punishment has undesirable side-effects whereas reward does not?

24 A reinforcement theorist may challenge what others consider to be common sense. Consider this remark of Skinner (1970, p. 99):

> . . . a natural mistake is to shift to a more interesting topic when a discussion or lecture appears to be boring the listener. A more interesting topic is a reinforcer, and by shifting to it we reinforce expression of boredom.

What would Skinner's theory require the teacher to do when signs of boredom surface?

---

## Personality and Goal Setting

Goal setting reflects personality. Personality differences between realistic, over-striving, and withdrawing students were apparent in Sears's study of goal setting (p. 605). Secure children set realistic goals, expecting slight but regular improvement. The realistic ones, Sears (1941) says,

> are self-confident in their attitude toward school subjects, assured in their performance, may show pressure and strong effort but in a realistic fashion which sets socially and self-approved limits on their achievement. They do not react with feelings of failure to poor performance on material which is clearly too difficult for them, nor on the other hand, do they gloat over good performance on easy material.

The emotionally mature, autonomous child (or adult) is more likely to supply his own motivational controls, and to need little external reinforcement. Thus, DiBartolo and Vinacke (1969) compared dependent and independent preschool children who were praised for completing jigsaw puzzles rapidly. When the teacher was permissive and encouraging, dependent and independent children did equally well. The highly dependent child did poorly when he had to work by himself, without emotional support or social reinforcement. The independent children remained effective. Baron and Ganz (1972) found that fifth-grade boys with a strong sense of efficacy learned more when checking their own responses than when they received the same feedback from the experimenter. The social reward produced a better result, however, in boys with a low sense of efficacy.

Should the teacher conclude that learners can be typed, and each given the motivational diet that fits his "type"? Certainly not. These experiments were all of short duration, and made little provision for helpful criticism or for praise that includes constructive advice. They do not apply directly to a continuing relation in the classroom. The studies do imply that no single balance of praise, criticism, and objective knowledge of results serves every learner and every situation.

**25** Account for the fact that Bill Chelten (p. 228) sometimes set high aspirations but at other times put forth little effort.

**26** How does a person's self-concept influence his reaction to thwarting?

# REACTIONS TO THWARTING

As a person confronts genuine problems, he experiences many a gap between his hopes and his attainments. Each time he falls short, he has to choose between acting once again to attain the same goal or shifting to a new goal. In a shift, he may abandon or lower the original aspiration, or he may withdraw from the situation. The withdrawal may be a shift to an activity in which he expects satisfaction, or it may be a retreat into moody inaction. The decision still to pursue the original goal may be a valid expression of confidence, or it may be a stubborn refusal to face reality. Some persons make constructive choices most of the time, others make self-defeating choices. The teacher does what he can to substitute effective coping responses for maladaptive patterns.

## Adaptive and Maladaptive Responses

REPETITIVE RESPONSE   At its best, repetition of a response is wise perseverance. Trying once again the very response that has been unsuccessful is sensible if the original interpretation was approximately correct. Minor variations in the situation or in the response will permit success on some subsequent trial. At its worst, repetition becomes rigid, mechanical action, continued because action is more comfortable than admitting defeat. A noteworthy example of blind repetition is the action of the parent who, failing to control his child with a particular tactic, becomes even more determined to make that tactic work. In such a heated contest of wills he damages his whole relation with the child (box). When the learner repeats his response without pausing to look for other interpretations, he perhaps overlooks superior courses of action. The Mitchells' belief that children are incomprehensible is a principal source of their failure. Instruction in problem analysis and socialization that develops security and autonomy liberate the person to use his judgment.

ALTERED RESPONSE   If the learner's original interpretation is wrong, the only way to solve the problem is to try something different. Adaptation based on reinterpretation is the common method of improving a response.

Altering the response is not necessarily the best reaction. If the goal is unattainable, lowering one's aim or shifting to a new goal is wiser. If the first interpretation was adequate, vacillating through alternative interpretations delays success. At the extreme, thoughtlessly "trying something different" degenerates into disorganized trial and error. The pilot jerks the controls to get out of a tailspin; the student guesses wildly in response to a teacher's question.

Repeating a response indicates some faith in one's plan and one's ability to execute it; altering the plan indicates faith that some better plan can be discov-

## The Mitchells

The Mitchells are farm parents who expect and demand obedience. When Charley or Diana does not give in, neither of the Mitchells stops to think through the specific situation. Diana has submitted to this pressure. The parents have made her into a plodding, lackluster, unhappy girl who, when nagged sufficiently, gives in to their demands. Charley completely defeats his parents by being tough enough to resist them. Thwarted, the Mitchells react by repetition rather than by reinterpretation. The observer (Baldwin et al., 1945, p. 28) reports:

> Mrs. Mitchell told of an incident which occurred recently—she had told Charles to go and stay in his room as punishment for some trivial offense. Charles flatly refused to go, and Mrs. Mitchell finally whipped him up the stairs with a fly swatter— Charley maintaining all the time that he wouldn't stay. The child did come straight downstairs, and the same thing happened again. About the third time he came down, Mrs. Mitchell grabbed him, said she knew one place where he couldn't get out, and locked him in the cellar. . . . Another time she spanked Charles seven times in succession because he wouldn't stay in his room and remarked hopelessly to the visitor that she can't lock him in the closet as punishment because Charles says he likes it in there.

Do not dismiss this as merely a bizarre family. The Mitchells are not unusual. Both parents have a college education and undoubtedly love their children when they are not exasperated. It simply never occurs to the Mitchells to re-examine their insistence on control and give the children more independence. When a sitter puts Diana's hair up in curls, Diana shows her good feelings next day by cheerfully volunteering for housework. This does not give Mrs. Mitchell any new ideas about how to handle the girl—it only proves that children are unpredictable!

ered. Thus, alteration may either imply confidence in one's adaptive powers, or mere lack of confidence in the previous try.

Repeated shifting of response almost invariably indicates lack of understanding. If a situation seems senseless, all one can do is guess. If a person feels incompetent, any action will be more comfortable than staring blankly at the difficulty. Who knows? *This* try might work. Random trial does little to promote self-reliance.

TABLE 14.3

Reactions to thwarting

| Reaction | Likely when | Desirable when | Undesirable when |
|----------|-------------|----------------|------------------|
| Repetitive response | Person expects response to succeed. Person cannot withdraw or reinterpret, or dislikes trying the more appropriate response. | Person re-examines situation before deciding to repeat. | Repetition is long continued, without re-examination of the interpretation or the goal |
| Altered response | Person has little faith in his original response. Person has confidence in his ability to reinterpret and carry out a new action. | The new response is based on reinterpretation; the old response is given due consideration. | The new response is chosen thoughtlessly. |
| Withdrawal | Person does not expect to succeed. Person finds trying unpleasant, or does not value the goal. | Person has little chance of succeeding. Goal is unimportant. | Person withdraws, when reasonable effort will bring success. |
| Substitution | Substitute is available. Other conditions as in withdrawing. | The new goal satisfies the same needs as the original goal. The new goal permits useful learning. Other conditions as in withdrawing. | Person fails to satisfy a basic need, so develops in unbalanced manner. The original situation is one the person should learn to cope with. The substitute undertaking is unrealistic. |

WITHDRAWAL   The least painful way out of many difficulties is to quit. Lowering one's aspiration is a sensible adaptation when the odds against success are great. At the extreme, the person may retreat into a corner to do nothing. Withdrawal gets him out of an intolerable situation, but leaves him defeated. Moreover, when he stops trying, he loses all chance of learning to handle the situation.

Freshmen who attempt premedical courses though they lack readiness for the work should withdraw into some more feasible program. A boy who has no chance to make the football team should use his afternoons in a more fruitful activity than riding the bench. Whether or not goals should be changed after thwarting is not a moral issue; it is a question of whether or not the person has accurately judged the possibility of eventual success. Withdrawal without a substitute endeavor is no improvement over the original inappropriate activity.

Withdrawal is less likely if a person is self-assured or places a high value on the goal. If the probability of success seems low and the goal is not important, the struggle is not worthwhile. To withdraw or not to withdraw is often more an emotional decision than a logical one. Fear of conspicuous failure will cause some people to abandon plans they very much want to carry off. The desire to put on a good show keeps others from withdrawing, when that is the sensible course.

PURSUIT OF A SUBSTITUTE GOAL   Steven, who cannot find material for a report on medieval weapons, makes a fine report on castles. John, who couldn't catch crawfish, prepared a basket for them instead (p. 158). This is compensation: finding satisfaction in a second place when it is denied in the first.

Shifting to a new goal has advantages and disadvantages. If the original goal is indeed beyond the person's reach, changing is the only possible constructive reaction. But often the original goal is attainable, even though hard to reach. Steven shifted from weapons to castles because he knew where to locate material on castles. He produced a good report, but he did not get practice at digging out material on obscure topics.

When a try is blocked, the person may substitute a new goal that will attain the *same* basic ends. If it rains, the picnickers go to someone's basement to eat and dance. The companionship, courtship, and eating are as satisfying as in the original plan. An undersized adolescent who wishes to be an athlete may satisfy the same need for approval by becoming the school's sports writer. A second type of substitution involves dropping the effort to obtain one sort of satisfaction and pursuing another. For example, the person denied sexual satisfaction can substitute no goal that will lead to the same satisfaction; he or she must find other rewards, perhaps in caring for children or taking pride in efficient work.

There are dangers in leaving a need unfulfilled. Replacing the hard-to-attain goal with a goal of an entirely different kind is likely to leave some ultimate developmental task unaccomplished. The student who cannot work smoothly with the committee because others disregard his suggestions goes off on an independent project. He gains independence and self-respect. Fine—but

## Substitute goal

he learns also to expect not to get along with his peers. Soon he is working by himself all the time.

Peculiarly difficult philosophical issues are involved in judging whether or not the substitution of one goal for another is desirable. A person who continually retreats to one area may develop great proficiency and self-confidence in it. He may make tremendous contributions, unbalanced though he is. Many brilliant and productive men have been socially maladjusted. The moodiness, eccentricity, and temperamental outbursts of Van Gogh, Beethoven, the scientist Cavendish are famous. These men achieved, but they appear to have been far from happy. A remarkable contemporary portrait of a discontented achiever is Ginzburg's (1962) interview with Bobby Fischer, who at 18 was being called the greatest chess player who ever lived. On the other hand, da Vinci, Brahms, and Jefferson are evidence that admirable social adjustment can accompany major contributions. The relation between adjustment and creative performance is ill understood.

Should the school pry a certain boy away from intellectual affairs because his social development will be handicapped by such concentration? The school ought surely to teach him skill in communicating with others. Beyond that, the teacher probably should try to bring the student out of his withdrawal into smoother social relations. Any other course is tantamount to saying that it is all right to leave his left arm paralyzed since he will develop exceptional dexterity with his right.

The preceding pages have mentioned conditions that make particular responses to thwarting especially likely. There is little to add regarding substitution of goals. Abandoning the original goal involves lack of confidence or lack of commitment. Taking up a substitute shows an expectation of satisfaction from it. Substitution, unlike withdrawal, implies that the person has self-confidence in at least one area.

## Implications for Teaching

Teachers can establish conditions that encourage appropriate persistence and appropriate change of plans. Consider Margaret, who felt rejected by her parents and adapted by becoming a model of the dutiful, unobtrusive, responsible child (Department of National Health and Welfare, 1947). She was seriously maladjusted, in the sense that she lacked self-acceptance and did not dare to act spontaneously; yet she was well able to meet the neatly structured demands of the school. We shall focus on an incident late in her elementary-school career, when she caught the enthusiasm of the others for the class play. If she had won a part in this great event she would have been prominent and happy for a time. Making a strenuous effort, Margaret tried for the central part of princess. Unsure of herself, and fearing that winning the part would cause her rival to dislike her, she made a miserable showing. The teacher was kind when deciding against Margaret, but that defeat was the end of Margaret's striving for attention. Margaret's life style was one of setting low aspirations. If the teacher could have found a way to reward her, the incident might have been a turning point. As it was, the thwarting simply intensified Margaret's habit of withdrawal.

What might the school better have done? The competition Margaret entered was disastrous because winning meant too much. If there is only one play, and only one stellar part in the play, only one child can triumph. If plays large and small had been common from the first grade, no one play would have been crucial to Margaret. If prepared by smaller successes *and partial failures* in other small performances, she would have done better. Also, because earlier participation would have built self-respect and the assurance that others thought well of her, this failure would have been less crushing.

Making appropriate goals available is the place to begin. If there are enough rewarding parts to go round, either in this play or in a series of plays, there is no need to choose one student ahead of another. If the students set goals that are within reach, few will fail. If all the girls seek to be the princess, most will fail.

I suggest three general rules to reduce frustration and conflict:

Eliminate blocking that has no educative aim (see also p. 817).

Reduce the emotional penalty attached to failure of a trial response.

Make it possible for the student to overcome the obstacles.

## Realistic aspirations

Drawing by Don Sibley

Blocking should be avoided except as it helps the student to learn. School tasks should be within the student's reach. When a school demands that every entering 6-year-old learn to read, many are confronted with a demand they cannot meet. Most of them could meet the demand easily if allowed to postpone reading for some months. Even with such a postponement, these pupils may be punished for their deficiency. If reading is the only "important" activity in the class, those in a nonreading group will feel as inferior as if they were being forced to try primer reading every day.

Excessively high standards increase the frequency of thwarting. When a student is learning for the first time to stand before a group and speak, criticizing his posture is much less important than encouraging him to state his main idea. "You did well *but—*" is all too likely to make him feel that he never can do right. Blocking multiplies as rules multiply. The teacher with fewer regulations to enforce is freer to teach. The student with fewer regulations to obey is less often tempted to break a rule.

Commitment to the goal in view is required if the person is not to give up at the first obstacle. Teachers increase the students' commitment by sound planning with the class. Acceptance of a goal is increased if the student perceives reasonable subgoals, recognizes how the specific learning fits into his long-range ambitions, and feels that his classmates want him to succeed.

The student who hopes to master a task can afford to persist or to reinterpret. He can see beyond any discouragement or frustration to the hope of success. At some points the most helpful way to reduce tension is to provide a clear explanation or demonstration; at other times, it is to diagnose and provide specific remedial treatment. When a student is making some progress, the teacher should help him recognize the progress he has already made. All too often, the student who is having difficulty is scolded for lack of effort or pushed to one side as hopeless.

Confidence is built up by accumulation of successes. Margaret was demoralized not because someone else was made princess, but because previous experiences had convinced her that she lacked ability. Teachers build confidence by introducing challenges gradually. A girl who delivers a single line in a first-grade skit is building readiness for a long part a few years later. What matter if she has to be prompted when she forgets a line in a fifth-grade tryout? That has happened to her before with no disastrous final outcome.

If a student fails at one thing, the teacher will often offer an alternative chance for success. Substituting costume making for acting contributes nothing to dramatic ability. Nonetheless, there are bound to be occasions when a student cannot achieve a particular goal. Then he is helped by a substitute goal that attains the same major ends. If he helps the group, he can enjoy the activity, learn something valuable through the duties themselves, and, more important, feel that others think him competent at something. Margaret, after her failure, could only think, "I'm no good, and the others know it." A substitute responsibility would have provided a sense of worth and belonging.

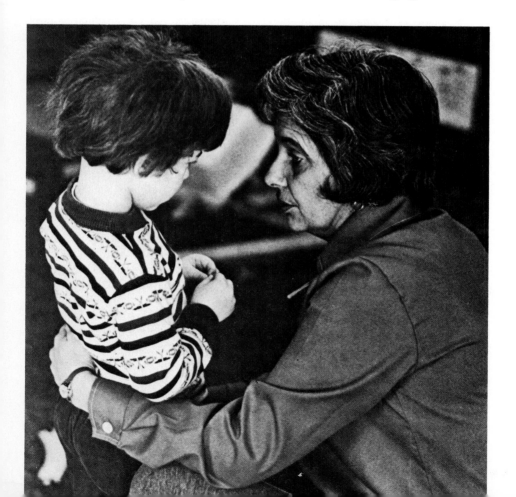

**27** In the incident described on p. 635, are Mrs. Mitchell's actions receiving reinforcement? Are Charley's?

**28** Describe a situation where repetition of a response after thwarting would be helpful, and one where it would be undesirable
  a. in sports
  b. in writing a composition
  c. in teaching reading

**29** Might a student find satisfaction in "proving" that chemistry is too difficult for him?

**30** In view of the conditions that foster repetition, what can a teacher do if a student persistently makes the same mistake?

## Defensive Motivation and Intellectual Performance

Certain personalities can be characterized as defensive. Trait labels such as anxious, dependent, and inhibited are used for various aspects of the defensive, fearful attitude. A person can be defensive in one segment of his life and not in another; thus, a distinction can be made between fear of failure in academic situations and anxiety in the face of other kinds of threats. Much in the following paragraphs is a paraphrase of statements made by J. Atkinson and N. Feather (1966, pp. 369–70). Ideas from Birney et al. (1969, pp. 199–200) also are included, along with research findings of others.

A student is dominated by the threat of failure when he looks on failure as a highly uncomfortable experience. This fear may have little to do with his *probability* of failure; rather, it is an attitude about failure if it should occur. A person fearing evaluation that *might* report failure avoids situations that will clearly expose his degree of competence. One route to emotional safety is to work in a collaborative group, where risks are shared.

Given definite material to learn, the defensive person makes the required effort and succeeds. The student who fears failure often seeks well-structured tasks. If he knows just what to do, he can be reasonably sure that careful effort will bring him through to success. Perversely, he may pick a task so excessively difficult that, when he does fail, the failure is no reflection on him. His hard work can be interpreted as compliance to social pressures. He tends to dislike intermediate risks, such as he encounters in the one-on-one competition, where only one person can win.

In Grade IV, when set to discover some principles of arithmetic experimentally, the anxious student does far worse than the nonanxious student. But when the teacher sets out the principles for the students to work with, the anxious students come up to a middling performance, and the nonanxious come down to the same level (Trown & Leith, 1975). The anxious student tends not to trust himself and turns to authority for guidance. Anxiety therefore tends to facilitate performance in a task where traditional answers pay off. It tends to interfere with original thought, as is suggested by the Wallach-Kogan report on children whose divergent performance is low. Tasks that require some degree of personal judgment are harder for the anxious person than tasks that demand self-critical conformity to rules (Sarason et al., 1960). In a college discussion on intellectual matters, the anxious student lets his mind wander; uncertainty about the standards for judging contributions is itself a source of threat (Gaier, 1952). The anxious person is more likely to "go to pieces" when the situation piles up stress or challenge. The nonanxious person frequently improves when stress is added.

The effects of arousal (intensified alertness) are not the same in every study, but it appears that there is an optimum level of tension for a particular task. Anxious persons come to the task with a built-in tension (Fig. 14.8). Their best performance is likely to come on a task set out with no special incentive or pressure—a noncompetitive game, for example. Stronger pressure or incentive pushes them into excessive tension. Pressure often brings the performance of the nonanxious person closer to the optimum. General predictions are hazardous, however, since exceptions to the rule turn up often. Preadolescents motivated to achieve did arithmetic problems pretty well under ordinary school motivation (C.P. Smith, 1966). When a five-dollar prize was offered for the best paper, their performance fell apart. We could interpret that as pressure beyond the optimum. The surprise was in an anxious group that lacked achievement motivation. They turned in a set of outstanding papers when the prize was offered!

FIGURE 14.8

Effect of stress in relation to initial tension level

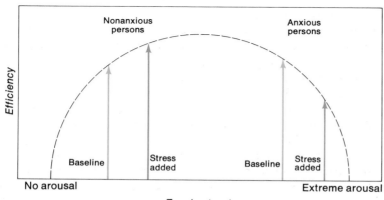

Robert C. Birney, Harvey Burdick, and Richard C. Teevan, "The Defense Against the Loss in Self-Estimate," in *Fear of Failure* (New York: Van Nostrand, 1969), pp. 210–20.

> Thwarting, especially in intellectual tasks, threatens self-esteem. These authors list and illustrate various defenses, from evasion of evaluation to intensified effort. Defenses make thwarting bearable, but many of them are substitutes for realistic adaptation.

Martin V. Covington and Richard G. Beery, "Success-Oriented Learning Structures," in *Self-Worth and School Learning* (New York: Holt, Rinehart and Winston, 1976), pp. 89–121.

> Describes briefly a number of techniques for increasing the student's commitment to success. Most of the techniques encourage each individual to set goals that are realistic for him, and to focus on his own growth in competence rather than to compete with others. Other chapters in the book amplify other topics in my Chapter 14.

Richard Farson, "Praise Reappraised," *Harvard Business Review* 41, no. 9 (1963), 61–65. Also in Hamachek (1976).

> Farson challenges the common belief that praise is a dependable method of motivation, with comments much like those of Ginott. Positive remarks that the person finds credible and that help him guide himself are useful; but most praise, Farson says, contributes little to autonomy and self-regulation and increases the social distance between the person who gives the praise and the person who gets it.

Robert L. Hamblin et al., "Changing the Game from 'Get the Teacher' to 'Learn'," in *Human Intelligence,* ed. J. McV. Hunt (New Brunswick, N.J.: Transaction Books, 1972), pp. 210–36.

> Describes how token economies are used with aggressive and autistic children in classrooms. Another section of the article tells about teaching 2-year-olds to read by reinforcement procedures.

Robert J. Havighurst, "Minority Subcultures and the Law of Effect," *American Psychologist* 25 (1970), 313–22.

> Havighurst sketches a developmental scale of motivations to which people in our society typically respond at various ages. (This may be regarded as an extension of his ideas on developmental tasks; see Table 5.1.) He then describes family and community patterns in lower-class and ethnic groups that alter the timing of this motivational development. Finally, he suggests practices by which teachers can set up productive motivational conditions for such students.

Frederic M. Levine and Geraldine Fasnacht, "Token Rewards May Lead to Token Learning," *American Psychologist* 29 (1974), 816–20. See also three comments on the article in *American Psychologist* 30 (1975), 780–83.

> The Levine-Fasnacht article and the three letters to the editor in the later issue provide a pro-and-con discussion of the use of token rewards and their limitations. The several authors seem to agree that token economies are a temporary expedient for getting the person to make responses he is capable of. They disagree sharply regarding the meaning of studies such as Lepper's, in which extrinsic rewards reduced the person's interest in the task.

Betty L. Mitton and Dale B. Harris, "The Development of Responsibility in Children," *Elementary School Journal* 54 (1954), 268–77.

> Responsibility is defined as taking goals seriously and accepting the consequences of one's own acts, hence as nearly synonymous with self-discipline. The authors review studies of this trait and extract ten principles regarding the practices by which it can be fostered.

Lauren B. Resnick and Betty H. Robinson, "Motivational Aspects of the Literacy Problem," in *Toward a Literate Society,* ed. John B. Carroll and Jeanne S. Chall (New York: McGraw-Hill, 1975), pp. 257–77.

> A psychologist and a school supervisor draw on their experience in improving reading performance of urban children, mostly from poor and black families. Among the motivational aspects discussed are expectation and goal setting, external reinforcers, and self-evaluation.

■ The teacher is responsible for establishing an enthusiastic and purposeful work atmosphere. Undirected activities tend to work out badly; students are often uncomfortable when given full responsibility and may be unwise in their decisions.

□ Some teachers make most of the decisions about purposes and plans. Others develop plans cooperatively with the group.

■ Having a clear plan promotes emotional security and morale. An elementary-school group that takes more responsibility for planning is more likely to maintain momentum.

□ Subject-matter learning proceeds equally well under either style of control. With less teacher direction students have more chance to develop skills of group membership.

□ The two teacher qualities that do most to elicit a positive response are warmth and orderliness. The style that works best with one student may not get best results with another; nor is any one style best for every teacher.

■ The well-disciplined classroom is one in which members work well; sound planning eliminates most problems. Skillful moment-to-moment management keeps activity properly targeted.

■ Motivational practices (including marking and use of competition) are to be judged in terms of four principles: clarity and attractiveness of goals, attainability of goals, provision for self-evaluation, and continuity with out-of-class motivation.

**CONCEPTS**

*classroom atmosphere*　　　　*warmth*
*undirected activities*　　　　*the teachable student*
*teacher-controlled activities*　　*classroom discipline*
*group control*　　　　　　　　*competition*
*rational authority*　　　　　　*group competition*

# THE TEACHER
# AS CLASSROOM
# LEADER

Students are always motivated; the question is, toward what ends? Their energies run off toward all points of the compass; they lack long-term vision and they lose sight of goals. But the energy is there to be mobilized. Healthy students are coiled springs ready to make something whirl. This may sound like an exaggeration to the teacher who prods and tugs at an indifferent class. Yet these same "indifferent" students work with endless commitment on a project that challenges them, whether its end is recreation or community service or social protest. The teacher's best hope is to direct energy into constructive channels and keep it there.

How can the teacher establish an enthusiastic and purposeful work atmosphere? Subordinate questions taken up in this chapter include: How can a working group be kept in order? How does the teacher's style affect the student's personal growth? How can students be led to take responsibility for planning, decisions, and conduct? All of these questions relate to the function of the teacher as a leader. The teacher is a good leader when he arranges conditions so that students want to do something worthwhile, have a chance to try it, and succeed. The benefits of good management are pleasant student-teacher relations, student conduct that facilitates rather than disrupts, more satisfaction with the work, and more learning.

We saw in Chapter 14 that schools have distinctive atmospheres, and that, within a school, classes vary in their spirit. As teachers and students work together, a "group personality" develops. Even two sections of the same high-school subject, taught by the same teacher in successive hours, may take on a different emotional climate. It is important for every teacher to think about the forces that shape a group, and in particular about the range of styles open to him as a leader.

There has been an enormous volume of research on differences in teacher behavior and the correlation of those differences with student gains in achievement. (For recent summaries, see Westbury & Bellack, 1971; Travers, 1973; Brophy & Good, 1974; and Dunkin & Biddle, 1974.) Studies have often set out to pin down simple generalizations: that democratic teaching is superior, that warm teachers are better, that inductive methods are superior (Chapter 13), or the like. Such broad generalizations are false to the facts. At most, one might be able to generalize about particular outcomes at a particular grade level. But teacher styles are highly individualized, and much depends on the kinds of students that come into the class; therefore, statistical summaries cannot possibly capture classroom dynamics.

Two aspects of teacher style in particular have been the subject of research: control and warmth. When I name three styles of control, and then contrast impersonal and supporting teachers, that may suggest that teachers fall neatly into six types. This is not so. Teachers who fit the same label are far from alike. When I present Miss Simmons (p. 655) as an example of a teacher who uses group planning, it should be obvious that her procedures are not the only way to go about group planning. Moreover, her procedures are responsive to the particular class, not fixed. When I suggest generalizations, in describing effects associated with the styles of control, you must bear in mind that all general statements in this chapter describe weak effects. And, as Dunkin and Biddle say (1974, p. 360), we simply do not know how widely the findings apply across subject-matter, grades, and cultural groups.

**1** Among the thousands of studies to date, probably none has systematically examined the relation between the style or specific actions of the teacher and the climate of the school as a whole. Why might the approach of a teacher work out well in one school and not in another?

## STYLES OF PLANNING AND CONTROL

Goals may be fully set out in advance or they may be left to the whim of the moment. Responsibility may be taken entirely by the teacher or it may be shared by everyone. Some groups learn to be docile, accepting a leader's proposals and control. Other classes learn techniques of initiating, planning, and cooperation—so they become more independent of superiors.

THREE STYLES    I shall contrast three styles of group operation: undirected activities, teacher-controlled activities, and group-controlled activities. The "group" is, in some instances, an intact class, and in other instances a subgroup. Sometimes more than one adult is engaged in the planning with the students. In groups large and small, the key question is: Who sets the goals for the group and evaluates performance? In the undirected program, no one defines the goals or lays out a work plan. The group is turned loose, like students freed to roam a museum. Under teacher control, the teacher sets goals and judges the progress made. Under group control, goals are selected through discussion, and the group as a whole reviews and assesses progress. The leader helps the group to govern itself.

UNDIRECTED ACTIVITIES    In a completely undirected activity, students are told, "You can do just what you want to do." Subsequent requests for advice are answered in such terms as, "Do whatever you think best." This utter permissiveness is sometimes intended to promote creativeness, learning "by discovery," and self-direction. It is often used in connection with activities (book reports, science projects, and so on) that the teacher sees as "outside the regular work" and therefore suitable for the expression of personal interests. Sometimes the tactic is intended to press the student to judge and plan for himself. Mr. Osborne (p. 652) is an example of this style.

TEACHER-CONTROLLED ACTIVITIES    It is hard to describe the second control pattern without arousing prejudices that interfere with observation. Calling it "teacher-controlled" raises visions of a schoolma'am rapping knuckles. To label it autocratic is to condemn it. But orderly, systematic, planful teachers—Mrs. Whittier and Mr. Wells (pp. 97ff.), for example—can be first rate. Even Gann's harsh flight instructor (p. 630) was highly effective with a committed student.

A teacher who seeks to maintain unwavering control will use his judgment at all points: in deciding what shall be done, who shall do it, when it is done well, and when reward or criticism are called for. He sets the goals, determines how the work is to proceed, and administers the social rewards. This teacher outlines the course in advance, selects the techniques of evaluation, and sets the standards that determine an A or a C grade. Strongly directive teaching is sensible when specific training is intended.

Fromm (1941) made a valuable distinction between rational authority and irrational authority. In rational authority, the superior directs so that both he and his subordinate satisfy their needs. In irrational authority, the superior attempts to satisfy his needs, at times sacrificing those of the subordinate. Many studies on leadership seem to assume that dominant leadership is harsh and irrational. But dominant teachers can be warm and considerate.

GROUP-CONTROLLED ACTIVITIES   A group that directs itself is often said to be "democratic." Actions commonly recognized as characteristic of the democratic teacher* are as follows:

> Encourages use of democratic procedures (discussing, voting, acting as chairman).
>
> Uses teacher-student planning.
>
> Encourages group members to accept responsibility after the group establishes goals.
>
> Has the group establish and enforce regulations for conduct.
>
> Does not directly supervise as students work.
>
> Speaks less than 50 per cent of the time.
>
> Welcomes questions.
>
> Encourages expression of more than one viewpoint.

* Adapted from Heil et al. (1960), Appendix, p. 70.

Similar tactics can be used at every level from preschool to adult education. The emotional climate must be such that the student is free to express opinions that conflict with those of others in the room. Group planning is less a matter of putting everything to a vote than of getting views out in the open.

The teacher does not simply give up control, as we see in Miss Simmons's class (p. 655). The teacher judges each plan to make sure that it accords with the mission of the school and with his own competence as instructor. He encourages the group to decide only those issues where he is willing to abide by the decision, and tries to make sure that the limits on group power are understood by everyone.

## Analysis

The undirected pattern can be pleasant. Students may find useful things to do, make friends, and teach themselves valuable lessons. But students do not by themselves fall into the most educative activities (p. 538); therefore this policy falls short. Moreover, as we shall see, students tend not to like the disorganized, utterly permissive setting. Often they feel that they are accomplishing little.

The arguments for intelligent teacher planning and teacher control are these:

> More time can go into the activity itself if no student time goes into planning.

> The teacher's decisions are wiser than those the group makes.

> The teacher represents the judgment of society, and cannot properly pretend that questions about what and how to study are open for the students to decide. Hence group control is actually a disguised form of teacher control.

Others conclude that:

> Those who share in setting goals are more eager to reach the goals.

> When activities reflect students' interests and when purposes are clarified through group planning, more intelligent cooperation results. Students are more likely to continue work "on their own" after the class ends.

> Learning to make group decisions and to plan for oneself is as important as mastering "lessons."

Both sides have a point; there is a time and a place for each style. Moreover, not every teacher is equally successful with each style, and no style fits all students equally well. The two classroom descriptions that follow will show some of the complexities of student response.

2 Do the arguments for group planning (if valid) apply only in a country with a democratic political system?

3 If teaching is to proceed largely through the use of exercises (p. 543), is teacher control the only appropriate style?

4 Is self-direction by the individual student a distinct style or a variant of one of the styles discussed above?

5 Among your own teachers you must have had many whose style was "teacher control." Consider one who generated good class morale and one who did not. How did their practices differ?

## An Undirected Class in Art*

Mr. Osborne had previously taught art to eighth-graders by spending the semester on watercolor painting. The assignments began with simple drawings of objects, then moved on to more complex still lifes, and ended with more imaginative painting. As the class did its work, Mr. Osborne watched and criticized, encouraged and explained.

After taking a summer-session course that urged development of independence, he set up a new plan. To his next class he said in effect, "You're here to learn about art. Art consists in working out ideas in pleasing and appropriate form. You can only do that by trying. We will use this semester in any way you wish. You can use any medium"—he displayed several—"and try any idea you want. I'm here to help and to answer your questions."

During his experimental semester, originality and individual differences blossomed as never before. The first weeks were wasted as the class waited for directions that never came. Then some of the students with more experience in art began sketches; someone else became fascinated with the potter's wheel and starting turning clay under Mr. Osborne's instruction. Working groups gradually began to form.

After six weeks, Mr. Osborne would normally have been looking over a lot of renderings showing two apples, with uniform composition and execrable coloring. This year, only a few finished works were in hand. These were sketches, bowls, a house exterior—the work of students who had an interest at the start or who sought the familiar groove of turning in a paper and getting a grade. Most of the class were midway into a project. Some had torn up two attempts and started over. Some had left their first medium for another. A few still wandered around watching. At the opposite extreme of purpose, one girl, who had been drawing as a hobby for several years, had begun a self-portrait in crayon.

Following his plan of letting students set their own goals, Mr. Osborne neither approved nor disapproved when Penny made six identical bowls, one

---

* This report is based in part on research by Herbert A. Thelen and John Withall.

after the other, nor when Ned and Herb spent a week without a trace of effort. The students who were busy were happy. They looked at each other's work and provided plentiful praise for each success. They crowded around Mr. Osborne to show him each step of Charlotte's miniature stage setting for *Romeo and Juliet*. Some asked how to get this effect or why that color was muddy or whether the sky should be blue or green. They were given assistance and saw Mr. Osborne's pleasure in their progress, without, however, being told that this product was fine or that one faulty.

Ned and Herb, out of the group entirely by now, had to be suppressed when they passed the limits of tolerable behavior and took to making and sailing paper airplanes. It required only the proof that Mr. Osborne meant his rule against disturbance to end that try for attention. The boys' next effort was a construction project (woodworking was allowed as art). During two weeks of sketching and conferring, the plan was a secret. Then, with the air of producing a magic rabbit, they announced that they were building a guillotine! Now they wanted Mr. Osborne's help. And he gave it gravely, however much he wondered whom the boys had in mind as symbolic victim. His invited criticisms of the design were accepted, and off the boys went to make their machine.

Report-card time could scarcely be handled by routine grading.* Mr. Osborne and the class agreed that what counted was working out creative ideas, making improvement rather than necessarily having a perfect product to show. (Here their procedures verged on group control.) Each student rated himself on such questions as "Have I used my time wisely?" and "Have I become more skilled in using some art medium?" Then Mr. Osborne talked over the ratings with the student. It was hard to accept some students' overestimates and others' self-depreciation. As much as he could, Mr. Osborne kept to provocative questions: "Do you think it was wise to try both modeling and drawing, or would you have gotten more out of staying with one?" "Even though you don't like this picture now, do you feel that you learned anything that will help you from here on?" Since the aim was to teach students to judge themselves, he did accept their answers and the summary grade they claimed. Ned and Herb created no problem here. They claimed only a D, and seemed pleased to be able to say that they had changed to a better use of time.

The work went on through the semester in the same way, most students finishing one project and starting another. Sometimes the new project was a redoing of the old one with a revised design; sometimes it was a shift of medium. Marcia's self-portrait proved to be a thorough unlikeness. Having tinkered with nose and eyes and chin and having followed Mr. Osborne's suggestions as well as she could without making it any more of a success, she came in one day with a grim look, tore the picture neatly into four pieces, and took her French book off into the corner while the class shrank back as if she had attempted suicide. After three days, Marcia came to Mr. Osborne with a grin, said she

---

* Merit rating (see pp. 686–88 and 722–25) is an impediment to creative teaching in almost any style. Schools are increasingly liberalizing their practices by substituting multidimensional ratings or descriptive reports for letter grades or by treating some courses as they have always treated extracurricular activities—that is, by requiring no report from the teacher.

# Teacher direction in the "open" classroom

Some educational reformers advocate an undirected style in elementary education and point to the "open classrooms" of the British schools as a successful example. That is misleading; activities in these schools (for ages 5–7) are not undirected. In most classes, Brandt (1975) observed, the teacher was continually managing. The teacher would move from a group weighing seashells and acorns (4 acorns = 5 shells!) to a table of children working quietly on notebooks, to the corner where a wooden airplane was being nailed together. Teachers were far from nonevaluative; they took care, however, to communicate standards through approval as much as possible. Brandt saw little direct expression of personal affection; the emphasis was on communication about tasks. His impressions show that leadership was firm:

- Children were generally expected to *have something to do*. The teacher would usually ask a child what he was doing if she noticed him wandering aimlessly around the room or holding an extended conversation with another child who was busy at his own task. At the beginning of independent activity periods the teacher almost always asked if anyone did not know what he planned to do, and then she discussed the options with him until one was selected.

- Children were generally expected to *finish something already started before starting something else*. If a child showed the teacher a picture he was painting of some flowers, for instance, she might ask him what color he wanted for the sky or what other kinds of things grew in his garden. Although questions were raised in this fashion, the teacher did not insist on particular details being added; but the child of his own volition often added to his picture items he had mentioned in response to her questions.

- Children were expected to *have something tangible to show or tell to account for time spent*. Notebooks were inspected frequently, and creative products were displayed before the group, with the teacher usually remarking about the progress made.

- Children were expected to *take care of materials being used and return items to their proper place and condition after using them*. Since it was late in the school year, I saw children already habituated to proper cleanup patterns; but occasionally, as a reminder of this expectancy, I heard the teacher ask who had been using something that was left out.

- Children were expected to *participate in group discussion and permit others to talk*. Many times when one child was telling about an experience that others had shared, the teacher would stop others from talking until the target child was finished.

was glad she'd torn it up, and what was wrong anyhow? Mr. Osborne silenced his thoughts about why an adolescent, concerned with her changing self, would xave special motives to do a self-portrait. He said instead that self-portraits are exceptionally difficult and require skill Marcia had not built up. His suggestion that she might work on some of the techniques of catching facial lines by making sketches from photographs appealed to her. Next day she brought in a publicity photo of a movie star who, not surprisingly, had Marcia's coloring and plumpness and a good deal more of mature sex appeal.

When the end of the course came, Mr. Osborne's feelings were mixed. Watching the unpredictable projects come to life had been much more fun than watching uninspired painters paint uninspired fruitbowls. Discipline problems had been few. Some of the students had discovered real intricacies in art and were mastering one or another medium. Some had done the best their talent permitted, others had settled for cheap and sketchy products. The boys finished their guillotine and showed it to everyone in the building. But there had been no follow-through, and their effort to make copper paper cutters during the last six weeks had no heart in it. Art meant no more to them than at the start of the term.

The student reactions were unanimous in praise of Mr. Osborne. They liked him, said he'd been helpful and patient and the other things one likes to hear. The majority said the same thing about art. It had been fine, they'd learned a lot, and they wished other courses gave them more chance to try things. Then some doubts crept in. "I wish," said Marcia, "you'd told me a self-portrait was too hard. I could have learned a lot more by starting with something easier." Penny thought she hadn't learned much, that if Mr. Osborne had made her do something harder she'd have achieved more. Many said it was unpleasant to not know what to choose. And Mr. Osborne should have told them if they were doing their projects well. Ned and Herb were violently negative. Mr. Osborne hadn't told them what to do; they'd have done it if he had. The guillotine was all right (defiantly)—they'd earned a C—but that wasn't what they were in school for.

All in all, Mr. Osborne felt that *he* had learned a lot. Enough so that he wouldn't teach the same way again. Accepting their ideas and letting students learn from mistakes had worked. They had begun to realize just what they could properly bite off. His method had done rather well in providing for the range of talent. Art was more original and much more meaningful than in the old fruitbowl days. Personal relations had been good, and fewer students found art frustrating. But his sphinx-like refusal to express his own ideas had left them feeling that he was concealing a negative opinion. He had offered a bewildering range of choices, and students had not chosen wisely in view of their talents. Too many had given up painting when, by starting to paint an easier subject, they would have had encouraging success. He had thrown them too abruptly on their own, made them act like mature art students.

## Group Planning in an English Class

Miss Simmons organizes things so that her class plans part of the work, but her style of teaching is orderly. She gets the group to make definite plans and sees to it that they are followed. Some teachers are more content to let activities work out as they go along. Within this businesslike procedure, Miss Simmons gives students a large measure of responsibility, establishes a pleasant and energetic group spirit, and responds flexibly to students' individual talents and problems.

In her school students expect a certain routine. A book is assigned as the text, a list of supplementary reading is passed out, and the class shuffles off down the track seeing no vista beyond tomorrow's assignment to "take pages 13 to 20 and be able to answer the questions on page 21." Miss Simmons, though, greets them the first day from behind a desk strangely free of a pile of texts to pass out, and says, "We're going to spend several days deciding what to work on this term." (Looks of puzzlement exchanged by students.) "Naturally, since this is an English class, we are going to study ways of using language. You have been learning in other grades to write clearly and to talk effectively. We will try to develop more of that skill. But we can do that while we work on other tasks. It is important to become familiar with the media of communication people use. For information and for entertainment, we use books, newspapers, plays, and so on. English courses in this school give you a chance to study these tools so you can enjoy them more and get more from them. Let's begin by listing the forms of communication you know of; we will select one of them as a topic for study for the next several weeks." Miss Simmons did not leave the choice of goals wide open. She stated firmly what she was there for. She assumed that the students would study. But she gave them latitude to voice interests before specific goals were fixed.

The choice that followed was not fixed by a quick vote among alternatives about which the class had little feeling. Discussion was used to warm up interests and awaken ideas. First there was the listing on the blackboard of communication media. The list ranged from magazines to skywriting, from commercial jingles to operas. Miss Simmons listed every medium mentioned, fearing that too critical a scrutiny of suggestions would make some members hesitant to talk.

On the second day, Miss Simmons asked the class what questions would be important to study in order to understand the media better. This inquiry, as she expected, brought bewildered silence. Having no experience in setting problems for themselves, the group could not respond. Miss Simmons then described learning as a process of solving problems, a new view to students who thought of schoolwork as soaking up statements from books. Consider communications, she went on. Some communications have little effect because no one pays attention to them. Some people do not know where to find interesting things to read, to see, or to listen to. She mentioned as a typical problem a current controversy about licensing a TV service that would reach only paying subscribers. "What other questions about any of these communication methods might be important?"

A somewhat dragging discussion followed, in which a total of four problems came out. "Shouldn't there be more good plays on television instead of such trashy stuff?" (This from Mary. Is she trying to curry favor?) "Why do some books get to be best sellers?" "Wouldn't we get better publishing and broadcasting if the government took charge?" "Why is it that all the literature and stuff they call 'good' is so dull?" (Thelma's offering is on the rebellious side. Accepting that loaded question should loosen up other members.)

After sufficient discussion to illustrate suitable questions, Miss Simmons divided the group into committees. Each student indicated which medium he wanted to work on. Committees on magazines, novels, radio, newspapers, television, and motion pictures were formed. Each group was to find important questions about its medium by talking about it and by reading in periodicals to identify current controversies. For the next few days the class hour was devoted to the work of these committees. Some groups went to the library. Others used reference books and magazines Miss Simmons had assembled.

Miss Simmons used discussion to start students on a process in which they had no experience. She steered a course between giving so many hints that she was doing the planning, and letting the discussion coast to a halt for lack of ideas. She payed out rather little rope at any time, showing how to accomplish each step. In a group that knew more about planning, she might have counted on more self-direction. The most fruitful suggestion proved to be having students go through issues of a news magazine, reading articles in the appropriate section (press, TV and radio, books, and so on). As each committee assembled to exchange reports on news items, some topics aroused genuine interest. An article on a famous comic strip pointed out how the writer conveyed his social attitudes in it. The newspaper committee was made uneasy by the idea that they had been absorbing this indoctrination without knowing it.

The motion-picture committee began to wrangle when a student read a review of a movie she had seen and thought just wonderful: the review was of a bitingly different opinion. "Who are these people who write reviews? Why does anyone care what they think when they are so wrong?" The evidence that reviewers disagree made the argument hotter.

Early in the second week the committees were ready to report to the class. Some committees had long question lists, others short. With so many questions now before the group, there was danger of losing the planning mission in scattered debates on the questions themselves.

Miss Simmons brought thinking to a focus by pointing out that one question came up in almost every committee: "Is censorship to elevate taste desirable?" The companion question, "Who sets standards of taste?", came up equally often. The class worked on consolidating the ideas under major headings. After two days the list included:

Should we have censorship?

Do stars make too much money?

How can we tell what is good in books or movies?

Should propaganda be allowed in entertainment?

Can educational communications be interesting?

As must be evident, Miss Simmons thought some of the questions far more significant than others. The spirit of the discussion showed that the planning sessions had succeeded.

Now a choice among the topics was due. The majority sentiment quickly lined up behind motion pictures, and the class turned to setting goals in that area. Most of the group wanted to debate, here and now, the issues of taste and censorship. Out of this, Miss Simmons suggested that the next four weeks be devoted to working out standards for judging a movie. As intermediate activities to help in setting the standards, she suggested viewing films as a class, writing reviews and comparing them to see if the writers' standards were similar, and viewing films by committees, to see whether films rated good or bad by the critics seemed to deserve those opinions. These activities were introduced by the teacher, and in that sense Miss Simmons was dominating the group. But the students had made a choice and their decision was being carried out.

In two weeks of stage setting, Miss Simmons had achieved several things. First, she built group spirit. These students had more social interaction than they would have had in months of some other classes. Everyone had become involved, talking about things he knew and saying things he wanted others to believe. Oral communication, then, was being used for a purpose. And she had demonstrated incidentally some of the techniques of keeping discussion to the point. In the movie reviews, the students would again be using language to convey ideas rather than to satisfy an arbitrary demand. The long-range plan would provide the motivation for weeks of activity.

The planning was not complete, as goals regarding language skills were left undefined. Miss Simmons would discuss the improvement of written language with the class after the first reviews had been done and after their content had been discussed. In the framework that "we are here to learn to use language better," she and the group could come to agree on the characteristics of a superior review. The class would also need criteria of good class discussion and of good group planning. So long as these were lacking, the students would not be fully capable of noting the consequences of their own performance and improving it. Miss Simmons properly did not stress these goals at the outset, when taking responsibility was new to the students.

---

**6** Often it is found that a teacher has a larger amount of direct interaction with abler students than with the weaker members of the class (Brophy & Good, 1974, pp. 14–17). Is this imbalance educationally appropriate?

**7** Insofar as you can judge from the case studies, did Mr. Osborne, Miss Simmons, and Mrs. Webster interact about equally with every member of his or her class?

---

# Factors Limiting the Teacher's Choice
## of Control Pattern

Is the teacher free to adopt any style? A role is inevitably controlled in part by the expectations of others; for the teacher, these expectations are defined by colleagues, students, and the community. Others expect a person to act in a certain way, and they prepare to respond in the appropriate manner. When the person does something unexpected, they are unprepared, insecure, sometimes antagonistic.

Student expectations include some idea of the teacher's *legitimate* power. The group accepts a decision seen as within the province of the teacher, whereas it may resent the same decision if it regards the decision as not legitimate. Students believe that the teacher's role legitimately includes a great deal of control and judging. Students expect the teacher to direct and to maintain standards. Where the school atmosphere is healthy, students expect teachers to treat them pleasantly and to listen to suggestions. In such a school, the teacher who exercises control in a nonarbitrary way will find his classes ready to cooperate. In some secondary schools, hostility between faculty and student body has become entrenched, and students expect only the worst of each new teacher.

In any student group, then, experience has developed readiness for certain styles, and this places a limit on the teacher's approach. He will have to prepare class members carefully if they are to take unaccustomed responsibility or to shift from fear and antagonism to mutual respect. Schmuck (box, p. 611), you will recall, found the shift far easier to accomplish with younger students.

Subject-matter limits the teacher. If his responsibility is to teach English as a second language, he cannot open the semester by letting students decide whether to study American culture, to learn to read, or to learn to converse. Students must reach a certain proficiency in reading and writing and speaking. The algebra teacher cannot let the group decide whether to take up factoring or spend additional time on solving equations; a later teacher in math or science or economics will expect them to be competent in all the fundamental skills of algebra. But even where the important general objectives are fixed—as in Miss Simmons's English course—alternative approaches to those objectives are open.

A third limitation is within the teacher. No one is equally comfortable in every style of teaching. Some professors dislike to face a class without a fully outlined lecture. Other professors are at their best when engaged in give-and-take. When the group takes responsibility, it is always possible that the plans will work out badly. Plan-as-you-go teaching keeps the teacher on his toes; some teachers enjoy this uncertainty and some find it upsetting.

Never is the teacher's role so specified that he must do precisely as everyone else does. The best evidence that the teacher is free to teach in his own way is the variety among classrooms. Teachers find many innovations possible, especially when they move slowly and when they help their students and other teachers to understand what they propose.

8 Does group planning serve only for instruction through what Chapter 13 called adventurous problem solving? Or can it be used in connection with exercises and expository teaching?

9 In what ways is group planning in the elementary school likely to differ from that in a high-school class?

10 Some teachers use a "contract" method in which the teacher lays out the topics to be covered in the course and the sequence in which activities are to be carried out, but the student is given considerable freedom to select his own pace and to decide when he is ready to take a test. What are the principal psychological differences between this method and the group planning illustrated in Miss Simmons's class?

11 Some persons challenge proposals to reduce the degree of teacher domination on the grounds that this is likely to reduce the standards of accomplishment. Is such a decline inevitable?

# CONSEQUENCES OF SYSTEMATIC PLANNING

The research in the following sections strongly favors planfulness as opposed to undirected activities. It will be seen that planning *with* the class has a function somewhat different from planning *for* the class. No general verdict for or against teacher control can be reached, in part because some controlling teachers do not have systematic plans.

EMOTIONAL SECURITY    Students who enjoy their activities put forth more effort and are less likely to develop antagonism toward school, the subject, or the teacher. Relations are friendlier when students have frequent occasion to work together. A teacher-controlled classroom may not permit much group activity, whereas friendly interaction is almost certain to occur when the group takes responsibility. Group planning can improve social relations. Cliques fade away as group members begin to work together. At the end of the work, friendship choices are likely to be spread thoroughly among the group. What is not so obvious is that friendliness grows more rapidly in a group working toward a common goal than in a group that is less work-oriented (Berkowitz et al., 1957; see also p. 779).

Students prefer thoroughly planned activities. In an undirected program, members do not know what is expected of them. Students have learned that unless they do what is expected they face unpleasant consequences; they are insecure until they know the expectations. Moreover, no one likes to feel that he may be wasting his time. In the teacher-controlled class, there is a definite goal and definite reinforcement. The price paid for such clarity is that students may never learn to set up goals for themselves or to trust their own judgment. Many students dislike group control. They feel insecure in taking responsibility and find it hard to be sure that they are doing what they should. Such students are often the ones who see themselves as excellent in meeting demands of others (p. 141).

EFFORT AND EFFICIENCY   There are theoretical reasons to expect planful teaching to get better results than undirected activities. If there is a definite goal and it is communicated to the students—whether they set it or not—they are in a better position to select provisional tries and judge the consequences. Students enjoy work that seems to be going someplace.

Ryans (1952) compared third- and fourth-grade classrooms that had high or low morale, taking into account the following student qualities: alert or uninterested, orderly or unruly, responsible or dependent, constructive or obstructive, participating or withdrawn, and initiating or passive. The teacher who obtained the desirable responses was more often observed to be democratic, understanding, kindly, systematic, consistent, responsive, and so on. The appearance in this list of *systematic, consistent,* and similar terms emphasizes the importance of planning (see also Fortune, 1967; and Spaulding, 1963). Disorganized, highly unpredictable teaching most often has bad effects. On the other hand, a teacher can follow a plan so rigidly that he is unresponsive to student ideas and difficulties.

In a comparable study of high-school classes (Ryans & Wandt, 1952; Ryans, 1960), high morale tended to occur in the classes of teachers who were understanding, systematic, stimulating, and responsive. Two teacher qualities relevant to morale in the lower grades—democracy and kindliness—had no statistical relation to work behavior in high school. Schmuck's report (p. 611) that it is difficult to build morale in an apathetic high-school class points in the same direction.

The foregoing reports are consistent with the theoretical expectation and with the Boys' Club study (box) in suggesting that definite planning is better than undirected activities. As for the choice between teacher control and group control, there is again reason to expect more effort and independence when the group participates in setting goals. Some evidence of this sort appeared in Chapter 14 (p. 610) and in the Boys' Club study. Ryans looked deeper into his elementary-school data and found a somewhat similar result. Among classes that were equally alert and interested, docile classes tended to have teachers who were more predictable, more responsible, but more autocratic. Student initiative was greatest when the teacher was more democratic, more understanding of pupils, and more original—but less responsible and less organized.

## The Boys' Club study: a famous victory for "democracy"

John Dewey (1938) was the person who spoke most forcefully of the need to take students into partnership in planning class activities, but the movement was given a powerful boost in the late 1930s by the work of the social psychologist Kurt Lewin. To demonstrate the effects of alternative styles of leadership, Lewin and his students (see R. White & R. Lippitt, 1960) established four clubs for 10-year-old boys.

Each club set to work on a project. For example, one club made plaster casts of footprints in the manner of Dick Tracy, and one worked on model planes. The groups that had little or no direction and planning spent little time on the work. The groups that worked out plans cooperatively used a much larger proportion of their time constructively. Reactions to a strong adult leader varied. An "aggressive" group ("Dominated A") resisted control. Another group ("Dominated S") submitted, and spent far more time than others at work.

When the leader left the room, a hidden observer recorded what happened. The colored lines in the figure show the dramatic change in efficiency that then took place. The group that had participated in goal setting did not need the leader. In the previously undirected group, efficiency went up, because some of the boys started to lead in the leader's absence.

From this study many educators concluded that teacher dominance is an unhealthy environment for learning. The experimenters were trying to demonstrate what group control could do, and did not demonstrate teacher direction at its best. As one of the group leaders (McCandless, 1967, p. 564) later said:

> The four leaders were graduate students . . . in . . . psychology. All were convinced and liberal equalitarians, living at a time when Hitler, the arch-authoritarian, was consolidating his power. . . . Each preferred and put his heart into his *democratic* leadership role, becoming perhaps the *warmest* and most dedicated democratic leader in recent history. But, when his turn came to play the authoritarian, he tended to become *cold* and *hard*. . . . In the *laissez-faire* role, [his] detachment [was] . . . profound. . . .

Quite possibly, a dominant but warm leader would have attained excellent results.

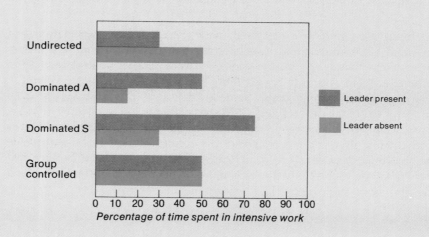

LEARNING OF COURSE MATERIAL    There is no basis for generalizing that teacher control or group control produces superior achievement. Insofar as any conclusion is to be drawn from the literature, the absence of consistent evidence is itself an indication that the many other variables at play swamp out any effect of this variable. Brophy and Good (1974, pp. 244–48) emphasize that some students do better under one plan and some better under another (p. 667). Dunkin and Biddle emphasize the confusion that enters the research because teacher control, or directiveness, or whatever it is called, is defined in many ways and combines many aspects of the classroom process. They did not find a substantial number of studies that focused on the planning and standard-setting process.

LEARNING TO BE AN EFFECTIVE GROUP MEMBER    Group planning has its greatest advantage in teaching how to make decisions and how to be effective in interaction. The socially effective person identifies relevant social cues, suggests appropriate actions in an acceptable way, and takes advantage of feedback. Being a skilled group member is in no way incompatible with being skilled in self-direction; indeed, planning and evaluation are much the same in both cases. Thus, cooperative planning led second-graders to greater self-control and improved comprehension of what self-control means (Kemp, 1961). I argued in Chapter 2 that the school should arrange activities that develop respect for others' views, concern for group goals, ability to settle disagreements amicably, and all the talents needed for living among people and for working in teams. Since attitudes and skills develop progressively, such activities should stretch over all the years of schooling.

Even successful group activities do not automatically teach desirable attitudes. For maximum transfer, generalizations should be firmed up through discussion of the group process. By reviewing a single session or a unit of work, a class can reflect on whether or not it planned wisely, what caused the discussion to ramble off the subject, and what fears kept some members from speaking up.

---

**12**  The Lewin-Lippitt-White study (box) was biased. Allowing for the bias, can you draw any definite conclusions from the study?

**13**  Chapter 5 discussed the changes in adolescent attitudes toward the older generation that have been observed in recent years. In view of these changes, is research done a decade ago on climates in high-school and college classrooms likely to be valid today?

**14**  Many writers on teaching have considered "amount of student talk" important. It was thought that students would learn more if they participated more actively. Dunkin and Biddle (1974, p. 372) and Rosenshine (in Westbury & Bellack, 1971, p. 156) find in the research no tendency of classes with more student talk to have higher achievement scores. How can this unexpected finding be explained?

---

# TEACHER WARMTH AND ITS CONSEQUENCES

Warmth consistently appears as one of the two most important qualities in teacher success (orderliness or planfulness being the other). Some teachers make a great deal of emotional contact; some teachers are remote and impersonal. One class is friendly and considerate, and one is businesslike. Emotional involvement does not depend on the method of control; teacher control is not to be identified with impersonality.

## The Impersonal and Supporting Styles

The impersonal teacher may like students but see himself as work-director. Other impersonal teachers are comfortable only when keeping their distance. The impersonal teacher expresses no more than perfunctory interest in what students do when it is not a part of "the schoolwork." He requires them to park friendships outside so they "do not interfere with the work." He may deliberately keep friendships from forming, for instance by seating students who support each other far apart.

**Warmth**

© 1974 United Feature Syndicate, Inc.

The impersonal approach offers little emotional assurance. Even if the teacher conscientiously dispenses praise when merited, the impersonal atmosphere quickly degenerates into a harsh and critical one for the student who lacks talent and interest (A. de Groat & G. Thompson, 1949).

What do writers who speak of "warm" teachers mean? The phrase may refer to any or all of these qualities:

- Spontaneous expression of feeling. The teacher colors classroom relationships with his expression of enthusiasm and liking for his students.

- Noncontingent support. The teacher responds positively whatever the student does, persuades him that he can reach his goal, and helps him past obstacles.

- Contingent social reinforcement. The teacher gives plentiful praise when it is earned, not otherwise.

- Tact and considerateness. Matter-of-fact criticism of work or conduct comes as deserved, in such a way that the student does not feel blamed or inferior.

- Acceptance of feelings. The teacher encourages the student to express his interests, fears, and so on, and takes them seriously.

On the whole, these kinds of support have positive results. But do not get the idea that support must be hearty and vocal. A quiet teacher who puts a

hand on this one's head and glows when that one brings up finished work may be fully as supporting as the bouncing extrovert.

Support is carried too far when reinforcement is liberal and noncontingent (p. 617). Learning is sacrificed when no standards of performance are maintained. The student dwells in a padded cell where he cannot hurt himself but where he does not face reality.

## Effects on Behavior

The supporting environment encourages the student to try. As likelihood of disapproval lessens, inhibitions disappear. Inventiveness and self-expression are released. This is supported by several findings: warm, considerate teachers get an unusual amount of original poetry and art from children (Cogan, 1958), generate a greater interest in schoolwork (Reed, 1961), and may produce superior achievement (Christensen, 1960; Soar, cited in Travers, 1973, p. 200).

An experiment on aspiration points to another motivational effect. Lehmusvuori (1958) separated the considerate teachers from those less concerned with student feelings. Each student of these teachers was tested on a simple intellectual task and then asked what score he expected to make on the next task. Before he stated his next goal, he was told that he had done well or badly on the task just finished, being alternately praised and criticized. Students who had been taught by the less supportive teachers changed goals on every trial. They were weather vanes with no firm self-concept, dependent entirely on evaluation by authority. The students of the supportive teacher paid little attention to what the investigator said on any one trial. They set a goal on the basis of experience over several trials, and stayed with that goal regardless of a momentary setback. The considerate teacher had confirmed the habit of independent self-evaluation.

Being responsive to feelings has another value. Unless feelings are brought into the open, the teacher has little insight into the student and is unable to help him. Merely enabling him to acknowledge weaknesses is an important step in bringing him to work on them. Sometimes the student refuses to admit need for help if he expects the teacher to be critical.

An isolated but suggestive finding comes from a study of two college psychology classes (McKeachie, 1951). Both groups saw and discussed *The Feeling of Rejection*. (This is the filmed treatment of the case of Margaret, the emotionally disturbed girl mentioned in Chapter 14.) Members of the group who had learned to work together freely had far more insight, and were better able to bring out their emotional reactions about the girl and her parents. Also, the students who participated most in the discussion changed most (Patton, 1955; see also p. 777).

---

**15** Can you recall, among your high-school and college teachers, exemplars of the supporting and impersonal styles? What effect did each have on your method of work, your interest, and your learning?

**16** It is said that some teachers sacrifice the needs of their students in order to satisfy their own emotional needs. Illustrate how this could occur.

---

## Interaction of Teacher Style and Student Needs

Domino (p. 141) showed that the effect of a certain style of teaching depends on the personalities of the students. Parent et al. (1975) provide further evidence. A two-hour unit on computer programming was taught to equated groups; one group was taught in a structured manner by an impersonal teacher who pressed for rapid progress. The other students, handed the same materials, were told to work in their own way. The teacher who had handled the first

## FIGURE 15.1

**Mastery of content as a function of teaching style and student sense of efficacy**

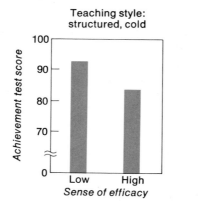
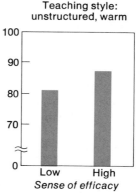

SOURCE: Data from Parent et al. (1975).

group formally handled the second group informally and receptively. The simple generalization that warmth and self-direction are desirable would lead one to expect consistently better results in the second group. In fact, there was a small average difference in the other direction. Students low in sense of efficacy (pp. 51–56) did much better under firm direction (Fig. 15.1). Results for those high in sense of efficacy were slightly better with informal teaching. Similar interactions have appeared in other studies of warmth and of teacher control (Brophy & Good, 1974; Cronbach & Snow, 1977).

Heil et al. (1960) studied 50 classrooms in Grades IV–VI. On the basis of personality questionnaires, Heil et al. classified the teachers into categories, which I shall label spontaneous, orderly, and fearful. The following descriptions fill out the picture of each type:

- Spontaneous. Self-expressive, turbulent, accepts own impulses, has strong preferences. Likes humor, dislikes routine. Satisfaction more from ideas than from relations with other persons. Low drive toward leadership, low self-aggrandizement, strong independence.

- Orderly. Severe self-control, avoids impulsive action, submissive to authority. Secure when things run smoothly. A planner de luxe, ambitious, and likes to lead.

- Fearful. Perceives environment as threatening. Dependent, dislikes being alone, severely conscientious. Protects self by adhering closely to rules and precedents.

Among teaching interns they studied, Heil et al. found 12, 15, and 23 (!) teachers in these respective categories. According to observations there was no great difference in use of democratic and flexible practices. Warmth did vary, so for analysis Heil split each group, calling "superior" the teachers who were warmer and more responsive.

The effect of each teacher was judged chiefly by the average changes on a standardized achievement test from October to June (after adjustment for school and neighborhood differences and for class differences in IQ). In Table 15.1, gains are expressed on a scale such that the average gain is 100 points. The "All students" column indicates the overall effectiveness of each type of teacher. The number of teachers of each type is small, hence not all the differences observed would reappear in another sample of teachers; cautious interpretation is advised. Fearful teachers were relatively ineffectual. Among spontaneous and orderly teachers, those who were warm and sensitive to student wishes got superior results.

The teachers affected students of different personality types differently. Heil et al. sorted students as follows:

Strivers: Strong need for self-respect or positive approval. Want to do well in school, concerned with the task more than with affectional relations.

Docile conformers: Concerned with maintaining smooth personal relationships and with avoiding adult disapproval.

Opposers: Anticipate rejection. Resistant to or withdrawn from authority. In a state of emotional conflict.

**TABLE 15.1**

**Interaction of teacher style and student personality**

| Teacher type | Number of teachers | Average achievement by students of each type | | |
| | | Strivers | Docile conformers | Opposers | All students |
| --- | --- | --- | --- | --- | --- |
| Spontaneous, superior | 6 | **130** | **162** | 75 | 101 |
| Spontaneous, inferior | 6 | 105 | 84 | 53 | 85 |
| Orderly, superior | 7 | 118 | 146 | **135** | **125** |
| Orderly, inferior* | 7 | 126 | 91 | 123 | 106 |
| Fearful, superior | 11 | 115 | 95 | 69 | 92 |
| Fearful, inferior* | 11 | 99 | 105 | 80 | 100 |
| All teachers | 48 | 113 | 111 | 86 | 100 |

SOURCE: Data from Heil et al. (1960), p. 51. The highest average in each column is shown in boldface.
* Two teachers who fell midway in the ratings of flexibility were omitted from the calculations.

The most noteworthy findings in the table are these: Strivers achieved about equally under all teachers. They did fairly well even under some of the fearful teachers. Conformers made extraordinary gains under the encouraging spontaneous teachers. They did badly under the spontaneous teachers whose classroom practices were less considerate and supporting. Opposers did best under the firm authority of the orderly teachers, and badly under the spontaneous and fearful teachers.

THE TEACHABLE STUDENT    Certain common themes run through the description of the effective learner in the preceding chapters: he accepts challenges, he enjoys achievement and competence, he has a positive approach to authority, he accepts himself. The box on the facing page speaks of such traits in describing "the teachable student." To obtain the data, Thelen (1967) first asked each of 15 high-school teachers to name students in his or her present class who seemed to be getting a lot out of it, and others who were not gaining much. ½ext, the research team assessed the attitudes and feelings of all those students. The box identifies some of the statements often endorsed by students judged teachable (by one or another teacher) and less often endorsed by students judged less teachable.

Thelen and his research team then gave the full list of items to the pool of students from which classes for the next year could be drawn. Thelen made up a "scoring key" to select students for a particular teacher, counting only the responses common among students whom *that* teacher had listed as successful in his past classes. According to Thelen, the traits that make a student "teachable" differ with the teacher. The teachable students of Teacher 5 in the report, for example, did fit the description in the box, but in addition they were emotionally expressive, vigorous and dominative in interpersonal relations, more interested in a strong and "useful" teacher than in a supportive one. Teacher 5 had had rather unsatisfactory experience with students who did not burst with energy and who tended to rely on others for decisions.

Thelen arranged a "teachable" class for each teacher—that is, one made up of students whose questionnaire responses fitted that teacher's key. The teacher also taught a control class—a random cross-section of those left over. The "teachable" classes worked out much better than the random classes, in these ways:

Teaching was more flexible.

Disruptive behavior was uncommon and was treated tolerantly by the teacher.

Work orientation was strong; there was little distraction.

Group solidarity was high.

The teacher was more openly enthusiastic in approving student work.

Both teacher and students in the teachable class found the experience satisfying. The teacher also gave higher grades in the teachable class—and the best grades were earned by the more teachable half of the class.

## The teachable student describes himself

"Teachable" high-school students responded positively to the following statements far more often than students judged to be not so "teachable" (Thelen, 1967, p. 96).

---

**I like to have the teacher lead a discussion in which basic principles are explained.**

**I like to get individual help and instruction from the teacher during class work.**

**I like being one of the more active persons during a lively class discussion.**

**I enjoy pointing out good ideas and attacking bad ideas during a class discussion.**

**I like to prepare a report to the class.**

**I think it is important to plunge courageously into the challenges of life.**

---

Having "his kind" of student, Teacher 5 was more free to be himself. In ordinary classes Teacher 5 kept his aggressive, challenging style in check. Given students who responded to that style, he became free-swinging, spontaneous, subjective, and personal in his interchanges with students. The teacher's "coming to life" as a person—the phrase is Thelen's—brought the students in the teachable class to life. The control class remained orderly and dutiful, no more.

Now what does all this imply? The student can be given a chance to select the teacher to whom he can respond. The multiteacher elementary classroom allows this. In the high school, it would not be out of the question to expose students to several math teachers during the first two weeks of the term, and then to consider student preference in making permanent assignments to classes. Another implication is that the teacher should study himself. As he learns what students his natural style can be expected to reach and which ones are likely to be turned off by it, he can either widen his range of tactics or put at least some of the students' work in other hands (a teacher aide? a student tutor? a shift to another teacher's class?).

---

**17** Can you make any connections between Heil's three types of teacher personality and Mead's three types of teachers (p. 42)?

**18** If you were selecting a teaching staff for Grades IV–VI, which of Heil's types of teacher would you prefer?

**19** Students successful with one teacher in Thelen's study (1967, p. 170) expect to work hard under adult supervision. In stress situations they are work-oriented; they try to cope. They have little wish to dominate. They do not feel much need for emotional support and they rather dislike authoritarian teachers.
   a. What teaching style is likely to fit this group?
   b. What would be missing in the education of these students if *all* their teachers had the style to which they respond?
   c. How would you expect a class with this pattern to respond to Teacher 5?

---

# DISCIPLINARY PROBLEMS AS FAILURE
# OF LEADERSHIP

The teacher who cannot establish classroom discipline cannot teach. Good discipline does not require every student in his place, every member of the group silent save one; in such a classroom, the listeners may be learning nothing. Kounin (box) found that even with one-by-one recitation, sound teacher tactics can bring bystanders psychologically "on stage."

Discipline has not failed when six eager children burst out with an idea at once. It is good for a class to break up into groups doing different things, all humming with busyness and work-related conversation. The noise level goes up, and that is usually to be welcomed as a sign of spirited involvement. Students can be given the job of controlling it when it exceeds their tolerance. Noise level is not the test of discipline; the test is whether behavior in the group permits everyone to work effectively.

Kounin studied videotapes of disciplinary incidents (box). One finding was that teachers with effective control were skilled in "time sharing"—that is, able to manage two activities at once. The teacher could, for example, monitor a class doing seatwork and if necessary nip a deviant act in the bud, without interrupting the work flow of a small group with which he was reading. Less effective teachers seemed unable to split their attention in this manner. Here are some additional techniques associated with effective class management in the elementary grades:

- Momentum. The effective teacher keeps up the tempo of stimulation, holding minor activities (reprimands, regrouping for a new task, and so on) to the shortest feasible time. The ineffective teacher gives too much attention to incidents that are off the main track of the learning activity.

- Variety. Student involvement in seatwork is high when the tasks change markedly in character in the course of the day. Variety is especially valuable in Grades I and II.

- Alerting of group. The effective teacher uses tactics (box, p. 674) that keep everyone in the act. Those not speaking at a given moment are nonetheless cued to remain alert and engaged.

Persistent disorder or confusion means that the group does not know what to do or does not want to do it. The teacher therefore should reexamine how goals have been established. If the goals are not valued, only continual cajoling and threats will keep students at work. Where the students cannot be convinced of the value of the goals, it may be that the goals have no real value. Possibly the goals are reasonable but have been poorly explained; if so, the teacher should find out what the students are trying to do and explain where

## The ripple effect

When a class rule is violated by a single child, the teacher may be wise to ignore the incident. But there is a risk that the misbehavior will prove to be contagious, in the sense that others will soon feel free to act out their impulses. Kounin (1970) set out to determine how to minimize this "ripple effect."

The teacher's technique in handling a particular incident did not have much influence on the group's level of effective work, Kounin found. His strongest finding echoes my emphasis on constructive motivation. A class characterized by a strong motivation to learn was likely to put a positive interpretation on whatever the teacher did to maintain order. The students said, for instance, that the reprimand of an offender made them attend more to their own work. In classes with low motivation, the opposite was true: more inclination to misbehavior and more hostile reactions to whatever the teacher did to restore order.

Kounin concluded that what distinguishes the orderly classroom from the classroom that gets out of hand is the students' sense that the teacher is on top of the situation. This is not a matter of directiveness, but of what we may call "keenness." (Kounin uses the term "withitness.") The keen teacher spots an action that may lead to a train of disorder as soon as it begins. The teacher may or may not react at once, but when he does act, the fact that he addresses the one who instigated the disorder lets the class know that he is fully aware. The less keen teacher may let the incident escalate; when he is finally forced to take action, he will speak sharply to the group as a whole or snap at the last child to enter the action. Kounin had videotapes from dozens of classrooms (Grade I–V), made with concealed equipment. Some teachers, he found, were consistently successful—not so much in preventing disruptive incidents as in stopping the disturbance promptly, without "ripples," or distracting aftereffects. The effective class manager "had eyes in the back of his head"—or at least convinced the students that he did.

**Keenness**

Drawing by Chon Day; © 1956 The New Yorker Magazine, Inc.

## How the teacher keeps bystanders attentive

Techniques used to keep nonreciters alert:

- Creating "suspense" before calling on one student. For example, looking over the whole group before calling on one student. Saying "Let's see now, who can . . ." before choosing.

- Picking reciters haphazardly, rather than in a predictable order.

- Calling for group activity from time to time: asking for a show of hands or response in unison.

- Giving an advance signal as to responsibility: "I want you to tell me if you hear a mistake." Or, "When Sarah is finished I'll ask you, Joe, to . . ."

Techniques that tend to turn off group alertness:

- Becoming preoccupied with the student who is speaking.

- Identifying who will be expected to respond before asking the question.

- Calling on students in predetermined order ("going down the row").

SOURCE: After Kounin (1970), pp. 117–18.

they are on the wrong track, or clarify the limits of allowable behavior. This applies both to the end in view and to the work methods employed.

The problems of individual misconduct are comparable to the problems of group disorder, and have similar causes. Does the student know where the group is heading? Does the goal seem worthwhile to him? Does he think he can do what is expected of him? If these questions are answered affirmatively, the only remaining explanation is that some individual need or habit is interfering. Unwanted habits can be suppressed by the behavior-modification techniques discussed elsewhere (pp. 628 and 748).

Coping with unwanted acts still leaves the problem of arousing interest in the class activities. To find the key to individual motivation is to make a study of the student as a person. Determine his readiness patterns, and the treatment will be determined accordingly. If penalties for misconduct are unthinkingly imposed on the student who deviates, the teacher may be adding new stresses where there were already too many.

 **20** Would the management tactics identified by Kounin be helpful in a high-school classroom?

# MOTIVATION FOR INSTRUCTION

Chapters 14 and 15 have developed four principles of motivation:

> Every activity should lead toward goals that the students are aware of and will want to attain.

> Goals should be within the students' reach, and should seem attainable to them.

> The students should be able to judge whether they are attaining their goals or how they are falling short.

> Classroom activities should lead to satisfactions that students will also seek outside the classroom, so that the learned actions will be used in nonschool situations.

This section serves to review these principles in the course of discussing practices teachers use to motivate students.

## Setting Definite Goals

Definiteness is particularly important in assignments. Some teachers end the class hour with such a statement as, "In tomorrow's work we will consider the rise of labor unions in relation to big business. Read the next five pages in the book." What reasons can the student have for doing this? Perhaps he has a chance interest in unions. Or he may be one of those omnivorous students who enjoys reading almost anything. Or he feels obligated to do as told and has the task on his conscience until he does it. Admittedly, a student is remotely aware of future praise and grades to be obtained, but if the question is whether to study or go to a show, it is easy to rationalize that he can strive for grades some other night. None of these motives seems to call for more than a cursory reading of the text.

More vital motives lie dormant. It is probable that many students really care about labor unions, whether they know it or not. They are not eager now to read about Sam Gompers and the ancient Haymarket riot, but Dad is a union member and everyone at home is strong for the union. A chance to argue about the matters Dad is always talking about will appeal to a student's interest in taking an adult role. The teacher might have turned the class loose on the topic of unions with a "what-do-you-think?" opening. One student asserts that labor unions are making it harder for high-school graduates to get jobs. This provokes another who identifies with skilled labor. Airing prejudices and counterprejudices promotes a willingness on the part of everyone to get to work on the topic.

Having aroused interest, the teacher must harness it to study. The student can listen to harangues about labor or business without any gain in insight. If the teacher helps the group summarize the discussion by listing major points of disagreement, the next question becomes how to settle specific disputes. Many issues will be factual; for instance, "Businessmen treat workers well" versus "Without unions, workers are exploited." This can be examined only by going to proper sources. Some will be magazine reports of current labor relations; some will be history books, which tell what conditions gave rise to unions. A labor leader or a businessman can visit the class, or the class can interview adults about local working relations. Students gather material for a purpose they have accepted as worth their effort. In contrast, the traditional manner of motivating assignments pointed only to goals far removed and indefinite: "when you know this you'll be ready for college," or "you'll understand history." A person trying to answer a question reads in a way different from that when he is trying to complete a chore. When a student wants to explain to the class what he has learned rather than just to appease the teacher, he will really strive to understand.

In a problem-oriented unit, the teacher does not merely inflate one day's topic into three weeks' talking. He uses the question about labor to get at fundamental matters: How to determine a fair return on capital? Should laborers have as high a living standard as owners and managers? Has government a proper place in business negotiations? These questions could not even be raised clearly in a one-hour discussion about the days of Sam Gompers.

**21** In the study of unions, how might the activities and goal-setting procedures provide for individual differences in ability and motivation?

**22** Seventh-graders became interested in a contemporary Sicilian bandit described in a news story. One student reported that the bandit was a Robin Hood helping the poor; another challenged the report. After considerable disagreement, because the class had few facts, they decided to hold a "trial for murder." A judge, a defendant, and a prosecutor were appointed, and a search for evidence began. For facts not available in published sources, the students wrote to news services, to Italian officials, to the Italian Embassy, even to the bandit's relatives in Italy. The "judge" visited courts to learn proper legal procedure, and the class prepared detailed reports on topics such as *habeas corpus* and the jury system in American law.

Discuss this activity considering responses that could be learned, student interest, clarity of purposes, practice with understanding, and provision for individual differences. In what ways might the method be inferior to more traditional lessons on trial by jury?

**23** How do the principles mentioned on p. 675 differ from the statement "The subject-matter for any class should be determined by what students are interested in"?

## Competition

Pitting students against one another is a frequent tactic intended to motivate—a prize for the best essay on liberty, gold stars for those who keep their desks neatest, grading on the curve, and so on.

Does competitive activity provide known and desired goals? Certainly the immediate goal is known; its attractiveness is another matter. Rewards offered are rarely of great value in themselves. They are mostly symbols of approval from authority or prizes in the game of testing one's powers. For some students, the threat of losing or the tension induced by working against classmates inhibits participation. Some of the most talented students like to express their ideas and to satisfy their curiosity, but care very little about the prizes an adult offers. Indeed, the Lepper research (box, p. 627) suggests that such incentives can wash out motivation.

Can everyone be confident of reaching the goal? No. When most participants are likely to lose, many students protect themselves by setting a low level of aspiration—that is, by not trying.

A competitive program tends to help only the better performers. The capital athlete is encouraged to train to his very peak. The average player gets little attention from the coach and may sit out the season on the bench. The topmost spellers stay in the spell-down competition, and some wind up in a national contest in Washington. The weaker spellers, eliminated early, become an audience while the others continue to practice and learn.

Competition usually provides little incentive or opportunity for the third principle of motivation—examining one's own performance. When prizes are awarded, the winner does not learn why he did well, and the losers have no idea how to do better the next time. Prizes are attached to products, not to processes. An art student who tries to satisfy contest judges may be sacrificing the development of his own style.

Winning a competition does teach pride in an accomplishment, but in focusing the spotlight on the very best performers, competition damages the self-respect and often the effort of the mediocre. The student whose craftsmanship is limited needs to practice and to believe in his capability just as much as the student who can win prizes. The student hopelessly outclassed in public-speaking competitions will avoid speech activities, taking no steps to develop skill and confidence as a speaker. Class discussions, panels, and noncompetitive talks would provide practice without threat. Competition is not the way to develop potentiality. Emphasizing the false standard that one should take pride where he excels, it discourages development of one's lesser talents.

Competition is socially disruptive. The student has no reason to help a classmate who is having trouble, and in fact will benefit from causing trouble for his fellows. Stories about one student's deliberate spoiling of another's laboratory notes—at the peak of competition for medical school—provide a case in point.

Competition has a place. Because competition plays a part in our culture, the person's socialization should include learning to be a good loser, to push to his limit when in competition, and to win gracefully. The crucial point is to keep the opportunities varied and the emotional pitch low. Then no single defeat counts for too much.

GROUP COMPETITION    Competition among groups is in many ways healthier than one-on-one competition. Many students profit when the music program emphasizes ensemble work and the interschool "competitions" are judged so that every chorus may go home with a first-class rating.

American grade-school teachers utilize group competition in small ways with such remarks as "Let's see which group can put its things away first." The Russian schools make this a starting point for a total system of academic motivation. Virtually all the work the student does is evaluated as a part of the effort of his "collective." In some contexts, the collective or "link" is his row in the classroom; in others, his class (which is compared with a neighboring class). The class performance, in turn, contributes to the standing of the school compared with other schools. As Bronfenbrenner (1970, p. 50; see also box) describes the system, it applies to academic work, community service projects, personal grooming, and moral conduct.

> As each child's status depends in part on the standing of the collective of which he is a member, it is to each pupil's enlightened self-interest to watch over his neighbor, encourage the other's good performance and behavior, and help him when he is in difficulty. In this system the children's collective becomes the agent of adult society and the major source of reward and punishment.

The child who leads the link makes formal oral reports regarding deficiencies he is aware of—"Valodya did the wrong problem, Alyosha had a dirty shirt collar." The teacher fosters competition between the link and the monitor; students are urged to detect their own shortcomings before the monitors do.

The system apparently brings about good conduct. Judging from Bronfenbrenner's account, it succeeds largely because of the consistent warmth the child experiences—pride and affection at home; encouragement and emotional warmth from the teacher (who stays with the same class for several years); mutual assistance and loyalty within various collectives, small and large. The emphasis is on shortcomings of *conduct.* Failure to understand is not a subject for criticism; failure to pay attention is. Also of considerable importance is the use of hierarchies of collectives. If competition simply pits one group steadily against another, antagonisms mount (Sherif et al., 1961). Where the competing units collaborate at the next level of competition, that danger is minimal.

At our distance, it is hard to evaluate the system as it works in the Soviet Union and even harder to guess what it might contribute in the United States. One needs to think about the reaction of children of low ability, children of ethnic minorities, and children with emotional maladjustments. The system risks encouraging conformity for the sake of conformity. In fact, the Russians themselves are attempting to modify the system. Novikova, whose manual was quoted above, has more recently written that unremitting task-oriented competition may impoverish personality.

## Collective competition in a Russian classroom

Here is a passage translated by Bronfenbrenner (1970; his pp. 59–60) from a manual for the third-grade teacher, *Socialist Competition in the Schools,* by Novikova.

> Two monitors at the desk silently observe the [third-grade] class. On their faces is reflected the full importance and seriousness of the job they are performing. . . .
>
> During the lesson, the teacher gives an exceptional amount of attention to collective competition between "links." Throughout the entire lesson the youngsters are constantly hearing which link has best prepared its lesson, which link has done the best at numbers, which is the more disciplined, which has turned in the best work.
>
> The best link not only gets a verbal positive evaluation but receives the right to leave the classroom first during the break. . . .
>
> "Work more carefully," says Olya to her girl friend. "See, on account of you, our link got behind today. You come to me and we'll work together at home."

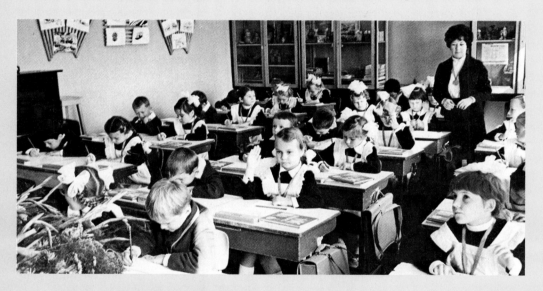

> . . . if every year we shall be obtaining more highly developed people but all of the same type, then this will be of little profit to society or to personality. Socialist society is interested in original persons capable of revolution in the spheres of science, technology, and the organization of production. And the personality is interested in developing to the full those capacities with which it is endowed by nature. And these capacities are by no means the same in all people. Thus we have an instance in which the interests of socialist society and personality completely coincide. (From Bronfenbrenner, p. 87.)

Just how the Soviet system of motivation through the collective will be changed to promote a responsible individuality—if indeed the trend takes root—is not yet clear.

American observations indicate that group self-discipline promotes desirable behavior. Children who have responsibility for enforcing a rule on others are much less likely to violate the rule themselves (Parke, 1974, pp. 127ff.). Moreover, giving the child greater opportunity to use judgment about the form of enforcement improves his own conduct. The American studies did not test the competitive aspect of the Russian system.

## Marking

The school needs an official record of the student's performance, particularly for guidance. Grades and report cards also fulfill the school's responsibility to tell parents how their child is getting along in the world. For those purposes, marks should be an emotionally neutral, factual account—but no one regards them that way. Students treasure them or worry over them; parents beam or scold. Teachers use marks deliberately to goad, reward, and punish.

Marks do meet the first of our criteria of motivational procedures; they serve as definite goals—for some students. The student has a level of expectation when he enters a course, and will work seriously to reach that level. The teacher who lists extra work that can be done to earn an A will get that work from these who regard themselves as potential A students. Those content to plug along at an average level will ignore the higher goal.

The motivating effect of marks is limited when the student feels that high grades are out of his reach. This is especially the case when everyone, without regard to initial ability, is judged against the same standard of acceptable performance. Where the mark is first and foremost a record of level attained, as it must be to serve its administrative purposes, the student who starts at a superior level is fairly certain to have a high final mark—whether or not he pushes himself. Marks are a sensible reward only if they measure progress during the course, which is not the same as level of final performance. That requires taking initial readiness into account in setting standards for individuals.

The teacher's marking practices may or may not promote self-judgment. At the worst, a teacher collects papers or observes students at work, makes records they never see, and at the end of the term issues marks with no explanation. Until the final blow falls, the student has no idea whether or not his work is satisfactory. If the student is continually judging his work in terms of standards that he understands, he is fully aware of the improvement desired. These frequent judgments, starting early in the course, arouse little tension and encourage a hopeful attitude.

A particular fault of traditional marks is that they grade the performance as a whole. A person who receives a B knows that he has done reasonably well but has not done everything perfectly. The mark tells him nothing about how to do better and is not an aid to further learning. A better evaluation is descriptive. It keeps the goals of the course in the foreground and gives a differentiated picture of the student's standing. Marks are discussed further in the next chapter.

Richard de Charms, "The Origin Classroom is Different," in *Enhancing Motivation* (New York: Irvington, 1976), pp. 161–76.

> De Charms's theory is that personal commitment arises when a person feels that he is an "Origin"—that he initiated and controls his assignment. This book describes procedures used by a consultant to raise morale in a school. The first step was to raise each teacher's sense of autonomy and responsibility; the chapter cited describes the kind of atmosphere a teacher so trained was able to develop.

David H. Hargreaves, "Discipline," in *Interpersonal Relations and Education* (London: Routledge & Kegan Paul, 1972), pp. 228–66.

> A British social psychologist advises teachers on "positive control techniques." Hargreaves takes the position that the teacher must establish dominance in his first encounters with the students; yet he sees initiation, self-direction, and self-evaluation by the learner as the heart of motivation. Hence he discusses transition techniques for relaxing control.

Jacob Kounin, "Withitness and Overlapping," in *Discipline and Group Management in Classrooms* (New York: Holt, Rinehart and Winston, 1970), pp. 74–91, 169–70.

> Summarizes evidence on practices of elementary teachers, such as keenness and time-sharing, which seem to produce an effective work atmosphere. Portrays differences between good and poor techniques through classroom incidents.

Carl R. Rogers, "The Interpersonal Relationship in the Facilitation of Learning," in *Humanizing Education: The Person in the Process,* ed. R. R. Leeper (Washington, D.C.: Association for Supervision and Curriculum Development, 1967), pp. 1–18.

> Sketches the practices and experiences of a number of teachers Rogers admires, emphasizing how they accept learners as persons. Teachers will be at their best, Rogers says, when they feel free to be themselves in classroom interchanges.

Herbert A. Thelen, "Patterns," in *Classroom Grouping for Teachability* (New York: Wiley, 1967), pp. 156–75.

> Describes the styles of four high-school teachers and the patterns of students they considered teachable. Do the teachers differ in needs that are hard to change? or in "styles" that can be changed at will?

■ Evaluation procedures serve to define the goals of instruction for teacher and student, to monitor the students' learning, to provide a record of individual competence or merit, and to guide improvement of the educational program.

■ A comprehensive procedure collects evidence on a wide range of outcomes and on a representative sample of the content to be mastered. Intellectual tasks range from simple recall to higher-level synthesis and judgment.

□ Evaluation becomes more useful to the student and teacher and less a source of tension when merit rating is minimized and when evaluation is a continuing process.

■ Choice-response tests, imaginatively designed and carefully reviewed, can measure both simple and complex outcomes. Only for special purposes are constructed-response questions more suitable. Performance observations provide superior evidence on a wide variety of educational outcomes.

■ A report of test scores or marks is generally less useful than a report of the kind and level of task the student can cope with. Much evaluation should be formative, taking place in the course of a unit of work.

□ End-of-course examinations should not dominate the process of evaluation. Standardized tests play a role in testing of readiness and in end-of-course evaluation, but interpretations based on norms are often incorrect.

**CONCEPTS**

*program evaluation*
*merit rating*
*content-by-process grid*
*Taxonomy of objectives*
*standard error*
  *of measurement*
*constructed-response test*

*performance observation*
*content-referenced scale*
*formative evaluation*
*mastery learning*
*summative evaluation*
*standardized test*
*grade-equivalent scale*

# 16

# ASSESSING
# PROGRESS
# IN LEARNING

Evaluation is the process of judging whether or not the goals of schooling are being attained by the individual, the class, or the school system. Whoever evaluates collects information as to what students have learned and makes a judgment about the results. The findings are applied in subsequent plans and decisions by the teacher, the school administration, and the public. The findings likewise have an important influence on the plans and actions of the students themselves.

Evaluation is not just testing. Every time the student performs a task or enters into a classroom discussion, evidence on competence and style becomes available. The beginning swimmers find themselves able to move away from the side of the pool after a few lessons; they know they are progressing. The civics teacher who hears students quoting authorities to prove points, rarely questioning the validity of such opinions, knows that students have failed to acquire a vital attitude.

Evaluation procedures will vary according to the maturity of the students, the subject taught, and the reason for collecting information. This chapter will center on evaluation in Grades IV–XII in the most common school subjects, and particularly on test construction and use. But the point of view applies to evaluation in preschool, where the teacher relies on observation and oral questioning. It applies also to examining in the university and in industrial training.

# FUNCTIONS OF EVALUATION

The student thinks of testing as an event that takes place after instruction is finished. But evaluation procedures—including tests—are a part of the instructional operation; they have good or bad effects on learning, depending on how the teacher uses them. I shall distinguish four broad functions of evaluation: motivation, monitoring, merit rating, and program evaluation. Each of these uses information differently and calls for a different information-collection strategy.

## Motivation

Tests need not be the primary means of getting students to take their work seriously, but the effect of tests is powerful even when they are only one among several motivating influences.

Testing procedures do much to define the goals of instruction. For a person learning to fly an airplane, the content of the instruction is quite literally set by a final examination. The pilot who obtains his license has gotten what he

**Evaluation specifies goals**

From *Psychology for Teaching: A Bear Always Usually Faces the Front,* Second Edition, by Guy R. LeFrancois. © 1975 by Wadsworth Publishing Company, Inc., Belmont, California 94002. Reprinted by permission of the publisher.

should from the instruction. Instruction in school, however, usually has goals the examination does not touch on. Even the teacher who starts with a broad set of goals is likely to find himself pointing the lessons more and more to the subset the final examination will cover. The student inevitably thinks that the responses the tests calls for or that the teacher criticizes are the ones he ought to concentrate on.

A main objective in history may be "to understand that present-day problems have a historical basis." If tests deal only with facts about the past and not at all with their present relevance, the objective is forgotten. Students then do not study by asking themselves, "How does this chapter bear on current problems?" They learn about Continental currency because it is in the book, never connecting it with contemporary inflation.

Donald performs an exercise in the laboratory. The lab manual calls for 10 ml. of silver nitrate. When Donald pours in an amount he guesses to be about right, he gets a bulky precipitate. He records the result in his notebook and writes the equation that explains it. The teacher circles in red where Donald wrote $Ag_2NO_3$ instead of $AgNO_3$ but makes no other comment. So Donald is confirmed in his neglect of laboratory procedure, but is warned that chemical formulas are important. Another teacher might have observed Donald's laboratory operations and cautioned him against guessing at amounts. That would put a different standard before Donald.


## Monitoring

The importance of monitoring during learning has been emphasized in earlier chapters. Coaching the tennis player, the instructor notes faulty strokes the player should work on. The geometry teacher who watches students try to support a conclusion or who inspects their completed proofs likewise gets information to guide instruction. Decisions about the pace of instruction and the need for review and choices among possible assignments are all based on impressions the teacher forms while monitoring.

Signaling what is wrong is itself a way to bring about improvement. High-school students took a multiple-choice test on an English lesson and were re-tested a week later. Those who had five minutes to look over their papers eliminated nearly half of their errors when they later took the retest. This occurred even though they had no reason to expect the retest. The review was effective because the teacher handed back not a score, not an identification of the items missed, but a paper marked to show the correct answer to each question (Plowman & Stroud, 1942; see also p. 462).

An important part of learning is learning to monitor oneself. Self-monitoring is needed as much in developing a philosophical argument as it is in driving a car. One has to foresee that what one is doing will work out badly, and correct it promptly. Sound evaluation does much to help the person become

aware of the significant aspects of a performance, and hence to monitor himself. "Am I communicating?" is a much better question for the student of language than "Am I making errors in grammar?" Similarly, "Do I understand why the equation is set up this way?" is a better question than "Does my work look like the model in the book?"

Duel (1958) had students in a technical school rate themselves on such questions as, "How proficient are you in using a multimeter to measure output voltages and currents of a vacuum tube?" Two groups were taught in precisely the same way, save that one group filled out this form at the start of the course and at the end of each unit of instruction. The students using the form did better throughout the course. A similar plan was used by Mr. Osborne (p. 652) to promote self-monitoring of proficiency not only in art but also in goal setting.

## Merit Rating

A merit rating reports how competent the student is. The report often is intended for persons outside the class (parents, prospective employers, other teachers, and so on). Whereas monitoring is analytic, merit rating is global. Performance is summed up in a letter grade or a passing mark or a ranking. Letters of recommendation, report cards, and marks given single pieces of work all imply merit or lack of merit. The emphasis is not on guiding further instruction; it is on rating the student's final performance as satisfactory or unsatisfactory, as A level or C level.

Statements about merit modify the student's self-concept and aspirations. They affect short-term motivation and shape long-range educational and vocational expectations. Scores, marks, and rankings thus have a guidance function. In adolescence and adulthood, moreover, a negative report is likely to close off educational and vocational options.

Quite properly, evaluation is used to certify that the person is indeed competent to fly an airplane, to teach school, to enter a college of engineering. Sometimes a special examination is used for certifying; sometimes the judgment is based on a cumulative grade record. The distinction between a summary judgment of merit and a factual report on competence is subtle—but the difference is there. "You failed" is not the same message as "I can't let you solo until you are better at recovering from a stall."

Whereas monitoring is forward-looking, the ratings of proficiency and merit that count most heavily are usually given after the chance for repair has passed. Everyone regards a poor mark as a blot on the record. The formal value judgment that goes on the record is thus inherently threatening. The threat is greatest when merit rating is competitive and only a certain number of high grades will be given.

Teachers find it distasteful to give marks and other merit ratings. Making close decisions is painful, especially where division points are arbitrary. The teacher feels defensive because his facts are often insufficient to warrant a confident judgment. A further complication is the conflict between the teacher's wish to give a truthful report and his desire to encourage the student.

The discomfort of teachers and students leads to various proposals for doing away with merit rating. Constructive steps in this direction can be taken. A college may allow students to work for credit in some courses without a grade being reported. Competition can be eliminated wherever it has no patent justification; thus it is normal—given the appropriate evidence—to certify as prepared to teach every person who completes a certain program of work. Likewise, a college may decide not to calculate rank in class for the graduating students.

Teachers must evaluate, but in my opinion they should do as little comparison and as little summary rating of individuals as the institutional setting allows. Devices discussed later in this chapter serve this purpose—for example, student self-evaluation, and keeping a record of the skills mastered rather than a composite score. Practice exercises and quizzes collect evaluative information with little or no tension when it is understood that they "do not count in the grade." The procedures and product of problem solving by the class as a whole can be evaluated without passing judgment on any individual.

Summary reports cannot be wholly eliminated. The counselor advising whether a student should take algebra wants a report from the most recent math teacher. The medical school wants a report from the applicant's college. It is unfortunate that not everyone can receive the highest recommendation, but the remedy is not to conceal inadequacies from those who have a need to know. The remedy is to determine what the student can do well in, and put *that* success on the record. The more valid and more complete the information the teachers use in arriving at their reports, the more likely it is that those receiving the reports will make sound decisions.

1  A prominent form of merit rating is the report to parents. Is it practical and desirable to reduce the extent to which these reports are perceived as a rating of individual merit?

2  The future farmer who has cared for a calf enters it in the stock show. Blue, red, and white ribbons go to the best animals. This is an evaluation of the young farmer as well as of the animal. Does it escape the faults of merit ratings in the school?

## Program Evaluation

Every time a teacher gives a test or listens to a class discussion, he has a chance to learn whether the teaching plan for the previous day or week was adequate. That is, he has a chance to monitor *his* performance. Evidence of student progress during a year permits an evaluation of the teacher's grand strategy. The teacher is shortsighted if he does not study these facts and jot down his ideas for improving his teaching of the same material the next time around.

Administrative officers need similar feedback on school system performance. Program evaluation is often carried out with a citywide test. The results are reported to the school staff and the school board, and a summary goes to the press. Other assessment programs are statewide or nationwide in scope. Sometimes special evaluative experiments or quasi experiments are conducted to validate a new program or course of study before it is widely adopted. The studies of compensatory education (pp. 355ff.) are examples.

To the school staff, an evaluation from outside is something of a threat. The solution is not to insist that neither teachers nor programs be evaluated; such a position would be irresponsible and politically unacceptable. Evaluation that chiefly judges the merit of teachers and school systems is understandably unpopular; evaluation that shows where the curriculum or classroom procedures can be improved pleases everyone.

The discussion to this point can be summed up as follows: Sound evaluation is evaluation that improves decisions made by the student, the teacher, the school administrator, or occasionally, by outsiders. The several functions of evaluation are served by different evaluation plans. Monitoring, for example,

## TABLE 16.1

## Roles of three kinds of evaluation in improving instruction

| *Preparative evaluation* | *Formative evaluation* | *Summative evaluation* |
|---|---|---|
| *To determine the attributes possessed by students before instruction commences* | *To provide continual feedback to students and teacher on their effectiveness as they proceed through the instructional sequence* | *Assessing the degree to which the instructional objectives have been attained by the end of the instructional sequence* |

### ROLES AT THE GROUP LEVEL

| | | |
|---|---|---|
| P1. Locating an appropriate starting point for group instruction. | F1. Identifying areas in which group attainment of the instructional objectives is less than desired. Planning remedial instruction. | S1. Evaluating the effectiveness of a unit of instruction and the instructional techniques employed. |
| P2. Planning remedial instruction. | F2. Planning subsequent instruction for the current group of students. | S2. Comparing the outcomes in different groups. |
| P3. Selecting instructional methods. | F3. Evaluating the effectiveness of the unit of instruction and the instructional techniques. | S3. Providing information for preparative evaluation in subsequent instruction of the same group of students. |
| P4. Assigning students to instructional groups. | F4. Quality control in the unit of instruction. | S4. Certifying skills and abilities attained. |
| P5. Collecting information on the effectiveness of previous instruction. | F5. Maintaining uniform grading of students each time a unit of instruction is presented. | S5. Predicting success in subsequent instruction. |

### ROLES AT THE INDIVIDUAL LEVEL

| | | |
|---|---|---|
| P6. Identifying and remedying specific deficiencies in an individual's preparedness for a particular unit of instruction. | F6. Diagnosis of learning difficulties of individuals. Planning remedial instruction. | S6. Providing feedback on deficiencies in attainment. |
| P7. Planning individualized instruction. | F7. Providing reinforcement for mastery. | S7. Providing reinforcement for attainment of objectives. |
| P8. Shifting the student to an alternative unit of instruction when appropriate. | F8. Pacing work of the individual. | S8. Motivating and directing effort during instruction, prior to the summative evaluation. |

SOURCE: Adapted from Mackay (1975), pp. 206 and 207.

should attend promptly to each day's performance and even to single acts within the day's work. Program evaluation usually takes the long view, summing up what has been accomplished by the group, not the individual, over months or even years of instruction.

In contrast to my scheme of four functions, Mackay (1975) discusses three kinds of evaluation (Table 16.1): *formative* and *summative,* terms in current American usage (see also p. 15), and *preparative,* which is what I have called "investigating readiness" (Chapters 7 and 9). Preparative evaluation takes place at the start of instruction (or a bit earlier); formative evaluation is carried on as instruction proceeds. When a unit or course ends, summative judgments are made.

---

**3** Consider the four functions of evaluation in turn. At what points does each appear in Table 16.1? What entries in the table seem to fit under none of the functions?

**4** To help a school choose among candidates for employment, a faculty member at the teacher-training institution writes a letter describing the candidates without referring to the file of their grade records. Is this preferable to the usual policy of referring to course grades in writing a letter of recommendation?

---

# QUALITIES DESIRED IN A TESTING PROCEDURE

Chapter 7 discussed the qualities desired in a test for assessing development or predicting future success. These charcterics are relevant also to evaluation instruments, but the emphasis shifts. In evaluation, one is most concerned with the content of the test and its fit to the curriculum. And evaluation should be concerned with describing what the person can do, as distinct from comparing him with others. Comprehensiveness, fairness, and interpretability are all aspects of validity. After discussing those topics and reliability, I shall take up the special purposes and qualities of standardized tests of achievement.

## Comprehensiveness

Are the right things being observed? The theoretical ideal is that an evaluation activity will check on all the outcomes desired from the instruction. (In practice, however, only a limited number of outcomes can be measured with care.) Program evaluation has to look beyond the fragmentary objectives of single lessons to assess the broad sweep of intellectual and personal development, even attending to outcomes such as character development or the dropout rate, which are the responsibility of no single course. It may be important to investigate something that could not properly be a basis for merit rating. The science teacher wants to interest a reasonable fraction of talented students in science as a possible career. Falling short in that implies a weakness in the program, one at least as serious as failing to get across the concept of electrolysis.

ADEQUATE SAMPLING OF CONTENT    A test can be only a sample of performance, as was said earlier (p. 265). The reading test presents a sample of paragraphs in a certain range of complexity. The year-end geography test asks the student to identify on a map a fraction of the rivers and cities he should know. For the broader educational objectives, such as critical thinking, the range of situations in which the ability could be displayed is virtually unlimited.

Sampling is simple when a spelling list is to be taught; the tester draws random words from the list. If the words are classifiable (–ie– words, –tted words, and so on), he draws randomly within sets to ensure that each source of difficulty is touched on. At first glance, it may seem that no sampling occurs when the novice cook is asked to turn out some pancakes. The ingredients and the recipe are indeed the same on every performance. Even so, if the cook were tested on many days, variations would occur in the cleanness and temperature of the griddle, the mixing of the batter, and so on; hence the cook's pancakes vary. The test pancakes are no more than a sample.

For broader skills, sampling has to be given more thought. In teaching comprehension of spoken French, should the test selections represent the conversations American tourists have in Paris? Should they include everyday conversations between French shoppers and salespersons? Should the test limit itself to the topics and vocabulary found in first-year textbooks? Further: Will the selections all be heard in the voice of the students' teacher? in the voice of a well-educated Parisian? or in voices sampled to cover the range of French social classes, ages, and sexes? These questions are not quibbles—a student who can easily grasp what his teacher says may be unable to follow some other intonation and rhythm. A test with several voices would detect the weakness.

What is to be sampled depends on the teaching objectives. Very likely the test for first-year French should be confined to passages the first-year students have a fair chance of understanding. The passages should not be restricted to the content of one textbook or one set of lessons.

Some objectives are stated in terms of typical behavior—for example, the habit of writing legibly. This is not evaluated by a "handwriting test." The best evidence would come from examining a broad sample of the student's written communications. Papers written for his English class are not representative enough, since he knows that the English teacher is likely to judge handwriting. This same concern for comprehensive sampling applies to objectives related to attitudes and conduct.

## A transfer item

---

**The water in a certain container would give off 800 calories of heat in cooling to 0°C. If 800 grams of ice are placed in the water, the heat from the water will melt**

   A.   all the ice

   B.   about 10 grams of the ice

   C.   nearly all the ice

   D.   between 1 and 2 grams of the ice.

---

Among high-school physics students responding to this test item, 35 per cent marked the correct choice: B. This is little better than the chance probability of 25 per cent. Yet 70 per cent of an equivalent sample responded correctly—"80 calories"—to the following item:

---

**How much heat is needed to melt one gram of ice at 0°C.?**

---

SOURCE: Adapted from Lindquist, in Hawkes et al. (1936), pp. 91–92.

RANGE OF RESPONSE PROCESSES    The evaluator samples response categories or processes as well as content or situations. The evaluation plan has to consider all the things the learner is supposed to do with the subject-matter. To test listening comprehension in French is not enough, since the course is intended to teach reading, writing, and speaking besides.

The outcomes desired from the teaching of literature are equally diverse: students are to know about certain periods or styles, to know certain pieces of literature and interpretations that have been given them, to read similar literature with understanding and pleasure, to recognize certain literary devices and to appreciate the effect achieved by them, to develop personal standards of taste and critical judgment, and so on. Some of these can be covered in a simple test of recall. To get evidence on the student's ability to read intelligently, responsively, and critically, one asks him to react to, say, a short story that has not been discussed in class. The book review and the tutorial interview are vehicles for such evaluation.

For a standardized achievement test or College Board test, a *content-by-process* grid is prepared. Figure 16.1, an example of such a grid, is a guide for preparing a test on the study of weather. Items will be written to fit the various cells of the grid, so that the test matches the intentions of the curriculum planners. Such a grid can help the classroom teacher in planning instruction and also in making a test. Note that procedures other than tests were recommended for two outcomes to inquire into the students' ability to deal with the unfamiliar. The proposal to test comprehension of literature by having students work on a fresh selection is of that type. Two teaching methods that are equally ex-cellent for putting across the explicit content of a certain lesson may be un-equal in their cultivation of transfer. (Recall the Brownell-Moser evidence, p. 122, and the studies of buoyancy, pp. 366 and 547.)

Many attempts to categorize responses have been made, but in practice most testers stop with simple rubrics such as those in Fig. 16.1.

In task analysis for instructional planning and in diagnosis of individual progress, it is necessary to subdivide complex performances. Yet performances are integrated wholes. If a person performs successfully, we know that he has a

## FIGURE 16.1
## Plan specifying a test on weather for a junior-high-school course

Numerals indicate number of items to be prepared; for example, there are to be two items regarding symbols and terms related to air pressure.

| Processes | Content areas | | | | | |
|---|---|---|---|---|---|---|
| | Air pressure | Wind | Temper-ature | Humidity | Clouds | All |
| Knows symbols and terms | 2 | 4 | 2 | 2 | 2 | 12 (24%) |
| Knows specific facts | 3 | 2 | 2 | 1 | 2 | 10 (20%) |
| Understands influence of factor on weather | 3 | 8 | 2 | 2 | 1 | 16 (32%) |
| Has skill in interpret-ing weather maps | 3 | 2 | 2 | 5 | 0 | 12 (24%) |
| Has skill in construct-ing weather maps | Observe students as they use measuring devices (rating scale) | | | | | |
| Has skill in use of measuring devices | Evaluate maps constructed by students (checklist) | | | | | |
| All | 11 | 16 | 8 | 10 | 5 | 50 (100%) |

SOURCE: Adapted from Gronlund, *Measurement and Evaluation in Teaching*, 2d. ed. (New York: Macmillan, 1971), p. 65.

reasonable command of a complete set of component responses. If he does not, we know that he lacked some component or that he failed in integration and self-monitoring. A test item, then, measures not one ability but many. As Diederich has said about reading comprehension (1969, p. 860):

> A diagnostic test usually tries to locate weaknesses by presenting different types of items: ten directed toward weakness A, ten toward weakness B, and so on. But as one listens to class discussions (of choices, after the test), it becomes apparent that it is not the type of item that discloses the weakness; it is the type of reasoning that students bring to these items.... It is these mistakes that need to be uncovered and corrected, not a tendency to go wrong on any particular type of item.

Tasks that fall at different levels of the *Taxonomy* (box) or in different cells of a content-by-process grid usually correlate substantially. One reason is that efficient learners make progress on all fronts at once if the teaching is suitably balanced. Another is that a task usually calls for a mixture of processes. Even "recall" of a fact is often a thinking process (p. 460). Burmester (box, p. 726) developed a test of ability to interpret data ("comprehension" in the *Taxonomy*). She was careful to reduce the demands upon knowledge. Even so, her test correlated about 0.50 with measures of knowledge and of analytic skills (after correcting for error of measurement). Tests of "different processes" usually correlate higher than that.

5  Would the same sample of reading passages in French serve for daily monitoring and for end-of-first-year measurement?

6  A beginning class is taught Spanish using tapes made by one very clear speaker. How early should other voices be introduced into the weekly tests?

7  If schools emphasize different regions, different periods, and different kinds of events, what should a published test for ninth-grade world history contain?

8  For high-school students who have been studying the short story, what would a task at the level of "analysis" be? Is analysis a unified ability or an aggregation of specific concepts and techniques? (Recall what was said about problem solving on p. 557.)

9  Do the two physics items (box, p. 692) measure different abilities?

10  How do the processes of problem solving (p. 551) relate to the levels of the *Taxonomy*?

11  In a student's first serious exposure to a subject—say, to the Greek and Roman myths, in Grade VII—is there a place for objectives higher than level 1 of the *Taxonomy*?

## Task taxonomies

A sort of dictionary of tasks to aid in planning tests is provided in the *Taxonomy of Educational Objectives.* Handbook I (Bloom et al., 1956) classifies tasks within "the cognitive domain." Handbook II (Krathwohl et al., 1964), on "the affective domain," has to do with feelings and motives. In addition, there are several alternative psychomotor taxonomies (for example, Harrow, 1972).

The cognitive taxonomy (Handbook I) is most widely used. It is a logical classification, with a loosely ordered system of six levels:

1. Knowledge. The student is to recall, define, or recognize some specific knowledge encountered during instruction. The knowledge may be a definition, a fact, a rule, a visual pattern, and so on.

2. Comprehension. The student is to add something to a communication or to make use of it: draw a picture, summarize, give an original example, trace an implication, and so on.

3. Application of abstract ideas and technical rules. The student is to use the knowledge to guide concrete acts in a particular situation: computing, constructing, classifying objects, and so on.

4. Analysis. The student is to identify parts in a communication or system and to detect their relations.

5. Synthesis. The student is to assemble elements into a structure or communication of his own.

6. Evaluation. The student is to apply standards, as in judging a work of art, a proposed law, or some personal conduct. (As used in the *Taxonomy, evaluation* refers to making a judgment about merit or suitability.)

The *Taxonomy* is not a psychological theory of learning or performance. It does not describe an order in which competence has to develop nor an order in which instruction should proceed. A learner can progress on all the levels at once. He can progress in irregular order. The 4-year-old is able to communicate a complex thought (synthesis) while violating rules of syntax (application). Instruction can and sometimes should develop the ability to apply a technique (for example, focusing a microscope) without attempting to promote comprehension of it at a verbal level.

## Fairness

The predominant student demand is that any test be "fair." A test is likely to be seen by students as unfair if the keyed answers do not seem right to them, if some items seem like "catch questions," or if the test does not cover what they expected.

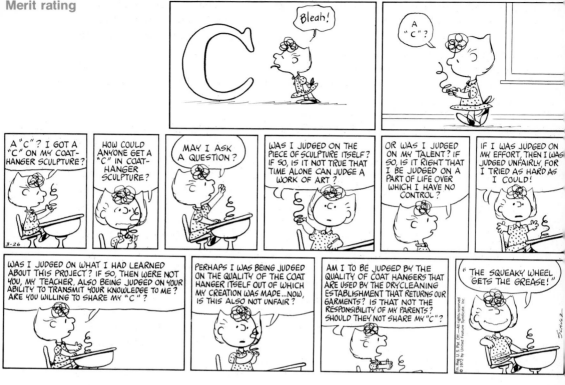

The kind of tension that blocks thinking is increased when teacher and student see the test as a sort of Last Judgment. A certain degree of relaxation on the part of both teacher and student is a great help. Tension is at its highest when merit rating is the center of attention; if the test is for monitoring or program evaluation, disputes over the occasional troublesome item will be brief and mild. A sense of proportion can be encouraged even when merit rating is at issue. One item here or there does not mean much, in a semester's work. And it fades into insignificance if students believe that due assessment is being made of work other than tests.

Teachers use various tactics to reduce the bugaboo of testing. One I find useful is to allow the students to censor items as they take the test. Each student is allowed to "protest" some number of items—say, six in a 30-item test—by circling the number of the item on the answer sheet. (I direct him, however, to attempt to answer the question he has protested.) I state in advance that any item frequently protested—say, by five or more of the students in a class of 35—will not be counted. Before papers are marked, I count up the circles, and remove the items that drew frequent protests. Students protest for many reasons: uncertainty as to meaning, belief that the content was not assigned, belief that the topic is unimportant, and so on. The number of protests allowed and the number required to knock out an item will depend on test length, class size, and other factors. The teacher has to experiment and has to teach students to use the procedure sensibly. In my college classes, few students use as many protests as they are allowed. Rarely are straightforward items protested, not even difficult ones. The few items actually knocked out of the test I, too, usually see as ambiguous or confusing—after the protest has forced me to reconsider them.

Students are especially distressed by what they see as "catch questions." Sometimes the phrase is misapplied to any item requiring subtle analysis, but the complaint is often legitimate. Students properly challenge items such as "The American author F. Scott Fitzgerald wrote *Tender as the Night.* True or false?" (The student who responds "True" is penalized for failing to note the replacement of *is* with *as* in the title.) The teacher can avoid most complaints about catch questions by drafting items around a definite focus, so that the student knows what judgment is the nub of the question. The item above would be much better in this form: "Who wrote *Tender is the Night*—F. Scott Fitzgerald or Ernest Hemingway?" (For more on item writing, see pp. 700ff.)

This brings us once again to the importance of letting the students know what they are to be tested on. Students rarely have the philosophical view of measurement that imbues this book—that detection of errors is necessary for reteaching. Seeing tests as part of merit rating, students believe that they ought to feel inadequate if they cannot answer a test question. Contrast this with the view that the teacher ought to find out how well students can handle situations *not* presented explicitly in their lessons.

Students can be led to see that the material covered by a test is proper and to their benefit. Other steps can be taken to abate the tension. The first is to separate merit rating from other functions of evaluation. Unfamiliar items can be given in the spirit of "Let's try this just to see how you do on new material." Students can understand the significance of transfer testing, and indeed are likely to favor it when the items are highly "relevant." (The exercises in the logic textbook are inevitably out of date—but items illustrating a logical fallacy can be based upon the front page of today's newspaper.) Complaints are reduced just by giving adequate advance notice of the evaluation plan. Specimen test questions of all kinds, including transfer questions, can be placed in an open file for consultation.

FAIRNESS IN MARKING   There is evidence of bias in teachers' marks. In particular, girls often receive marks higher than is warranted by their proficiency. For example, R. Carter (1952) examined the algebra marks given by six experienced teachers in the same high school. As seen in Table 16.2, the boys and girls were much the same on a standardized end-of-semester achievement test. But girls received significantly higher marks than boys. Girls' marks, and marks given by women teachers, had relatively little correlation with achievement. Male teachers graded more rigorously than women. Carter did not find out why the marks were inaccurate, but it is well known that teachers often grade on conduct, neatness, and other matters far removed from course achievement. Any form of credit for docility (for example, credit for consistently prompt and

**TABLE 16.2**

Teacher bias in giving marks in algebra

| Group | IQ Mean | IQ Superiority of girls | Achievement test Mean | Achievement test Superiority of girls | Teacher mark Mean | Teacher mark Superiority of girls | Correlation of marks with achievement |
|---|---|---|---|---|---|---|---|
| Girls taught by men | 109 | | 29.1 | | 79.5 | | 0.57 |
| | | 2.0 | | −1.7 | | + 2.9 | |
| Boys taught by men | 107 | | 30.8 | | 76.6 | | 0.78 |
| Girls taught by women | 107 | | 30.5 | | 86.7 | | 0.35 |
| | | −1.0 | | + 1.0 | | + 4.1 | |
| Boys taught by women | 108 | | 29.5 | | 82.6 | | 0.37 |
| All girls | 108 | | 29.7 | | 82.5 | | 0.45 |
| | | 1.0 | | −0.5 | | + 3.2 | |
| All boys | 107 | | 30.2 | | 79.3 | | 0.59 |

SOURCE: Data from R. Carter (1952).

complete homework) will favor girls. Hess et al. (1969) found no evidence that first- and second-grade teachers overrated girls, but did find that objective achievement agreed well with teachers' reports on boys and poorly with their reports on girls.

A study at the college level (Hartnett & Stewart, 1965) contrasted 144 students whose final examinations were consistently better than the marks assigned by their instructors with 153 whose marks exceeded their test scores. The students that instructors appeared to undervalue averaged much higher on a mental test than the grade-getters. A personality test showed them to be less rigid and conforming.

It is reasonable to employ evaluation procedures to motivate: to define educational goals for the learner, and to provide feedback and encouragement. But this is motivation toward an *educational* outcome. When marks are used to "motivate" students to follow prescribed procedures—punctuality, neat margins, or politeness—they subvert education *and* evaluation. Marks that rest in part on these factors fail to tell the truth about ability. Hence they do not perform the merit-rating function.

**12** Some teachers "allow students to raise their grades" by turning in extra work (for example, an extra book report). Assume that this option is clearly announced and open to all students. Is there any unfairness or invalidity in the procedure?

**13** A psychology department provides an open file of 1000 or more choice-response items for the introductory psychology course, with the understanding that all tests that count in the course mark will consist of items from this set. (The set is brought up to date at the start of each year.) What can be said for and against this procedure?

## Reliability

Any one test is a sample; a student's score on a second sample—on another day and with another set of items—would differ. Chapter 7 discussed how information on error of measurement, published in test manuals, is interpreted. This section explains how teachers may appraise their own tests.

ESTIMATING THE ERROR   The teacher can calculate a standard error of measurement (p. 267) by taking two independent samples of the behavior in question, preferably by administering equivalent test forms on different occasions. One calculates the difference (Form A minus Form B) for each student, and gets its standard deviation (p. 117). If the forms are similar, the mean of the differences will be near zero. The standard deviation of these differences is divided by 1.41 (the square root of 2) to get the standard error of measurement, whose interpretation was discussed in Chapter 7.

If it is not feasible to measure twice, the teacher can learn something by splitting a test, obtaining one score for odd-numbered items and another for even-numbered items. *Multiplying* the standard deviation of differences by 1.41 gives a standard error. Although this tells how much two samples of items disagree, it cannot say anything about how much performance fluctuates from day to day.

The preceding paragraphs consider the standard error for individual scores. In assessing the performance of a class or school, the standard error of the group average is important. If this group were to be retested under similar conditions, how much would the group average shift? To answer this question, the standard error for individuals is divided by the square root of the number of persons in the group.

REDUCING THE ERROR   Lengthening a test improves accuracy. In a test scored by percentage correct, for example, doubling the number of items reduces the standard error by 30 per cent. When the intent is to get an accurate reading on the individual student, fairly extensive testing is necessary. To get an accurate reading on the group, for program evaluation, a short test will suffice. A test of a few items is not a convincing sample of content, however. Matrix sampling solves the problem. In this technique, several short tests are given—one to each of several fractions of the class. For instance, pages of five items each are distributed at random, each student receiving one page. If there are ten different pages, four students in a class of 40 will receive the same questions. Thus, only a few students respond to any one item, but the average score for the class covers a good spread of content. Group performance over many objectives can be assessed efficiently.

14   Matrix sampling is now routinely used in the National Assessment of Educational Progress (p. 68). Assuming that about 40 minutes per student, once each year, is allowable for such an assessment, what is gained by using matrix sampling?

15   It is suggested that a college instructor in economics administer two or three items per student on a matrix-sampling basis at the end of each class hour, checking on topics covered in that day's lecture. How would the benefits compare with the cost in time and trouble?

16   If two forms of a test are given to determine a standard error of measurement, should they be given on the same day? In the same week? In the same month?

# TEST DEVELOPMENT

There are two basic kinds of test items: those offering alternative answers, which can be scored by a key, and those where the person constructs a response that has to be judged. The former includes true-false, multiple-choice, and several other forms. I shall discuss multiple-choice items only and then go on to constructed-response tests.

    The test item is perhaps the most difficult of all literary forms to produce. It has to be almost as brief as a haiku, yet, unlike the haiku, it has to be open to only one interpretation. The ideal item is so clear that even the student who does not know the subject-matter knows what he is being asked. In a choice-response item, the right choice ought to fit so well that even those who selected the wrong answer will agree with the keyed answer when the item is discussed in the next class meeting.

# Can multiple-choice tests elicit high-level thinking?

In the humanities in particular, many instructors have a distrust of objectively scorable test items. The exercise below, from a test used with undergraduates in a humanities course at the University of Chicago, demonstrates the possibility of asking challenging questions in multiple-choice form. The complete exercise quoted a second critic, and after asking questions about each set of comments separately, went on to pose questions about the disparity between their criticisms.

---

DIRECTIONS: The following statements are taken from ... book reviews written at the time of the first publication of *A Farewell to Arms.* . . .

*Critic I*

In its depiction of war, the novel bears comparison with its best predecessors. But it is in the hero's perhaps unethical quitting of the battle line to be with the woman he has gotten with child that it achieves its greatest significance. Love is more maligned in literature than any other emotion, by romantic distortion on the one hand, by carnal diminution on the other. But Author Hemingway knows it at its best to be a blend of desire, serenity, and wordless sympathy. His man     5
and woman stand incoherently together against a shattered, dissolving world. They express their feelings by such superficially trivial things as a joke, a gesture in the night, an endearment as trite as "darling." And as they make their escape from Italy in a rowboat, survey the Alps from their hillside lodgings, move on to Lausanne where there are hospitals, gaze at each other in torment by the deathbed of Catherine, their tiny shapes on the vast landscape are expressive of the     10
pity, beauty, and doom of mankind.

(1) Critic I finds the "significance" of the novel to lie especially in
    A. its account of the psychology of a deserter
    B. its evocation of pity and fear
    C. its representation of the true nature of love
    D. its combination of realistic fatalism and symbolic beauty
(2) In support of this view, Critic I directs attention to certain details in the novel. When he describes the characters' methods of expressing their feelings as "superficially trivial," one understands that he must mean that
    A. these "things" are trivial only on the surface
    B. the characters are mediocre and lacking in depth
    C. the novelist has been deficient in invention
    D. there is a clear, but unimportant, weakness in the diction of the novel
(3) The last sentence of the passage implies that
    A. the human figures are distorted by the romantic setting of the action
    B. the emotions of the characters, being the common experience of all men, are shared by the reader
    C. the particulars of the novel stand for universal propositions about life
    D. the inevitable consequence of errors in conduct is symbolized in the outcome of this action
(4) Consequently, it is apparent that Critic I is judging the novel primarily as
    A. an imitation of life
    B. an interpretation of life
    C. a means to the end of good conduct
    D. an extension of the reader's experience

---

SOURCE: Adapted from Bloom et al. (1971), p. 213.

## Choice-Response Tests

A teacher is sure to draft a faulty item now and then, but he can guard against some mishaps by a careful editorial job. The worst practice is to make up items at the last minute. If you leave items in a drawer for a week you discover faults when you read the items afresh. Having a student work through the test "thinking aloud" is informative. Having another teacher go over the items also locates faults, but this is harder to arrange. It is wise to file items that have been used, after discussing them with the class and editing them to remove unintended sources of confusion. Sprinkled into tests in future years, veteran items will serve better than new ones that have never run the gantlet of student criticism.

PROCEDURAL SUGGESTIONS   A test ought to allow sufficient time for students to attempt all items. In practice, time limitations may require some compromise with this ideal; if the limits could lead to time pressure, items should be arranged roughly in order of difficulty. In reading, speed is a significant outcome; separate speeded and nonspeeded tests are needed to separate reading level from efficiency.

I favor "correction for guessing." If a test contains 40 items, each with four choices, the student who answers every item blindly gets somewhere near ten correct. His true ability on these items is represented by a score of zero, and his ten credits for good guesses ought to be offset by a penalty. We charge him for one-third of his 30 wrong guesses; thus his ten credits are offset by a −10. The rationale is that for every lucky guess there will be three wrong guesses, on the average. In general, if items offer $k$ choices, the scoring formula is

$$\text{Number right} - \frac{\text{Number wrong}}{k-1}.$$

Unless the correction formula is used, the student who takes more chances has an advantage. His advantage is particularly great when others obey an injunction to respond only when confident that their answers are correct. When I give a course examination, I tell students to attempt every item, selecting what seems to be the best answer when uncertain. Some teachers prefer to give "never guess" instructions. Admittedly, guessing brings a random element into scores, but there is no clear line between guessing and partial knowledge. Some students hesitate to respond when slightly uncertain; others, told never to guess, nonetheless mark every item. Even when the formula is used, the student who attempts more items is likely to earn more points, because the correction formula compensates for truly blind guessing only. Intelligent judgment based on partial knowledge produces many right answers (Frary, 1969). Differences among students reflect competence rather than daring if everyone tries every item. (For more on this recommendation, see R. Thorndike, 1971.)

"Testwiseness"—skill in taking tests—undoubtedly affects scores on choice-response tests. Marking every item is just one example of point-getting technique.

# A test of comprehension

Getting the most out of charts and graphs is not limited simply to reading off "25 per cent of the cotton was exported." This task, prepared for use in elementary-school social studies, tests subtle aspects of comprehension and can also be used in teaching.

*Directions:* **Use the following letters to indicate your answer.**

    **A. The statement is supported by the evidence given in the chart.**
    **B. Whether the statement is correct or incorrect cannot be determined by the evidence in the chart.**
    **C. The statement is contradicted by the evidence given in the chart.**

1. **The total farm economy of the United States depends upon exports.**
2. **Percentage-wise, we export more of our rice than any other crop shown above.**
3. **The American farmer would suffer great loss of income if other countries stopped importing our agricultural products.**
4. **The United States consumes about three-fifths of the tobacco produced.**
5. **The graph demonstrates that economic health in the United States depends upon the economic health of the countries that import our products.**
6. **Growers of corn would suffer most from the cessation of exports.**
7. **The United States keeps for its own use over half of the soybeans and wheat grown.**
8. **Americans consume a greater proportion of their cotton than any other agricultural product shown in the above graph.**

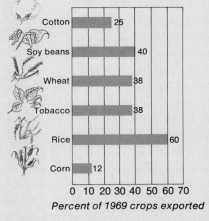

*Percent of 1969 crops exported*

SOURCE: Adapted from *Yearbook of Agriculture* (1970).

SOURCE: Adapted from Morse & McCune, *Selected Items for the Testing of Study Skills and Critical Thinking,* 5th ed. (Arlington, Va.: National Council for the Social Studies, 1971), pp. 46–47. Reproduced by permission; chart somewhat reduced.
The answers are keyed as follows: B,A,B,A,B,C,A,C.

(There are also skills in taking essay tests.) Millman et al. (1965) offer 15 pages of "principles of testwiseness" with examples of their application. These should interest every teacher and student. Millman et al. argue that testwise students exhibit their ability more fully than test-naive students, hence they favor teaching the principles of test taking. Such training is feasible, and it stands to reason that it will improve validity even if (or perhaps because) it makes it harder for the test constructor to fool examinees.

ITEM WRITING  A multiple-choice item consists of a *stem* followed by alternatives. The stem states the topic and the problem. Consider these two stems:

| | |
|---|---|
| **The correction for guessing:** | (Poor) |
| **A chief reason for recommending a correction for guessing is:** | (Good) |

The poorer stem names a topic but does not pose a problem. The second is so pointed that it could be used as it stands as a sentence-completion task.

Stems should be readable *and* to the point. Excess detail and unnecessary words should be cut out. It may be wise to break a long stem into two or more sentences, ending with the incomplete sentence that points the question. This allows the item to describe, for instance, a complex scientific observation, and ask for an explanation. A complex item requires more time than an elementary item (box, p. 701), but it usually is better to ask one significant question than three trivial ones.

A set of items can require students to interpret data about the balance of foreign trade, to predict what will happen in an experiment with plants, to choose among proposed revisions of a paragraph, and so on. Test items that illustrate varied techniques are scattered through the boxes and questions of this chapter.

The alternative answers offered should be genuine alternatives; they should have to do with the same issue and should all seem reasonable to a person who has not studied the material. A useful check is to try out items on beginners; an alternative that no beginner picks is pointless. One good way to generate alternatives for multiple-choice items is to present stems as sentence-completion tasks; the wrong answers provide the alternatives. As a general rule, 3- and 4-choice items are most efficient.

A maxim for editing items is that there should be no *irrelevant* difficulty. The tester should know what competence the item is trying to get at, and should frame the item so that students who possess that competence will choose the answer. Excessive reading demand is perhaps the most prominent source of irrelevant difficulty. A test item should use words and sentences as simple as the theme of the item allows. I suggest this rule of thumb: A student two grades behind the class for which the test is intended should be able to comprehend the question. He will not know the technical terms, of course, and he probably cannot answer correctly.

Some experimental test formats allow instant feedback. Typically, an elaborate, realistic problem is posed, with several questions to be answered in turn. The technique was first applied in testing electronics trainees. The trainee was shown the diagram of a piece of equipment and a report of the malfunction (as in Duncan's task, p. 572). He also had a list of repairs he could recommend, such as replacing this condenser or that transistor, and a list of diagnostic procedures such as finding out if current was reaching a certain junction. He "or-

## Test items need not be dull

> "Psychoanalytical theories suggest that man is essentially a battle-field, he is a dark cellar in which a maiden aunt and a sex-crazed monkey are locked in mortal combat, the affair being refereed by a rather nervous bank clerk."[*]
>
> Consider the Freudian terms (a) id, (b) ego, and (c) superego. To which does each of the following refer?
> (1) maiden aunt
> (2) sex-crazed monkey
> (3) nervous bank clerk

This illustration of the "master-list" test was offered by Hall (1969). An initial list of terms supplies choices for several items. Hall advises the tester to use some terms more than once, and perhaps not to use one of them, so that the student cannot find answers by elimination alone.

[*] D. Bannister, "A New Theory of Personality," in B. M. Foss, ed., *New Horizons in Personality* (New York: Penguin, 1966).

dered" any test he thought pertinent, and received a report (for example, "test lamp glows" or "does not glow"). He could make his final recommendation at any time, or could ask for further diagnostic information. A record was kept of his responses and the order in which he made them. The total performance indicated whether he proceeded systematically, making no irrelevant tests and interpreting symptoms sensibly. The series of questions teaches as well as tests. Ability to do such problems, which call for integrating information and making sequential judgments, has little correlation with success on conventional unconnected multiple-choice items (McGuire & Babbott, 1967).

Rarely will a teacher have the opportunity to use these sequential-response techniques in their most elaborate form, but simple versions can readily be invented where students should deal with complex wholes. Consider a test in comprehension of French, for example. One might have the student read a complete essay, but check his comprehension after each paragraph or two with questions that he scores immediately, a key providing the correct meaning wherever he has gone astray. (Short constructed responses would serve as well as choice-response questions.) With this device, a student can be led through an argument or story far more complex than those included in the usual test.

ITEM ANALYSIS  To detect faults, professional test constructors try out an item before using it in a published test. Statistical analysis of the results picks out many of the faulty items. The teacher can profitably do something similar after a test is given. What he learns about student errors will guide his future teaching, and what he learns about the items will help in revising the items for future use and in developing his test-making skill. The basic technique is to tabulate how many

In a large university, the following item was used as part of an educational psychology examination given to a total of 615 students in various sections (Lange et al., 1967, p. 66).

---

**Motivation is an internal state. Yet we continually talk as though it were a tangible, measurable quality. As a teacher you would most likely be able to best judge the motivation of a particular student by**

A. giving him an intelligence test.

B. having his mother in for a parent-teacher conference.

C. observing his behavior in the classroom and drawing your own conclusions.

D. McClelland's tests of internal motivation.

E. reviewing his past and present academic record.

---

The item analysis gave the response percentages shown below.

|  | Response | | | | | |
|---|---|---|---|---|---|---|
|  | A | B | C | D | E | None |
| Best 27% | 0 | 10 | 63 | 5 | 21 | 1 |
| Poorest 27% | 2 | 9 | 52 | 11 | 26 | 0 |

Dissatisfied with these values, the instructors revised the item as shown below. For the new statistics on the item, see Question 21 on p. 707.

---

**Motivation is an internal state. Yet we continually talk as though it were a tangible, measurable quality. As a teacher you would most likely be able to best judge the motivation of a particular student by**

A. giving him an interest inventory.

B. having him write an autobiography.

C. observing his behavior in the classroom and drawing your own conclusions.

D. McClelland's tests of internal motivation.

E. reviewing his past and present academic record.

---

times each response is given, making separate tallies for the "Highs" (who did well on the test) and the "Lows."

The first result of interest is the information on difficulty. The teacher should think especially about any subtopic for which the items prove to be difficult for the high fraction of the class. The choice-by-choice tally indicates just where difficulty arises. If most of the students who miss an item select one of the alternatives, that is a rather clear signal of a misconception to be removed.

The next matter to consider is the relative success of the Highs and Lows. As the box indicates, it is usual to contrast the highest and lowest fractions of the class. (Disregarding those in the middle saves time and also makes for a clear-cut contrast.) An alternative no one selected may be trivial. An alternative such as *E* (box), which Highs and Lows selected with about the same frequency, ought to be reexamined.

---

**17** Educators formerly spoke of choice-response tests as "recognition" tests, and of constructed-response tests as "recall" tests. Why are those designations not usually appropriate?

**18** Characteristics that parents acquire are not passed to children by heredity. Prepare a choice-response item to measure comprehension of that principle. (Indicate the grade level for which you intend the item.)

**19** Which of these aspects of appreciation of poetry can be measured by a choice-response test?
   a. Knowledge of forms: sonnet, iambic meter, epic
   b. Judgment of the originality and artistic appropriateness of meta-phors
   c. Ability to point out similarities in style among poems
   d. Enjoyment of poems of different types

**20** Which of these two contrasting styles of stem is preferable?

---

**An amphibian is an animal that**
A. **lives in marshes and swamps**
B. **has a spinal column**
C. **can live in both air and water**
D. **has its skeleton on the outside of its body**

**An animal that can live in both air and water is called**
A. **an amphibian**
B. **a crustacean**
C. **a vertebrate**
D. **a reptile**

---

**21** In a large educational psychology class (*N* = 560), the responses of the top and bottom 27 per cent of the class were distributed in the percentages shown below.

| | *Response* | | | | | |
| --- | --- | --- | --- | --- | --- | --- |
| | *A* | *B* | *C* | *D* | *E* | *None* |
| Best 27% | 3 | 21 | 53 | 3 | 20 | 0 |
| Poorest 27% | 5 | 27 | 32 | 9 | 26 | 0 |

What do these statistics suggest about the worth of the item and its improvability? The correct answer was C.

**22** Eighth-graders' understanding of Celsius temperature readings is to be tested. Which of these styles of response alternative is preferable?

A reading of 19°C. equals _____°F. To answer this question, one would calculate:

A. 1.8 (19) + 32    B. $\frac{212}{100}$ (19) + 32    C. $\frac{5}{9}$ (19) + 32

A reading of 19°C. equals

A. 61.4°F.    B. 66.2°F.    C. 91.8°F.    D. 94.6°F.

A reading of 19°C. equals about

A. 30°F.    B. 50°F.    C. 70°F.    D. 90°F.

**23** The statistics given in Question 21 are for the second version of an item whose first and second versions are shown in the box, along with statistics for the first version. Which changes had a good effect? Can you suggest further changes?

## Constructed-Response Tests

Questions that call on the examinee to supply his own words range from completion items, where one word is missing, to assignments that call for several pages of writing. I shall not discuss simple completion items; much of what was said about choice-response items applies. Questions requiring longer answers can be treated together for our purposes. For the average student in Grade VIII or thereabouts, "Give six adjectives that describe Shylock" is not all that different from "Write an essay on Shylock's personality."

Constructed-response questions are a normal part of assignments in most subjects, and the responses provide evaluative information. In formal tests, such questions have advantages and disadvantages.

Consider first the motivational function. Essay questions serve well in this respect. They can be written to emphasize almost any objective. The English teacher, for example, wants the student to develop his own literary taste. He cannot express this in answering choice-response questions to which the teacher will apply a fixed scoring key. An essay question can ask the student to apply his personal standards.

Tests shape activities during study. When items are confined to details, students prepare by cramming on minor points, to the neglect of main ideas and deeper interpretations. College classes that rank highest on a fact-loaded objective test are likely to have average or below-average standings on an essay test measuring reflective understanding and integration (McKeachie, 1959).

The following questions are of kinds used in high-level measurement.

---

**How well did the author of this poem achieve his purpose? Why do you think so?**

---

**Here is a passage that criticizes the American foreign-aid program of the 1950s as wasteful and unnecessary. What information is required to determine whether or not the criticisms are justified?**

---

**This map shows the physical geography of a region, and these diagrams [or better, actual specimens] show the nature of the soil and rocks. What hypotheses about the geographical history of the region seem reasonable?**

---

Similar but simpler questions can be used in elementary grades. An interview or group discussion is often preferable to a written test, unless one requires a numerical score for each individual.

A person solving a problem outside the classroom has sources available; for advanced students especially, the open-book test is realistic. Good open-book questions call for interpretation, not mere look-up. It may be appropriate to set a problem requiring several days of work, in or out of class.

Open-end questions sample topics less thoroughly than choice-response questions do and may not serve the monitoring function well. Since the student selects the content of the response, such a question is not targeted to check on particular misconceptions. Choice response is generally to be preferred for appraising low-level outcomes. Only free responses show why students go wrong in analysis, and expose values and styles. When tests are reviewed in class, open-end questions are most likely to stimulate discussion at a high level.

From a score alone, the student is not likely to understand what he did wrong. The score does little to teach self-evaluation. The teacher's descriptive comment, pointing out where improvement is needed, also shows the student how to judge himself. (For example, on the Shylock item, a list consisting only of unfavorable adjectives misses the depth of Shakespeare's characterization.)

Constructed-response questions are rarely advantageous for merit rating. Scoring them is arduous, subject to bias, and imprecise. The practical advantage is all on the side of choice-response questions.

The fourth function, program evaluation, may require evidence from constructed responses. However, since free responses are awkward to collate into a summary, open-end questions should not be used to assess outcomes for which choice-response questions can serve.

ACCURACY AND UNIQUENESS    The inevitable inaccuracy in grading essays is seen in a report by Swineford (see Coffman, in R. Thorndike, 1971, pp. 280ff.). As the graders followed all the precautions usual in College Board testing, the

## Essay questions for before-and-after testing of critical thinking

Munro (1975, p. 228) offers this pair of questions as "opportunities for pupils to display the attitudes associated with the scientific temper." One can be used at the start of a science course (about Grade IX) and one at the end. Formal scoring rules would be used to obtain scores for soundness of thought and for critical attitude. For program evaluation, the order in some classes might be reversed, just to make sure that question difficulty did not contribute to the pretest-posttest difference.

---

A church in a small town which is built of grey limestone is in good preservation and the stone is unweathered. In a neighbouring town where there are steelworks and mines, the same stone has been used in some of the older buildings, but it has weathered badly. Some reasons which have been put forward to account for the weathering are:

  i   It is caused by rain
  ii  It is caused by soot
  iii It is caused by wind
  iv  It is caused by acid fumes

(a) Very briefly discuss each of these possibilities.
(b) Suggest what you think is a most likely explanation.
(c) How could you test the truth of your explanation?

---

The two northbound lanes of a bridge are paved with the same surface material. The surface on the left-hand lane, nearest the edge of the bridge, is beginning to become worn and pitted. The right-hand northbound lane shows few signs of wear. Some reasons which have been put forward to account for the wear are:

  i   It is caused by exhaust fumes
  ii  It is caused by engine oil
  iii It is caused by the weight of traffic
  iv  It is caused by the speed of the traffic

(a) Very briefly discuss each of these possibilities.
(b) Suggest what you think is a most likely explanation.
(c) How could you test the truth of your explanation?

---

Responses to sections (a) are marked for the ability to analyse data; those for sections (b), for the ability to select or formulate testable hypotheses and sections (c) are scored for the ability to devise experiments to test hypotheses.

scoring was close to the best possible. Even though the scorers were well qualified, they disagreed quite a bit. Also, student scores varied markedly from question to question. The following correlation coefficients indicate the accuracy of measurement on an Advanced Placement Examination in American history:

| Independent scorings for same essay paper (three questions totaled) | about 0.74 |
| Independent scorings for two 135-minute tests, each with three questions | about 0.65 |
| Three essay questions (135 minutes) versus a choice-response test (45 minutes) | about 0.65 |

These essay scores did not agree with each other better than the essay agreed with an objective test. Moreover, each essay exam required 90 additional minutes of testing time and was costly to score. One would like a coefficient close to 0.90 when an important comparative decision, such as admission to college, is being made. Coffman calculates that every student would have to write 15 essay responses (45 minutes each, nearly 12 hours in all) for the score to have that degree of precision.

Do some students show up better on choice-response tests, others on constructed-response tests? In the ranking of individuals, the essay test agreed with the objective test as well as it did with another essay, according to Swineford's data. Research in mathematics, science, and language supports much the same conclusion. Note this point, however: Tests that agree in ranking individuals may not tell the same story about the level of class accomplishments.

Swineford's correlation of 0.65 for individual history scores is fairly typical. All such correlations are held down by inconsistency in scoring. If we were to obtain "true" marks for the essay questions by having each response scored by many scorers, then the two three-question tests would correlate 0.87 (estimated), and the essay score would correlate 0.74 with the objective test. Though the two types of test agree well, they do not fully coincide in what they measure. The disparity arises partly because qualities such as grammar and spelling enter the score even when graders are urged to judge content only (J. C. Marshall & J. M. Powers, 1969). Those qualities are not relevant to merit in history.

RECOMMENDATIONS    Most course examinations should include constructed-response questions along with choice-response questions. This capitalizes on the value of constructed-response questions in pointing the student toward more reflective study. But if a choice-response test can assess learning of a particular kind, the student should not be asked to construct a response. The time saved in test construction does not offset the excess time taken for marking.

Constructed-response questions can be much more valid than they usually are (Diederich & Link, 1967; Coffman, in R. L. Thorndike, 1971, pp. 285ff.). One principle is to make the question explicit:

---
**Discuss the causes of World War II.**

---

What is wanted? One student thinks it wise to list all the events that had any effect on the war. Another mentions two or three causes and tells why he thinks them

**Essay question**

important. One writes about the years just before the war; another goes back 20 years. Some students cover economic pressures; some stress political and diplomatic maneuvers from Munich to the invasion of Poland.

A discussion question ought to indicate both the content to be covered and the form or style wanted. This gives the student a chance to satisfy the grader and makes it more likely that scorers will agree. To assess understanding of the roots of World War II, one can pose this task:

> **State four continuing economic or political problems on which the aims of the German and French governments differed. Consider the time span from 1925 to 1939. Tell what each government desired.**

Such a clear statement as to what is important makes it more likely that scorers will agree.

The merits of the following marking procedures should be obvious.

- Judge papers without knowing who wrote them.

- Score Question 1 on every paper before reading Question 2, and so on. For Question 2, take up the papers in a different order (and without looking at the score given on Question 1).

- Exchange papers among members of a department, so that no teacher marks papers of his own class.

- Choose a few responses of varying quality in advance, have teachers assign a mark to each in conference, and provide copies of each paper for all graders to use as a common reference scale.

- Prepare an explicit guide for allocation of credit. For example:

  Full credit will be allowed if the student mentions four of the following five points.
  Out of 20 points for the question, 0 to 3 points will be given for organization.

The procedures taken together are excessively elaborate and are not to be followed literally. Once aware of the sources of bias these precautions guard against, the teacher will use his own devices to avoid them when grading essays.

Comparing students on a numerical scale is not the significant aim in using discussion questions. If nothing is desired but a grade, the short-answer test is likely to serve much better. The payoff from the elaborate constructed response is in the descriptive information it provides (and the motivational effect). To know that Albert's writing style is conventional and colorless, that his generalizations are cautious and qualified, that he sees a problem in a very narrow context, and so on—these findings are ripe with suggestions for Albert and his teacher. Albert needs to be freed to experiment with metaphor. He should be encouraged to make vigorous, sweeping statements. If his inhibitions can be relaxed, he will hereafter be able to choose between a forceful and a qualified style, suiting his subject-matter and his audience. For many characteristics revealed by the essay, any rating of merit is arbitrary. Who can say that a "light" style is better than a weighty style? that sensitivity to political problems is more creditable than sensitivity to economic implications? that a pessimistic conclusion is wiser than a cheerful one? Yet these preferences, habits, and blind spots are educationally significant, and, with proper written or oral feedback, the teacher's review helps the student understand himself.

24 English teachers emphasize different qualities in marking a paper. No doubt each teacher has his own view of what to stress in teaching. Are discrepancies in marking then to be regarded as "errors of measurement"? As "unfair" to the student whose style would be graded higher by teachers other than his own? Should teachers in a department agree to a single basis for grading?

25 When an essay is to be used to obtain qualitative information rather than a numerical score, which of the recommendations given in this section are pertinent?

## Performance Observation

Observing the student at work is often the natural way to collect information. On the athletic field, in the library, behind the wheel, in the shop, or in the classroom where practice teaching is taking place, the student goes about the task for which he is being trained. Instead of observing work on ordinary assignments and practice, one can devise "performance tests." Observation of everyday work may not be sufficiently analytic. Recall how Lindahl modified disk-cutting machinery (p. 402). The tracing of movements helped the worker (and his instructor) understand what he was doing wrong. A standardized artificial task is set up when accurate comparison is desired—for showing the student his progress, for merit rating, or for program evaluation. When it is impractical to observe the work, one can evaluate the product: a specimen of handwriting, a poem, or a broom holder made in the shop.

## Have students learned to speak out on public issues?

The National Assessment of Educational Progress periodically surveys how adequately persons are educated in various areas (p. 68). The assessment in citizenship reported in 1970 used a matrix-sampling plan (p. 700) to check on many kinds of knowledge and performance. One objective of instruction is that students learn to "communicate honestly with others, willingly expressing their own views even on controversial issues."

The procedure at ages 13 and 17 was to bring ten persons together in a classroom and let each one draw a slip of paper on which a controversial issue was described. For example: "Should the police be able to listen in on telephone calls in order to catch lawbreakers?" "Should the owner of a house have the right not to rent to someone just because the person is black?"

The student had a minute to think whether he would or would not speak on the issue he drew; a count was made of those who raised their hands to volunteer. Then at least five students had time to say what they thought. After each student spoke, there was an opportunity for the listeners to raise their hands to volunteer a contrary opinion, and some of these opinions were heard. The nationwide results were as follows:

|  | Age 13 | Age 17 |
|---|---|---|
| Initially volunteered to speak (raised hand after looking over the slip drawn) | 42% | 56% |
| Volunteered at least one contrary opinion after another student spoke | 63% | 31% |
| Volunteered to speak at either first or second opportunity | 69% | 62% |

SOURCE: National Assessment (1970), p. 69.

Chapter 10 had much to say about the contribution the instructor's observations can make to the learning of motor skills. Here I illustrate the kind of feedback possible in art. The content is different, but the principles are the same: Teach the criteria of good performance and show what to do to improve. Brent Wilson (in Bloom et al., 1971, p. 555) quotes a forceful but supportive instructor to illustrate the point:

> Actually, I think you have a very good start. The use of reds in both the head and the guitar help pull together the opposing art styles, as does the repeat of brown and yellow in both sides of the painting. The pencil shading in the head is good and could be left as is. It forms a nice contrast with the paint. It would also be a good idea to leave charcoaling along the edge of the pitcher, and in the neck of the guitar, because it turns the charcoaling into an integrating force.
>
> There are a couple of things I want you to work on now. The area below the chin of the king's head is very unclear. Think about it for a while before doing anything else to it. How can you integrate this one part with the rest of the painting and define it at the same time?
>
> You have two different paint consistencies here too. The guitar's red is very strong and thick, but the red in the man's face is watery and lacking force. Try

## Proficiency in cooperative work

The Russell Sage Social Relations Test was given in two classrooms. One group of students (Browning) had been taught in a conservative manner, with a set curriculum, individual recitation, and a large degree of teacher dominance. The other class (Conrad) had been accustomed to group work.

### Browning

This group was marked by the greatest tension and competition, the greatest rigidity of group structure, and the highest proportion of nonparticipants. Planning was hasty, with little interplay among participants. Once building began, a division of the class into three groups quickly emerged: a small central ring of builders, an outer ring who watched, and a remaining group of children who were completely excluded. At no time during the session were there any girls in the central group and few were in the ring of watchers. The building activity was accompanied by much bickering, tension release in the form of shouting, and a preoccupation among principal performers with claiming major credit for the accomplishment. ("I did most of it, with Harry"; "You did it, but I had to fix it.") The children completed the second construction accurately, but were not able to complete the first within the time limit.

### Conrad

The performance of the Conrad children had the qualities of an effective group effort, carried through with considerable *esprit de corps*. Planning was vigorous and relevant; building was self-propelled, effective, and technically accurate.

There were central, active figures here, as in the other schools, but less active members were also involved in the general effort. All the children found roles—some to analyze and communicate about patterns, some to spot the current needs, some to build. The general mood was less tense and competitive than in the other schools. The group saw itself as a working unit, dependent on the cooperative efforts of all members. Furthermore, they accepted the responsibility for reviewing their own work and finding their errors; they conducted a systematic check of the correspondence between their construction and the model before declaring it finished. They completed both models accurately within the time limits.

The spontaneous activity which followed completion of the second construction bears mention. The children re-formed the test blocks to fashion the figure of a man, likened it to George Washington, and finished by adding a "wig" which they shaped out of cotton lying on a nearby shelf. The activity was characterized, as was most of the session, by a sense of productive autonomy, a flow of ideas that built on each other, harmonious relations among the children, and general pleasure in what they were doing.

The differences among these groups, while not expressed in quantitative form, are striking enough to indicate that group functioning and group problem solving constitute a completely distinct dimension of school impact.

The Browning students had been dominated by the teacher, not very warmly. The Conrad group, somewhat smaller, had been taught supportively and flexibly, with activities that left much responsibility to the child. Tested *individually,* the Browning students were distinctly superior to the Conrad students on a standardized achievement test and somewhat inferior on a block-design test that measured fluid ability.

 SOURCE: Minuchin et al. (1969), pp. 204–05. See also my pp. 82–83.

keeping all your paint the same consistency. If you want lighter red, mix white with the red instead of adding water.

You should also start thinking about a background color. Do you want to leave it white? Try to be very consistent in your use of color—keep it strong as in the guitar. The washed-out brown is very weak.

Performance tests can be designed even for socioemotional development. The Russell Sage Social Relations Test (Damrin, 1954) asks a class to build a house according to a pattern, using variously shaped pieces. Each child is handed a piece or two. After stating the task, the teacher or examiner retires to the sidelines and leaves the students to work. Classes differ. Some decide early that they need to organize their efforts, name a chairman, and have him systematically call for pieces as they are needed. Some classes break into competitive clusters, each cluster trying to beat the others by somehow fitting its random handful of pieces together. Some classes remain lost and aimless without the teacher. Inefficient social behavior is not confined to the young; some adult

## FIGURE 16.2

**Evaluation form for sociodramatic play of preschool children**

| Behavior | Not at all | A little | Medium amount | A lot | Specify: roles, objects, situation, roles child interacts with |
|---|---|---|---|---|---|
| 1. Make-believe<br>a. Manipulation of toys | | | | | |
| b. Using toys to enact roles | | | | | |
| c. Using "nothing" to enact roles | | | | | |
| d. Using props to enact roles | | | | | |
| 2. Imitative play<br>a. Actions | | | | | |
| b. Roles | | | | | |
| c. Situations | | | | | |
| 3. Persistence within a role (specify approx. time) | | | | | |
| 4. Interaction<br>a. Nonverbal | | | | | |
| b. Verbal | | | | | |

Comments:

SOURCE: After Kamii, in Bloom et al. (1971), p. 328. Reduced.

groups take longer than children to build the house, because every person is thinking about his individual contribution.

From many points of view, the performance sample is an ideal basis for evaluation. It embodies the main objective and so has the best possible motivating effect. A poor merit rating based on performance is easier to accept as fair than a poor rating from a written test. And it puts proof-of-the-pudding evidence at the disposal of program evaluation.

Where discriminations, timing, and motor coordination are relevant, observations give sounder evidence than pencil-and-paper tests. On a written test regarding repair of machinery, the high scorers are more often workers with superior verbal ability than workers superior at the bench (Stuit, 1947, p. 307).

Even when observations are informal and the situation is not standardized, the observer needs a clear idea of what to look for and record. Kamii uses the grid of Fig. 16.2 as an observer's guide and record sheet. The preschool child who is observed may be playing spontaneously or pursuing a theme someone has suggested. Interpretation can be subtle. Kamii points out that using "nothing" as a thematic prop—"driving a car" without using something resembling a car—evidences more powerful imagery than acting *with* a prop. Likewise, taking a role—Daddy driving the car to take a sick child to the hospital—is an advance over simply turning the wheel of the car.

---

**26** The Russell Sage test (box, p. 716) measures the behavior of the group, not of the individual. In what sense is change in the behavior of a particular group an objective of instruction?

**27** The "speak out" task (box, p. 715) is a way of getting information on typical behavior and, indirectly, on student confidence and concern.
   a. Do you consider this an appropriate objective against which to judge the adequacy of education in citizenship?
   b. Could a classroom teacher make good use of this procedure?
   c. For which functions of evaluation would it be appropriate to consider performance of this kind in evaluating individual students?

---

# CONTENT-REFERENCED SCALES FOR REPORTING PERFORMANCE

Observations often have to be compressed into a number, but the educator does not have units such as pounds and meters. Raw test scores are not very satisfactory because they depend on the choice of items and the marking standards. A report in the school file that Fred scored 33 in English usage is altogether uninterpretable. If the report is converted to, say, 82 per cent, it still conveys little—until one inspects the test from which the number is derived.

For these reasons the raw score is often translated into a comparative report (p. 269 and p. 726). Illustrations of such *norm-referenced* interpretations are:

Fred is at the national 40th percentile for his grade.

Fred performs at the fifth-grade level.

Fred is at the median for this school.

The alternative is a "content-referenced"* interpretation. Content reference points to a scale of easy-to-hard tasks or a scale of lenient-to-demanding quality standards. Content scales take many forms, and the inference from the raw test score may be direct or indirect. Consider these estimates of proficiency:

Mark throws a football 50 feet; Angela throws it 46 feet.

Matt can spell 74 per cent of the six thousand words most used in business correspondence.

The football test presents a single task, and the raw-score scale itself describes the performance adequately. To establish the spelling scale, someone had to prepare a standard word list. If Matt was tested on representative words, the percentage score directly indicates his ability to handle the content. The information might be obtained indirectly. A score of 88 on an easy test might be converted (by a prepared table) to the report that the student can spell 74 per cent of the master list.

The spelling scale may describe the level of difficulty the student can handle, the levels being represented by specimen words:

---

LEVEL C: prepare, counter, profit

LEVEL F: committee, metaphor, precede

LEVEL J: exchequer, munificent, basilisk

---

When it is reported that Agnes can spell most Level F words, the reader can refer to the scale to decide whether this is good enough. The level of spelling good enough for learning shorthand may be fine also for a job as clerk-typist, but not nearly good enough for a court reporter.

A content-referenced scale or a checklist of subskills can be employed as a report card (see Fig. 16.3).

It is comparatively difficult to "check off" mastery of intellectual achievements that develop gradually. In trying to record the student's success in detecting

---

* Educators also use the term *criterion-referenced*. Some distinction can be made between them (Cronbach, in R. L. Thorndike, 1970, p. 85), the term *criterion* being pertinent in military training, where studies of such interpretations originated.

FIGURE 16.3

A report card based on content-referenced measurement in Grade II mathematics

| Skill | Date |
|---|---|
| **Concepts** | |
| Understands commutative property of addition (e.g., 4 + 3 = 3 + 4) | 9/27 |
| Understands place value (e.g., 27 = 2 tens + 7 ones) | 10/3 |
| **Addition** | |
| Supplies missing addend under 10 (e.g., 3 + ? = 5) | 10/8 |
| Adds three single-digit numbers | _____ |
| Knows combinations 10 through 19 | _____ |
| *Adds two 2-digit numbers without carrying | _____ |
| *Adds two 2-digit numbers with carrying | _____ |
| **Subtraction** | |
| Knows combinations through 9 | 10/4 |
| *Supplies missing subtrahend—under 10 (e.g., 6 − ? = 1) | _____ |
| *Supplies missing minuend—under 10 (e.g., ? − 3 = 4) | _____ |
| *Knows combinations 10 through 19 | _____ |
| *Subtracts two 2-digit numbers without borrowing | _____ |
| **Measurement** | |
| Reads and draws clocks (up to quarter hour) | _____ |
| Understands dollar value of money (coins up to $1.00 total) | _____ |
| **Geometry** | |
| Understands symmetry | _____ |
| Recognizes congruent plane figures—that is, figures which are identical except for orientation | _____ |
| **Graph reading** | |
| *Knows how to construct simple graphs | _____ |
| *Knows how to read simple graphs | _____ |

*In Jefferson Elementary School, these skills are usually learned toward the end of grade two. Some children who need more than average time to learn mathematics may not show proficiency on tests of these skills until they are in grade three.

SOURCE: Adapted from Millman (1970), p. 228. Reproduced by permission.

particular fallacies in propaganda, a proper description would have to recognize that he rejects such-and-such a logical trap 60 per cent of the time, not that he has achieved immunity to that particular appeal. Note also that a content-referenced report makes most sense when the measure is confined to a single integrated performance. A scale of quality is much more sensible for handwriting than for punctuation. Excellence in writing short stories would embrace so many kinds of performance that a scale would be useless. One *could* check off subskills: ability to find an intriguing opening, for example.

**28** Among the examples of content-referenced measurement given above, which is most similar to each of the following?

    a. The standard eye chart with type ranging from large to small, which gives a report such as "20/40 vision," meaning that the person can read at 20 feet what normal eyes read at 40.

    b. Typing tests that report scores for typing nontechnical material in words per minute. (Disregard the usual penalty for errors.)

    c. A rating scale for judging muffins baked in a cooking class that identifies several levels of quality, the highest of which is "Uniform, moist, breaks raggedly with a fork; lightly browned on top." Intermediate and lower levels would have poorer texture and, at the extreme, might be underdone or otherwise inedible.

**29** If a set of content-referenced scales for mastery of Russian were set up, there could be one for Russian-into-English vocabulary, one for English-into-Russian vocabulary, one for spelling words from dictation, and so on. Assuming that scales are applied monthly to help college students chart their progress, how many separate scales would be advisable?

# EVALUATION PLANS

Let us now put the teacher's evaluation activities in context. Evaluation has two faces: the forward-looking attempt to judge what instruction a student or a class should next receive, and the backward-looking attempt to sum up experience. The first is formative, the latter summative.

## Formative Evaluation

The forward-looking activities, an intimate part of the instruction, ought to continue from the first day of the year to the last. They should be concerned with the micro-objectives of particular lessons and with the gradual social, emotional, and intellectual development of the student.

TESTS AS AN ADMINISTRATIVE DEVICE IN MASTERY LEARNING  Many of today's systems for flexible instruction rely on formal tests to regulate lessons (p. 384). The tests are given when appropriate for the student, not on a fixed schedule. Thus, an arithmetic course may have a unit on reading decimal fractions, followed by one on adding them. A student does the worksheets on the first unit with the help of his teacher, and if he is having considerable difficulty, the teacher gives him extra lesson material. Two other students go straight through the worksheets; when they finish, they are handed a content-referenced test. One student will do well enough to move to the second unit; the other perhaps does less well and is assigned review tasks, aiming toward a second test on the unit a few days later. After a few weeks, the students are spaced over several units, each following a prescribed review or moving on to a fresh unit once a test has certified his mastery of the prerequisites.

The mastery plan is highly structured. According to one of the advocates of the method (J. H. Block, 1971, pp. 64ff.), it is suitable primarily when the subject-matter is sequential or hierarchical (p. 532) so that good knowledge of one unit is the foundation for later ones. (Chemistry is more likely to be sequential in this sense than literature or sociology.) Second, the subject-matter to be taught should be "closed"—a definite body of content with well-defined right answers. (The plan, therefore, does not apply to developmental objectives, such as self-expression or ability to draw conclusions from experiments. Progress along these lines is gradual; the curriculum-maker cannot chop out distinct stages for the student to "master" one by one.) Third, Block advises using the procedure for courses where all students begin at the beginning. In ninth-grade algebra, the first lessons are new to everyone, even though some students have superior readiness. In eighth-grade arithmetic, however, the students start with some command of most of the subskills to be used, and each is making gradual progress in consolidating his subskills. This kind of broad-front learning also is hard to break into segments.

EVALUATION OF INDIVIDUALIZED ACTIVITIES    Flexible testing can be used in informal curricula. The ISIS science program consists of dozens of units among which the student can select. Each unit comes with an evaluation plan; the student is to prepare an exhibit (for example, showing the parts of a flower), take a test, or be interviewed by the teacher. The student presents himself for evaluation when he feels ready (box). The teacher, of course, ought to guide the student to choose a unit appropriate for him, and will have to press the laggard to come in for evaluation.

Where students pursue independent projects, as well as in classrooms where everyone stays in step, there ought to be continuous evaluation. The teacher need not wait until the term paper is complete to evaluate it. If he does, he and the student lose all the benefits of monitoring. The teacher can monitor artistic activities as they proceed (p. 715) and learn about work habits and about stumbling blocks that might not be detected in end-of-unit evaluation.

FORMATIVE USE OF INFORMATION    Information should be integrated into a value judgment and a plan for action. A low score in arithmetic might by itself seem to say that immediate concentration on that subject is urgently required. Seeing

# Resolving the marking problem
# in a flexible course

Allen D. Dawson (1975) recounts his practices in teaching a semester-long course in ninth-grade science using minicourses from ISIS (Individualized Science Instructional System):

I let my students choose [as an initial unit] either the *Buying and Selling* or the *Things That Last* minicourse. I chose those two because they're very different. The former is less laboratory oriented and requires few materials. The latter is full of science laboratory work. Thus both science-prone and nonscience-prone students could begin with something that quickly caught their interest. . . . They were then directed to go to work either in teams of two or as individuals.

The management of materials was less difficult than I had imagined. This was probably helped by student monitors and cleanup teams, which were rotated weekly. I also numbered each of the minicourse booklets and recorded the number for each student. Part of each student's responsibility was to notify me immediately if his or her booklet was missing. To date, I've lost three booklets and no more supplies than I did in my traditional science classrooms.

The management of materials became more complicated after several students had completed their first minicourse. At that point, they were allowed to select any one of the other twelve titles available in the classroom. One class ended up by working on nine different minicourses at the same time. Instead of chaos, things went along rather smoothly. Because of differences in self-pacing and minicourse selection, I always seemed to have enough time to stay ahead of the game and still work with individual students encountering problems. I found that I could handle all of the evaluation and management tasks without putting in any more time than I had in my traditional classes. One of the reasons for this is that the program provided the daily lesson plans and tests that I had previously had to design myself.

With few exceptions, student self-pacing worked well. At the start, I told my students that each minicourse should be completed in two to three weeks and that three must be completed within the ten-week marking period to qualify for a grade of C or better. However, completing three or more minicourses did not guarantee a passing grade. Only the total points earned on all minicourses determined the final achievement grade. With these guidelines and a few progress reports to parents on foot-dragging individuals, the students worked at least as well as students in my group-centered classes.

Grading is subjective and messy in any classroom. In my ISIS classes, grades were based on a point system with a required project and notebook for each minicourse worth fifty points each. The notebook was to contain self-explanatory answers to core and completed excursion self-check questions. At least two excursions were required. In addition, the notebook was to contain simple answers to questions for any activities completed by the student. Test percentage scores were added in as points to determine the student's final ten-week grade. A set scale was used to assign grades. Although I had my doubts about using a set scale, it worked out rather well. Students were not required to repeat a minicourse if they failed the test, but I have not ruled out this possibility for future use.

The large majority of my students whom I had graded on group-centered work in the first ten weeks of the fall semester either maintained or improved their earlier grades. One pleasant surprise was that most of the improvement came from students in the lower ability range.

this fact in relation to others, the teacher might conclude that, because the student is at this time making rapid strides toward gaining acceptance by the group, playfulness during the arithmetic period is, for the moment, more important. A very fine drawing might in one child be something to encourage without reservation; in another child, the teacher would wonder about a one-sided interest. Persistence is normally healthy—but when a usually perfectionist student gives up on some half-done project, he may be seeing his efforts in better perspective. Ruth Munroe tells of the college teacher who had the good sense to congratulate one overcontrolled girl on "attaining a little confusion" in one of her papers. Similarly, an elementary teacher set down the following plan for an excessively inhibited girl:

> One of the goals for Yvonne is to get her to relax and have a little more fun in life. Therefore, I decided to seat her in a rather lively social setting. At first she resisted the temptations all about her, but slowly she has loosened up a bit and once or twice I have watched her pass a note or whisper (rather self-consciously). When she notices me watching her she looks very guilty and waits for my reaction. She seems to be waiting for some censure but I have been merely smiling and letting her enjoy some of the social goings on in the classroom. (P. Sears, 1957, p. 324.)

Much of the evaluation the teacher keeps to himself. Barry is offered a book in which he can get the facts about airplanes the group needs for its project; the teacher need not mention that the task was chosen to increase his interest in reading. Paul is asked to work with the teacher in arranging the class visit to the newspaper office—without any open statement that evaluation showed that he needed to feel accepted by adults.

## Summative Evaluation of Student and Program

Periodic comprehensive tests of generalized abilities will remain useful. A student who works through units on compound sentences may not retain all that was essential. A student who works enthusiastically on a large number of science units may somehow escape those that would teach him to organize and make sense of experimental data (box, p. 726). So some survey of each student's broad educational development is called for.

Tests given at the end of the course ought rarely to be the prime means for carrying out a backward-looking evaluation. When tests are elevated into the one important index of accomplishment, they distort the learning process. The student crams for the final examination because he wants his record to be unrepresentative of his learning during the semester. The test under these circumstances is not particularly valid. Information loaded aboard at the last minute is likely to be poorly integrated, and if so it will not be retrievable after the test is past. Performance under do-or-die pressure, moreover, is not often optimum. The test ought to be no more than a way of judging formally what has been judged informally all along. Periodic, low-pressure evaluation gives the truest picture of attainment.

The typical end-of-course examination loses the main educative values of an evaluation procedure. It sets no goals for future learning; the student puts the course behind him when he turns in the test paper. It does not guide re-teaching. It gives no diagnostic report to augment self-knowledge; the student never sees his paper, never tries to determine what his grade means. Such tests tend to hold all students to the same standard. Everyone is asked the same questions, which implies that each student is expected to perform the same tasks as everyone else. This negates all the high-sounding principles about setting goals in line with individual readiness and enhancing everyone's self-respect.

When the teacher takes full advantage of the information flowing in from daily and weekly activities, the tensions and distortions occasioned by back-ward-looking, merit-rating evaluations are much reduced. Students have seen continuous evidence of their progress relative to their own starting point and they know the teacher is taking this into consideration in the final judgment of merit. Where the system permits the final report to be multidimensional or de-scriptive rather than a single score or letter grade, the student is even better able to accept a systematic assessment.

STANDARDIZED TESTS   Research at the turn of the century showed that perfor-mance standards in different schools were not comparable. For superintendents pressed by their school boards to report what the school system was accom-plishing, the solution was the standardized test. Such a test covers whatever content schools typically teach in a particular subject and grade level. The test is tried out in a sample of schools, and tables of norms summarize performance in these representative schools.

No test can cover every outcome, and a test that fits the common denomi-nator of curricula will rarely fit the curriculum of any one school. Because they are to be administered on a large scale, standardized tests generally use the choice-response format. Widely accepted outcomes that cannot fit into the choice format are left out. In mathematics and language, schools accept much the same goals and there is strong public interest in comparative data. The published test is well prepared and probably does a better job than a home-made one. A published test that attempts to cover elementary science or social studies is much less likely to match the local curriculum.

Standardized tests have a limited role in evaluation. If they influence the teacher's distribution of effort, they very likely persuade him to spend his time on the commonplace outcomes. They do not encourage imaginative extension of the curriculum or adaptation to local concerns. Administered only once or twice a year and global in outlook, they do not help in detailed planning of les-sons. In merit rating, they can supplement other information primarily in sub-jects such as mechanics of English expression, for which schools have much the same objectives. In program evaluation (for which they were originally in-vented), they should play their role in tandem with program-specific measures.

These tests, with their norms, are probably more useful in "needs assess-ment" than in after-the-fact evaluation. Given early in the year, they provide

## Interpreting experimental data

Burmester (1951) developed several tests measuring the ability of college freshmen to reason scientifically. The set of items below is a portion of the test on ability to interpret data; the actual test had about twice as many questions as this chart, and others covering other types of research.

---

This test was designed to measure your ability to interpret data. Following the data you will find a number of statements. You are to assume that the data as presented are true. Evaluate each statement according to the following key. . . .

A. **True:** The data alone are sufficient to show that the statement is true.

B. **Probably true:** The data indicate that the statement or hypothesis may be correct, that it is logical on the basis of the data but the data are not sufficient to say that it is definitely true.

C. **Insufficient evidence:** There are no data to indicate whether or not the statement is true.

D. **Probably false:** The data indicate that the statement or hypothesis is probably false, that is, it is not logical on the basis of the data but the data are not sufficient to say that it is definitely wrong.

E. **False:** The data alone are sufficient to show that the statement or hypothesis is incorrect.

The questions refer to the graph. Use the key above to answer the items. The lizard is considered to be cold-blooded, the others warm-blooded.

1. When the external temperature is 50°C., the temperature of the lizard is also 50°C.
2. The body temperature of warm-blooded animals is unaffected by the external temperature.
3. At an external temperature of 50°C., the temperature of the cat is 50°C.

---

information on the readiness of individual students and give the teacher a general sense of what program he can expect to carry out successfully. It will be recalled that the Iowa Test of Work-Study Skills was described (p. 261) as a measure of readiness. It is a standardized test measuring how far students have progressed toward an educational outcome, and it can be used at either the beginning or the end of the year.

USE AND MISUSE OF NORMS IN PROGRAM EVALUATION  The norms for a published test ought to be representative of a significant population of schools and students. The better current tests conscientiously sample school systems, but not all nationally published tests have good norms. It is not unknown for two

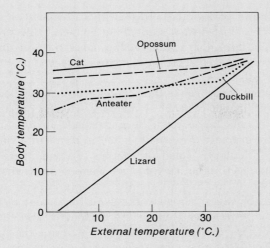

4. When the external temperature is 50°C., the temperature of the anteater would be higher than the temperature of the cat.
5. The temperature of a mouse would be about halfway between that
   of the cat and the anteater.
6. The ability of the cat to maintain its temperature is due to its coat
   of hair.
7. There is a close correlation between the body temperature of the
   lizard and that of the external environment.
8. Warm-blooded animals can withstand cold better than cold-
   blooded animals.
9. If the temperature of other cold-blooded animals were plotted, it
   would resemble that of the lizard.

SOURCE: Abridged from Burmester (1951; copyright 1953). Reproduced by permission, with minor editorial changes, including some suggested by Leo Klopfer.

reading tests to draw their samples differently, so that a class averaging above the national norm on one test is below the norm on the other (Millman & Lind-lof, 1964). Norms for all kinds of schools mixed together are uninformative. A suburban school will not learn much by comparing itself against norms unless they are norms for suburban schools. It makes little sense for a school whose enrollment includes many children of migrant workers to try to match the national norm. Yet norms for such separate kinds of community are rarely available.

Bringing norms into the interpretation is often confusing. "The schools in Mixville are ahead of the national average," the superintendent reports cheerfully. But that is perhaps not to the school's credit if the system draws students with a superior home background. Moreover, too many of the hearers will think that the norm indicates what students in a given grade *ought* to be accomplishing. Few people think that today's national norm in reading or mathematics is at a satisfactory level. Norms are a historical record of what schools have been doing, not an ideal.

When the annual report ranks the schools within Mixville, and shows that Coyote Park is seventh out of eight elementary schools, public complaints are inevitable. This sign of "inadequacy" is misleading. In the first place, differences among school averages are usually small in terms of a content-referenced scale; the ranking dramatizes small differences. Second, there is no adequate way to adjust for the fact that in Coyote Park there is much absenteeism arising from sickness or family indifference, or that Coyote Park drew an exceptional number of children of migrant farm workers. Further, some of the schools may have put on a drive to improve reading and arithmetic, and consequently their average is good in those subjects. An evaluation covering the whole curriculum would possibly show that they are neglecting some educational aims where Coyote Park is strong.

How reference data help in evaluating a system, and some of the cautions necessary in making interpretations, can be illustrated with a report from the California Assessment Program (Fig. 16.4). The California legislature, wanting information on progress and problems, has required that every sixth-grader be given a test.* The annual report for 1975 displays the findings for consecutive years. (There were companion charts in three other subjects, and charts for certain other grades.) The median sixth-grader in California reads as well as the 48th percentile in the publisher's national sample, up from 44th percentile in 1973–1974. The same slight rise appears at the one-quarter mark of the distribution, reversing a drop from 1969 to 1974. This drop may seem trivial—it amounts to only about two raw-score points—but even a small shift may reflect a distressing trend. The trend had aroused added concern because scores in Grade II were creeping *up* over the same period, and reading scores in Grade III had held level. Reading instruction was perhaps being neglected in California's upper-elementary schools.

The trend might spring from several causes, and hence it cannot by itself yield a single conclusion. Students migrate into California, and it is possible that their primary training was comparatively poor on the average. Perhaps California has a more liberal promotion policy than other states, so that poor readers reach Grade VI more rapidly in California. Finally, the proportion of urban schools is large and increasing in California, and urban norms tend to be low. If the national norms were divided so that schools in like communities could be compared, California might look better. But the fact remains: California legislators want their schools to be superior to the national norm, and in 1970–1975 they were not, according to these tests.

---

* Currently, the report is generated by matrix sampling rather than by giving a single uniform test, 1974–1975.

## FIGURE 16.4

### Results in California statewide reading tests for Grade VI in six successive years

Broken horizontal lines represent distribution of scores in a national sample (tested when the test was being developed, in the late 1960s). The shaded area locates the central half of the California distribution in each year. The double line shows the California median.

| Year administered | 1969-70 | 1970-71 | 1971-72 | 1972-73 | 1973-74 | 1974-75 |
|---|---|---|---|---|---|---|
| Number of pupils tested | 328,754 | 333,734 | 341,035 | 342,946 | 336,054 | 201,723 |

**A.** Interquartile ranges (25th, 50th, and 75th percentile scores) compared to publishers' norms

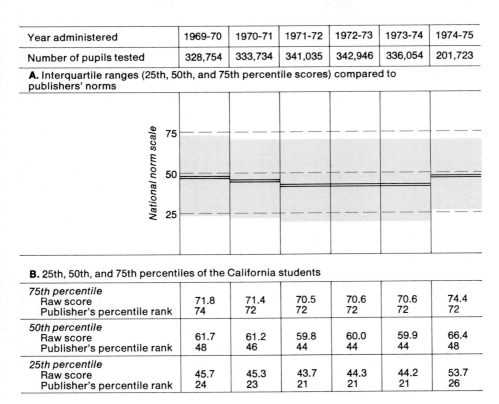

**B.** 25th, 50th, and 75th percentiles of the California students

| | | | | | | |
|---|---|---|---|---|---|---|
| **75th percentile**<br>Raw score<br>Publisher's percentile rank | 71.8<br>74 | 71.4<br>72 | 70.5<br>72 | 70.6<br>72 | 70.6<br>72 | 74.4<br>72 |
| **50th percentile**<br>Raw score<br>Publisher's percentile rank | 61.7<br>48 | 61.2<br>46 | 59.8<br>44 | 60.0<br>44 | 59.9<br>44 | 66.4<br>48 |
| **25th percentile**<br>Raw score<br>Publisher's percentile rank | 45.7<br>24 | 45.3<br>23 | 43.7<br>21 | 44.3<br>21 | 44.2<br>21 | 53.7<br>26 |

SOURCE: Adapted from California Assessment Program, *Profiles of School District Performance, 1973–1974*.

I add a technical note to end this chapter. In the 1920s, a "grade-equivalent" system was invented for reporting scores on educational tests in the principal school subjects. With this system, if the median score of students entering Grade III is 33 points on a certain reading test, then a child who earns 33 points is said to be "reading at the third-grade level." This same statement is made whether he is in Grade II or Grade V. Similarly, a score of 42 points might be interpreted as a "grade equivalent" of 4.0. Because its message seems to be clear, the grade-equivalent score is much used in surveys and program evaluations. (For example: "In this district, 20 per cent of the students entering Grade VII are reading at the third-grade level.") Grade equivalents are natural enough in teachers' and parents' conversations, but for technical purposes the grade-equivalent scale is fallacious (Angoff, in R. Thorndike, 1971, pp. 523ff.). Only a few examples of the difficulties the scale causes can be given here.

The New York City schools applied a standard test to students in each grade and tabulated the scores on Paragraph Reading. The second column of Table 16.4 indicates precisely when the children were tested; for example, 2.7 indicates that the test was given in the spring, seven-tenths of the way through Grade II. If the performance of these children matched the national norms, they would earn, on the average, a "grade-equivalent score" of 2.7. In fact, as column 3 shows, they came out almost equal to the nationwide sample. In other grades, however, the New York median was below the norm. When the *New York Times* reported the finding, the writer said: "The city's second-graders as a group now register [at] . . . the national norm, while all other levels lag behind. This overall picture is so dismal because this lag worsens from grade to grade." The trend after Grade V is not all that regular, but there *is* a trend. The writer

**TABLE 16.4**

**New York City data on reading reported in two ways**

| Grade | Point of testing | New York median on grade-equivalent scale | Difference | Position of New York median on national percentile scale* |
|-------|------------------|-------------------------------------------|------------|-----------------------------------------------------------|
| II    | 2.7  | 2.6 | —0.1 | 49 |
| III   | 3.7  | 3.4 | —0.3 | 36 |
| IV    | 4.6  | 4.0 | —0.6 | 35 |
| V     | 5.8  | 4.7 | —1.1 | 32 |
| VI    | 6.5  | 5.6 | —0.9 | 32 |
| VII   | 7.8  | 6.0 | —1.8 | 30 |
| VIII  | 8.4  | 7.4 | —1.0 | 39 |
| IX    | 9.1  | 8.4 | —0.7 | 37 |

SOURCE: Data from Davis (1972).
* The percentile figures are approximate.

failed to realize that students spread out in achievement as they go through school, just as runners in a distance race gradually spread out. A runner who maintains his position in the pack will see the leaders pulling further away from him. The percentile values in the last column of Table 16.4 show that the New York City students held roughly the same standing nationally in Grades III through IX. The percentile scale also indicates a substantial drop in standing from Grade II to Grade III, perhaps because an intensive effort had been made in Grades I and II during the two years preceding the survey.

Teachers and parents are often distressed to find that a student who was below average when the year began makes "less than a year's progress" from beginning to end of the grade. But that is normal. On the Metropolitan Test of Paragraph Reading, the national median is 5.0 at the start of Grade V and 6.0 at the start of Grade VI. So the students who start even with the norms will, on average, finish even with them, making gains of around 1.0. The 25th percentile corresponds to 4.0 at the start of Grade V and 4.8 at the start of Grade VI. On the average, we can expect those who start at the 25th percentile to remain at about that level. (*Someone* has to be in the bottom fourth!) The students who hitherto have been comparatively slow to learn progress less rapidly than the average.

"A year's work" sounds like a proper unit of measurement, but in many basic subjects the progress is great in early years and small later. When an entering seventh-grader earns a grade-equivalent of 9.0 in Language Usage, this does not mean that he knows what is taught in Grades VII and VIII. Although the precocious reader in Grade VII who earns a top score may be reported as reading at the twelfth-grade level, he "cannot make head or tail" of actual books for Grade XII (Diederich, 1969). It is entirely possible for a child who is not much above the median for his grade to be as much as two years "ahead" on the grade-equivalent scale.

**30** What are some approaches to evaluating artwork in kindergarten? Present arguments for and against making the effort to evaluate formally.

**31** Knowing that grammatical usage in a fifth-grade class (punctuation, capitalization, tenses, and so on) is below the national norm for that grade, what facts would you look for in deciding whether to increase emphasis on developing that ability?

**32** In assembling norms for a test in Spanish for the elementary school (with both printed and tape-recorded questions), what would be a suitable reference population?

**33** In fourth-grade science or social studies, are the desired outcomes sufficiently uniform from school to school for standardized testing to have any value? Would it make sense for a publisher to prepare a standard test for a single broad topic such as the metric system?

**34** How could a school principal judge whether or not a fourth-grade teacher is effective? Should standardized tests play a part in the judgment?

**35** There is some evidence that the down-then-up trend found in California statewide tests was found in other states during the same years (R. Zajonc, personal communication). If that is the case, how might the trend be explained? What does it suggest regarding the use of national norms collected in any one year?

READING LIST

Paul B. Diederich, "What Does Research in Reading Reveal About Evaluation in Reading?" *English Journal* 58 (1969), 853–68.

> An experienced teacher and test developer discusses how teachers can best use tests and other evaluation procedures in instruction, particularly in secondary school. While the illustrations have to do with reading skill and literary interpretation, the advice can be used in many other areas.

Stanford C. Ericksen, "Grading or Evaluation," in *Motivation for Learning: A Guide for the Teacher of the Young Adult* (Ann Arbor: University of Michigan Press, 1974), p. 194–218.

> Ericksen addresses the concerns of the college teacher, but what he says will also apply in high schools and in formal adult programs. He sees the functions of evaluation about as this text does. He makes suggestions for various kinds of tests and for decisions about assigning grades that supplement those given here.

Jason Millman, Carol H. Bishop, and Robert Ebel, "An Analysis of Test-Wiseness," *Educational and Psychological Measurement* 25 (1965), 707–26.

> A long list is given of tactics by which a sophisticated student could legitimately "beat the test" or at least show his knowledge to advantage. Two questions for the teacher arise. How can one modify a test's items, directions, and so on so that scores will reflect knowledge of the subject-matter and not test-wiseness? Should students be taught these tricks of the trade?

Gilbert Sax, "Disseminating and Reporting Test Information and Data," in *Principles of Educational Measurement and Evaluation* (Belmont, Calif.: Wadsworth, 1974), pp. 506–53.

A textbook chapter covering two main topics: planning an adequate school testing program and reporting student progress to students and parents. Describes various reporting practices—including "grading on the curve" and "behavioral mastery reports"—and notes the advantages and disadvantages of each.

Herbert A. Thelen, "The Triumph of 'Achievement' over Inquiry in Education," *Elementary School Journal* 60 (1960), 190–97. Also in Sprinthall (1969).

A clever—and subversive—argument that present methods of testing and grading interfere with the student's education.

A. G. Wesman, "Writing the Test Item," in *Educational Measurement,* ed. R. L. Thorndike (Washington, D.C.: American Council on Education, 1971), pp. 81–129.

Advice on writing and editing choice-response test items, including items on interpretation of complex reading materials.

# PART FIVE

## Beliefs, Feelings, and Character

■ Attitudes form systems of meanings that have emotional and intellectual components. An attitude developed in one situation generalizes to a class of similar situations.

■ Appraising attitudes of groups plays an important role in program evaluation. Observation and self-report are used in monitoring attitudinal development.

■ Attitudes develop continuously. Existing attitudes determine what experiences the person seeks and how he interprets them.

■ Models suggest interpretations and responses. Competent and supportive models who embody the learner's aspiration are most likely to influence him. The school offers a biased selection of models that sometimes communicate stereotyped attitudes.

■ Factual information does little to change belief unless implications are discussed.

■ A persuasive communication may or may not change belief; an argument that considers both sides of a controversy often has more lasting effect than a one-sided statement.

■ Interacting with the attitude-object influences attitudes, but the experience may consolidate unwanted attitudes instead of replacing them.

---

**CONCEPTS**

*attitude*  
*prejudice*  
*generalization*  
*desensitization*  
*dogmatism*  
*self-report*  
*situational variation*

*model*  
*persuasion*  
*identifying figure*  
*sex stereotypes*  
*credibility*  
*role playing*

# 17

# ATTITUDE DEVELOPMENT AND ATTITUDE CHANGE

The earlier chapters on school learning concentrated on the acquisition of skills, knowledge, and understanding. Now, at last, we examine formation of the belief systems and emotional reactions that influence what a person chooses to do. Obeying the law is not learned as a habit in itself; it derives from hopes, beliefs, and fears. On the surface, Mack's behavior (p. 127) was admirable; but it derived from a fear of weakness and for that reason rested on a maladaptive and even dangerous belief system. These two final chapters will again stress the unity of development. What the student takes away from a lesson, a course, or a school career depends on what the experience means to him as a person. I reserve character-as-a-whole for Chapter 18 and devote this chapter to the learning of more specific attitudes (for example, toward the music of John Cage, fluoridation of water, or freedom of speech).

Every course aims to develop attitudes closely related to its subject-matter: respect for accuracy in bookkeeping, for conservation in biology, for individuality in psychology, for orderly social processes in government. Another set of attitudes concerns teachers of all courses: a positive yet realistic self-concept, appreciation of excellence, appreciation of human interdependence, and so on.

## What is prejudice?

Three distinct ideals are mixed together in writings on prejudice (Harding et al., 1969, p. 5). The three suggest somewhat different educational objectives.

- Rationality. "This norm enjoins a persistent attempt to secure accurate information, to correct misinformation, to make appropriate differentiations and qualifications, to be logical in deduction and cautious in inference. Prejudice . . . may occur in the form of hasty judgment or prejudgment [the root meaning of *prejudice*], . . . thinking in stereotypes, . . . and refusal to admit or take account of individual differences."

- Justice. "The standard of justice here is one of equal treatment. . . . [It] requires that in all areas of public concern individuals be treated equally except insofar as unequal treatment is based on abilities . . . functionally relevant to the . . . situation." Prejudice takes the form of discriminatory acts and insensitivity to discriminatory conditions.

- Human-heartedness. This norm "enjoins the acceptance of other individuals in terms of their common humanity, no matter how different they may be from oneself." It is a standard of direct personal response. Indifference—as well as overt hostility or intolerance—is prejudice, from this point of view.

The opportunity for teaching personal-social attitudes never ends. An instructor in a graduate school perceives that a student holds an attitude the instructor considers unwise. Then, with all respect for the student's right to be himself, the teacher sets out to alter the attitude—or holds back, and lets the fault entrench itself deeper. There is no middle ground. Mack will serve as an example. If one of Mack's English teachers had sensed that he was uncritical of persons in power and hostile to minorities, that teacher would inevitably be concerned—as educator, representative of society, and admirer of Mack's potential.

1  List attitudes to be promoted by teachers of
   a. primary reading.
   b. band.
   c. high-school economics.

2  Many adults know that physical exercise will contribute to their physical well-being, but do not exercise often. What attitudes might account for this?

# ATTITUDES AS MEANINGS

## Action, Affect, and Cognition

A psychological analysis might look only at overt acts. In driver training, producing conformity to the speed limit is one aim. An evaluator might, therefore, observe the speed with which graduates of the course usually drive. But this would be superficial information. Among the internal attitudes that affect driving are a love of daring, a wish to save time, a concept of oneself as a law-abiding citizen, a fear of unpleasantness if an accident occurs, and so on. Hidden attitudes cannot be inferred from usual actions. A driver who dislikes legal restrictions may conform just because he has an exaggerated fear of the law's reprisal. Changes in surface behavior are likely to be temporary unless the underlying attitudes change. The person who does not approve the speed limit usually conforms—when on public view. Stricter enforcement has more effect on the number of times he looks in his rear-view mirror than on his speed. When driving within the limit becomes part of the person's concept of safe driving and he accepts safe driving rather than daring as an ideal, the desired action is likely to follow. But there is a contrary to the proposition that the belief system shapes behavior: Situational constraints and pressures also count. The patrol car does hold the daring driver in check. In the absence of the patrol car, the expectations of the driver's passengers may push him toward caution—or toward recklessness.

Obviously, social pressures may be in harmony with personal beliefs or in opposition to them. Warner and DeFleur (1969) collected evidence on the way social and individual factors interact, arriving at Fig. 17.1 as a synthesis of the information available.

It may be useful to distinguish cognitive and affective objectives of education, but the two are intertwined. Educators have at times treated beliefs as if they were acquired intellectually, assuming, for example, that the study of factual American history will in itself teach American ideals. The same historical facts, however, can be accommodated in contradictory belief systems—witness the attitudes toward military glory that have been accepted in one generation and rejected in the next.

The following definition embraces both the cognitive and the affective aspects of attitudes: An attitude toward an object or concept consists of the interpretations a person makes regarding its value for various purposes.

What is your attitude toward coffee? You drink several cups a day. But you drink it regularly at breakfast; never in midmorning, except as a social ritual when there is a chance to chat over it; never at night, except at a company dinner. Moreover, you add low-fat milk if you can, often going to some trouble to obtain it. The attitude is complex. Perhaps you do not care for the taste of

FIGURE 17.1

Presumed relation of prejudiced behavior to situation and internal attitude

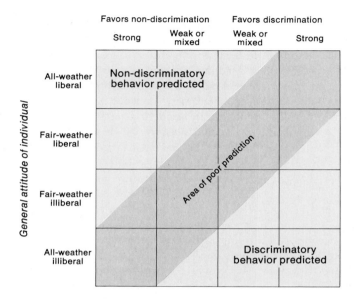

*Support provided by sociocultural context*

SOURCE: Adapted from Warner & De Fleur (1969).

coffee alone; you find it acceptable with milk; your start in the morning feels incomplete without it; it seems "more sociable" than a glass of cold milk.

A person's beliefs may be inconsistent. Americans have learned to reject totalitarianism, yet these same people—some of them—endorse propositions that are totalitarian in spirit. It is not enough to develop loyalty to the abstractions "democracy" and "free speech." These attitudes will not produce democratic judgments unless the concept is a developed system of meanings. A verbal principle does not direct action unless the student can and does match the concrete event to the abstractions he has learned (box, and Question 26, p. 140).

---

3 Describe fully your attitude toward comic strips or toward vegetable gardening.

4 The self-concept falls within the definition of attitude. List four or five questions that, if answered frankly, would give a reasonably complete picture of a 12-year-old's self-concept.

---

## Testing attitudes at a functional level

In Chapter 16 (box, p. 692), we saw that many students who could respond correctly when questioned directly about a verbal principle responded incorrectly or not at all when the question required application in a concrete context. Something similar is true of attitudes. Acceptance of the abstract idea of free speech, for example, is not always carried over into concrete judgments.

The chart shows results representative of what has been found in many studies of children (Zellman, 1975). In the "select" sample—third-graders through sixth-graders, all from well-to-do homes—an overwhelming majority endorsed civil liberties in both the abstract and concrete questions. But note the change: the number of intolerant responses was many times as great when the questions became more concrete. In the unselected sample—fifth-graders through ninth-graders (unselected as to type of home)—there was an equally drastic drop in tolerance. Findings with adults are much the same.

As Zellman and Sears (1971, pp. 122 and 123) say in interpreting one of these studies:

> Attitudes regarding free speech for dissenting or nonconforming political groups are acquired by a socialization process wholly different from that involved in the acquisition of the abstract principle of free speech. In brief, the abstract belief in "free speech for all" simply mimics the dominant adult political norm; it is learned as a slogan bearing no concrete implications. In contrast, most children's attitudes toward rights of free expression for specific dissenting political groups depend more upon their attitudes toward the groups than upon their acceptance of the general principle of free speech. Children do not deduce from an abstract principle to concrete situations, and there is no evidence that free speech in concrete situations is taught as a dominant norm of the adult political world.

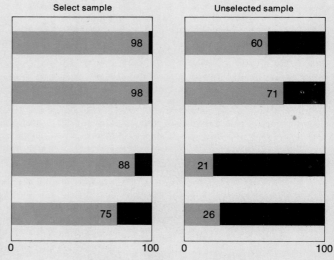

ABSTRACT STATEMENTS

I believe in free speech for all no matter what their views might be.

People who hate our way of life should still have a chance to talk and be heard.

CONCRETE STATEMENTS

Allow a Communist Party member to make a speech in this city?

If a Communist were legally elected mayor of this city, the people should not allow him to take office.*

Select sample | Unselected sample

98 | 60
98 | 71
88 | 21
75 | 26

*Percentage of tolerant responses*

* Percentage is of those *rejecting* the statement.

## Generalization of Attitudes

An attitude that develops out of experience with one concrete object is likely to generalize to similar objects. Sometimes an attitude is formed initially by the conditioning process that Gagné refers to as signal learning (p. 95): Couple a stimulus with a pleasant or unpleasant consequence. This sets up an expectation, so that soon the stimulus alone is enough to trigger the emotional reaction. And the reaction generalizes.

John B. Watson, the founder of behaviorism, and Rosalie Watson demonstrated this long ago (Watson & Watson, 1920). They taught a 2-year-old to fear a rat just by clanging a bar every time the child touched the animal. The infant was startled and agitated by the violent sound. Soon the mere sight of the rat was enough to cause the child to shrink into a corner and cry. The rat had come to mean "horrible sound about to happen." The child responded just as emotionally to other furry animals and even to a fur collar. That is, he seemed to perceive the "furry" aspect of the situation when the noise occurred. All situations with that characteristic signaled the same threat.

Ordinarily, when a trial interpretation is not confirmed, a new interpretation is made. The fur collar was not accompanied by a loud sound, and indeed no sound accompanied the rat until it was touched. But since the child was

shrinking from the object and not touching it, he never tested his expectation—"fur plus touching means horrid sound."

Fortunately, false interpretations can be overcome. Mary Cover Jones (1924, 1974) applied what is today called "desensitization," introducing the rat at a distance while the child was happily occupied, and then gradually bringing it closer. Such techniques are used practically to overcome fears of snakes, for example, or public speaking (Bandura, 1969).

Here, learning and generalization were nonverbal. A verbal label can crystallize an attitude by identifying situations to avoid or accept. An obvious example is the voter prepared to distrust all officeholders from a particular political party. Some schoolchildren avoid books they can identify as "classics" or tasks they recognize as "mathematics." A generalized attitude toward another ethnic group is a particularly important example. Even persons who have friends in other ethnic groups have an attitude regarding blacks or Anglos or Japanese as an abstract category. Such specific attitudes fit into a system. Mack's suspicion of ethnic minorities reflected his personal insecurities. Self-acceptance tends not to go with racial prejudice, and the person who has one strong racial prejudice also has others (Glock et al., 1975, pp. 71 and 143). Indeed, Lundberg and Dickson (1972) observed that white students holding discriminatory attitudes toward alien ethnic groups were also inclined to discriminate against various subgroups of whites in the student body. The person with ethnic prejudices also is likely to have dogmatic views on scientific questions and on social policy (Rokeach, 1960; Martin & Westie, 1971). When college students were asked for advice regarding changes in examination procedures, the ethnically prejudiced students opposed any change in procedure and did not even want to be interviewed about possible changes. Giving tests is the job of authority, they said; they wanted to be told the rules, not to take any responsibility (Jacob, 1957, pp. 11 and 121ff.).

Open-mindedness is essential for learning and growth, but, to the dogmatic person, anything strange is threatening. Consider Mikol's (1960) observation of the reaction of dogmatic and nondogmatic students to modern music. The students were classified according to their beliefs about politics, authority, achievement, and so on. The groups did not differ in their reactions to the conventional music of Brahms and Saint Saëns, nor in their initial dislike for the strange music of Schönberg. But on a *second* hearing of the Schönberg selection, the open-minded students became more favorable while the dogmatic ones rejected it more harshly than they had at first.

---

**5** Is the advice to shape attitudes toward a broad class of objects consistent with the statement that developing an attitude toward an abstraction is not enough?

**6** Is interest in physical exercise highly generalized? A set of unrelated, situation-specific attitudes? Part of a system of beliefs?

---

# APPRAISING ATTITUDES

The following discussion gives background for the research on attitudes treated below, and also supplements Chapter 16, on evaluation, where intellectual growth was emphasized. All the techniques for appraising attitudes listed here can be employed in evaluating educational programs; some can properly be used in evaluating the individual student.

## Techniques for Collecting Data

The methods fall into three broad groups: observation of everyday behavior, controlled experimental tests, and self-report.

OBSERVATION    Some attitudes are inferred from consistencies (and inconsistencies) in what the person does. A few pages back we inferred an attitude regarding coffee from the observed responses in many incidents. In Chapter 6 we inferred Bill Chelten's attitude toward authority from observations. Attitudes in a student body or community can be inferred from routine records—a count of missing library books, for example, or cafeteria sales of diet beverages. Many causes lie behind such figures, and inferences should be cautious. Nonetheless, when a message on carbohydrate consumption is used to test the effectiveness of some method of persuasion, a change in cafeteria sales would be better evidence of impact than what the students *say* they now believe.

CONTROLLED TESTS    When observations are made in everyday situations (for example, of interaction with minority-group classmates), it is hard to separate individual differences from situational differences. The advantage of everyday observation is that the information *is* representative of the person's own life space.

A performance test of proficiency (p. 714) places the person in a standard situation and records what he does. Standard situations are also used to assess typical behavior and attitudes, chiefly in formal research. The method is not intended to give accurate information on individual students. Lepper and his colleagues (p. 627) wanted to know whether offering rewards raised or lowered interest in an activity; they arranged a choice of activities for the child and recorded his choices before and after the experimental treatment. The ray-gun test of honesty (p. 135) and the Russell Sage Social Relations Test (p. 717) are other examples. Self-report questions (below) disguised to overcome bias fall into this category (Webb et al., 1966). Consider these two statements:

**Scientists say that Americans eat too much sugar.**

**Some people say that Americans eat too much sugar.**

Half the students in a group are asked if they agree with the first, and 60 per cent say yes. Of the other half, asked if they agree with the second statement, 47 per cent (let us suppose) say yes. The 13 per cent difference suggests the extent to which the students trust scientists more than others on such matters.

SELF-REPORT    The terms *self-report* refers most often to questionnaires and interviews, including the depth interview, such as Sanford used with Mack (p. 127), and self-concept measures (p. 240). The sociometric survey (p. 189) is another self-report procedure relevant to appraisal of attitudes.

Attitude questionnaires are comparatively simple. Sometimes one question at a time is analyzed, as in the Gallup poll. Alternatively, a dozen or more questions may refer to the same object from various angles. This produces a scale on attitude toward classical music, attitude toward foreign aid, and so on. (For a collection of such scales, see Robinson and Shaver, 1973.) Some investigators rely on overall scores, some interpret the pattern of responses. Either analysis could be made of the questions on sense of efficacy presented in Fig. 6.5 (p. 222) and the self-concept measure seen in Fig. 6.6 (p. 240).

The kinds of items often used are shown in the box (p. 746). The ecology questions fall into three groups: reports of feelings (affect); statements of position (verbal commitment); and reports of behavior (actual commitment). The affect score correlated only 0.41 with the score on actual behavior. This is one bit of evidence for the conclusion that the persons who report the strongest emotions are not always on the front lines of social action.

Questionnaire results do not correlate highly with observed behavior (Wicker, 1969; Liska, 1975). The person may say what will please the questioner. He may not be fully aware of his own feelings. And broad questions may not elicit a true picture of his responses to specific events, with their particular situational pressures.

LaPiere (1934) traveled across the country with a Chinese colleague and his wife, and on only one occasion were they refused accommodations or a meal. (Such discrimination did not violate the laws of that time.) A few months after his trip, LaPiere mailed a questionnaire to the restaurants and motels at which the party had stopped. One question was: "Will you accept members of the Chinese race as guests . . . ?" Over 90 per cent of the responses were negative. Self-report may be defensive: "If I say yes, what am I letting myself in for?" Actual behavior responds to details of the event—LaPiere's smiling friends on the doorstep constituted no threat. In race relations, in particular, generalized verbal answers are often more extreme than face-to-face conduct (Triandis, 1971, Chap. 1).

## Three aspects of an ecological attitude

Maloney et al. (1975) assessed ecological attitudes by asking subjects to indicate agreement or disagreement with the following statements:

AFFECT SCALE

I feel people worry too much about pesticides on food products.*
It genuinely infuriates me to think that the government doesn't do more to help control pollution of the environment.
I'm usually not bothered by so-called "noise pollution."*
When I think of the ways industries are polluting, I get frustrated and angry.

VERBAL COMMITMENT SCALE

I'd be willing to ride a bicycle or take the bus to work in order to reduce air pollution.
I would probably never join a group or club which is concerned solely with ecological issues.*
I'm not willing to give up driving on a weekend due to a smog alert.*
I would donate a day's pay to a foundation to help improve the environment.

ACTUAL COMMITMENT (REPORT OF BEHAVIOR)

I have switched products for ecological reasons.
I have never attended a meeting related to ecology.*
I don't make a special effort to buy products in recyclable containers.*
I keep track of my congressman's and senators' voting records on environmental issues.

* Items scored in the reverse direction.
All items copyright 1975 by the American Psychological Association. Reprinted by permission.

CONSISTENCY AND SITUATIONAL VARIATION This brings us back to the topic of the consistency of attitudes. To formulate a question about "attitude toward the Chinese" is to impose an abstract category on a complexly textured reality. The reaction to a Chinese person in a situation depends on the particular Chinese, on the role the reactor is expected to play, and other specifics. Much the same is to be said about such traits as anxiety; whether a person becomes anxious depends on the challenge he faces, the emotional support immediately available, and the gains or losses in prospect.

This specificity sometimes makes it seem that prediction of behavior is impossible, as every situation has unique aspects. Or, at best, it suggests that one has to know the respondent's attitude in each narrow kind of situation. On the other hand, summary statements about broad attitudes suggest that people are more consistent than they really are. The conflict is resolved if one speaks of probabilities covering classes of situations.

Fishbein and Azjen (1974) asked college students about acts reflecting religious attitudes. Do you say grace regularly? Pray? Attend Sunday services? Contribute financially to the church? And so on. The individual student's responses showed only slight consistency. For example, the ones who prayed might or might not attend church, according to the reports. Some students gave many yes responses. However, some gave few. These differences were not accidental. The data showed that students with many yes responses would also score high on a second, equally diverse list of situations related to the same subject—religion. Thus, although response in any *one* situation is hard to predict, the person with "a positive attitude toward religion" accepts more of the opportunities available to him for religious observance. His probability of positive response in this class of situations is above average.

Likewise with anxiety. Fear of heights has little correlation with tendency to become tense before an exam or to be anxious in a social situation (Endler, in Magnusson & Endler, 1976). Put into 50 situations that might generate tension, some students experience tension in 20 or more; and those 20 are likely to have common elements (for example, a threat that merit will be judged). Behavior is thus fairly consistent over a class of situations that appear similar to the person. Over a wider assortment of possible threats, reaction is less consistent. To speak of a general trait or attitude, then, is not to speak of an invariable reaction.

---

7  In judging whether 15-year-olds have developed an interest in physical exercise, what would be the comparative advantages of observation and self-report?

8  Show that each of the following questions about the coherence or consistency of behavior is best answered by speaking of probabilities covering classes of situations.
   a. Is reading comprehension a unified ability (p. 694)?
   b. Is concrete operational thought a unified intellectual development or a set of responses to particular situations (p. 336)?
   c. Is the expert skier more consistent than the average skier (pp. 396ff)?
   d. A person fearful of flying becomes accustomed to flying and then does not react emotionally; is his fear truly gone?

9  Among popular singers issuing records nowadays, what proportion do you like? Could you describe a subclass of singers toward which your attitude would be highly consistent (proportion near 1.00 or .00)?

---

## Evaluation in the Affective Domain

Now how can educational evaluation use information on attitudes, feelings, and habits? Consider in turn the four functions of evaluation (p. 684).

Merit rating is quickly disposed of. Habits of work ought to be taken into account in merit rating. A surgeon obviously ought not to be certified if he knows what to do but cannot be counted on to perform at his best. A similar argument can be given for other skilled performances. Evidence on typical behavior for use in merit rating probably should come from observations under normal conditions of work.

Merit rating of students ought not to consider beliefs, life style, and personality. When attitudes count in the student's mark, the mark is not communicating what it is expected to—namely the student's level of competence and performance. Even in music appreciation, where attitude change is a central objective of the course, it is inappropriate to pressure the student to pretend to like music he does not care for. The student is invited to falsify when a show of liking the music the teacher admires can raise his mark.

Let us consider the motivational, directing function of evaluation and the monitoring function together. Teachers should monitor habits directly related to the school subject; in doing so, they help the student understand what a good performance is. Teachers cannot monitor attitudes on a regular basis. There are many attitude objects to consider, valid evidence is hard to obtain, and change comes slowly and indirectly.

It is often reasonable to have the student monitor his own conduct. For example, a set of standards can describe the desirable style of work in the kitchen: measuring ingredients, cleaning up the work space periodically, and so on. Having the student rate his own acts against that checklist keeps him mindful of the goal (as with the rating on skills discussed on p. 686). When a student wants to modify one of his habits, he can keep track of his progress. The teacher may loan the student a wrist counter and let him press it every time he catches himself in the unwanted act, or every time he acts as he wishes to act (Thoresen & Mahoney, 1974, Chap. 3). Thus, a college student who is shy about speaking up in class could chart the number of times he did (or did not) voice what was on his mind. The day-to-day record not only emphasizes the goal, but underlines whatever small progress the student makes. He sees himself grow.

A warning: Only a qualified therapist can safely undertake to make the student highly conscious of his beliefs and feelings about personal matters. Making a student self-conscious can be damaging. Thus, it would not have been proper for Mack's teachers to tell him that he had a fear of weakness and should overcome it. There is a place for the adolescent or the advanced student to examine closely his philosophy of life; such a systematic review is not undertaken in the spirit of short-term feedback.

Composite information on beliefs and feelings of the class or student body is used in program evaluation. The teacher of music appreciation can inquire

## Three kinds of instruction: student reactions

One reasonable question in program evaluation is: How well do the learners like the instruction? The texture of such information is illustrated in reactions of junior-high-school students who had been receiving remedial drill in arithmetic on a computer terminal (Hess & Tenezakis, 1973). The students were asked a large number of questions about "computer," "teacher," and "textbook." The questions were phrased to ask about teachers or texts in general, not about particular instances. Several classes are represented in the sample.

Each question was answered on a 1-to-5 scale, with 1 representing the strongest positive answer. The figure includes just a few of the items. All are in the *semantic differential* format, except the last question which had a conventional agree/disagree format: "I believe a computer (teacher) will always be right." (This was not asked regarding the textbook.)

If only the like-dislike question had been asked, the report would have been: These students, on the average, are neutral about teachers and textbooks; they have a favorable impression of the computer even though, as poor students, they probably do not enjoy math lessons. The chart enables the evaluator to answer, in addition, questions such as these: Did the students find the machine more remote and cold than the teacher? In what respect was the computer seen as especially superior to the teacher? Was the computer judged poorer than the teacher in any respect?

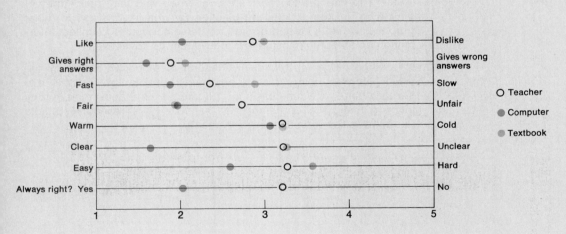

how students respond emotionally to music before and after his course. Without investigating that, the teacher may badly misjudge the effectiveness of what he is doing. Anonymous responses usually provide the best information. The teacher might have students rate a number of musical selections (probably not the ones studied in the course) on a semantic differential scale somewhat like that illustrated in the box. Students are less likely to falsify unsigned responses. An alternative—less anonymous and less objective, but also rich in information—is to encourage a class as a group to discuss their reactions to a selection they hear for the first time.

Such variables as sense of efficacy, aspirations, and interests are also significant to consider. The poll on efficacy (p. 222) said much about the morale of the student body questioned. Too often, especially after about Grade VI, evaluation concentrates on outcomes specific to one or another school subject and ignores the objectives of schooling as a whole.

A high school can reasonably compile information on the educational and vocational aspirations within the student body. The anonymous questionnaire usually should include questions on sex, home background, and grade average (B or better? lower?), to allow cross-tabulations. That girls set lower aspirations than boys of the same ability and background, for example, is a significant discovery. When the school takes steps to reduce the disparity, later evidence will show whether its new procedures are working.

**10** Which of the following questions comes closer to expressing the objective appropriate in a high-school civics course?
"How strong is his belief in a free press?"
"What are his attitudes regarding a free press?"

**11** Those who educate teachers are concerned with the "philosophy of education" of the prospective teacher. By what means and for what purposes would it be appropriate for those educators to collect information on student philosophies, individually or collectively?

**12** One could judge the musical education of American adults by behavior (concert-going, record purchases, and so on). Is this evidence a better or worse basis for judgment than that from an inquiry into the intellectual and emotional reactions of representative adults to opportunities for musical experience?

## ATTITUDE FORMATION: A DEVELOPMENTAL PROCESS

Rarely is an attitude formed from scratch. When a new object swims into the person's ken, he brings to it relevant meanings from past experience. The newspaper carries a story of someone's plan for a solar-power station to orbit far above the earth. New as the idea is, the reader promptly judges it exciting or dull, credible or incredible. He reacts according to his conception of the trustworthiness of scientists and of newspaper accounts of brave new ideas. Similarly, a newly created sculpture elicits responses built up in encounters with other sculpture. Attitudes do not descend solely along "subject-matter" lines; an adolescent's enjoyment of his first evening of folk dancing will depend on how secure he is with his peers as much as it does on his associations with music or dancing.

Over the years, attitude formation is continuous. Out of the infant's security or insecurity comes an attitude of trust or distrust that influences what he learns a year or so later (Erikson, 1968). Concepts of self, of authority, and of adults take form.

A generalized trust in other persons predisposes the 7-year-old to think well of persons in other countries, when he hears about them in stories. Differentiation follows. Around age 8, children become fully conscious of their own national identity and are ready to form different views of other nations. Representative American 6-year-olds had nothing in particular to say when asked, "What foreign peoples are just like you?" (Lambert & Klineberg, 1967). By age 10, the British were mentioned with some frequency, and "What would you least like to be?" elicited a pronounced anti-Russian bias. Likes and dislikes emerged in other parts of the world also, though the children's responses were not the same as the Americans'. Such reactions are based on stereotypes, not information; 10-year-olds have precious little genuine information about foreigners.

Refinement of concepts, with consequent shift in attitudes, is illustrated by other surveys (D. Easton & J. Dennis, 1969; Tapp & Kohlberg, 1971; Gallatin &

Adelson, 1971). As students move from Grade IV to VIII, for example, their perception of government decisions changes. The childish notion that the policeman is a major political actor fades. The President is less powerful in the eyes of the more mature student. Reasoning about a proposed law requiring citizens to paint their houses every five years, students in their early teens are more likely to emphasize the concrete benefit (and cost) of painting. By age 18, the respondents are much more likely to refer to the threat to individual freedom implied in such specific controls. Thus, the judgments of the more educated person involve more reference to abstract principles.

Emotional responses are attached to objects and concepts long before the child's ideas about them are definite. (See box, and pp. 170 and 775.) The adolescent has the possibility of accumulating information and making more subtle judgments. Knowing more, he is under some constraint to work out logically defensible positions. In Chapter 13 we saw that the influence is rather the other way around, that even in judging syllogisms the person's logic is swayed by his beliefs.

## Political sentiments take shape early

Judith, a slim, alert, pony-tailed 10½-year-old . . . is a somewhat-better-than-average student. She lives in a modest, middle-class neighborhood. (Her father owns and operates a small hardware store.) She chatted easily, sitting with me in a vacant classroom. . . .

[Interviewer]: How about the word "democracy," what does that mean?

[Judith]: Democracy . . . oh. Well, democracy is really a kind of—well, what the people have—well, I can't explain it!

I: Say the words that come to your mind.

J: Well, democracy is sort of what the people should have . . . well, you should have democracy and be . . . well, it's like . . . uh!

I: You're not exactly sure what it is?

J: I'm not exactly sure but in a way I am—it's what the people should have, they should have democracy, like be a good citizen, or something like that—I can't explain it.

I: Uh huh—it's something good at any rate.

J: Yes.

I: You're not completely sure about the details.

J: No, I'm not.

I: Did I ask you what sorts of things you thought of when you heard the word "communism"?

J: Communism? No, you didn't.

I: What does it mean to you offhand?

J: Well, communism is sort of—it's a different way of people; well, sort of like . . . to me it's *bad*. I can't explain it, just like democracy—it's sort of the opposite.

SOURCE: Greenstein (1969), pp. 18–26.

## Techniques Used to Shape Attitudes

Educators can affect attitudes by various tactics, used singly or in combination:

- Simple conditioning (p. 94). The attitude object is accompanied by some event that causes pleasure or pain. Teachers make some use of this technique (for example, when they try to make classroom events pleasant), but it is not a principal way of instilling attitudes.

- Making experience rewarding. The curriculum engages the student with works of art, scientific equipment, shop tools, team sports, and so on. The school can set up activities such as a project to clean up a neighborhood eyesore. Apart from the curriculum, attitudes are being shaped and reshaped every day by the student's contacts with teachers and classmates, including those with social backgrounds unlike his. In this direct experience the person interprets, sets up an expectation, and finds it confirmed (or disconfirmed). The process is subtler than conditioning.

- Promoting understanding and differentiation. As one comes to know more about a class of objects, one's attitudes take form. Young people get their start toward an interest in hunting mushrooms when shown how to recognize one or two safe species. They develop an interest in abstract art by being shown "what is there." Their lessons on the structure of city government equip them to comprehend the news about the upcoming election; seeing more in the events, they can react more. Intellectual lessons can also open the belief system to change. The science student hears about the kinds of tryout on animals and human patients that the FDA requires of a drug. Merely knowing of this makes him less willing to trust the next tale he hears of a newly discovered wonder drug.

- Providing a model. The learner copies provisional tries from those around him. The views that teachers, in particular, express and the ways they act suggest attitudes to adopt.

- Persuasive communication. Persuasive communications are deliberate attempts to mold a belief. They are not readily distinguished from strictly informative lessons. For example, the teacher who talks with a class about a cubist painting of a woman's head surely wishes to persuade them to take such art seriously. A communication is persuasive in function (if not in intent) when some hearers reject the message—"I don't believe it" or "That isn't the full story." When the topic is controversial, that reaction could follow a statement the teacher thinks of as well-grounded information. If so, the psychology of response to persuasion—not merely the psychology of factual learning—becomes relevant.

All these avenues work, and none works every time it is tried. People resist some propaganda appeals and succumb to others. The experience of attending a university in a foreign country may leave the student warmly sympathetic to citizens of that country or antagonistic to their way of life. Research sheds some light on the conditions that facilitate attitude change, and so offers some warnings and suggestions to the teacher.

**13** Americans differ in their attitudes toward eating Chinese food. Are such attitudes explained adequately by whether they liked the taste of the first Chinese meal they ate? Could that attitude have developed out of other attitudes?

**14** In many places in the western United States, forest fires and brush fires are a danger. To make preadolescents sensitive to this danger, which of the types of instruction listed above might be used?

**15** Trial and confirmation "is subtler than conditioning." Illustrate how this statement applies to a college sophomore working part-time as an aide in a hospital ward. Assume that his work is judged satisfactory by superiors, and occasionally praised.

**16** Which of the instructional approaches listed above can be used by the preschool teacher?

**17** Most teachers nowadays desire to make students sensitive to threats to the ecology. How far is it legitimate for them to use persuasion? Can you distinguish between persuasion and indoctrination? Why is indoctrination considered undesirable by commentators on education?

**18** In 1971, American schoolchildren were asked a number of questions about the Vietnam war (Tolley, 1973). Percentages of children answering yes to the question, "Should the United States use atom bombs to win in Vietnam?" were: Grades III and IV, 41; Grades V and VI, 21; Grades VII and VIII, 12. How can this trend be explained? (Assume that the school was giving no lessons directly on this topic.)

**19** A psychologist writes: "Attitudes are shaped more by communications from others (face to face and in media) than from contact with the object." What do you think?

## LEARNING FROM MODELS

Other persons do much to shape attitudes. In this section the emphasis is on learning from observation of how others act, but the content also bears on verbal communications. To say that the child learns by copying and that the way to teach is to set a good example oversimplifies. No child imitates every action he sees. Sometimes he ignores the model his parent sets and he takes over contrary patterns from someone else.

Look at it from the learner's point of view. He is in a new situation, lacking a ready response and seeking a response that will gain certain ends. If he cannot reason out what to do, he observes a model who seems able to get the right result. He looks for an authority or expert to imitate. The point is charmingly illustrated by Nevitt Sanford's story of the 2-year-old, initially terrified of a new puppy, who within a few hours was crawling about, barking, and threatening to bite people—and less charmingly illustrated by Bettelheim's (1960) description of concentration camp inmates adopting the mannerisms of the all-powerful guards. The child sees other persons attaining goals or suffering penalties; these observed consequences to others modify his subsequent tries much as the consequences of his own behavior do. Thus, the experience of seeing another child approach an animal fearlessly can extinguish fear just as direct desensitization does (p. 743; Bandura, 1969, pp. 167–96).

Models suggest a style of action. Aggression is or is not an acceptable style of life; youngsters decide as they observe real persons and television characters. Hostile, militant language is accepted by their group or rejected; they shape their own speech accordingly (Ditrichs et al., 1967). The effect is not so much to teach a specific action as to suggest the range of behavior that will be tolerated.

## Figures with Whom the Learner Identifies

Many who influence behavior are models at that instant only, never to be encountered again. Other individuals—real or fictional—are repeatedly used as guides. Such persons are identifying figures.

The child's first identification is normally with his parents. They increase his happiness and take care of things that go wrong. The child's gratification broadens into identification, identification being stronger in a warm home (Mussen & Packer, 1965; McCord et al., 1963). By the age of 5, the child frequently picks playmates and older members of the family as models: "Johnny showed me how to ride the scooter" or "Why don't we have the kind of cake I had at Johnny's house?"

Other adults become identifying figures. Students come to pursue the teacher's example, some so strongly that in the upper grades they are estranged from their peers. Others come to feel that the teacher "isn't my kind of person." (Witness the girl who names a playmate as her ideal, because "she is not too smart and not too dumb, not too rich and not too poor, because she is just an average girl.")

CHARACTERISTICS OF INFLUENTIAL MODELS   According to Bronfenbrenner (1970, pp. 131ff.), a person who might affect an attitude has greater influence if:

The learner considers the model competent. The model who is rewarded or attains his goal(s) has more influence.

Other models say or do the same things.

The learner sees the model as powerful, capable of providing him with rewards. Parents and playmates—the everyday sources of support and control—are especially influential.

The model has previously rewarded or encouraged the learner.

The learner sees the model as similar to himself.

The model represents a group that the learner belongs to or anticipates joining.

These characteristics fall into three groups. The first two relate to the model's perceived excellence: the model followed is one who seems to have the right ideas. The next two refer to the social relation between model and learner, and the last two reflect the learner's self-concept and aspirations.

MODELS CONSISTENT WITH THE SELF-CONCEPT    If Allen's parents have rewarded him for being quiet and passive, he cannot, on the schoolground, see himself becoming like tough and energetic Rudy. Rudy's conduct would be accepted as an ideal only if Allen were willing to reject everything he had been trying to be.

As the child grows into an adult, his identifying figures represent successive differentiations of his ideal. By the time he is of school age, some adults seem more "his type" than others. As a boy begins to take pride in his own physique and his ability to hold his own in conflict, he is ripe to idolize people who represent a high development of those assets: athletes, daredevil lawmen, stronger boys at school (Bailyn, 1959, p. 15). Eron et al. (1974) report that boys who at age 9 favored TV programs showing much violence were much more aggressive not only at age 9 but also on a follow-up at age 19. Munroe (1942) has described how adolescents with unsatisfied needs gorge themselves on stories whose central figures have conflicts like their own. The medical student who admires a teacher may yet reject him as a model, if he sees the teacher's preoccupation with research on animals as inconsistent with his own ideal of serving patients directly (Hughes, 1959).

The autobiography of former Justice William O. Douglas illustrates how a person seeks a model consistent with his needs and self-concept and takes his provisional tries from this model. Polio at an early age had left Douglas with weak and spindly legs. Tactless comments from boys, plus the solicitous comments of his mother, made him sensitive and determined to prove himself capable. One response was to plunge into study, driving for grades of 100 in all his courses. His school record was impressive, but he remained dissatisfied with his inability to be like other boys. He stumbled on the story of Sparta in his reading and found that "they were rugged and hardy people, the kind that I aspired to be. So I searched out the literature that described their habits and capacities to see if I could get some clues to their toughness." Douglas abandoned the Spartans as models, for in Plato he read the devastating information that the Spartans did away with their weaklings. Then came the model Douglas was ready for (1950, pp. 34–35):

> One day I met another boy, whom I had known at Sunday school, coming in on a fast walk from the country. He was a husky, long-legged chap, to me a perfect physical specimen. I asked him where he'd been, and he replied that he had been climbing the foothills north of town. I asked him why he did it. He told me that his doctor had advised it; that he was trying to correct certain difficulties following an illness. He was climbing the foothills every day to develop his lungs and legs.
>
> An overwhelming light swept me. My resolution was instantaneous. I would do the same. I would make my legs strong on the foothills. Thus I started my treks, and used the foothills as one uses weights in a gymnasium. . . . By the time the next spring arrived, I had found new confidence in myself. My legs were filling out. They were getting stronger. . . . Following these hikes the muscles of my knees would twitch and make it difficult for me to sleep at night. But I felt an increasing flow of health in my legs, and a growing sense of contentment in my heart.

Upon this success and satisfaction, Douglas built a lifelong interest in mountain climbing and the outdoor life.

READINESS TO USE MODELS    Some students are more influenced by models than others, as shown in the famous pressure-for-conformity experiment (p. 214). Laboratory studies on imitation indicate that a child is more likely to follow a model if the child's social experiences have been predominantly successful. Those who have had difficulty in social relations are not so readily influenced (Hartup & Coates, 1967). This is in keeping with the generalized distrust we saw in Bandura's aggressive delinquents (p. 212; see also pp. 789-80).

During the college years also, it is the students emotionally secure at entrance who are most free to change (Newcomb, 1943; Webster, 1958). Here is Newcomb's summary (pp. 155 and 156):

> Those who are capable of considerable independence from parents find no great obstacle in the fact that dominant attitudes at college differ from those of parents. Those who are particularly ripe for parental emancipation find in social attitudes a ready symbol. Over-dependence upon parents prevents attitude change.... For some, conflict between home and college standards is simply intolerable; to embrace the latter would be an act of excessive disloyalty. For others the tie is so all-absorbing that the college influences are scarcely felt; hence there is no conflict.
>
> As to adjustment toward contemporaries, ... those who are most susceptible to community influences orient ... toward a total community rather than toward a limited group within it. Those who choose the latter orientation are almost invariably those whose sense of personal inadequacy in competing with their peers has prevented them from entering the larger arena. Hence they are not influenced by the dominant community attitudes.

Another characteristic of students more likely to change was the realistic nature of their aspirations. The person who is meeting his own standards in an environment can identify with his fellows; the person who considers himself a failure—for good or bad reason—cannot identify easily with teachers or successful peers.

These college studies turn up another finding that very likely holds true in high school and in out-of-school life. The students who shift most are those already inclined toward the attitudes of the college community (Feldman & Newcomb, 1969, p. 142). The entering student who is set toward scientism or social criticism or whatever will find his models among those who speak a similar language. When those voices are in the majority, his opinions move further as conversations and reading erase his uncertainties. But when he and those like him are in the minority, they support each other and so can resist most of the social inducement to consider another view (Newcomb et al., 1967).

There is no universal law in these matters; an occasional conservative or liberal "sees the light" and reverses the attitudes he formerly held. When the student's general philosophy fits that of his environment, it is more likely to influence particular attitudes on which he deviates from the group. "At home" in the environment, he is prepared to listen to messages on specific issues that run counter to his prior beliefs. Thus Levin (1967) found a large change in authoritarianism among those college students who were intellectually oriented and interested in discussion of human problems, even though their initial authoritarianism was in conflict with the college norm.

School experience has lasting effects. Newcomb et al. (1967) were able to track down Bennington College alumnae who had been observed as students. Though they came from well-to-do and mostly conservative families, most of them shifted to liberal views while attending college; and they were predominantly liberal 20-odd years later. That most graduates change their political outlooks little after college (though of course their views of particular issues develop) is found in other studies also (Feldman & Newcomb, 1969, Chap. 10).

## Models Offered by the School

TEACHING MATERIALS AS A SOURCE OF MODELS    A lesson offers models whenever it describes people. One of the long-appreciated reasons for studying literature, history, and religion is the possibility of following examples they offer. The content suggests ways of living that the students might otherwise not encounter.

Books communicate the value system of writers, intentionally or otherwise. Textbooks convey the approved attitudes of each adult generation (de Charms & Moeller, 1962).

Sometimes the textbook communicates prejudices without intending to. (So may the teacher.) Stories in readers have often shown children getting rewards when they carry out the ideas of superiors, but getting into difficulty by acting independently (Child et al., 1946). Acquiring knowledge by asking an authority has been consistently shown as good to do; unrealistically, the authorities asked always give a sound answer. The outcome for the child who sets out to discover things on his own is often bad. Time after time, the child gets help on a difficult project by appealing to adults. In the books Child et al. analyzed, the stories showed no models of peers helping each other to complete a job without relying on adults.

Books used in school have stereotyped the sexes. Women and girls have rarely been shown as achieving or striving for recognition; the females are sociable, timid, inactive, unambitious, and uncreative, and have an air of helplessness. The males, on the other hand, have a near-monopoly on giving information, on effort, and on productivity. According to Child et al., "being female is a pretty bad thing" in the books they examined. If girls have not resigned themselves to an inferior position, it is because other social examples and their own experience are more encouraging.

THE TEACHER    Teachers most admired by students—the ones who most often function as models—are those who show personal interest. When students are asked which teachers have helped them most, and why, responses like these are common: "She approaches us as if she considers us intelligent." "He makes you feel you can do the work." "The class is like a happy family." Other favored traits are patience, wide interests, fairness, and a sense of humor. Does this imply that a teacher has to be easy, or that a teacher's success is to be judged by his popularity?

It's not a rocket.
It's a bus.
Get in.

Dan! Ben! Where are you?

Here we are, Tony.
We are in the rocket.

Where can we go?

SOURCE: *Tigers* (Houghton Mifflin Readers) by Durr et al. Copyright © 1971, 1974 by Houghton Mifflin Company. Reproduced by permission of the publisher.

Neither of these follows. The teacher the students admire is generally also highly regarded by the principal who knows how much the teacher is accomplishing. Students respect teachers who keep them pointed toward significant goals, even if the goals require effort. They do not mind insistence on their best effort, but they want the teacher also to recognize their difficulties and help them meet the standards. There is a vast difference between a nagging taskmaster and a teacher who sets the student's eyes on a peak and helps him select a path that gets there.

## FIGURE 17.3

Text material that avoids sex stereotypes

Dan! Ben! Where are you?

Here we are, Jenny.
We are in the rocket.

IS THIS A ROCKET?

It's not a rocket.
It's a bus.
Get in.

Where can we go?

Each teacher appeals to some students more than to others. Miss Shannon—red-haired, bouncing, full of ideas—becomes the envy and idol of half the girls in the high school. They swarm to her play tryouts, they cluster round her at dances, they grasp a suggestion tossed out in class and come in the next week with a dozen original "folk ballads" describing school events. For the girl who envisions herself as potentially a dazzling woman, who wants to make splash in her crowd, Miss Shannon is a tremendously influential model whose word on necklines or Nabokov carries great weight. But to retiring, dainty Celia, who would rather be shot

## Advice for the educator

The Macmillan Publishing Company commissioned a set of recommendations to help textbook authors avoid presentations that convey bias regarding race and gender. The writer of the final document was Nancy Roberts. It is appropriate for teachers to ponder the guidelines since, insofar as they are judged to be valid, they apply to all communications in the classroom.

*What Is Sexism?* Sexism is anything that limits a person's role in life according to gender (other than actual reproduction). Usually it takes the form of assigning girls and women to subordinate passive roles, limiting their participation in the areas most valued intellectually and economically in our society, and reinforcing dominant roles and activities outside the home for men and boys.

*What Is Racism?* Racism is anything that assigns to people an inferior or limited role based on ethnic or national origin, race, religion, or skin color, with the assumption that these characteristics are related to a person's capacities and behavior. The glorification of one race over others, or the consistent omission of certain races, is also racist.

*Commission and Omission:* Modern textbooks rarely offend groups of people by direct statements. More often, the social judgment is implied, making it all the more damaging for its subtlety. Black children may get the message that there is something wrong with them when all the people in their textbooks are white. Girls may be conditioned to feel instinctively that the creed "all men are created equal" does not apply to them; children may accept society's rejection of aged people when they show up only in subordinate roles in their reading materials. . . .

*What About Different Grade Levels?* With varying degrees of sophistication, the guidelines here presented will apply on every grade level. In the lower grades, we should concentrate on giving children the message that people of both sexes and all races are important in our culture, with no one group esteemed more than another. This is accomplished indirectly much of the time, through our choice of stories, examples, and illustrations. With this foundation, children will be prepared to deal more directly with social issues in the higher grades. There, we will be examining material that *is* sexist and racist—as in literature and history—along with material that confronts these issues in the light of today's egalitarian standards.

Sexual and racial balance must be maintained in every item we publish, whether or not it is part of a series.

*"Accurate Portrayal" Versus Ideal Situations:* Except in the social studies field, we are more interested in emphasizing what can be, rather than the negatives that still exist. "Reality" itself is subject to slanted interpretations. The fact that black persons do not yet hold a proportionate share of executive positions should not prevent us from depicting a sizable number of blacks as executives. Realistically, persons from any group can sometimes be stupid, make mistakes, ask for help; but no one group of people should have a corner on negative attributes.

SOURCE: *Guidelines for Creating Positive Sexual and Racial Images in Educational Materials* (New York: Macmillan, 1975), pp. 3–4.

The following is a passage from the Macmillan guidelines for textbook writers (see box on facing page).

> *"Mother said, 'I can't get Mike. I will get Daddy. Daddy can go up the tree. He will get Mike down.'"*

> *"Their guide from here on was an amazing Shoshoni Indian woman, Sacajawea. . . . Promised her freedom as a reward for getting the party through the Rockies, she did just that, with a young baby strapped to her back."*

It is a myth that women are fragile. In real life, some women frequently climb ladders, carry heavy weights, perform rescue operations, split logs for the fireplace, drive cars and trucks, and otherwise belie the stereotype of female weakness. Also, despite popular images, women and girls are not naturally reduced to quivers at the sight of bugs and snakes, or in need of male protection in all challenging circumstances. Children are sometimes weak and uncertain when learning a new skill or facing a difficult situation, but this should bear no relationship to their sex.

The passage about Sacajawea is a more subtle example of how the myth of feminine fragility is reinforced. The book from which it was taken abounds with stories of male guides, explorers, and other rugged heroes who toted many a heavy load. Sacajawea was the only person of this ilk described as "amazing." Why? The implication is that only a very unusual woman would possess the courage and stamina to perform a feat commonplace for male guides during that time in history.

GUIDEPOST:

> Show women and girls as strong, enterprising, competent, and courageous as often as you do males. Allow males to be occasionally self-doubting, in need of reassurance and support.

SOURCE: *Guidelines for Creating Positive Sexual and Racial Images in Educational Materials* (New York: Macmillan, 1975), pp. 10–11.

than speak before an audience, identification with Miss Shannon would be hitching herself to a rocket. Celia may envy Miss Shannon and those who follow her lead, but she cannot picture herself growing into such a person. She will seek a model more consistent with her concept of herself. Perhaps Mrs. van Ness, deliberate and orderly and sensitive, is the one with whom Celia can be comfortable. Mrs. van Ness just teaches French—no dramatics, no chorus, no Athletic Association. But she also is a person, gracious and receptive. If her quiet manner and respect for Celia's concerns encourages Celia just once to voice a personal problem or an opinion, the experience leaves Celia ready to unfold more the next time. Such a relation grows gradually into a firm identification. Mrs. van Ness may be the identifying figure for one pupil to Miss Shannon's twenty, but she reaches

## Encouragement—in what?

The late distinguished physicist J. Robert Oppenheimer was the son of a well-to-do, reserved New York couple. His health and strength were not good and he was isolated from other children. For these and other reasons he became bookish and socially awkward. Significantly, his one nonacademic passion in early adolescence was the largely solitary sport of sailing. His biographer, Peter Michelmore (1969, p. 7), tells us something about his teachers' response to him:

> Robert spent as much time as possible at school. His Greek teacher, a Miss Alberta Newton, kept him after class so they might read together Homer, a little Plato, and fight again the Trojan War. They loved the Greeks but rooted for the Trojans. A chemistry tutor named Augustus Klock, destined to become the Mr. Chips of the place, drew out Robert's talent for science to the extent that he spent one entire summer helping Klock set up a small laboratory.

Another teacher later played a different role. Because of ill health, Oppenheimer had to delay his start in college, and he became increasingly moody. His parents sent him off for the following summer with one of the high-school English teachers, who happened to be as muscular as Robert was scrawny and awkward. Robert resisted the idea of a "nursemaid" but in the end had a fine summer in New Mexico, most of it on horseback. As in Douglas's case, this led to lifelong pleasure in the life of the trail.

some who could never get close to Miss Shannon. A balanced faculty has a variety of personalities to serve as models, so that each student has a good chance of forming an allegiance.

A faculty should include in its number people who exemplify various social roles. The child who lacks a father, or who finds his father unacceptable as a model, will perhaps be greatly helped by a supporting masculine figure. Quiet and intellectual boys may be unable to affiliate with a rugged male, and for them other men are needed as models.

To teach the student to value learning and to respect his own potential, a teacher "of his own kind" is sometimes helpful, as Labov (p. 33) suggested. To the lower-class child whose home has not taught motives associated with achievement, the teacher who obviously belongs to a different community offers a seemingly foreign set of values. The student should be exposed to alternative models, at least one of whom has characteristics that mark him as "my own kind of person." Having mothers, fathers, and radically diverse older students as teacher-aides connects the child's own group with the attitudes the school is teaching. As a by-product, the parent learns techniques effective at home.

Similar advantages are to be found in procedures that make older children in a school responsible for supervising and guiding the activities of the younger ones. Such participation enhances the lessons of the older children (and may provide a worthwhile review of lessons they only half-learned). For the children they assist, the scheme provides models easy to identify with. The fact that per-

**TABLE 17.1**

Generous actions following exposure to a child model

| Example set by model | Time of test | Average number of tokens given to charity | | |
|---|---|---|---|---|
| | | Model's remarks favored generosity | Model's remarks irrelevant | Model's remarks favored selfishness |
| Generous | Immediate | 7.6 | 7.6 | 6.1 |
| | Two months later | 5.2 | 6.8 | 3.3 |
| Selfish | Immediate | 1.8 | .9 | 1.7 |
| | Two months later | 3.2 | 2.8 | 2.4 |

SOURCE: Adapted from Rushton (1975), pp. 463 and 464.

sons like them have become tutors proves that by mastering school tasks one can become a powerful, significant individual.

The force a peer model has is seen in Rushton's data (Table 17.1). In the study, a child earned tokens according to his score in bowling. The tokens could be used to get prizes, and they could also be donated to a charity. Children performing alone (control group) gave to the charity 4.1 tokens, on the average. The generous models won 16 tokens, in accord with the plan, and put 8 of them in the charity bowl; the selfish models gave away none. A different set of children was exposed to each combination of modeled behavior and remarks. The children who observed a generous-acting model themselves acted generously, even after a two-month interval. Verbal persuasion by the model seemed to make a difference only at one point. When the model donated tokens but also muttered things like "It's not right to share tokens with kids like them," his long-term effect was slightly negative.

**20** Feldman and Newcomb (1969) conclude that students with the same major become more like one another in their attitudes, and so diverge somewhat from the rest of the campus as they proceed through college. Through what processes can this occur?

**21** Was it wise of Oppenheimer's teachers to work with him personally in the way they did?

22  I have argued for realism in models. The Macmillan guidelines (box) object to realism. Is there real conflict? If so, is the correct resolution to be unrealistic with younger children and realistic in the higher grades?

23  Some primary-grade readers try to avoid stereotypes of race and gender by using only animals as characters in their stories. What do you think of this approach?

24  Do *you* think the Sacajawea passage (box) tends to "reinforce the myth of feminine fragility"?

25  In this book, what instances do you see where the writing and illustrations break down or avoid stereotypes? What instances do you see where sex stereotypes persist? Would any of the latter suggest to a prospective teacher that "being female [or, for that matter, male] is a pretty bad thing"?

## TEACHING FACTS ABOUT THE ATTITUDE-OBJECT

Some teachers assume that students will reconsider illogical prejudices if given facts about racial groups, including the fact that most so-called races have no biological homogeneity. This same view is seen in claims that historical knowledge teaches patriotism, and that studying French promotes goodwill toward other nations.

Beliefs and actions do not always match a person's knowledge. On page 746 a scale of attitudes regarding ecology was illustrated. The three attitude scores had only negligible correlations with information questions about, for example, the chief source of lead in the atmosphere (Maloney & Ward, 1973; see also box p. 138). Persons can *know* more about threats to the environment without *caring* about them.

Facts have relatively little impact on the person who has made up his mind. Suppose the daily paper tells you that Senator X, whom you admire, made a deal to pay off an opponent and keep him from running in the next election. The chances are that you will shake your head over this but decide that that is what X had to do to stay in office and carry out his program. Most of those who are horrified by the disclosure, and instantly say so, were already opposed to X and welcome this added justification for their attitude. It takes an overpowering array of facts to change the minds of people who are once set in a belief that has emotional significance.

Factual information or persuasive arguments are often distorted to fit the old scheme of beliefs. Put into Lincoln's mouth a statement such as, "Negroes are unfit for leadership." The liberal reader will find an explanation that restores consistency: "He means that blacks of his time were handicapped and so could not take their proper station unless given greater opportunities for development." By this device, which is not always legitimate, the reader maintains his views (H. Lewis, 1941). Another defense against unpleasant evidence is to intensify one's challenged belief. Batson (1975) exposed adolescent church members who were committed to a belief in the divinity of Jesus to information that the whole story of the resurrection was faked. (The information came in the form of a news story, ostensibly suppressed by the World Council of Churches, about some new Dead Sea scrolls in which early followers of Jesus justified preaching and writing a false gospel. Batson explained the hoax to the subjects when the test was over.) Many of the believers rejected the news report. Those who credited it as true shifted, from pretest to posttest, in the direction of *more* emphatic belief in Jesus and the infallibility of the Bible. When threatened, a true believer digs in for a siege.

Factual information does color emotional reactions when one starts with a blank slate. Choose an event that students have not made up their minds about, focus them on facts that support one point of view, and they take on that viewpoint—regarding the causes of the American Revolution, say, or the value of tonsillectomy. But blank slates are not the usual thing. The child who knows nothing about tonsils probably already trusts doctors, or fears strange experiences; this sets his mind for or against tonsillectomy. And the high-school student may be too patriotic to take in facts about Revolutionary firebrands like Sam Adams, who made peaceful resolution of British-American conflicts unlikely. Most instruction related to attitudes, then, has the task of dealing with the conflict between feelings already present and the attitude the educator seeks to promote.

Discussing the implications of facts and getting conflicts out in the open facilitate attitude change (p. 777). Austin Bond (1940) made one of the most careful field tests of the rational, factual approach. Bond prepared a unit in genetics for college freshmen, as a part of their introductory science course. Certain scientific generalizations were selected for emphasis, such as, "Because of the nature of the process of mutation and the operation of chance, most racial differences are trivial." Students began by defining "race" and classifying groups on measurable characteristics. In discussion, students commented freely on differences that, they thought, made some groups inferior or hard to assimilate. This led to distinguishing between biological and cultural qualities, at the end of the third class hour. The work of Mendel was then introduced, with discussion of theories and examination of hybrid corn specimens. This scientific evidence was connected to intermarriage and other questions that had come into the original discussion, so that the facts were seen by the students as significant. The classwork moved into a study of variability and overlap of groups and applied the concepts to skin color, height of Japanese and American soldiers, and other examples. Cultural sources of variation were considered in detail. The final summary at the end of the 15-hour unit was: "Evaluation of an individual should be in terms of individual worth, not of racial or national worth."

Meanwhile, a control group studied genetics in the traditional way. They learned the same generalizations, examining more detailed scientific material, but made no deliberate application to racial questions. Both groups read the same sources.

Bond gave 19 tests of attitudes and understanding; the experimental method gave positive results on 17 of them. To illustrate:

The experimental group was less favorable to imperialism.

The experimental group was more favorable toward Orientals, Jews, and Italians.

The experimental group was significantly better in reasoning about one set of problems on genetics and heredity, particularly human heredity, but the control group had a slight (insignificant) advantage on a second form of this test.

The experimental group was markedly superior in analyzing and drawing conclusions from an experimental study of mouse heredity.

The experimental method not only improved understanding and reasoning, but also carried over into changed opinions on social problems.

---

 **26** In the light of Bond's study, how might a course in French develop appreciation of and respect for French civilization?

---

# PERSUASION

A communication has to try to persuade when some part of its audience resists the message (p. 753). McGuire (1969, p. 151) put it more formally. If a message intended to alter attitudes is not incorporated into the hearer's belief system, it may be because he does not comprehend the message intellectually, or it may be that he comprehends it and rejects it.* Hence the speaker who would alter a belief has two tasks: explanation and persuasion. When most hearers understand the message, the persuader has succeeded in his task of informing; if they then fail to adopt the communicator's conclusion, it is the persuasive task at which he has failed. Most of this book has considered the first aspect—communication. Here the question is, What causes hearers to yield to a message or resist it?

The hearer does not passively absorb a message; he makes an active intellectual response. He entertains the message as a possible interpretation. Something like Piagetian assimilation and accommodation (p. 329) go on. If he can assimilate the new message to his existing belief structure, he is likely to adopt it. Sometimes a hearer will accept beliefs that do not fit with others he holds. Sometimes he distorts the communication or rejects it outright; either tactic keeps the existing system intact. Sometimes he works out an accommodation, altering his old views enough to make them compatible with the new ideas or

---

* For simplicity I refer to speaker and hearer, but the statements apply also to writer and reader.

accepting an ideal at the verbal level yet acting in concrete instances without taking it into account.

The voluminous research on persuasion has usually studied single messages—speeches, or films, or other isolated appeals. Moreover, the message has usually been delivered by an anonymous stranger. This is not much like the persuasion that occurs in the classroom, when a familiar teacher expresses certain viewpoints over an extended period. Even so, the experiments have turned up pertinent information; but they have not identified trustworthy means for changing beliefs and conduct.

Investigators have asked questions such as "Does it help if the persuader recognizes arguments on the other side, in addition to presenting the arguments on his side?" Here, as much as in any section of this book, a conclusion from the body of research must start with the words "It depends." Because many aspects of subject-matter, situation, and listener influence what happens, the technique that gives a solid positive result in one study may show no effect in another, or may even backfire, setting the audience against the message. The maturity and sophistication of the audience, the emotional security of individual listeners, the social cohesion of the group, the degree to which the person's ego is involved in the topic of discussion—these factors and more condition the outcome. This section can only draw attention to aspects of the communication process that often make a difference.

Getting arguments in mind need not change belief. Conversely, belief can change even when the person does not retain the supporting arguments. Tested some time after exposure to a communication, persons who did shift toward the position advocated often have forgotten the facts the advocate presented and the logic behind his conclusions (Watts & McGuire, 1964; Greenwald, 1968). Once the person has yielded, he retains his new view, though he forgets much of the argument that persuaded him. A new structure of concepts and feelings forms in the hearer's mind. The steps of thought by which he tested and discarded his old belief are lost, along with the old structure. This resembles the growth in a concept that Piaget describes (p. 336). Once a conservation law is locked in place, the child forgets his older, conflicting views.

## The Persuasive Communication

CHARACTERISTICS OF THE COMMUNICATOR    Who it is that communicates the message makes a difference. The differences are often summed up by reference to the credibility of the communicator and the hearer's identification with him. This is little more than an echo of the characteristics that make a model influential (p. 756). Other things being equal, a message has more impact if the hearer regards the speaker as well informed. And, other things being equal, a speaker carries more weight if liked by the hearer, or perceived as similar to him or as representing a role the hearer aspires to.

A propagandist who condemns *all* your beliefs is clearly no friend; self-respect demands that his arguments be rejected. The communicator who establishes that he and his hearer are agreed on basic values can become a model. "This fellow thinks as I do. He and I are on the same side." Mead (1955) tells of the public health nurse in Mexico who found the native diet extremely unsuitable and condemned it in order to persuade mothers to feed their babies milk. The mothers refused to follow the suggestion. When the nurse dropped her negative tone, and suggested only that babies be fed water in which the family beans had been cooked—a recommendation in harmony with the mothers' beliefs—the suggestion was adopted. The babies did noticeably better, and now the mothers started feeding their babies milk, without further urging. The nurse had become a trusted guide instead of a hostile, uncomprehending outsider.

BOTH SIDES OR ONE SIDE?  A communicator who tells both sides of the story before throwing his weight toward one side, or who otherwise makes a show of objectivity, might seem to have greater credibility. Not so, according to the evidence (McGuire, 1969, p. 185). Presenting both sides can inoculate against future propaganda (Lumsdaine & Janis, 1953; McGuire, 1964).

Even being required to memorize arguments on one side may not shift beliefs when the student is aware that counterarguments exist. Greenwald (1968) had four groups of students read one or both of two sets of six arguments—one set for and one set against foreign aid. Then they studied one set. The first group described in Table 17.2 read and studied pro arguments only; the second read and studied anti arguments only. Among those who read all twelve arguments, some studied the pro arguments and some studied the anti arguments. The latter two groups tended to retain only the arguments studied. And their beliefs did not change. Merely making it evident that opposing arguments exist was enough to strip persuasive power from the arguments studied, Greenwald concluded. The groups who saw arguments on only one side remembered more, *and* beliefs shifted.

The communicator may set up the arguments on the opposing side for the purpose of knocking them down. Thus, a biology teacher might state the creationist position alongside the case for evolutionary theory. The student whose biology teacher took up creationism is not likely to be so ready to accept creationist counterpropaganda in the future. To examine both sides and then come down in favor of one of the two is more persuasive for an educated audience. It is less persuasive to a less able audience; the back-and-forth flow of argument can confuse.

A decision requires commitment. One effect of introducing both sides, including unpalatable or threatening information, is to enable the person to work through his discomfort with the alternative positions before he commits himself to one of them. Decisions worked through in this way are firmer (box, p. 774).

The teacher who makes clear his stand on an issue can be expected to have more influence than one who leaves the students to draw their own con-

## TABLE 17.2

### Effects of exposure to pro and anti arguments

| Arguments read | Arguments studied | Mean recall score | | Change of belief |
| | | Arguments read and studied | Arguments read only | |
| --- | --- | --- | --- | --- |
| Pro<br>Anti | Pro<br>Anti | 3 | — | Toward position studied |
| Pro and anti<br>Pro and anti | Pro<br>Anti | 1.8 | 0.3 | None |

SOURCE: Data from Greenwald (1968).

## Working through a conflict produces firmer decisions

As Janis and Mann (1969) see it, the person deciding whether to undergo a surgical operation, or whether to continue to smoke, works out a balance sheet. If he "anticipates the worst" before choosing his course, he is more likely to take later unpleasant consequences in stride. The following passage is adapted from their pages 340–42.

Several hundred young men who had recently undergone a surgical operation were studied. Before deciding to have the surgery, some of them had heard from their physician about the postoperative pains and stresses to be expected. The less advance information they had been given, the less tension the men showed prior to the operation. During the recovery period, however, the ill-prepared men were hostile toward the medical staff and less cooperative in routine hospital procedures.

A controlled experiment was made on a later group of adult patients. Half of them received considerable information about probable unpleasant consequences. On the day of the operation, both groups required about the same amount of drugs to kill pain. On the next five postoperative days, the experimental group asked for only half the amount of narcotics the Controls called for. The well-informed patients were released from the hospital about 2–3 days earlier than the Control patients, on the average, indicating that the Experimentals recovered faster. (The surgeons authorizing release did not know who was in the experimental group.) Painting a fairly complete picture of the attitude-object (the operation) before the event immunized the experimental group not against counterpropaganda but against reality itself. Approximately similar results were found in a study of mothers in childbirth (Levy & McGee, 1975).

clusions. Students willing to listen to his expertise will find it hard to do so if he conceals his views. Martin (1975) thus reported that study of Eskimo culture in Grade V reduced ethnocentrism most in those classes where teachers suggested the justification for Eskimo cultural practices. Equally important, the influential teachers let students voice their own negative reactions to Eskimo practices such as leaving the very old to die.

In view of the fact that the learner must somehow assimilate the persuasive message to his old beliefs, it might seem that the persuader would be most effective if he were to advocate just a small change. The evidence is to the contrary. A communication that sharply challenges your views may move your attitude only a fraction of the distance toward the communicator's position, but such challenges are likely to change it more than messages that advocate small changes. A communication may be so extreme as to be rejected as untrue. This risk is not great—the Big Lie is a notably effective propaganda device. The educator can use the Big Truth with equal boldness, even though his hearer will not swallow it whole.

EMOTIONALITY IN PRESENTATION  Dramatic appeals are effective persuaders. Television and motion pictures can glamorize an occupation or a nationality, capturing the attention and emotions of the viewer. He lives in the characters on the screen for a while, sympathizing with the hero and hating the villain. He learns new meanings.

The classic evidence is the Peterson-Thurstone study of 1933, in which students checked statements they believed regarding various ethnic groups. The statements ranged from extremely favorable to unfavorable. Then the class was shown one of several films. In *The Birth of a Nation,* a bestial slave freed by the Civil War attacks a fair-haired child and is hunted down by a heroically portrayed Ku Klux Klan. After seeing this, the students' attitudes toward blacks became less favorable. This shift persisted on a retest five months later. In *Son of the Gods,* they saw the story of Sam Lee, an admirable young Chinese growing up in a Chinese community in the United States, not fully accepted by whites because of his race. Much of Chinese life was shown. Before the film, the typical attitude was expressed in such statements as:

**Some Chinese traits are admirable but on the whole I don't like them.**
**I have no particular love or hate for the Chinese.**

After the film, opinions shifted, and the typical response was more favorable:

**The Chinese are pretty decent.**
**The Chinese are different but not inferior.**

Likewise, in reading a powerful novel, a person practices certain interpretations and emotional responses as if he were living the experiences of the character with whom he identifies.

Should an advocate of attitude change try to give his presentation more impact by a strong emotional appeal? Messages intended to persuade students to brush their teeth carefully have been favorite material for research. The results in Fig. 17.4 came from a study in junior-high physical education classes. The message was presented in five ways:

R      Recommended procedures stated compactly, without emotion.

RE      Recommendation elaborated with considerable detail, without emotion.

R+      R supplemented by positive appeal (being illustrated by stories of people whose attractive teeth helped their social success).

F      R supplemented by a weak appeal to fear (case histories being reported where neglect of teeth had bad effects).

F!      R supplemented by a strong appeal to fear (case histories of damage being presented vividly and emotionally).

## FIGURE 17.4

Behavioral change and change in self-report resulting from each of five forms of persuasion

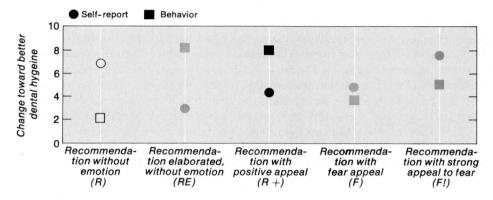

SOURCE: Data from Evans et al. (1970).

Five days after the message, students were questioned. It was found that the R+ group had retained the most information, followed by the RE group, with R in third place. Asked how often they had brushed their teeth, the F! and R groups said they were doing as they had been told. But Evans et al. also tested each student with a "disclosing wafer." (When chewed, it stains the teeth vividly at any dirty spot.) According to the evidence obtained this way, the fear appeals and the deadpan R appeal had comparatively little effect on behavior.

Whether arousing emotion interferes with acceptance of the communication depends on the degree of arousal. In the Evans study, stronger fear seemed to be somewhat more effective. In an attempt to reduce frequency of smoking among college students, however, moderate arousal gave better results than either no arousal or strong arousal. Strong arousal had more effect than no arousal. In that study, a lasting effect on smoking was produced only when the appeal was supplemented by suggested methods of stopping smoking (Leventhal et al., 1967).

**27** The Janis-Mann report on the effect of information about adverse consequences (box) is remote from the school situation. Describe a decision made by students to which the Janis-Mann conclusion might be expected to apply.

**28** The findings regarding the effects of comparatively strong arousal in the Leventhal study disagreed with those in the Evans study. Does this suggest that worthwhile conclusions are unlikely to be reached by experimental studies?

## Active Response to the Issue

DISCUSSION AND ROLE PLAYING   A communication can be expected to have more influence when the recipient makes some sort of overt response and that response has satisfactory consequences for the speaker. In a group discussion, remarks consistent with the persuasive communication are usually well received by the rest of the group. In one study, a film designed to combat racial prejudice was shown to high-school students; in some classes the film was followed by a discussion directed to support the effect of the film. Tests of prejudice were given before and after the teaching, and again a month later. The average scores shifted as shown in Table 17.3. No attempt was made to influence the control group; their increased prejudice came from uncontrolled influences such as the current news. In the experimental groups there was a large immediate change in opinion, but—as often in studies of this kind—a later return toward the initial beliefs. Without discussion, two-thirds of the impact of the film was gone a month later. With discussion, only one-fourth of the gain was lost. The effect of discussion here seems rather small, however, and there are other studies in which discussion shows no effect or inconsistent effects. A truly open discussion may even reduce the intended influence. A member of the group tends selectively to listen to those people whose views he finds congenial; thus, a two-sided discussion may help him to resist persuasion (Brodbeck, 1956).

The student who takes an active part in the discussion may change more (pp. 663, 800). In laboratory experiments, indeed, the student seems to be his

**TABLE 17.3**

**Effect of discussion on response to persuasion**

|  | Amount of prejudice | | | |
|  | Initial test | After teaching | One month later | Net change |
| --- | --- | --- | --- | --- |
| Film plus discussion | 70 | 62 | 64 | −6 |
| Active participants | 67 | 59 | 62 | −5 |
| Passive class members | 76 | 68 | 70 | −6 |
| Film only | 70 | 61 | 67 | −3 |
| Neither (control group) | 72 | 77 | 75 | + 3 |

SOURCE: Data from Mitnick & McGinnies (1958).

own best persuader (Greenwald, 1968). Students have been assigned to make speeches on one or the other side of the issue, or to write one-sided arguments. Playing an artificial role in this way often alters attitudes. Having to give the best argument you can *against* your prior beliefs forces you to take seriously the other side of the story. Acting a part in a skit or project (for example, simulating the role of a labor or management representative in a bargaining situation) enables the actor to see that his is not the only perspective. I remind you, however: "It depends." Discussion and role-playing do not always work.

**29** The members of the passive group (those who did not speak during the discussion of the film) were more prejudiced initially than those who spoke (Table 17.3). They changed more than those who only saw the film. Suggest explanations for these observations.

## LEARNING THROUGH ACTIVITIES

Direct experience with the attitude-object obviously builds meanings, and activities that provide such experience sometimes work powerful changes. "Students," says Jacob (1957, p. 10), "are often deeply affected by participation in experiences which vividly confront them with value issues, and possibly demand decisions on their part whose consequences they can witness."

In junior-high-school general science, for example, students often study trees. Conventional activities might include learning the parts of trees, examining a cross-section of a trunk, naming trees on lantern slides, talking about the economic value of lumber and conservation, and possibly making a collection of leaves. All this could be done at a high level of understanding and interest. An activity approach to environmental education in quite different.

W. French et al. (1948) report how a class in the South set out to determine how landscaping improves the community. From pictures of homes in magazines the students identified attractive trees. They learned from the county agent what trees would grow in their locality and what soil conditions were needed. Then they surveyed the school grounds to identify needed improvements and themselves made many of the improvements. Deciding that flowers and lawn were especially needed, they dug a bed for roses, removed the clay top and substituted forest soil, and nourished rose cuttings to the blooming stage the next year. They leveled the ground where lawn was needed, removed rubbish, and used the extra dirt and clay to fill gullies where soil was being washed away. In addition, students surveyed their own homes, and many made improvements there.

The merit of this activity can be judged in terms of the often-repeated principle: Interpretations confirmed through trial are learned. It was fun to be outdoors. Students probably learned to handle a shovel and how deep to set a rose cutting. Understanding about erosion, fertilizer, and soil surely was promoted. If generalizations were explicitly developed, they might have learned about organizing for community improvement or caring for plants. In addition, as they planned the activity, deciding that grass was desirable, for example, they were expressing and confirming attitudes. The students took pride in contributing to the community. Their satisfaction was strengthened by the common spirit of the group and by the praise of adults. As such projects become a tradition, the visibly growing results of previous classes' work are additional confirmation that community improvement pays. The students in the class learn about conservation problems they can come to grips with. This is more useful than studying the laws that might conserve trees in the distant Pacific Northwest.

It is not enough to provide a pleasant experience in which planting is fun; conscious verbal judgment and generalization are important if students are to identify similar challenges in the future. One risk in a "real" project is that the work will consume time far beyond its educative value. When students spend most of their time loading wheelbarrows, intellectual growth is slight. Projects are justified when the student is continually improving his interpretations of important situations. As George Stoddard put it, "We learn not by doing, but by thinking about what we are doing."

Are attitudes toward a minority benefited by close contact with members of the minority group? Contact may produce favorable attitudes or it may intensify prejudices. If white students have opportunities to engage with black students in a shared task, this may break down barriers (Sherif et al., 1961; Cook, 1970). A competitive interaction, however, can raise the level of prejudice (Silverthorne et al., 1974). When a student body includes both blacks and whites, students sometimes associate freely only with those of their own race, having formal and guarded contacts with the other group. Then they practice, at best, only formal politeness, not human friendliness. At worst, overt conflict breaks out between racially defined subgroups and antagonisms harden. Contact is more likely to intensify an attitude the person already holds than to change its direction (McGuire, 1969; Amir, 1969).

Some of the clearest work on what makes contact educative was done in a summer camp to which New York City boys were sent by a social agency (Mussen, 1950). During a four-week period, they worked, played, and lived with other campers, some of whom were black. Subtle and indirect tests showed no average change in the attitude score of white boys. Individuals changed in one direction or the other.

The ones who came to the camp with the most prejudice had more need to be dominant and aggressive, and seemed possibly to have more hostility to their parents. Perhaps hostility toward parents had generalized to targets safer to attack (p. 212). The boys who increased in prejudice were the ones who rather disliked the camping experience, who did not fit in and did not receive social rewards from the mixed group, and who no doubt felt all the more abused and antagonistic as a result. The ones who became less prejudiced were those who fitted into the camp, got along with others, and—as in the Bennington study (p. 758)—found it rewarding to accept group standards. Their personalities were marked by less aggression, less feeling of being mistreated, and more friendliness toward others. Both the boys who changed and the boys who did not change tested and confirmed attitudes, but only the boys secure in the situation confirmed socially desirable beliefs. (See also H. P. Smith, 1955.)

It is inappropriate here to make a concluding statement on methods of attitude education, as the research on character development in the next chapter continues the story. At the end of that chapter, methods of instruction are more fully discussed.

READING LIST

Kenneth A. Feldman and Theodore M. Newcomb, "The Impact of College: Epilogue," in *The Impact of College on Students* (San Franciso: Jossey-Bass, 1969), pp. 325–38.

> Draws, from a large body of research, nine generalizations about the degree to which attitudes change and the conditions under which they change. Small, homogeneous campuses have the greatest influence. The authors consider how large institutions of higher education might provide a climate in which students will work out new attitudes.

William J. McGuire, "The Nature of Attitudes and Attitude Change," in *Handbook of Social Psychology,* 2nd ed., ed. G. Lindzey and E. Aronson (Reading, Mass.: Addison-Wesley, 1969), pp. 136–314.

> This massive chapter is a handbook in itself, extracting the main ideas from several decades of research on attitude change and persuasion.

Muzafer Sherif et al., "Intergroup Relations: Reducing Friction," in *Intergroup Conflict and Cooperation: The Robbers Cave Experiment* (Norman, Okla.: University Book Exchange, 1961), pp. 151–96.

> Hostility between two groups of normal, well-adjusted boys was generated in a series of competitive activities. Sherif et al. here describe the experimental procedure that overcame hostility—"introducing superordinate goals."

Howard P. Smith, "Do Intercultural Experiences Affect Attitudes?" *Journal of Abnormal and Social Psychology* 51 (1955), 469–77.

Smith questioned college students who visited Europe to learn why some changed to more world-minded attitudes while others did not.

Russell H. Weigel, Patricia L. Wiser, and Stuart W. Cook, "The Impact of Cooperative Learning Experiences on Cross-Ethnic Relations and Attitudes," *Journal of Social Issues* 31, no. 1 (1975), 219–43.

When students in a desegregated group were asked to do assignments and projects in cooperating groups of four to six students rather than individually, it was hoped that intergroup relations would be improved. The study illustrates good evaluation practice; in some respects there were desirable changes, but not all outcome measures confirmed this impression. The article as a whole gives a good picture of social psychologists' thinking about desegregation today.

# CHARACTER

18

Perhaps you have thought of character as a moral quality separate from intellect and emotional maturity. Character, however, is evidenced in the way a person handles dilemmas, especially those where his wishes run counter to the interests of other persons. And the choice he makes depends on his concepts, attitudes, needs, and feelings. For this reason, a discussion of character gives an opportunity to review and integrate principles developed in earlier chapters.

This chapter assumes that the school has a responsibility to promote character development. Some parents hold that the child's character is the parent's responsibility, and no concern of the school. Without repeating all that was said in Chapter 2 on the broad responsibility of the school, I remind you of three points: First, the public does assign the school part of the blame for deviancy in society—for vandalism, dropping out, drug abuse—and also for failure to teach "ethical" practices in law and business. (Even the parents who want the school to keep hands off *their* children's character want social intervention to straighten out children "from the other part of town.") Second, liberal education—in teaching literature, philosophy, and social science particularly—has been intended to develop insight into the human condition that will improve judgment and conduct. Third, the educational program that never looks beyond its lessons to think about the effects of its practices on the student's sense of security and responsibility is likely, inadvertently, to hinder his development.

Character education is a particularly crucial "collateral learning" in the school. Having said this, I add that educators sometimes do intrude into the privacy of the student and his family. Attempts to pick out potential delinquents in advance, for example, run grave risks of making it more likely that those so identified will become delinquent. Another kind of intervention, the "encounter" techniques that invite children to bare their feelings and self-doubts in a group setting, may intensify the emotional problems of some of them.

## CHARACTER STRUCTURES

Character is not a cumulation of separate habits and ideas. Character is an aspect of the personality. Beliefs, feelings, and actions are linked; to change character is to reorganize the personality. Tiny lessons on principles of good conduct will not be effective if they cannot be integrated with the person's system of beliefs about himself, about others, and about the good community.

With no pretense of settling finally what are the best values and the best forms of living, character can be defined here in terms of the choices the individual makes when his actions affect the welfare of others: the person of good character generally tries to choose acts that promote the welfare of others as well as of himself. As character develops, a person learns to take pride in considerate action and to hold in check impulsive, selfish behavior. "Good" behavior is motivated by its connections with affection, self-respect, and other needs.

It is exceedingly difficult to evaluate character. It is necessary to know how a person makes his judgments and what motivates them. The goodness of an act has to be judged by what it means to the individual. Behavior that conforms perfectly to the standards of a particular community may occur *because* the person made no moral judgment.

When interviewed, persons describe different reasons for the same action; the same act is to be judged differently in each case. When the crowd at a football game erupts into unruly postgame behavior, some teenagers are going to hang back from the mob and go their own ways. Some may do so without thinking of any choice to be made; their minds are on other plans, or they drift off in the wake of their own crowd. Some hang back because of fear of a crackdown; that too may be self-centered or conforming. Among the conscientious, some consider the possibility of trying to stop the mob, and then decide not to interfere on the grounds that this could make matters worse. Staying out of the action is for them a complex decision.

Classifying character is not enough; one must look for causes, especially those that arise out of a person's life situation. The community is prepared to condemn delinquent acts, but the label "delinquent" is a legal classification, not

*"You wait here and I'll bring the etchings down."*

a psychological description (H. Quay, in Hobbs, 1975b, vol. 1, p. 377). As behavioral scientists see it:

> Delinquency is no small part of the total stream of the individual's life activities and represents, equally with all other behavior, a response to inner and outer pressures. In common with all voluntary activities, it is a variety of self-expression.
>
> The terms by which delinquency is designated—larceny, truancy, breaking and entering, and so on—are descriptions of behavior which do not in the least indicate what is expressed by the offender in the delinquent act. . . .
>
> Contrast cases of the simple offense, truancy. One boy may be avoiding a situation in which he feels inadequate and discouraged; another has developed out of family life antagonism to all forms of authority—school representing one form; another has such need of recognition that, even though he does not dislike school, he truants in order to be "a regular fellow" with his companions; still another is the victim of peculiar anxieties which make the classroom hateful to him. (Healy & Bronner, 1936.)

**1** Does this book's definition of character neglect any values that present-day Americans should teach to their children?

**2** Show that each of the following character traits requires sacrifice of some gratification: loyalty to friends, honesty, defense of an unpopular principle.

**3** Could truthfulness sometimes be motivated by a desire to hurt another person? Would it then be a virtue?

**4** Men who went to Canada to escape from the military draft during the Vietnam war were violating the law. What does it mean to say that, for different men, this act expressed different things?

**5** Could the act of contributing to a charity drive mean different things to different students?

## Five Levels of Character

Insofar as roles (Chapter 5) and intellectual processes are mastered gradually (Chapter 8), there must be a developmental progression toward complexly organized character. Psychologists and moral philosophers have developed many systems for describing character. Lawrence Kohlberg's (1973) system, a direct extension of ideas of Piaget, is particularly prominent in current discussion. Kohlberg emphasizes the cognitive aspect of choice. Although Kohlberg's ideas and findings are prominent in this chapter, I adopt a simpler system. Kohlberg has seven levels and subdivisions within levels, whereas I speak of five levels. The scheme I use grew out of the studies of personality development by Robert Havighurst and his colleagues, from which the concept of developmental tasks (p. 178) also came.

A list of stages implies a logical sequence or direction of development, but there is no moment when the child leaps from one box to the next. Development proceeds unevenly, across a broad front; from one choice to another and from day to day, the maturity of judgment rises and falls (Turiel, in Travers, 1973, pp. 737 and 748). To say that a person has reached a particular level of character is to speak of the highest level observed frequently in his behavior, not a level he consistently maintains. When a person discusses moral dilemmas verbally, he does take a similar stance most of the time, according to Kohlberg.

Peck and Havighurst (1960) discuss character in terms of these levels:

1. the amoral                          (0)
2. the self-centered, expedient        (1, 2)
3. the conforming, conventional        (3)
4. the irrational-conscientious        (4)
5. the rational, considerate           (5, 6)

The numbers in parentheses refer to corresponding states in Kohlberg's system. He counts his Stages 2 and 3 as "conventional," speaking of 0 and 1 as "preconventional" and of 4 to 6 as "postconventional." The important reason for distinguishing among the levels is that educators who propose to develop character have to be clear about their aims, both short-term and long-term.

A person acts amorally when he does not recognize the good or bad effects of his choice on other persons. In a self-centered act, the person does what he prefers, considering others only in order to attain his ends. An act is called conventional when the person does what his group usually does, without reflecting whether the action is good or bad. Behavior is classified as conscientious when the person follows some rule of good conduct that he firmly believes in. At the fourth level of development the application of the formal rule is rigid, without intelligent recognition of variation in circumstances. In rational self-control, conscience dictates an aim or policy rather than a rule of action. At this highest level the "rational person" is not rational in all his acts and judgments, but he acts and thinks at this level in most of the important conflicts he faces.

The stages can be used to classify a single action, or a verbal judgment about a single moral dilemma. They can also be used to classify a person; a person considers possible actions from many sides and decides what action will produce the most satisfactory result for all concerned.

The following sections discuss each level in turn.

THE AMORAL LEVEL    Behavior is amoral when the performer is unaware of or disregards the effect his act has on others. The infant, with no concept of good or bad, is amoral. He reaches for attractive objects on impulse and is outraged when his will is blocked. If a 3-year-old pulls up a flower from someone's yard, he probably does not know that the act causes stress to whoever planted it. The child, lacking that knowledge, is making no choice between self-interest and considerateness.

Everyone is thoughtless at times. But few persons past the age of 6 consistently act in an amoral manner. A preadolescent who is purely egocentric and hedonistic, out for every gratification he can get, is emotionally retarded. Amoral disregard of others is a serious abnormality in an adult; in a significant respect his socialization has failed. A psychiatrist would class him as "antisocial."

THE EXPEDIENT LEVEL    The expedient person is also self-centered, but his behavior is far more controlled. He knows the importance of considering others' reactions in order to come out ahead in the long run. Indeed, according to Peck and Havighurst,

> his outward behavior may often be honest and responsible, in the main, so far as others can see. The key to his low-level morality is his "me-first" attitude in a critical situation, where an unmoral act may bring advantages that outweigh any disapproval. . . .

## Expedient reasoning in three cultures

In his research, Kohlberg confronts young people with moral dilemmas. For example, the shopkeeper in a town is greedy, setting prices out of reach. A poor man, whose wife is starving to death, is tempted to steal food. Should he? Kohlberg (in Beck, 1971, p. 33) reports the following answers, all of which he sees as reflecting the same level of moral judgment.

In Taiwan the child at the expedient stage says: "He should steal the food for his wife because if she dies, he'll have to pay for the funeral and that costs a lot."

Funerals count for little in the aboriginal Atayal culture of Malaysia. There the answer is: "He should steal because he needs his wife to cook for him."

In the U.S. the archetype answer for this stage comes from the 13-year-old boy who says: "If a pet dies, you can get along without it—it isn't something you really need. Well, you can get a new wife, but it's not really the same."

Despite his IQ of 102, this boy's moral reasoning was slow to develop, Kohlberg says. The reasoning is parallel in each culture.

> . . . many very young children . . . have learned to behave correctly when an adult is around. . . . In the absence of such controls, they immediately relapse into doing what they please, even if this involves shoving other people around, taking what they want, or otherwise gratifying their self-centered desires. (1960, pp. 5–6.)

An older expedient person gratifies his impulse even when he knows the action is not "good." He sizes up the risk of detection and the penalties that might follow. If these are small, he goes ahead. It is not the impulse to do something unwise that shows immaturity; at any age a person has impulsive desires. A person may acknowledge such wishes without guilt, and still know that to act on them would be unwise.

THE CONVENTIONAL LEVEL   A person who usually makes the choices that are normal in his group is said to be acting conventionally. When distressed, we hide our tears more out of an attempt to behave properly than for any moral reasons. How fast we drive is determined mostly by how fast we see others driving. There is a strong element of expediency in conventional behavior. Following the pack protects one from disapproval. The conformer gratifies fewer of his impulses than the expedient person does, but he too is looking out for himself.

Responsibility calls for more than obedience. The person should learn why a certain group norm is desirable to imitate, and when to violate even that norm. Many "good citizens" do operate at the conventional level. Faced with a choice between what the group wants and what their judgment tells them is best, they are more likely to go along with the group. They follow the fads in political opinion, in what they buy, and in child rearing. When, carried on the tide of changing popular sentiment, they find themselves acting in a way inconsistent with their old beliefs, they feel discomfort rather than guilt.

THE IRRATIONAL-CONSCIENTIOUS LEVEL    Conscience is the name given to internal self-criticism that makes the person dissatisfied with some act even though it attains his external goals. Freud distinguished two types of self criticism—that originating in the Ego and that in the Superego. Ego may be thought of as the seat of attitudes that keep a person realistic, so that he tries to foresee consequences. It is through the Superego that he judges whether his plans are morally worthy or unworthy. Ego knows that buying votes is a way to win elections but Superego keeps a candidate from using that route to win. Thus, Superego (the conscience or system of values) judges any provisional try against a high moral standard, whereas Ego judges the proposed behavior in terms of efficiency. Bannister (box, p. 705) says that Freud pictures the choosing of responses as a contest among the impulsive monkey Id, the spinster Superego and the bank clerk Ego. However fanciful the metaphor, it helps distinguish moral learning from purely factual or rational learning. Before our discussion ends, you will see that Ego and Superego do not have to be in opposition.

Behavior is irrational-conscientious when a person's values have been emotionally conditioned. It is easier to illustrate this style than to define it. Consider the person who cannot tell a lie. Many people learn just this attitude in early childhood from a parent who insists on truthfulness. The child whose first innocent alterations of the truth bring severe punishments is likely to feel fearful when the thought of falsehood tempts him later. The temptation to untruth is threatening for him as Watson's rat was threatening for the child who came to associate it with loud noise (p. 742). His anxiety will bar him from lying even when there is no possibility of his being detected and punished. It will bar him from lying when lying might serve others well. If, because of some strong temptation, he does lie, he will feel guilty. Guilt is a sense of unworthiness, "of having violated one's own moral integrity." (Peck & Havighurst, 1960, p. 7). It is quite different from the feeling of the person who believes he has made a mistake and can act more wisely next time. The latter person is learning to discriminate where lying is bad. The first person, subjected to severe punishment on some occasions, develops a conflict that prevents discrimination (p. 211).

Some might contend that inviolable standards represent the best in character. The person who is irrevocably attached to truth-telling, however, is limited. He will lack the gracious social lies that make it possible to get along with others. "How did you like my daughter's performance in the school play, Mr. McGee?" If McGee cannot evade or stretch the truth, his candid comment will make him unpopular and will needlessly wound the matron and her daughter. McGee could never fill a role where "the whole truth and nothing but the truth" is not a prime value. An irrational value system may be self-defeating

"IT'S FAKE-FUR, HONEY."   "FAKES GOT A RIGHT TO LIVE, TOO, Y'KNOW!"

"Dennis the Menace" used courtesy of Hank Ketcham and
© 1976 by Field Newspaper Syndicate, T.M. ®

because it insists on a single principle of action regardless of circumstances. One value competes with others. The person has no way to solve a problem where his irrationally held values do not all lie on one side.

Irrational values contribute to neurotic maladjustment. It is neurotic, for example, for a person to drive himself toward a perfection he can never attain. Yet such behavior is seen in intelligent people, as in the man who never completes a report on time because he is always dissatisfied with the loose ends. The person who violates a deeply conditioned value pays the penalty afterward in feelings of guilt. Self-acceptance and guilt are incompatible.

The values that parents pound into children do aid in social living. Nothing is to be said against truthfulness, cooperation, generosity, and neatness. As habits, they combine into a comfortable and useful style of life. It is in the exceptional situation that conventional values are inadequate guides. It may be necessary to attack others boldly to bring a community problem into the open; then to not assert oneself is a vice.

THE RATIONAL LEVEL   Most standards of conduct are encountered first at the conventional level, then verbalized into a policy to be followed with a clear reason, and finally, much later, understood. Upon entering school the child finds it the custom to spend a certain period each day picking up materials. He conforms, first to be sure of approval, then because he is pleased to fill his role as class member. The teacher criticizes a piece of work as untidy. The student council sends out the word that there is too much trash on the school ground. Such incidents coalesce into an abstract concept of neatness. If the student accepts teacher and peers as models, this abstract ideal will become a value. Skilled teaching can gradually bring him to question why neatness is desirable, and how one can decide what is "neat enough."

He will recognize that an untidy paper is hard to read, that an untidy school yard is ugly. But he will not have impulses to square the corners of the papers on his desk. On occasion, he can subordinate neatness to other, greater ends.

Transition from the irrational to the rational level is slow. As one becomes more rational, he becomes more aware of conflicts among values and more conscious that different cultures assign different priorities to the values. The person is never so relativist as to give up his convictions: one hears an adolescent denouncing in one breath the "arbitrary traditions" his elders hold up as standards for him and, in the next, fervently pressing some value of his own on everyone. Kohlberg's highest level of moral judgment is marked by commitment to key principles (for example, to enhancing the dignity of all persons), not by a wishy-washy readiness to see all points of view as equal.

To arrive at rational solutions to conflict, one must be clear which values are subordinate. Destruction of life is undesirable, so war is undesirable; but oppression is undesirable and willingness to make war may sometimes be the only way to prevent oppression. A person's system of beliefs can be organized so that he knows which ends are the most important and why; such a person is integrated. Wish, knowledge, and conscience are allies rather than antagonists. The ideal of moral education is to free a person's mind so that it can serve his highest values.

A value is a principle. It is an aid to interpretation. One understands a value if one knows what consequences (for himself and others) are likely to follow its application. One understands a conflict between values when one sees what remote ends each value serves and what it leaves out of account. Thus, in the long run, having a philosophy makes one's conduct consistent. If a person is clear about what is of highest importance and knows that he must sacrifice minor values in order to achieve it, both Ego and Superego are satisfied.

Surely no one becomes totally rational about his conduct. Personal needs have sufficient force to keep us from carrying out some moral decisions. The pressures of a social situation may override personal judgment, making a conformer of even a highly mature individual. One can be rational in some areas more than in others, and at some times more than at others. The rational character is an ideal to be approached, to be attained only in myth.

One might distinguish among the five levels in this way. The amoral person ignores values beyond immediate pleasure and displeasure. The expedient person has become aware of ethical values or group standards but does not use them to judge himself. Conformity may be a means for him, not an end. The conventional person wants to do as others do, and this aim is more compelling for him than any abstract moral idea. When the group abandons some value, he also abandons his attachment to it. Conscientious individuals want to do right. They are emotionally attached to value ideals, which they use to judge proposed actions. The irrational conscience is emotionally bound to principles that are likely to be incompatible.

The person with rational character is concerned with real effects. He is firmly committed to some basic values, but he knows how they fit together and holds few standards inviolable. The rational person adheres neither to the group example nor to abstract "laws" of morality; for him, a conflict situation calls for intellectual analysis. Fromm (1947, p. 130) has argued cogently that the person who most considers others is also the one who has the deepest self-acceptance.

Character, as defined here, contains a large intellectual element; the rational-conscientious person recognizes moral dilemmas, analyzes them, and thinks his way through to a resolution. It is not surprising, then, to discover a correlation of character with measured ability. Among 36-year-old women who were rated after lengthy interviews, the ones classed as "thoughtful" in their daily activities tended to have above-average verbal ability, and those classed as "conventional" tended to be below average (Bayley, in Mussen, 1970, vol. 1, p. 1201). The child's mastery of concrete operational thought about objects is strongly correlated with ability to make judgments about equity in human affairs; tests of the two kinds correlate as high as 0.80 at ages 7 and 8 (Damon, 1975). Both kinds of judgment require that one take multiple points of view into account. In another study, Grim et al. (1968) found cheating most frequent among schoolchildren who are restless, impulsive, and inattentive; they are weak in "taking and maintaining a mental set" (p. 275).

---

**6** Classify the following statements or actions according to the level of character development the action represents:
  a. James, 11, thinks that criminals are crazy because "crime does not pay."
  b. Martha insists on inviting a Japanese schoolmate to her party because if she is not invited her feelings will be hurt.
  c. Martha's mother suggests that Martha limit her list to children of her own class and ethnic group, on the grounds that people in her neighborhood don't usually mix with people from other parts of town.

d. Sunny, a white girl age 4, goes to nursery school and immediately starts playing with a black girl.
e. To teach responsibility, a college formulates with the students an "honor principle" that replaces all other rules. The students are free to do what they choose, "consistent with the welfare of the entire community." After five years of successful operation, with a few cases of honor violations disposed of by a student-faculty review committee, the system is threatened with breakdown. Reserve books are taken from the library without being signed out. Equipment is broken in dormitory scuffles for which no one admits blame. Though the persons responsible are known to many fellow students, these students choose not to report them as "honor violators."
f. In one of the famous episodes of the Watergate affair, President Nixon directed his Attorney General to discharge the Special Prosecutor for excessive zeal. The Attorney General refused to do so and resigned, apparently believing that the prosecutor had been acting legitimately, but not denying the President's constitutional right to discharge a subordinate. His deputy did the same. The Solicitor General, who was third in line, carried out the order, apparently believing that the order was lawful, that anyone holding the office of President should be able to command the cooperation of his subordinates, and that refusal and resignation on his part would be only a gesture that would not long delay the dismissal.

7 Reread the case of Mack (p. 127) and answer these questions:
a. Which of Mack's expectations or attitudes may have been confirmed in school classrooms?
b. Which of Mack's attitudes may have been confirmed in his attaining election and serving as a student-body officer?
c. Sanford speaks of Mack's "rigid adherence" to the standards of authority, but adds that Mack does not accept these authorities "in any fundamental way." What does he mean?

8 Would it be possible to have a rational, selfish character?

9 The correlation of adult rational character and verbal ability might be explained in many ways. Do any of the following explanations seem plausible? Which?
a. The rational person appreciates the value of education and develops his abilities.
b. The person who has a larger vocabulary and greater reasoning ability avoids error; rational character is just another name for reaching sound conclusions.
c. Some third factor in development, such as parental attitude, is the link that causes superiority in these traits to go together.

# HOW UNIFIED IS CHARACTER?

Chapter 17 discussed the consistency of attitudes and personality traits. We saw that a particular person has his own pattern of response to situations related to religion, and yet can be summed up by a statement about the probability, over a large class of situations, of his adopting certain religious practices. Much the same is to be said about the consistency of traits of character. A person who makes honesty a conscious principle will act honestly in the face of most temptations. But "most" is not "all." Whether, on a particular occasion, he acts honestly depends on the reward dishonesty can bring, on the probability that dishonesty will be detected, on his view of the person or institution his dishonesty will hurt, and on the community standards—in particular, on how *his* associates respond to comparable temptations. Recall Mark Twain's story "The Man Who Corrupted Hadleyburg."

There are three ways to study character formally. One is the case study, which collects information not only on what the person does but also how he feels about himself, about others in his life, about various kinds of impulse, and so on. This method was exhibited in the case of Mack (p. 127), and we need say little more about it. The second procedure is the controlled experimental test, like those discussed on p. 744. The ray-gun test of honesty (p. 135) is an example; a temptation is set up, and what the person actually does is recorded. Third are tests of judgment, which can be thought of as an extension of verbal tests of mental ability. General tests like Wechsler's ask, for example, "What should you do if you see someone leave his book. . . ?" Tests of moral judgment pose a sharper dilemma, and the tester usually interviews the person in some depth to find out how he defends his choice.

CONTROLLED EXPERIMENTAL TESTS The Character Education Inquiry (Hartshorne & May, 1928, 1929, 1930) was distinguished from virtually all previous attempts to find out about character because the investigators actually observed character in action. Although later research goes beyond Hartshorne and May, their facts have been confirmed repeatedly. Most judgments of character are based on reputation, or on the casual impressions of teachers and other acquaintances. The C.E.I. instead built tests that confronted students with conflicts. The behavior sample gave an indisputable (if incomplete) indicator of character in that setting. Here are C.E.I. tests of honesty, generosity, and cooperation:

- Students were asked to do as well as they could on an impossible task, such as placing dots in small circles while blindfolded. This is so difficult that any student who succeeded certainly peeked.

- In an arithmetic game, each student experimented at his seat with a box of coins. Afterward, while placing his coins in the box and returning them to the front of the room, the student had a chance to sneak out some money. Hidden marks on the box told the research workers which children took money.

- Each student was given as a present a pencil box full of attractive things. A box was provided into which he could deposit, unobserved, whatever objects (if any) he wished to donate to poor children. Covert markings allowed the investigators to record the child's generosity.

- Each student took some arithmetic tests when working "for himself"— that is, with his name on the paper and a prize offered for high score. In another set of tests his scores were to be counted in the group's score, but he did not sign his individual paper. The similarity in the two scores presumably represented how much effort he put out for the group good.

Other tests dealt with self-control and persistence. The tests were used only for research.

The value of using measurements instead of opinions is suggested by the differences found between boys and girls. Two comparisons were made: how honestly the boys and the girls behaved, and how teachers rated their honesty. As Table 18.1 shows, more boys than girls resisted temptation on most of the tests. In contrast, teachers rated girls as more honest than boys by a wide margin. Girls' measured conduct was slightly better than boys' in some traits, but in reputation they were undeservedly far above the boys. This is reminiscent of the bias found in teacher's academic marks (p. 697).

On tests of honesty, many scores are close to 50 per cent. A middling score gives no basis for predicting the person's response to the next temptation. Some children took coins because they wanted money badly and felt that they

**TABLE 18.1**

**Performance of boys and girls on character tests**

| Test | Percentage who cheated | | |
| --- | --- | --- | --- |
| | Boys | Girls | Difference |
| Peeping in dotting test | 79 | 85 | 6* |
| Peeping in a party game | 38 | 68 | 30* |
| Cheating in grading own school papers | 31 | 34 | 3 |
| Cheating in grading own schoolwork at home | 28 | 37 | 9* |

SOURCE: Adapted from Hartshorne & May (1928).
*Difference too large to be attributed to chance.

hurt no one in stealing school money. The same children might never take another child's unguarded lunch money. Others no doubt enjoyed daring to take money under the teacher's nose; they found no such thrill in the dotting test. If two situations present different goals and different threats, it is unreasonable to expect a person to react to them in the same way. A change in response is not inconsistency.

TESTS OF JUDGMENT    The character tests described above are behavioral, focusing on acts. To test the deeper aspect of character, we need to investigate how the person thinks when facing a moral dilemma.

Durkin (1959a and b), following the lead of Piaget, presented questions like these in an interview:

---

**One morning in school a boy named Keith took a ruler off Russell's desk and wouldn't give it back to him. What should Russell do? Why? What if Keith had taken the ruler and broken it in two? What should Russell have done then? Why?**

---

Piaget, you will recall, has been interested in "reversibility" of operations as a sign of advancing intellectual development. The child learns to adjust quantities, weights, and the like to restore balance. Piaget suggested that the childish behavior of "getting even" can be looked on as a similar restoration of equilibrium. But a more mature response is to turn the situation around and perceive it through the other person's eyes. Durkin classified children's responses according to whether or not they used the reciprocity principle—"treat him as he treated you." The results (Table 18.2) show a marked advance beyond reciprocity over the grades, and marked differences from one type of conflict to another. (See also Turiel, in Travers, 1973, p. 741.)

**TABLE 18.2**

Children's judgments according to age and kind of injury

| Type of Injury | Percentage of pupils recommending "reciprocal" action | | |
|---|---|---|---|
| | In Grade II | In Grade V | In Grade VIII |
| Refusal to share property | 72 | 39 | 17 |
| Defaming one's character | 50 | 21 | 6 |
| Taking one's property | 7 | 5 | 3 |
| Destroying one's property | 11 | 10 | 0 |

SOURCE: Data from Durkin (1959b), p. 292.

## Dilemma

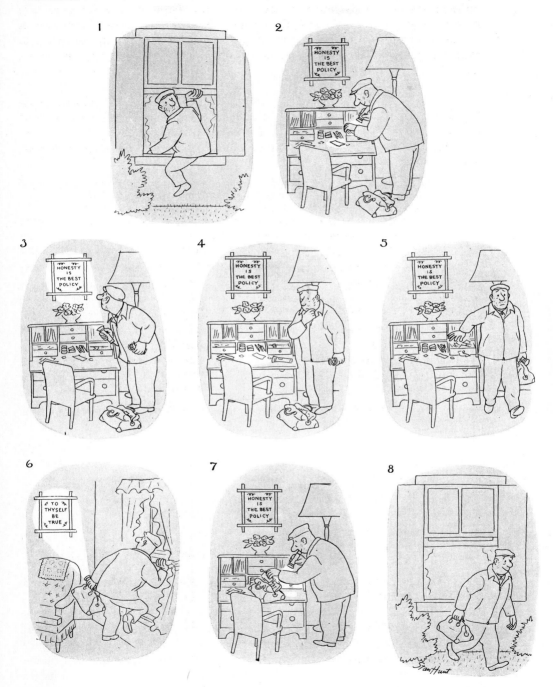

Drawing by Stan Hunt; © 1957 The New Yorker Magazine, Inc.

## Should Holly climb the tree?

A moral-judgment test for first-graders tells the simple story:

Holly is an eight-year-old girl who likes to climb trees. She is the best tree-climber in the neighborhood. One day while climbing down from a tall tree, she falls off the bottom branch but doesn't hurt herself. Her father sees her fall. He is upset and asks her to promise not to climb trees any more. Holly promises.

Later that day, Holly meets Shawn. Shawn's kitten is caught up a tree and can't get down. Something has to be done right away or the kitten may fall. Holly is the only one who climbs trees well enough to reach the kitten, but she remembers her promise to her father.

Responses to this story were scored at three levels (Selman & Lieberman, 1975, p. 714; see also p. 812):

*Level 0.* Confused response. No single perspective, dilemma left unresolved.

Julie (4 years 1 month): What should Holly do? *Save the kitten.* Why is that right? *Kittens are nice. She doesn't want it to get hurt.* What will Holly's father do when he finds out? *Be angry.* Why? *She broke her promise.* Was it right to climb the tree? *No.* Why not? *Because her father could punish her.*

*Level 1.* Simple emphasis on goodness or badness of intentions.

Tom (6 years, 8 months): Should the father punish her for climbing the tree? *He could, but it wouldn't be right.* Why not? *Because she didn't mean to do anything wrong. She was trying to save the kitty.*

Sarah (7 years, 4 months): Do you think Holly's father would understand if she told him why she climbed the tree? *Yes. Because she got the kitten down instead of just climbing it for fun.*

*Level 2.* Reciprocal perspectives. Dilemma seen from perspective of other persons.

Ann (8 years, 1 month): Do you think that Holly should climb the tree? *No.* Why not? *She might think she should because she's saving the kitten but she is afraid her father would think she didn't care about him.*

Allan (9 years, 2 months): Do you think Holly will climb the tree? *Yes.* Why? *To save the kitten.* Won't she be worried that her father will punish her? *No. She knows her father will understand why she did it.*

---

The heart of judgment is not the action selected but the reasons offered (box). Mature thinkers may choose different actions, each justified by a balanced argument. Kohlberg, testing older persons, presses the reasoning to its limits by a series of questions, each built on the person's previous answer. Should the husband steal a drug for his hopelessly ill wife? If the drug doesn't work, should the doctor put her out of her pain? If he did, would you blame him? Should the doctor be sentenced to death? And (at each juncture): Why do you think so? (Porter & Taylor, 1972.)

Moral judgment is to be distinguished from moral knowledge, just as beliefs about the ecological movement are distinct from knowledge about ecology (p. 745). On tests that simply ask the person to classify "right" and "wrong" conduct, verbally described, scores decrease (!) with increasing age.

> High scores on these tests are achieved by the time children reach first grade, which indicates that they are relatively aware of the moral cliches of their culture at an early age. The decrease in test scores we observed after age 10 does not mean that these children forgot what they once knew.... The test scores decreased because as children grow older they think about the same issues in a different way. (Turiel, in Travers, 1973, p. 735.)

An example would be the child who, with greater maturity, comes to reject the statement "One should always speak the truth."

Intellectual beliefs are not always expressed in action (Chapter 17), hence it is no surprise that conduct often falls below the level of verbal judgments. Nelsen et al. (1969) found that the sixth-grader's level of moral judgment did not predict whether he would cheat on tests like the ray-gun. Kohlberg (in Beck et al., 1971, p. 75; see also p. 813) goes so far as to say: "People's verbal moral values about honesty have nothing to do with how they act"—but he doesn't really mean it. People who stop to think about values often do act as they think best (his p. 79). A person with strong needs and little self-control, however, often acts contrary to his best judgment even if his understanding is good (Nelsen et al., 1968). This is a common finding among delinquents (p. 96). Conversely, those whose thinking is superficial may act in an approved manner because they are not tempted or because group standards hold them in line.

Personal motives are part of the picture. Schwartz et al. (1969) found that male college students low in moral judgment *and* low in need for achievement were most likely to cheat on a challenging intellectual task. (See also Fig. 18.1.) The person

## FIGURE 18.1

### Relation of cheating to motivation to achieve and to anxiety

Motivation to achieve was measured by a picture-interpretation technique. These results are for male college students; data on women showed no clear pattern.

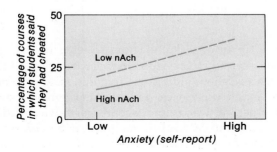

SOURCE: Data from C. P. Smith et al. (1972).

with a need to achieve is not so much tempted; he gains satisfaction only through genuine accomplishments. A second test measured helpfulness—willingness to help another person at a sacrifice of one's own earnings and rewards. Helpfulness went with high need for affiliation and low need for achievement; moral judgment correlated only very weakly with helpfulness.

Haan (1975) investigated the thinking of Berkeley students in a crisis situation and compared it to their thinking about hypothetical dilemmas. The real event was a sit-in to protest campus restrictions on political activity; in the end, police arrested the protesters. Statements about this event tended to be more mature than those made about the hypothetical event. Of the persons actually arrested, 21 per cent had been scored as expedient on the hypothetical test; but risking arrest was an act above the expedient level, and so was their thinking about the real event. The protest was a community affair, and the group's discussion of policy probably increased the insight of all participants. But community can reduce the level of rationality, as is evidenced in the witch hunts of Salem and of the McCarthy period.

10  One investigator found that students who cheated on an arithmetic test were not the ones who cheated on a spelling test. How could this be explained?

11  In one character test, students check a list of words, marking those whose meaning they know. Then a test is given to see if they really know the words. Does the number of words checked but not truly known indicate the same sort of dishonesty that the dotting and coin tests show?

12  Consider the following true-false statement: "To divide a cake fairly, you should make everyone's piece the same size." Assume that more 8-year-olds than 12-year-olds say "True." How can this be explained?

# CHARACTER FORMATION AS A DEVELOPMENTAL PROCESS

The child cannot be expected to develop character faster than he develops comprehension of human relations. Judgment requires insight, and that insight is achieved through social experience and the developing powers of logical thought. Likewise, the child who cannot accept frustration or delay of gratification is certain to act contrary to his best judgment. Kohlberg and his associates suggest that progress in moral judgment among American city children speeds up at certain ages:

> The first [spurt] is the preadolescent period (age ten to thirteen) at which time the transition from preconventional [expedient] to conventional morality occurs.... Those who do not reach ... [the conventional level] by age thirteen are unlikely to attain principled thinking in adulthood. The second transitional period appears to be late adolescence, ages fifteen to nineteen. Our results suggest that those who do not use some (at least twenty per cent) principled thinking by the end of high school are unlikely to develop principled thinking in adulthood. (Kohlberg & Turiel, in Lesser, 1971, p. 448.)

If being able to see a problem from various angles is the key to maturity on the intellectual side, coming to terms with authority is the key on the emotional side. The authority of adults and the authority of the peer group are likely to be equally significant.

A child may reject either kind of authority if he cannot receive rewards by doing as that authority demands. Lacking identification with representatives of society, he may never become committed to moral values, and may defy them. At the other extreme of reaction, a person may find conformity (to peers or to power figures) so necessary that he has no freedom to be himself.

As at many points in this book, I emphasize side by side the continuity of development and the possibility of altering its course. Chapter 6 cited some facts on the way character grows out of home experience, and more evidence on the continuity of development appears in this chapter. For example, cheating in the ray-gun test (Table 18.3) is forecast by lack of conscientiousness five years earlier. Although continuity is undeniable, the chapter will also include evidence that development of character is an active process to which the school can contribute.

## TABLE 18.3
### Early character development and later behavior

| Strength of conscience at age 6 (mother's report) | Behavior on the ray-gun test at age 11 | |
| --- | --- | --- |
| | Number who cheated | Number who did not cheat |
| Strong | 19 | 18 |
| Moderate or weak | 79 | 23 |

SOURCE: Data from Grinder (1962).

## Defiance and Delinquency

Delinquents live in the present, in a world of immediate gratifications and annoyances. They are typically expedient, looking toward short-run consequences. In an academic setting where few students cheat, the cheaters are students who expect the world to impose on them and who express resentment against the system.

Not all delinquents are emotionally disturbed; some—especially among the very poor—are simply conforming to a subcommunity where delinquency is the norm. Typically, however, delinquents have had the dice loaded against them from the start. Their homes are more likely to be disorganized and lacking in coherent discipline (Ahlstrom & Havighurst, 1971; Conger et al., 1975; McCord et al., 1959). Most have had a history of poor relations with peers (Roff et al., 1972). Many began early to distrust others (p. 211). And their school histories have been discouraging.

In an urban, poor neighborhood, a third of the boys have concluded as early as age 10 that their chances of finishing high school are poor. This early pessimism—which is not warranted by abnormally low achievement—is a forerunner and probably a cause of delinquency in the teen years (Caplan, 1972). In the Ahlstrom-Havighurst study and the Conger study, elementary-school teachers had complained particularly of the lack of self-control or responsibility of boys who later were delinquents; such complaints entered the school records of many boys as early as Grade I and increased through the years. There is some dispute about the extent of actual academic failure. Ahlstrom and Havighurst say that 60 per cent of their boys had academic deficiencies, whereas in Caplan's sample delinquency was not associated with poor achievement. Academic failure certainly does not "explain" delinquency; many failing students and dropouts avoid delinquency. Alienation and low morale are the crucial developmental failure.

## Conformity

The conformer adapts to his group; getting along with others is his principal guide to conduct. Such a personality is obviously formed by successful experience in gaining acceptance from others. A child who feels secure with his parents will expect to be approved when he follows their example. If he has been consistently accepted by his social group, he will expect satisfying consequences when he adopts their standards. Some persons never grow beyond a conforming level. Their moral complexion changes as they go from group to group. The permissive home seems especially to foster a pliable, group-oriented style (Devereux, 1969). When value standards are not truly a part of the person's belief system, conduct is regulated largely by the rewards and sanctions expected from other persons.

The other persons may encourage socially desirable conduct, or the opposite. Bronfenbrenner (1970, p. 78) asked Russian and American 12-year-olds what they would do in the face of various temptations—for example, to cheat on a test. Students were tested under three conditions:

- The scientific condition, under which the responses would be reduced to group statistics and these would be seen only by far-away scientists. No one would know what any individual said.

- The "PTA" condition, under which information on what each student said would be posted. The findings would be discussed at a meeting of parents and teachers.

- The class condition, under which information on what each student said would be posted in his classroom (and only there). The findings would be discussed by the class.

Under all three conditions, far more of the Soviet children said they would resist temptation than American (or English or West German) children did. They have been socialized in a manner that makes the peer group a powerful moral force (p. 611). What their classmates would think of them influenced them as much as what adults would think. Classmates also had a strong effect on American 12-year-olds, but not a moral one. Under the condition where peers were to be informed, *more* of the Americans said they would violate the rules than under the condition where they had only themselves to satisfy.

The commitment of Russian children to community standards is further indicated by a second Bronfenbrenner study (his p. 79). He asked Russian and Swiss 12-year-olds how they would react if they observed another child in some misdeed. A full 75 per cent of the Russian children said that they would talk to the violator and tell him he should not do it; nearly all the others said they would report the offense to an adult or to other members of the group. About a third of the Swiss children would speak directly to the offender, and equal numbers would tell an adult or do nothing. The Russian children identify with the community so strongly, even by age 12, that they are enforcers rather than obeyers alone. The person who is his brother's keeper must keep watch also on his own conduct.

The American adolescent of the pliable, conforming type is likely to be optimistic, confident, socially accepted, and active in school affairs (Havighurst & Taba, 1949; Devereux, 1967). Such youngsters tend not to strive to achieve, though on average they get along fairly well in school. Because they are aware of fewer problems, conformers can be more contented. The fact that conformers are usually at ease is not entirely a good sign; conformity easily becomes irresponsibility. For a current interpretation of what conformity means in different emotional contexts, see L. Ross et al. (1976).

---

 **13** According to Devereux (1967), a classroom as a whole develops a moral orientation that can be observed when members individually judge moral dilemmas. Some classes give much the same answers under all three experimental variations of the Bronfenbrenner study. Others endorse adult-approved responses in the "PTA" condition, and, in the other conditions, swing far over to selfish responses or responses calculated to please classmates. Can the teacher influence this aspect of the class spirit?

---

## Rational Self-Discipline

The rational adolescent shuttles between conformity and independence. He has enough self-respect to think for himself, but enough respect for others to feel uncertain when he disagrees with them. Typically, his home is harmonious, reasonably lenient, democratic, and highly consistent, all of which help him learn discriminations between good and bad conduct. He has identified with parents and learned to want to do right. He has not become so dependent on parent approval or peer approval that he fears to disagree (Havighurst & Taba, 1949; Peck & Havighurst, 1960; Becker, 1964; Haan et al., 1968; Devereux, 1967).

How the treatment children and adolescents receive in the home influences their moral judgment and conduct has been investigated in many studies, and this work is comprehensively reviewed by M. Hoffman (in Mussen, 1970, vol. 2, pp. 282ff.). The mother who asserts power and uses punishment tends to have bad effects; the mother who treats the child warmly and reasons with him to shape his conduct has positive effects. Hoffman did not review case studies, and in correlational studies he did not find any consistent relation of the child's moral development to how his father had treated him. It is in case studies that we find the evidence on effects of authoritarian fathers discussed earlier. Another matter mentioned earlier, particularly in the Mussen study (p. 137), is that the same parental style may affect boys and girls differently. Hoffman's review (and later reports by Baumrind, 1973, and Hoffman, 1975) show clearly that complex sex-related effects remain to be pinned down, but other studies do not find the same effect as Mussen reported.

Kohlberg (1971, pp. 349–50) echoes Barker (p. 174) and the Commission on Youth (p. 197) in emphasizing the "role-taking opportunities" found in the culture. Figure 18.2 shows Kohlberg's classification of the moral judgment of

**FIGURE 18.2**

**Moral judgment exhibited by American and Israeli youth**

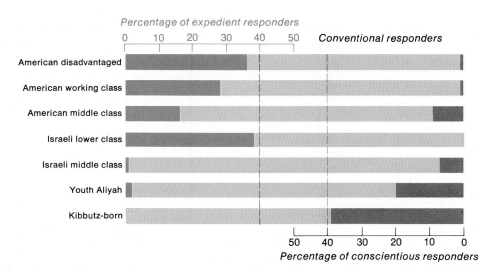

SOURCE: Data from Kohlberg (1971a), p. 349.

**TABLE 18.4**

**Summary of common constellations of adolescent character**

| Level of character integration | Factors predisposing to this pattern |
|---|---|
| Self-centered, expedient | Rejecting or neglecting home |
| Conventional, conforming | Pleasant appearance and good physique |
| Irrational-conscientious | Any handicap that might arouse inferiority feelings<br>Dominant, severe home |
| Rational, considerate | High mental ability<br>Parents democratic or mildly dominant, but warm<br>Bases for approval and disapproval made clear |

several hundred adolescents in two countries. The high scores of the kibbutz-niks is perhaps not surprising; they were reared in an intellectually intense, morally committed communal group. The scores of the Youth Aliyah sample, however, are remarkable. These are Jews who migrated to Israel from countries outside the Western world, carrying most of the stigmata of cultural disadvantage. The youths in Kohlberg's sample had been assigned to kibbutz living; just a few years in that setting brought their thinking almost to the level of the born kibbutznik.

To summarize: The self-centered adolescent has failed to accomplish developmental tasks of relating to authority and winning self-respect in normal ways. The conformer places too much importance on peer approval. The irrational-conscientious person has wanted adult or community approval, and finds self-respect in following the code. He remains dependent on the rules set down by his identifying figures, even after they have left the scene. The rational person acts according to his appreciation of the value issues at stake in a particular choice. Such a person finds self-respect in self-direction.

As a way of bringing the preceding sections together, Table 18.4 provides a brief outline. It is important to remember that it indicates only a few common combinations. Each individual works out a relationship all his own. One can certainly not conclude that every person with high ability and a democratic home will have a rational character in adolescence.

| Feeling about parents | Feeling about peers | Feeling about self |
| --- | --- | --- |
| Feels rejected and rejecting | Rejects most of group but may find some supporters | Discontented, strives actively for power, independence, or short-run goals |
| Feels loved and secure | Feels loved and secure | Self-satisfied No apparent anxiety |
| Feels likely to be rejected if conduct is bad Little open conflict | Not close to peers Thinks of them as vaguely threatening | Secure if able to live within his code, but anxious when values conflict |
| Respects and loves parents but feels safe in acting independently | Often feels somewhat isolated | Believes in own ability but not complacent |

14  What changes in conduct would you anticipate if an adolescent of each of the four common types moved from a strict, religious small town to a large city high school where group standards are much less strict?

15  In a small community, adolescents were asked individually to name adults who represented desirable qualities. Those at the lower levels of character development appear to select less admirable persons as models; some adults named are shiftless and a bit disreputable (Peck & Havighurst, 1960, p. 153). How is this choice of models to be explained?

## EDUCATING FOR CHARACTER

In both Chapters 17 and 18 I have discussed the interplay between intellectual beliefs and understandings, emotional commitments and fears, and overt action. Some educational methods are designed to improve just one of these, some are more comprehensive. We can consider first the methods that try to modify behavior directly, and then the methods that try to influence character through verbal instruction (with and without accompanying activities). The direct forms of character education have their place, but character formation is to a large extent a collateral learning, a part of the total development of the person. It follows that character is influenced by the student's entire life in school, and not just by the moments set aside for "moral education." The developmental supports the school provides or fails to provide are therefore a part of the program of character education.

## Practice to Shape Habits of Conduct

One prominent conception is that character is formed through action, that it consists of specific habits that can be strengthened through practice, or reshaped by techniques that encourage more desirable acts and reinforce them. The idea that character development is simply the solidification of habits has never been put more eloquently than in the famous essay on habit of William James:

> Habit is thus the enormous flywheel of society, its most precious conservative agent. It alone is what keeps us all within the bounds of ordinance, and saves the children of fortune from the envious uprisings of the poor. It alone prevents the hardest and most repulsive walks of life from being deserted by those brought up to tread therein. . . . It is well for the world that in most of us, by the age of thirty, the character has set like plaster, and will never soften again. . . . (1890, I, pp. 121ff.)

What the person is at age 30—what he fears, what he admires, what standards he sets for himself—has been consolidating throughout his history, and dramatic changes after age 30 are not to be expected. But to say that character is "set like plaster" goes too far. Attitudes regarding particular dilemmas—regarding tolerance, and trust in government, for example—continue to evolve, and new-found security or progressive disappointment can alter even the emotional foundations on which key values or anxieties rest. A person can grow in insight throughout life, attach himself to new ideals, and throw new energy into social action—if at his core he likes the world, feels that the world likes him, and believes in the power of his own intelligence.

Simply providing opportunities to engage in desirable actions, encouraging them by setting forth a model, and administering suitable rewards is a limited tactic at best. We saw in Chapter 17 that arranging for interracial contacts is not a dependable way to overcome prejudice, and the educator who sets out to "form the habit of generosity" in the child is likely to be similarly disappointed. The educator would give the child occasions to contribute to charity drives, to prepare Thanksgiving baskets, and so on. Supposedly, his "habit of giving" is strengthened each time he places his dime or can of food on the class pile.

But what response is the child practicing? The student usually gets the money by asking at home; he faces no conflict and makes no moral choice. Giving acquires no positive value for him. Consider, however, the one who knows that his father will be angry at the request, or embarrassed by a lack of funds. In the end, to avoid embarrassment at school, the child gets the money if he can. This try is confirmed: no one bothers him until the next drive. His contribution was not gratifying to him, however, and he does not learn to enjoy generous acts for their own sake.

The *idea* of self-sacrifice can be developed without drill. Discussions communicate values to those who identify with the teacher. Some activities that serve others the child can do and will enjoy. This is better than using him as an intermediary to collect money from home. Proper experiences make contributing a source of pleasure, not an act of forced compliance.

Trained patterns of conduct may not transfer. In the Boys' Club (p. 662), where strongly directed boys "practiced" persistence and cooperation, the orderly atmosphere disintegrated as soon as the leader left. For the expedient, an act loses its point when the promise of reward or the threat of punishment is removed. The conformers and the conscientious are more likely to continue to act as they did during the activity, not because of extensive practice but because a new aim was communicated. Often, disapproval for noncompliance is more prominent in attempts to reshape habits than positive encouragement. As we saw in Chapter 14, negative consequences may suppress unwanted acts temporarily, but their effects are not educative. Punishing children who yield to temptation is much less effective in producing lasting change than giving some reason—even a weak one—for resisting the temptation (Aronfreed, 1968). Giving a reason leads the child to think of the act as wrong rather than merely risky.

Interplay between experience and verbalization is as crucial for development of social and moral reasoning as for the development of reasoning about objects. Some of the earliest experiments on character education confirmed this. Voelker (1921) divided 57 boys into six small patrols. Two were given the usual Boy Scout training, which mentioned honesty and other such concepts but primarily provided "practice" in group activities. For experimental purposes two patrols were given many opportunities to discuss moral principles along with their activities. A continual effort was made to clarify and emphasize a code of good conduct. Two control groups received no Scout practice and did not discuss conduct. By far the greatest gains on experimental tests of character were made by the experimental group. Patrols that engaged in group activities without broader discussion made only slight gains over the controls. Ruediger (1908) similarly demonstrated that requiring students to do arithmetic lessons neatly did not improve their other work. When the practice was supplemented by discussion of the value of neatness, students began to judge their work in all situations against this ideal.

R. Miller et al. (1975) add a modern twist to these long-standing findings. Second-graders were exposed to eight days of "persuasion" or of "attribution."

FIGURE 18.3

**Reduction of littering as a consequence of an attribution treatment and of a persuasion treatment**

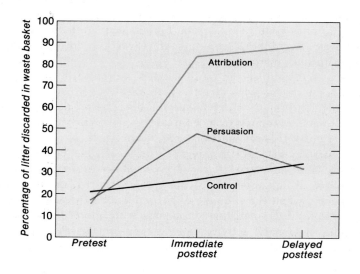

SOURCE: R. Miller et al. (1975), p. 433. Copyright 1975 by the American Psychological Association. Reproduced by permission.

The persuasion group heard a great deal about littering in connection with each field trip and with many schoolroom events. The recurrent message was, "You should be careful about litter." In the attribution group the activities were much the same, but the message was an attempt to change the self-concept: "We are a clean class; we are careful about litter." (The message, indeed, was so saccharine that some of the children protested: "We do litter sometimes.") The investigator gave littering tests on three occasions. For example, he handed out individually wrapped candies and later counted the wrappers found in proper containers, or on the floor and playground. Figure 18.3 displays the results. The attribution condition evidently did most to establish neatness as an ideal for the self.

**16** Describe school procedures that employ repetitive practice to teach
a. patriotism.
b. responsibility in carrying out duties.

## Verbal Teaching

Talking and reading about good behavior have been relied on by both religious and secular educators of character. Educators have always hoped that history, literature, and other subjects would contribute to character, though nothing beyond anecdote indicates that such hopes are often realized. Here we add to the discussion of verbal education in attitude formation in Chapter 17.

Just as the child taught conservation principles verbally fails to take them in, so direct presentation of advanced moral arguments is likely to have little impact. The child progresses toward conservation gradually; as he begins to carry in mind how an object looks from two points of view, he becomes aware of inconsistencies in his thinking and forms a more inclusive, more flexible interpretation. So with moral reasoning; becoming conscious of conflicts within one's belief system accelerates forward movement. A person who hears an argument with a theme far above his present level of moral judgment does not grasp what is being said (Kohlberg, in Beck et al., 1971, p. 49; Rest, 1973). The conformer, for example, can scarcely make sense of the assertion that a certain long-established law is morally wrong. As shown in the box, hearers reinterpret messages to fit their own ideas (Piagetian assimilation). But every person's thinking does include some elements of the level immediately above his cus-

### Growing into the Golden Rule

Kohlberg and Turiel (in Lesser, 1971, pp. 451–52) describe the difficulty of communicating moral content that is at a stage beyond the person's stage of development. Persons between the ages of 10 and 16 were questioned. In reading the passage, keep in mind that Kohlberg's Stage 2 is "expedient, self-centered," and Stage 3 is a conventional orientation to good conduct—winning approval, having good intentions. (The study was conducted by Selman.)

Almost all of the children in the study were able to repeat the Golden Rule as the formula, "Do unto others as you would have them do unto you." They were then asked, "Why is it a good rule?" and "What would it tell you to do if someone just came up and hit you on the street?" To the latter question, most of the ten-year-olds said, "Hit him back, do unto others as they do unto you." They interpreted the Golden Rule as Stage-2 reciprocity of actual exchange or revenge, instead of in terms of Stage-3 ideal reciprocity involving a consideration of what you would wish if you were in the other's place. Furthermore, they would justify the Golden Rule in Stage-2 terms: "If you follow the Golden Rule other people will be nice back to you." Only children at Stage 3 or above on the moral-judgment scale were able to interpret the Golden Rule correctly. The intellectually active effort required for an understanding of the formula is indicated in the following response by a ten-year-old Stage-3 boy: "Well, the Golden Rule is the best rule because like if you were rich, you might dream like that you were poor and how it felt and then the dream would go back in your own head and you would remember and you would help make the laws that way."

tomary level; if those elements are brought to consciousness by a message just one stage above his own, he accommodates by amending his system.

A suggestive experiment by Arbuthnot (1975) had college students play two conflicting roles in Kohlberg's scenario of conflict (box, p. 788). One student acted the part of a man desperate for a drug whose price was beyond his reach; the other acted the part of the druggist. Each tried to persuade the other to accept his position. Whereas reading morally advanced arguments had a negligible effect, the role-playing experience did advance the judgment of whichever partner started at a lower level than the other.

Discussion promotes change of belief even without role playing, as we saw in Chapter 17. Second-graders discussed moral dilemmas during a five-week period (Selman & Lieberman, 1975). The dilemmas dealt with promise keeping, truth telling, and the like, each dilemma being within the child's experience. The pictorial filmstrips offered no "right answers"; rather, they presented for discussion several reasons, mature and immature, such as children might offer. Moral judgment was assessed by an interview procedure—once before the training, again at midyear when the training program had been completed, and once more at year-end. On the scale used, 100 represents an emphasis on avoiding punishment (expediency) and 200 represents a more comprehensive awareness of consequences. In the control classes, the passage of time produced a little movement: from 110 at pretest, to 115 in midyear, to 125 at year-end. A typical experimental class went from 110 to 125 to 160. The gain continued through the year, partly because the experimental teachers discussed additional moral issues with the class during the spring (without filmstrips).

Blatt and Kohlberg (1975; box) reported a 12-week program of experimental teaching at age 11 and above. Here, also, lasting but modest gains were reported. Only a fraction of the trained group moved as much as one stage on Kohlberg's scale. Although there were gains in moral judgment, scores on a behavioral test of honesty did not change.

The emphasis in the Selman and the Blatt training was on seeing a problem from all sides, not on teaching moral rules. It was thus a step toward rational, conscientious behavior. A good deal of moral education is concerned with making the learner conscious of general principles with which to guide his behavior. Framing verbal generalizations is an important supplement to activities—"thinking about what one is doing," Stoddard called it.

Effects of moral education usually are weak, according to Turiel (in Travers, 1973, pp. 738ff.). As a prime example, he describes a year-long experiment in seventh- and eighth-grade classes (V. Jones, 1936). The students given an activity program did such things as planning a safe and sane Halloween. In a second treatment, students engaged in discussion of an abstract kind about, for example, Halloween traditions and the ethics of various pranks. A third group had both kinds of experience. Only the third procedure produced change on tests of conduct beyond that found in a control group; the changes varied from test to test, and Turiel seems right to say that the changes were not large. Partly, the poor results have to do with the mismatch between the lessons and the behavioral tests. Jones gave no test of judgment about property rights, for example. Seemingly, Jones was aiming for an unrealistic degree of transfer.

In the light of current theory, the deficiency of Jones's training was that the discussion amounted to indoctrination, not to argument about a genuinely recognized dilemma. For such argument to occur, according to the experiments of the Kohlberg-Turiel group, the student must be exposed to views just one (Kohlberg) stage in advance of his own, as happens in classroom debates such as Selman's kitten story (box, p. 798) precipitated.

The Kohlberg-Turiel argument that learning comes primarily through wrestling with dilemmas is consistent with the psychology of intellectual development, but it is too narrow. The Blatt-Kohlberg training failed to raise behavioral honesty. Beliefs and commitments must precede action; forming them is an emotional as well as an intellectual process. Verbal education runs a great risk of being verbal*istic* education.

The learner should surely try his principles in real situations. Students who set out to change the city bicycle ordinance learn a great deal about what civic participation is like and the consequences to be expected. They experience the good feeling of potency that builds up in a civic-action group. They learn that a moment of dabbling does not get results, that civic change comes only with persistent endeavor. Students thus acquire a level of aspiration that fits the facts. When, as adults, they perceive a civic problem, there is a good chance of their attacking it realistically (Douvan & Walker, 1956).

*(text continues on p. 816)*

## "You got to have a reason for what you steal"

This dilemma was presented to disadvantaged 15-year-old boys for discussion:

There was a case in court the other day about a man, Mr. Jones, who had an accident in his house. His child, Mike, was wounded in the chest. He was bleeding heavily, his shoes and pants were soaked with blood. Mike was scared. He began screaming until he finally lost consciousness.

His parents were scared, too. His mother began screaming, crying. She thought her child was dying. The father no longer hesitated; he lifted Mike up, ran down the stairs and went outside in hopes of getting a cab and going to the hospital. He thought that getting a cab would be quicker than calling an ambulance. But, there were no cabs on the street and Mike's bleeding seemed worse.

Suddenly, Mike's father noticed a man parking his car. He ran up and asked the man to take him to the hospital. The man replied, "Look, I have an appointment with a man about an important job. I really must be on time. I'd like to help you but I can't." So Mr. Jones said, "Just give me the car." The man said, "Look, I don't know you. I don't trust you." Mr. Jones told Mrs. Jones to hold Mike. She did. Then Mr. Jones punched the man, beat him up, took his keys and drove away toward the hospital. The man got up from the street, called the police, and took them to the hospital. The police arrested Mr. Jones for car theft and aggravated battery.

Here are excerpts from the discussion:

Student A: He should have called the ambulance. He can't make nobody do something he don't want to do. (Inaudible rejoinder.)

Teacher: Was the man who refused to give Mr. Jones the car, was he perfectly okay in what he did?

Student B: He could do anything he wanted to do with his own car. (Agreements.) . . . .

Teacher: All right. Mr. Jones stole the car. Does Mr. Jones have the legal right to beat up the man and take his car?

Student B: He doesn't have the legal right, no.

Teacher: No. Because this guy has a right to property and Mr. Jones obviously has no right to hurt this guy. Now, what was involved on this side? What was Mr. Jones' problem? (Chorus of "the boy.") And there was a case of life, right? (Chorus of "right.") This guy's right to property conflicts with this guy's right to life.

Student C: Yes, but the law doesn't say you can't steal unless somebody's life is involved. The law says you can't steal.

Teacher: So what you're saying is, according to the law it doesn't make any difference when you steal. Stealing is stealing, and wrong. Okay? (Chorus of "right.")

Student A: He was wrong to take the car.

Student C: You got to have a reason for what you steal.

| | |
|---|---|
| Teacher: | Suppose you steal when you're hungry. You steal food, you're hungry, you don't have any money. |
| Student A: | That's against the law. |
| Student C: | There's a reason for it. |
| Student A: | You get caught, I bet you get put in jail, don't you? Stealing a car, that's the same thing. |
| Student B: | But this man had a real good reason for stealing the car. |
| Student A: | What is a good reason for you doesn't have to be a good reason for somebody else. |
| Student B: | If you were bleeding and your father was running around with you trying to get somebody to take you to the hospital and you know good and well that you want your father to hit that dude and take that car, wouldn't you? |
| Student A: | No! |
| Student B: | Yes, you would. You'd be laying there, bleeding to death, wouldn't you? You'd let your own self die? |
| Student A: | But I'm saying that it's against the law. You took something that wasn't yours. |
| Teacher: | All right, let me ask you, "What is the purpose of the law?" (Two or three answer, "To protect.") To protect people and their property. In this case suppose you have here a person whose life is in danger. You say the function of the law is to protect the people. All right. Now, it has to protect life— |
| Student A: | But what about the property part? What about the other person. He has to be protected, too. |
| | . . . . |
| Teacher: | Okay, but suppose this guy's right to property interferes with this guy's right to life. Is property and life the same? |
| Student A: | That car may depend on that other man's life, too. He has to get a job. If he don't get it, he might die. You have to see what a person thinks is more valuable, a life or a car. |
| Teacher: | So what you're saying is, circumstances don't make a difference. Stealing is stealing, no matter what. (Chorus of "No." Another chorus of "Yes.") |

In this class, the discussion centers around Student A's position that taking the car was unjustified. . . . His view is that apart from law and punishment everything is arbitrary. . . . The teacher as well as the other students attempt to convince him that there are good reasons independent of the law which may be formulated at a . . . [practical or conventional level], and that you should think of the "morally right" and of "good reasons" as well as the legally right. . . . Student A, though unwilling to shift the content of his choice seems to move toward accepting the notion that there are good reasons. . . .

SOURCE: Blatt & Kohlberg (1975).

Verbal principles have only a surface influence unless the person incorporates them into his ideal. What people say is often nobler than what they do. Corey (1937) asked college students what they thought about cheating on tests, and to no one's surprise they stated that cheating is sinful and contrary to the cheater's best interests. The next step was to find out if they would cheat, given a good chance. After collecting each Friday quiz, Corey left the papers unmarked. In class on Monday each student graded his own quiz paper. Corey compared the scores with the grades he had secretly recorded before returning the quiz sheets on Monday. In five weeks, only one-quarter of the class consistently refrained from changing answers to raise their scores. Whether or not a person was honest had no relation to the attitude he expressed (correlation of 0.02).

**17** Does having a student government insure that students will practice democratic attitudes? that they will acquire these attitudes as conscious ideals?

**18** Can the study of great literature teach character? Comment on this answer by Kohlberg:

> There are three educational theories of the moral effects of literature. The first is that literature is valuable because it . . . conveys true moral and political doctrines and stimulates virtuous habits and emotions. . . . The second doctrine, that of Aristotle, retains part of this notion, but stresses "practical wisdom" as opposed to moral ideology and "catharsis" as opposed to stimulation of virtuous emotions. As stated by [E.] Olson: "Tragedy promotes . . . a temporary alignment of passion, emotion and desire with right principle." The cognitive-developmental, the third doctrine, stresses that literature stimulates new stages, qualitatively new forms, of moral and aesthetic thought and feeling. The value of tragic literature is that it invests life with a meaning beyond conventional morality and conventional emotion, that it gives a new meaning to morality rather than supporting the old meanings of conventional moral or religious ideologies. (In Weintraub and Young, 1973, p. 47.)

**19** Blatt considers Student A (box) to be somewhere near the expedient / conforming borderline. What in A's remarks supports that classification in the face of his "irrational" emphasis on obeying the law?

## Promoting Adjustment

A large part of the behavior society considers undesirable is a reflection of tension and insecurity. Hence anything the school does to enhance self-acceptance promotes considerate action.

REDUCING FRUSTRATION   The first concern of the school should be to make sure that its policies and techniques do not intensify emotional strains. Those who *cause* difficulty in school are those who have *had* difficulty in school. Among students aged 9 to 16 who had upset classroom discipline or who had been truants, an impressive number suffered from remediable physical and educational handicaps (Mullen, 1950). The two types of maladjustment to school seemed to have different determinants. The truants came from unsatisfactory home situations: families on welfare, broken homes, crowded homes, and the like. The students who caused disciplinary problems were merely restless and impulsive.

Students from reasonably well-to-do homes, especially those bound for college, receive much more emotional support in school and much teacher approval; they capture the class offices, and they predominate in the extracurricular activities (except athletics). For the less favored students, school life is a source of irritation rather than support much of the time.

Esther is 16, beginning to date boys and to hold a part-time job. She had been merely an obscure and average participant in school, but as juniors she and a friend tried out as cheerleaders. Three popular girls went out for the activity, helped each other practice, and easily won the tryout from Esther and her friend. This one thwarting could not have been the sole cause of Esther's irritation, but it was soon followed by truancy, which resulted in complaints from the school to her parents. At this point a field worker interviewed Esther and obtained this comment:

> The way a lot of us girls are treated here, you just can't blame us for the way we feel. Frankly, for a lot of us, there's nothing but just coming to classes, and listening to the teacher, and reciting our lessons, and studying, and going home again. We're just pushed out of things. There are a group of girls here who think they're higher than us, and they look down on us. I won't mention any names, but they're a group of girls from the wealthier families. They have a club that's supposed to be outside the school, but it's really in the school. They can do things that we can't afford, and they hog all the offices and are in all the activities. They just won't pay any attention to us. I've almost quit going to church because some of this same group go to the church that I used to go to, and there's only one girl besides myself who goes there that's not in that group. They snub us, and they won't talk to us. Now, I know that we're not rich. Dad's only a factory worker, and we can't afford to do a lot of things, but we'd like to be in the school activities and the school games, and things like that. But they just make us feel like we're not wanted. I went to some of the activities when I first started high school, but they just ignored us. . . . They just dance among themselves and have a good time, and we're just nobody. We're made to feel out of place, and that's just the way it is. (Havighurst & Taba, 1949, p. 39.)

Programs that are good in principle, like clubs, offices, and dances, can intensify the emotional difficulties of some students unless teachers continually promote the educational values of the programs. Making the instructional program more meaningful and better suited to student readiness, diagnosing the problem and helping the individual to remove his handicaps, adopting an accepting teaching style—all practices that teach more—lead to greater success and thereby contribute to mental health.

HELPING STUDENTS ACCOMPLISH DEVELOPMENTAL TASKS   Failure in a developmental task makes the person a misfit. Anything the school can do to help satisfy the basic needs promises to improve adjustment. A teacher on friendly terms with the student can hold him responsible for worthwhile activity and for judging himself. For the child or adolescent who has always been in trouble with authorities and who feels that no one at home understands him, finding someone who expects him to do well offers him his first hope. Devereux (1967, p. 131) found moral judgments more mature in classes where teachers were "supporting, demanding, and controlling, but not punitive or nagging."

If school regulations seem arbitrary, or if the demands seem always to be out of reach, the student must regard authority as an enemy. He may come to terms by giving up his own aims and waiting to be told what to do, or he may become a rebel. Either attitude retards development of moral judgment and independent thought.

Reasoning about values is to be encouraged throughout schooling. Teaching is never neutral. Either the school from the start encourages independence of thinking, security, and maturity, or it teaches the opposite: irrational dependence and anxiety. Whenever the sincere question, "What do *you* think?" is asked, the student who thinks for himself is rewarded. Whenever a conflict in values or interests is settled by open discussion rather than by a flat-footed decision from on high, the student is helped toward the precious idea that reason, not power, makes standards for conduct.

To reach a truly central educational ideal, the entire institution should line up behind that goal. Lessons in critical thinking during an isolated hour in the student's day will do little to promote a rational approach to controversy if in his other classes and out-of-class discussions he can get by with uncritical and even blatantly prejudiced statements. Several colleges and a few universities have established a climate of discussion that presses continually upon each member to think through whatever he is about to say on a serious topic, and their graduates show this. Feldman and Newcomb (1967, p. 331) suggest that close day-to-day interaction with a community the learner takes seriously is the

source of impact. An example of total institutional press at the other end of the educational scale is the successful preschool. The teacher's acts and words and, insofar as possible, the interactions of the children are shaped to promote the child's success, self-satisfaction, and cooperation with others. The Soviet system, which arranges every activity of the young members to support an ideal of service to the collective, is a third example. American schools do not often develop a coherent institutional program. The diversity of interests and attitudes among teachers, a respect for self-determination among students, the tendency to compartmentalize lessons and to give attitudinal learning second place—all work against effective influence on basic attitudes. The result is to leave the graduate's thoughts less analytical, more determined by the prejudices of his home, and often not in line with school objectives.

Instruction is not accomplished through concentrated doses of indoctrination. Ideas and ideals are developed in personal contacts with peers outside any deliberate program. They are picked out of the casual remarks of a respected teacher. A quite minor story may teach that Indians are cruel, ignoble, and ungrateful. These glimmering, tentative meanings, if not contradicted, become a fixed part of the student's interpretative system. Formal instruction can crystallize concepts and beliefs already forming. Sometimes it can help the student recognize fallacies or conflicts. In the long run, though, a philosophy of life is established by living; interpretations are tried, confirmed, and retained accordingly. Each person takes on, for the most part, the attitudes of the people to whom he is loyal.

Therefore the aim of the school is to make the student loyal to his society and to develop a commitment to act responsibly. If in his school years he becomes committed to this ideal, he can be trusted thereafter to learn what he needs to know about a new problem and to reach a balanced judgment.

18   READING LIST

Erich Fromm, "The Emergence of the Individual and the Ambiguity of Freedom," in *Escape from Freedom* (New York: Rinehart, 1941), pp. 24–39.

> A thoughtful attempt to distinguish good conduct from conformity. Freedom, says Fromm, is "freedom to"—not "freedom from." Be sure as you read that you know what common definitions of good character he would disagree with. Then decide which you yourself accept—a philosophical, not a scientific, choice.

Robert J. Havighurst and Hilda Taba, "Objectives for Prairie City," in *Adolescent Character and Personality* (New York: Wiley, 1949), pp. 190–204.

> After studying adolescents in a midwestern high school, the authors propose a program of character education that would contribute to emotional, social, and intellectual growth. Detailed procedures are suggested. Other chapters in the volume offer descriptions of character tests, case studies of character types, and statistical findings.

Lawrence Kohlberg and Elliot Turiel, "Moral Development and Moral Education," in *Psychology and Educational Practice,* ed. Gerald Lesser (Chicago: Scott Foresman, 1971), pp. 410–65.

> Illustrates how children reason at various stages of development and argues for teaching by means of moral dilemmas.

Nevitt Sanford, "Developmental Status of the Entering Freshman," Chapter 6 in *The American College,* ed. Nevitt Sanford (New York: Wiley, 1962), pp. 253–82.

> Sanford discusses typical character patterns of college freshmen, finding in most of them the irrational-conscientious pattern. They lack a mature sense of their own identity. Sanford discusses aspects of college life that can promote or hinder future growth of character.

Simpson, Elizabeth Léonie, "Moral Development Research: A Case Study of Scientific Cultural Bias," *Human Development* 17 (1974), 81–106.

> A carefully argued attack on the stage theory of Kohlberg, and, by implication, an attack on any character education that seeks autonomy and rationality as end-products. Such moral reasoning, Simpson says, "bids fair to destroy man." Moreover, the effort to intellectualize decisions defines character in a way that is unfair to other cultures and to most of the persons in our culture.

# BIBLIOGRAPHY

Adams, J. A. Response feedback and learning. *Psychological Bulletin* 70, 1968, 486–504.

———. A closed-loop theory of motor learning. *Journal of Motor Behavior* 3, 1971, 111–49.

Adams, R. M. Haunted landscape. *New York Review of Books* 22 (16), 1975, 6–9.

Adelson, J., Green, B., & O'Neil, R. Growth of the idea of law in adolescence. *Developmental Psychology* 1, 1969, 327–32.

Adorno, T. W., et al. *The authoritarian personality.* New York: Harper, 1950.

Ahlstrom, W. M., & Havighurst, R. J. *400 losers.* San Francisco: Jossey-Bass, 1971.

Ainsworth, M. D. The development of infant-mother attachment. In B. M. Caldwell & H. Ricciuti, eds., *Review of child development research,* vol. 3. Chicago: University of Chicago Press, 1973. Pp. 1–94.

American Psychological Association. *Standards for educational and psychological tests.* Washington, D.C.: APA, 1974.

Amir, Y. Contact hypotheses in ethnic relations. *Psychological Bulletin* 71, 1969, 319–42.

Amos, R. T., & Washington, R. M. A comparison of pupil and teacher perceptions of pupil problems. *Journal of Educational Psychology* 51, 1960, 255–58.

Anastasi, Anne. *Differential psychology,* 3d ed. New York: Macmillan, 1958.

Anderson, R. C. Concretization and sentence learning. *Journal of Educational Psychology* 66, 1974, 179–83.

———, & Myrow, D. L. Retroactive inhibition of meaningful discourse. *Journal of Educational Psychology* 62, 1971, 81–94.

---

NOTE: Numbers preceded by the letters ED (as in the entry "Brophy, J. E." on p. 827) refer to the ERIC microfiche system.

Anderson, T. A study of the use of visual aids in basket shooting. *Research Quarterly of the American Association for Health, Physical Education, and Recreation* 13, 1942, 532–37.

Andrews, I. R. Wage inequity and job performance: An experimental study. *Journal of Applied Psychology* 51, 1967, 39–45.

Aquino, M. The validity of the Miller-Coleman readability scale. *Reading Research Quarterly* 4, 1969, 342–57.

Arbuthnot, J. Modification of moral judgment through role playing. *Developmental Psychology,* vol. II, 1975, 319–24.

Aronfreed, J. M. *Conduct and conscience; the socialization of internalized control over behavior.* New York: Academic Press, 1968.

Aronson, E., & Carlsmith, J. M. Performance expectancy as a determinant of actual performance. *Journal of Abnormal and Social Psychology* 65, 1962, 178–82.

Arrow, K. J. *The limits of organization.* New York: Norton, 1974.

Ashton-Warner, S. *Spinster, a novel.* London: Secker & Warburg, 1958.

Atkinson, J. W., & Feather, N., eds. *A theory of achievement motivation.* New York: Wiley, 1966.

Atkinson, R. C. Ingredients for a theory of instruction. *American Psychologist* 27, 1972, 921–31.

————. Teaching children to read using a computer. *American Psychologist* 29, 1974, 169–78.

————, & Paulson, J. A. An approach to the psychology of instruction. *Psychological Bulletin* 78, 1972, 49–61.

————, & Wescourt, K. T. Some remarks on long-term memory. In P. M. A. Rabbitt & S. Dornic, eds., *Attention and Performance V.* New York: Academic Press, 1975. Pp. 485–98.

————, & Wickens, T. D. Human memory and the concept of reinforcement. In R. Glaser, ed., *The nature of reinforcement.* New York: Academic Press, 1971.

Ausubel, D. P., & Robinson, F. D. *School learning.* New York: Holt, Rinehart and Winston, 1969.

Babikian, Y. An empirical investigation to determine the relative effectiveness of discovery, laboratory, and expository methods of teaching science concepts. *Journal of Research in Science Teaching* 8, 1971, 201–09.

Bailyn. L. Mass media and children: A study of exposure habits and cognitive effects. *Psychological Monographs* 73 (1), 1959.

Baldwin, A. L. The effect of home environment on nursery-school behavior. *Child Development* 20, 1949, 49–62.

————, Kalhorn, J., & Breese, F. H. Patterns of parent behavior. *Psychological Monographs* 58 (3), 1945.

Ball, S., & Bogatz, G. A. *Reading with television: An evaluation of "The Electric Company."* Princeton: Educational Testing Service, 1973.

Baller, W., Charles, D., & Miller, E. Mid-life attainment of the mentally-retarded: A longitudinal study. *Genetic Psychology Monographs* 75, 1967, 235–329.

Bandura, A. *Principles of behavior modification.* New York: Holt, Rinehart and Winston, 1969.

————. Vicarious and self-reinforcement processes. In R. Glaser, ed., *The nature of reinforcement.* New York: Academic Press, 1971. Pp. 228–79.

————. Behavior theory and the models of man. *American Psychologist* 29, 1974, 859–69.

————, Grusec, J. E., & Menlove, F. L. Observational learning as a function of symbolization and incentive set. *Child Development* 37, 1966, 500–06.

————, & Walters, R. H. *Adolescent aggression.* New York: Ronald Press, 1959.

Bannister, D. A new theory of personality. In B. M. Foss, ed., *New horizons in personality.* New York: Penguin, 1966.

Barclay, A., & Cusumano, D. R. Father absence, cross-sex identity, and field dependent behavior in male adolescents. *Child Development* 38, 1967, 243–50.

Barker, R. G., & Schoggen, P. *Qualities of community life.* San Francisco: Jossey-Bass, 1973.

Baron, R. M. Social reinforcement effects as a function of social reinforcement history. *Psychological Review* 73, 1966, 527–39.

————, & Ganz, R. L. Effects of locus of control and type of feedback on the task performance of lower-class black children. *Journal of Personality and Social Psychology* 21, 1972, 124–30.

Barrett, B. B. Training and transfer in combinatorial problem-solving. *Developmental Psychology* 11, 1975, 700–04.

Barrington, H. An evaluation of the effectiveness of instructional television presentation variables. *British Journal of Educational Psychology* 41, 1971, 219–20.

Barron, F. *Artists in the making.* New York: Seminar Press, 1972.

Barth, J. W., et al. *Experiences in inquiry.* Boston: Allyn & Bacon, 1974.

Barth, R. S. *Open education and the American school.* New York: Agathon, 1970.

Bartlett, F. C. *Remembering: A study in experimental and social psychology.* Cambridge, England: Cambridge University Press, 1932.

————. The measurement of human skill. *Occupational Psychology* 22, 1948, 30–38, 83–91.

————. *Thinking.* London: George Allen & Unwin, 1958.

Batson, C. D. Rational processing or rationalization? The effect of disconfirming information on a stated religious belief. *Journal of Personality and Social Psychology* 32, 1975, 176–84.

Baumrind, D. The development of instrumental competence through socialization. In A. D. Pick, ed., *Minnesota Symposium on Child Psychology,* vol. 7. Minneapolis: University of Minnesota Press, 1973. Pp. 3–46.

Bayley, N., & Schaefer, E. S. Correlations of maternal and child behaviors with the development of mental abilities: Data from the Berkeley Growth Study. *Monographs of the Society for Research on Child Development* 29 (6), 1964.

Bearison, D. J. Role of measurement operations in the acquisition of conservation. *Developmental Psychology* 1, 1969, 653–60.

————, & Cassel, T. Z. Cognitive decentration and social codes: Communication effectiveness in young children from differing family contexts. *Developmental Psychology* 11, 1975, 29–36.

Beck, C. M., Crittenden, B. S., & Sullivan, E. V., eds. *Moral education: Interdisciplinary approaches.* Toronto: University of Toronto Press, 1971.

Becker, W. C. Consequences of different kinds of parental discipline. In M. L. Hoffman & L. W. Hoffman, eds., *Review of child development research,* vol. 1. New York: Russell Sage Foundation, 1964. Pp. 169–208.

————, Engelmann, S., & Thomas, D. R. *Teaching 2: Cognitive learning and instruction.* Chicago: Science Research Associates, 1975.

Belmont, J. M., & Butterfield, E. C. The relations of short-term memory to development and intelligence. In L. P. Lipsett & H. W. Reese, eds., *Advances in Child Development and Behavior,* vol. 4, 1969. Pp. 29–82.

Bem, S. L. The role of comprehension in children's problem solving. *Developmental Psychology* 2, 1970, 351–58.

Bennett, G. K., Seashore, H. G., & Wesman, A. G. *Counseling from profiles. A casebook for the Differential Aptitude Tests,* 2d ed. New York: Psychological Corporation, 1977.

Berkowitz, L., Levy, B. I., & Harvey, A. H. Effects of performance evaluations on group integration and motivation. *Human Relations* 10, 1957, 195–208.

Berlyne, D. E. *Conflict, arousal, and curiosity.* New York: McGraw-Hill, 1960.

Bernstein, B. A sociolinguistic approach to socialization: with some reference to educability. In F. Williams, ed., *Language and poverty.* Chicago: Markham, 1970. Pp. 25–61.

Bettelheim, B. The evaluation of the appreciation of art. In E. R. Smith, R. W. Tyler, et al. *Appraising and recording student progress.* New York: Harper, 1942. Pp. 276–306.

————. *The informed heart.* Glencoe, Ill.: Free Press, 1960.

————. Violence: A neglected mode of behavior. *Annals of the American Academy of Political and Social Science* 364, 1966, 50–59.

Biehler, R. F., ed. *Psychology applied to teaching: Selected readings.* Boston: Houghton Mifflin, 1972.

Bilodeau, E. A., & Bilodeau, I. McD. Motor-skills learning. *Annual Review of Psychology* 12, 1961, 243–80.

Bindra, D. A motivational view of learning, performance, and behavior modification. *Psychological Review* 81, 1974, 199–213.

Birch, H. G., & Lefford, A. Visual differentiation, intersensory integration, and voluntary motor control. *Monographs of the Society for Research in Child Development* 32 (2), 1967.

Birney, R. C., et al. *Fear of failure.* New York: Van Nostrand, 1969.

Blatt, M. M., & Kohlberg, L. The effects of classroom moral discussion upon children's level of moral judgment. *Journal of Moral Education* 4, 1975, 129–61.

Blau, P., & Duncan, O. D. *The American occupational structure.* New York: Wiley, 1967.

Block, J. *Lives through time.* Berkeley: Bancroft, 1971.

Block, J. H., ed. *Mastery learning: Theory and practice.* New York: Holt, Rinehart and Winston, 1971.

Bloom, B. S. *Stability and change in human characteristics.* New York: Wiley, 1964.

————. Mastery learning and its implications for curriculum development. In E. W. Eisner, ed., *Confronting curriculum reform.* Boston: Little, Brown, 1971. Pp. 17–49.

————. Affective consequences of school achievement. In M. K. Pringle & V. P. Varma, eds., *Advances in educational psychology 2.* London: University of London Press, 1974.

————. *Human characteristics and school learning.* New York: McGraw-Hill, 1976.

————, & Broder, L. J. *Problem-solving processes of college students.* Chicago: University of Chicago Press, 1950.

————, Hastings, J. T., & Madaus, G. F. *Handbook of formative and summative evaluation of student learning.* New York: McGraw-Hill, 1971.

————, Krathwohl, D. R., & Masia, B. B. *Taxonomy of educational objectives, Handbook I.* New York: Longmans, 1956.

Boeck, C. H. The inductive-deductive compared to the deductive-deductive approach to laboratory instruction in high-school chemistry. *Journal of Experimental Education* 19, 1951, 247–54.

Boehm, L. The development of independence: A comparative study. *Child Development* 28, 1957, 85–102.

Boker, J. R. Immediate and delayed retention effects of interspersing questions in written instructional passages. *Journal of Educational Psychology* 66, 1974, 96–98.

Bolton, N. *The psychology of thinking.* London: Methuen, 1972.

Bond, A. *An experiment in the teaching of genetics. Teachers College Contributions to Education,* no. 797. New York: Teachers College, Columbia University, 1940.

Bond, G. L., & Tinker, M. A. *Reading difficulties: Their diagnosis and correction.* New York: Appleton-Century-Crofts, 1973.

Boucher, J.-L. Higher processes in motor learning. *Journal of Motor Behavior* 6, 1974, 131–38.

Bower, G. H. Selective facilitation and interference in retention of prose. *Journal of Educational Psychology* 66, 1974, 1–8.

————, Clark, M. C., Lesgold, A. M., & Winzenz, D. Hierarchical retrieval schemes in recall of categorized word lists. *Journal of Verbal Learning and Verbal Behavior* 8, 1969, 323–43.

Brackbill, Y., & O'Hara, J. The relative effectiveness of reward and punishment for discrimination learning in children. *Journal of Comparative and Physiological Psychology* 51, 1958, 747–51.

Bradburn, N. M. Achievement and father dominance in Turkey. *Journal of Abnormal and Social Psychology* 67, 1963, 464–68.

Brainerd, C. J. Neo-Piagetian training experiments revisited: Is there any support for the cognitive-developmental stage hypothesis? *Cognition* 2, 1973, 349–70.

Brandt, R. M. Observational portrait of a British infant school. In B. Spodek & H. J. Walberg, eds., *Studies in open education.* New York: Agathon, 1975. Pp. 101–25.

Bransford, J. D., & Franks, J. J. The abstraction of linguistic ideas. *Cognitive Psychology* 2, 1971, 331–50.

Briggs, G. E., & Naylor, J. C. The relative efficiency of several training methods as a function of task complexity. *Journal of Experimental Psychology* 64, 1962, 505–12.

Brodbeck, M. The role of small groups in mediating the effects of propaganda. *Journal of Abnormal and Social Psychology* 52, 1956, 166–70.

Bronfenbrenner, U. Socialization and social class through time and space. In E. E. Maccoby, T. M. Newcomb, & E. L. Hartley, eds., *Readings in social psychology,* 3rd ed. New York: Holt, Rinehart, and Winston, 1958. Pp. 400–25.

————. The changing American child. *Journal of Social Issues* 17, 1961, 6–18.

————. *The two worlds of childhood: U.S. and U.S.S.R.* New York: Russell Sage Foundation, 1970.

————. *Is early education effective?* Washington, D.C.: Office of Human Development, 1974a.

————. The origins of alienation. *Scientific American* 231 (8), 1974b, 3–9.

————. Unpublished presidential address, Division 7, American Psychological Association, 1974c.

————. Alienation and the American psychologist. *APA Monitor* 6 (9), 1975, 2.

Bronson, W. C. Dimensions of ego and infantile identification. *Journal of Personality* 27, 1959, 532–45.

Brophy, J. E. A study to determine if teachers communicate differential expectations to students. Unpublished report, University of Texas, Austin, 1972. ED 067 379.

————, & Good, T. L. *Teacher-student relationships.* New York: Holt, Rinehart and Winston, 1974.

Brown, B. B. *The experimental mind in education.* New York: Harper & Row, 1968.

Browne, R. J., & Anderson, O. R. Lesson kinetic structure analysis as related to pupil awareness and achievement. *Journal of Educational Psychology* 55, 1964, 864–71.

Brownell, W. A. & Moser, H. E. *Meaningful versus mechanical learning: A study in grade III subtraction. Duke University Research Studies in Education,* no. 8, 1949.

Bruner, J. S. Learning and thinking. *Harvard Educational Review* 29, 1959, 184–92.

————. *The process of education.* Cambridge, Mass.: Harvard University Press, 1960.

————, Olver, R. S., & Greenfield, P. M. *Studies in cognitive growth.* New York: Wiley, 1966.

————, Wallach, M., & Galanter, E. The identification of recurrent regularity. *American Journal of Psychology* 72, 1959, 200–09.

Bunderson, C. V., & Faust, G. W. Programmed and computer-assisted instruction. In N. L. Gage, ed., *The psychology of teaching methods.* Seventy-fifth yearbook of the National Society for the Study of Education. Chicago: University of Chicago Press, 1976. Pp. 44–90.

Burmester, M. A. The construction and validation of a test to measure some of the inductive aspects of scientific thinking. Unpublished doctoral dissertation, Michigan State University, 1951.

Buros, O. K., ed., *The seventh mental measurements yearbook.* Highland Park, N.J.: Gryphon Press, 1972.

California Assessment Program. *Profiles of school district performance, 1973–74.* Sacramento, Calif.: California State Department of Education, 1974.

Campbell, D. T. Reforms as experiments. *American Psychologist* 24, 1969, 409–29.

Campbell, J. D. Peer relationships in childhood. In M. L. Hoffman & L. W. Hoffman, eds., *Review of child development research,* vol. 1. New York: Russell Sage Foundation, 1964. pp. 289–322.

Cantoni, L. J. Guidance: Four students ten years later. *Clearing House* 28, 1954, 474–78.

Cantril, H., & Allport, G. W. *The psychology of radio.* New York: Harper, 1935.

Caplan, N. Delinquency and the perceived chances for conventional achievement. Unpublished paper, Institute for Survey Research, University of Michigan, 1972.

Carroll, J. B. A model of school learning. *Teachers College Record* 64, 1963, 723–33.

————. *Learning from verbal discourse in educational media: A review of the literature.* Princeton: Educational Testing Service, 1971. RB 71–61.

————, & Sapon, S. M. *Modern language aptitude test.* New York: Psychological Corporation, 1959.

————. *Modern language aptitude test—elementary.* New York: Psychological Corporation, 1967.

Carter, H. D. *The California study methods survey.* Los Angeles: California Test Bureau, 1958.

Carter, R. S. How invalid are marks assigned by teachers? *Journal of Educational Psychology* 43, 1952, 218–28.

Case, R. Structures and strictures: Some functional limitations on the course of cognitive growth. *Cognitive Psychology* 6, 1974, 544–73.

Cattell, R. B. *Abilities: Their structure, growth, and action.* Boston: Houghton Mifflin, 1971.

Cazden, C. B. *Child language and education.* New York: Holt, Rinehart and Winston, 1972a.

————, ed. *Language in early childhood education.* Washington, D.C.: National Association for the Education of Young Children, 1972b.

————, John, V. P., & Hymes, D. *Functions of language in the classroom.* New York: Teachers College Press, 1972.

Chance, E. *Families in treatment.* New York: Basic Books, 1959.

Chapanis, A. Interactive human communication. *Scientific American* 232 (3), 1975, 36–42.

Chase, W. G., ed. *Visual information processing.* New York: Academic Press, 1972.

Child, I., Potter, E. H., & Levine, E. M. Children's textbooks and personality development: An exploration in the social psychology of education. *Psychological Monographs* 60 (3), 1946.

Christensen, C. M. Relationships between pupil achievement, pupil affect-need, teacher warmth, and teacher permissiveness. *Journal of Educational Psychology* 51, 1960, 169–74.

Christina, R. W. Movement-produced feedback as a mechanism for the temporal anticipation of motor responses. *Journal of Motor Behavior* 3, 1971, 97–104.

Clarizio, H. F., Craig, R. C., & Mehrens, W. A. *Contemporary issues in educational psychology.* Boston: Allyn & Bacon, 1974.

Clark, C. A., & Walberg, H. J. The influence of massive rewards on reading achievement in potential urban dropouts. *American Educational Research Journal* 5, 1968, 305–10.

Clausen, J. A. The social meaning of differential physical and sexual maturation. In S. Dragastin & G. H. Elder, eds., *Adolescence in the life cycle: Psychological change and social context.* Washington, D.C.: Hemisphere, 1975. Pp. 25–46.

Coelho, G. V., Hamburg, D. A., & Adams, J. A., eds. *Coping and adaptation.* New York: Basic Books, 1974.

Cogan, M. L. The behavior of teachers and the productive behavior of their pupils. *Journal of Experimental Education* 27, 1958, 89–124.

Coleman, J. S. Social climates in high schools. *Cooperative Research Monograph* No. 4. Washington, D. C.: U.S. Office of Education, 1961a.

————. *The adolescent subculture.* Glencoe, Ill.: Free Press, 1961b.

————. The children have outgrown the schools. *Psychology Today* 5 (9), 1972, 72–75, 82.

————, et al. *Equality of educational opportunity.* Washington, D.C.: U.S. Government Printing Office, 1966.

Coleman, R., & Neugarten, B. *Social status in the city.* San Francisco: Jossey-Bass, 1971.

Collins, A. M., & Loftus, E. F. A spreading-activation theory of semantic processing. *Psychological Review* 82, 1975, 407–28.

————, & Quillian, M. R. Retrieval time from semantic memory. *Journal of Verbal Learning and Verbal Behavior* 8, 1969, 240–47.

Colville, F. M. The learning of motor skills as influenced by knowledge of mechanical principles. *Journal of Educational Psychology* 48, 1957, 321–27.

Condry, J. C., Jr., Siman, M. L., & Bronfenbrenner, U. Characteristics of peer and adult-oriented children. Unpublished manuscript, Cornell University, 1968.

Conger, J. J., et al. Antecedents of delinquency: Personality, social class, and intelligence. In P. H. Mussen et al, eds., *Basic and contemporary issues in developmental psychology.* New York: Harper & Row, 1975. Pp. 433–50.

Cook, S. A. Motives in a conceptual analysis of attitude-related behavior. In W. J. Arnold and D. Levine, eds., *Nebraska Symposium on Motivation, 1969.* Lincoln: University of Nebraska Press, 1970. Pp. 179–97.

Cooley, W. W. *Career development of scientists.* Cambridge, Mass.: Harvard Graduate School of Education, 1963.

————, & Lohnes, P. R. *Predicting development of young adults.* Pittsburgh: American Institutes for Research, 1968.

Cooper, R., & Zubek, J. Effects of enriched and restricted environments on the learning ability of bright and dull rats. *Canadian Journal of Psychology* 12, 1958, 159–64.

Corey, S. M. Professed attitudes and actual behavior. *Journal of Educational Psychology* 28, 1937, 271–80.

Costantini, A. F., & Hoving, K. L. The effectiveness of reward and punishment contingencies on response inhibition. *Journal of Experimental Child Psychology* 16, 1973, 484–94.

Covington, M. V., Olton, R. M., & Crutchfield, R. S. *The Productive Thinking Program,* 2d ed. Columbus, Ohio: Merrill, 1974.

Cox, C. M. *Genetic studies of genius, II.* Stanford: Stanford University Press, 1926.

Cox, J. W. Some experiments on formal training in the acquisition of skill. *British Journal of Psychology* 24, 1933, 67–87.

Crandall, V. C. Achievement behavior in young children. In B. C. Rosen, H. J. Crockett, Jr., & C. Z. Nunn, eds., *Achievement in American society.* Cambridge, Mass.: Schenkman, 1969.

————, & Battle, E. S. The antecedents and adult correlates of academic and intellectual achievement effort. In J. P. Hill, ed., *Minnesota symposia on child psychology,* vol. 4. Minneapolis: University of Minnesota Press, 1970. Pp. 36–93.

Cronbach, L. J. The meanings of problems. *Supplementary Educational Monographs,* no. 66, 1948. Pp. 32–43.

———. *Essentials of psychological testing,* 3d ed. New York: Harper & Row, 1970.

———. Beyond the two disciplines of scientific psychology. *American Psychologist* 30, 1975a, 116–27.

———. Five decades of public controversy over mental testing. *American Psychologist* 30, 1975b, 1–14.

———. Equity in selection—where psychometrics and political philosophy meet. *Journal of Educational Measurement* 13, 1976, 31–41.

———, & Drenth, P. J. D., eds. *Mental tests and cultural adaptation.* The Hague: Mouton, 1972.

———, Rogosa, D., Floden, R. E., & Price, G. Analysis of covariance—angel of salvation, or temptress and deluder? Occasional papers of the Stanford Evaluation Consortium, 1976.

———, & Snow, R. E. *Aptitudes and instructional methods.* New York: Irvington, 1977.

Cunningham, R., Elzi, A., Hall, J. A., Farrell, M., & Roberts, M. *Understanding group behavior of boys and girls.* New York: Bureau of Publications, Teachers College, Columbia University, 1951.

## D

Dahllöf, U. S. *Ability grouping, content validity, and curriculum process analysis.* New York: Teachers College Press, 1971.

Damon, W. Early conceptions of positive justice as related to the development of logical operations. *Child Development* 46, 1975, 301–12.

Damrin, D. E. The Russell Sage social relations test. *Proceedings, 1954 invitational conference on testing problems.* Princeton: Educational Testing Service, 1955. Pp. 75–84.

Davies, D. R. The effect of tuition upon the process of learning a complex motor skill. *Journal of Educational Psychology* 36, 1945, 352–65.

Davis, F. B. Reporting test data in the media: two case studies. *Reading Teacher* 26, 1972, 305–10.

Dawson, A. D. Notes from the real world. *Newsletter,* Individualized Science Instructional System, no. 4, May, 1975.

Dearborn, W. F. Experiments in learning. *Journal of Educational Psychology* 1, 1910, 373–88.

DeBacy, D. Effect of viewing video tapes of a sport skill performed by self and others on self-assessment. *Research Quarterly* 41, 1970, 27–32.

de Bono, E. *Children solve problems.* London: Allen Lane, 1972.

DeCecco, J. P., Richards, A., Summers, F., et al. Civic education for the seventies, vol. 1. Unpublished report, Teachers College, Columbia University, 1970. ED 041 810.

de Charms, R., & Moeller, Gerald H. Values expressed in American children's readers. *Journal of Abnormal and Social Psychology* 64, 1962, 136–42.

———, et al. *Enhancing motivation: Change in the classroom.* New York: Irvington, 1976.

de Groat, A. F., & Thompson, G. G. A study of the distribution of teacher approval and disapproval among sixth-grade pupils. *Journal of Experimental Education* 18, 1949, 57–75.

DeLawter, J. A., & East, M. J. Focus on oral communication. *Elementary English* 43, 1966, 880–91, 901.

Del Rey, P. Appropriate feedback for open and closed skill acquisition. *Quest* 17, 1972, 42–45.

Dennis, W. Causes of retardation among institutional children. *Journal of Genetic Psychology* 96, 1960, 47–59.

———, & Dennis, M. G. The effect of cradling practice upon the onset of walking in Hopi children. *Journal of Genetic Psychology* 56, 1940, 77–86.

Department of National Health and Welfare. *The feeling of rejection.* Ottawa, Canada: the Department, 1947.

Deutsch, C. P. Social class and child development. In B. M. Caldwell & H. Ricciuti, eds., *Review of child development research,* vol. 3. Chicago: University of Chicago Press, 1973. Pp. 233–82.

Deutsch, M., & Deutsch, C. P. Intelligence, heredity, and environment. *New York University Education Quarterly* 5 (2), 1974, 4–12.

_____, & Solomon, L. Reactions to evaluations of others as influenced by self-evaluation. *Sociometry* 22, 1959, 93–112.

Devereux, E. C. The role of peer-group experience in moral development. In J. P. Hill, ed., *Minnesota symposia in child psychology,* vol. 4. Minneapolis: University of Minnesota Press, 1967. Pp. 94–140.

Dewey, John. *Experience and education.* New York: Macmillan, 1938.

DiBartolo, R., & Vinacke, W. E. Relationship between adult nurturance and dependency and performance of the preschool child. *Developmental Psychology* 1, 1969, 247–51.

Diederich, P. B. What does research in reading reveal about evaluation in reading? *English Journal* 58, 1969, 853–68.

_____, & Link, F. R. Cooperative evaluation in English. In F. T. Wilhelms, ed., *Evaluation as feedback and guide.* Washington, D.C.: Association for Supervision and Curriculum Development, 1967. Pp. 181–223.

Ditrichs, R., Simon, S., & Greene, B. Effect of vicarious scheduling on the verbal conditioning of hostility in children. *Journal of Personality and Social Psychology* 6, 1967, 71–78.

Di Vesta, F. J., & Gray, G. S. Listening and note taking. *Journal of Educational Psychology* 63, 1972, 8–14.

Dobzhansky, T. *Genetic diversity and human equality.* New York: Basic Books, 1973.

Doland, D. J., & Adelberg, K. The learning of sharing behavior. *Child Development* 38, 1967, 695–700.

Domino, G. Differential prediction of academic achievement in conforming and independent settings. *Journal of Educational Psychology* 59, 1968, 256–60.

_____. Interactive effects of achievement orientation and teaching style on academic achievement. *Journal of Educational Psychology* 62, 1971, 427–31.

Douglas, W. O. *Of men and mountains.* New York: Harper, 1950.

Douvan, E., & Adelson, J. *The adolescent experience.* New York: Wiley, 1966.

_____, & Walker, A. M. The sense of effectiveness in public affairs. *Psychological Monographs* 70 (22), 1956.

Drews, E. M. Student abilities, grouping patterns, and classroom interactions. Unpublished report, Michigan State University, 1963. ED 002 679.

Droege, R. C. Sex differences in aptitude maturation during high school. *Journal of Counseling Psychology* 14, 1967, 407–11.

Duchastel, P. C., & Brown, B. R. Incidental and relevant learning with instructional objectives. *Journal of Educational Psychology* 66, 1974, 481–85.

_____, & Merrill, P. F. The effects of behavioral objectives on learning: A review of empirical studies. *Review of Educational Research* 43, 1973, 53–69.

Duel, H. J. Effect of periodic self-evaluation on student achievement. *Journal of Educational Psychology* 49, 1958, 197–99.

Duncan, K. D. Retention and transfer of search skill. *British Journal of Psychology* 62, 1971, 439–48.

_____, & Gray, M. J. An evaluation of a fault-finding training course for refinery process operators. *Journal of Occupational Psychology* 48, 1975, 119–218.

Duncan, O. D., Featherman, D. L., & Duncan, B. *Socioeconomic background and achievement.* New York: Seminar Press, 1972.

Dunkin, M. J., & Biddle, B. J. *The study of teaching.* New York: Holt, Rinehart and Winston, 1974.

Durkin, D. Children's concepts of justice: A comparison with the Piaget data. *Child Development* 30, 1959a, 59–67.

————. Children's acceptance of reciprocity as a justice principle. Ibid., 1959b, 289–96.

————. *Children who read early.* New York: Teachers College Press, 1966.

Dusek, J. B., & Dietrich, D. M. Informational and motivational components of social reinforcement. *Journal of Experimental Child Psychology* 16, 1973, 267–77.

————, & O'Connell, E. J. Teacher expectancy effects on the achievement test performance of elementary school children. *Journal of Educational Psychology* 65, 1973, 371–77.

Dvorak, A., Merrick, N. L., Dealey, W. L., & Ford, G. C. *Typewriting behavior.* New York: American Book, 1936.

Easton, D., & Dennis, J. *Children in the political system.* New York: McGraw-Hill, 1969.

Edwards, D. W. Blacks versus whites: When is race a relevant variable? *Journal of Personality and Social Psychology* 29, 1974, 39–49.

Egan, D. E., & Greeno, J. G. Acquiring cognitive structure by discovery and rule learning. *Journal of Educational Research* 55, 1962, 453–60.

Eichorn, D. H., & Jones, H. E. Maturation and behavior. In G. J. Seward & J. P. Seward, eds., *Current Psychological Issues.* New York: Holt, 1958. Pp. 211–48.

Eimas, P. D., et al. Speech perception in infants. *Science* 171, 1971, 303–06.

Elardo, R., Bradley, R., & Caldwell, B. M. The relation of infants' home environments and mental test performance from six to thirty-six months. *Child Development* 46, 1975, 71–76.

Elashoff, J., & Snow, R. E., eds. *Pygmalion revisited.* Worthington, Ohio: C. A. Jones, 1971.

Elkind, D. The development of quantitative thinking: A systematic replication of Piaget's studies. *Journal of Genetic Psychology* 98, 1961a, 37–46.

————. Children's discovery of the conservation of mass, weight, and volume. Ibid. 1961b, 219–27.

————. Developmental studies of figurative perception. In L. P. Lipsett & H. W. Reese, eds., *Advances in child development and behavior,* vol. 4. New York: Academic Press, 1969. Pp. 2–28.

————. Two approaches to intelligence: Piagetian and psychometric. In D. R. Green et al., eds., *Measurement and Piaget.* New York: McGraw-Hill, 1971. Pp. 12–28.

————. Recent research on cognitive development in adolescence. In S. Dragastin & G. H. Elder, eds., *Adolescence in the life cycle: Psychological change and social context.* Washington, D.C.: Hemisphere, 1975. Pp. 49–60.

————, Koegler, R. R., & Go, E. Effects of perceptual training at three age levels. *Science* 137, 1962, 3532.

English, Horace B. Chronological divisions of the life span. *Journal of Educational Psychology* 48, 1957, 437–39.

Ericksen, S. C. *Motivation for learning.* Ann Arbor: University of Michigan Press, 1974.

Erikson, E. H. *Childhood and society,* 2d ed., rev. New York: Norton, 1964.

————. *Identity: Youth and crisis.* New York: Norton, 1968.

Erikson, K. T. *Wayward Puritans.* New York: Wiley, 1966.

Erlenmeyer-Kimling, L., & Jarvik, L. F. Genetics and intelligence: A review. *Science* 142, 1963, 169–76.

Eron, L. D. How learning conditions in early childhood—including mass media—relate to aggression in late adolescence *American Journal of Orthopsychiatry* 44, 1974, 412–23.

Ervin, S. M., & Foster, G. The development of meaning in children's descriptive terms. *Journal of Abnormal and Social Psychology* 61, 1960, 271–75.

Eskridge, T. J., Jr. Growth in understanding of geographic terms in grades IV to VII. *Duke University Studies in Education,* no. 4, 1939.

Espenshade, A., & Eckert, H. Motor development. In W. R. Johnson & E. R. Buskirk, eds., *Science and medicine of exercise and sports,* 2d. ed., New York: Harper & Row, 1973.

Estes, W. K. Learning theory and intelligence. *American Psychologist* 29, 1974, 740–50.

Evans, R. I., Rozelle, R. M., et al. Fear arousal, persuasion, and actual versus implied behavior change. *Journal of Personality and Social Psychology* 16, 1970, 220–27.


Faust, M. S. Developmental maturity as a determinant in prestige of adolescent girls. *Child Development* 31, 1960, 173–84.

Fein, S. *Heidi's horse.* Pleasant Hill, Calif.: Exelrod, 1976.

Feldman, K. A., & Newcomb, T. M. *The impact of college on students*. San Francisco: Jossey-Bass, 1969.

Feldman, K. V., & Klausmeier, H. J. The effects of two kinds of definition on the concept attainment of fourth- and eighth-grade students. *Journal of Educational Research* 67, 1974, 219–23.

Festinger, L. Wish, expectation, and group performance as factors influencing level of aspiration. *Journal of Abnormal and Social Psychology* 37, 1942, 184–200.

Findley, W. G., & Bryan, M. W. *Ability grouping: 1970. Status, impact, and alternatives*. Athens, Ga.: Center for Educational Improvement, 1971. ED 048 381–384.

Fishbein, M., & Azjen, I. Attitudes towards objects as predictors of single and multiple behaviorial criteria. *Psychological Review* 81, 1974, 59–74.

Fisher, M. D., Blackwell, L. R., Garcia, A. B., & Greene, J. C. Effects of student control and choice on engagement in a CAI arithmetic task in a low-income school. *Journal of Educational Psychology* 67, 1975, 776–83.

Fitts, P. M. & Posner, M. I. *Human performance*. Belmont, Calif.: Brooks-Cole, 1967.

Flacks, R. Social and cultural meaning of student revolt. *Social Problems* 17, 1970, 340–57.

Flanagan, J. C. Stability of career plans. In J. C. Flanagan et al., *Project TALENT: One-year follow-up studies*. Pittsburgh: University of Pittsburgh, School of Education, 1966. Pp. 171–81.

———, Davis, F. B., Dailey, J. T., Shaycoft, M. F., et al. *The American high school student*. Pittsburgh: University of Pittsburgh, 1964.

Flavell, J. H. *The developmental psychology of Jean Piaget*. Princeton: Van Nostrand, 1963.

Fleishman, E. A. Toward a taxonomy of human performance. *American Psychologist* 30, 1975, 1127–49.

Fleming, E. S., & Antonen, R. G. Teacher expectancy as related to the academic and personal growth of primary-age children. *Monographs of the Society for Research on Child Development* 36 (5), 1971.

Flesch, R. The marks of a readable style. *Teachers College Contributions to Education,* no. 897. New York: Teachers College, Columbia University, 1943.

Fodor, J., Bever, T. G. & Garrett, M. F. *The psychology of language*. New York: McGraw-Hill, 1974.

Ford, J. B. Some more on the Samoans. *American Psychologist,* 12, 1957, 751.

Fortune, J. C. A study of the generalities of presenting behaviors in teaching. Unpublished report, Memphis State University, 1967.

F

Fouracre, M. H. Physically handicapped children. In C. W. Harris, ed., *Encyclopedia of Educational Research.* New York: Macmillan, 1960. Pp. 995–1008.

Fowler, W. Cognitive learning in infancy and early childhood. *Psychology Bulletin* 59, 1962, 116–52.

Frary, R. B. Elimination of the guessing component of multiple-choice test scores: effect on reliability and validity. *Educational and Psychological Measurement* 29, 1969, 665–80.

Freeberg, N. E., & Payne, D. T. Parental influence on cognitive development in early childhood: A review. *Child Development* 38, 1967, 65–89.

French, E. G. Effects of the interaction of motivation and feedback on task performance. In J. W. Atkinson, ed., *Motives in Fantasy, Action, and Society.* Princeton: Van Nostrand, 1958. Pp. 400–08.

French, J. R. P., Jr., Israel, J., & Ås, D. An experiment in a Norwegian factory. *Human Relations* 13, 1960, 3–20.

French, J. W. Aptitude and interest score patterns related to satisfaction with college major field. *Educational and Psychological measurement* 21, 1961, 287–94.

French, W. W. et al. Secondary school programs for improved living. *Bulletin of the National Association of Secondary School Principals* 32, May, 1948, 3–100.

Frenkel-Brunswik, E. Differential patterns of social outlook and personality in family and children. In M. Mead and M. Wolfenstein, eds. *Childhood in contemporary cultures.* Chicago: University of Chicago Press, 1955, Pp. 369–405.

Friedenberg, E. Z. Childhood, society, and Erik Erikson. *New York Review of Books* 4 (7), 1965, 1–7.

Fromm, E. *Escape from freedom.* New York: Farrar and Rinehart, 1941.

_____. *Man for himself.* New York: Rinehart, 1947.

Gaa, J. P. Effects of individual goal-setting conferences on achievement, attitudes, and goal-setting behavior. *Journal of Experimental Education* 42, 1973, 22–28.

Gage, N. L. *Teacher effectiveness and teacher education.* Palo Alto, Calif.: Pacific Books, 1972.

Gagné, R. M. *The conditions of learning,* 2d ed. New York: Holt, Rinehart and Winston, 1970.

_____. Learning and instructional sequence. *Review of Research in Education* I, 1973, 3–33.

_____, & Briggs, L. J. *Principles of instructional design.* New York: Holt, Rinehart and Winston, 1974.

_____, & Smith, E. C., Jr. A study of the effects of verbalization on problem solving. *Journal of Experimental Psychology,* 63, 1962, 12–18.

Gaier, E. L. Selected personality variables and the learning process. *Psychological Monographs* 66 (17), 1952.

Gallatin, J., & Adelson, J. Legal guarantees of individual freedom: A cross-national study of the development of political thought. *Journal of Social Issues* 27 (2), 1971, 93–108.

Gann, E. K. *Fate is the hunter.* New York: Simon and Schuster, 1961.

Gardner, J. W. *Excellence.* New York: Harper, 1961.

Gates, A. I. Recitation as a factor in memorizing. *Archives of Psychology* 40, 1917.

_____. The necessary mental age for beginning reading. *Elementary School Journal* 37, 1937, 497–508.

Gavurin, E. I. Anagram solving and spatial aptitude. *Journal of Psychology* 65, 1967, 65–68.

Getzels, J. W., & Jackson, P. W. The study of giftedness: A multidimensional approach. In *The gifted student.* Cooperative Research Monograph no. 2. Washington, D. C.: U. S. Office of Education, 1960. Pp. 1–18.

Gewirtz, H. B. Generalization of children's preferences as a function of reinforcement and task similarity. *Journal of Abnormal and Social Psychology* 58, 1959, 111–18.

Ghilain. J. Note sur le testing de l'educabilité dans une groupe de Noirs congolais. *Bulletin de l'academie Royale des Sciences d'Outre-Mer* 6, 1960, 292–321. (Excerpted and translated in F. B. Wickert, ed., *Readings in African psychology from French language sources.* East Lansing: Michigan State University, 1967. Pp. 29–30.

Ghiselli, E. E. *The validity of occupational aptitude tests.* New York: Wiley, 1966.

Gibbon, S. Y., Jr., & Palmer, E. L. Pre-reading on "Sesame Street." Unpublished report, Children's Television Workshop, New York, 1970. ED 047 825.

Gibson, E. J. *Principles of perceptual learning and development.* New York: Appleton-Century-Crofts, 1969.

_____, Gibson, J. J., Pick, A. D., & Osser, H. A developmental study of the discrimination of letter-like forms. *Journal of Comparative and Physiological Psychology* 55, 1962, 897–906.

Ginott, H. Even praise has its pitfalls. *Early Years* 3 (1), 1972, 43–45.

Ginzburg, R. Portrait of a genius as a young chess master. *Harper's Magazine* 224, 1962, 49–55.

Gladwin, T. *East is a big bird.* Cambridge, Mass.: Harvard University Press, 1970.

Glaser, R., ed. *The nature of reinforcement.* New York: Academic Press, 1971.

Glock, C. Y., Wuthnow, R., Piliavin, J. A., & Spencer, M. *Adolescent prejudice.* New York: Harper & Row, 1975.

Glucksberg, S., Krauss, R., & Higgins, E. T. The development of referential communication skills. In F. D. Horowitz, ed. *Review of child development research*, vol. 4. Chicago: University of Chicago Press, 1975. Pp. 305–45.

Goldschmid, M. L. The role of experience in the rate and sequence of cognitive development. In D. R. Green et al, eds., *Measurement and Piaget.* New York: McGraw-Hill, 1971. Pp. 103–110.

Gordon, C. Social characteristics of early adolescence. *Daedalus* 100, 1971, 931–60.

Gordon, C. W. *The social system of the high school.* Glencoe, Ill.: Free Press, 1957.

[Goslin, D. A.] *Guidelines for the collection, maintenance, and dissemination of pupil records.* New York: Russell Sage Foundation, 1970.

Gotkin, L. *Matrix games.* New York: Appleton-Century-Crofts, 1966.

Gottman, J., Gonso, J., & Rasmussen, B. Social interaction, social competence, and friendship in children. *Child Development* 46, 1975, 709–18.

Goulet, L. Training, transfer, and the development of complex behavior. *Human Development* 13, 1970. 212–40.

Green, D. R., Ford, M. P., & Flamer, G. B., eds. *Measurement and Piaget.* New York: McGraw-Hill, 1971.

Greene, D., & Lepper, M. Effects of extrinsic rewards on children's subsequent intrinsic interest. *Child Development* 45, 1974, 1141–45.

Greenstein, F. I. *Children and politics,* rev. ed. New Haven: Yale University Press, 1969.

Greenwald, A. G. Cognitive learning, cognitive response to persuasion, and attitude change. In Greenwald et al., eds., *Psychological foundations of attitudes.* New York: Academic Press, 1968.

Greenwood, C. R., Hops, H., Delquadri, J., & Guild, J. Group contingencies for group consequences in classroom management. *Journal of Applied Behavioral Analysis* 7, 1974, 413–26.

Gregg, L. W., ed. *Cognition in learning and memory.* New York: Wiley, 1972.

_____. *Knowledge and cognition.* Potomac, Md.: Erlbaum, 1974.

Gregory, R. L., & Wallace, J. G. Recovery from early blindness—a case study. *Experimental Psychology Monographs,* no. 2, 1962.

Grim, P. F., Kohlberg, L., & White, S. H. Some relationships between conscience and attentional processes. *Journal of Personality and Social Psychology* 8, 1968, 239–52.

Grinder, R. E. New techniques for research in children's temptation behavior. *Child Development* 32, 1961, 679–88.

————. Parental child-rearing practices, conscience, and resistance to temptation of sixth-grade children. *Child Development* 33, 1962, 803–20.

Gronlund, N. E. *Sociometry in the classroom.* New York: Harper, 1959.

————. *Measurement and evaluation in teaching.* New York: Macmillan, 1971.

Gross, R., & Murphy, J. *Educational change and architectural consequences.* New York: Educational Facilities Laboratories, 1968.

Guilford, J. P., & Hoepfner, R. *The analysis of intelligence.* New York: McGraw-Hill, 1971.

Haan, N. The adolescent antecedents of an ego model of coping and defense and comparisons with Q-sorted ideal personalities. *Genetic Psychology Monographs* 89, 1974, 273–306.

————. Hypothetical and actual moral reasoning in a situation of civil disobedience. *Journal of Personality and Social Psychology* 32, 1975, 255–70.

————, Smith, M. B., & Block, J. Moral reasoning of young adults. *Journal of Personality and Social Psychology* 10, 1968, 183–201.

Haber, R. N. How we remember what we see. *Scientific American* 222 (5), 1970, 104–12.

Haggard, E. A. Socialization, personality, and academic achievement in gifted children. *School Review* 65, 1957, 388–414.

Hall, E. Item writing in empirical studies. *Educational Research* 11, 1969, 223–25.

Hall, V., & Turner, R. R. The validity of the "different language explanation" for poor scholastic performance by black students. *Review of Educational Research* 44, 1974, 69–81.

Hall, V. C., Turner, R. R., & Russell, W. Ability of children from four subcultures and two grade levels to imitate and comprehend crucial aspects of standard English: A test of the different language explanation. *Journal of Educational Psychology* 64, 1973, 147–58.

Hall, W. S., & Freedle, R. O. A developmental investigation of standard and nonstandard English among black and white children. *Human Development,* 16, 1973, 440–64.

Hamachek, D. E., ed. *Human dynamics in psychology and education,* 3d ed. Boston: Allyn & Bacon, 1976.

Hammond, K. R. Computer graphics as an aid to learning. *Science* 172, 1971, 903–08.

Haney, C., & Zimbardo, P. G. The blackboard penitentiary: It's tough to tell a highschool from a prison. *Psychology Today* 9 (7), 1975, 26–30, 106–08.

Hanna, G. S., Bligh, H. F., Lenke, J. M., & Orleans, J. B. Predicting algebra achievement with an algebra prognosis test, IQs, teacher predictions, and mathematical grades. *Educational and Psychological Measurement* 29, 1969, 903–07.

Hanson, N. R. *Patterns of discovery.* Cambridge, England: Cambridge University Press, 1958.

Harding, J., et al. Prejudice and ethnic relations. In G. Lindzey & E. Aronson, eds., *Handbook of social psychology,* 2d ed., vol. 5. Reading, Mass.: Addison-Wesley, 1969.

Haring, N. G., & Phillips, E. L. Analysis and modification of classroom behavior. Englewood Cliffs, N.J.: Prentice-Hall, 1972.

Harlow, H. F. The formation of learning sets. *Psychological Review* 56, 1949, 51–65.

————. Mice, monkeys, men, and motives. *Psychological Review* 60, 1953, 23–32.

————, Harlow, M. K., Rueping, R. R., & Mason, W. A. Learning motivated by a manipulation drive. *Journal of Experimental Psychology* 40, 1950, 228–34.

Harmon, L. R. High school backgrounds of science doctorates. *Science* 133, 1961, 679–88.

Harmon, J. M., & Miller, A. G. Time patterns in motor learning. *Research Quarterly of the American Association for Health, Physical Education, and Recreation* 21, 1950, 182–86.

Harrow, A. J. *A taxonomy of the psychomotor domain.* New York: David McKay, 1972.

Harter, S. Pleasure derived by children from cognitive challenge and mastery. *Child Development* 45, 1974, 661–69.

_____. Mastery motivation and the need for approval. . . . *Developmental Psychology* 11, 1975, 186–96.

Hartnett, R. T., & Stewart, C. T. Personality rigidity of students showing consistent discrepancies between instructor grades and term-end examination grades. *Educational and Psychological Measurement* 25, 1965, 1111–15.

Hartshorne, H., & May, M. A. *Studies in deceit.* New York: Macmillan, 1928.

_____. *Studies in service and self-control.* New York: Macmillan, 1929.

_____. *Studies in the organization of character.* New York: Macmillan, 1930.

Hartup, W. W., & Coates, B. Imitation of a peer as a function of reinforcement from the peer group and rewardingness of the individual. *Child Development* 38, 1967, 1003–16.

Harvey, A. L. Goal setting as compensator for fear of success. *Adolescence* 10, 1975, 137–42.

Havighurst, R. J. *Human development and education.* New York: Longmans, 1953.

_____. A social-psychological perspective on aging. *The Gerontologist* 8, 1968, 67–71.

_____. Minority subcultures and the law of effect. *American Psychologist* 25, 1970, 313–22.

_____, & More, D. M. Recommended objectives in personal development and social maturation. In *Supplement to "Elementary school objectives."* Princeton: Educational Testing Service, 1953. Pp. 84–102.

_____, & Taba, H. *Adolescent character and personality.* New York: Wiley, 1949.

Hawkes, H. E., Lindquist, E. F., & Mann, C. R. *The construction and use of achievement examinations.* Boston: Houghton Mifflin, 1936.

Hawkins, P. R. Social class, the nominal group and reference. *Language and Speech* 12, 1969, 125–35.

Healy, W., & Bronner, A. *New light on delinquency and its treatment.* New Haven: Yale University Press, 1936.

Hebb, D. O. *A textbook of psychology.* Philadelphia: W. B. Saunders, 1958.

Heil, L. M., Powell, M., & Feifer, I. Characteristics of teacher behavior related to the achievement of children in several elementary grades. Unpublished report, Brooklyn College, 1960. ED 002 843.

Henderson, R. L. A comparison of three methods of organizing and administering child-study programs in rural twelve-grade schools. Unpublished doctoral thesis. University of Chicago, 1949.

Hendrickson, G., & Schroeder, W. H. Transfer of training in learning to hit a submerged target. *Journal of Educational Psychology* 32, 1941, 205–13.

Henle, M. On the relation between logic and thinking. *Psychological Review* 63, 1962, 366–78.

Henry, J. Education of the Negro child. In M. L. Wax et al., eds., *Anthropological perspectives in education.* New York: Basic Books, 1971.

Hermans, H. J. M., ter Laak, J. J. F., & Maes, P. C. J. M. Achievement motivation and fear of failure in family and school. *Developmental Psychology* 6, 1972, 520–28.

Hertzig, M. E., Birch, H. G., Thomas, A., & Mendez, O. Class and ethnic differences in the responsiveness of preschool children to cognitive demands. *Monographs of the Society for Research in Child Development* 33 (1), 1968.

Hess, R. D. Social competence and the educational process. In K. Connolly & J. Bruner, eds., *The growth of competence*. New York: Academic Press, 1974.

_____, & Shipman, V. C. Cognitive elements in maternal behavior. In J. P. Hill, ed., *Minnesota Symposia on Child Psychology,* no. 1. Minneapolis: University of Minnesota Press, 1967.

_____, Shipman, V. C., Brophy, J. E., & Bear, R. M. Cognitive environments of urban preschool children. Unpublished report, University of Chicago, 1968. ED 039 264.

_____, Shipman, V. C., Brophy, J. E., & Bear, R. M. The cognitive environment of urban preschool children: Follow-up phase. Unpublished report, University of Chicago, 1969. ED 039 270.

_____, & Tenezakis, M. D. Selected findings from "The computer as a socializing agent: Some socioaffective outcomes of CAI." *AV Communication Review* 21, 1973, 311–25.

Higgins, E. T. Social class differences in verbal communicative accuracy. *Psychological Bulletin* 83, 1976, 695–714.

Higgins, J. R., & Angel, R. W. Correction of tracking errors without sensory feedback. *Journal of Experimental Psychology* 84, 1970, 412–16.

Highet, G. *The art of teaching.* New York: Knopf, 1950.

Hilgard, E. R. *Theories of learning.* New York: Appleton-Century-Crofts, 1956.

_____, & Atkinson, R. C. *Introduction to psychology,* 6th ed. New York: Harcourt Brace Jovanovich, 1975.

_____, & Bower, G. H. *Theories of learning,* 4th ed. Englewood Cliffs, N.J.: Prentice-Hall, 1975.

Hilgard, J. R. Learning and motivation in preschool children. *Journal of Genetic Psychology* 41, 1932, 36–56.

Hilton, T. L., Beaton, A. E., & Bower, C. P. *Stability and instability in academic growth—A compilation of longitudinal data.* New Jersey: Educational Testing Service, 1971. ED 072 075.

Hobbs, N. *The futures of children.* San Francisco: Jossey-Bass, 1975a.

_____, ed. *Issues in the classification of children.* 2 vols. San Francisco, Jossey-Bass, 1975b. Pp. 130–58.

Hoffman, L. W., Rosen, S., & Lippitt, R. Parental coerciveness, child autonomy, and child's role at school. *Sociometry* 23, 1960, 15–22.

Hoffman, M. L. Sex differences in moral internalization. *Journal of Personality and Social Psychology* 32, 1975, 720–29.

Holt, J. *How children fail.* New York: Pitman, 1964.

_____. *How children learn.* New York: Pitman, 1967.

Honzik, M. P. Environmental correlates of mental growth: prediction from the family setting at 21 months. *Child Development* 38, 1967, 337–64.

Horner, M. S. Sex differences in achievement motivation and performance in competitive and non-competitive situations. Unpublished doctoral dissertation, University of Michigan, 1968.

Horton, R. E., Jr. American freedom and the values of youth. In H. Remmers, ed., *Anti-democratic attitudes in American schools.* Evanston: Northwestern University Press, 1963. Pp. 18–61.

House, B. J., & Zeaman, D. The transfer of a discrimination from objects to patterns. *Journal of Experimental Psychology* 59, 1960, 298–302.

Howe, M. J. A. Repeated presentation and recall of meaningful prose. *Journal of Educational Psychology* 61, 1970, 214–19.

_____. *Understanding school learning.* New York: Harper, 1972.

Hughes, E. C. Stress and strain in professional education. *Harvard Educational Review* 29, 1959, 319–29.

Hunt, D. E., & Sullivan, E. V. *Between psychology and education.* Hinsdale, Ill.: Dryden, 1974.

Hunt, J. McV. *The challenge of incompetence and poverty.* Urbana, Ill.: University of Illinois Press, 1969.

Huntley, R. M. C. Heritability of intelligence. In J. E. Meade & A. S. Parkes, eds., *Genetic and environmental factors in human ability.* Edinburgh: Oliver & Boyd, 1966. Pp. 201–18.

Husband, R. W. Positive transfer as a factor in memory. *Proceedings of Iowa Academy of Sciences* 54, 1947, 235–38.

Husén, T. The influence of schooling upon IQ. *Theoria* 17, 1951, 61–88.


Inhelder, B., & Piaget, J. *The growth of logical thinking from childhood to adolescence.* New York: Basic Books, 1958. (Originally published in French, 1955.)

Inkeles, A. Social structure and socialization. In D. A. Goslin, ed., *Handbook of socialization theory and research.* Chicago: Rand McNally, 1969.

———, & Smith, D. H. *Becoming modern.* Cambridge: Harvard University Press, 1974.

Irion, A. L. Historical introduction. In E. A. Bilodeau, ed., *Principles of skill acquisition.* New York: Academic Press, 1969. Pp. 1–31.


Jacob, P. E. *Changing values in college.* New York: Harper, 1957.

James, W. *The principles of psychology.* New York: Holt, 1890.

———. *Talks to teachers on psychology.* New York: Holt, 1907.

Janis, I. L., & Mann, L. A conflict-theory approach to attitude change and decision making. In A. G. Greenwald et al., eds., *Psychological foundations of attitudes.* New York: Academic Press, 1969. Pp. 327–60.

Jencks, C. *Inequality.* New York: Basic Books, 1972.

———, & Riesman, D. On class in America. *The Public Interest* 10, 1968, 68–85.

Jensen, A. R. *Educability and group differences.* New York: Harper & Row, 1973.

———. How much can we boost IQ and scholastic achievement? *Harvard Educational Review* 39, 1969, 1–123.

Johnson, D. M. *A systematic introduction to the psychology of thinking.* New York: Harper & Row, 1972.

Johnson, G. O. Special education for the mentally handicapped—a paradox. *Exceptional Children* 29, 1962, 62–69.

Johnson, H. W. Skill = speed × accuracy × form × adaptability. *Perceptual and Motor Skills* 13, 1961, 163–70.

Johnson, N. J., & Sanday, P. R. Subcultural variations in one urban poor population. *American Anthropologist* 73, 1971, 128–43.

Johnson, R. E. Abstractive processes in the remembering of prose. *Journal of Educational Psychology* 66, 1974, 772–79.

Jones, B. Is proprioception important for skilled performance? *Journal of Motor Behavior* 6, 1974, 33–45.

Jones, M. C. The elimination of children's fears. *Journal of Experimental Psychology* 7, 1924, 382–90.

———. The later careers of boys who were early- or late-maturing. *Child Development* 28, 1957, 113–28.

———. Psychological correlates of somatic development. *Child Development* 36, 1965, 899–911.

———. Albert, Peter, & J. B. Watson. *American Psychologist* 29 (8), 1974, 581–83.

———, & Bayley, N. Physical maturing among boys as related to behavior. *Journal of Educational Psychology* 41, 1950, 129–48.

———, & Mussen, P. H. Self-conceptions, motivations, and interpersonal attitudes of early- and late-maturing girls. *Child Development* 29, 1958, 491–502.

Jones, P. A. Home environment and the development of verbal ability. *Child Development* 43, 1972, 1081–86.

Jones, V. *Character and citizenship training in the public school.* Chicago: University of Chicago Press, 1936.

Jucknat, M. Leistung, Anspruchsniveau, und Selbstbewusstsein. *Psychologische Forschung* 22, 1938, 89–179.

Judd, W., & Glaser, R. Response latency as a function of training method, information level, acquisition, and overlearning. *Journal of Educational Psychology* 60, 1969, 1–30.

Justin, N. Culture conflict and Mexican-American achievement. *School and Society* 98, 1970, 27–28.

Kagan, J. Acquisition and significance of sex typing and sex role identity. In M. L. Hoffman & L. W. Hoffman, eds., *Review of child development research,* vol. I. New York: Russell Sage Foundation, 1964. Pp. 137–67.

———, & Coles, R. *Twelve to sixteen: Early adolescence.* New York: Harcourt Brace Jovanovich, 1972.

———, & Moss, H. A. *Birth to maturity.* New York: Wiley, 1962.

———. The stability of passive and dependent behavior from childhood through adulthood. *Child Development* 31, 1960, 577–91.

Kaplan, E. S. "Head Start" experience and the development of skills and abilities in kindergarten children. *Graduate Research in Education and Related Disciplines* 2 (1), 1966, 4–28.

Kaplan, S. N., Kaplan, J. B., Madsen, S. K., & Taylor, B. K. *Change for children: Ideas and activities for individualizing learning.* Pacific Palisades, Calif.: Goodyear, 1973.

Karabenick, S. Valence of success and failure as a function of locus of control. *Journal of Personality and Social Psychology* 21, 1972, 101–10.

Katz, I. The socialization of academic motivation in minority group children. In D. Levine, ed., *Nebraska Symposium on Motivation, 1967.* Lincoln, Nebraska: University of Nebraska Press, 1967. Pp. 133–91.

Kaufman, A. S. Factor analysis of the WISC-R at 11 age levels. *Journal of Consulting and Clinical Psychology* 43, 1975, 135–47.

Kavanau, J. L. Behavior of captive white-footed mice. *Science* 155, 1967, 1623–39.

Kay, H. Learning and retaining verbal material. *British Journal of Educational Psychology* 44, 1955, 81–100.

Keislar, E. R., & McNeil, J. D. Teaching scientific theory to first grade pupils by auto-instructional device. *Harvard Educational Review* 31, 1961, 73–83.

Kelly, R. T., Rawson, H. E., & Terry, R. L. Interaction effects of achievement need and situational press on performance. *Journal of Social Psychology* 89, 1973, 141–45.

Kemp, C. G. Children's perception of and performance in self-control. Paper presented to American Educational Research Association, 1961.

Keniston, K. Youth, a (new) stage of life. *American Scholar* 39, 1970, 631–54.

Keyes, D. Flowers for Algernon. In J. Merrill, ed., *The year's best S-F.* New York: Simon and Schuster, 1960.

Kirchner, E. P. Vividness of adjectives and the recall of meaningful verbal material. *Psychonomic Science* 15, 1969, 71–72.

Kirk, S. A. *Early education of the mentally retarded.* Urbana: University of Illinois Press, 1958.

Klausmeier, H. J., Beeman, A., & Lehmann, I. J. Comparison of organismic age and regression equations in predicting achievements in elementary school. *Journal of Educational Psychology* 49, 1958, 182–86.

_____, & Feldman, K. V. Effects of a definition and a varying number of examples and nonexamples on concept attainment. *Journal of Educational Psychology* 67, 1975, 174–78.

_____, Ghatala, E. S., & Frayer, D. A. *Conceptual learning and development.* New York: Academic Press, 1974.

Knezevich, S. J. The constancy of the IQ of the secondary school pupil. *Journal of Educational Research* 39, 1946, 506–16.

Kohl, H. R. *Math, writing, and games in the open classroom.* New York: The New York Review, 1974.

Kohlberg, L. Cognitive-developmental theory and the practice of collective moral education. In M. Wolins & M. Gottesman, eds., *Group care: The education path of Youth Aliyah.* New York: Gordon & Breach, 1971. Pp. 342–71.

_____, ed. *Collected papers on moral development and moral education.* Cambridge, Mass.: Harvard University Press, 1973.

Kohn, M. L. *Class and conformity: a study in values.* Homewood, Ill.: Dorsey, 1969.

Kohn, M., & Rosman, B. L. Relationship of preschool social-emotional functioning to later intellectual achievement. *Developmental Psychology* 6, 1972, 445–52.

Konishi, M. The role of auditory feedback in the control of vocalization in the White-crowned Sparrow. *Zeitschrift für Tierpsychologie* 22, 1965, 770–83.

Kounin, J. *Discipline and group management in classrooms.* New York: Holt, Rinehart and Winston, 1970.

Kounin, J. S., & Gump, P. V. The ripple effect in discipline. *Elementary School Journal* 59, 1958, 158–62.

_____. The comparative influence of punitive and non-punitive teachers upon children's concepts of school misconduct. *Journal of Educational Psychology* 52, 1961, 44–49.

Krasner, L., & Krasner, M. Token economies and other planned environments. In C. E. Thoresen & H. G. Richey, eds., *Behavior modification in education: The seventy-second yearbook of the National Society for the Study of Education.* Chicago: University of Chicago Press, 1973.

Krathwohl, D. R., Bloom, B. S., & Masia, B. B. *Taxonomy of educational objectives: Handbook II.* New York: McKay, 1964.

Krauss, R. M., & Weinheimer, S. Changes in the length of reference phrases as a function of social interaction. *Psychonomic Science* 1, 1964, 113–14.

Krueger, W. C. F. Further studies in overlearning. *Journal of Experimental Psychology* 13, 1930, 152–63.

Krumboltz, J. D., & Krumboltz, H. B. *Changing children's behavior.* Englewood Cliffs, N.J.: Prentice-Hall, 1972.

Kulhavy, R. W., & Swenson, I. Imagery instructions and the comprehension of text. *British Journal of Educational Psychology* 45, 1974, 47–57.

Kuvshinov, N. I. Reshenie prakticheskikh zadach uchashchimisia nachal'nykh klassov na urokakh truda. *Voprosy Psikhologii* 5, 1959, 48–58.


Labov, W. *The social function of English in New York City.* Washington, D.C.: Center for Applied Linguistics, 1966.

_____. Some sources of reading problems for Negro speakers of nonstandard English. In A. Frazier, ed., *New directions in elementary English.* Champaign, Ill.: National Council of Teachers of English, 1967. Pp. 140–67.

L

_____. The logic of nonstandard English. In F. Williams, ed., *Language and poverty*. Chicago: Markham, 1970.

_____, & Robins, C. A note on the relation of reading failure to peer-group status in urban ghettos. *Teachers College Record* 70, 1969, 395–405.

Lambert, W. E., & Klineberg, O. *Children's views of foreign peoples*. New York: Appleton-Century-Crofts, 1967.

_____, & Tucker, G. R. *Bilingual education of children: The St. Lambert experiment*. Rowley, Mass.: Newbury House, 1972.

Lane, H. *The wild boy of Aveyron*. Cambridge, Mass.: Harvard University Press, 1976.

Lange, A., Lehmann, I. J., & Mehrens, W. A. Using item analysis to improve tests. *Journal of Educational Measurement* 4, 1967, 65–68.

LaPiere, R. T. Attitudes versus actions. *Social Forces* 13, 1934, 230–37.

Latham, G. P., & Baldes, J. J. The "practical significance" of Locke's theory of goal setting. *Journal of Applied Psychology* 60, 1975, 122–24.

Lawrence, David H. *Selected essays*. London: Heinemann, 1950.

Lawrence, Douglas H., & Goodwin, W. R. Transfer in tracking behavior between two levels of speed. *Research Bulletin* 54–70, San Antonio: Air Force Personnel and Training Research Command, 1954.

Lefrancois, G. R. *Psychology for teaching*. Belmont, Calif.: Wadsworth, 1975.

Lehmusvuori, H. The effect of teachers' authoritarian and democratic attitudes on the children's level of aspiration after success and failure. *Research Reports, Department of Psychology, Jyvaskyla Institute of Pedagogics,* no. 13, 1958, 7–20.

Lepper, M. R., Greene, D., & Nisbett, R. E. Undermining children's intrinsic interest with extrinsic reward. *Journal of Personality and Social Psychology* 28, 1973, 129–37.

Lesser, G. S. Applications of psychology to television programming. *American Psychologist* 31, 1976, 135–36.

_____, ed. *Psychology and educational practice*. Glenview, Ill.: Scott-Foresman, 1971.

Lessing, E. E., Beiser, H., Krause, M., Dolinko, P., & Zagorin, S. W. Differentiating children's symptom checklist items on the basis of judged severity of psychopathology. *Genetic Psychology Monographs* 88, 1973, 329–50.

Lester, B. M., & Klein, R. E. The effect of stimulus familiarity on the conservation performance of rural Guatemalan children. *Journal of Social Psychology* 90, 1973, 197–205.

Leventhal, H., Watts, J. C., & Pagano, F. Effects of fear and instructions on how to cope with danger. *Journal of Personality and Social Psychology* 6, 1967, 313–21.

Levin, M. M. Congruence and developmental changes in authoritarianism in college students. In J. Katz, ed., *Growth and constraint in college students*. Unpublished, Institute for the Study of Human Problems, Stanford University, 1967. Pp. 422–71. ED 016 264.

Levy, J. M. & McGee, R. K. Childbirth as crisis. *Journal of Personality and Social Psychology* 31, 1975, 171–79.

Lewin, K. Behavior and development as a function of the total situation. In L. Carmichael, ed., *Manual of child psychology*. New York: Wiley, 1946. Pp. 791–844.

_____. Group decision and social change. In E. Maccoby et al., eds., *Readings in social psychology*. New York: Holt, 1958. Pp. 197–211.

Lewis, H. B. Studies in the principles of judgment and attitudes: IV. The operation of "prestige suggestion." *Journal of Social Psychology* 14, 1941, 229–56.

Lindahl, L. G. Movement analysis as an industrial training method. *Journal of Applied Psychology* 29, 1945, 420–46.

Linn, M. W., et al. A social dysfunction rating scale. *Journal of Psychiatric Research* 6, 1969, 299–306.

Linn, R. Fair test use in selection. *Journal of Educational Research* 43, 1973, 139–61.

Linton, M. Memory for real-world events. In D. A. Norman & D. E. Rumelhart, eds., *Explorations in cognition.* San Francisco: Freeman, 1975. Pp. 376–404.

Liska, A. E., ed. *The consistency controversy.* New York: Schenkman, 1975.

Locke, E. A. Toward a theory of task motivation and incentives. *Organizational Behavior and Human Performance* 3, 1968, 157–89.

Locke, L. F. Implications for physical education. *Research Quarterly* 43, 1972, 374–86.

Loehlin, J. C., Lindzey, G., & Spuhler, J. N. *Race differences in intelligence.* San Francisco: Freeman, 1975.

Lorton, P., Jr. Computer-based instruction in spelling. Unpublished doctoral dissertation, Stanford University, 1972.

Lowell, F. E. A study of the variability of IQ's in retest. *Journal of Applied Psychology* 25, 1941, 341–56.

Luchins, A. S. Mechanization in problem solving—the effect of Einstellung. *Psychological Monographs* 54 (6), 1942.

Lumsdaine, A. A., & Janis, I. L. Resistance to "counterpropaganda" produced by one-sided and two-sided "propaganda" presentations. *Public Opinion Quarterly* 17, 1953, 311–18.

Lundberg, G. A., & Dickson, L. Selective association among ethnic groups in a high school population. In A. R. Brown, ed., *Prejudice in children.* Springfield, Ill.: C. C. Thomas, 1972. Pp. 96–118.

McCall, R. B., Applebaum, M. I., & Hogarty, P. S. Developmental changes in mental performance. *Monographs of the Society for Research in Child Development* 38 (3), 1973.

McCandless, B. R. *Children: Behavior and development.* New York: Holt, Rinehart and Winston, 1967.

McCarthy, D. Research in language development: retrospect and prospect. *Monographs of the Society for Research in Child Development* 24 (5), 1959, 3–24.

———. *Manual for the McCarthy Scales of Children's Abilities.* New York: Psychological Corporation, 1972.

McClelland, D. C. Testing for competence rather than for "intelligence." *American Psychologist* 28 (1), 1973, 1–14.

———, Atkinson, J. W., Clark, R. A., & Lowell, E. L. *The achievement motive.* New York: Appleton-Century-Crofts, 1953.

———, & Watson, R. I., Jr. Power motivation and risk-taking behavior. *Journal of Personality* 41, 1973, 121–39.

McClintock, C. G. Development of social motives in Anglo-American and Mexican-American children. *Journal of Personality & Social Psychology* 29, 1974, 348–54.

Maccoby, E. E., & Jacklin, C. N. *The psychology of sex differences.* Stanford: Stanford University Press, 1974.

———, & Zellner, M. *Experiments in primary education: Aspects of Project Follow-Through.* New York: Harcourt Brace Jovanovich, 1970.

McCord, J., McCord, W., & Howard, A. Family interaction as antecedent to the direction of male aggressiveness. *Journal of Abnormal and Social Psychology* 66, 1963, 239–42.

McCord, W., McCord, J., & Zola, I. K. *Origins of crime.* New York: Columbia University Press, 1959.

Macfarlane, J. W. From infancy to adulthood. *Childhood Education* 39, 1963, 336–42.

M

_____, Allen, L., & Honzik, M. P. A developmental study of the behavior problems of normal children between twenty-one months and fourteen years. *University of California Publications in Child Development,* vol. 2. 1954.

MacGinitie, W. H. Language comprehension in education. In J. R. Davitz & S. Ball, eds., *Psychology of the educational process.* New York: McGraw-Hill, 1970. Pp. 101–56.

McGuire, C. H., & Babbott, D. Simulation technique in the measurement of problem-solving skills. *Journal of Educational Measurement* 4, 1967, 1–10.

McGuire, W. J. Inducing resistance to persuasion: Some contemporary approaches. In L. Berkowitz, ed., *Advances in experimental social psychology,* vol. 1. New York: Academic Press, 1964. Pp. 191–229.

_____. The nature of attitudes and attitude change. In G. Lindsay & E. Aronson, eds., *Handbook of social psychology,* vol. 3. Reading, Mass.: Addison-Wesley, 1969. Pp. 136–314.

Mackay, L. D. The role of measurement and evaluation in science courses. In P. L. Gardner, ed., *The structure of science education.* Hawthorne, Victoria, Australia: Longman Australia, 1975. Pp. 190–219.

McKeachie, W. J. Anxiety in the college classroom. *Journal of Educational Research* 45, 1951, 153–60.

_____, ed. *The appraisal of teaching in large universities.* Ann Arbor: University of Michigan Press, 1959.

_____. Instructional psychology. *Annual Review of Psychology* 25, 1974, 161–93.

_____, & Kulik, J. A. Effective college teaching. In F. N. Kerlinger, ed., *Review of Research in Education,* vol. 3. Itasca, Ill.: Peacock Publishers, 1975. Pp. 165–209.

McKenzie, G. R. Some effects of frequent quizzes on inferential thinking. *American Educational Research Journal* 9, 1972, 231–40.

McNeill, D. Developmental psycholinguistics. In I. Smith & G. A. Miller, eds., *The genesis of language.* Cambridge, Mass.: MIT Press, 1966. Pp. 15–84.

Madsen, C. H., Jr., et al. An analysis of the reinforcing function of "sit down" commands. In R. K. Parker, ed., *Readings in educational psychology.* Boston: Allyn & Bacon, 1968. Pp. 265–78.

Magnusson, D. & Endler, N. S., eds., *Personality at the crossroads: Current issues in interactional psychology.* Hillsdale, N.J.: Erlbaum, 1976.

Mahoney, M. J., & Thoresen, C. E. *Self-control: Power to the person.* Monterey, Calif.: Brooks/Cole, 1974.

Majasan, J. K. College students' achievement as a function of the congruence between their beliefs and their instructor's beliefs. Unpublished doctoral disseration, Stanford University, 1972.

Malina, R. M. Effects of varied information feedback practice conditions on throwing speed and accuracy. *Research Quarterly, American Association for Health, Physical Education and Recreation* 40, 1969, 134–45.

Maloney, M. P., & Ward, M. P. Ecology: Let's hear from the people. *American Psychologist* 28, 1973, 583–86.

_____, & Braucht, G. N. A revised scale for the measurement of ecological attitudes and knowledge. *American Psychologist* 30, 1975, 787–90.

Manahan, J. E. Formulation of the motor plan. *Quest* 17, 1972, 46–51.

Marjoribanks, K., & Walberg, H. J. Ordinal position, family environment, and mental abilities. *Journal of Social Psychology* 95, 1975, 3–9.

Marks, J. B. Interests, leadership and sociometric status among adolescents. *Sociometry* 17, 1954, 340–49.

Marshall, J. C., & Powers, J. M. Writing neatness, composition errors, and essay grades. *Journal of Educational Measurement* 6, 1969, 97–101.

Martin, D. S. Ethnocentrism toward foreign culture in elementary school social studies. *Elementary School Journal* 75, 1975, 381–88.

Martin, J. G., & Westie, F. R. The tolerant personality. In A. R. Brown, ed., *Prejudice in children.* Springfield, Ill.: C. C. Thomas, 1972. Pp. 121–32.

Maslow, A. What is a Taoist teacher? In L. J. Rubin, ed., *Facts and feelings in the classroom.* New York: Walker, 1973. Pp. 150–67.

May, M. A. The psychology of learning from demonstration films. *Journal of Educational Psychology* 37, 1946, 1–12.

————, & Lumsdaine, A. A. *Learning from films.* New Haven: Yale University Press, 1958.

Mayer, M. *The schools.* New York: Harper, 1961.

Mayer, R. E. Some conditions of meaningful learning for computer programming. *Journal of Educational Psychology* 68, 1976, 143–50.

————, Stiehl, C. C., & Greeno, J. G. Acquisition of understanding and skill in relation to subjects' preparation and meaningfulness of instruction. *Journal of Educational Psychology* 67, 1975, 331–50.

Mead, M. *The school in American culture.* Cambridge, Mass.: Harvard University Press, 1951.

————. *Culture and commitment.* New York: Doubleday, 1970.

————, ed. *Cultural patterns and technical change.* New York: Mentor, 1955.

Mechner, F. Science education and behavioral technology. In R. Glaser, ed., *Teaching machines and programed learning, II.* Washington: Department of Audiovisual Instruction, National Education Association, 1965. Pp. 441–507.

Mellon, J. C. Transformational sentence-combining. *Research Reports* no. 10. Champaign, Ill: National Council of Teachers of English, 1969.

Merrill, M. D., & Boutwell, R. C. Instructional development: Methodology and research. *Review of Research in Education* 1, 1973, 95–131.

Meyer, O. E., & Schvaneveldt, R. W. Meaning, memory structure, and mental processes. *Science* 192, 1976, 27–33.

Michelmore, P. *The swift years: The Robert Oppenheimer story.* New York: Dodd, Mead, 1969.

Mikol, B. The enjoyment of new musical systems. In M. Rokeach, ed., *The open and closed mind.* New York: Basic Books, 1960. Pp. 270–84.

Miles, D. T. Affective goals in open education. In B. Spodek & H. J. Walberg, eds., *Studies in open education.* New York: Agathon, 1975. Pp. 79–97.

Miller, G. A. The magic number seven, plus or minus two: Some limits on our capacity for processing information. *Psychological Review* 53, 1956, 81–97.

————, Galanter, E., & Pribram, K. H. *Plans and structure of behavior.* New York: Holt, Rinehart and Winston, 1960.

Miller, R., Brickman, P., & Bolen, D. Attribution versus persuasion as a means for modifying behavior. *Journal of Personality and Social Psychology* 31, 1975, 430–41.

Millman, J. Reporting student progress: A case for a criterion-referenced marking system. *Phi Delta Kappan* 52, 1970, 226–30.

————, Bishop, C. H., & Ebel, R. An analysis of test-wiseness. *Educational and Psychological Measurement* 25, 1965, 707–26.

————, & Lindlof, J. The comparability of fifth-grade norms of the California, Iowa, and Metropolitan achievement tests. *Journal of Educational Measurement* 1, 1964, 135–37.

Minuchin, P., Biber, B., Shapiro, E., & Zimiles, H. *The psychological impact of school experience; a comparative study of nine-year-old children in contrasting schools.* New York: Basic Books, 1969.

Mischel, W. Toward a cognitive social learning reconceptualization of personality. *Psychological Review* 80, 1973, 252–83.

Mitnick, L. L., & McGinnies, E. Influencing ethnocentrism in small discussion groups through a film communication. *Journal of Abnormal and Social Psychology* 56, 1958, 82–90.

Moely, B. E., Olson, F. A., Halwes, T. G., & Flavell, J. H. Production deficiency in young children's clustered recall. *Developmental Psychology* 1, 26–34.

Morris, C., & Small, L. Changes in conceptions of the good life by American college students from 1950 to 1970. *Journal of Personality and Social Psychology* 20, 1971, 254–60.

Morse, A. D. *Schools of tomorrow—today.* Garden City: Doubleday, 1960.

Morse, H. T., & McCune, G. H. *Selected items for the testing of study skills and critical thinking.* Washington: National Council for the Social Studies, 1971.

Moser, A. C., & David, B. B. I pledge a legion. *Journal of Educational Sociology* 9, 1936, 436–40.

Moser, H. E. The concept of arithmetic readiness; an investigation on the second-grade level. Unpublished doctoral thesis, Duke University, 1947.

Mowrer, O. H. *Learning theory and behavior.* New York: Wiley, 1960.

Mueller, P. Doing it the hard way. *School Arts* 74 (5), 1975, 40–42.

Mullen, F. A. Truancy and classroom disorder as symptoms of personality problems. *Journal of Educational Psychology* 41, 1950, 97–109.

Munro, R. Curriculum evaluation. In. P. L. Gardner, ed., *The structure of science education.* Hawthorne, Victoria, Australia: Longman Australia, 1975. Pp. 220–35.

Munroe, R. L. *Teaching the individual.* New York: Columbia University Press, 1942.

Munsinger, H. The adopted child's IQ: A critical review. *Psychological Bulletin* 82, 1975, 623–59.

Mussen, P. H. Some personality and social factors related to changes in children's attitudes toward Negroes. *Journal of Abnormal and Social Psychology* 45, 1950, 423–41.

————, ed. *Carmichael's manual of child psychology,* 3d. ed. 2 vols. New York: Wiley, 1970.

————, & Distler, L. Child-rearing antecedents of masculine identification in kindergarten boys. *Child Development* 31, 1960, 89–100.

————, & Jones, M. C. The behavior-inferred motivations of late and early maturing boys. *Child Development* 29, 1958, 61–67.

————, & Kagan, J. Group conformity and perceptions of parents. *Child Development* 29, 1958, 57–60.

————, & Parker, A. L. Mother nurturance and girls' incidental imitative learning. *Journal of Personality and Social Psychology* 2, 1965, 94–97.

————, Rutherford, E., Harris, S., & Keasey, C. B. Honesty and altruism among preadolescents. *Developmental Psychology* 3, 1970, 169–94.

Myrdal, G. *An American dilemma; the Negro problem and modern democracy.* New York: Harper, 1944.

————. The case against romantic ethnicity. *The Center Magazine* 7 (4), 1974, 26–30.


N

National Assessment of Educational Progress. *Science objectives.* Denver: NAEP, 1972.

————. *Citizenship: national results. Report 2.* Washington, D.C.: Government Printing Office, 1970.

National Commission on Resources for Youth. *New roles for youth.* New York: Citation Press, 1974.

Naylor, J. C. Parameters affecting the relative efficiency of part and whole training methods: A review of the literature. Technical report no. 950–1. Naval Training Devices Center, 1962.

————, & Briggs, G. E. Effects of task complexity and task organization on the relative efficiency of part and whole training methods. *Journal of Experimental Psychology* 65, 1963, 217–24.

Nelsen, E. A., Grinder, R. E., & Biaggio, A. M. B. Relationships among behavioral, cognitive-developmental, and self report measures of morality and personality. *Multivariate Behavioral Research* 4, 1969, 483–500.

Nelson, C. D. Subtle brain damage: Its influence on learning and language. *Elementary School Journal* 61, 1961, 317–21.

Nelson, R. O., & Wein, K. S. Training letter discrimination by presentation of high-confusion versus low-confusion alternatives. *Journal of Educational Psychology* 66, 1974, 926–31.

Nesselroade, J. R., & Baltes, P. B. Adolescent personality development and historical change: 1970–1972. *Monographs of the Society for Research in Child Development* 39 (1), 1974.

Newcomb, T. M. *Personality and social change.* New York: Dryden Press, 1943.

————, et al. *Persistence and change: Bennington College and its students after twenty-five years.* New York: Wiley, 1967.

Newell, A., & Simon, H. A. *Human problem solving.* Englewood Cliffs, N.J.: Prentice-Hall, 1972.

Newman, H. H., Freeman, F. N., & Holzinger, K. J. *Twins: A study of heredity and environment.* Chicago: University of Chicago Press, 1937.

Nolen, P. S. Reading nonstandard dialect materials: A study at grades two and four. *Child Development* 43, 1972, 1092–97.

Norman, D. A. Cognitive organization and learning. In P. M. A. Rabbitt & S. Dornic, eds., *Attention and performance,* V. New York: Academic Press, 1975. Pp. 530–46.

Nottebohm, F. Ontogeny of birdsong. *Science* 167, 1970, 950–56.


O'Donnell, R. C., Griffin, W. J., & Norris, R. C. Syntax of kindergarten children: A transformational analysis. *Research Reports* no. 8, *National Council of Teachers of English,* 1967.

Offer, D. *The psychological world of the teen-ager.* New York: Basic Books, 1969.

O'Leary, K. D., & Becker, W. C. Behavior modification of an adjustment class: A token reinforcement program. *Exceptional Children* 33, 1967, 637–42.

————, & Drabman, R. Token reinforcement programs in the classroom: A review. *Psychological Bulletin* 75, 1971, 379–98.

Olson, D. R. Language and thought: Aspects of a cognitive theory of semantics. *Psychological Review* 4, 1970, 257–73.

Osherson, D. N., & Markman, E. Language and the ability to evaluate contradictions and tautologies. *Cognition* 3, 1975, 213–26.

Otto, W., McMenemy, R. A., & Smith, R. J. *Corrective and remedial teaching.* Boston: Houghton Mifflin, 1973.

Oxendine, J. B. *Psychology of motor learning.* New York: Appleton-Century-Crofts, 1968.


Palardy, J. M. What teachers believe—what children achieve. *Elementary School Journal* 69, 1969, 370–74.

Palmer, D. E. The play's the thing. *English Journal* 38, 1949, 568–71.

Palmer, E. L. Formative evaluation in the production of television for children. In D. R. Olson, ed., *Media and symbols. Yearbooks of the National Society for the Study of Education* 73 (part I), 1974, 303–29.

Palmer, F. H. Inferences to the socialization of the child from animal studies: A view from the bridge. In D. A. Goslin, ed., *Handbook of socialization theory and research.* Chicago: Rand McNally, 1969. Pp. 25–55.

————. Socioeconomic status and intellective performance among Negro preschool boys. *Developmental Psychology* 3, 1970, 1–9.

Palmer, H. O. Tachistoscopic training for beginning typing students in a secondary school. Unpublished doctoral dissertation, Oregon State College, 1955.

Panel on Youth, President's Science Advisory Committee. *Youth: Transition to adulthood.* Chicago: University of Chicago Press, 1974.

Parent, J., Forward, J., Canter, R., & Mohling, J. Interactive effects of teaching strategy and personal locus of control on student performance and satisfaction. *Journal of Educational Psychology* 67, 1975, 764–69.

Parke, R. D. Rules, roles, and resistance to deviation. In A. D. Pick, ed., *Minnesota Symposia on Child Psychology,* vol. 8. Minneapolis: University of Minnesota Press, 1974. Pp. 111–43.

Paton, S. M., Walberg, H. J., & Yeh, E. G. Ethnicity, environmental control, and academic self-concept in Chicago. *American Educational Research Journal* 10, 1973, 85–92.

Patrick, C. Creative thought in artists. *Journal of Psychology* 4, 1937, 35–73.

Patrick, J. R. Studies in rational behavior and emotional excitement, II. The effect of emotional excitement on rational behavior in human subjects. *Journal of Comparative Psychology* 18, 1934, 153–95.

Patton, J. A. A study of the effects of student acceptance of responsibility and motivation on course behavior. Unpublished doctoral dissertation, University of Minnesota, 1955.

Pavan, B. N. Good news: Research on the nongraded elementary school. *Elementary School Journal* 73, 1973, 333–42.

Peck, R. F., & Havighurst, R. J. *The psychology of character development.* New York: Wiley, 1960.

Pei, M. *The story of language,* 2d ed. Philadelphia: Lippincott, 1960.

Penfield, W., & Roberts, L. *Speech and brain-mechanisms.* Princeton: Princeton University Press, 1959.

Penrose, L. S. *The biology of mental defect.* London: Sidgwick and Jackson, 1963.

Pentony, P. Home environment and nursery school behavior. *Australian Journal of Psychology* 8, 1956, 61–65.

Perry, W. G., Jr. Students' use and misuse of reading skills: A report to a faculty. *Harvard Educational Review* 29, 1959, 193–200.

Peskin, H., & Livson, N. Pre- and postpubertal personality and adult psychologic functioning. *Seminars in Psychiatry* 4, 1972, 343–53.

Peters, W. *A class divided.* New York: Doubleday, 1971.

Peterson, R. C., & Thurstone, L. L. *Motion pictures and the social attitudes of children.* New York: Macmillan, 1933.

Piaget, Jean. *The psychology of intelligence.* London: Routledge and Kegan Paul, 1950. (Originally published in French, 1947.)

————. *The construction of reality in the child.* New York: Basic Books, 1954. (Originally published in French, 1937.)

————. Logique et équilibre dans les comportements du sujet. *Études d'épistémologie génétique* 2, 1957, 27–72.

————. *To understand is to invent.* New York: Grossman, 1973.

————, & Inhelder, B. *The child's conception of space.* London: Routledge and Kegan Paul, 1956. (Originally published in French, 1948.)

Plowman, L., & Stroud, J. B. The effect of informing pupils of the correctness of their responses to objective test questions. *Journal of Educational Research* 36, 1942, 16–20.

Poliakova, A. G. Analysis of the process of acquiring habits by means of imitation in children of preschool age. *Voprosy Psikhologii* 4, 1958, 88–97.

Polya, G. *Mathematics and plausible reasoning.* Princeton: Princeton University Press, 1954.

Porter, N., & Taylor, N. *How to assess the moral reasoning of students.* Toronto: Ontario Institute for Studies in Education, 1972.

Postman, L. Verbal learning and memory. *Annual Review of Psychology* 26, 1975, 291–335.

Poulton, E. C. Tracking behavior. In E. A. Bilodeau, ed., *Acquisition of skill.* New York: Academic Press, 1966. Pp. 361–410.

Prescott, D. A. *The child in the educative process.* New York: McGraw-Hill, 1957.

Pronko, N. H. On learning to play the violin at the age of four without tears. *Psychology Today* 2 (12), 1969, 52–53, 66.

Purdy, B. J., & Lockhart, A. Retention and relearning of gross motor skills after long periods of no practice. *Research Quarterly* 33, 1962, 265–72.

Q

Quartermain, David, & Scott, T. H. Incidental learning in a simple task. *Canadian Journal of Psychology* 14, 1960, 175–82.

Quay, L. C. Language, dialect, reinforcement, and the intelligence-test performance of Negro children. *Child Development* 42, 1971, 5–15.

R

Radin, N. Father-child interaction and the intellectual functioning of four-year-old boys. *Developmental Psychology* 6, 1972, 353–61.

Raguse, F. W. Qualitative and quantitative achievements in first grade reading. *Teachers College Record* 32, 1931, 424–36.

Rathbone, C. H. Examining the open education classroom. *School Review* 80, 1972, 521–49.

Rawlings, E. I., Rawlings, I. L., Chen, S. S., & Yilk, M. D. The facilitating effects of mental rehearsal in the acquisition of rotary pursuit tracking. *Psychonomic Science* 26, 1972, 71–73.

Raynor, J. O., & Rubin, I. S. Effects of achievement orientation and future orientation on level of performance. In J. W. Atkinson & J. O. Raynor, eds., *Motivation and achievement.* Washington, D.C.: Winston, 1974. Pp. 181–87.

Read, C. Preschool children's knowledge of English phonology. *Harvard Educational Review* 41, 1971, 1–34.

Reed, H. B., Jr. Teacher variables of warmth, demand and utilization of intrinsic motivation related to pupils' science interests. *Journal of Experimental Education* 29, 1961, 205–29.

Reed, S. K., & Abramson, A. Effect of the problem space on subgoal facilitation. *Journal of Educational Psychology* 68, 1976, 243–46.

Reeves, B. F. The first year of "Sesame Street": The formative research. Unpublished report. New York: Children's Television Workshop, 1970. ED 047 822.

Reinfeld, F. *Win at chess.* New York: Dover, 1945.

Reitman, W. R. *Cognition and thought, an information-processing approach.* New York: Wiley, 1965.

Rest, J. R. The hierarchical nature of moral judgment. *Journal of Personality* 41, 1973, 86–109.

Reynolds, N. J., & Risley, T. R. The role of social and material reinforcers in increasing talking of a disadvantaged preschool child. *Journal of Applied Behavior Analysis* 1, 1968, 253–62.

Richardson, A. Mental practice: A review and discussion. *Research Quarterly* 38, 1967, 95–107.

Rickards, J. P., & Di Vesta, F. J. Type and frequency of questions in processing textual material. *Journal of Educational Psychology* 66, 1974, 354–62.

Riecken, H., & Boruch, R. *Social experimentation.* New York: Academic Press, 1974.

Riesen, A. Effects of stimulus deprivation on the development and atrophy of the visual sensory system. *American Journal of Orthopsychiatry* 30, 1960, 23–36.

Risley, T., & Wolf, M. Establishing functional speech in echolalic children. *Behaviour Research and Therapy* 5, 1967, 73–88.

Rist, R. C. Student social class and teacher expectations: The self-fulfilling prophecy in ghetto education. *Harvard Educational Review* 40, 1970, 411–51.

Robb, M., & Teeple, J. Video tape and skill learning: An exploratory study. *Educational Technology* 10, 1969, 79–82.

[Roberts, N.] *Guidelines for creating positive sexual and racial images in educational materials.* New York: Macmillan, 1975.

Robinson, J. P., & Shaver, P. R. *Measures of social psychological attitudes.* Ann Arbor: Institute for Social Research, 1973.

Roff, M. F., Sells, S. B., & Golden, M. M. *Social adjustment and personality development in children.* Minneapolis: University of Minnesota Press, 1972.

Rogers, C. R. Learning to be free. In S. M. Farber & R. H. L. Wilson, eds., *Man and civilization: Conflict and creativity.* New York: McGraw-Hill, 1963. Pp. 268–89.

Rohwer, W. D., Jr. Prime time for learning: Early childhood or adolescence? *Harvard Educational Review* 41, 1971, 316–41.

Rokeach, M. *The nature of human values.* New York: Free Press, 1973.

_____. *The open and closed mind.* New York: Basic Books. 1960.

Rosen, B. C. Race, ethnicity, and the achievement syndrome. *American Sociological Review* 24, 1959, 47–60.

_____. Socialization and achievement motivation in Brazil. *American Sociological Review* 27, 1962, 612–24.

_____, & d'Andrade, R. The psychosocial origins of achievement motivation. *Sociometry* 22, 1959, 185–218.

Rosenbaum, M. E. The effect of verbalization of correct responses by performers and observers on retention. *Child Development* 38, 1967, 615–22.

Rosenblith, J. F., Allinsmith, W., & Williams, J. P., eds. *Readings in educational psychology.* Boston: Allyn & Bacon, 1973.

Rosenhan, D. L. Effects of social class and race on responsiveness to approval and disapproval. *Journal of Personality and Social Psychology* 14, 1966, 253–59.

Rosenthal, D. J. A., & Resnick, L. B. Children's solution processes in arithmetic word problems. *Journal of Educational Psychology* 66, 1974, 817–25.

Rosenthal, R., & Jacobsen, L. *Pygmalion in the classroom.* New York: Holt, Rinehart and Winston, 1968.

Ross, D. Relationship between dependency, intentional learning and incidental learning in preschool children. *Journal of Personality and Social Psychology* 4, 1966, 374–81.

Ross, L., Bierbrauer, G., & Hoffman, S. The role of attribution processes in conformity and dissent: Revisiting the Asch situation. *American Psychologist* 31, 1976, 148–57.

Rothkopf, E. Z. Structural text features and the control of processes in learning from written material. In J. B. Carroll & R. O. Freedle, eds., *Language comprehension and the acquisition of knowledge.* New York: Wiley, 1972. Pp. 315–35.

_____, & Johnson, P. E., eds. *Verbal learning research and the technology of written instruction.* New York: Teachers College Press, 1971.

Ruediger, W. G. The indirect improvement of mental function thru ideals. *Educational Review* 36, 1908, 364–71.

Rushton, J. P. Generosity in children: Immediate and long-term effects of modeling, preaching, and moral judgment. *Journal of Personality and Social Psychology* 31, 1975, 459–66.

Ryan, J. IQ—the illusion of objectivity. In K. Richardson & D. Spears, eds., *Race and intelligence.* Baltimore: Penguin, 1972. Pp. 36–55.

Ryans, D. G. A study of criterion data. *Educational and Psychological Measurement* 12, 1952, 333–44.

_____. *Characteristics of teachers.* Washington, D.C.: American Council on Education, 1960.

_____, & Wandt, E. A factor analysis of observed teacher behaviors in the secondary school. *Educational and Psychological Measurement* 12, 1952, 574–86.

Ryder, R. G. Birth to maturity revisited: A canonical reanalysis. *Journal of Personality and Social Psychology* 7, 1967, 168–72.

Sabers, D. L., & Feldt, L. S. The predictive validity of the Iowa Algebra Aptitude Test for achievement in modern mathematics and algebra. *Education and Psychology Measurement* 28, 1968, 901–07.

Sadker, D., Sadker, M., & Cooper, J. M. Elementary school—through children's eyes. *Elementary School Journal* 73, 1972, 289–96.

Sandiford, P. *Educational psychology.* New York: Longmans, Green, 1928.

Sanford, N. *Self and society.* New York: Atherton Press, 1966.

_____, ed. *The American college.* New York: Wiley, 1962.

Sarason, S. B., Davidson, K. S., Lighthall, F. F., Waite, R. R., & Ruebush, B. K. *Anxiety in elementary school children.* New York: Wiley, 1960.

Sassenrath, J. M. Theory and results on feedback and retention. *Journal of Educational Psychology* 67, 1975, 894–99.

Sawuda, R. J. *Psychological testing of American minorities.* New York: Dodd, Mead, 1975.

Scannell, D. P., & Tracy, D. B. *Testing and measurement in the classroom.* Boston: Houghton Mifflin, 1975.

Schaie, K. W., & Labouvie-Vief, G. Generational versus ontogenetic components of change in adult cognitive behavior. *Developmental Psychology* 10, 1974, 305–20.

Schmidt, R. A. *Motor skills.* New York: Harper & Row, 1975a.

_____. A schema theory of discrete motor skill learning. *Psychological Review* 82, 1975b, 225–60.

Schoeppe, A., & Havighurst, R. J. A validation of developmental and adjustment hypotheses of adolescence. *Journal of Educational Psychology,* 43, 1952, 339–53.

Schonfield, D., & Robertson, B. A. Memory storage and aging. *Canadian Journal of Psychology* 20, 1966, 228–36.

Schroder, H. M., & Rotter, B. Rigidity as learned behavior. *Journal of Experimental Psychology* 43, 1952, 141–50.

Schultz, C. B., & Sherman, R. H. Social class, development, and differences in reinforcer effectiveness. *Review of Educational Research* 46, 1976, 25–59.

Schwab, J. J. Inquiry, the science teacher, and the educator. *School Review* 68, 1960, 176–95.

Schwartz, S. H., Feldman, K. A., Brown, M. C., & Heingartner, A. Some personality correlates of conduct in two situations of moral conflict. *Journal of Personality* 37, 1969, 41–57.

Scottish Council for Research on Education. *Social implications of the 1947 Scottish mental survey.* London: University of London Press, 1953.

S

Scribner, S., & Cole, M. Cognitive consequences of formal and informal education. *Science* 182, 1973, 553–59.

Sears, D. O. Political behavior. In G. Lindzey and E. Aronson, eds., *Handbook of Social Psychology* 2d ed., vol. 5. Reading, Mass.: Addison-Wesley, 1969. Pp. 315–458.

Sears, P. S. Levels of aspiration in academically successful and unsuccessful children. *Journal of Abnormal and Social Psychology* 35, 1940, 498–536.

―――. Level of aspiration in relation to some variables of personality: Clinical studies. *Journal of Social Psychology* 14, 1941, 311–36.

―――. Problems in the investigation of achievement and self-esteem motivation. In M. R. Jones, ed., *Nebraska symposium on motivation, 1957.* Lincoln: University of Nebraska Press, 1957. Pp. 265–339.

―――, & Sherman, V. S. *In pursuit of self-esteem.* Belmont, Calif.: Wadsworth, 1964.

Sears, R. R. Ordinal position in the family as a psychological variable. *American Sociological Review* 15, 1950, 397–401.

―――, Maccoby, E. E., & Levin, H. *Patterns of child rearing.* Evanston: Row-Peterson, 1957.

Sebald, H. *Adolescence: A sociological analysis.* New York: Appleton-Century-Crofts, 1968.

Segall, M. H., Campbell, D. T., & Herskovits, M. J. *The influence of culture on visual perception.* Indianapolis: Bobbs-Merrill, 1966.

Seligman, C. K., Tucker, G. R., & Lambert, W. E. The effects of speech style and other attributes on teachers' attitude toward pupils. *Language in Society* 1, 1972, 131–42.

Selman, R. L., & Lieberman, M. Moral education in the primary grades: An evaluation of a developmental curriculum. *Journal of Educational Psychology* 67, 1975, 712–16.

Shalemon, E. O vozrastnykh osobennostiakh èlementarnogo konstruirovaniia u schkol'nikov I, III, V klassov. *Voprosy Psikhologii* 5, 1959, 100–06.

Shantz, C. U., & Wilson, K. E. Training communication skills in young children. *Child Development* 43, 1972, 693–98.

Shaycoft, M. F., Dailey, J. T., Orr, D. B., Neyman, C. A., & Sherman, S. E. *Studies of a complete age group—age 15.* Pittsburgh: Project TALENT, 1963.

Sherif, M., Harvey, O. J., White, B. J., Hood, W. R., & Sherif, C. *Intergroup conflict and cooperation: The robbers cave experiment.* Norman, Okla.: University Book Exchange, 1961.

Sherwood, G. G., & Gray, J. E. Two "classic" behaviour modification patients: A decade later. *Canadian Journal of Behavioural Science* 6, 1974, 420–27.

Shiffrin, R. M. Short-term store: The basis for a memory system. In F. Restle et al., eds., *Cognitive theory, vol. 1.* Hillsdale, N.J.: Erlbaum, 1975. Pp. 193–218.

Shulman, L. S., & Elstein, A. S. Studies of problem solving, judgment, and decision making: Implications for educational research. *Review of Research in Education* 3, 1975, 3–42.

―――, & Keislar, E., eds. *Learning by discovery.* Chicago: Rand McNally, 1966.

Siegler, R. S., & Liebert, R. M. Acquisition of formal scientific reasoning by 10- and 13-year-olds. *Developmental Psychology* 11, 1975, 401–02.

Silberman, H. F., et al. Use of exploratory techniques for the development of programming methods. Unpublished report. Santa Monica, Calif.: Rand Corporation, n.d. ED 003 210.

Silverthorne, C., Chelune, G., & Imada, A. The effects of competition and cooperation on level of prejudice. *Journal of Social Psychology* 92, 1974, 293–301.

Simon, H. A. How big is a chunk? *Science* 183, 1974, 482–88.

Sinclair, R. L., & Sadker, D. *Through the eyes of children.* Bedford, Mass.: Institute for Educational Services, 1973.

Singer, R. N., & Dick, W. *Teaching physical education; a systems approach.* Boston: Houghton Mifflin, 1974.

Skinner, B. F. *The technology of teaching.* New York: Appleton-Century-Crofts, 1968.

————. Contingency management in the classroom. *Education,* 1970, 93–100.

Slater-Hammel, A. T. An action current study of contraction movement relationships in the tennis stroke. *Research Quarterly* 20, 1949, 424–31.

Smith, C. P. *Achievement-related motives in children.* Princeton: Van Nostrand, 1966.

————, Ryan, E. R., & Diggins, D. R. Moral decision making: Cheating on examinations. *Journal of Personality* 40, 1972, 640–60.

Smith, H. P. Do intercultural experiences affect attitudes? *Journal of Abnormal and Social Psychology* 51, 1955, 469–77.

Smith, K. U. Cybernetic theory and analysis of learning. In E. A. Bilodeau, ed., *Acquisition of skill.* New York: Academic Press, 1966. Pp. 425–82.

Smith, M. B. Competence and socialization. In J. A. Clausen, ed., *Socialization and society.* Boston: Little, Brown, 1968. Pp. 270–320.

Smith, S. G., & Sherwood, B. A. Educational uses of the PLATO computer system. *Science* 192, 1976, 344–52.

Smith, W. M., McCrary, J. W., & Smith, K. U. Delayed visual feedback and behavior. *Science* 132, 1960, 1013–14.

Smode, A. F., Beam, J. C., & Dunlap, J. W. *Motor habit interference.* Stamford, Conn.: Dunlap, 1959.

Smothergill, N. L., Olson, F., & Moore, S. G. The effects of manipulation of teacher communication style in the preschool child. *Child Development* 42, 1971, 1229–39.

Solley, C. M., & Murphy, G. *Development of the perceptual world.* New York: Basic Books, 1960.

Solomon, R. L. Punishment. *American Psychologist* 19, 1964, 239–53.

Sontag, L. M., Baker, C. T., & Nelson, V. L. Mental growth and personality development: A longitudinal study. *Monographs of the Society for Research in Child Development,* vol. 23, no. 68, 1958.

Spaeth, R. K. Maximizing goal attainment. *Research Quarterly* 43, 1972, 337–61.

Sparks, H. L., & Blackman, L. S. What is special about special education revisited: The mentally retarded. *Exceptional Children* 31, 1965, 242–47.

Spaulding, R. L. Achievement, creativity, and self-concept correlates of teacher-pupil transactions in elementary school classrooms. Unpublished report, University of Illinois, Urbana, 1963.

Spear, P. S. Motivational effects of praise and criticism on children's learning. *Developmental Psychology* 3, 1970, 124–32.

————, & Spear, S. A. Social reinforcement, discrimination learning, and retention in children. *Developmental Psychology* 7, 1972, 220.

Spielberger, C. D. Conceptual and methodological issues in anxiety research. In *Anxiety: Current trends in research and theory,* vol. 2. New York: Academic Press, 1972. Pp. 281–494.

————, ed. *Anxiety: Current trends in theory and research.* New York: Academic Press, 1972.

Sprinthall, R. C., & Sprinthall, N. A. *Educational psychology: Selected Readings.* New York: Van Nostrand Reinhold, 1969.

Staats, A. W. Behavior analysis and token reinforcement in educational behavior modification and curriculum research. In *Seventy-second yearbook of the National Society for the Study of Education,* part 1, 1973. Pp. 195–229.

Staffieri, J. R. Body build and behavioral expectancies in young females. *Developmental Psychology* 6, 1972, 125–27.

Staub, E. Effects of persuasion and modeling on delay of gratification. *Developmental Psychology* 6, 1972, 166–77.

Stephens, J. M. *Educational psychology: The study of educational growth,* rev. ed. New York: Holt, Rinehart and Winston, 1956.

Sterrett, M. D., & Davis, R. A. The permanence of school learning. *Educational Administration and Supervision* 40, 1954, 449–60.

Strang, H. Pictorial and verbal media in self-instruction of procedural skills. *AV Communication Review* 21, 1973, 225–32.

Strodtbeck, F. L. The hidden curriculum in the middle-class home. In J. D. Krumboltz, ed., *Learning and the educational process.* Chicago: Rand McNally, 1967. Pp. 91–112.

Strunk, W., & White, E. B. *The elements of style,* 2d. ed. New York: Macmillan, 1972.

Stuit, D. B., ed. *Personnel research and test development in the Bureau of Naval Personnel.* Princeton: Princeton University Press, 1947.

Suedfeld, P., Glucksberg, S., & Vernon, J. Sensory deprivation as a drive operation: Effects upon problem solving. *Journal of Experimental Psychology* 75 (2) 1967, 166–69.

Sullivan, J. Open—traditional—what is the difference? *Elementary School Journal* 74, 1974, 493–500.

T

Taba, H. *School culture.* Washington, D.C.: American Council on Education, 1955a.

_____. *With perspective on human relations.* Washington, D.C.: American Council on Education, 1955b.

Taffel, S. J., O'Leary, K. D., & Armel, S. Reasoning and praise: Their effects on academic behavior. *Journal of Educational Psychology,* 60 (3), 1974, 291–95.

Tanner, J. M. Physical aspects of adolescence. In M. K. Pringle & V. P. Varma, eds., *Advances in educational psychology, 2.* London: University of London Press, 1974. Pp. 248–65.

Tapp, J. C., & Kohlberg, L. Developing senses of law and legal justice. *Journal of Social Issues* 27 (2), 1971, 65–91.

Terman, L. M. *The measurement of intelligence.* Boston: Houghton Mifflin, 1916.

Thayer, J. A. Johnny could read—what happened? *Journal of Reading* 13, 1972, 501–06.

Thelen, H. A. *Classroom grouping for teachability.* New York: Wiley, 1967.

Thomas, L. E. Political generation gap. *Journal of Social Psychology* 84, 1971, 313–14.

_____. Generational discontinuity in beliefs: An exploration of the generation gap. *Journal of Social Issues* 30 (3), 1974, 1–22.

Thoresen, C. E., & Mahoney, M. J. *Behavioral self-control.* New York: Holt, Rinehart and Winston, 1974.

Thorndike, E. L. Mental discipline in high school studies. *Journal of Educational Psychology* 15, 1924, 1–22, 83–98.

Thorndike, R. L., ed. *Educational measurement.* Washington, D.C.: American Council on Education, 1971. Pp. 59–61.

_____. *Stanford-Binet Intelligence Scale: 1972 norms tables.* Boston: Houghton Mifflin, 1973.

_____. Mr. Binet's test 70 years later. *Educational Researcher* 4 (5), 1975, 3–7.

_____, & Hagen, E. *10,000 careers.* New York: Wiley, 1959.

_____. Examiner's manual, Cognitive Abilities Test. Boston: Houghton Mifflin, 1971.

_____. Technical manual, Cognitive Abilities Tests. Boston: Houghton Mifflin, 1974.

Thune, L. C., & Ericksen, S. C. Studies in abstraction learning: IV. The transfer effects of conceptual vs. rote instruction in a simulated classroom situation. Mimeographed. Nashville: Vanderbilt University, 1960.

Tobias, S. *The effect of creativity, response mode, and subject matter familiarity on achievement from programmed instruction.* New York: MSS Information Corporation, 1968.

Tolley, H., Jr. *Children and war*. New York: Teachers College Press, 1973.

Torrance, E. P. *Education and the creative potential*. Minneapolis: University of Minnesota Press, 1963.

_____. *Rewarding creative behavior*. Englewood Cliffs, N.J.: Prentice-Hall, 1965.

_____, & Myers, R. E. *Creative learning and teaching*. New York: Dodd, Mead, 1970.

_____, & White, W. F., eds. *Issues and advances in educational psychology,* 2d ed. Itasca, Ill.: Peacock Publishers, 1975.

Travers, R. M. W., ed. *Second handbook of research on teaching*. Chicago: Rand McNally, 1973.

_____, Van Wagenen, K. R., Haygood, D. H., & McCormick, M. Learning as a consequence of the learner's task involvement under different conditions of feedback. *Journal of Educational Psychology* 55, 1964, 167–73.

Triandis, H. C. *Attitude and attitude change*. New York: Wiley, 1971.

Trown, E. A., & Leith, G. O. M. Decision roles for teaching strategies in primary schools: Personality-treatment interactions. *British Journal of Educational Psychology* 45, Part 2, 1975, 130–41.

Tryon, C. M., & Henry, W. E. How children learn personal and social adjustment. In N. B. Henry, ed., *Learning and instruction*. Yearbook of the National Society for the Study of Education, vol. 49, part 1. Chicago: University of Chicago Press, 1950. Pp. 156–82.

Tulving, E. Cue-dependent forgetting. *American Scientist* 62 (1), 1974, 74–82.

Tyler, L. The stability of patterns of primary mental abilities among grade school children. *Educational and Psychological Measurement* 18, 1958, 769–74.

Tyler, R. W., Permanence of learning. *Journal of Higher Education* 4, 1933, 203–04.

Vaillant, G. E., & McArthur, C. C. Natural history of male psychologic health, I. The adult life cycle from 18–50. *Seminars in Psychiatry* 4, 1972, 415–27.

Vander Meer, A. W. The economy of time in industrial training. *Journal of Educational Psychology* 36, 1945, 65–90.

Venn, E. G. Unpublished Master's thesis, State College of Washington, 1946.

Vesell, E. S. Induction of drug-metabolizing enzymes in liver microsomes of mice and rats by softwood bedding. *Science* 157, 1967, 1057–58.

Voelker, P. F. The function of ideals and attitudes in social education. *Teachers College Contributions to Education,* no. 112. New York: Teachers College, Columbia University, 1921.

von Senden, M. *Space and sight*. Glencoe. Ill.: Free Press, 1960. (Originally published in German, 1932.)

von Wright, J. M. A note on the role of "guidance" in learning. *British Journal of Psychology* 48, 1957, 133–37.

Wallach, M. A., & Kogan, N. *Modes of thinking in young children*. New York: Holt, Rinehart and Winston, 1965.

Wardrop, J. L., Goodwin, W. L., Klausmeier, H. J., et al. The development of productive thinking skills in fifth-grade children. *Journal of Experimental Education* 37 (4), 1969, 67–77.

Wargo, M. I., Tallmadge, G. K., Michaels, D. D., et al. *ESEA Title I: A reanalysis and synthesis of evaluation data from fiscal year 1965 through 1970*. Palo Alto, Calif.: American Institutes for Research, 1972. ED 059 415.

Warner, L. G., & DeFleur, M. L. Attitude as an interactional concept. *American Sociological Review* 34, 1969, 153–69.

V

W

Wason, P. C., & Johnson-Laird, P. N. *Psychology of reasoning: Structure and content.* Cambridge, Mass.: Harvard University Press, 1972.

Watson, J. B. *The psychological care of the infant and child.* New York: Norton, 1928.

―――, & Watson, R. R. Conditioned emotional reactions. *Journal of Experimental Psychology* 3, 1920, 1–14.

Watts, G. H., & Anderson, R. C. Effects of three types of inserted questions on learning from prose. *Journal of Educational Psychology* 62, 1971, 387–94.

Watts, W. A., & McGuire, W. J. Persistence of induced opinion change and retention of the inducing message contents. *Journal of Abnormal and Social Psychology* 68, 1964, 233–41.

Weatherley, D. Self-perceived rate of physical maturation and personality in late adolescence. *Child Development* 35, 1964, 1197–1210.

Webb, E. J., et al. *Unobtrusive measures: Nonreactive research in the social sciences.* Chicago: Rand McNally, 1966.

Weber, G. *Uses and abuses of standardized testing in the schools.* Washington, D.C.: Council for Basic Education, 1974.

Webster, H. Change in attitudes during college. *Journal of Educational Psychology* 49, 1958, 109–17.

Weinstein, E. A. Development of the concept of flag and the sense of national identity. *Child Development* 28, 1957, 167–74.

Weintraub, S., & Young, P. *Directions in literary criticism.* University Park, Pa.: Pennsylvania State University Press, 1973.

Welford, A. T. *Fundamentals of skill.* London: Methuen, 1968.

―――. The obtaining and processing of information. *Research Quarterly* 43, 1972, 295–311.

Werner, E. Report of the stress study. Unpublished manuscript, Institute of Child Development and Welfare, University of Minnesota, 1959.

Wertheimer, M. *Productive thinking.* New York: Harper, 1959.

Wesley, F. Silents, please. *Audio-Visual Communications Review* 10, 1962, 102–05.

West, L. J. Development of marketable typing skill: Sensory processes underlying acquisition. Unpublished report, City University of New York, 1966.

―――. Vision and kinesthesis in the acquisition of typewriting skill. *Journal of Applied Psychology* 51, 1967, 161–66.

Westbury, I., & Bellack, A. A. *Research into classroom processes.* New York: Teachers College Press, 1971.

Westin, Alan F. *Privacy and freedom.* New York: Atheneum, 1967.

Westinghouse Learning Corporation. *The impact of Head Start.* Washington, D.C.: Office of Economic Opportunity, 1969.

Wheeler, L. R. The intelligence of East Tennessee mountain children. *Journal of Educational Psychology* 23, 1932, 351–70.

―――. A comparative study of the intelligence of East Tennessee mountain children. Ibid., 33, 1942, 321–34.

Wheeler, R., & Ryan, F. L. Effects of cooperative and competitive classroom environments. *Journal of Educational Psychology* 65, 1973, 402–07.

Whipple, G. M., ed. *Intelligence: Its nature and nurture.* Yearbook of the National Society for the Study of Education, vol. 39, part 2. Bloomington, Ill.: Public School Publishing Co., 1940.

White, B. L. An experimental approach to the effects of experience on early human behavior. In J. P. Hill, ed., *Minnesota symposia on child psychology,* vol. 1. Minneapolis: University of Minnesota Press, 1967. Pp. 201–26.

―――, & Watts, J. C. *Experience and environment,* vol. 1. Englewood Cliffs, N.J.: Prentice-Hall, 1973.

White, R., & Lippitt, R. *Autocracy and democracy: An experimental inquiry.* New York: Harper, 1960.

White, R. W. Competence and psychological stages. In M. R. Jones, ed., *Nebraska symposium on motivation, 1960.* Lincoln: University of Nebraska Press, 1960. Pp. 97–141.

White, S. H. A contemporary perspective on learning theory and its relation to education. In. J. I. Goodlad, ed., *Human behavior and childhood education.* Waltham, Mass.: Blaisdell, 1969.

_____, Day, M. C., Freeman, P. K., et al. Federal programs for young children: Review and recommendations. Washington, D.C.: Department of Health, Education, and Welfare, 1973. ED 092 230–233.

Whyte, W. F. *Money and motivation.* New York: Harper, 1955.

Wicker, A. W. Attitudes versus actions: The relationship of verbal and overt behavioral responses to attitude objects. *Journal of Social Issues* 25 (4), 1969, 41–78.

Wicker, F. W. Photographs, drawings, and nouns as stimuli in paired-associate learning. *Psychonomic Science* 18, 1970, 205–06.

Wilkins, M. C. The effect of changed material on the ability to do formal syllogistic reasoning. *Archives of Psychology* 16 (102), 1928.

Williams, F., ed. *Language and poverty.* Chicago: Markham, 1970.

_____, & Naremore, R. C. On the functional analysis of social class differences in modes of speech. *Speech Monographs* 36, 1969, 77–102.

_____, Whitehead, J. L., & Miller, L. Relations between language attitudes and teacher expectancy. *American Educational Research Journal* 9, 1972, 263–77.

Williams, J. Training children to copy and to discriminate letterlike forms. *Journal of Educational Psychology* 67, 1975, 790–95.

Williams, R. R. *Toward the conquest of beriberi.* Cambridge, Mass.: Harvard University Press, 1961.

Willie, C. V. The black family and social class. *American Sociological Review* 44, 1974, 50–60.

Willis, J. Effects of systematic feedback and self charting on a remedial tutorial program in reading. *Journal of Experimental Education* 42 (4), 1974, 83–85.

Winger, F. E. The determination of the significance of tachistoscopic training in word perception as applied to beginning typewriting instruction. Unpublished doctoral dissertation, University of Oregon, 1951.

Wittrock, M. C., & Carter, J. F. Generative processing of hierarchically organized words. *American Journal of Psychology* 88, 1975, 489–502.

Wohlwill, J. F. Developmental studies of perception. *Psychological Bulletin* 57, 1960, 249–88.

Wolcott, H. F. The teacher as an enemy. In G. D. Spindler, ed., *Education and cultural process.* New York: Holt, Rinehart and Winston, 1974. Pp. 411–25.

Wolf, R. M. The identification and measurement of environmental process variables related to intelligence. Unpublished doctoral dissertation, University of Chicago, 1964.

Wood, B. D., & Freeman, F. N. *An experimental study of the educational influence of the typewriter in the elementary school.* New York: Macmillan, 1932.

Wood, K. S. Parental maladjustment and functional articulatory disorders. *Journal of Speech Disorders* 11, 1946, 255–75.

Woodrow, H. The effect of type of training upon transference. *Journal of Educational Psychology* 18, 1927, 159–72.

Wright, H. F. How the psychology of motivation is related to curriculum development. *Journal of Educational Psychology* 39, 1948, 149–56.

Wrightstone, J. W. Demonstration guidance project in New York City. *Harvard Educational Review* 30, 1960, 237–51.

————, Forlano, G., Frankel, E., et al. Evaluations of the Higher Horizons program for under-privileged children. Unpublished report. New York: Bureau of Educational Research, 1964. ED 001 787.

Wyatt, R. F. Improvability of pitch discrimination. *Psychological Monographs* 58, 1945.

## Y

Yakovlev, P. I., & Lecours, A. R. The myelogenetic cycles of regional maturation of the brain. In A. Minkowski, ed., *Regional development of the brain in early life.* Oxford: Blackwell, 1967. Pp. 3–71.

Yankelovich, D. *Generations apart.* New York: Columbia Broadcasting System, 1969.

————. *The new morality: A profile of American youth in the 70's.* New York: McGraw-Hill, 1974.

Young, M. *The rise of meritocracy.* London: Thames & Hudson, 1958.

## Z

Zacharias, L., Rand, W. M., & Wurtman, R. J. A prospective study of sexual development and growth in American girls. *Obstetrical and Gynecological Survey* 31, 1976, 325–37.

Zellman, G. L. Antidemocratic beliefs: A survey and some explanations. *Journal of Social Issues* 31 (2), 1975, 31–53.

————, & Sears, D. O. Childhood origins of tolerance for dissent. *Journal of Social Issues* 27 (2), 1971, 109–36.

Zigler, E. Social class and the socialization process. *Review of Educational Research* 40, 1970, 87–110.

————. Has it really been demonstrated that compensatory education is without value? *American Psychologist* 30, 1975, 935–37.

# PICTURE CREDITS

# AUTHOR INDEX

---

NOTE: Some entries refer to authors who are one of a group. In such cases, the text cites only the main author, "et al." For the full listing, see the Bibliography.

Tolley, H., Jr., 754, 855
Torrance, E. Paul, 34, 35, 558, 563, 589, 621, 855
Tracy, D. B., 59, 851
Travers, R. M. W., 144, 367, 405–07, 467, 541, 544, 618, 648, 666, 786, 796, 799, 813, 855
Triandis, H. C., 745, 855
Trown, E. A., 643, 855
Tryon, C. M., 158, 855
Tucker, G. R., 371, 499, 842, 852
Tulving, E., 453, 469, 855
Turiel, Elliot, 367, 786, 796, 799, 801, 811, 813, 824
Turnbull, W. W., 347
Turner, R. R., 502, 836
Tyler, L., 312, 855
Tyler, R. W., vi, 456, 826, 855

# V

Vaillant, G. E., 187, 858
Vander Meer, A. W., 421, 855
Van Wagenen, K. R., 618, 855
Venezky, Richard L., 305
Venn, E. G., 512, 855
Vernon, J., 557, 854
Vesell, E. S., 567, 855
Vinacke, W., 633, 831
Voelker, P. F., 809, 855
von Senden, M., 162, 855
von Wright, J. M., 421, 855

# W

Waite, R. R., 242, 643, 851
Walberg, H. J., 216, 222, 621, 828, 844, 845, 848
Walker, A. M., 813, 831
Wallace, J. G., 162, 835
Wallach, Michael A., 466, 560, 563–64, 855
Walters, R. H., 212, 824
Wandt, E., 661, 851
Ward, M. P., 746, 767, 844
Wardrop, J. L., 575, 855
Wargo, M. I., 361, 855
Warner, L. G., 739, 855
Warwick, D. P., 758

Washington, R. M., 8, 823
Wason, P. C., 559, 568, 856
Watson, John B., 49, 742, 856
Watson, R. I., Jr., 608, 843
Watson, Rosalie R., 742, 856
Watts, G. H., 465, 856
Watts, Jean Carew, 67, 171, 776, 842, 856
Watts, W. A., 771, 856
Weatherley, D., 157, 856
Webb, E. J., 744, 856
Weber, George, 257, 305, 856
Webster, H., 758, 856
Wechsler, D., 276
Weigel, Russell H., 781
Wein, K. S., 475, 847
Weinheimer, S., 493, 841
Weinstein, E. A., 171, 856
Weintraub, S., 816, 856
Welford, A. T., 421, 436, 439, 856
Werner, E., 214, 856
Wertheimer, Max, 558, 560, 856
Wescourt, K. T., 448, 824
Wesley, F., 512, 856
Wesman, A. G., 296, 733, 825
West, Leonard J., 107, 400, 420, 856
Westbury, I., 648, 663, 856
Westie, F. R., 743, 845
Westin, Alan F., 236, 856
Westinghouse Learning Corporation, 357, 856
Wheeler, L. R., 320, 856
Wheeler, R., 120, 856
Whimbey, Arthur, 541
Whimbey, Linda Shaw, 541
Whipple, G. M., 353, 856
White, B. J., 678, 779, 852
White, Burton L., 67, 162, 171, 856
White, E. B., 516, 854
White, Ralph, 662, 857
White, Robert W., 198, 857
White, S. H., 20, 360, 836, 857
White, W. F., 34, 35, 589, 835
Whitehead, J. L., 499, 857
Whyte, W. F., 611, 857
Wickens, T. D., 621, 824
Wicker, A. W., 745, 857
Wicker, F. W., 457, 857
Wilkins, M. C., 569, 857

Williams, F., 499, 857
Williams, Joanna, 110–19, 850, 857
Williams, R. R., 567, 857
Willie, Charles V., 223, 251, 857
Willis, J., 621–23, 857
Wilson, Brent, 716
Wilson, K. E., 496, 852
Winger, F. E., 414, 857
Winzenz, D., 470, 827
Wiser, Patricia L., 781
Withall, John, 652
Wittrock, M. C., 470, 857
Wohlwill, J. F., 523, 857
Wolcott, H. F., 223, 857
Wolf, M., 21, 850
Wolf, R. M., 215, 857
Wood, B. D., 374, 857
Wood, K. S., 207, 857
Woodrow, H., 435, 446, 857
Woodruff, Asahel D., 487
Wright, H. F., 597, 857
Wrightstone, J. W., 358–60, 857, 858
Wurtman, R. J., 153, 858
Wuthnow, R., 743, 835
Wyatt, R. F., 22, 858

# Y

Yakovlev, P. I., 159, 858
Yankelovich, D., 179, 194, 220, 858
Yeh, E. G., 222, 848
Yilk, M. D., 114, 849
Young, Michael, viii, 72, 858
Young, P., 816, 856

# Z

Zacharias, L., 153, 858
Zagorin, S. W., 246, 842
Zajonc, R., 732
Zeaman, D., 444, 838
Zellman, G. L., 741, 858
Zellner, M., 365–69, 843
Zigler, E., 354, 620, 858
Zimbardo, Phillip, 84, 145, 836
Zimiles, H., 177, 715, 845
Zola, I. K., 802, 843
Zubek, J., 317, 829

# SUBJECT INDEX

effect of experience on, 166–68, 311, 327–40, 441–47
heredity and, 315–19
home influences on, 137, 171, 214–16, 279, 324, 494
kinds of, 284–90, 554, 562
measuring, 271–90, 560
stability of, 292–94, 307–13
in subcultures, 315, 323–26
Mental age, 269
Mental health. *See* Adjustment; Emotion; Thwarting
*Mental Measurements Yearbook,* 265
Mental practice, 114, 426, 465–66
Merit rating, 686–88, 696, 697f., 748
Minority groups. *See* Black students; Chicano students; Ethnic background; Ethnic groups; Indian cultures
Mnemonic devices, 470–71
Mobility, social, 70ff.
Models, 57, 172, 421–24, 490, 507, 754–66, 807
*See also* Demonstration; Template
Modernity, 53f.
Monitoring, 426ff., 685f., 748
Mooney Problem Checklist, 9, 241
Moral judgment, 788, 792, 796–800, 811–15
*See also* Character
Motion pictures, learning from, 406, 419, 421, 428, 775, 777
Mother. *See* Parents
Motivation, 79, 85ff., 105, 174–75, 205–51, 271, 506, 557–65, 593–645, 648–80, 684
*See also* specific motivations
Multiple-choice tests. *See* Choice-response tests
Music, learning in, 320, 400, 407, 412, 429, 743

# N

Needs, 185–202
*See also* specific needs
Neobehaviorism, 22
Neural maturation, 159ff.
Nongraded school, 382f.
Normal distribution, 117f., 154, 267, 270
Norms: in goal setting, 610ff.
for tests, 269f., 294, 318, 725–31

# O

Objectives, 16, 57–69, 362, 466, 599, 685, 690–95
Observation of students, 232ff., 717, 744
*See also* Monitoring; Performance tests
Occupations, aptitude for, 288–90, 298–303, 379
Open classroom, 18, 40, 382, 654
Operational thought, 328–39, 365, 509, 792
Oppenheimer, J. Robert, 765
Organization: in associative learning, 453–54, 461, 469–71
in instructional communications, 522–25, 533–37
Originality. *See* Divergent thinking
Overlearning, 437, 467
Overt response. *See* Practice; Provisional try

# P

Parents: effect on child's ability, 137, 171, 214–16, 279, 321–24; 494
handling of child, 136ff., 188, 205–26, 635, 801, 802, 804–07
identification with, 755
Parts versus wholes, 415–18, 480, 522–24, 536
Pascal, Blaise, 200
Peers: approval by, 181, 189ff., 818
influence on attitudes and conduct, 172, 611, 754–59, 765–66, 777, 800, 803–04
ratings by, 237–39
Percentile, 269
Perception, 86, 162f., 334, 477–80, 511
Perceptual learning, 110ff., 162f., 334, 365, 414, 443–45
Performance: effects of stress or arousal on, 165, 409, 437, 642–43
records of, 403, 426, 622, 748
Performance tests: of achievement, 493, 714–18
of attitude, personality, or character, 744, 794–96
of mental ability, 277
Personality: and abilities, 136, 563
and achievement, 53ff., 143, 248–49, 539, 604, 667–71, 743, 804
appraisal, 227–46, 744–46, 794–800
and attitude change, 743, 751, 758, 779–80
consistency of, 130, 189, 190, 198, 234, 247ff., 746–47, 795–96, 801
and goal setting, 604–09, 633f.
related to physique, 128
Persuasion, 144, 753, 766, 777–78, 809
Physical development, 151–63, 167, 180
Physical education, 158, 417, 429
Piagetian theory, 144, 166, 328–39, 342, 364–69, 512, 796
Pictorial. *See* Audio-visual methods; Visual cues
Planning, 569–70, 596–99, 647–63
*See also* Goals
Political socialization, 32, 46, 171, 183, 193, 484, 715, 739–41; 751–52
*See also* Attitudes; Ethnic groups
Practice, 413–30, 463–68, 526ff., 808ff.
mental, 114, 426, 465–66
Praise. *See* Reinforcement
Prediction of achievement, 73, 140, 248, 290–303
Prejudice, 484, 738, 762
Preschool. *See* Early education
Preverbal understanding, 332–37, 481, 509ff., 552
Principles, teaching of, 28, 95, 367, 473–75, 512–14, 525–37
Privacy, 236, 784
Problem checklist, 9, 241
Problems, as distinct from exercises, 527
Problem solving: as aim of socialization, 45f., 543–84
improvement of, 28, 443, 563, 570–75
individual differences in, 144, 285, 562–65
processes in, 550–71
as type of learning, 95, 549–75
Production deficiency, 272, 324, 557ff.
Profile interpretation, 284ff., 296, 298, 304, 312
Program, executive, 398, 408
Program, neural, 167, 398